Manipulation of Flowering

Proceedings of Previous Easter Schools in Agricultural Science, published by Butterworths, London

*SOIL ZOOLOGY   Edited by D.K.McE. Kevan (1955)
*THE GROWTH OF LEAVES   Edited by F.L. Milthorpe (1956)
*CONTROL OF THE PLANT ENVIRONMENT   Edited by J.P. Hudson (1957)
*NUTRITION OF THE LEGUMES   Edited by E.G. Hallsworth (1958)
*THE MEASUREMENT OF GRASSLAND PRODUCTIVITY   Edited by J.D. Ivins (1959)
*DIGESTIVE PHYSIOLOGY AND NUTRITION OF THE RUMINANT   Edited by D. Lewis
(1960)
*NUTRITION OF PIGS AND POULTRY   Edited by J.T. Morgan and D. Lewis (1961)
*ANTIBIOTICS IN AGRICULTURE   Edited by M. Woodbine (1962)
*THE GROWTH OF THE POTATO   Edited by J.D. Ivins and F.L. Milthorpe (1963)
*EXPERIMENTAL PEDOLOGY   Edited by E.G. Hallsworth and D.V. Crawford (1964)
*THE GROWTH OF CEREALS AND GRASSES   Edited by F.L. Milthorpe and J.D. Ivins (1965)
*REPRODUCTION IN THE FEMALE MAMMAL   Edited by G.E. Lamming and E.C. Amoroso
(1967)
*GROWTH AND DEVELOPMENT OF MAMMALS   Edited by G.A. Lodge and G.E. Lamming
(1968)
*ROOT GROWTH   Edited by W.J. Whittington (1968)
*PROTEINS AS HUMAN FOOD   Edited by R.A. Lawrie (1970)
*LACTATION   Edited by I.R. Falconer (1971)
*PIG PRODUCTION   Edited by D.J.A. Cole (1972)
*SEED ECOLOGY   Edited by W. Heydecker (1973)
HEAT LOSS FROM ANIMALS AND MAN: ASSESSMENT AND CONTROL   Edited by J.L.
Monteith and L.E. Mount (1974)
*MEAT   Edited by D.J.A. Cole and R.A. Lawrie (1975)
*PRINCIPLES OF CATTLE PRODUCTION   Edited by Henry Swan and W.H. Broster (1976)
*LIGHT AND PLANT DEVELOPMENT   Edited by H. Smith (1976)
PLANT PROTEINS   Edited by G. Norton (1977)
ANTIBIOTICS AND ANTIBIOSIS IN AGRICULTURE   Edited by M. Woodbine (1977)
CONTROL OF OVULATION   Edited by D.B. Crighton, N.B. Haynes, G.R. Foxcroft and G.E.
Lamming (1978)
POLYSACCHARIDES IN FOOD   Edited by J.M.V. Blanshard and J.R.Mitchell (1979)
SEED PRODUCTION   Edited by P.D. Hebblethwaite (1980)
PROTEIN DEPOSITION IN ANIMALS   Edited by P.J. Buttery and D.B. Lindsay (1981)
PHYSIOLOGICAL PROCESSES LIMITING PLANT PRODUCTIVITY   Edited by C. Johnson
(1981)
ENVIRONMENTAL ASPECTS OF HOUSING FOR ANIMAL PRODUCTION   Edited by J.A.
Clark (1981)
EFFECTS OF GASEOUS AIR POLLUTION IN AGRICULTURE AND HORTICULTURE
Edited by M.H. Unsworth and D.P. Ormrod (1982)
CHEMICAL MANIPULATION OF CROP GROWTH AND DEVELOPMENT   Edited by J.S.
McLaren (1982)
CONTROL OF PIG REPRODUCTION   Edited by D.J.A. Cole and G.R. Foxcroft (1982)
SHEEP PRODUCTION   Edited by W. Haresign (1983)
UPGRADING WASTE FOR FEEDS AND FOOD   Edited by D.A. Ledward, A.J. Taylor and R.
A. Lawrie (1983)
FATS IN ANIMAL NUTRITION   Edited by J. Wiseman (1984)
IMMUNOLOGICAL ASPECTS OF REPRODUCTION IN MAMMALS   Edited by D.B. Crighton
(1984)
ETHYLENE AND PLANT DEVELOPMENT   Edited by J.A. Roberts and G.A. Tucker (1985)
THE PEA CROP   Edited by P.D. Hebblethwaite, M.C. Heath and T.C.K. Dawkins (1985)
PLANT TISSUE CULTURE AND ITS AGRICULTURAL APPLICATIONS   Edited by Lyndsey
A. Withers and P. G. Alderson (1986)
CONTROL AND MANIPULATION OF ANIMAL GROWTH   Edited by P.J. Buttery, D.B.
Lindsay and N.N. Haynes (1986)
COMPUTER APPLICATIONS IN AGRICULTURAL ENVIRONMENTS   Edited by J.A. Clark.
K. Gregson and R.A. Saffell (1986)

These titles are now out of print but are available in microfiche editions

Manipulation of Flowering

J. G. ATHERTON
University of Nottingham School of Agriculture

Butterworths
London   Boston   Durban   Singapore   Sydney   Toronto   Wellington

First published 1987

© The several contributors named in the list of contents, 1987

British Library Cataloguing in Publication Data

Manipulation of flowering.—(Easter
    schools of agricultural science)
    1. Plants, Flowering of 2. Plant
    regulators 3. Crops—Growth
    I. Atherton, J.G. (Jeffrey Gordon)
    II. Series
    631.5'4 SB126.8

    ISBN 0–407–00570–6

Library of Congress Cataloging in Publication Data

Manipulation of flowering.

    Proceedings of the 45th University of Nottingham
Easter School in Agricultural Science held at Sutton
Bonington, April 7–10, 1986.
    Bibliography: p.
    Includes index.
    1. Plants, Flowering of—Congresses. I. Atherton,
J.G., 1948–   . II. Easter School in Agricultural
Science (45th: 1986: Sutton Bonington, Nottinghamshire)
SB126.8.M36 1987   635.9'1544   86–23301

    ISBN 0–407–00570–6

Photoset by Latimer Trend & Company Ltd, Plymouth
Printed and bound by Robert Hartnoll Ltd, Bodmin, Cornwall

PREFACE

Genetic, environmental and chemical means of manipulating flowering are used extensively in agriculture and horticulture. Promotion of flowering is required by growers of early flower, seed and fruit crops and by plant breeders, whilst suppression of flowering is particularly important to sugar producers and growers of vegetables and late crops. Considerable research effort has been expended on the elucidation of processes that regulate flowering. The 45th University of Nottingham Easter School in Agricultural Science held at Sutton Bonington from 7–10 April 1986 brought together crop researchers, plant physiologists, geneticists and other interested parties from industry and academia to consider the results from this research that were most relevant to agriculture and horticulture. Considerable mutual benefits were derived from this interaction and consequently more effective manipulation of flowering can now be expected.

This book presents the edited proceedings of the Easter School. The first main section examines measurement and prediction of flowering. It addresses problems of how best to measure flowering when the aim is either to construct predictive models or to assist physiological interpretations. This integrated assessment of flowering provides a useful perspective for the detailed analyses of particular stages in flowering which follow. Juvenility and the nature of determination in meristems are examined, followed by aspects of vernalization, photoperiodic induction and flower evocation, initiation and development to anthesis. Each section opens with an extensive review and continues with a number of research orientated chapters. The main sections are preceded by an analysis of the flowering problems and followed by a critical view of how to achieve a better understanding and use of the physiology of flowering.

The success of the Easter School was a credit to the contributors and delegates alike, and I thank them all most sincerely. The splendid organization of the School was largely due to the skill and hard work of Mrs Marion Wilton and I am particularly grateful to her. I would like also to thank Charles Wright, David Hand, Trevor Lord, Carol Williams and other members of my department for their capable management of the visual aids and visits. Finally I wish to thank the Session Chairmen—John Monteith, Alan Longman, Ian Sussex, Dick Whittington, Lloyd Evans, Ken Cockshull and Peter Harris.

The Easter School could not have taken place without the generous financial support kindly donated by many commercial organizations. They are listed separately in the Acknowledgements. I would also like to acknowledge here the grant aid received from the Royal Society and the British Council.

Jeff Atherton

ACKNOWLEDGEMENTS

Donations are gratefully acknowledged from the following:
  Asmer Seeds Limited
  BASF United Kingdom Limited
  Bayer UK Limited
  British Petroleum Company plc
  Ciba-Geigy Agrochemicals
  Dow Chemical Company Limited
  FBC Limited
  Imperial Chemical Industries plc
  Marks and Spencer plc
  May and Baker Limited
  Miln Marsters Group Limited
  Monsanto Europe SA
  Nickerson RPB Limited
  Sandoz Products Limited
  Sharpes (Charles Sharp and Company, plc)
  Shell Research
  Tozer Limited
  Unilever Research
  Yoder Toddington Limited

CONTENTS

I

Introduction

1

THE FLOWERING PROBLEM

W.W. SCHWABE
Department of Horticulture, Wye College,
University of London, Nr. Ashford, Kent

In introducing the topic of flowering for this book, it would not be appropriate merely to review the latest literature nor is it the place to present fresh results on some narrow aspect of the wide field, which anticipate the detailed research reports that follow. An attempt is made here to pinpoint some crucial areas which would justify inclusion under the heading of 'The flowering problem'. These are not new, but are discussed in order to focus attention on areas where progress has been made, or would be useful. Of these topics the one referred to as 'evocation' is morphogenetically perhaps the most striking aspect and may deserve rather more attention.

Apical change

Basically, the problem of flowering is to discover the underlying causes for the relatively sudden transition of a vegetative growing point from the production of leafy organs to the formation of floral organs. The floral organs themselves almost certainly represent homologies with leaves, e.g. sepals, petals, stamens and carpels. They are of bilateral symmetry, and this is also borne out by their vascular anatomy—cf. the 'gonophyll theory' of Melville (1962, 1963). Thus the production of lateral organs still continues the foliar pattern on a cauline structure, which itself continues to exhibit radial symmetry. The reasons why lateral organs should be formed at all on such cauline structures clearly goes back to the Psilotalean organization pattern and a consideration of possible mechanisms is beyond the scope of this discussion on flowering.

The switch to the formation of a new type of lateral organ is nearly always associated with general changes at the growing point itself, often in both the so-called 'bare apex' and the primordial initiation zone, the 'anneau initial'. This could be via the operation of a series of quite specific morphogens, but the kind of lateral organ being formed on the cauline structure may itself be a consequence of the size of the cauline axis (e.g. diameter, or surface area)—cf. Bernier and Nougarède (e.g. in Bernier, 1979)—and, for instance, a smaller meristem than the normal vegetative apex might entail *ipso facto* the development of sepals or anthers rather than leaves, though this is still in the realm of speculation. Moreover, in many instances there is an associated change in apical dominance, nearly always a weakening. This is usually temporary, and when the new type of organ, homologous with leaves, is formed, dominance is often re-established—in as much as this is still possible. There are

3

several distinct types of development: apices ending in a single flower (e.g. *Viscaria*, apices ending in an inflorescence terminated by a single inflorescence (e.g. the terminal spikelet in the wheat ear) or with a compound inflorescence (e.g. in the compositae).

There are only relatively few examples where the terminal apex itself normally reverts again to the formation of leaves, in a continuation of vegetative growth (e.g. *Ananas comosa*). As a teratological phenomenon, however, this is not uncommon.

Another factor that is of significance in this respect is the apparent antagonism (or competition) between foliar growth and cauline development. While a discussion of the possible mechanism of such antagonism and the reasons for the development of axillary buds, i.e. cauline structures in the axils of leaves, would again take this review beyond its confines, there is little doubt about the existence of this competition. It is seen very clearly in the Hop apex (*Humulus lupulus*), where at the onset of flowering cauline development gradually predominates (Thomas and Schwabe, 1970). Another excellent example is afforded by the development of the cereal ear, where the shoot apex, as seen soon after seed germination, is a relatively short cylindrical, cauline, structure with single ridges (leaf initials). The latter weaken and their developmental period becomes progressively curtailed, while the development of the axillary buds in their axils (cauline structures) becomes *pari passu* greater, until only the upper ridge (spikelet) develops at all, the cauline development having totally suppressed foliar 4 development (*Figure 1.1*) (Hutley-Bull and Schwabe, 1980). Subsequently the development of the spikelet axis itself, with the formation of glume initials (i.e. foliar type structures) repeats this pattern of development.

Similarly, in the development of the composite flower, foliar development is increasingly reduced until the first inflorescence bracts are formed and then it is suppressed either completely, or reduced to minute scales when floret initiation occurs on the much enlarged receptacle. In those members of the Compositae family where total suppression is the rule (Chrysantheminae—according to Rendle, 1925) a partial reversal from the flowering condition can involve their reappearance (Schwabe, 1951).

The temporary lapse of apical dominance referred to above would appear to coincide with this temporary supremacy of cauline development, but this dominance is re-established as soon as foliar structures arise on the new axillary cauline meristem; the new 'foliar' type of development being represented by the floral organs themselves. Although the underlying mechanism is, obviously, not yet understood, even in part, it would seem likely that auxin production and transport may be causally involved. If the young, bilaterally symmetrical, organs (usually leaves) are the source of the apical auxin production, perhaps especially in their earlier stages of development (e.g. Snow, 1937), a lapse in their formation would explain a 'wave trough' of reduced auxin flow, and consequently reduced apical dominance, and this may then be followed by a new surge when floral organs are being formed in large numbers, such as in the composite inflorescence. A closely similar situation might obtain in the cereal ear between the stages of spikelet initiation and the formation of the glumes. A resulting expression of this behaviour may also be found in the relative internode lengths below an inflorescence in the Compositae. Thus in the Chrysanthemum one, or more commonly several, relatively short internodes are formed below the inflorescences, followed again by very long ones. The length of these latter internodes, however, depends on the presence of the developing florets, and when these are removed the internodes fail to elongate, unless an exogenous auxin supply (IAA in lanolin) replaces them, in which case normal elongation is restored (Schwabe, 1968).

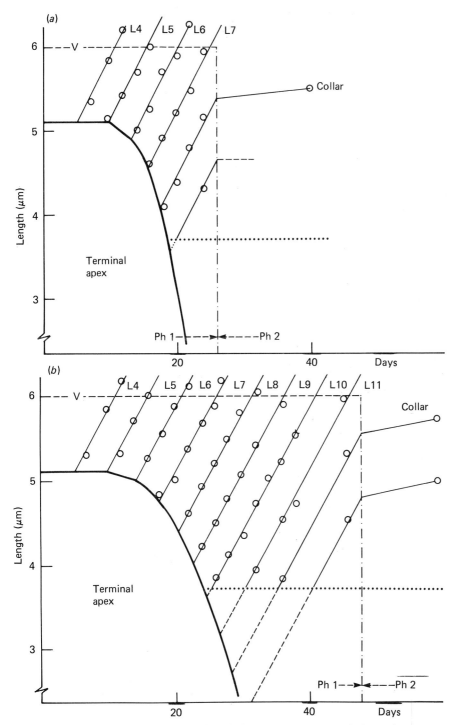

Figure 1.1 Growth rates of successive leaves of wheat cv Timmo on terminal apex in relation to spikelet development in (*a*) long (16 h) and (*b*) short (8 h) days at 15 °C.

The change to floral organ production is nearly always preceded by shape changes of the meristem. This may, at its simplest, be assessed by a ratio of two measurements (e.g. as in the hop plant: *Figure 1.2*) or in terms of size as in the Chrysanthemum, where receptacle formation causes an enlargement of some 400 times the area of the vegetative meristem, and this breaks up into hundreds of small floret apices at that stage.

The transition to floral development thus seems to involve a series of correlative events and changes that occur before, during and after evocation is initiated—generally as a consequence of a signal from the leaves.

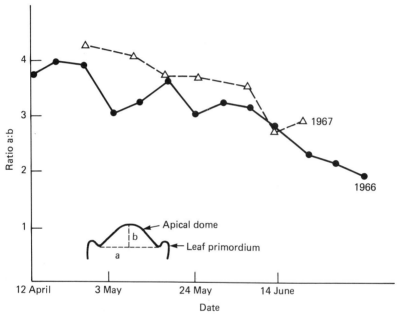

Figure 1.2   Changes in apical diameter (μm) and the ratio of diameter: height of apical dome with time in the hop, *Humulus lupulus* cv Fuggle.

The interaction of the meristem and the signal received

The initial stimulus causing this morphological switch appears to originate generally in the leaves, at least where photoperiodic control is involved, although in such plants as *Rafflesia* there must be other sources.

There have been many attempts during the long search for the flowering mechanism to identify the first site of response in the meristem. It may not have seemed unreasonable to regard the meristem in the vegetative state as relatively undifferentiated biochemically, as an agglomeration of more or less identical cells metabolically, with perhaps differing degrees of activity. The stimulation of some target cells, or tissues, by a fairly non-specific trigger could then set off the chain reaction (cascade). However, more probably there are metabolically different tissues in the shoot meristem even though less obvious than the 'quiescent centre' which is often obvious in the root. These may be stimulated into 'action' (possibly faster rates of cell division, or changed planes of division and/or cell expansion). This would suggest that the stimulus could be non-specific, but with a specific target. Equally, it may be that only a specific 'flowering stimulus' could pass along this route and reach the tissue concerned.

The work of Bernier and his group in determining what these changes are and equally Lyndon and co-workers' studies are clearly of the greatest significance here (Bernier *et al.*, 1981; Lyndon and Francis, 1984). As they contribute themselves to this book (Chapters 21 and 24), only a brief reference to their work must suffice. They have shown that there are changes that occur very rapidly in response to the leaf stimulus being received, but do not necessarily lead to the irreversible shift to a new morphogenetic pathway. However, the hope that they could be simply equated with a synchronization of cell cycles has been proved wrong by Lyndon and Francis (1984). While this may not be generally true, it does appear that there are target tissues in the meristem, i.e. groups of cells that become differentially activated and are often referred to as the 'prefloral meristem', which may then be responsible for the shape and/or size changes, temporary loss of apical dominance and for the changed type of organ produced, i.e. floral differentiation. Much effort has gone into discovering the possible changes initiated in terms of nuclear activation and hormonal (cytokinin) effects and also soluble sugar levels, and, if nothing else, they have demonstrated the complexity of the sequence of responses at that stage. As always in these situations, it is far from easy to discern the true sequence of events and to distinguish between cause and effect.

The signal reaching the meristem and its pathway

In all those many species where flowering is triggered, and thereby synchronized, by the external environment, it is an inevitable hypothesis that some stimulus passes from the area, or site of perception, to the growing point where the changes are initiated; hence the search for the very first effects. What kinds of stimulus could reach the meristem? There is the possibility of a physical stimulus, as suggested by Milburn (1979), e.g. hydraulic pressure changes, perhaps with rhythmic fluctuations, in the phloem which could be rapidly transmitted over long distances. The probability of this is, however, slight, firstly because of the rather non-specific nature of such a signal, and secondly because numerous disparate environmental effects may have the same action. It would also be difficult to envisage the operation of such a mechanism when a prolonged period of favourable cycles is needed to reach a threshold. The possibility of electrical charges or potential differences is equally unsatisfactory for similar reasons. This brings one back to the old hypothesis that the signal is a chemical one, and there are then numerous possibilities. It could be a quantitative change in any of several major compounds, e.g. carbohydrate (soluble sugars), amino-acids, or lipids or other components, or combinations of any of them. Once again the non-specificity of such signals argues against their having a primary role, though they may be involved perhaps as a secondary message. The transport of more specific, hormone-like substances still seems more probable. Here, the choice has hovered for many years between the possibility of quantitative changes in one or more of the five known hormones, or by the intervention of an unknown flowering hormone, long-since named 'florigen' by Chailakhyan (1936). There is no need to reiterate the mass of evidence for a graft-transmissible stimulus. The latter suggestion may still be said to have general acceptance. If we put the blame not on hormonal changes themselves but on sensitivity changes of the responding cells and tissues, a possibility that has been stressed again recently (e.g. Hanson and Trewavas, 1982), we need to look for a graft-transmissible signal to modify sensitivity.

The actual pathway and translocation system must permit acropetal transport from the leaf (e.g. against any polar auxin flow) to the meristem. Also it would seem that there must be a quantitative relation, in that a minimum 'amount' of signal is needed—to overcome a threshold. We still know relatively little about the route, though what evidence there is points to phloem transport, probably co-transport with sucrose.

It should be recalled that in many short-day plants there is a need for CO_2 to be available to leaves in the light period. Flowering fails if the leaf is in CO_2-free air. Carbon dioxide cannot be substituted in *Kalanchoe* and *Xanthium* by the major photosynthetic products or amino-acids, etc. None the less, it appears that the effect operates via photosynthesis since substances such as DCMU prevent flowering as well as photosynthesis and *Xanthium* leaves bleached with streptomycin fail to perceive the photoperiodic stimulus.

Inhibition of induction

Inhibition of inductive processes can occur in the leaf where, under favourable conditions, the photoperiod is perceived and the stimulus made; i.e. (1) there may be interference with the establishment of the manufacturing process in the leaf ('factory'); or (2) the interference may be with the working of the factory, i.e. with the production of the end product; or (3) inhibition may result if the export of the stimulus to the target meristem is somehow prevented; and finally (4) the promotive stimulus may be destroyed again, either in the leaf itself or en route to the meristem.

It seems that the establishment of the promoter-producing system in the leaf, so convincingly shown by Zeevaart's (1957a, b) grafting experiments with *Perilla* can be negated by inhibitor effects produced in unfavourable daylengths.

The evidence for such inhibition of the production system by specific inhibitor(s) is strong in numerous short-day plants (Harder *et al.*, 1949; Schwabe, 1959), and the facts established for *Kalanchoe* may be listed here:

1. Each unfavourable long-day (or light break) intercalated among inductive short-days can negate $1\frac{1}{2}$–2 short days.
2. The inhibition acts on the inductive cycles succeeding the inhibitory long day.
3. There is a maximum to the amount of inhibition that may be accumulated (usually reached after two long-day cycles).
4. The effect seems to act in the induced leaf itself.
5. The inhibitor is soluble and can be transferred from one leaf of *Kalanchoe* to another by injection of 'sap' into the intercellular spaces of another leaf undergoing inductive treatment. The natural inhibitor is powerful since no concentration is required for it to have an effect, and it is likely to be a relatively small molecule.

A somewhat similar system of inhibition for long-day plants has been demonstrated by Lang *et al.* (1977), but the evidence is somewhat less detailed than for short-day plants.

Inhibition by preventing the transport of the promoter to the meristem has often been claimed on the basis of interference with the carbohydrate transport from the leaf to the tip, involving the co-transport of promoter and 'sucrose'. This has been supported by evidence from experiments on translocation of labelled carbohydrate which showed correlation with floral stimulus transport (Zeevaart *et al.*, 1977). This situation is being re-investigated in experiments using Chailakhyan's 'half-leaf' method, or situations where a leaf in the unfavourable daylength is situated between the induced leaf and the meristem, and the results reported later in this book (Chapter 25) make it seem less likely that interference with carbohydrate transport is the complete answer.

The basic conclusion that may be drawn from these experiments is that both promoter (florigen?) and inhibitors are involved, but probably *not* in the way of a *balance*, but rather on the basis of an interaction (interference) with the promoter-forming capacity.

Juvenility

A possible definition of juvenile behaviour in relation to flowering would be that the plant is unable to respond to a promotory stimulus from the environment in spite of all external conditions being favourable for sexual reproduction. This condition will persist until maturity is attained—or as has been said, a 'phase change' has occurred. What is this change? It has been suggested (Robinson and Wareing, 1969) that some change must occur in the meristem, but what this change consists of has not been elucidated as yet. Nor is this change always irreversible: partial reversion of scions from mature fruit trees, olives, etc. grafted onto seedling rootstocks has been observed. In this context, it may be suggested that vernalization, known to be perceived by the meristem itself, may be regarded as another method for bringing about this change. A different hypothesis is concerned with the effect of roots on flowering (Schwabe, 1976). In the blackcurrant and the ivy, and probably numerous other species, it would appear that a root-produced gibberellin ascends the stem, but not very rapidly or over a great length, and that this gibberellin is inhibitory to flowering (Schwabe and Al-Doori, 1973; Wareing and Frydman, 1976). Increasing the distance between the apical meristem from its own roots then permits flowering, as does root removal (Krekulé and Seidlova, 1973).

If this root effect can be shown to be widely applicable to juvenile behaviour it would then indicate that failure of plants in the juvenile state to respond to inductive stimuli could be due to the arrival of conflicting messages at the target meristems, i.e. a promotory one and a more powerful inhibitory effect of a gibberellin.

Phytochrome and rhythmic phenomena

Despite the recognition of the enormous importance of phytochrome and its 'setting' to the leaf response and stimulus formation and the probably closely related internal circadian rhythmic changes, it is still not clear how the production of the leaf message is controlled and regulated. However, this topic receives detailed attention later in the book (Chapters 17 and 18).

A synthesis

In seems that over the last decade individual aspects of the physiology of flowering have been pursued in some depth, but no real attempt seems to have been made to integrate the accumulated information, except by the model makers. Mostly, these are represented by combinations of black boxes which help to draw attention to areas of ignorance.

Attempts to synthesize the information from the behavioural patterns gained from numerous different species into one coherent scheme or model would seem to be a forlorn hope were it not for the fact that the final product, stimulus, or 'florigen' (anthesin) appears to be a common end-product in many species. The evidence for 10 this seems strong, when successful graft transmission has been demonstrated between different species, genera and even members of different families. Moreover, the taxonomic proximity of opposite reaction types, even including cultivars of the same species, suggests that a common mechanism, with only quantitative, rather than qualitative reaction differences may be operative in all behavioural types ranging from obligate to quantitative short-day requirements to quantitative and obligate long-day types passing through day-neutral behaviour. A model of this type in terms of biochemical reactions in the leaf leading to the transferable message was put forward by Schwabe and Wimble (1976), in which two bottlenecks were envisaged. In the case of short-day plants this would involve the formation of an enzyme catalysing the final step in the production of the stimulus and its inhibition by an inhibitor, while for long-day plants the limitation was suggested to be concerned with the rates of substrate production. It may be permissible to refer to this schema again, which then seemed to accommodate all the hard, identifiable facts of photoperiodic behaviour (some 30 items). Despite the greatly increased sophistication of our knowledge in some respects, it still does not seem to have been invalidated, and predictions made from the scheme have yielded confirmatory results. These include a shortening of the critical dark period in short-day plants and, perhaps more significantly, the demonstration of a transmissible inhibitor produced in unfavourable daylengths (*Figure 1.3*).

Figure 1.3   A model for the control of flower initiation in long-day and short-day plants (after Schwabe and Wimble, 1976).

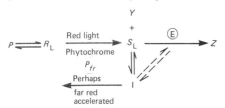

Three important assumptions are made.
1. An intermediate substance R is produced at an accelerating rate from the precursor, $P \rightarrow R$ is then transformed by light to serve as substrate S for an enzyme reaction which ultimately results in the production of the flowering promoter (Z). The light reaction is probably phytochrome (P_{fr})-mediated. There is also an upper limit (R_L) of precursor which can be accumulated and when this is reached production falls to zero, which also results in a maximum level for S, i.e. S_L.
2. Enzyme E is believed to be adaptive—increasing in amount with activity.
3. The inhibition required is produced from S either by a rapid but reversible reaction to the inhibitor I which blocks E (equilibrium being tilted heavily in favour of I), or more simply by excess S acting through substrate inhibition of E. If a molecular change of S to I is adopted, then inhibitor I would competitively block enzyme E and thus stop it from operating. Also, inhibitor I will be lost again at a steady rate not specifically dependent on light or dark or any other condition.

Conditions for each reaction step, rates of each reaction and limitations on product accumulation

Reaction	Condition for reaction	Rate of reaction	Limitation on product accumulation
$P \rightleftharpoons R_L$	none	Sigmoid	Up to maximum R_L
$R \rightarrow S$	Red light, phytochrome P_{fr}	Generally very rapid	S/I equilibrium with I predominating heavily
$S \rightleftharpoons I$	none	Very rapid	S_L and I_L
Loss of I	Perhaps far red light accelerated	Roughly constant	Until I exhausted
$Y + S \rightarrow Z$	Presence of free enzyme E	Dependent on amount of E	As E increases Z will exceed threshold level and accumulate until full flowering
$E + I \rightleftharpoons EI$	none	Rapid, constant	Competitive combination and reversal as level of I declines in dark
E increase	Free E functioning	Dependent on activity	Increasing with activity until full induction
Y	Perhaps dependent on photosynthesis	Unspecified	May become limiting in very long dark periods

Applied aspects

In spite of well over a half-century of research we are still far from having achieved the full potential of flowering control that may one day be possible. In a few valuable 'crops', mainly decorative plants, we can actually manipulate photoperiod, and in a few cases treatment with auxin or with ethylene-generating substances, as in the *Bromeliaceae*, can be commercially applied in controlling onset of flowering. Nevertheless, hope remains that sooner or later a chemical substitute may be found which can simulate endogenous florigen and trigger the floral response. Perhaps the hopes for *inhibition of flowering* may be nearer realization, and this 'negative' control would also have considerable benefits; a few examples suffice: delay of flowering until a larger-sized vegetative plant is reached could have large consequences on seed yield on a per plant basis, and probably also on a per acre basis. Complete prevention of flowering in, say, forage grasses would yield a leafy herbage or hay, and would yield a more nutritional material. Recent studies on early cereal treatment with gibberellin and anti-gibberellins for tiller manipulation have suggested another promising approach. The prevention of bolting in such crops as sugar beet might allow different cultural patterns of sowing, etc. which could affect the establishment of a higher leaf area index at an earlier time in the season and greatly affect yield. Indeed, there are many more possibilities where such morphogenetic control would have large beneficial effects.

References

BERNIER, G. (1979). The sequences of floral initiation. In *La Physiologie de la Floraison* (P. Champagnat and R. Jaques Eds) Paris, Editions du Centre de la Recherche Scientifique

BERNIER, G. and NOUGAREDE. (1979). In *La Physiologie de la Floraison* (P. Champagnat and R. Jaques, Eds), Paris, Editions du Centre de la Recherche Scientifique

BERNIER, G., SACHS, R.M. and KINET, J.M. (1981). *The Physiology of Flowering*, Vol. 2. Boca Raton, Florida, CRC Press

CHAILAKHYAN, M.C. (1936). On the hormonal theory of plant development. *C.R. (Doklady) Acad. Sc. URSS*, **3**, 443–447

HANSON, J.B. and TREWAWAS, A.J. (1982). Regulation of plant cell growth; the changing perspective. *New Phytologist*, **90**, 1–18

HARDER, R., WESTPHAL, M. and BEHRENS, G. (1949). Hemmung der Infloreszenbildung durch Langtag bei der Kurztagspflanze. *Kalanchoe blossfeldiana. Planta*, **36**, 424–438

HUTLEY-BULL, P.D. and SCHWABE, W.W. (1980). Some physiological features in Bread Wheat (*Triticum aestivum L.*) with special reference to the influence of photoperiod and applied gibberellic acid. *British Plant Growth Regulator Group Monograph*, **5**, 111–125

KREKULE, J. and SEIDLOVA, F. (1973). Treatments that enhance flowering in the post-inductive period of a short-day plant, *Chenopodium rubrum. Annals of Botany*, **37**, 615–623

LANG, A., CHAILAKHYAN, M.C. and FROLOVA, J.A. (1977). Promotion and inhibition of flower formation in a day-neutral plant in grafts with a short-day plant and a long-day plant. *Proceedings of The National Academy of Science USA*, **74**, 2412–2416

LYNDON, R.F. and FRANCIS, D. (1984). The response of the shoot apex to light-generated signals from the leaves. In *Light and the Flowering Process* (D. Vince-Prue, B. Thomas and K.E. Cockshull, Eds), pp. 171–189. London and New York, Academic Press

MELVILLE, R. (1962/1963). A new theory of the angiosperm flower. *Kew Bulletin*, **16**, 17(1)

MILBURN, (1979). In *La Physiologie de la Floraison* (P. Champagnat and R. Jaques, Eds), Paris, Editions du Centre de la Recherche Scientifique

RENDLE, A.B. (1925). *The Classification of Flowering Plants*. London, Cambridge University Press

ROBINSON, L.W. and WAREING, P.F. (1969). Experiments on the juvenile-adult phase change in some woody species. *New Phytologist*, **68**, 67–78

SCHWABE, W.W. (1951). Factors controlling flowering in the Chrysanthemum. II. Daylength effects on the further development of inflorescence buds and their experimental reversal and modification. *Journal of Experimental Botany*, **2**, 223–237

SCHWABE, W.W. (1959). Studies of long-day inhibition on short-day plants. *Journal of Experimental Botany*, **10**, 317–329

SCHWABE, W.W. (1968). Effects of photoperiod and temperature on flowering of the Chrysanthemum. *Scientific Horticulture*, **20**, 89–94

SCHWABE, W.W. (1976). Applied aspects of juvenility and some theoretical considerations. *Acta Horticulturae*, **56**, 45–56

SCHWABE, W.W. and AL-DOORI, A. (1973). Analysis of a juvenile-like condition affecting flowering in the blackcurrant (*Ribes nigrum*). *Journal of Experimental Botany*, **24**, 969–981

SCHWABE, W.W. and WIMBLE, R.H. (1976). Control of flower initiation in long- and short-day plants—a common model approach. In *Perspectives in Experimental Biology*, Vol. 2. (N. Sunderland, Ed.), pp. 41–57, Oxford, Pergamon Press

SNOW, R. (1937). On the nature of correlative inhibition. *New Phytologist*, **36**, 283–300

THOMAS, G.G. and SCHWABE, W.W. (1970). Apical morphology in the hop (*Humulus lupulus*) during flower initiation. *Annals of Botany*, **34**, 849–859

WAREING, P.F. and FRYDMAN, V.M. (1976). General aspects of phase-change with special reference to *Hedera helix L. Acta Horticulturae*, **56**, 57–69

ZEEVAART, J.A.D. (1957a). Studies on flowering by means of grafting. I. Photoperiodic induction as an irreversible phenomenon in *Perilla*. *Proceedings, Koniglijke Nederlands Academie van Wetenschapen, Series C*, **60**, 325–331

ZEEVAART, J.A.D. (1957b). Studies on flowering by means of grafting. II. Photoperiodic treatment of detached *Perilla* and *Xanthium* leaves. *Proceedings, Koniglijke Nederlands Academie van Wetenschapen, Series C*, **60**, 332–337

ZEEVAART, J.A.D., BREDE, J.M. and CETAS, C.B. (1977). Translocation patterns in *Xanthium* in relation to long-day inhibition of flowering. *Plant Physiology*, **60**, 747–753.

II

Measurement and prediction of flowering

2

MEASUREMENT AND PREDICTION OF FLOWERING IN ANNUAL CROPS

E.H. ROBERTS and R.J. SUMMERFIELD
*University of Reading, Department of Agriculture, Plant Environment Laboratory,
Shinfield Grange, Reading, Berkshire, UK*

Environmental control of development and behaviour

In most regions where crops are grown the year is divided into at least two seasons—one during which conditions are relatively benign for growth and survival, and the other when they are inimical. Many species of plants have evolved strategies which allow them to minimize or avoid the problems of inclement seasons by adopting dormant and hardy forms—e.g. spores, seeds, underground organs of perennation, and a deciduous habit. Reproduction is often also timed so that vulnerable offspring are not subject to the worst elements of climate.

In cool temperate climates winter is the rigorous season with cold or freezing weather exacerbated by dull and short days. In Mediterranean, sub-tropical and seasonally arid tropical climates it is typically the season of drought and extreme heat which it is more important to avoid. Plants rely on environmental signals to trigger their seasonal responses—either to minimize or to avoid potentially lethal stress or, when conditions are favourable, to become fruitful and multiply. But often it would not be an effective survival strategy to respond directly and immediately to the adverse (cold or dry) or favourable (warm or wet) characteristics of the environment. Although such characteristics may be statistically associated with particular seasons, they are also subject to unseasonal fluctuations. It would not do, for instance, for hardy buds to lose dormancy in response to an unseasonably warm day in mid-winter; the new growth would result in non-hardy tissues susceptible to frost and so likely to be damaged or killed when more seasonably cold conditions returned.

The only completely reliable environmental signal with respect to calendar date at any given latitude (except at the equator) is day-length; and it is therefore not surprising that plants have evolved mechanisms which enable them to respond to photoperiod. But plants make use of temperature signals too—either as a precondition for a subsequent photoperiodic response, as in vernalization, or as a modifier of their photoperiodic response. Thus, although day-lengths have identical durations in autumn and spring, cold-temperature vernalization ensures that winter annuals, biennials and some perennials respond only to long days in the spring. Warm temperature modification of the photoperiodic response enables timing to be finely tuned so that, for example, flowering can occur earlier or later if the season is warmer or cooler than usual.

Types of flowering response to photoperiod

Although it is the duration of the dark period in each diurnal cycle which is of paramount importance, it is conventional to describe photoperiodic responses in terms of day-length. Three main categories of response are recognized: photoperiod-insensitive or day-neutral plants (DNPs), and then two types of photoperiod-sensitivity, short-day plants (SDPs) and long-day plants (LDPs). In addition, within both SDPs and LDPs there are species with obligate (or absolute or qualitative) responses to photoperiod and others with quantitative (or facultative) responses (Vince-Prue, 1975). Several variants additional to these five basic patterns have been reported but it is only necessary to add one of them here, i.e. short-long-day plants (SLDPs), in order to include the photoperiod responses of the major world crops. SLDPs flower soonest if short days are followed by long.

There is not complete unanimity in the definitions of response types and some of the associated terms, and so it is necessary to specify those adopted here. Since, as we have discussed, the ecological essence of photoperiodic responses is in the timing of biological events, we shall define flowering responses in terms of time taken to flower.

For this purpose it is simplest to begin with the responses of plants grown in artificial environments in which the photoperiod in any one environment does not vary with date. Examples of the two major types of photoperiod sensitivity are shown in *Figures 2.1(a)* and *2.1(b)* in which the times taken for a soyabean (*Glycine max*; an SDP) and a chickpea (*Cicer arietinum*; an LDP) genotype to come into flower (f) are shown as functions of photoperiod. Later, we shall show that these typical forms of the photoperiodic response curves both of SDPs and LDPs are a consequence of a linear relationship between photoperiod and rate of progress towards flowering (the reciprocal of the time taken to flower, $1/f$). These linear relationships are of negative slope in the case of SDPs (*Figure 2.1(c)*) and positive for LDPs (*Figure 2.1(d)*). Accordingly, when data are plotted as days to flower (f) in relation to day-length, there is a typical L-shaped curve for obligate LDPs (*Figure 2.1(b)*) while that for an obligate SDP is an L-shape in mirror image (*Figure 2.1(a)*). An obligate SDP is capable of flowering only when the day-length is shorter than a particular value and conversely, an obligate LDP is only capable of flowering when the day-length is longer than a particular value. What these respective values are can be most clearly seen in *Figures 2.1(c)* and *2.1(d)*. The abscissa intercepts are those photoperiods in which rates of progress towards flowering are zero, i.e. when plants would take an infinite time to flower (or, in other words, they would be permanently vegetative).

Interestingly, in these two examples the photoperiod that it is necessary to exceed for flowering to occur in the LDP is just under 8 h (*Figures 2.1(d)*) and in the SDP the photoperiod that must not be exceeded for flowering to occur is just under 14 h (*Figure 2.1(c)*). These examples make it clear that, despite some misleading statements to the contrary, SDPs can often flower in relatively long days and LDPs can often flower in relatively short days. The essential difference between an obligate LDP and an obligate SDP is whether it is necessary for flowering for a particular night length to be exceeded or for it not to be exceeded, respectively: the fact that a species is categorized as either LDP or SDP tells us nothing about the duration of this critical night period.

In contrast to the obligate responses to photoperiod shown in *Figures 2.1(a)* and *2.1(b)*, a quantitative response is one in which flowering is delayed but not prevented in less inductive photoperiods. Such a quantitative response can be conceived as a secondary limitation placed upon a standard obligate response curve in which there is

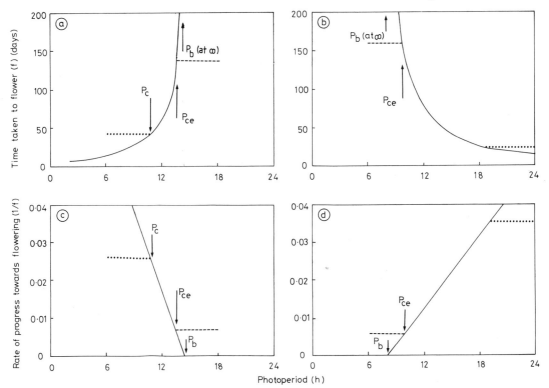

Figure 2.1 Typical photoperiodic responses of SDPs (*a, c*) and LDPs (*b, d*) when grown continuously in constant photoperiods. The upper graphs (*a, b*) show the time taken to flower (*f*) as a function of photoperiod, whereas the lower graphs show the same data (*c, d* respectively) when rate of progress towards flowering (1/*f*) is shown as a function of photoperiod. The SDP example (*a, c*) was calculated for a soyabean accession TGx 46-3C in photoperiods from 8 h:20 min to 15 h at a mean temperature of 22.5°C (Hadley *et al.*, 1984). The LDP example was calculated for chickpea cultivar JG62 in photoperiods from 12 to 15 h at a mean temperature of 15°C (from Roberts *et al.*, 1985). The solid curves in each case show the underlying response; the dotted line shows the minimum time taken to flower the height of which is dependent on temperature; the broken line shows the maximum time taken to flower in plants with quantitative responses only, the height of which is independent of temperature and photoperiod (plants with obligate responses do not have this limitation). Whereas the dotted and broken lines in (*a*) and (*c*) represent the actual response of TGx 46-3C, the corresponding lines in (*b*) and (*d*) are arbitrary and hypothetical since the experimental photoperiods did not cover these extremes. The base (P_b), critical (P_c) and ceiling (P_{ce}) photoperiods are defined in the text.

an overall maximum delay in flowering which is never exceeded (broken line in *Figures 2.1(a)* and *2.1(b)*, which can, alternatively, be thought of as a minimum rate of progress towards flowering (broken line in *Figures 2.1(c)* and *2.1(d)*).

One further complication to the basic patterns needs to be mentioned. In the description so far it has been implied that the whole time from sowing to flowering is subject to photoperiodic control. In fact, during the vegetative period there is typically a pre-inductive phase (sometimes known as a juvenile or basic vegetative phase; Vergara and Chang, 1976) and a post-inductive phase, neither of which is sensitive to photoperiod. Between these two is an inductive phase which is sensitive to photoperiod and varies in duration (number of diurnal cycles required to complete it) depending on the photoperiod experienced (Roberts *et al.*, 1986). The analyses of these three phases will be discussed later but their relevance here is that, strictly speaking, the responses described so far probably refer to the inductive phase rather than the whole period from sowing to flowering. This would not significantly affect the form of the response curves illustrated in *Figure 2.1* except in the most strongly inductive photoperiods where the actual duration of the inductive phase is very short and so the respective durations of the pre- and post-inductive phases are relatively long. The main effect of this is that in the response curves shown in *Figure 2.1* there will be minimum times to flower (dotted lines) which override the basic response curves (solid lines). The period represented by the values of these horizontal dotted lines on the ordinate is determined largely by mean temperature (which may affect all phases of development) and is known to occur in the SDP cowpea (Hadley *et al.*, 1983a) as well as in the specific example of soyabean illustrated in *Figures 2.1(a)* and *2.1(c)* (Hadley *et al.*, 1984). The corresponding dotted line (i.e. the minimum time to flowering) in LDPs typically intercepts the basic response curve at photoperiods between 17 and 20 h, as shown by investigations on wheat, barley, oats, rye, rape and flax (Major, 1980). Thus in most LDPs this limitation is often well outside the range of photoperiods which the crops normally experience during the pre-flowering period.

A concept commonly used in photoperiodism is that of critical day-length. Different definitions have been proposed by various authors; others have assumed that it is generally understood what is meant without definition. Hence there is some confusion. If obligate photoperiodic response curves of the type shown in *Figures 2.1(a)* and *2.1(b)* were truly L-shaped, or the mirror image (i.e. if they were exact right-angles) there would be no problem: the definition of critical day-length for an SDP would be that day-length which, if exceeded, prevents flowering; and the converse would apply to an LDP. But the curves in reality are not of this form (with a horizontal line at some point changing abruptly to a vertical line) and so other definitions must be sought.

In previous papers (Hadley *et al.*, 1983a; 1984) we have defined the critical photoperiod, P_c, in SDPs as the interface between a temperature response surface and a photoperiodic response surface, which will be explained with respect to *Figures 2.4(b)* and *2.4(c)*; the corresponding point has been marked in *Figures 2.1(a)* and *2.1(c)*. It can be seen that, according to this definition, the critical photoperiod is that photoperiod at or below which the time to flower is minimal and is not affected by variations in day-length; photoperiods longer than P_c delay flowering. This seems a logical definition and we advocate it since there are objections to some of the more obvious alternatives. For example, in a quantitative SDP one could have chosen the ceiling photoperiod, P_{ce}, i.e. that photoperiod at and above which the greatest delay in flowing occurs or, put another way, below which flowering is hastened; but this definition can only apply to quantitative SDPs and not to those with an obligate response, and it is therefore of limited application (*Figures 2.1(a)* and *2.1(c)*). An alternative would be the base photoperiod, P_b, i.e, that photoperiod at which, if exceeded, progress towards flowering is zero so that the plant remains permanently vegetative; but this only applies to obligate responses and therefore is also of limited application (*Figures 2.1(a)* and *2.1(c)*).

It might be considered that analogous arguments should apply to LDPs, i.e. that the critical photoperiod should be considered as that photoperiod above which time to flowering is minimal and not affected by further increases in photoperiod, and below which flowering is delayed. However, as we have already mentioned, where there is evidence of such a point, its value is typically greater than the maximum day-lengths experienced by crop species (especially between sowing and flowering) in the regions where crops are commonly grown (*see Table 2.2*). And so, it may not be of great practical significance in LDPs. Furthermore, since the angle enclosed by the two lines which define the critical photoperiod is often very obtuse (e.g. *Figure 2.1(b)*) then its determination experimentally may be somewhat imprecise.

An alternative definition of critical photoperiod in LDPs could be the ceiling photoperiod, i.e. that photoperiod in which there is maximum delay in flowering (*Figure 2.1(d)*). But this would also often lie outside the normal range of photoperiods experienced by crops and, in any case, is only applicable to quantitative LDPs.

The base photoperiod, P_b, in LDPs is that photoperiod below which progress towards flowering is zero, so that the time taken to flower would be infinite, i.e. the plants remain vegetative. This point can only be a reality in plants with an obligate response to photoperiod; but a 'nominal' base photoperiod can be calculated by extrapolation in LDPs with quantitative responses and, as we shall show later, this proves to be a useful concept in predicting times to flower in natural environments.

Recently (Roberts *et al.*, 1986), we have used the term critical photoperiod in LDPs to describe the equivalent of the base photoperiod but specifically when its value is calculated in relation to the inductive phase since this, it is argued, could be considered to be a physiological definition. But, since the examples shown in *Figure 2.1* are based on total times from sowing to flowering (rather than on the inductive phase), we have not indicated a critical photoperiod for the LDP, but the analogy would be P_b which, when based on the total period from sowing to flowering, we have called 'nominal base photoperiod' (Roberts *et al.*, 1986).

Types of flowering response to temperature

Temperature may affect times from sowing to flowering in three distinct ways:

1. There may be a specific cold-temperature hastening of flowering known as vernalization.
2. Over a wide range of temperatures the rate of progress towards flowering increases with increasing temperature to an optimum temperature at which flowering is most rapid (responses over this sub-optimal range of temperatures may be modified by photoperiod or vernalization).
3. At supra-optimal ('stressful') temperatures flowering is progressively delayed as temperatures get warmer.

GEOGRAPHICAL ORIGINS AND ADAPTATIONS OF VERNALIZATION AND PHOTOPERIODIC RESPONSES

Vernalization typically occurs at temperatures between -5 and $16\,°C$ but with maximum effect between 0 and $8\,°C$ (Whyte, 1946). The duration of the cold treatment needed to saturate the vernalization response can vary from a few to about 60 days, or much longer, depending on species and genotype and presumably also on temperature; but comprehensive quantitative data are lacking. Nevertheless, the literature suggests that, as with photoperiodism, there are obligate and quantitative responses to vernalization (Thomas and Vince-Prue, 1984).

The term vernalization was originally applied to treatments given to imbibed seeds or to seedlings, but eventually it was extended to include cold treatments which have similar effects when applied to plants during later stages of development—or even to earlier stages of development when the seed is still attached to the mother plant. It is often applied, for example, to cold treatments given to some biennials and perennials which may be unresponsive to similar treatments imposed on seeds or seedlings.

In temperate climates the growing season is centred around the spring and summer months when days are warm and long. It is usually during this period when it is ecologically most appropriate for flowering to occur. Accordingly, the vast majority of crop species that originate from the temperate latitudes are LDPs. Some are also sensitive to vernalization and only respond to long days after they have experienced a cold period. This dual response presumably evolved to combat premature flowering in plants derived from seeds shed in the summer and which would experience relatively long days in early autumn. Such a dual response is common to many winter cultivars (i.e. autumn-sown cultivars) of all the temperate cereal species. But, in some of these winter forms, a period of short days may substitute for, or may be required instead of, or may enhance, the effect of cold temperatures. Because short photoperiods applied during the early stages of crop development can have similar effects on flowering to cold-temperature vernalization, this response is sometimes referred to as 'short-day vernalization', and gives rise to the photoperiodic category of short-long-day plants (SLDPs), i.e. plants in which earlier flowering is dependent on exposure to short followed by long days.

As mentioned earlier, in more tropical climates the growing season is generally delimited by lack of rain. The rainy seasons are a consequence of the adiabatic cooling of the warm rising air in the Inter-Tropical Convergence Zone, which tends to coincide with those latitudes where heat from the sun is more intense, i.e. regions where the sun is overhead at midday (Dennett, 1984). And so, within those regions approaching the Tropics of Cancer and Capricorn, say typically between latitudes 10–30 °N and 10–30 °S, the annual distribution of rainfall tends to be monomodal, with the wettest period coinciding roughly with the longer day-lengths—except, of course, in the desert areas which encroach into these regions. Rainy seasons, and so growing seasons, start in advance of the longest day and crops become reproductive towards the end of the wet season when day-lengths are shortening (e.g. Wien and Summerfield, 1980). So far as we are aware, and not surprisingly, all tropical and sub-tropical annual crops are SDPs. Of course, DNPs also occur, as they do in temperate crops, but these tend to be the products of selection for special agricultural purposes.

The known responses of some of the major field crops of temperate and tropical origin are shown in *Table 2.1* (the thirteen major grain legume crops have been excluded since these have been classified in the same way in *Table 15.1* of Chapter 15).

We conclude, therefore, that most crops of temperate origin are LDPs or DNPs, with or without a vernalization response; and that all crops of tropical or sub-tropical origin are SDPs or DNPs and, as expected since they do not normally experience cold temperatures, are insensitive to vernalization. The only exceptions to these generalizations of which we are aware are *Chrysanthemum morifolium* a native of China (Purseglove, 1968) but a complex hybrid derived from several wild species (Cathey, 1969), and *Allium cepa* which is only known in cultivation but thought to have a primary gene pool in Afghanistan (McCollum, 1974). Both of these species have been classified as quantitative SDPs in which flowering is nevertheless accelerated by vernalization (Vince-Prue, 1975). However, in *Allium cepa* the response is somewhat equivocal: flower initiation is apparently unaffected by day-length or, in one genotype at least, may even show a quantitative long-day response; but further floral development can be indirectly inhibited by long days because they stimulate bulbing

Table 2.1 PHOTOTHERMAL RESPONSES OF MAJOR FIELD CROPS (RESPONSES OF THE GRAIN LEGUMES ARE SHOWN IN CHAPTER 15)

Species	Common name	Centre of origin	Latitude	Short day DN O	Short day DN Q	Long day O	Long day Q	Vernalization response O	Vernalization response Q
Dactylis glomerata	Cocksfoot	West Europe	40–55°N			*			*
Lolium perenne	Ryegrass	West Europe	40–55°N			*	*	*	*
Trifolium repens	White clover	West Europe	40–55°N			*			*
Avena sativa	Oats { spring	Central Europe	45–50°N			*			
	winter					*			*
Secale cereale	Rye { spring	Turkey, NW Iran, Armenia	35—45°N			*	*		
	winter					*		*	*
Triticum aestivum	Bread wheat { spring	Fertile crescent	30–37°N				*		
	winter						*	*	*
Hordeum vulgare	Barley { spring	Fertile crescent	30–37°N				*		
	winter					*	*	*	*
Papaver somniferum	Poppy	Turkey	37–42°N				*		*
Brassica oleracea	Cauliflower	Mediterranean/Asia Minor	30–45°N				*		*
Brassica napus	Rape	East Mediterranean	30–45°N				*		*
Beta maritima	Beet	Mediterranean?	30–45°N			*	*		*
Spinacia oleracea	Spinach	SW Asia	30–45°N			*	*	*	*
Lactuca sativa	Lettuce	Mediterranean	30–45°N		*	*	*	*	*
Allium cepa	Onion	Afghanistan	30–35°N	*	*	*	*	*	*
Daucus carota	Carrot	Afghanistan	30–35°N			*			*
Raphanus sativus	Radish	East Mediterranean	30–45°N		*		*		*
Linum usitatissimum	Flax	India/Afghanistan	25–35°N				*		*
Helianthus annuus	Sunflower	SW USA	30–45°N	*	*		*		
Stylosanthes guianensis	Stylo	S America	5°N–30°S	*			*		
Chrysanthemum morifolium	Chrysanthemum	China	20–35°N	*	*				*
Nicotiana tabacum	Tobacco	South Bolivia, North Argentina	15–30°S	*	*				
Capsicum annuum	Chilli pepper	Central America	10–30°N	*	*				
Desmodium spp.	Desmodium	Tropics		*	*				
Amaranthus caudatus	Grain amaranth	Central Andes	10–30°S	*					
Solanum tuberosum	Potatoes	Central Andes	10–30°S	*	*	*			
Gossypium hirsutum	Cotton	Central America	10–25°N	*	*				
Sesamum indicum	Sesame	Ethiopia or India	5–24°N	*	*				
Ricinis communis	Castor	Ethiopia or India	5–24°N	*	*				
Coffea arabica	Arabica coffee	Ethiopia	5–15°N	*	*				
Pennisetum americanum	Bulrush millet	West Africa	10–15°N	*					
Sorghum bicolor	Sorghum	Ethiopia or W Africa	5–15°N	*	*	*			
Zea mays	Maize	Central America	10–30°N	*	*	*			
Oryza sativa	Rice	SE Asia	15–25°N	*	*	*			
Saccharum spp.	Sugar cane	New Guinea	0–10°S	*					

O = obligate response; Q = qualitative response.

which, through the ensuing mechanical compression, can physically restrict the enlargement of floral parts (Rabinowitch, 1985).

There are two other apparent exceptions in which SDPs appear to have originated at higher latitudes than is typical. *Table 2.1* suggests that it is rare for SDPs to originate outside the 30 ° parallels. But the reputed centres of origin of soyabean and sunflower, north China and south-west USA respectively, are north of this area. However, we suspect that these apparent exceptions are more the result of regional perturbations in climate than biological anomalies. Because of the special continental land configurations, the summer monsoon areas in China are pushed further north than is typical so that there is a marked monomodal rainfall distribution in north China with a peak in July and August preceded by a dry winter and spring. Consequently the growing season is severely limited by water and crops tend to flower during shortening days. The climatic constraints are therefore not dissimilar from the tropics. In the south-west of the USA where sunflower is said to have originated, the pattern is less clear. There is less rainfall and more variation in it so that conditions vary more from site to site and season to season. The arguments are therefore less clear but again there tends to be more rain during the summer months; consequently similar arguments could apply to the selection of the short-day reponse in sunflower.

Finally the case of *Stylosanthes guianensis* is interesting. It has a very wide latitudinal distribution in South America, at least 5 °N to 30 °S, and types from about 25 °S are LDPs whereas those from nearer the equator are SDPs (Cameron and Mannetje, 1977). Thus unusually, within a single species, both responses are found, possibly selected during the early spread and adaptation of the species.

THE GENERAL EFFECT OF TEMPERATURE IN THE SUB-OPTIMAL RANGE

The second and more general effect of temperature appears to be fundamental to the majority of plant species and affects almost all developmental processes. Most simply stated it is that, in the absence of other complicating factors such as photoperiodism or vernalization, the rate of development increases linearly with temperature. Furthermore, as we seek to show later, such responses are also evident in photoperiod-sensitive species when the separate effects of photoperiod and vernalization are disentangled from those of post-vernalization temperatures.

Before discussing this fundamental response further, it has to be pointed out that rates of development cannot be observed or measured directly. And so, the end-point of a developmental process has to be timed and, as with determining the rate of movement (speed) of a vehicle or the rate of an enzyme reaction, it is the reciprocal of the time taken to reach the destination or end-point which is a measure of the rate of progress. The relation between the time taken to reach an end-point and rate of progress towards it is not linear. Therefore, if the effect of temperature on rate of progress towards flowering is linear, then the relation between temperature and the time taken to flower cannot be (*Figure 2.1*).

It is not clear why the relationship between temperature and the rate of development processes should be linear (Monteith, 1981). Most chemical reactions on which developmental processes must depend conform to the Arrhenius relationship in which the logarithm of the rate of reaction is a linear function of the reciprocal of absolute temperature. We suggest that a possible (albeit, perhaps, only partial) explanation for a linear relationship between temperature and rate of developmental processes is the consequence of two underlying principles. First, over the range of temperatures within which plant development typically occurs, the relation between temperature (°C) and the reciprocal absolute temperature (°C + 273) would not be detectably different from linear in biological experiments; and so it would not matter whether temperature or the reciprocal of absolute temperature is taken as the independent variable. Secondly, relative growth rates and rates of plant development often relate linearly to the logarithm of the concentrations of limiting substances (e.g. of growth substances or of minor elements at sub-optimal concentrations). Thus, if a linear change in temperature affects the logarithm of the concentration of some limited factor, as implied by the Arrhenius relation, and if a logarithmic change in concentration of the limiting factor causes a linear change in rate of development, then it would be expected that the effect of temperature on rate of development would also be linear.

Whether or not this speculation is correct, it is a fortunate circumstance that the rate of developmental processes is usually a linear function of temperature, because upon this depends the concept of temperature-sum or thermal time, which enables developmental progess to be monitored and forecast in fluctuating temperatures such as occur in natural environments.

The concept of thermal time was, and still is, often referred to as the summation of 'heat units' but this terminology is misleading since it is temperature and not heat which is measured. The idea probably originated more than 250 years ago, with Réaumur in 1735 (Abbe, 1905; Aitken, 1974), but it was not exploited significantly until it was applied to the climatic zoning of crops on a continental scale in North America at the end of the nineteenth century. The notion is that the fulfilment of a developmental process in a plant requires that it experience a certain number of units (day-degrees) of thermal time above a base temperature characteristic of that process. Thermal time is calculated as the sum of daily mean temperatures above a given base temperature (Monteith, 1981). When temperature summations were first used, base temperatures were either not subtracted from mean daily values or it was assumed for no special reason—which amounts to the same thing—that the base temperature was 0 °C (Abbe, 1905). Also, it was and still is, apparently, not always realized that the validity of the concept depends on there being a linear relationship between temperature and rate of development (reciprocal of the time taken for the developmental process to be completed). It is also this relationship that enables the base temperature and thermal time (temperature-sum) to be defined accurately.

For example, there are many circumstances in which the time taken to flower (f) can be considered as a rate ($1/f$) and then related linearly to mean temperature $\bar{T}$ (°C) as follows:

$$1/f = a + b\bar{T} \tag{2.1}$$

where a and b are constants. The base temperature, T_b, is the maximum temperature at or below which the rate of progress towards flowering ($1/f$) is zero (or the time to flower, f, is infinity); its value is given by the relation:

$$T_b = -a/b \tag{2.2}$$

And the thermal time (°C d) required for flowering, θ_f, is given by:

$$\theta_f = 1/b \tag{2.3}$$

In practice, the main interest is usually in predicting times taken to flower, rather than rates of progress towards it. Although the one value may be readily transformed to the other, analysing responses in terms of rate has at least three advantages. First, a consideration of rate rather than time is probaby one step closer to the basic cause of developmental processes: the reason why an event happens in a short time is because the rate of progress was rapid, and not vice versa. Secondly, because the relation between temperature and rate is typically linear, data from only a few environments (theoretically only two) are required to define and quantify it. Thirdly, the two constants that define the rate relation (Equation 2.1) can be applied, via thermal time (Equations 2.2 and 2.3), to predict times of flowering in natural environments in which temperatures fluctuate.

In spite of these advantages, the concept of thermal time has been little used until recently, except by growers contracted to the vegetable processing industry who have used various systems of 'heat units' to predict dates of harvest and the timing of successive plantings of crops such as peas, beans (*Phaseolus* spp.) and maize destined for canning or freezing. A preoccupation with 'dates' in the traditional 'heat unit' approach to the management of what are often relatively minor crops (or minor uses of otherwise major crops), coupled with a neglect of photoperiodic effects on development in these crops, probably contributed to the proliferation of rather vague or arbitrary temperature summation methods (e.g. *see* Arnold, 1959; Wang, 1960; Cross and Zuber, 1972). Furthermore, in the case of major world crops, it seems that the discovery of photoperiodism by Tournois (1914) and its rediscovery by Garner and Allard (1920) probably drew attention away from temperature as a factor modulating development. Also, because of the influence of photoperiodism and vernalization on flowering there are many circumstances in which the concept of thermal time will not apply without some modification.

The concept of thermal time, which depends on the application of Equation 2.1, is most clearly seen in developmental processes unaffected by photoperiod. One process in which the most detailed analyses have been made concerns rates of seed germination (e.g. Garcia-Huidobro *et al.*, 1982a, b; 1985; Covell *et al.*, 1986; Ellis *et al.*, 1986). These studies have shown clearly that the concept can be used not only to analyse the times taken for seeds to germinate from a base to an optimum temperature, but that there is also a linear decrease in rate of germination with increase in temperature above the optimum temperature to a ceiling temperature at which the rate of germination is again zero. We shall return to the latter concept later when dealing with supra-optimal temperatures for flowering, after concluding our discussion of the effects of sub-optimal temperatures in circumstances when photoperiodism does not interfere.

In those species classified as SDPs (*Tables 2.1* and *15.1*) there are two circumstances in which photoperiodism does not obscure the effects of temperature on flowering: first, in photoperiod-insensitive genotypes (*see Figure 2.4(a)*), and secondly in photoperiods shorter than the critical value in SDPs (*see Figures 2.4(b)* and *2.4(c)*) (Hadley *et al.*, 1983a, b; 1984). In each of these cases the flowering response is modulated solely by mean temperature according to Equation 2.1. Analogous examples occur in LDPs. For example, some barley and non-vernalized faba bean genotypes are insensitive to photoperiod and respond to temperature as indicated by Equation 2.1 (Cooper *et al.*, 1987; Ellis *et al.*, 1987e). And similar responses are found in LDPs in photoperiods longer than the ceiling value (*see Figure 2.5(a)*; recalculated from data in Berry and Aitken, 1979). The concept of thermal time can also be applied, with some modification, as we discuss later, in circumstances where photoperiod also affects flowering. But before dealing with such situations, the special effects of very warm temperatures, which may be stressful, need to be considered.

THE EFFECT OF TEMPERATURE IN THE SUPRA-OPTIMAL RANGE

There is obviously an upper temperature limit above which Equation 2.1 is no longer valid. Beyond some point on the response curve, which may be defined as the optimum temperature, T_O, it would be expected that further increases in temperature would be detrimental and would decrease the rate of progress towards flowering. Although there is much less quantitative information on the effects of supra-optimal temperatures on rates of progress towards flowering than there is for effects on rates of germination mentioned earlier, that evidence which is available suggests that the

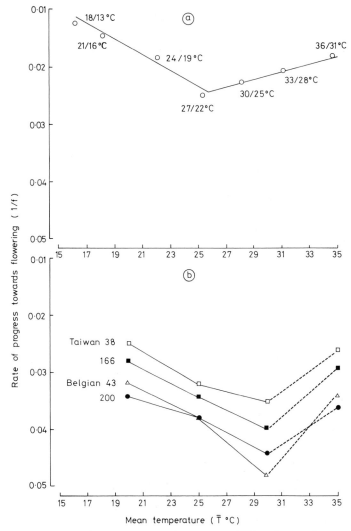

Figure 2.2 Relations between mean temperature ($\overline{T}$°C) and rates of progress towards flowering ($1/f$) of: (*a*) the photoperiod-sensitive soyabean cultivar Wayne grown in long (16 h) days in the various day and night temperatures indicated (calculated from data presented in Shibles *et al.*, 1975); and (*b*) four photoperiod-insentitive soyabean genotypes grown in natural days which varied in duration from 13 h 30 min to 14 h 20 min (calculated from data presented in Inouye *et al.*, 1979).

effect is similar: i.e. at supra-optimal temperatures the rate of progress towards flowering is linearly related to mean temperatures but, instead of the relation being positive as.it is at sub-optimal temperatures, it is now negative. An example is shown for the soyabean cultivar Wayne in *Figure 2.2(a)* (calculated from the data of Shibles *et al.*, 1975), which has an optimum mean temperature close to 26 °C, and for diverse genotypes of soyabean in *Figure 2.2(b)* (calculated from data presented in Inouy *et al.*, 1979) where the optimum mean temperature, in each case, is close to 30 °C. Wayne is a cultivar recognized to be well adapted to the 'Corn Belt' states in the USA (and

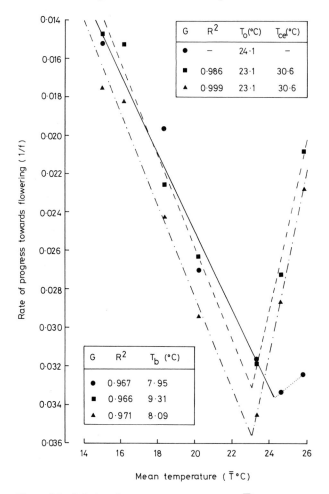

Figure 2.3 Relations between mean temperature ($\overline{T}$°C) and rates of progress towards flowering ($1/f$) of three cultivars of *Phaseolus vulgaris* said to be (Wallace, 1985) either lowland adapted (JU-80-13; ● — ●) or highland adapted (San Martin; ■ – – – ■ and Negro Patzicia; ▲ —·— ▲) when grown at elevations from 50 to 1800 m in Guatemala. The fitted lines are based on Equation 2.1 for $\overline{T} < T_0$ and for $\overline{T} > T_0$. Tabulated information within the body of the figure are, bottom left, genotype symbol (G), coefficient of multiple determination (R^2) for each fitted line when $\overline{T} < T_0$, and the base temperature for flowering (T_b) calculated from Equation 2.2; top right, the r^2 values are for the fitted lines when $\overline{T} > T_0$, the optimum mean temperature for flowering (T_0), and the ceiling temperature for flowering (T_{ce}), as described in the text. All data (recalculated from Wallace, 1985) are mean values of experiments conducted in 1982 and 1983.

especially within the approximate range of latitudes from 40 ° to 42 °N; Scott and Aldrich, 1970) whereas the genotypes investigated by Inouye *et al.* are of tropical or sub-tropical origin.

The fact that optimum mean temperatures for flowering vary, not only within species for genotypes of different origin, but also between species is illustrated by comparisons of *Figures 2.2(a)* and *2.2(b)* with *Figure 2.3*. Here, we have replotted the data on *Phaseolus vulgaris* reported by Wallace (1985) for three cultivars, two said to be highland adapted and the other said to be lowland adapted when grown at various elevations in Guatemala. It is clear from *Figures 2.3* that the optimum mean temperature (T_O) for flowering in all three cultivars is within 0.9 °C of 24 °C. Furthermore, the base (T_b) and ceiling (T_{ce}) temperatures (i.e., the cooler and warmer values at which extrapolations indicate that rates of progress towards flowering would be zero) are also apparently very similar, and close to 8.5 °C and 30.6 °C, respectively.

Effects of photoperiod on rates of progress towards flowering and interactions with temperature

The previous section has shown several advantages in considering the effects of temperature in terms of the rate of progress towards flowering. It is therefore somewhat surprising that, until recently, an analogous approach has seldom, if ever, been used to quantify the effects of photoperiod on flowering. Furthermore, since both temperature and photoperiod can modulate flowering of a given genotype, it is important to quantify the response to each factor in the same way for it is only then that the possibility of interactions can be explored. Moreover, there is a school of thought which maintains that the concept of biological interactions is only valid with respect to rate processes (Drury, 1980).

These were the arguments that led us to the approach which we are using in experiments designed to quantify flowering responses to the combined effects of temperature and photoperiod in controlled environments. So far, seven species have been investigated—two SDPs, cowpea (Hadley *et al.*, 1983a) and soyabean (Hadley *et al.*, 1984) and four LDPs, chickpea (Roberts *et al.*, 1985), lentil (Summerfield *et al.*, 1985a), barley (Cooper *et al.*, 1987) and faba bean (Ellis *et al.*, 1967). Furthermore, we have begun to reanalyse published data for several other species, including both SDPs (e.g. *Phaseolus vulgaris; Figure 2.3*) and LDPs (e.g. *Pisum sativum; see Figure 2.5(a)*). Our reanalyses, in terms of $1/f$, usually simplify the traditional approach, which uses f, and we believe offer a more plausible explanation of photo-thermal effects on flowering. A similar approach, i.e. one based on rate processes, has been used for the analysis of field data by Gallagher *et al.* (1983) and advocated by France and Thornley (1984); but it is difficult, if not impossible, to discern the separate effects of temperature and photoperiod from field data without supporting evidence from investigations in controlled environments.

The details of the experimental design of our investigations in controlled environments have varied according to species, but several principles underlie them all. First, preliminary investigations are undertaken to identify cultural techniques, especially light quality (combination of lamp types), which ensure that pot-grown plants closely resemble those grown in the field in terms of morphology, phenology and, in the case of grain legumes, in their relative reliance on symbiotically fixed and inorganic nitrogen (e.g. Summerfield *et al.*, 1985b). Secondly, different day and night temperatures are used and, in order not to depart too far from the typical phase-shift in the natural diurnal temperature cycle, which lags asymmetrically behind the natural photoperiod, the switch from 'night' to 'day' temperature in the controlled environments is programmed to occur 2 h after lights-on, while the switch to 'night' temperature coincides with lights-off. Thus, although thermoperiod does not coincide precisely with photoperiod it is deliberately partially confounded with it.

Of course, when photoperiods differ as well as day and night temperatures within the same experiment, then confounding of some sort between photoperiod and temperature is inevitable; but deliberate confounding can be exploited.

A typical orthogonal design may consist of 3 photoperiods × 2 day temperatures × 2 night temperatures. Such a design will reveal whether there are separate specific effects of day temperature or night temperature and thermoperiod and, if not (as has been found in each of the seven species investigated so far), the flowering response can be analysed as a function of mean temperature. And, because of the variation in thermoperiod as well as in both day and night temperatures implicit in the design, there are twelve different mean temperatures which are sufficient to quantify accurately the response surface for the effects of mean temperature on flowering. Such designs are therefore powerful and economical. In each species, several genotypes, selected to represent a wide geographical range of origin, are simultaneously investigated; and when LDPs are investigated, two additional treatments, vernalized and non-vernalized seeds, are normally included.

Figures 2.4 and *2.5* show typical examples to illustrate the range of responses encountered in these investigations; each column of graphs shows the response of a single genotype of each species. The results for any one genotype are presented in four different ways, since different presentations emphasize different features. The upper graphs in each example (*Figures 2.4(a–c)* and *2.5(a–c)* are isometric three-dimensional displays and gives the most comprehensive view of rates of progress towards flowering as functions of both photoperiod and mean temperature. (Note that the ordinate scales are drawn so that $1/f$ increases downwards, and accordingly times taken to flower (f) increase upwards.) The second series of graphs in each example (*Figures 2.4(d–f)* and *2.5(d–f)*) are the relations between photoperiod and $1/f$ at three different mean temperatures (this convention corresponds to that used in *Figures 2.1(c)* and *2.1(d)* but where the results for only one mean temperature were shown). Below (*Figures 2.4(g–i)* and *2.5(g–i)*) the same data are replotted so that f is the ordinate scale instead of $1/f$ (corresponding to the convention used in *Figures 2.1(a)* and *2.1(b)*). Finally, the bottom series (*Figures 2.4(j–l)* and *2.5(j–l)*) show the relations between $1/f$ and mean temperature at three different photoperiods.

The first example is for a photoperiod-insensitive genotype of cowpea (*Figure 2.4(a,d,g,j)*) but similar examples could have been illustrated for other photoperiod-insensitive genotypes of different species, e.g. the soyabean cultivar Fiskeby V (Hadley *et al.*, 1984). In these photoperiod-insensitive genotypes it is clear that rate of progress towards flowering is a linear function of mean temperature and that this

---

Figure 2.4   Photo-thermal effects on flowering in three SDPs: (*a*), (*d*), (*g*) and (*j*), a photoperiod-insensitive genotype of cowpea (TVu 1009); (*b*), (*e*), (*h*) and (*k*), a photoperiod-sensitive genotype of cowpea (TVu 1188); and (*c*), (*f*), (*i*) and (*l*), a photoperiod-sensitive genotype of soyabean (TVx 46-3C). Data for cowpea (*Vigna unguiculata*) are from Hadley *et al.* (1983a); those for soyabean are from Hadley *et al.* (1984). In figures other than the isometric projections (*a*, *b* and *c*), broken lines indicate individual responses to photoperiod at different values of mean temperature or vice versa; solid lines indicate where the responses overlap.

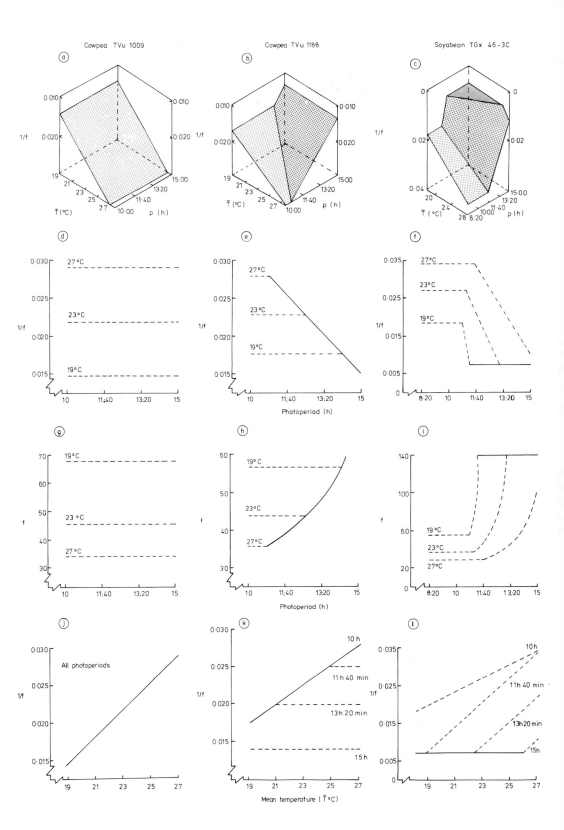

response is unaffected by day-length. Is is also unaffected by total radiation receipts because, in the experimental design used, photoperiod is confounded with total radiation.

Accordingly, in this and similar examples the concept of base temperature and thermal time (Equations 2.1–2.3) may be applied without complications in natural environments where both temperature and photoperiod vary—a proposition confirmed by comparisons made between data from controlled environments and the field (Summerfield and Roberts, 1985).

Figures 2.4(b,e,h,k) show a typical example of a photoperiod-sensitive cowpea genotype. This probably represents the simplest type of a SDP response. Clearly, there is an underlying (or basic) temperature response similar to that shown by photoperiod-insensitive genotypes (*Figure 2.4(a)*). But this basic temperature response is overlaid with a photoperiodic response in which rate of progress towards flowering is a linear negative function of photoperiod and so can be described as:

$$1/f = a' + c'P \tag{2.4}$$

where P is photoperiod (h) and a' and c' are constants. Once the values of the constants in Equations 2.1 and 2.4 have been determined for genotypes of this response category, the time taken to flower in any given constant environment can be predicted by solving both Equations 2.1 and 2.4 for that environment and taking whichever is the larger value of f given by either equation. In other words, in this type of response the time taken to flower is determined *either* by temperature *or* by photoperiod (whichever calls for the greater delay in flowering) but in no circumstances by both factors.

If the critical photoperiod (P_c) is defined in SDPs as that photoperiod which, if exceeded, causes a delay in flowering, then it will be seen that geometrically it corresponds with the line of intersection of the basic temperature-determined plane and the photoperiod-determined plane in *Figure 2.4(b)*. This line can be defined algebraically as:

$$P = P_c \text{ when } a + b\overline{T} = a' + c'P$$

and so:

$$P_c = (a + a' + b\overline{T})/c' \tag{2.5}$$

Note that, since c' has a negative value in SDPs, the critical photoperiod *decreases* with increase in temperature (in this genotype by about 27 min per °C increase in mean temperature). The extent to which P_c varies is a simple geometric consequence of the relative sensitivity of the genotype to temperature (b) and to photoperiod (c'). In genotypes that are very sensitive to photoperiod (where the photoperiodic plane in a three-dimensional projection of the type shown in *Figure 2.4(b)* is almost vertical), there is very little variation in P_c with temperature.

Figure 2.5　Photo-thermal effects on flowering in three LDPs: (*a*), (*d*), (*g*) and (*j*), a photoperiod-sensitive genotype of pea (MU 35); (*b*), (*e*), (*h*) and (*k*), a photoperiod-sensitive genotype a lentil (ILL 4605); and (*c*), (*f*), (*i*) and (*l*), a photoperiod-sensitive, vernalized land race of barley (Arabi Abiad). Data for pea are from Berry and Aitken (1979); those for lentil (*Lens culinaris*) are from Summerfield *et. al.* (1985a); and those for barley (*Hordeum vulgare*) are from Cooper *et al.* (1987). Otherwise, explanation as for *Figure 2.4*.

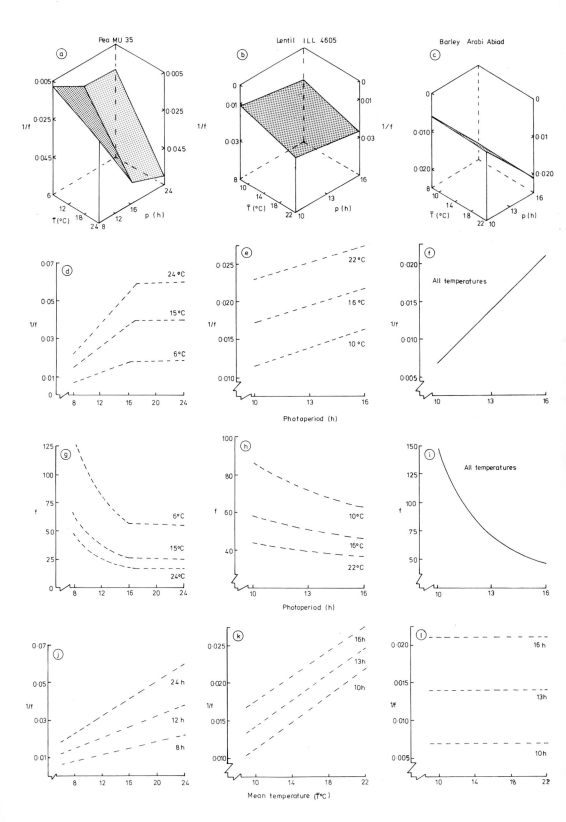

If a natural environment were such that the day-length experienced was always shorter than the critical photoperiod (which is improbable) then time to flower in a fluctuating environment could be determined entirely on the basis of thermal time. On the other hand, if the environment were such that the photoperiod experienced was always longer than the critical photoperiod (which is more probable) then time to flower could be determined by an approach analogous to the thermal time concept, namely by calculating a base photoperiod, P_b, as follows:

$$P_b = -a'/c' \tag{2.6}$$

and so the photoperiodic time ($h\ d$) for flowering, φ_f, which is the number of hours of light in excess of the base photoperiod which has to be accumulated before flowering occurs, is given by:

$$\varphi_f = 1/c' \tag{2.7}$$

Equations 2.6 and 2.7 offer a practical approach to predicting flowering in natural environments in which photoperiod varies, providing the day-length is always longer than the critical photoperiod. Although this approach involves an assumption which is almost certainly incorrect (Roberts *et al.*, 1986), i.e. that plants are sensitive to photoperiod throughout the period from emergence to flowering, in practice this will not necessarily lead to serious problems in applying the concept to natural environments. However, we shall discuss this difficulty later. Here, we simply recognize that P_b and φ_f probably have less fundamental significance than T_b and θ_f since it is probable that temperature affects rates of development throughout the life of plants and so no similarly questionable assumption is involved.

A final implication of the type of response illustrated in *Figure 2.4(b)* is that it is possible to estimate the values of the four constants that define the entire response surface from experiments in only four different environments. (Indeed, just three environments could be used provided that they included two different photoperiods *and* two different mean temperatures.) *Figure 2.4(b)* shows that data obtained from two environments with different photoperiods and a temperature regime which is warm, but not necessarily controlled, will define the photoperiodic constants (a' and c') without interference from temperature. While two environments of different mean temperature in photoperiods, again not necessarily constant, shorter than the critical value, will define the thermal constants (a and b) without interference from photoperiod. By these means the separate genetically controlled photoperiodic and temperature responses can be isolated and so germplasm can be screened for relative sensitivity of both responses using very simple schemes involving field experiments (Hadley *et al.*, 1983a, b; 1984).

Figure 2.4(c) shows a typical example of a photoperiod-sensitive soyabean genotype. In photoperiods shorter than the critical value the type of response is very similar to cowpea, i.e. it conforms to Equation 2.1. And, like cowpea, it also shows a negative linear relationship between photoperiod and rate of progress towards flowering in photoperiods longer than the critical value. But, unlike cowpea, temperature also has some effect on rate of progress towards flowering in regimes where $P > P_c$, although there is no evidence of interaction between P and $\overline{T}$ in this response plane. Accordingly, this photoperiodic response plane for soyabean is only slightly more complicated than that described for cowpea (Equation 2.4), and may be written as:

$$1/f = a' + b'\overline{T} + c'P \tag{2.8}$$

where a', b' and c' are the constants which apply when day-lengths are longer than the critical photoperiod. (Equation 2.4 for cowpea can be considered as a special case of Equation 2.8 in which the value of b' is zero.)

Finally, in some soyabean genotypes there appears to be a minimum rate of progress towards flowering (or a maximum time to flower) irrespective of photo-thermal conditions; in other words they have a quantitative rather than an obligate response to photoperiod. This limitation is represented by a horizontal plane in *Figure 2.4(c)* (and *see* Major, 1980).

The fact that temperature also has a positive effect on rates of progress towards flowering in photoperiods longer than P_c results in a slight rotation of the photoperio-dic-response plane with respect to the ordinate compared with the response in cowpea. In turn, this alters the angle of intersection with the basic temperature-response plane (which is exposed in photoperiods shorter than P_c) such that variations in temperature in soyabean have smaller effects on the value of the critical photoperiod as compared with cowpea. Furthermore, in contrast to cowpea, the value of the critical photoperiod *increases* in warmer environments (often by about 11 min °C^{-1}). Algebraically, the photoperiod becomes critical when the value of f given by Equation 2.1 is equal to that given by Equation 2.8. Hence, the critical photoperiod, P_c, in soyabean is given by:

$$P_c = [a - a' + \overline{T}(b - b')]/c' \tag{2.9}$$

These arguments are considered in greater detail elsewhere (Hadley *et al.*, 1984).

Another consequence of temperature having an effect on progress towards flower-ing in day-lengths longer than the critical photoperiod is that the base photoperiod is not independent of temperature and neither is the base temperature for this plane independent of photoperiod. The implications of this complication are discussed later in relation to LDPs, where temperature can have relatively greater effects on the form of the photoperiodic response plane.

Whilst it is clear that mean temperature can strongly modulate rates of progress towards flowering in soyabean in photoperiods both shorter and longer than the critical photoperiod, many accessions and cultivars are so extremely sensitive to photoperiod (their relative sensitivity is given by the value of the photoperiod slope constant, c', in Equation 2.8) that this factor is the major determinant of the timing of flowering. Cregan and Hartwig (1984) emphasized the importance of these differences in relative sensitivity to photoperiod for soyabean adaptation and cultivar develop-ment. They quantified the effect of photoperiod on the time from sowing to flowering, f, using linear and quadratic models. Their approach was statistically successful (R^2 values between 0.87 and 0.97) but not easy to relate to the biology of photoperiodism. Moreover, when the original responses (*Figure 2.6(a)*) are replotted in the form of rates of progress towards flowering in relation to photoperiod (*Figure 2.6(b)*), a much simpler, and biologically more plausible, model emerges, i.e. Equation 2.4 applies; with R^2 values for different genotypes of between 0.87 and 1.00. (Equation 2.4 rather than Equation 2.8 was applied since the cultivars were grown under similar temperature conditions.) We have also found that a re-analysis (not shown here) of the times to flowering of diverse genotypes of mung bean (*Vigna radiata*) in a wide range of photoperiods (Bashandi and Poehlman, 1974) is as successful as that illustrated in *Figure 2.6*.

It is interesting to note the relative sensitivity to photoperiod of flowering in the soyabean cultivar Biloxi (*Figure 2.6(b)*)—one of the classical genotypes used in studies of photoperiodism (Garner and Allard, 1923; Hamner, 1969). This cultivar has the

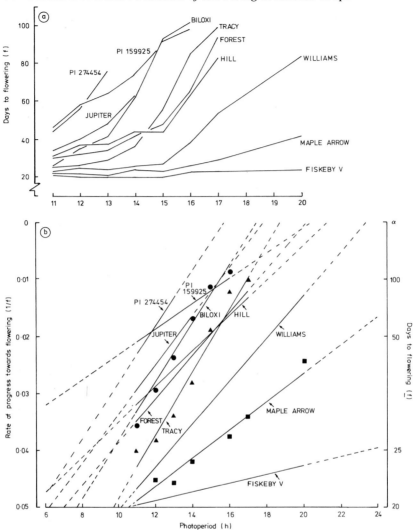

Figure 2.6 (*a*) Relations between photoperiod and days from emergence to flowering (*f*) in each of ten diverse genotypes of soyabean, i.e. cultivars adapted to various regions in the USA and Canada, plant introductions and experimental lines (data replotted from Cregan and Hartwig, 1984); and (*b*) the same data as in (*a*) replotted in the form of 1/*f* in relation to photoperiod. The lines for each genotype are linear regressions based on Equation 2.4; original data points are shown for three genotypes (● Biloxi; ▲ Tracy; ■ Maple Arrow) to indicate the typical goodness of fit of the model (R^2 values of between 0.87 and 1.00). Extrapolations to the abscissa for PI 274454, Hill and PI 159925 are 5.6, 5.2 and −2.0 h, respectively.

largest photoperiod constant, c′, of the ten genotypes tested—supporting our earlier suggestion that such dramatic responses to photoperiod, being assumed (incorrectly) to be typical of the species, have probably led to the neglect of temperature as a factor that also controls development in the major world crops. Whether this speculation is correct or not, the observations of Garner and Allard more than 60 years ago (1923) and, more recently, of Salisbury (1982), have not been sufficiently heeded: 'temperature is undoubtedly the most important environmental factor in relation to the action of the light period on plant growth'; and 'In virtually every case where studies have been extensive enough, photoperiodic response has been readily modified in one way or another by changing temperature'.

Among the nine soyabean genotypes evaluated by Hadley *et al.*, 1984, critical photoperiods decreased from 10–12 h at a mean temperature of 24 °C to 9–10.5 h at a mean temperature of 20 °C. And so, with the prevailing monthly mean temperature experienced during the investigation by Cregan and Hartwig (1984), i.e. 18.6–24.9 °C, the conditions were probably always on that part of the photo-thermal response surface which is modulated mainly by photoperiod and never on that part modulated solely by temperature (except for Fiskeby V and, perhaps, Maple Arrow).

The fact that critical photoperiod varies with mean temperature—as described by Equations 2.5 and 2.9—does not support the traditional viewpoint that P_c 'remains relatively resistant to changing temperatures' (Schwabe, 1971; Vince-Prue, 1975; Salisbury, 1982). A reappraisal of earlier data on species such as *Xanthium* and *Pharbitis* (where changes in f have often been related to the temperature experienced during darkness) in terms of $1/f$ and $\overline{T}$ would seem to be justified.

We now turn to photo-thermal responses of LDPs (*Figure 2.5*). Data published by Berry and Aitken (1979) for a photoperiod-sensitive genotype of pea are reanalysed in *Figure 2.5(a)*. This response is essentially a mirror-image of the example shown of a photoperiod-sensitive genotype of soyabean (*Figure 2.4(c)*) except that, within the range of photoperiods studied (which more than covers the range of photoperiods experienced by the pea crop in natural environments), a plateau of maximum delay in flowering is not evident. Indeed it is possible that this cultivar would have been shown to be an obligate LDP if sufficiently short photoperiods had been included in the experiment. That part of the response surface which responds to photoperiod is described by Equation 2.8, except that in the case of pea the value of the photoperiodic constant, c', is positive, since it is an LDP, rather than negative as it is in SDPs. The fastest rate of progress towards flowering in this example is achieved with a ceiling photoperiod of just over 16 h. In photoperiods longer than P_{ce}, i.e. in the most inductive conditions, the rate of development is now limited by temperature and accordingly the underlying temperature response is revealed which, again, is described by Equation 2.1.

In passing, it is worth noting that flowering data for the pea cultivar, Alaska, obtained over the same range of photoperiods and temperatures, showed complete insensitivity to photoperiod (Berry and Aitken, 1979) so that the form of the three-dimensional isometric projection is identical with that in *Figure 2.4(a)* except that, of course, the numerical values are different.

Figure 2.5(b) shows the response typical of the lentil crop. In this species we are not yet aware of a genotype that is either completely insensitive to photoperiod or to temperature (Summerfield *et al.*, 1985a)—but 400 genotypes will be evaluated in 1986. The wide ranges of each of photoperiod and mean temperature which have been comprehensively investigated to date (10–16 h and 9–20 °C) cover most, and perhaps all, agricultural situations but are not as great as the ranges investigated for pea (8–24 h and 6–24 °C). And so, it may be for this reason that a ceiling photoperiod has not been reached exposing a response plane for lentil where only temperature has an effect. Certainly, had this narrower range of conditions been applied to the pea example, a ceiling photoperiod would not have been revealed. Nevertheless, we have chosen to illustrate lentil as an example, since later we use experiments on this species to analyse the photoperiod-sensitive and insensitive phases of development. Furthermore, over a similar range of conditions, the type of response shown for lentil appears to be common in other LDPs, e.g. in chickpeas (Roberts *et al.*, 1985) and in some, but not all, cultivars of barley (Cooper *et al.*, 1987) and of faba bean (Ellis *et al.*, 1987).

Barley has proved to be an extremely variable species within which a wide range of response types has been identified from the diverse range of genotypes examined in factorial experiments including day-lengths from 10 to 16 h and mean temperatures from 9° to 22 °C (Cooper *et al.*, 1987). For example, we have identified cultivars that are apparently completely insensitive to photoperiod, to temperature and to vernalization; others that are sensitive to photoperiod and not to mean temperature, but in which the photoperiod response only becomes marked after vernalization; and yet others that are insensitive to vernalization but their response to both photoperiod and temperature is reminiscent of that in the pea example shown in *Figure 2.5(a)* (Berry and Aitken, 1979). It is not possible to give examples of all these response types here, and so we have chosen to illustrate that of a land-race which, after imbibed seeds have been vernalized for 30 h at 1 ±0.5 °C, is sensitive to photoperiod but not to mean temperature (*Figure 2.5(c)*). This response provides a contrast to that of cowpea TVu 1009 shown in *Figure 2.4(a)*, which is sensitive to mean temperature but not to photoperiod.

Taken altogether, the first impression of *Figures 2.4* and *2.5* might be that the effects of photoperiod and temperature on flowering are dauntingly complex. However, we believe that, once the responses to both temperature and photoperiod are conceived as rates of progress towards flowering, several simplifying principles emerge which may be summarized as follows:

1. Rates of progress towards flowering, almost without exception, tend to be linear functions of either temperature, or photoperiod, or both.
2. The responses to both environmental determinants can be expressed simultaneously as response surfaces. It then becomes apparent that one plane is sufficient to describe the response of photoperiod-insensitive plants (DNPs); whereas in photoperiod-sensitive species (both SDPs and LDPs), a second plane is also required to describe obligate responses; and to these a third plane has to be added to describe quantitative responses.
3. The first of these planes, the basic temperature response, is probably common to almost all annual crops; it is not affected by photoperiod (at least over the range of day-lengths which cover all agricultural situations) and describes the underlying response of flowering to mean temperature when photoperiod does not interfere. Accordingly, Equation 2.1 describes the typical response of DNPs, and also of photoperiod-sensitive species when photoperiods are sufficiently inductive for the limiting factor to become temperature. This occurs in photoperiods shorter than the critical day-length in SDPs and in the photoperiods longer than the analogous ceiling photoperiod in LDPs.
4. The second plane, the photoperiod-temperature sensitive response, is common to all photoperiod-sensitive species, whether SDPs, LDPs obligate or quantitative. This plane emerges in photoperiods longer than the critical photoperiod in SDPs or in day-lengths shorter than the ceiling photoperiod in LDPs. Within this plane there is a positive response to photoperiod in LDPs and a negative response to photoperiod in SDPs; at the same time there is normally a positive response to mean temperature—although this may vary in magnitude, even to zero (as in the case of cowpea; *Figure 2.4(b)*). The magnitude of the c' constant which describes

the slope of the plane with respect to day-length, i.e. the photoperiod sensitivity, varies among species and cultivars; but the highest values are found amongst tropical (short-day) plants, presumably since it is these that need to respond to relatively small differences in day-length (*Table 2.2*).

5. The third plane, which may be considered as an environment-insensitive plane, describes the minimum rate of progress towards flowering (or, if preferred, the maximum delay in flowering) in quantitative photoperiod-sensitive plants. There is generally no response to either mean temperature or to photoperiod, and so the plane is horizontal in the case of the three-dimensional projections shown in *Figure 2.4*.

6. The generalizations above refer to 'non-stress' temperatures; at supra-optimal temperatures there is a negative linear relation between mean temperature and rate of progress towards flowering. It is not yet known how this response is affected by photoperiod.

7. Since the three possible components of the overall response surface for rates of progress towards flowering are normally planes, the implication is that there are no interactions between mean temperature (up to the optimum) and photoperiod when photo-thermal responses are expressed as rates within the range of combinations of mean temperature and photoperiod described by any one of the planes. (Interactions would, however, occur if data were analysed in the traditional manner, i.e. in terms of days to flowering.) When dealing with rates, interactions only emerge when intersections between planes are transgressed.

8. Because responses to mean temperature and to photoperiod with respect to rates of progress towards flowering can be described as planes, it follows that variable daily contributions of the environment towards the induction of flowering can be treated as additive increments. This has already been discussed in terms of thermal time for the contribution of temperature; we later discuss how photoperiod can be similarly treated (i.e. in terms of photoperiodic time) and combined with mean temperature to predict durations to flower under natural and therefore variable conditions.

Table 2.2 VARIATION IN DAY-LENGTH WITH LATITUDE

Latitude	Day-length, sunrise to sunset			Day-length, including civil twilight*		
	Longest day	*Shortest day*	*Annual variation in day-length*	*Longest day*	*Shortest day*	*Annual variation in day-length*
(°N or S)	*(h:min)*	*(h:min)*	*(h:min)*	*(h:min)*	*(h:min)*	*(h:min)*
0	12:07	12:07	0:00	12:50	12:50	0:00
10	12:43	11:33	1:10	13:29	12:19	1:10
20	13:21	11:14	2:07	14:11	11:44	2:27
30	14:05	10:34	3:31	15:01	11:04	3:57
40	15:01	9:46	5:15	16:01	10:22	5:39
50	16:23	8:42	7:41	17:53	9:20	8:33
60	18:52	5:53	12:59	22:25	7:48	14:37
70	24:00	0:00	24:00	24:00	0:00	24:00

* Civil twilight begins before sunrise and ends after sunset when the true centre of the sun is 6 degrees below the horizon; it corresponds to an illuminance of about 3–4 lux. Day-length defined in this way is that which is probably perceived by most but not all species (*see* Chapter 15).

In these descriptions of the combined effects of mean temperature and photoperiod on flowering, we have avoided discussing how the responses are modified by vernalization in the case of LDPs. This is because, so far, insufficient data are available for a clear picture to have emerged (e.g. compare Murneek and Whyte, 1948 with Napp-Zinn, 1984). In a few species (e.g. celery) plants may be virtually insensitive to photoperiod after vernalization (Salisbury, 1982), but in general it seems that vernalization tends to allow subsequent stimulatory effects of photoperiod, or of warm temperatures, or of both, to be expressed. In lentils, at least, the resulting response surfaces for flowering of plants grown from vernalized seeds may still be described as planes (Summerfield *et al.*, 1985a). And with faba beans and barley, some genotypes become acutely sensitive to photoperiod and/or mean temperature only after vernalization; when grown from non-vernalized seeds they are either insensitive or far less sensitive to photo-thermal conditions during vegetative growth (Ellis *et al.*, 1987b and Cooper *et al.*, 1987, respectively).

Changes in photoperiod sensitivity during development

Whereas it is known that temperature may affect rates of development throughout the life of a plant, it has generally been acknowledged that there is a 'juvenile' phase in most plants during which they are unresponsive to day-length. It is often claimed that after this juvenile phase has ended plants tend to become increasingly sensitive to photoperiod. For example, the number of long days required to elicit flowering response in the LDP *Lolium temulentum* decreases as the plants get older: for example, when plants were grown in 8 h days, after they were 1 week old, then six 24 h diurnal cycles of continuous light (i.e. six 24 h photoperiods) were needed for all the replicates to respond whereas when they were 6 weeks old only a single 24 h cycle was required (Evans, 1960). However, unless it is also shown that an 8 h day is shorter than the base photoperiod, this interpretation is open to question because, as we have shown earlier, any photoperiod longer than the base photoperiod can have some inductive effect, as least up to the ceiling photoperiod. Within the range from base to ceiling photoperiod, although longer photoperiods are more inductive than shorter ones, all photoperiods are inductive to some extent. Furthermore, it follows from Equations 2.4 and 2.6–2.8 that the effects of consecutive photoperiodic cycles which are longer than the base photoperiod in LDPs, or shorter than the critical photoperiod in SDPs, are additive. And so in many experiments it could appear as though plants become more sensitive to photoperiod as they age, whereas this apparent increase in relative sensitivity may be a product of the number of cycles already received and the relative inductiveness of those cycles. We believe, however, that this is not a function of plant age but of the sum total of inductive stimulus the plants have experienced.

This argument does not preclude the existence of a photoperiod-insensitive juvenile phase. Furthermore, it also seems probable that once the flowering stimulus has been irreversibly induced there will be an inevitable delay from the completion of induction until the appearance of the first flower. This implies the existence of a post-inductive phase which is also insensitive to photoperiod.

In order to test these ideas, a series of reciprocal-transfer treatments were imposed on three genotypes of lentil of diverse origin. The experiments comprised 22 photoperiodic treatments in which plants were transferred from short days (normally 10 h) to long days (16 h) or vice versa at 4-day intervals and the consequences for flowering were recorded. All three genotypes responded similarly to the treatments and differed only in relative sensitivity: *Figure 2.7* shows the response of the most sensitive genotype, the land-race Syrian Local Large (Roberts *et al.*, 1986).

After sowing, there was an initial pre-emergence phase, g, during which the seedlings were in the dark. This was followed by a pre-inductive phase after the seedlings had emerged, *j*, and which lasted about 8 days (i.e. from time E_m to X in *Figure 2.7*) during which time photoperiod had no significant effect on the time taken to flower: compare the similarity of the results of treatments **I** and **J** (which either had no long days (**I**) or only 4 long days (**J**) during this period) with those of treatments **K** to **Q** (in which this first phase consisted entirely of long days).

The pre-inductive phase was followed by a period during which the plants were very sensitive to photoperiod, and which therefore may be called the inductive phase, *i*. It began at time X and its duration depended on the photoperiodic regimes experienced thereafter. In a continuous succession of 16 h photoperiods the inductive phase was completed at time Y; and so in *Figure 2.7* the inductive phase in treatments **I** to **Q** is from X to Y. This can be deduced by noting the similarity of the results of treatment **Q** (in which 12 days of 16 h photoperiodic cycles immediately following the

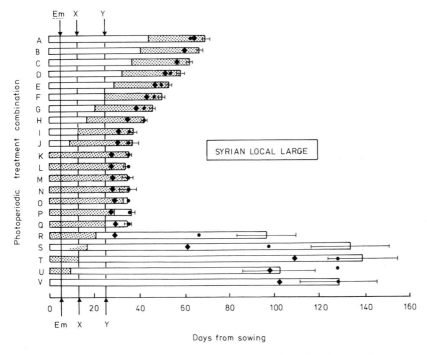

Figure 2.7 Effects of various photoperiod treatments (**A–V**) on days from sowing to the appearance of first flowers (complete histograms) and to first flower buds detectable by eye ( ) in the lentil land race Syrian Local Large grown at a mean temperature of 21.25°C. Open and stippled areas within individual histograms are 10 h and 16 h photoperiods, respectively. Horizontal lines spanning times to first flowers are standard deviations. *Em* and *X* denote seedling emergence and the end of the pre-inductive phase, respectively; *Y* marks the end of the inductive period in continuous 16 h photoperiods (i.e. in treatments **I–Q**; *see* text). Theoretical times from sowing to first flower (days from emergence to first flower + 5 days) calculated according to the method described in the text are shown as ● within or adjacent to individual histograms.

pre-inductive phase were sufficient to minimize the time taken to flower) with those of treatments **I** to **P** (in which the 16 h cycles after the pre-inductive phase were continued after time *Y*). It is therefore clear that 12 days of 16 h photoperiods satisfy the inductive phase in this genotype when grown at a mean temperature of 21 °C. This conclusion is confirmed by the fact that when 10 h days were substituted for 16 h cycles during any part of the period *X* to *Y*, then flowering was delayed (i.e. in treatments **F**, **G** and **H**, or even more dramatically if one compares treatments **R**, **S** and **T** with treatment **Q**).

Although 12 days of 16 h photoperiods are required to induce flowering in the shortest time when they immediately follow the pre-inductive phase, a flower bud takes time to develop and open, and so there is a delay after induction is completed until the first flower appears. The duration of this post-inductive phase, *d*, can be estimated by calculating the time taken to the appearance of the first flower after the inductive phase has been completed. This is most clearly seen in those treatments where the pre-inductive phase was immediately followed by 12 cycles of 16 h photoperiods, i.e. in treatments **I** to **Q**. In all these treatments the post-inductive phase (which started at time *Y*) was of almost exactly the same duration—10 days— despite large variations amongst the treatments in the number of 10 h and 16 h cycles given during this final phase. It follows that the post-inductive phase is not affected by photoperiod.

In *Figure 2.7*, the duration of the inductive phase, *i*, can be calculated by subtracting the durations of the pre-emergence phase (5 days), the pre-inductive phase (8 days), and the post-inductive phase (10 days) from the total time taken to flower. From this calculation it can be shown that the inductive phase lasted for 12 days when 16 h photoperiods were applied throughout it; whereas its duration was 105 days in continuous 10 h photoperiods. These values can be applied in an equation, based on Equation 2.8, but in which the temperature can be ignored (since it did not vary between treatments), as follows:

$$1/i = k + c''P \tag{2.10}$$

where k and c″ are constants, the values of which were calculated as -0.113491 and 0.012302, respectively, by simultaneous equations.

From these results the base photoperiod, P_b, was calculated (by analogy with Equation 2.6) using the relation $-k/c''$, and has a value of 9.23 h. The total number of inductive hours of light, i.e. the photoperiodic time, required to be accumulated above the base photoperiod each day in order to complete the inductive phase, i.e. to induce flowering, is given (by analogy with Equation 2.7) by $1/c''$ and, in this case, has a value of 81 h.

Having calculated the base photoperiod and the photoperiodic time for flowering, the expected durations of the inductive phase can then be calculated for all the treatments in *Figure 2.7*. For example, in treatment **A**, where the plants were transferred from 10 h photoperiods to 16 h photoperiods 45 days after sowing, the first 13 days will have occurred during the pre-emergence and pre-inductive phases and so will have no effect, leaving 32 days of 10 h photoperiods which would have been inductive. To calculate their contribution to photoperiodic time, 9.23 h has to be subtracted from the photoperiod experienced each day; thus their total contribution will have been $32 \times (10 - 9.23) = 24.6$ h. Since the photoperiodic time for flowering is 81 h, this leaves 56.4 h to be contributed after transfer of the plants to the 16 h photoperiods. The number of days required to complete induction in this regime is therefore given by $56.4/(16 - 9.23) = 8$ days.

Finally, the total number of days to flower, *f*, is calculated by adding the following components: a pre-emergence phase of 5 days; a pre-inductive phase of 8 days; an inductive phase comprising 32 days of 10 h photoperiods followed by 8 days of 16 h photoperiods, i.e. a total of 40 days; and a post-inductive phase of 10 days. Accordingly, the total calculated time to first flower is 63 days, whereas the observed time was 70 days. It is clear that while there are minor discrepancies between observed and calculated durations to flowering, as in the example just described, the values calculated on this basis are generally very close to those observed (*Figure 2.7*). It is also clear that these simple assumptions also account very adequately for what otherwise would be a rather perplexing distribution of *f* amongst the various treatments as indicated by the histograms.

This evidence suggests that there is no change in photoperiod-sensitivity *per se* during the inductive phase, and that its duration is a simple consequence of the number and duration of the photoperiodic cycles which are required to complete the induction stimulus. Futhermore, similar conclusions may also apply to barley (Roberts *et al.*, 1987).

The development of predictive models for flowering in natural environments

As the example for lentils illustrates, large experiments are needed to quantify the duration of the inductive phase. And so, in order to evaluate the photo-thermal characteristics of flowering in large numbers of genotypes—a common objective in crop breeding—we have suggested a cruder approach based on Equation 2.8 in which the duration of the inductive phase is not separately identified and quantified. In this case, when the analysis of flowering responses in natural environments is based on the whole of the time taken to flower, *f*, instead of on the inductive phase, *i*, we suggest that, in order to avoid confusion, a different terminology is used because the analogous values obtained will be different from the base photoperiod and photoperiodic time as calculated on the basis of the inductive phase. Thus we now recommend the terms 'nominal base photoperiod' and 'nominal photoperiodic time' when calculations are based on the entire period from sowing to flowering.

Calculations show that when Equation 2.8 is used, nominal base photoperiods can often have negative values at ambient temperatures and so cannot easily be related to photoperiodic theory; they are, instead, simply arbitrary values which result from the inclusion of non-photoperiodically modulated entities (*g, j* and *d*) in their calculation. This fact, we suggest, is a plausible explanation for the 'negative base temperatures (which are) not feasible in the physiological sense' which have been calculated for flowering in sunflowers (Goyne *et al.*, 1977) and elsewhere (Arnold, 1959).

We have shown (Roberts *et al.*, 1986a) that when Equation 2.8 applies, the nominal base photoperiod is given by $-(a' + b'\overline{T})/c'$. This value, subtracted from the actual photoperiod experienced in any day will give the contribution of that day to nominal photoperiodic time. And so:

$$l_d = P_d + (a' + b'\overline{T_d})/c' \tag{2.11}$$

where l_d is the contribution each day to nominal photoperiodic time, P_d is the photoperiod experienced, which is sunrise to sunset in lentils (*see* Summerfield and Roberts, chapter 15), $\overline{T_d}$ is the mean temperature that day, and a', b' and c' are the constants whose values are obtained from Equation 2.8 (Roberts *et al.*, 1986).

It follows from Equations 2.8 and 2.11 that in this case the nominal base photoperiod varies with temperature; but the nominal photoperiodic time which has to be accumulated above this nominal base photoperiod for flowering to occur is given by $1/c'$ and thus is independent of temperature. This model has been shown to predict time of flowering with considerable accuracy for spring sowings of lentils at Tel Hadya in Syria and at Leonessa in Italy. It has yet to be tested for winter sowings (which can, in some years, lead to severe frost damage during the vegetative period) and further work is necessary to quantify the effects of vernalization in lentils and other LDPs more accurately.

WHEAT MODELS

Since bread wheat is the most important world crop it is not surprising that many attempts have been made to model the growth and development of this species (e.g. Robertson, 1968; Halsse and Weir, 1970; Porter, 1983; Weir *et al.*, 1984; French and Hodges, 1985; Porter, 1985). Despite these intensive efforts internationally, and the advances that have been made, 'consistent accurate prediction is not yet a reality . . . remaining anomalies, which require further experimental work and a better understanding, concern the early stage of crop development' (Porter, 1985). It is not possible here to consider all of these models but, since Equations 2.8 and 2.11 appear to describe the responses common to several LDPs, it is interesting to consider briefly those wheat models which appear to include assumptions which have some similarities with those implicit in these equations.

In order to facilitate comparisons, it is necessary first to point out that Equation 2.11 states the implications of Equation 2.8 in terms of calculating the photoperiodic time in excess of a nominal base photoperiod which is contributed towards the completion of flower induction, and it indicates that the nominal base photoperiod (and not the photoperiodic time required, given by $1/c'$) is modified by mean temperature. Furthermore, it is possible to state exactly the same concept in terms of the thermal time required for flowering in excess of a base temperature. Then, it is evident that the base temperature (and not the thermal time required) varies with photoperiod. The expression for calculating the daily contribution to thermal time (which can be used as an alternative to calculating nominal photoperiodic time as in Equation 2.11) is as follows:

$$t_d = \overline{T}_d + (a' + c'P_d)/b' \tag{2.12}$$

where t_d is the daily contribution to thermal time, $\overline{T}_d$ is the mean temperature that day, and a', b' and c' are the constants for the genotype being considered and which apply in Equation 2.8.

In some wheat models which have been developed on the basis of field data, it is assumed that it is the thermal time in excess of a given constant base temperature which is modified by photoperiod (e.g. Gallagher *et al.*, 1983; Weir *et al.*, 1984). This contrasts with the variation in base temperature according to photoperiod as Equations 2.8 and 2.12 imply. The response described by Equation 2.8 is shown in *Figure 2.5(b)* and, more clearly for the present purpose, in *Figure 2.5(k)*. In contrast with *Figure 2.5(k)*, the wheat models imply lines of common origin on the abscissa, with slopes that vary according to photoperiod.

While the distinction between the two models may appear fundamental, in practice in field experiments, where mean temperatures for the most part are warmer than the base temperature and where mean temperature and photoperiod tend to be confounded, it may not be easy to distinguish between the two. To confirm that the assumptions on which the field models of wheat are based are indeed the most appropriate would require factorial experiments in controlled environments.

Epilogue

We would like to end where logically we might have begun—by quoting Bernier *et al.* (1981) who, in the first chapter of their twin-volume work on *The Physiology of Flowering*, point out that, '... despite manifold attempts to achieve a universally accepted system, the measurement of flowering remains as varied as the species under investigation.'

There is no reason, of course, why there should be a single system; the system chosen should be that most appropriate to the purpose of the investigation. However, in their discussion of the various measurement systems that have been used in studies on the environmental control of flowering, it emerges that Bernier *et al.* consider three types have been predominant:

1. Those in which the number of days taken from sowing or emergence are recorded for plants to reach a particular and defined stage in their reproductive development—days to double ridge formation in cereals or to first open flower or anthesis in many dicotyledons are traditional examples.
2. Those where an index of vegetative development prior to flowering is recorded—the number of nodes or leaves below that subtending the first flower being a common example.
3. Treatments in which plants are sampled after specified times and scored according to some arbitary system which depends on the stage of development each replicate has reached.

We believe that for most purposes the last system is the least useful; the second has a number of virtues; but it is the first that is the most useful—hence our exclusive concentration upon it. It is the time taken to flower which is usually of greatest ecological and agricultural interest and which therefore needs to be predicted. But, between measurements of the time taken to flower in experimental treatments and its reliable prediction in various other circumstances, comes analysis and synthesis, and for these intermediate steps we have argued that it is usually helpful if times of development are transformed into rates. Furthermore, when this approach is combined with the concepts of thermal time (e.g. Monteith, 1981) and of photoperiodic time it seems probable that the modelling of crop phenology will be simplified, more reliable, and more biologically plausible. Models which, on the other hand, seek to correlate dates of flowering (or days to flowering, f) with various states of environmental factors such as temperature or photoperiod using formal statistical procedures seem, inevitably, destined towards increasing complexity; these models can become so bulky and unwieldy that, ultimately, they may suffer the same fate as the dinosaurs (Monteith, 1977). Reevaluations of previous efforts to predict the flowering and/or maturity of both soyabeans (e.g. Brown, 1960; Major *et al.*, 1975; and Meyer *et al.*, 1979) and maize crops (e.g. Gilmore and Rogers, 1958; Coligado and Brown, 1975; and Rinne, 1984) in terms of rates of progress towards these events and the concepts of thermal and photoperiodic time might well be fruitful (and *see* Angus *et al.*, 1981a, b).

Finally, two practical applications of the approach advocated here also merit comment. Plant breeders recognize the importance of matching crop phenology to cropping seasons and that an understanding of the environmental and genetic control of development is central to their efforts to improve and stabilize yields (e.g. Wallace, 1985). However, unless phenology can be predicted accurately, then extensive (and expensive) testing of germplasm in different locations is seen as the only practical alternative. Furthermore, in seeking to utilize both exotic and local germplasm in their hybridization programmes, rates of progress can be limited if the flowering of diverse genotypes cannot be synchronized or manipulated (e.g. Hellmers and Burton, 1972). We have described elsewhere in this volume how artificial manipulations of photoperiod using incandescent lamps in the field can help to synchronize (or, if required, to delay) the onset of flowering in LDPs (Summerfield and Roberts, Chapter 15). What is now clear is that a knowledge of response surfaces for flowering (e.g. *Figures 2.4* and *2.5*) can be exploited—by reducing the number of field locations required for evaluating phenological responses to climate (as we have discussed earlier) and to ensure the meaningful genetic analysis of these responses in SDPs and LDPs by evaluating the outcome of hybridization in locations known to lie within particular planes of the overall response surface. When this approach is taken actual or variable rather than mean weather parameters can be converted more simply to phenological statistics. Practical utility demands both simplicity and a proven ability to anticipate biological events (Waggoner, 1974).

Acknowledgements

We thank the Overseas Development Administration of the UK Foreign and Commonwealth Office for their generous financial support of successive research programmes. The scientific contribution of Dr P. Hadley, Department of Horticulture, University of Reading to the formulation of the models for soyabean, cowpea and chickpea, and that of our colleagues Dr R. H. Ellis and Professor J. P. Cooper FRS to the models for lentil, faba bean, barley and other crops is gratefully acknowledged. We have greatly benefited from stimulating dialogue and cooperation with scientists in the Grain Legume Improvement Program at IITA, Nigeria; in the Pulses Improvement Program at ICRISAT, India; and in the Food Legume and Cereal Improvement Programs at ICARDA, Syria. The dedicated technical assistance of Miss C. Chadwick and Mr M. Craig and the engineering assistance of Messrs D. Dickinson, A. C. Richardson, K. Chivers and S. Gill has been the foundation for our research programmes.

References

ABBE, C. (1905). *The Relations Between Climates and Crops*, USDA Weather Bureau Bulletin No. 36. Washington, Government Printing Office

AITKEN, Y. (1974). *Flowering Time, Climate and Genotype*, Carlton, Victoria, Melbourne University Press

ANGUS, J.F., CUNNINGHAM, R.B., MONCUR, M.W. and MACKENZIE, D.H. (1981a). Phasic development in field crops. I. Thermal response in the seedling phase. *Field Crops Research*, **3**, 365–378

ANGUS, J.F., MACKENZIE, D.H., MORTON, R. and SCHAFER, C.A. (1981b). Phasic development in field crops. II. Thermal and photoperiodic responses of spring wheat. *Field Crops Research*, **4**, 269–283

ARNOLD, C.Y. (1959). The determination and significance of the base temperature in a linear heat unit system. *Proceedings of the American Society of Horticultural Science*, **74**, 430–445

BASHANDI, M.M.H. and POEHLMAN, J.M. (1974). Photoperiod response in mung beans (*Vigna radiata* (L.) Wilczek). *Euphytica*, **23**, 691–697

BERNIER, G., KINET, J. and SACHS, R.M. (1981). *The Physiology of Flowering. Vol. 1 The Initiation Process*. Baton Rouge, Florida, CRC Press

BERRY, G.J. and AITKEN, Y. (1979). Effect of photoperiod and temperature on flowering in pea (*Pisum sativum* L.). *Australian Journal of Plant Physiology*, **6**, 573–587

BROWN, D.M. (1960). Soyabean ecology. 1. Development temperature relationships from controlled evironment studies. *Agronomy Journal*, **52**, 493–496

CAMERON, D.F. and MANNETJE L.'T (1977). Effects of photoperiod and temperature on flowering of twelve *Stylosanthes* species. *Australian Journal of Experimental Agriculture and Animal Husbandry*, **17**, 417–424

CATHEY, H.M. (1969). *Chrysanthemum morifolium* (Ramat.) Hemsl. In *The Induction of Flowering* (L.T. Evans, Ed.), pp. 268–290. Melbourne, Australia, Macmillan

COLIGADO, M.C. and BROWN, D.M. (1975). A bio-photo-thermal model to predict tassel-initiation time in corn (*Zea mays* L.). *Agricultural Meteorology*, **15**, 11–31

COOPER, J.P., SUMMERFIELD, R.J., ELLIS, R.H. and ROBERTS, E.H. (1987). Effects of temperature and photoperiod on flowering in barley (*Hordeum vulgare* L.). *Annals of Botany*, **37**, 705–715

COVELL, S., ELLIS., R.H., ROBERTS, E.H. and SUMMERFIELD, R.J. (1986). The influence of temperature on seed germination rate in grain legumes. I. A comparison of chickpea, lentil, soyabean and cowpea at constant temperatures. *Journal of Experimental Botany* (in press)

CREGAN, P.B. and HARTWIG, E.E. (1984). Characterization of flowering response to photoperiod in diverse soyabean genotypes. *Crop Science*, **24**, 659–662

CROSS, H.Z. and ZUBER, M.S. (1972). Prediction of flowering dates in maize based on different methods of estimating thermal units. *Agronomy Journal*, **64**, 351–355

DENNETT, M.D. (1984). The tropical environment. In *The Physiology of Tropical Crops* (P.R. Goldsworthy and N.M. Fisher, Eds), pp. 1–38, Chichester, John Wiley and Sons

DRURY, R. (1980). Physiological interaction: its mathematical expression. *Weed Science*, **28**, 573–579

ELLIS, R.H., COVELL, S., ROBERTS, E.H. and SUMMERFIELD, R.J. (1986). The influence of temperature on seed germination rate in grain legumes. II. Intraspecific variation in chickpea, lentil, soyabean and cowpea at constant temperatures. *Journal of Experimental Botany* (in press)

ELLIS, R.H., SUMMERFIELD, R.J., ROBERTS, E.H. and ROBERTSON, L.D. (1987). Effects of temperature and photoperiod on flowering in faba bean (*Vicia faba* L.). *Annals of Botany* (in preparation)

EVANS, L.T. (1960). Inflorescence initiation in *Lolium temulentum* L. I. Effect of plant age and leaf area on sensitivity of photoperiodic induction. *Australian Journal of Biological Science*, **13**, 123–131

FRANCE, J. and THORNLEY, J.H.M. (1984). *Mathematical Models in Agriculture*, London, Butterworths

FRENCH, V. and HODGES, T. (1985). Comparison of crop phenology models. *Agronomy Journal*, **77**, 170–171

GALLAGHER, J.N., BISCOE, P.V. and DENNIS-JONES, R. (1983). Environmental influences on the development, growth and yield of barley. In *Barley Production and Marketing* (Wright, G. M., Ed.), Agronomy Society of New Zealand

GARCIA-HUIDOBRO, J., MONTEITH, J.L. and SQUIRE, G.R. (1982a). Time, temperature and germination of pearl millet (*Pennisetum typhoides* S. & H.). I. Constant temperature. *Journal of Experimental Botany*, **33**, 288–296

GARCIA-HUIDOBRO, J., MONTEITH, J.L. and SQUIRE, G.R. (1982b). Time, temperature and germination of pearl millet (*Pennisetum typhoides* S. & H.). II. Alternating temperature. *Journal of Experimental Botany*, **33**, 297–302

GARCIA-HUIDOBRO, J., MONTEITH, J.L. and SQUIRE, G.R. (1985). Time, temperature and germination of pearl millet (*Pennisetum typhoides* S. & H.). III. Inhibition of germination by short exposure to high temperature. *Journal of Experimental Botany*, **36**, 338–343

GARNER, W.W. and ALLARD, H.A. (1920). Flowering and fruiting of plants as controlled by the length of day, *Yearbook of Agriculture*, p. 377. USDA

GARNER, W.W. and ALLARD, H.A. (1923). Further studies in photoperiodism, the response of the plant to relative length of day and night. *Journal of Agricultural Research*, **23**, 871–920

GILMORE, E.C. and ROGERS, J.S. (1958). Heat units as a method of measuring maturity in corn. *Agronomy Journal*, **50**, 611–615

GOYNE, P.J., WOODRUFF, D.R. and CHURCHETT, J.D. (1977). Prediction of flowering in sunflowers. *Australian Journal of Experimental Agriculture and Animal Husbandry*, **17**, 475–481

HADLEY, P., ROBERTS, E.H., SUMMERFIELD, R.J. and MINCHIN, F.R. (1983a). A quantitative model of reproductive development in cowpea [*Vigna unguiculata* (L.) Walp.] in relation to photoperiod and temperature, and implications for screening germplasm. *Annals of Botany*, **51**, 531–543

HADLEY, R., SUMMERFIELD, R.J. and ROBERTS, E.H. (1983b). Effects of temperature and photoperiod in reproductive development of selected grain legume crops. In *Temperate Grain Legumes: Physiology, Genetics and Nodulation* (D.G. Jones and D.R. Davies, Eds), pp. 19–41, London, Pitman

HADLEY, P., ROBERTS, E.H., SUMMERFIELD, R.J. and MINCHIN, F.R. (1984). Effects of temperature and photoperiod on flowering in soyabean [*Glycine max* (L.) Merrill.]: a quantitative model. *Annals of Botany*, **53**, 669–681

HALSE, N.J. and WEIR, R.N. (1970). Effects of vernalization, photoperiod and temperature on phenological development and spikelet number of Australian wheat. *Australian Journal of Agricultural Research*, **21**, 383–393

HAMNER, K.C. (1969). *Glycine max* (L.). Merrill. In *The Induction of Flowering* (L.T. Evans, Ed.), pp. 62–89, Melbourne, Macmillan

HELLMERS, H. and BURTON, G.W. (1972). Photoperiod and temperature manipulation induces early anthesis in pearl millet. *Crop Science*, **12**, 198–200

INOUYE, J., SHANMUGASUNDARAM, S. and MASUYAMA, T. (1979). Effects of temperature and daylength on the flowering of some photo-insensitive soyabean varieties. *Japanese Journal of Tropical Agriculture*, **22**, 167–171

McCOLLUM, G.D. (1974). Onion and allies. In *Evolution of Crop Plants* (N.W. Simmonds, Ed.), pp. 186–190, London, Longmans

MAJOR, D.J. (1980). Photoperiod response characteristics controlling flowering of nine crop species. *Canadian Journal of Plant Science*, **60**, 777–784

MAJOR, D.S., JOHNSON, D.R., TANNER, J.W. and ANDERSON, I.C. (1975). Effects of daylength and temperature on soybean development. *Crop Science*, **15** 174–179.

MEYER, G.E., CURRY, R.B., STREETER, J.G. and MEDERSKI, H.J. (1979). SOYMOD-OARDC: A dynamic simulator of soybean growth, development and seed yield. *Ohio Agricultural Research and Development Center Research Bulletin* 1113

MONTEITH, J.L. (1977). Climate. In *Ecophysiology of Tropical Crops* (P. Alvim, Ed.), pp. 1–27, London, Academic Press

MONTEITH, J.L. (1981). Climatic variation and the growth of crops. *Quarterly Journal of the Royal Meteorological Society*, **107**, 749–744

MURNEEK, A.E. and WHYTE, R.O. (1948). *Vernalization and Photoperiodism*, Waltham, USA, Chronica Botanica Company

NAPP-ZINN, K. (1984). Light and vernalization. In *Light and the Flowering Process* (D. Vince-Prue, B. Thomas and K.E. Cockshull, Eds), pp. 75–88, London, Academic Press

PORTER, J.R. (1983). Modelling stage development in winter wheat. *Aspects of Applied Biology*, **4**, 449–455

PORTER, J.R. (1985). Models and mechanisms in the growth and development of wheat. *Outlook on Agriculture*, **14**, 190–196

PURSEGLOVE, J.W. (1968). *Tropical Crops, Dicotyledons 1*, London, Longmans

RABINOWITCH, H.D. (1985). Onions and other edible *Alliums*. In *A Handbook of Flowering* (A.H. Halevy, Ed.), pp. 398–409, Boca Raton, Florida, CRC Press

RINNE, J. (1984). Effect of temperature and day-length on the development of sweet corn in Finland. *Agricultural and Forest Meteorology*, **31**, 261–271

ROBERTS, E.H., HADLEY, P. and SUMMERFIELD, R.J. (1985). Effects of temperature and photoperiod on flowering in chickpeas (*Cicer arietinum* L.). *Annals of Botany*, **55**, 881–892

ROBERTS, E.H., SUMMERFIELD, R.J., MUEHLBAUER, F.J. and SHORT, R.W. (1986). Flowering in lentil (*Lens culinaris* Medic.): the duration of the photoperiodic inductive phase as a function of accumulated day-length above the critical photoperiod. *Annals of Botany*, **58**, 235–248

ROBERTS, E.H., SUMMERFIELD, R.J. and COOPER, J.P. (1986b). Flowering in barley (*Hordeum vulgare* L.): The duration of the photoperiodic inductive phase as a function of photoperiodic time. *Annals of Botany* (in press)

ROBERTSON, G.W. (1968). A biometeorological time scale for a cereal crop involving day and night temperature and photoperiod. *International Journal of Biometeorology*, **12**, 191–223

SALISBURY, F.B. (1982). Photoperiodism. *Horticultural Reviews*, **4**, 66–105

SCHWABE, W.W. (1971). Physiology of vegetative reproduction and flowering. In *Plant Physiology—A Treatise*, Vol. 6 (F.C. Steward, Ed.), pp. 233–411, New York, Academic Press

SCOTT, W.O. and ALDRICH, S.R. (1970). *Modern Soybean Production*, Illinois, S & A Publications

SHIBLES, R.M., ANDERSON, I.C. and GIBSON, A.H. (1975). Soybean. In *Crop Physiology: Some Case Histories* (L.T. Evans, Ed.), pp. 151–190, Cambridge, Cambridge University Press

SUMMERFIELD, R.J. and ROBERTS, E.H. (1985). Photo-thermal regulation of flowering in soybean. In *Proceedings of the World Soybean Research Conference III* (R. Shibles, Ed.), pp. 848–857, Colorado, Westview Press

SUMMERFIELD, R.J., ROBERTS, E.H., ERSKINE, W. and ELLIS, R.H. (1985a). Effects of temperature and photoperiod on flowering in lentils (*Lens culinaris*). *Annals of Botany*, **56**, 659–671

SUMMERFIELD, R.J., PATE, J.S., ROBERTS, E.H. and WIEN, H.C. (1985b). The physiology of cowpeas. In *Cowpea: Research, Production and Utilization* (S.R. Singh and K.O. Rachie, Eds), pp. 65–102, Chichester, John Wiley and Sons

THOMAS, B. and VINCE-PRUE, D. (1984). Juvenility, photoperiodism and vernalization. In *Advanced Plant Physiology* (M.B. Wilkins, Ed.), pp. 408–439, London, Pitman

TOURNOIS, J. (1914). Études sur de la sexualité du houblon. *Annales des Sciences Naturelles (Botanique)*, **19**, 49–191

VERGARA, B.S. and CHANG, T.T. (1976). *The Flowering Response of the Rice Plant to Photoperiod*, pp. 75, The Philippines, IRRI

VINCE-PRUE, D. (1975). *Photoperiodism in Plants*, Maidenhead, McGraw-Hill

WAGGONER, P.E. (1974). Using models of seasonality. In *Phenology and Seasonality Modelling* (H. Lieth, Ed.), pp. 401–405, London, Chapman & Hall

WALLACE, D.H. (1985). Physiological genetics of plant maturity, adaptation and yield. *Plant Breeding Reviews*, **3**, 21–166

WANG, J.Y. (1960). A critique of the heat unit approach to plant response studies. *Ecology*, **41**, 785–790

WEIR, A.H., BRAGG, P.L., PORTER, J.R. and RAYNER, J.H. (1984). A winter wheat crop simulation model without water or nutrient limitations. *Journal of Agricultural Science*, **102**, 371–382

WHYTE, R.O. (1946). *Crop Production and Environment*, London, Faber and Faber

WIEN, H.C. and SUMMERFIELD, R.J. (1980). Cowpea adaptation in West Africa: photoperiod and temperature responses in cultivars of diverse origin. In *Advances in Legume Science* (R.J. Summerfield and A.H. Bunting, Eds), pp. 405–418, London, HMSO

3

MEASUREMENT AND PREDICTION OF FLOWERING IN CLONAL PLANTS

A.J. DAVY

School of Biological Sciences, University of East Anglia, Norwich, UK

Introduction

The fundamental mechanisms of the flowering process have remained extremely intractable, despite an immense amount of research effort (Bernier, Kinet and Sachs, 1981a, b; Kinet, Sachs and Bernier, 1985). The problem discloses itself in the apparently bewildering diversity of flowering responses to variations in the environment of plants. Investigators naturally have tended to seek out and concentrate on the simplest model systems available. We know most about the responses of a small and eccentric group of species that is not even representative of herbaceous plants: experimental subjects are predominantly annuals, with more or less determinate growth and rapidly satisfied inductive requirements (Schwabe, 1971). The responses in question are mainly those of isolated individuals to straightforward combinations of conditions in otherwise static, controlled environments.

Many plant species, including certain important crops, exist as clones of reiterated modules with varying degrees of physiological integration and varying longevity. Modular clonal growth is essentially indeterminate in nature and raises conceptual and practical problems for both the measurement and prediction of flowering. Measurements are confounded because flowering is at the same time a property of the genetic individuals (genets) and their component clonal modules (ramets): prediction, on the other hand, requires knowledge of the often quite distinct influences on flowering attributable to ramet and genet levels of organization. Prediction of flowering in natural communities or crops implies an understanding of the possibly overriding influences of neighbouring individuals (of both the same and different species), herbivores, mycorrhizal symbionts and parasites. It also involves responses to field environments, with their continually changing combinations of conditions. Protracted conditioning may be required in the field to induce, evoke and allow development of inflorescences. The outcome is often dramatic, unexplained variations in flowering from year to year, and from population to population (Schemske *et al.*, 1978; Wells, 1981; Inghe and Tamm, 1985).

The purpose of this chapter is to address the issues raised by clonal plants, particularly as they behave in the field. Work is described for two herbaceous species that have contrasting variations on a very common growth form: initiation of an inflorescence terminates the main axis of the semelparous (monocarpic) module, and clonal growth proceeds sympodially from axillary buds. One, *Deschampsia cespitosa*, is a grass that forms densely packed tussocks of tillers interconnected by very short rhizomes; tiller apices require extended low-temperature vernalization, followed by long days, for flowering. The other, *Hieracium pilosella*, is a rosette-forming dicotyledon that produces daughter rosettes at the ends of long stolons; it has no strict temperature requirement for flowering, although its phenology suggests evocation under long days.

The measurement problem

Even in unitary plants the measurement of flowering is not straightforward. They normally have a juvenile phase, during which induction cannot take place, and a floral development phase, during which the environment can modify the expression of the inductive response. Induction cannot yet be recognized biochemically and so a morphological index of induction must be used: for instance, apex length, flower bud production or node of flower bud production. Any plant capable of producing more than a single flower obviously raises further problems for quantification of the flowering response.

Each ramet of a clonal plant usually has the potential to initiate at least one inflorescence. Accordingly, the number of flowers in an inflorescence, the number of inflorescences per ramet and the total number of ramets in the clone are all separate components of the flowering response of that clone. These components are by no means independent, as will be seen later.

The most intricate problems of measurement are presented by plants in which the ramets show a high degree of physiological integration. Four different measures of flowering performance may be exemplified with a single clone of *Deschampsia cespitosa*. Tussocks of approximately 120 tillers, in 127 mm pots, were exposed to the natural temperature regime from mid-September; replicate tussocks were transferred to a heated glasshouse with long (14 h) days, each week until the following April.

For a tussock, as for any individual, flowering is a qualitative event with a particular probability (*Figure 3.1(a)*). Flowering began in the sample from week 8 (mid-November). There was a 4-week transition period before the probability of flowering reached 1.0 in the sample from week 12 (mid-December). From then on all tussocks flowered. Such an analysis clearly displays the onset of flowering; it will, however, be sensitive to the number of tillers in a tussock, and undoubtedly masks the within-tussock quantitative responses. This is evident if the mean number of inflorescences per tussock is examined (*Figure 3.1(b)*). Not surprisingly, the mean number of inflorescences increased until all replicate tussocks achieved flowering but, with prolonged exposure to winter, it increased a further three-fold, apparently reaching saturation some 8 weeks later (week 20 sample, mid-February). The mean inflorescence height (*Figure 3.1(c)*) also increased, markedly during the transition period and then rather modestly for the subsequent 8 weeks. Taller inflorescences within a clone tend to bear more branches and hence more spikelets (cf. *Table 3.1*). The mean development time of the inflorescences, timed from removal to the glasshouse to emergence of the panicle from the flag leaf sheath, adds a further dimension (*Figure 3.1(d)*). It reveals three more or less distinct phases: the first corresponds reasonably well with the transition period, where development time decreased rapidly from 63 days to about 26 days; in the second phase it remained nearly constant and this presumably reflects the intrinsic time for the glasshouse conditions; after week 17 apparent development time again declined because the day-length threshold for development had been exceeded in the field, and progressively

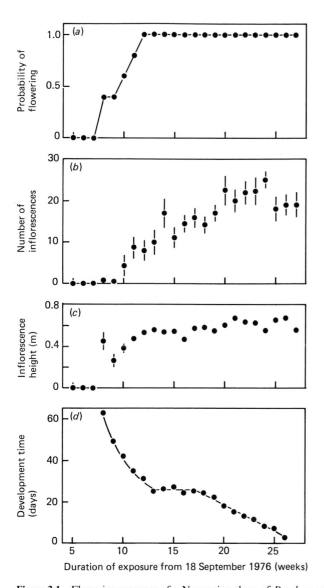

Figure 3.1 Flowering response of a Norwegian clone of *Deschampsia cespitosa* ssp. *alpina* after exposure to increasing periods of natural temperature regime from 18 September 1976, at Norwich: (*a*) probability of a tussock flowering (*n* = 5); (*b*) mean number of inflorescences per tussock; (*c*) mean inflorescence height; (*d*) mean development time (to panicle emergence), after transfer to a heated, illuminated glasshouse. Vertical bars in (*b*) and (*c*) represent ± SE, where this is large enough to be shown.

less of the development occurred in the glasshouse. The importance of this is that the first phase clearly identifies a period in which induction was marginal. None of these different measures alone describes adequately the flowering behaviour of whole tussocks.

In *Hieracium pilosella* the problems of physiological integration are less acute. A stolon senesces and dies as soon as it has served to place the daughter rosette, closely followed by the parent rosette. Only a single capitulum can normally be evoked from a rosette. The difficulty with *Hieracium* comes rather in identifying the intermingled clones, given the great mobility conferred by the stolons and the estimated half-lives of rosette populations in the field of up to 2.3 years (Bishop and Davy, 1984).

Clearly there is no universally applicable measure of flowering in clonal species. For many purposes flowering corresponds with the idea of reproductive effort (Willson, 1983), although it remains to determine the most appropriate common currency in which express the reproductive allocation. Conventionally, carbon (dry mass) or an important inorganic nutrient element have been favoured. Variations in growth form and uncertainty as to what resource is actually constraining growth and development at any time suggests that a morphological unit should be sought. Numbers of ovules, flowers and inflorescences are all attractive candidates. But for the prediction of flowering the concern is essentially with the fates (reproductive or vegetative) of particular meristems, the units that actually respond to inductive environments.

Accordingly, attention will be focussed on the apical meristem of the ramet and the subordinate axillary meristems generated by it. The important issues can be framed as three sequential questions representing successive stages on the path to flowering:

1. What are the morphogenetic constraints on apex availability for flowering?
2. Which of these apices produce floral primordia and what are the influences on induction and evocation?
3. What constrains the development of inflorescences from apices with floral primordia?

Morphogenetic constraints on apex availability for flowering

Reproductive and vegetative growth compete for the same pools of resources available to a plant such that the promotion of one is likely to be at some cost to the other (Willson, 1983; Watson and Casper, 1984). Only recently has the principle been extended to meristem availability. Tripathi and Harper (1973) showed that the greater flowering in the non-rhizomatous *Elymus caninus*, compared with *E. repens* which is strongly rhizomatous but otherwise very similar, could be attributed to the different partitioning of a limited pool of meristems; axillary buds directed to become rhizomes reduce the number available to become flowering tillers. The converse argument has been used to explain the marked reduction in clonal growth in flowering populations of *Eichhornia crassipes*, a stoloniferous rosette-forming aquatic plant. Under favourable conditions every axillary bud produces a stolon and new rosette. A logistic curve closely fitted the increase in rosette numbers in a culture of a non-flowering population; in contrast, a flowering population fell short of the logistic curve progressively from the onset of flowering (Watson, 1984). When a terminal bud initiates floral primordia the uppermost axillary bud continues the vertical growth of the flowering ramet sympodially, thus depleting the pool of meristems for clonal growth. Watson (1984) showed that the rate of lateral meristem production and differentiation was not affected by flowering. The disposition of the meristems is all important.

Despite some striking similarities in growth form, there is no evidence that

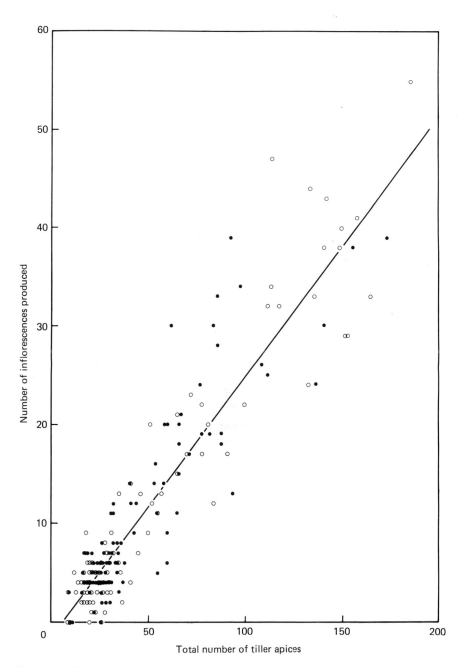

Figure 3.2 Relationship between the number of tillers, in tussocks of a Norwegian clone of *Deschampsia cespitosa* ssp. *alpina*, present at the end of two periods of exposure to the natural temperature regime at Norwich from 18 September 1978, and the number of inflorescences produced after transfer to a heated, illuminated glasshouse; transfers were made on 8 January ($\bigcirc$) and 15 March 1979 ($\bullet$). $y = 0.265x - 1.553$ ($r^2 = 0.86$; $P < 0.001$; $n = 207$).

Hieracium pilosella is similarly constrained. Three major reasons for this are: firstly, there is no continuation of the growth of a ramet axis after floral evocation, although it is not uncommon for a daughter ramet to develop in an axil without an interposing stolon. Secondly, stolon or axillary daughter production are always concomitant on floral evocation in a rosette; vegetative apices appear to maintain complete dominance over their axillary meristems and so there is no clonal growth without floral evocation. The same correlation pertains to *Hieracium floribundum* (Thomas and Dale, 1974). Furthermore, on the nutrient-poor soils of Breckland the production of more than two stolons by a ramet is rare, even though up to nine axillary meristems may be present (Bishop and Davy, 1984). Likewise, the average probability of floral evocation in the field is low (0.12–0.26); but all ramets flower when cultivated on fertile soil (cf. *Figure 3.6*) and a single rosette may bear 14 primary stolons (Bishop and Davy, 1985). Far from depriving clonal growth of meristems, flowering releases meristems that otherwise would not differentiate into stolons.

Quite different considerations apply to the integrated clones of *Deschampsia cespitosa*, in which new tillers arise predominantly from the axillary meristems of vegetative apices. This behaviour raises the question of whether there is a limitation on the number of inflorescences that can be produced by a tussock of a particular size; the perennial nature of the clone depends on the failure of at least some tiller apices to flower. The relationship between the number of flowering tillers and the total number of tillers in a tussock at the end of the vernalization period is shown in *Figure 3.2*. Tussocks of a clone of *D. cespitosa* in pots appropriate to their tiller numbers were exposed to the natural temperature regimen, as before, but transferred to a heated glasshouse (14 h photoperiods) in two batches: in January and March. All plants were regularly watered with nutrient solution in the glasshouse until there was no further flowering.

The number of inflorescences was linearly related to the total number of tillers in tussocks ranging in size from 9 to 186 tillers (*Figure 3.2*). Furthermore, the regressions for the two samples did not differ significantly. The overall probability of an apex present at the end of the vernalization period producing an inflorescence was only 0.25 and additional vernalizing temperatures between January and March did not affect this probability. As the rate of tillering in winter is exceedingly slow, the probability of flowering for a tiller present at the beginning of the vernalization period was only marginally higher.

Young (1984) reports average probabilities for flowering in the field of 0.02–0.04, which were also independent of clone size, in integrated clones of *Lobelia keniensis* ranging from 2 to 16 rosettes. The limitation on flowering in both cases is apparently not morphogenetic. The failure of apices to flower may be due to their more demanding requirements for induction, or alternatively it could arise from some resource limitation affecting the development of evoked apices.

The induction and evocation of flowering apices

The induction of flowering can be recognized only after subsequent evocation of double-ridged primordia, often under quite different conditions to those for induction. In clonal plants even evocation *per se* can be difficult to determine. The apices may be small and prohibitively labour intensive to dissect out on a scale appropriate to the investigation of whole clones, especially in the field. Two practical approaches to the quantification of evocation offer themselves. The provision of optimal conditions for the development of inflorescences until they become recognizable should maximize the development of evoked apices (and the evocation of induced ones). This is the approach adopted in the work with *D. cespitosa*. An alternative is to exploit a morphogenetic correlate of evocation as a marker; in the case of *H. pilosella* stolon differentiation appears to work well.

VERNALIZATION

Where there is a protracted vernalization requirement, such as in *D. cespitosa*, the quantitative relationship between temperature and flowering is of cardinal import-ance for the prediction of flowering competence. Numerous studies have defined the inductive requirements for flowering, of a wide range of species, in terms of constant temperatures and photoperiods (e.g. Chouard, 1960; Evans, 1969; Zeevaart, 1976). In fluctuating field environments complications may arise that make extrapolations from constant environments hazardous: short days may substitute partially for low temperatures in long-day plants (Vince-Prue, 1975); the effectiveness of vernalization varies greatly with temperature and the duration of treatment (Purvis, 1961)—the optimum temperature may even be higher for short treatments than long ones; devernalization can take place at temperatures as low as 18 °C (Bernier, Kinet and Sachs, 1981a).

Deschampsia cespitosa exemplifies the effects of the problems well. It is possible to characterize the response of a northerly (Norwegian) clone of ssp. *alpina* in a growth cabinet at 6 °C with 16 h photoperiods. Full flowering was achieved after between 6 and 12 weeks of treatment and there was evidence that pretreatment with warm 8 h days slightly enhanced induction. But these results are exceptional. Other genotypes (ssp. *cespitosa*) have failed to respond to up to 25 weeks of similar treatment. Plainly, realistic prediction demands an analysis of the response to field winter conditions.

The effects of temperature and photoperiod in the field can be largely separated by examining the responses of particular clones to year-to-year variations in temperature (Davy, 1982). Tussocks of three different clones of ssp. *cespitosa* were exposed to the natural winter conditions of Norwich, UK, each September from 1974 to 1977. Five replicate tussocks of each clone were sampled each week during the winter, and transferred to the heated glasshouse with 14 h photoperiods, as described previously. The subsequent incidence and intensity of flowering were recorded (*Figure 3.3*). In every case the number of inflorescences produces per tussock continued to increase with prolonged exposure, after 100% flowering in the replicates had been reached. This accords with the findings for ssp. *alpina* shown in (*Figure 3.1(b)*). The implication is that the apices in a tussock have a distribution of vernalization requirements with a wide range. A precedent for this model was reported by Chouard (1960) for *Geum urbanum*. The axillary buds were vernalized by 5–15 weeks at 4 °C, whereas the terminal apex could only be vernalized by 30–50 weeks of treatment, a circumstance never likely to be realized in the field. Hence it is a perennial.

The number of weeks of exposure (from 18 September) required to achieve 100% flowering in *D. cespitosa* was regressed on daily mean air temperature (average of minimum and maximum) at a meteorological station 15 km from the experimental garden. The running mean temperature, over periods increased successively by increments of 10 days, accounted for progressively more of the year-to-year variation in flowering up to 60 days (*Figure 3.4(a)*), when the coefficient of determination reached 98–99% (*Figure 3.4(b)*). Beyond 80 days there was a rapid decline in the proportion of variance accounted for (*Figure 3.4(a)*).

The critical period, during which temperature appeared to determine variations in flowering competence, was between mid-September and mid-November or early December. It represents the unreliable part of the year: earlier in the season temperatures are always predominantly non-vernalizing and later they are always predominantly vernalising, for the years examined (Davy, 1982). Clearly, mean temperature *per se* is not the determinant of vernalization in a rapidly and unpredictably changing temperature regimen; rather, it is itself correlated with a complex integral of the distribution of time spent at different temperatures with varying efficacies in promoting vernalization. Nevertheless, mean temperature over the critical period is an extremely good predictor of flowering competence. The relationships for the three clones were quite distinct, which suggests that we need to take account of genotype and provenance.

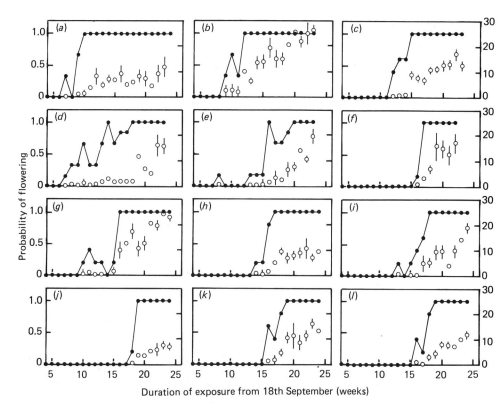

Figure 3.3 Probability of a tussock of *Deschampsia cespitosa* ssp. flowering (●) and the mean number of inflorescences produced per plant (○) after exposure to increasing periods of natural temperature regime from 18 September each year at Norwich. (*a*)–(*c*) 1974/75; (*d*)–(*f*) 1975/76; (*g*)–(*i*) 1976/77; (*j*)–(*l*) 1977/78; (*a*), (*d*), (*g*), (*i*) Moorhouse clone; (*b*), (*e*), (*h*), (*k*) Knock Fell clone; (*c*), (*f*), (*i*), (*l*) Chiltern clone. Vertical bars represent ± SE for inflorescence number, where this is large enough to be shown (*n* = 5). (Reproduced from Davy (1982), with kind permission of author and publishers.)

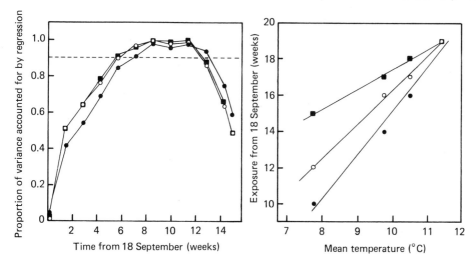

Figure 3.4 (*a*) Proportion of the year-to-year variance in exposure time required for
100% flowering (*n* = 5) in *Deschampsia cespitosa* spp. *cespitosa* that was accounted for by
regression on overall running mean temperature, for increasing periods from 18
September. The horizontal broken line represents P = 0.05. (*b*) Regression of exposure
time requirement for 100% flowering on overall mean temperature for 60 days from 18
September. (●) Moorhouse clone; (○) Knock Fell clone; (□) Chiltern clone.
(Reproduced from Davy (1982), with kind permission of author and publishers.)

GENOTYPE AND PROVENANCE EFFECTS

Plant populations frequently become genetically differentiated from one another, as
evolutionary responses to their local environments. Flowering, a prerequisite for
reproduction and therefore fitness, is directly susceptible to these pressures and there
is considerable evidence for intra-specific differentiation in flowering responses to
photoperiod and vernalization (Murfet, 1977). If differentiation is to be of predictive
value, variation in flowering response must be related quantitatively to the relevant
aspects of the environment. Ketellapper (1960), for instance, found an exact negative
relationship between the length of cold treatment required to induce flowering in
populations of *Phalaris tuberosa* and the average temperature of the coldest month in
their habitats.

Deschampsia cespitosa is certainly a genetically very diverse species (Davy, 1980;
Rothera and Davy, 1986). The implications of this for its inductive requirement were
examined by comparing the flowering responses, to a common environment, of nine
clones that represent a latitudinal transect from Iceland to the Pyrenees. The method
was as described for the previous experiment, except that the comparison was made
over a single winter (1976/77).

A highly significant relationship (*Figure 3.5*) emerged between the period of
exposure in the experimental gardens at Norwich that was needed to achieve 100%
flowering and the latitude of origin of the clones. The more northerly clones were the
less demanding, irrespective of whether they were diploid or tetraploid. Equivalent
regressions on the altitude and average temperatures of their sites of origin were not

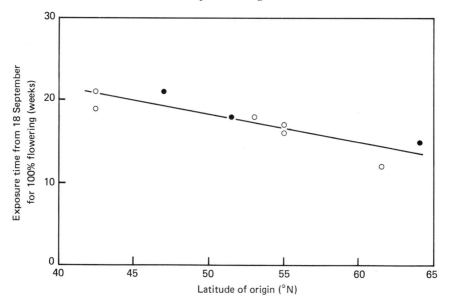

Figure 3.5 Relationship between exposure time required for 100% flowering ($n = 5$), from 18 September 1976, in *Deschampsia cespitosa* ssp. *cespitosa* at Norwich and latitude of origin for 9 clones on a transect from Iceland to the Pyrenees. Diploid clones, $2n = 26$ (●); tetraploid clones, $2n = 52$ (○). $y = 34.97 - 0.334x$ ($r^2 = 0.77$).

significant. This suggests a photoperiodic involvement but in a single season experiment it is necessarily confounded with vernalization. Heide (1986) has recently found similarly less stringent vernalization requirements in Norwegian populations of *Alopecurus pratensis* than are usual in more southerly populations.

NEIGHBOUR EFFECTS

In less integrated clones, where the ramets separate, they still influence each other's capacity to flower. *Hieracium pilosella* genets sown at a very wide range of density in pots of nutrient-rich compost in a glasshouse showed a remarkable attenuation in the probability of evoking an inflorescence with increasing density (*Figure 3.6*). The same phenomenon has been observed in the nutrient-poor grass heaths of the Breckland, where the population of *H. pilosella* is embedded in a matrix of grasses and numerous other species. The presence of other species appears to shift the response to rather lower density; in rabbit grazed areas, where the grasses and other palatable species are removed in preference to the *H. pilosella*, the displacement is less than in exclosed areas (*Figure 3.6*; Bishop and Davy, 1984).

   The regulation of inflorescence evocation by density may operate through limitation of the number of rosettes able to reach a threshold size for flowering. Kachi and Hirose (1985), however, report a precise linear relationship between the probability of flowering of *Oenothera glazioviana* and the logarithm of its rosette diameter in May, in a sand dune system. Competition for inorganic nutrients, both intra- and inter-specifically, is likely to be important. The addition of nitrogen and phosphorus to Breckland plots strongly stimulates flowering of *H. pilosella* in the first summer,

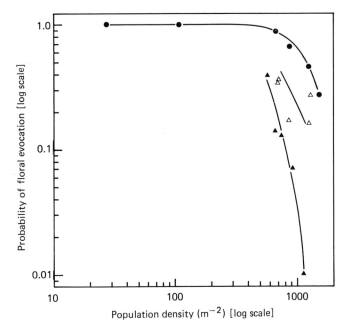

Figure 3.6 Probability of floral evocation in *Hieracium pilosella* in relation to population density. Genets grown from seed as a monoculture in 216 mm pots of Levington compost in a heated, illuminated glasshouse (●) (after Bishop and Davy, 1985); Ramet populations in 0.5 × 0.5 m quadrats in ungrazed (▲) and grazed (△) Breckland grass heath (after Bishop and Davy, 1984).

although without grazing it leads subsequently to reduced flowering and extinction, through the promotion of more vigorous competitors (Davy and Bishop, 1984).

The development of flowering apices

Any modification of the flowering response of a clone of *Deschampsia cespitosa* after vernalization in the field and removal to the glasshouse can be attributed to the differential development of induced apices. The potential for such modification was investigated in an experiment in the winter of 1984/85. Tussocks were returned to the glasshouse on 19 February and subjected to factorial combinations of treatments: 0, 50 or 83% shade; 76 or 127 mm pots; + or − nutrient supplementation. A minimum day-length of 15 h was maintained.

Shading was of overriding importance with virtually no inflorescences in 83% shade. The probability of an apex present at the end of the vernalization treatment producing an inflorescence was greatly reduced by 50% shade, relative to the unshaded plants (*Table 3.1*). In full light, failure to increase the rooting volume also reduced this probability, as did the absence of nutrient supplementation after repotting. These effects are compounded by parallel ones on the number of spikelets borne by the inflorescences (*Table 3.1*). Ong, Marshall and Sagar (1978) were able to modify the probability of flowering of a tiller (per plant) much less than this after double-ridge formation in *Poa annua*; a 50-fold increase in nutrient supply at double-

62

Table 3.1   THE EFFECT OF SHADE, NUTRIENT SUPPLY AND ROOTING VOLUME,
AFTER TRANSFER TO THE GLASSHOUSE, ON THE PROBABILITY OF AN APEX OF
Deschampsia cespitosa PRESENT AT THE END OF THE FIELD VERNALIZATION PERIOD (20
SEPTEMBER 1984–19 FEBRUARY 1985) DEVELOPING INTO AN INFLORESCENCE, AND
ON THE NUMBER OF SPIKELETS IN THE INFLORESCENCES PRODUCED (MEAN ± SE
FOR (n) INFLORESCENCES). UNPUBLISHED DATA OF A.D.A. WHITE.

Shade (%)	Pot size (mm)	Nutrient addition	Probability of an apex flowering	Number of spikelets per inflorescence
0	127	+	0.21	164 ± 6.5 (30)
		−	0.15	152 ± 8.5 (23)
	76	+	0.07	120 ± 11 (15)
		−	0.08	109 ± 7.0 (19)
50	127	+	0.02	86 ± 2.5 (4)
		−	0.04	100 ± 3.9 (7)
	76	+	0.07	79 ± 5.2 (14)
		−	0.04	96 ± 5.7 (13)

Shade screens were of neutral density Rokolene mesh; plants were grown in Fison's Levington potting
compost, with or without repotting from 76 to 127 mm pots on transfer to the glasshouse; complete
nutrient supplements were given weekly.

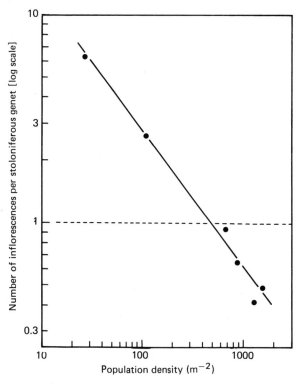

Figure 3.7   The mean number of inflorescences produced per stoloniferous genet (i.e.
genet showing floral evocation) in relation to surviving genet density in *Hieracium
pilosella*. $\ln y = 1.75 - 0.657 \ln x$ ($r^2 = 0.98$). (Reproduced from Bishop and Davy (1985),
with kind permission of authors and publishers.)

ridge formation increased the proportion from 0.17 to 0.22, whilst the reciprocal treatment reduced it from 0.33 to 0.31.

There is also evidence of an effect at the development stage in *Hieracium pilosella*. *Figure 3.7* shows the mean number of inflorescences per stoloniferous genet, at a range of surviving densities, in the glasshouse experiment described previously. As stolon development is the marker for floral evocation a theoretical value of unity would be expected, whereas in fact there was strong negative density dependence. The higher values, up to 6.25 at low density, result from a propensity of stolon apices to flower precociously, whilst still attached to the parent rosette, in response to artificially sustained long days in the glasshouse. But values of less than 1.0 presumably represent the abortion of a proportion of the evoked apices. This assumption yields an abortion probability of up to 0.58 at high density; at a density corresponding with the average in the a field, the probability of abortion was 0.36, strikingly similar to long term field estimates of 0.30–0.35.

Conclusions

There is scant evidence for the idea of a morphogenetic constraint on meristem availability for flowering in either of the contrasting sympodial species examined. Experimental manipulations of *Deschampsia cespitosa* suggest that a maximum of 25–30% of interconnected apices will flower after exposure to the vernalizing effects of a whole winter. *Hieracium pilosella* rosettes achieve 100% flowering only under exceptional conditions; as flowering enables clonal growth, the effect is generally to increase the bank of meristems with flowering potential. The outcome of monopodial clonal growth may be similar in the many species where the flowers are axillary and the ramets potentially iteroparous (polycarpic). The apex of *Trifolium repens*, for instance, responds to long days or vernalizing temperatures by cutting off axillary meristems that develop into floral primordia, whilst itself remaining vegetative (Thomas, 1962). An analysis of the consequences of growth-form for flowering is nevertheless important for prediction; closely related species may differ greatly.

Limitation of flowering at the induction stage is precisely predictive in *D. cespitosa*, at least in relation to year-to-year variation in field temperature. The increasing number of inflorescences following more prolonged exposure to early winter conditions also suggests that apices within a clone may vary considerably in their requirements for induction; the distribution of requirements within a tussock would be of considerable predictive value.

There can be little doubt that resource limitation exerts a powerful and predictable influence on flowering. Restriction of photosynthates or inorganic nutrients either directly, or indirectly through density/competition effects, reduces the probability of a ramet flowering. Effects on inflorescence development are important, although a clear separation of stages is not possible (cf. Ong *et al.*, 1978). Reduced flowering might involve failure of double-ridge formation or, more probably, abortion of apices with floral primordia. The uncertainties do underline the dependence of our ability to make specific, quantitative predictions on empirically determined relationships. Advances in understanding the mechanism of flowering will allow the development of more predictive theory for clonal organization, as for unitary organization.

References

BERNIER, G., KINET, J-M. and SACHS, R.M. (1981a). *The Physiology of Flowering. I The Initiation of Flowers.* Florida, CRC Press

BERNIER, G., KINET, J-M. and SACHS, R.M. (1985). *The Physiology of Flowering. III The Development of Flowers.* Florida, CRC Press

BISHOP, G.F. and DAVY, A.J. (1984). Significance of rabbits for the population regulation of *Hieracium pilosella* in Breckland. *Journal of Ecology*, **72**, 273–284

BISHOP, G.F. and DAVY, A.J. (1985). Density and the commitment of apical meristems to clonal growth and flowering in *Hieracium pilosella*. *Oecologia (Berlin)*, **66**, 417–422

CHOUARD, P. (1960). Vernalization and its relations to dormancy. *Annual Review of Plant Physiology*, **11**, 191–238

DAVY, A.J. (1980). *Deschampsia caespitosa*: Biological flora of the British Isles. *Journal of Ecology*, **68**, 1075–1096

DAVY, A.J. (1982). Flowering competence after exposure to naturally fluctuating winter temperatures in a perennial grass, *Deschampsia caespitosa* (L.)Beauv. *Annals of Botany*, **50**, 705–715

DAVY, A.J. and BISHOP, G.F. (1984). Response of *Hieracium pilosella* in Breckland grass-heath to inorganic nutrients. *Journal of Ecology*, **72**, 319–330

EVANS, L.T. (Ed.) (1969). *The Induction of Flowering*, Melbourne, MacMillan

HEIDE, O.M. (1986). Primary and secondary induction requirements for flowering in *Alopecurus pratensis*. *Physiologia Plantarum*, **66**, 251–256

INGHE, O. and TAMM, C.O. (1985). Survival and flowering of perennial herbs. IV. *Oikos*, **45**, 400–420

KACHI, N. and HIROSE, T. (1985). Population dynamics of *Oenothera glazioviana* in a sand-dune system with special reference to the adaptive significance of size-dependent reproduction. *Journal of Ecology*, **73**, 887–901

KETELLAPPER, H.J. (1960). Growth and development in *Phalaris*. I. Vernalization response in geographic strains of *P. tuberosa* L. *Ecology*, **41**, 298–305

KINET, J-M., SACHS, R.M. and BERNIER, G. (1981b). *The Physiology of Flowering. II Transition to Reproductive Growth.* Florida, CRC Press

MURFET, I.C. (1977). Environmental interaction and the genetics of flowering. *Annual Review of Plant Physiology*, **28**, 253–278

ONG, C.K., MARSHALL, C. and SAGAR, G.R. (1978). The effects of nutrient supply on flowering and seed production in *Poa annua* L. *Journal of the British Grassland Society*, **33**, 117–121.

PURVIS, O.N. (1961). The physiological analysis of vernalization. In *Encyclopedia of Plant Physiology* XVI (W. Rühland Ed.), pp. 76–122. Berlin, Springer-Verlag

ROTHERA, S.L. and DAVY, A.J. (1986). Polyploidy and habitat differentiation in *Deschampsia caespitosa*. *New Phytologist*, **102**, 449–467

SCHEMSKE, D.W., WILLSON, M.F., MELAMPY, M.N., MILLER, L.J., VERNER, L., SCHEMSKE, K.M. and BEST, L.B. (1978). Flowering ecology of some spring woodland herbs. *Ecology*, **59**, 351–366

SCHWABE, W.W. (1971). Physiology of vegetative reproduction and flowering. In *Plant Physiology. VIA* (F.C. Steward, Ed.), pp. 233–411, New York, Academic Press

THOMAS, A.G. and DALE, H.M. (1974). Zonation and regulation of old pasture populations of *Hieracium floribundum*. *Canadian Journal of Botany*, **52**, 1451–1458

THOMAS, R.G. (1962). The initiation and growth of axillary bud primordia in relation to flowering in *Trifolium repens* L. *Annals of Botany*, **26**, 329–344

TRIPATHI, R.S. and HARPER, J.L. (1973). The Comparative biology of *Agropyron repens* (L.) and *A. caninum* (L.) Beauv. 1. The growth of mixed populations established from tillers and from seeds. *Journal of Ecology*, **61**, 353–368

VINCE-PRUE, D. (1975). *Photoperiodism in Plants*, Maidenhead, McGraw-Hill

WATSON, M.A. (1984). Developmental constraints: effects on population growth and patterns of resource allocation in a clonal plant. *The American Naturalist*, **123**, 411–426

WATSON, M.A. and CASPER, B.B. (1984). Morphogenetic constraints on patterns of carbon distribution in plants. *Annual Review of Ecology and Systematics*, **15**, 233–258

WELLS, T.C.E. (1981). Population ecology of terrestrial orchids. In *The Biological Aspects of Rare Plant Conservation* (H. Synge, Ed.), pp. 281–295, Chichester, Wiley

WILLSON, M.F. (1983). *Plant Reproductive Ecology*, New York, Wiley

YOUNG, T.P. (1984). The comparative demography of semelparous *Lobelia telekii* and iteroparous *Lobelia keniensis* on Mount Kenya. *Journal of Ecology*, **72**, 637–650

ZEEVAART, J.A.D. (1976). Physiology of flower formation. *Annual Review of Plant Physiology*, **27**, 321–348

4

MODELLING FLOWER INITIATION

J.H.M. THORNLEY
Animal and Grassland Research Institute, Hurley, Maidenhead, Berkshire, UK

Introduction

Development and flowering present a challenging problem to the plant scientist—much work has been done yet much remains to be understood. The four principal phases of plant development are germination, vegetative growth, flower development and fruit growth; these phases are punctuated or delimited by events such as sowing, emergence, flower initiation, anthesis and maturity. Of these developmental events, flower initiation is of especial interest because it presents, perhaps more so than the other events, an example of a genuine bifurcation or choice of developmental pathway.

The task for the scientist is to describe, predict, understand and apply, not necessarily in that order. Prediction and application may precede understanding; and much of our understanding may be inapplicable to current problems. For plant developmental events in general, and for flower initiation in particular, prediction of the macroscopic phenomena in relation to environmental influences has proved to be quite easy, and of considerable practicable value. For example, the computation of temperature sums—perhaps modified for the effects of radiation, photoperiod and vernalization—provides an accurate predictor of many developmental events. In this chapter some of the modelling approaches that have been used in this area will be surveyed.

Understanding is the proper long-term goal for some research, and it may useful to ask what type of understanding is sought for developmental phenomena. The predictive models referred to in the last paragraph are simply input–output relations and may be termed empirical or phenomenological; while such models can work well and are very useful, it would be unusual to claim that they lead to understanding. Plant biology is notable for the existence of a pronounced hierarchy of organization—crop, plant, organ, tissue, cell and macromolecule, for example. Different phenomena and spatial–temporal relations can be attached to each level. A model of phenomena at the ith level in this organizational hierarchy provides understanding if it relates these ith level phenomena to other processes or phenomena at a lower organizational level—say the $(i-1)$th and/or $(i-2)$th level (for example, Thornley, 1976, 1980). Such models have been termed 'mechanistic' or 'explanatory', and they can be integrative in several ways: they bring several processes or mechanisms together (photosynthesis, transport, chemical conversion) to give a coherent picture of the ith level system; they often relate fast processes (biochemical, metabolic) to slower processes (tissue, organ); they sometimes relate spatially distinct entities to each other (root, shoot). For the purpose of understanding, models of developmental pheno- mena, including flower initiation, are required that include internal variables of the plant, that is, tissue, cell or biochemical characters. Such models are few, are mostly of a speculative nature, and are not well connected to the observational data that are available. I shall describe some of the models in which I have recently taken an interest: these models should be viewed as attempts to develop ideas, rather than as hypotheses to be falsified.

In addition to these two broad categories of model, empirical and mechanistic, there is a third type of model that should be considered. Mechanistic models follow the enormously successful reductionist tradition of directing one's attention downwards in the organizational hierarchy and representing increasing amounts of detail. Empirical models operate at a single level in the hierarchy. There is a category of models which has been termed 'teleonomic' or 'teleological', or 'goal-seeking'. These models may be empirical or phenomenological, and are based at a given level. They are upward looking in the organizational hierarchy; they consider the constraints that are imposed from above, how the plant may respond to them, and how the response may affect survival. Especially they are concerned with the often complex mechanisms that have evolved over long periods of time, and which provide efficient (in terms of survival) responses to environment. If we say that a plant initiates reproductive growth when an increasing day-length reaches a particular value because the plant 'knows' that favourable growing conditions are ahead, this is a teleonomic view of the response of the plant. If we say that a plant regulates its root:shoot ratio in order to maintain a certain nitrogen:carbon ratio, then this is a goal-seeking model of root:shoot partitioning. A goal-seeking model can always be represented mechanisti- cally, and mechanistic models are objective in their operation (as with Newton's laws, a set of given initial conditions, plus the equations of motion governing the system, lead to a calculable outcome). However, a teleonomic model can give a useful and simpler view of the system, and lead to valuable insights. Some empirical models of aspects of plant response lend themselves to a teleonomic interpretation whereas others do not. There is an excellent discussion of this topic by Monod (1972).

EMPIRICAL MODELS

Empirical models of flower initiation are equally applicable, at least in principle, to other developmental phases. This approach is based on the idea that it is possible to associate a scalar (singled-valued) variable, h (say), with the phase of development being considered, and to use the value of h to denote progression through that phase. If a scalar variable describes development, then a single rate constant, k, denotes the rate of development. Assuming $h = 0$ at the beginning of the phase of development when time $t = 0$, then at time t (days), h is given by:

$$h = \int_0^t k \, dt \tag{4.1}$$

h increases with increasing time t, if k is non-zero and positive. The units of h/k are of course days, but otherwise the units of h can be chosen for convenience. When h attains a particular value, h_i, at time $t = t_i$, then flower initiation occurs and that phase of development is complete. It is assumed in this approach that the plant, or part of the plant, possesses a developmental process or clock which proceeds at the rate k during the given phase. I am not aware that anyone has addressed the problem, experimentally, of whether a single variable is sufficient to define the developmental status of an apex. Some of the theoretical models do require more than one variable for this purpose.

Ideally, some of the internal variables of the system, the vegetative apex, would allow the developmental index h to be calculated directly from them, so that:

$$h = h(\text{internal state variables of system}) \tag{4.2}$$

Using the usual rate:state formalism (e.g. France and Thornley, 1984, pp. 15–19) the differential equations of the model determine how the state variables change with time, and Equation 4.2 then defines how the developmental index changes. The environmental variables would appear in the differential equations, where they affect the dynamics of the internal variables, but would not appear directly in the calculation of h. This could provide a mechanistic approach to the problem.

However, the very successful empirical approach has been to assume that the rate constant k and also h through Equation 4.1 depend directly upon the environmental variables, E, so that:

$$k = k(E) \tag{4.3}$$

The next part of the discussion is concerned with how the developmental rate constant k depends upon temperature, radiation, and day-length, which are the principal environmental variables for flower initiation.

Threshold models using environmental sums

Assuming a finite time interval Δt, then Equation 4.1 can be aproximated by:

$$h = \sum_{j=1}^{j=n} k\Delta t \tag{4.4}$$

where the index j runs over the n intervals of Δt in time t.

The temperature–sum method is obtained by assuming that the rate constant k depends linearly on temperature T alone, according to:

$$k = k_0(T - T_0) \text{ for } T \geqslant T_0, \tag{4.5}$$
$$= 0 \text{ otherwise}$$

k_0 is a constant; T_0 is a base temperature below which development does not proceed at all. If it is assumed that the time interval Δt is 1 day, and using T_j to denote the mean temperature on the jth day, combining Equations 4.4 and 4.5 gives:

$$h = \sum_{j=1}^{n} \Delta t k_0 (T_j - T_0)_+ \tag{4.6}$$

The + subscript on the expression in brackets indicates that terms only contribute if they are positive; otherwise they are set to zero. Since the scale attached to the values of h is arbitrary, Equation 4.6 is usually further simplified by taking k_0 equal to unity, so that:

$$h = \sum_{j=1}^{n} \Delta t (T_j - T_0)_+ \tag{4.7}$$

The units of h are day °C. Some workers prefer to define the expected value of h over a particular phase of development as unity, and this fixes the value of k_0. In either case, the operation of Equations 4.6 and 4.7 is straightforward. Deputat (1974), working with spring wheat for the developmental period from emergence to earing, found that $h = 533$ day °C and $T_0 = 4$°C in Equation 4.7.

Equations 4.6 and 4.7 have been extended or modified in many ways by Nuttonson (1955), Robertson (1968), Angus *et al.*, (1981) and others. For example, it may be assumed that the response to temperature is non-linear giving:

$$h = \sum_{j=1}^{n} [a(T_j - T_0)_+ + b\,(T_j - T_0)_+^2 + c(T_j - T_0)_+^3], \tag{4.8}$$

where a, b and c are constants, and each term only contributes to the sum if positive. Taking account of other environmental factors, such as daily radiation receipt J, and day-length g, and assuming these factors are linear and non-interacting, leads to:

$$h = \sum_{j=1}^{n} [a(T_j + T_0)_+ + b(g_j - g_0)_+ + c(J_j - J_0)_+], \tag{4.9}$$

where a, b and c are constants [not the same as in Equation 4.8], g_j and J_j denote the day-length and radiation receipt on the jth day, and g_0 and J_0 are threshold values of g and J. Again the terms only contribute to the sum if positive. A general equation where the three factors of temperature, radiation and day-length interact is:

$$h = \sum_{j=1}^{n} f_T(T_j)f_J(J_j)f_g(g_j) \tag{4.10}$$

where f_T, f_J and f_g represent functions of temperature T, radiation receipt J and day-length g. A 'photothermal' index may take the form:

$$h = \sum_{j=1}^{n} J_j(T_j - T_0)_+ \tag{4.11}$$

Equation 4.11 is able to allow for the experimental observation that higher temperatures are more effective in promoting development if the plant is supplied with high radiation levels, presumably ensuring plentiful substrate availability. After considering several expressions, Angus *et al.* (1981) found that a negative exponential function gave satisfactory results with wheat development, and they used:

$$f_T(T) = [1 - e^{-b(T - T_0)_+}],$$
$$f_g(g) = [1 - e^{-c(g - g_0)_+}], \tag{4.12}$$

to describe the multiplicative effects of temperature and day-length.

Equation 4.11 suggests a way in which these empirical approaches might be made more mechanistic. For example, one could replace the daily radiation receipt on the jth day, J_j, by a mean daily substrate level, S_j, giving instead of Equation 4.11:

$$h = \sum_{j=1}^{n} S_j(T_j - T_0)_+ \tag{4.13}$$

A plant growth model, representing the response of substrate supply to radiation, and the effects of different competing sinks on the substrate level at the apex being considered, could be used in conjunction with Equation 4.13 to compute the developmental index.

MECHANISTIC SWITCHES FOR FLOWER INITIATION

The models of the last section have been of the form:

While $h < h_i$, continue vegetative development
but if $h \geqslant h_i$, then initiate and carry out reproductive development.

Rather than relate the developmental index h directly to environmental variables as hitherto, we now wish to explore ways in which h and its threshold value h_i might be related directly to internal variables of the plant Not enough is known to do this other than speculatively, and some of the variables we shall use (e.g. vegetative and flowering morphogens) are hypothetical.

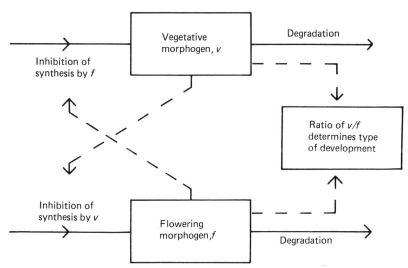

Figure 4.1 Scheme for a two-morphogen switch to control flowering. The dashed lines indicate control paths, the continuous lines denote fluxes.

A two-morphogen switch

Figure 4.1 shows a scheme is shown which is able to have two stable steady-state solutions given suitable parameter values. v is a vegetative morphogen whose synthesis may be inhibited by the presence of a flowering morphogen f according to a sigmoidal inhibition response. Similarly the synthesis of f may be inhibited by v. Both morphogens v and f are degraded linearly. These assumptions lead to two differential equations (see Thornley, 1972, 1976, for further detail):

$$\frac{dv}{dt} = \frac{1}{1+(f/c)^q} - v, \quad \frac{df}{dt} = \frac{1}{1+(v/c)^q} - f \tag{4.14}$$

c is an affinity constant, and q determines the sigmoidicity of the inhibition curve. The equations have been non-dimensionalized for convenience.

The steady-state solutions are obtained by equating Equation 4.14 to zero, giving:

$$v = \frac{1}{1+(f/c)^q}, \quad f = \frac{1}{1+(v/c)^q} \tag{4.15}$$

These two equations, which are symmetric in v and f, are shown in *Figure 4.2*, and the points of intersection give the steady-state solutions. There are one or three points of intersection, depending upon the values of q and c. For the three-solution symmetric case shown in *Figure 4.2*, U is unstable, and V (vegetative) and F (flowering) are stable; if the system point is placed above the line $v=f$, application of Equation 4.14 moves the (v, f) point to V, and *vice versa*.

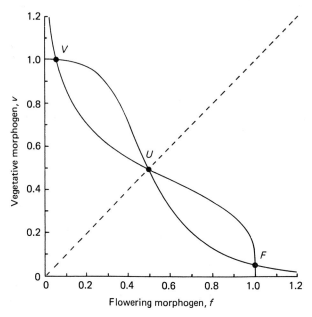

Figure 4.2   Two-morphogen switch. Equations 4.15 are plotted for $c=0.5$, $q=4$, showing the three steady-state solutions, V, U and F, to Equations 4.14. V and F are stable points, and hypothetically correspond to vegetative and flowering development; U is unstable. The dashed line is $v=f$, dividing the system space into two regions, in which either V or F is the attractor.

There are several ways in which Equations 4.14 can be made to simulate the response of a switch. Perhaps the simplest is to assume that a flowering stimulus s applied over a short period of time has the effect of reducing the level of the vegetative morphogen v and increasing that of the flowering morphogen f, according to:

$$\Delta v = -s, \qquad \Delta f = s, \tag{4.16}$$

this shifts the system point toward the dashed line $v=f$ in *Figure 4.2*, and once the system point crosses this line, it then moves towards F rather than towards V.

However, it may be conceptually more satisfactory to assume that hormonal or other influences gradually change the affinities in the regulation system. Suppose we replace Equations 4.14 by:

$$\frac{dv}{dt} = \beta[\frac{1}{1+(f/(1-c))^q} - v], \frac{df}{dt} = \beta[\frac{1}{1+(v/c)^q} - f] \tag{4.17}$$

here it is assumed that the affinity constants are reciprocally related, that is are $(1-c)$ and c, so that if one becomes smaller, then the other becomes larger; β is simply a number (for example, 100) that scales up the time derivatives so that integration of Equations 4.17 maintains the system point (v, f) close to a steady-state solution, that is, one of the intersections shown in *Figures 4.2* and *4.3*. *Figure 4.3* shows the solutions obtained when Equations 4.17 are equated to zero, so that $dv/dt = df/dt = 0$, for three values of c, namely c = 0.3, 0.5 and 0.7. For c = 0.3 there is a single solution that can be equated with vegetative growth: for c = 0.5 there are (as in *Figure 4.2*) three solutions with the possibilites of vegetative growth or flowering growth; for c = 0.7, there is again a single solution, this time corresponding to reproductive growth.

To obtain switch behaviour, it is next assumed that c is a slowly varying quantity, given by:

$$\frac{dc}{dt} = g,$$

(4.18)

where g is a constant. As c increases over the range from 0.3 to 0.7, then inspection of *Figure 4.3* shows that at a certain value of c there is a sudden (catastrophic) change in the nature of the solution: this change is equated with the transition to flowering. This is shown more explicitly in *Figure 4.4*, where the morphogen ratio, v/f, is drawn as a function of time, t, assuming that the rate of change of c, g, is constant at g = 0.02, and that c(t = 0) = 0.3; at time t = 20, c = 0.7.

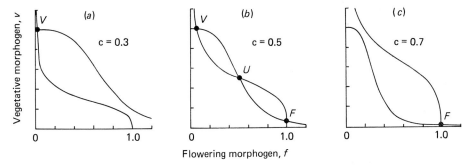

Figure 4.3 Steady-state solutions to Equations 4.17 are shown for values of c as shown. In (a), the single solution at V is equated with vegetative growth; in (b), the three solutions to the symmetric equations allow either vegetative growth (V) or flowering growth (F); in (c) the single solution corresponds to flowering growth (F).

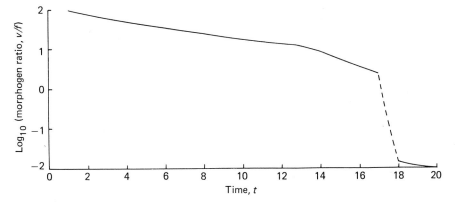

Figure 4.4 Switched development using the scheme of *Figure 4.1*. The time course shown was obtained by integrating Equations 4.17 and 4.18 with β = 100, g = 0.02, and initial values at time t = 0 of v = f = 1, and c = 0.3; the fourth-order variable-step Runge–Kutta method was used with a △t (maximum) of 0.005.

A substrate supply-demand switch

It is possible to construct a model that will lead to a sudden change in apical behaviour solely in terms of the supply of substrate to the shoot apex and the utilization of substrate. To many scientists such a hypothesis will be more acceptable than a hypothesis based on morphogens, whose existence is totally speculative at the present time.

Let x denote some measure of apex size. Assume that the substrate flux into the shoot apex, F, depends non-linearly on x, is polar (always into the apex), and is independent of substrate level s. In particular we assume that:

$$F = c + \frac{x^2}{1+x^2},$$

(4.19)

where c is a constant giving the flux into a very small apex. Assume also that the rate of substrate utilization, U, is proportional to apex size, according to:

$$U = kx,$$

(4.20)

where k is a constant. When the rates of supply and demand are in balance, $F = U$, and:

$$kx = c + \frac{x^2}{1+x^2}$$

(4.21)

Equation 4.21 is cubic in x, with one or three real solutions: however, we prefer to graph each side of the equation, as in *Figure 4.5*, and consider the points of intersection.

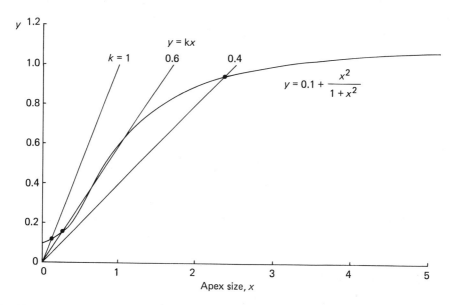

Figure 4.5 Graphical representation of solutions of Equation 4.21. The sigmoid curve denotes the supply of substrate to the apex of Equation 4.19; the demand function of Equation 4.20 is shown for three values of k as indicated. The switch occurs between $k = 0.6$ and $k = 0.4$; the relevant steady-state solution is shown by ●.

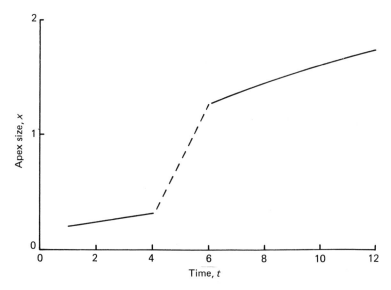

Figure 4.6 Substrate supply–demand switch. The time course shown was obtained by integrating Equations 4.22 and 4.23 with $\beta = 100$, $c = 0.1$, $\alpha = 0.1$, $k_f = 0.4$, and initial values at time $t = 0$ of $x = 0.1$ and $k = 0.7$; the fourth-order variable-step Runge–Kutta method was used with a $\triangle t$ (maximum) of 0.005.

Figure 4.5 shows a constant supply function with c constant, but with a varying demand function, simulated by varying k. It can be seen that a reducing k can produce a switch in the operating point of the system, to a larger value in the apex size variable x. In contrast to the switch of the last section which required three differential equations for its definition (Equations 4.17 and 4.18), two equations are sufficient for a simple supply-demand switch. From the above considerations, we can write down:

$$\frac{\mathrm{d}x}{\mathrm{d}t} = \beta(c + \frac{x^2}{1+x^2} - kx), \tag{4.22}$$

$$\frac{\mathrm{d}k}{\mathrm{d}t} = \alpha(k_f - k) \tag{4.23}$$

As earlier after Equations 4.17, β is a large number to ensure that x remains close to a stable solution of Equation 4.21; α determines how rapidly k changes from its initial value at time $t = 0$ towards its final value of k_f. The results of integrating Equations 4.22 and 4.23 are shown in *Figure 4.6*, and they exhibit the now familiar switch behaviour. This supply–demand switch has been written in terms of apex size, because this seems to be an important variable associated with flower initiation; a switch of substrate concentrations could equally easily be constructed.

A spatially constrained switch

Small vegetative apices tend to produce large primordia, and larger reproductive apices tend to produce smaller floral primordia. This suggests that there may be constraints present in the system that relate primordial size (and type) to apical size in some sort of 'equation of state', to use the physicochemical term for an equation like van der Waal's equation for the pressure–volume–temperature relations of a pure substance. The problem of superconductivity may be a useful analogy to what is being described in this section. The phase transition, or change in state, involved in superconductivity has long been described in a phenomenological manner with considerable success; yet attempts to relate the responses to atomic or molecular level parameters have been far less successful. However, the phenomenological theory has been exceedingly useful, even though the parameters of this theory are not thoroughly understood. Is it then possible, borrowing these ideas, to construct a theory that will at least describe the events that occur in flower initiation on a macro level? If this is achieved, the relationship of the parameters of such a theory to underlying properties at the cellular or biochemical levels may perhaps usefully be regarded as a separate problem.

The elements of a possible phenomenological theory of flower initiation were proposed by Thornley and Cockshull (1980), who adapted the cusp catastrophe equation from catastrophe theory to relate primordial size to apex size, and married this to the inhibitor approach to primordial initiation (Thornley, 1975; Charles-Edwards *et al.*, 1979). We describe the salient features of this approach below; for further details and background, the original papers should be consulted.

The model has three state variables: W_a is the mass of the apex just before primordial initiation takes place; W_p is the mass of a primordium just after its initiation; and I is the level of concentration of an inhibitor of primordial initiation. It is convenient to write parts of the model in terms of variables x and y which are related to W_a and W_p by:

$$x = \frac{W_p}{W_a} \text{ and } y = \alpha(W_a - C_a)$$

(4.24)

where x now denotes the fraction of the apex which will be donated to the next primordium, y is linearly related to apex size, α and C_a are constants. The 'equation of state' relating x and y, and therefore primordial size to apical size, is taken to be:

$$0 = 4b(x - x_0)^3 - 2a(x - x_0) + fy + \frac{h(2x - x_{min} - x_{max})}{(x_{max} - x)^2(x - x_{min})^2}$$

(4.25)

where b, a, x_0, f, h, x_{min} and x_{max} are constants. Apart from the last term, this equation denotes the intersection of a cubic term with a linear term and gives the type of catastrophe shown in *Figure 4.5*; the last term limits the allowed values of x to the range x_{min} to x_{max}, that is, the new primordium cannot occupy the whole of the apex and also it has a minimum size.

Using the inhibitor approach to primordial initiation, the plastochron t_p (the time between the initiation of successive primordia), and the specific growth rate of the apex R (R is an overall specific growth rate, measured from initiation event to the next initiation event), are given by:

$$t_p = \frac{1}{\mu + k_d} \ln(1 + \frac{\lambda x}{I_c}) \text{ and } R = \mu + \frac{1}{t_p} \ln(1 - x)$$

(4.26)

where μ is the intrinsic apex specific growth rate (between primordial initiation events), k_d is the decay rate of the inhibitor I, λ defines how much inhibitor is produced at each primordial initiation (a new primordium of mass W_p gives rise to λW_p units of inhibitor) and I_c is the critical value of inhibitor concentration for primordial initiation.

The rate equation which drives the system determines the increase in apex size, according to:

$$\frac{dy}{dt} = R_w(y + \alpha C_a)$$

(4.27)

As apex size (that is, y) increases, the solution to Equation 4.25 determines x and primordial size. Following the procedure used earlier, we can obtain a good approximation to the solution of Equation 4.25 by assuming that:

$$\frac{dx}{dt} = -\beta[4b(x - x_0)^3 - 2a(x - x_0) + fy + \frac{h(2x - x_{min} - x_{max})}{(x_{max} - x)^2(x - x_{min})^2}]$$

(4.28)

where β is a large constant.

In *Figure 4.7*, the time responses from this model are shown. At least qualitatively, this model is able to simulate successfully many of the changes that occur at the shoot apex when flowering is initiated.

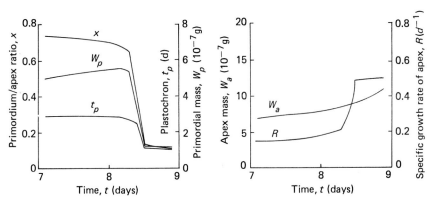

Figure 4.7 A vegetative–reproductive switch based on spatial constraints between apex size and primordial size, using equations from catastrophe theory. The results were obtained by integrating Equations 4.27 and 4.28 by Euler's method with $\Delta t = 0.001\ d$, and with $a = 0.2$, $b = 1$, $f = 1$, $h = 0.0001$, $x_0 = 0.5$, $x_{min} = 0.05$, $x_{max} = 0.8$, $c_a = 6 \times 10^{-7}$, $\alpha = 2 \times 10^5$; and at $t = 0$, $x = 0.72$ and $y = -0.062$. (For further details *see* Thornley and Cockshull (1980).).

Discussion

This chapter began by suggesting that there are three significant types of model relevant to flower initiation: empirical, mechanistic and teleonomic.

The empirical models have been steadily improved over the years, and they now work very satisfactorily; little more is wanted from them that they are not already capable of delivering; the approach has a distinctly 'mature' appearance, and it is difficult to imagine what breakthroughs if any are required or possible.

While the empirical models have a much appreciated immediate utility, it is not possible to explore the full range of options (such as environmental manipulation, genetic modification and so on), without a mechanistic understanding of the system. Mechanistic models, because they encompass more phenomena, can always reveal more possibilities than an empirical model. Our account of mechanistic approaches has been totally speculative—I believe that not enough is currently known to be otherwise. These models are at present mostly concerned with developing possible relevant ideas and approaches. Also, an important class of mechanistic switching models has been omitted—those involving genetically mediated mechanisms, epigenesis and other regulatory machinery (for example, Kauffman, 1973; Sibatani, 1978).

There are few teleonomic models of flower initiation, unless one is to regard the attainment of a particular value of a temperature sum as teleonomy, which most would not. Much has been said and written about the value of particular responses in ensuring survival, whether by vernalization, day-length, temperature sums, or the control of leaf orientation. Teleonomy may be regarded as a sophisticated response to environment that frequently anticipates the future. The best single example of teleonomy in biology is possibly that of the response of the gut bacterium *Escherichia coli* to a β-galactoside substrate; the teleonomic view of this response is underpinned by an objective mechanistic model at the molecular level. For root–shoot dry matter partitioning, a teleonomic approach to the problem has been suggested which operates via control of C:N ratios (Reynolds and Thornley, 1982; Johnson, 1985). As discussed earlier, teleonomic mechanisms may arise from the juxtaposition of the myriad regulatory possibilities offered by the biological machinery, and the constraints imposed by a higher level in the organizational hierarchy, which may favour (genetically) a particular type of response. Paltridge and Denholm (1974) investigated the switch from vegetative to reproductive growth in terms of the yield over the whole life cycle for the wheat crop. Their model, neither empirical nor mechanistic, is perhaps the only example of an overtly teleonomic approach to flower initiation.

Acknowledgements

The Animal and Grassland Research Institute is financed through the Agricultural and Food Research Council; the work is in part commissioned by the Ministry of Agriculture, Fisheries and Food.

References

ANGUS, J.F., MACKENZIE, D.H., MORTON, R. and SCHAFER, C.A. (1981). Phasic development in field crops. II. Thermal and photoperiodic responses of spring wheat. *Field Crops Research*, **4**, 269–283

CHARLES-EDWARDS, C.E., COCKSHULL, K.E., HORRIDGE, J.S. and THORNLEY, J.H.M. (1979). A model of flowering in chrysanthemum. *Annals of Botany*, **44**, 557–566

DEPUTAT, T. (1974). The influence of temperature on the length of the development periods between the phases of spring wheat. *Pamietnik Pulawski*, **60**, 129–146

FRANCE, J. and THORNLEY, J.H.M. (1984). *Mathematical Models in Agriculture*, London, Butterworths

JOHNSON, I.R. (1985). A model of the partitioning of growth between the shoots and roots of vegetative plants. *Annals of Botany*, **55**, 421–431

KAUFFMANN, S.A. (1973). Control circuits for determination and trans-determination. *Science*, **181**, 310–318

MONOD, J. (1972). *Chance and Necessity—An Essay on the Natural Philosophy of Modern Biology*, London, Collins

NUTTONSON, M.Y. (1955). *Wheat—Climate Relationships and the Use of Phenology in Ascertaining the Thermal and Photothermal Requirements for Wheat*, Washington, D.C., American Institute of Crop Ecology

PALTRIDGE, G.W. and DENHOLM, J.V. (1974). Plant yield and the switch from vegetative to reproductive growth. *Journal of Theoretical Biology*, **44**, 23–34

REYNOLDS, J.F. and THORNLEY, J.H.M. (1982). A shoot:root partitioning model. *Annals of Botany*, **49**, 585-597

ROBERTSON, G.W. (1968). A biometerological time scale for a cereal crop involving day and night temperature and photoperiod. *International Journal of Biometeorology*, **12**, 191–223

SIBATANI, A. (1978). A bifurcation model for developmental processes. *Journal of Theoretical Biology*, **75**, 149–166

THORNLEY, J.H.M.(1972). A model of a biochemical switch, and its application to flower initiation. *Annals of Botany*, **36**, 861–871

THORNLEY, J.H.M. (1975). Phyllotaxis. I. A mechanistic model. *Annals of Botany*, **39**, 491–507

THORNLEY, J.H.M. (1976). *Mathematical Models in Plant Physiology*, London, Academic Press

THORNLEY, J.H.M. (1980). The role of mathematics in plant science research. *Plant, Cell and Environment*, **3**, 233–236

THORNLEY, J.H.M. and COCKSHULL, K.E. (1980). A catastrophe model for the switch from vegetative growth to reproductive growth in the shoot apex. *Annals of Botany*, **46**, 333–341

III

Juvenility

5

JUVENILITY AND CELL DETERMINATION

P.F. WAREING
*Department of Botany and Microbiology, University College of Wales,
Aberystwyth, UK*

Introduction

Seedlings of both woody and herbaceous plants commonly pass through a 'juvenile' phase marked by various characteristic differences in form and behaviour from the mature stages of the species, but the most consistent of these differences relates to flowering behaviour. As is well known, the seedlings of tree species lack the ability to flower during a juvenile period which may last many years.

Herbaceous species, both annual and perennial, show analogous behaviour; thus it is exceptional for flowering of annual plants to occur at a very early stage following germination, and usually there is a vegetative period of variable duration before the plants achieve the ability to initiate flowers. This phenomenon is seen not only in day-neutral species, such as sunflower, but also in species in which flower initiation is regulated by day-length. Thus, seedlings of the short-day plant, *Perilla ocymoides*, will initiate flowers only after they have formed three pairs of leaves (Zeevaart, 1958). Similarly, among plants with a chilling requirement for flowering, certain species, such as Brussels sprouts (*Brassica oleracea*) cannot be vernalized at the seed stage and will respond only when they have undergone a period of vegetative growth and attained a certain minimum size (Stokes and Verkerk, 1951).

Both in woody and in herbacecous plants there would seem to be adaptive advantages in the delay of sexual reproduction and fruiting until a certain size has been attained. The adaptive significance of the woody habit lies in the ability to attain a large size and hence an advantage in the competition for light. Clearly, the rate of vegetative growth will be diminished if appreciable proportions of dry matter are diverted into fruits and seeds at an early stage, and there would appear to be competitive advantages in the inhibition of flowering during the early phases of growth. Similar arguments can be applied to herbaceous species, since seed yield will be reduced if flowering occurs in very small seedlings, before an adequate leaf area and capacity for dry matter production has been attained. Thus the juvenile phase should apparently be regarded as one in which precocious flowering is actively inhibited.

Although the adaptive significance of a juvenile phase appears to lie in the prevention of precocious flowering, the two phases (juvenile and adult) are frequently distinguishable also by differences in various vegetative characters, such as leaf shape and size, phyllotaxy, rooting ability, pigmentation, etc., as seen, for example, in ivy (*Hedera helix*) (Doorenbos, 1954; Wareing and Frydman, 1976).

Although the functional significance of a non-flowering juvenile phase would appear to be similar in both woody and herbaceous species, it is not known whether the physiological and molecular bases of juvenility are the same in both groups. The phenomenon has been the subject of much more attention in woody plants, because of the practical problems arising from a long juvenile phase in tree-breeding, and much more information is thus available on the phenomenon in woody than in herbaceous plants. Since the literature on the subject has been reviewed extensively (Brink, 1962; Doorenbos, 1954; Hackett, 1985; Zimmerman, Hackett and Pharis, 1985) only the salient features need be summarized here.

Phase change in woody plants

In considering the phenomenon of juvenility in woody plants it is necessary to make a distinction between two major problems (Wareing and Frydman, 1976):

1. What factors control the stage at which the transition from the juvenile to the adult stage occurs within the tree?
2. What is the molecular basis of the differences between juvenile and adult shoots and how are these differences transmitted through cell division?

Although the juvenile phase may extend over several years, it is now well established that *time* is not the primary controlling factor and neither is the number of annual cycles of growth and dormancy; rather it appears that the transition occurs when a certain *size* has been attained regardless of whether this is achieved by rapid or slow growth (Longman and Wareing, 1959). However, it is still not clear whether it is size *per se* which is the controlling factor, or some other variable with which size is correlated. The problem is complex and has been discussed at length by Hackett (1985).

The adult, flowering phase, once attained, is remarkably stable and is not normally reversed by grafting an adult scion on to a juvenile stock, a fact which, of course, forms the basis of much horticultural and forestry practice.

Although adult shoots show reduced ability to form adventitious roots, it is possible to root cuttings of adult ivy, which can retain their adult characters for many years, if grown out-of-doors. Conversely, if juvenile shoots are grafted into adult parts of a tree or vine, the juvenile characters persist for several years (Schaffelitsky de Muckadell, 1954; Robinson and Wareing, 1969).

The occurrence of two distinct and stable phases in ivy and other woody species is very striking, so that it is appropriate to apply the term *phase-change* (Brink, 1962) to the phenomenon.

Although the two phases are remarkably stable, nevertheless phase-change is not irreversible and indeed, reversal from the adult to the juvenile condition occurs during normal sexual reproduction, since juvenile embryos are formed in fruits borne on adult shoots. Moreover, phase reversal may occur if rooted cuttings of adult ivy shoots are maintained at high temperatures or treated with repeated applications of gibberellic acid (Robbins, 1957; Frydman and Wareing, 1974). Thus it is clear that phase change does not entail irreversible changes in the genome, but stable differences in *gene expression* which are transmitted through repeated cycles of cell division, and it is the primary purpose of this chapter to discuss the phenomenon in a more general context.

Cell determination in apical meristems

The totipotency of many plant cells has rightly attracted a great deal of attention and has been the subject of an enormous amount of experimental work, because of its practical importance, but this has led to the almost total neglect of the phenomenon of *determination* in plant cells. Indeed, at first sight, the occurrence of totipotency would appear to negate the possibility of cell determination, but the two concepts are not mutually incompatible, since it is not suggested that the same cell can, *at the same time*, be both totipotent and determined—they are alternative states.

When a cell is determined, it is *committed* to a certain pathway of development. Meristematic cells are thought of as being totally uncommitted, because they are 'undifferentiated', but there are good reasons to question the validity of this assumption (Wareing, 1978, 1979).

It is clear that the form of juvenile and adult shoots of *Hedera*, involving differences in leaf shape, phyllotaxis, growth habit and other characters must reflect differences in the properties of the shoot apical meristems from which the respective mature tissues are derived. Thus the shoot apical meristems of the two phases occur in different states. This conclusion is supported by the results of an experiment in which very small pieces of apical meristem of adult shoots of *Citrus*, consisting of only the apical dome and two leaf primordia, were grafted into the hypocotyls of *Citrus* seedlings (Navarro, Roistacher and Murashige, 1975). These grafted meristems gave rise to adult shoots which bore fruit. Isolated apices of adult *Hedera helix*, consisting of the apical dome and two leaf primordia, continued to produce leaves with the phyllotaxy of adult shoots when cultured aseptically (Hackett, 1985). Thus it is clear that the shoot apical meristems of woody plants showing phase-change exist in either the 'juvenile' or 'adult' state. Moreover, it would appear that the meristem cells exist in these alternative states and are committed as either 'juvenile' or 'adult' cells.

That apical meristem cells can be committed in this way is also indicated by the experiments on vernalization of rye embryos carried out by Purvis (1940). Shoot apices of rye embryos were cultured on a nutrient medium and either chilled or unchilled. These apices regenerated whole plants and the plants from the chilled apices flowered in due course. Evidently, changes occurred in the apical meristems as a result of chilling, which were transmitted by cell lineage and only expressed many cell generations later. That is to say, the cells of the chilled apical meristems had become committed (determined) to the flowering pathway.

Thus there seems to be clear evidence that apical meristem cells can be determined along alternative pathways of development, and that the determined state is stable and can be transmitted through successive cell divisions. What is the basis of this stability?

Three alternative hypotheses can be postulated (Wareing and Frydman, 1976):

1. The structure and properties of the shoot apices are controlled by influences from pre-existing, differentiated tissue or from more remote parts of the plant.
2. The properties of the apex are determined by the structure and organization of the apex as a whole, and the differences between the two phases arise from the different organization of their apices.
3. There are intrinsic differences in the meristematic cells of the juvenile and adult apices, and the differences in their properties and structure arise from intrinsic differences in the cells.

The first hypothesis would appear to be excluded by the evidence presented above that (1) a grafted adult *Citrus* apex gives rise to an adult shoot and (2) isolated rye apices can be vernalized and regenerate vernalized plants. Thus the second and third hypotheses remain.

Now it was shown by Stoutemeyer and his co-workers that callus cultures established from petiole or stem tissue of juvenile and adult *Hedera* differ in their growth rates and ability to produce adventitious roots (Stoutemeyer and Britt, 1965). This observation indicates that differences in actively dividing cells of callus from stem tissue of the two phases can persist even when grown on the same medium. More recently Polito and Alliata (1981) have shown that similar differences were observed when callus cultures were established from apical meristems of juvenile and adult *Hedera* shoots. This latter observation suggests that there are, indeed, intrinsic differences in the meristem cells of the two phases of *Hedera*.

Cell determination as an epigenetic phenomenon

It was suggested above that phase change indicates the existence of stable differences between meristematic cells with respect to *gene expression*, which can be transmitted through repeated cycles of cell division. Persistent differences in gene expression, without permanent changes in the genome, are said to be *epigenetic* (Meins, 1983).

Very little is known about the nature of epigenetic variation, but in recent years Meins has produced much experimental evidence that the well-known phenomenon of 'habituation' in cell cultures probably involves epigenetic changes (Meins, 1982, 1983). Meins has pointed out that epigenetic changes differ from genetic changes involving mutation in the following respects:

1. Epigenetic change is directed—it occurs regularly in response to inducing conditions. The rate of change is higher than 10^{-15} per cell generation and thus is greater than the normal rate of mutation.
2. The variant phenotype, though stable, is reversible. Reversal is directed and at a high rate.
3. By definition epigenetic changes are not transmitted through meiosis.

Meins has shown that habituation in cultures of tobacco pith cells shows the characteristics of epigenetic variation.

Experimental results have been obtained recently which indicate that apical meristem cells do indeed show determination and which are consistent with the view that the variation in their state of determination is of an epigenetic nature (Wareing and Al-Chalabi, 1985; Wareing and Al-Ani, unpublished observations). These experiments did not involve a comparison of juvenile and adult shoot apices, but differences between shoot and root apices. It has been argued (Wareing, 1979) that the remarkable stability of the shoot and root apical meristems of a given plant suggest that they are determined either as shoot meristem or root meristem cells, and the experiments were carried out to test this hypothesis.

In preliminary experiments, root tips 1 mm in length and shoot tips consisting of the apical dome and two leaf primordia were excised from seedlings of *Euphorbia heterophylla* germinated under aseptic conditions and cultured on Murashige and Skoog medium containing benzylaminopurine (BAP) 10^{-6} mol l^{-1} and naphthalene acetic acid (NAA) 10^{-6} mol l^{-1}. The cultures were maintained under 8 hours of light per day at 25 ± 1 °C. Callus was formed from both types of meristem, and was subcultured through several passages. The callus formed from the shoot apical meristems was green and readily regenerated buds, whereas the callus from the root tips was non-green and formed no buds in the first four passages. However, on further subculture green patches were formed on the root callus, from which buds later regenerated.

Although the explants used in these first experiments were small, they would have contained various meristematic zones and consequently there was the possibility that the derived calluses were mixtures of cells from which there was unintentional selection during subculturing. In further experiments, therefore, cell clones were first established from meristem cultures. After obtaining callus cultures from shoot and root meristems as before, liquid cell suspension cultures were established from both types of callus for a short time (13–14 days), after which the cell suspensions were passed through filters which only allowed the passage of clumps comprising not more than three cells. The filtered suspension was plated on to solid medium and clones were established from the separate cell colonies that developed. As before, the callus from shoot meristem colonies was green and readily regenerated buds, whereas the 'root' callus remained non-green and formed roots, for three passages. Root callus was then transferred to Murashige and Skoog medium containing cytokinin only (BAP 10^{-6} mol l^{-1}), on which it turned green and initiated buds, from which whole plants were successfully regenerated.

These results provide strong evidence that (1) the cells of the two types of meristem are determined as 'shoot' or 'root' cells, respectively and (2) that the observed differences disappear after repeated subculture or in response to appropriate hormone treatment, and therefore do not involve irreversible genetic changes, but are probably of an epigenetic nature. The results are clearly relevant to the problem of phase change, and taken together with the observations of Polito and Alliata (1981) on cell cultures established from juvenile and adult shoot meristems of *Hedera* (*see* page 86), give credence to the suggestion that the apical meristem cells of *Hedera* shoots are intrinsically determined as juvenile or adult.

Reversal of determination

Evidence which, at first sight, appears to be inconsistent with the conclusion that there are intrinsic differences between juvenile and adult cells is provided by the work of Banks (1979), who observed that embryos regenerated from 'adult' callus of *Hedera* showed juvenile characters, suggesting that the cells were not intrinsically determined as adult. However, as Hackett (1985) points out, there is much evidence that adventitious bud and embryo formation causes rejuvenation (Mullins and Srinivasan, 1976; Krul and Worley, 1977; Barlass and Skene, 1980) and hence the production of adventive embryos from adult *Hedera* callus may quite probably have caused reversion to the juvenile state. There is, indeed, other evidence which indicates that changes in epigenetic states may be associated with switches in development. Thus, as we have seen (*see* page 86) Meins has shown that when whole tobacco plants are regenerated from habituated cells, the pith cells of these plants are no longer habituated, indicating a repression of the habituated state during the normal processes of tissue differentiation in developing shoots. A similar conclusion is suggested from the following experiments with *Euphorbia heterophylla* (Al-Ani and Wareing, unpublished observations).

As reported above (*see* page 86), whole plants were regenerated from the buds formed on 'cloned' calluses derived from both shoot and root meristems, and fresh cultures were established from the shoot and root meristems of these plants. Again it was found that on a medium containing BAP 10^{-6}M/NAA 10^{-6} mol l^{-1} the callus from shoot tips was green and freely regenerated buds, whereas 'root' callus remained non-green for several passages.

Thus there were differences between the cultures from stem and root tissue, regardless of whether the parent plants themselves had been regenerated from 'shoot' or 'root' callus. It is clear, therefore, that the state of determination as 'root' cells is reversed during bud formation on root-derived callus, but that during the processses of regeneration of adventitious roots from stems of the regenerated plants, the state of determination as root tissue is re-established.

This latter observation might be interpreted alternatively to indicate that stem tissues are *not* determined as such, otherwise they would not regenerate root tissue. However, it may be that the renewal of cell division in a vacuolated, mature stem cell leads to the 'scrubbing out' of the previous state of determination and the establishment of a new epigenetic state. This conclusion is consistent with Hackett's suggestion that adventitious bud formation by adult tissue leads to a reversion to the juvenile state (*see* page 87).

There are clearly considerable differences in the degree of stability of the determined state in different systems. In animal tissues, determination is, in general, irreversible, but this is less so in plant tissues. It is possible to reverse the vernalized state in rye embryos by applying high temperatures within 4 days of termination of chilling, but thereafter reversal becomes impossible, except during sexual reproduction. Although adult shoots of *Hedera* can be induced to revert to the juvenile state by certain treatments, in general the adult phase of woody plants is remarkably stable, a fact that is exploited in vegetative propagation by grafting in horticulture and forestry.

The habituated state in tissue cultures is relatively stable, but is completely reversed during the regeneration of tobacco shoots (*see* page 86). Determination as shoot or root tissues appears to be less stable than in phase change and vernalization, but although the determination can ultimately be reversed *in vitro*, the states of determination as shoot or root meristem cells are clearly maintained *in vivo*, in the intact apical meristems. Reversal at certain developmental stages or in response to certain experimental treatments is not incompatible with a state of determination at other developmental stages or under other conditions.

The molecular basis of phase change

If the differences between juvenile and adult tissues are of an epigenetic nature, how can such differences be maintained through nuclear and cell division? If phase change does not involve permanent, irreversible changes in the genome, it would be expected that the DNA content of 'juvenile' and 'adult' cells would not be different. Millikan and Ghosh (1971) and Kessler and Reches (1977) reported that the DNA content of nuclei of adult *leaf tissue* of *Hedera* was lower than that of juvenile leaf tissue, but analysis of the nuclei of cells of apical meristems showed no differences in DNA content between juvenile and adult shoots (Wareing and Frydman, 1976; Domoney and Timmis, 1980). Similarly, calluses established from juvenile and adult meristems of *Hedera* showed no differences in DNA content (Polito and Alliata, 1981; Polito and Chang, 1984).

However, the possibility exists that the DNA of somatic cells may be modified during development. Thus, it is known that a high proportion of cytosine in the DNA of higher plants is methylated to form 5-methylcytosine (Grierson and Covey, 1984). It has been suggested that this methylation process may be involved in the control of gene expression, since there appears to be a correlation between low methylation and activity of specific DNA sequences (Hepburn *et al.*, 1983). A mechanism has been proposed whereby a methylation pattern, once established in somatic cells, could be inherited by progeny cells (Holliday and Pugh, 1975). Thus the possibility that stable epigenetic effects may involve reversible modification of the DNA in somatic cells cannot be excluded.

Juvenility in herbaceous plants

As has already been noted (*see* page 83), herbaceous plants show juvenility, in the sense that following germination there is normally a vegetative phase during which flower initiation does not occur. It has been recognized since the early work of Klebs (1918) that the attainment of the state of 'ripeness-to-flower' is necessary before many species become capable of responding to inductive conditions. The situation is more complex in herbaceous perennials, where flowering is usually preceded each year by a stage of vegetative growth, even after emergence from an initial juvenile phase in the first year.

In addition to differences in flowering behaviour, there are frequently observable differences in leaf size and form and other vegetative characters between the seedling and mature stages. The occurrence of such differences in leaf characters is referred to by the general descriptive term *heteroblasty*. Since there is frequently a progressive change in leaf characters from the seedling to the mature stage, it is clear that heteroblasty is often an ontogenetic phenomenon, but several other factors, including the size of the apical meristem and nutrition, also affect leaf form (Allsopp, 1965).

Phase change in certain woody species, such as *Hedera helix*, is frequently, but not always, accompanied by differences in leaf characters between the juvenile and adult phases, so that in these species phase change is accompanied by heteroblasty. However, it is important not to fall into the logical trap of concluding that whenever heteroblasty is observed, this automatically indicates that the plant has undergone phase change, or that reversion to juvenile type leaves implies phase reversal. There is, indeed, at present no direct evidence that herbaceous species show a type of phase change identical with that in woody plants, since there is little evidence that there are persistent differences between the tissues of juvenile and adult stages of herbaceous plants, although the absence of evidence in no way excludes the possibility of such differences. Therefore, it is better to restrict the use of the term phase-change to instances where there are stable differences between the tissues of juvenile and adult shoots which are maintained through vegetative propagation. 'Juvenility' and 'heteroblasty' should be used only in descriptive senses, so that their occurrence does not constitute evidence for phase change in herbaceous plants.

There is very little information on the physiological and molecular aspects of juvenility in herbaceous plants. It has been shown that callus cultures from pith explants of day-neutral cultivars of tobacco show an increasing capacity to regenerate flowers *de novo*, with increasing height of stem from which the explants are derived (Aghion-Prat, 1965). It would appear that the potential for flower initiation becomes determined in stem tissues of day-neutral tobacco plants at a certain stage of development, since calluses established from stem tissue retain the capacity to flower through three passages (Chailakhyan *et al.*, 1975).

Floral determination in axillary buds of tobacco has been studied by Dennin and McDaniel (1985) and the subject is further discussed in Chapter 8.

One of the very few studies on juvenility in a non-woody plant was carried out by Zeevaart (1962) on *Bryophyllum daigremontianum*, a long–short day plant, which apparently requires to have developed at least 10–12 pairs of leaves before it is capable of responding to photoperiodically inductive conditions (transfer from long days to short days). It was shown that the growing points of young plants are induced to flower by grafting on to flowering donor stocks, indicating that the shoot apices of juvenile plants are capable of responding to a floral stimulus, which their own leaves are incapable of producing. However, this observation does not necessarily exclude the possibility of intrinsic differences between juvenile and adult apices, since the leaves are produced by the shoot apical meristem, which evidently undergoes a change from an initial phase of juvenile leaf production to one in which it produces leaves capable of responding to photoperiodic signals.

A similar experiment was carried out with the woody species *Mangifera indica* by Singh (1959), in which seedlings approach-grafted to shoots of mature trees flowered if the leaves were removed from the seedlings. However, these results do not imply that the adult stock caused phase change in the juvenile seedling, since there is no evidence that it continued to flower if detached from the mature stock.

Conclusion

The primary objective of this chapter has been to present evidence suggesting that phase-change in woody plants involves intrinsic differences in the meristem cells of juvenile and adult shoots and that these differences are epigenetic in nature. It is argued that vernalization and the differences between shoot and root apices also indicate that meristem cells may be determined and that such cell determination is an epigenetic phenomenon, involving persistent differences in gene expression which are transmitted through mitosis. Nevertheless, these stable cell differences are reversed at critical stages in the life-cycle, notably during sexual reproduction, but also during the formation of adventitious buds and roots. Such reversal is not incompatible with determination at other stages of development.

Although it is argued that the meristems of woody species, such as *Hedera helix*, are determined along broad alternative routes, i.e. the 'juvenile' and 'adult' developmental pathways, it is not suggested that this implies determination at the tissue level; that is to say, commitment as juvenile or adult meristem cell does not necessarily imply that there is also determination of their derivatives to form vascular or cortical tissue.

It has been argued that phase change must involve intrinsic differences in juvenile and adult apical meristems, but this does not exclude the possibility of influences from the mature parts of the plant, especially hormonal factors arising in the leaves or roots. In particular, influences from other parts of the plant may be important in promoting or inhibiting phase-change or its reversal, but phase-change is an inductive phenomenon and once it has taken place the conditions that promoted the change need not continue to operate—as seen, for example, in the experiment in which adult *Citrus* shoot apices were grafted on to seedling stocks (*see* page 85).

In spite of its practical importance, the problem of phase change has proved very intractable and relatively little progress in understanding its physiological and molecular basis has been made for some years. However, the problem is now susceptible to approach by the techniques of molecular biology, and the time is now ripe for such approaches.

References

AGHION-PRAT, D. (1965). Néoformation de fleurs *in vitro* chez *Nicotiana tabacum* L. *Physiologie Végétale*, **3**, 119–303

ALLSOPP, A. (1965). Heteroblastic development in cormophytes. In *Encyclopedia of Plant Physiology XV/1* (W. Ruhland, Ed.), pp. 1172–1221, Berlin, Springer

BANKS, M.S. (1979). Plant regeneration from callus from two growth phases of English ivy *Hedera helix* L. *Zeitschrift für Pflanzenphysiologie*, **92**, 349–353

BARLASS, M. and SKENE, K.G.M. (1980). Studies on the fragmented shoot apex of grapevine. II. Factors affecting growth and differentiation *in vitro*. *Journal of Experimental Botany*, **31**, 489–495

BRINK, R.A. (1962). Phase change in higher plants and somatic cell heredity. *Quarterly Review of Biology*, **37**, 1–22

CHAILAKHYAN, M.KH., AKSENOVA, N.P., KONSTANTINOVA, T.N. and BAVRINA, T.V. (1975). The callus model of plant flowering. *Proceedings of Royal Society, Series B*, **190**, 333–345

DENNIN, K.A. and MCDANIEL, C.N. (1985). Floral determination in axillary buds of *Nicotiana sylvestris*. *Developmental Biology*, **112**, 377–382

DOMONEY, C. and TIMMIS, J.N. (1980). Ribosomal RNA gene redundancy in juvenile and mature ivy (*Hedera helix*). *Journal of Experimental Botany*, **31**, 1093–1100

DOORENBOS, J. (1954). Rejuvenation of *Hedera helix* in graft combinations. *Proc. Koninkl. Nederl. Akademie van Wetenschappen Series C*, **57**, 99–102

FRYDMAN, V.M. and WAREING, P.F. (1974). Phase change in *Hedera helix* L. III. The effects of gibberellins, abscisic acid and growth retardants on juvenile and adult ivy. *Journal of Experimental Botany*, **25**, 420–429

GRIERSON, D. and COVEY, S. (1984). *Plant Molecular Biology*, Glasgow, Blackie

HACKETT, W.P. (1985). Juvenility, maturation and rejuvenation in woody plants. *Horticultural Reviews*, **7**, 109–155

HEPBURN, A.G., CLARKE, L.E., PEARSON, L. and WHITE, J. (1983). The role of cytosine methylation in the control of nopaline synthase gene expression in a plant tumour. *Journal of Molecular and Applied Genetics*, **2**, 315–329

HOLLIDAY, R. and PUGH, J.E. (1975). DNA modification mechanisms and gene activity during development. *Science*, **187**, 226–232

KESSLER, B. and RECHES, S. (1977). Structural and functional changes in chromosomal DNA during ageing and phase change in plants. *Chromosomes Today*, **6**, 237–246

KLEBS, F. (1918) Über die Blütenbildung von *Sempervivum. Flora (Jena)*, **111**, 128–151

KRUL, W.R. and WORLEY, J.F. (1977). Formation of adventitious embryos in callus cultures of 'Seyval', a French hybrid grape. *Journal of American Society of Horticultural Science*, **102**, 360–363

LONGMAN, K.A. and WAREING, P.F. (1959). Early induction of flowering in birch seedlings. *Nature (London)*, **184**, 2037–2038

MEINS, F. (1982). The nature of the cellular, heritable, change in cytokinin habituation. In *Variability in Plants Regenerated from Tissue Culture* (E. D. Earle and Y. Demarley, Eds), pp. 202–210, New York, Praeger

MEINS, F. (1983). Heritable variation in plant tissue culture. *Annual Review of Plant Physiology*, **34**, 327–346

MILLIKAN, D.F. and GHOSH, B.N. (1971). Changes in nucleic acids associated with maturation and senescence in *Hedera helix*. *Physiologia Plantarum*, **24**, 10–13

MULLINS, M.G. and SRINIVASAN, C. (1976). Somatic embryos and plantlets from an ancient clone of the grapevine (cv. Cabenet-Sauvignon) by apomixis *in vitro*. *Journal of Experimental Botany*, **27**, 1022–1030

NAVARRO, L., ROISTACHER, C.N. and MURASHIGE, T. (1975). Improvement of shoot tip grafting *in vitro* for virus-free *Citrus*. *Journal of American Society of Horticultural Science*, **100**, 471–479

POLITO, V.S. and ALLIATA, V. (1981). Growth of calluses derived from shoot apical meristems of adult and juvenile ivy (*Hedera helix* L.). *Plant Science Letters*, **22**, 387–393

POLITO, V.S. and CHANG, Y.C. (1984). Quantitative nuclear cytology of English ivy. *Plant Science Letters*, **34**, 369–373

PURVIS, O. (1940). Vernalization of fragments of embryo tissue. *Nature (London)*, **145**, 462

ROBBINS, W.J. (1957). Gibberellic acid and the reversal of adult *Hedera* to a juvenile state. *American Journal of Botany*, **44**, 743–746

ROBINSON, L.W. and WAREING, P.F. (1969). Experiments on the juvenile-adult phase change in some woody species. *New Phytologist*, **68**, 67–78

SCHAFFELITZKY DE MUCKADELL, M. (1954). Juvenile stages in woody plants. *Physiologia Plantarum*, **7**, 782–796

SINGH, L.B. (1959). Movement of flowering substances in the mango leaves (*Mangifera indica* L.). *Horticultural Advances*, **3**, 20–28

STOKES, P. and VERKERK, K. (1951). Flower formation in Brussels sprouts. *Mededelingen van de Landbouwhogeschool Te Wageningen*, **50**, 141–160

STOUTEMEYER, V.T. and BRITT, O.K. (1965). The behaviour of tissue cultures from English and Algerian ivy in different growth phases. *American Journal of Botany*, **52**, 805–810

WAREING, P.F. (1978). Determination in plant development. *Botanical Magazine, Tokyo, Special Issue*, **1**, 3–17

WAREING, P.F. (1979). What is the basis of stability of apical meristems? *British Plant Growth Regulator Group Monograph*, **3**, 1–3

WAREING, P.F. and AL-CHALABI, T. (1985). Determination in plant cells. *Biologia Plantarum*, **27**, 241–248

WAREING, P.F. and FRYDMAN, V.M. (1976). General aspects of phase change, with special reference to *Hedera helix*. *Acta Horticulturae*, **56**, 57–70

ZEEVAART, J.A.D. (1958). Flower formation as studied by grafting. *Mededelingen van de Landbouwhogeschool Te Wageningen*, **58**, 1–88

ZEEVAART, J.A.D. (1962). The juvenile phase in *Bryophyllum daigremontianum*. *Planta*, **58**, 543–548

ZIMMERMAN, R.H., HACKETT, W.P. and PHARIS, R.P. (1985). Hormonal aspects of phase-change and precocious flowering. In *Encyclopedia of Plant Physiology (NS)* (R.P. Pharis and D.M. Reid, Eds), Vol. **11**, pp. 79–115, Berlin, Springer.

6

APICAL MERISTEM CHARACTERISTICS AND ACTIVITY IN RELATION TO JUVENILITY IN *HEDERA*

W.P. HACKETT, R.E. CORDERO**
Department of Horticultural Science and Landscape Architecture, University of Minnesota, St Paul, USA

C. SRINIVASAN*
Department of Environmental Horticulture, University of California, Davis, USA

Marked morphological differences between the juvenile and mature phases of *Hedera helix* (*Table 6.1, Figures 6.1* and *6.2*; Robbins, 1957) and the stability of these differences in clonally propagated plants present unique opportunities for morphogenetic analysis of phase determination. These opportunities are greatly enhanced because juvenile characteristics may be induced in mature phase plants by treatment with relatively small doses of gibberellins A_3, $A_{4/7}$ or A_1 (Robbins, 1957; Rogler and Hackett, 1975).

Stein and Fosket (1969) made the first systematic effort to describe the anatomical characteristics of the two phases. They found that although the shoot apical meristem was very much larger in the mature plants, cells in the tunica, corpus and cortex of internodes were somewhat longer and wider in the juvenile plants. They also noted that the timing of internode elongation was different in the two forms and speculated that the more rapid elongation of juvenile internodes as they were formed was due to more active cell division in the subapical region. Polito and Chang (1984) found differences between the nuclei of cells of the pith rib meristem (PRM) in the two forms. The PRM of the juvenile apex had smaller and more dense nuclei than the mature shoot apex. They suggested that these differences were probably related to differential rates of cell division.

Based on observations of increases in cell numbers in cross-sections of the apex during a plastochron and their assumption that a plastochron was twice as long in the juvenile as mature apex, Stein and Fosket (1969) concluded that increase in cell number was much greater and more rapid in the mature than in the juvenile apex. Phyllotaxis for the juvenile phase is distichous (1,2) whilst for the mature phase it is spiral (2,3) (Maksymowych and Erickson, 1977).

These results indicate that there are probably differences in both cell division and cell expansion activities of the two phases in both the apical and subapical regions of the shoot apex. A detailed analysis of these activities is described in this chapter. Particular interest was attached to how these activities were related to the dynamics of internode elongation and the spacial placement of leaf primordia on the apical dome, both of which are very different for the two forms.

*Current address: HyClone Inc., PO Box 3190, Conroe, TX 77305 USA.
**Current address: Dept. of Biology, St. Joseph Univ., Philadelphia, PA 19131 USA.

Table 6.1 CHARACTERISTICS OF JUVENILE AND MATURE *Hedera helix*

Juvenile	Mature
5-lobed palmate leaves	Entire, ovate leaves
Distichous (1, 2) phyllotaxis	Spiral (2/3) phyllotaxis
Anthocyanin stem pigmentation	No anthocyanin pigmentation
Stem aerial roots	No aerial roots
Plagiotropic growth habit	Orthotropic growth habit
Absence of flowering	Presence of flowering

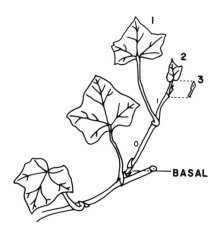

Figure 6.1 Typical juvenile *H. helix* shoot 3–4 plastochrons old.

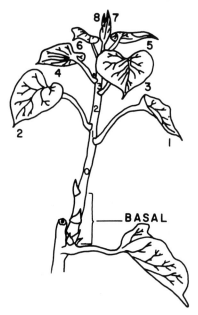

Figure 6.2 Typical mature *H. helix* shoot 8 plastochrons old.

Materials and methods

Single stem plants of juvenile and mature *H. helix* were raised from cuttings and grown in 13 cm clay containers. They were then decapitated to leave a shoot with four or five fully expanded leaves remaining. Buds were removed from the axils of all leaves except the most distal one. The shoot developing from this axillary bud was the experimental unit used for various measurements. For most of the work plants were grown under long (16 h) days either in a greenhouse (15 °C dark, 21 °C light) where natural days were supplemented with light from high-pressure sodium vapour lamps or in a growth chamber (21 °C dark, 26 °C light) with light ($200\,\mu E\,m^{-2}\,s^{-1}$) from a mixture of fluorescent and incandescent lamps. In one experiment, short (12 h) days were used to ensure continued vegetative growth of mature plants.

For GA_3 experiments, decapitated plants were prepared for treatment by drilling a 1 mm hole through the stem below the petiole subtending the single, remaining distal bud. A 5 µl drop containing 50 µg GA_3 (potassium gibberellate) was placed in the hole immediately. In the case of control plants, 5 µl of distilled water was placed in the hole. Apices from control and treated plants were sampled weekly for preparation for scanning electron micrography (SEM) using standard procedures. The leaf primordia free cross-sectional area of the apical dome was measured from SEMs using a leaf area meter. The angle of divergence of leaf insertion from the centre of the apical dome for the two most apical primordia was also obtained from the micrographs.

Results

PLASTOCHRON AND APICAL ACTIVITY

Although Stein and Fosket (1969) assumed that plastochron was twice as long for the juvenile (1 leaf per week) as the mature shoot (2 leaves per week), they did not measure it. Based on semi-log plots of lengths of successive leaves through the exponential growth stage and use of a reference leaf length of 13 mm, plastochrons were determined for the two forms under long days (Cordero *et al.*, 1985). For the juvenile shoot, leaf emergence was very regular with a plastochron of 4.2 days. For the mature shoots, leaf emergence was initially very rapid for the first five or six leaves with a plastochron of 0.83 days and then considerably slower with a plastochron of 3.2 days for the remaining leaves. The first appearing leaves with the short plastochron correspond to leaf primordia which were preformed in the axillary bud at the time of shoot decapitation. The plastochron for non-flowering, mature plants grown in short days was at first very similar to that of long day plants but a second cycle of initially short (2.5 days) and then longer (3.2 days) plastochrons occurred with a total of 25–30 leaves being formed. Short photoperiods maintain vegetative growth in mature plants and are therefore the preferred experimental conditions under which to study morphogentic characteristics and factors influencing phase change in *Hedera*.

These results suggested that whereas the rates of both the initiation and emergence of leaves are very uniform and regular in the juvenile form, this is not the case for the mature shoot. The rates of leaf (node, internode) initiation and macroscopic leaf appearance (emergence) were compared in shoots of various plastochron ages. These apices were sampled at intervals and sectioned longitudinally (juvenile) or transversely (mature) to measure the rates of node initiation and node emergence. As noted earlier, mature axillary buds contain about six leaf primordia (day 0). Between day 0 and day 10 (budbreak), 8 more leaf primordia were produced at a rate of 0.8 per day. For 33 days after budbreak the rate of node initiation slowed to 0.4 per day. Unlike node initiation, node emergence was delayed although the apical meristem was actively producing new leaves. Ten days after budbreak no new internodes were visible but there were about 14 leaf primordia in the bud. From day 13 to 15, five nodes emerged at a rate of 2.5 per day. After day 15, the rate of node emergence in mature shoots was 0.30 per day. This rate of node emergence yielded a value close to the plastochron for later appearing leaves (3.2 days).

In contrast to mature shoots, rates of initiation and appearance of nodes for juvenile shoots are similar with values of 0.254 and 0.248 per day, respectively. These rates of internode initiation or appearance yield a value close to the plastochron for appearance of juvenile leaves (4.2 days).

Mature shoots therefore produced nodes much more rapidly after decapitation than juvenile shoots. At budbreak (day 10), 14 leaf primordia were counted in mature buds whereas juvenile buds contained only 4.5. Mature shoots produce nodes more rapidly than they emerge. This results in a rosette-like telescoping of internodes and nodes just below the apical meristem. In contrast, juvenile internodes appear to be elongated in a repetitive, sequential manner resulting in nodes and internodes emerging in the same orderly manner.

INTERNODE ELONGATION AND SUBAPICAL ACTIVITY

Different rates of internode elongation in the two forms were confirmed by counting nodes and internodes in cross- and longitudinal sections starting at the vertex of the apical dome to various distances below it. At 50 μm below the vertex, mean internode length was 1.4 times greater in the juvenile apex than in the mature. By 200 μm, internode length was 1.7 times greater in the juvenile; and by 500 μm, 3.0 times greater. This showed that leaf primordia and internodes did not accumulate just below the apical meristem in juvenile apices because internodes began to elongate immediately below the apical dome. Internode elongation in mature apices was significantly slower and this contributed to the telescoping of leaf primordia in the apex.

These results suggested markedly different subapical as well as apical meristem activity in the two forms. Further evidence for this came from studies on the relative meristematic activity of the two forms, estimated from counts of division figures in 10 μm cross-sections of the apical dome and pith at various distances below the vertex of the apical dome. When the total number of division figures *per section* are considered, there is a peak of activity both in juvenile and in mature apices extending from 20 to 150 μm below the vertex with maximum activity at about 60–70 μm. The number of division figures in this zone was more than twice as great in the mature as in the juvenile. In contrast, when division figures are expressed *per unit cross-sectional area*, the peaks of activity occur at about 120 μm below the vertex and the peak number of division figures is almost 10 times as great in the juvenile as in the mature apex. These results suggest that the greater total number of division figures in the mature apex is at least partially due to its much larger diameter. They also suggest that cell division at 60–70 μm below the vertex in both forms is contributing significantly to radial growth. The greater cell division figures per unit area basis, at 120 μm below the vertex in the juvenile form suggests that at this level, cell division contributes mainly to axis elongation and that there is much greater activity in that direction in the juvenile apex.

This interpretation is confirmed by examination of longitudinal sections of the subapical region. The PRM initials are first evident 120 μm below the vertex in the mature shoot apex whereas in the juvenile form they appear 70 μm below it. Intense axial cell division in juvenile shoots is reflected by their pith files comprising about twice as many cells as mature internodes. Maximal pith cell length is only slightly greater in the juvenile than the mature shoot.

INFLUENCE OF GA$_3$ ON SHOOT APEX ACTIVITY AND PHYLLOTAXIS

It is known that stable juvenile characteristics can be induced in mature plants by treatment with GA$_3$ (Robbins, 1957). Because phyllotaxis is the morphological characteristic most closely associated with apical meristem activity and because dome size is much smaller in the juvenile than mature apices (*Figure 6.3*), phyllotaxis was chosen here for study in relation to GA$_3$ treatment and dome size.

Figure 6.3 Scanning electron micrographs of actively growing shoot apices of juvenile (above) and mature (below) *H. helix* × 125. Note larger area of leaf primordia free dome in mature than in juvenile apex. Phyllotaxis is distichous (1, 2) in juvenile apex and spiral (2, 3) in the mature.

After bud burst the apical dome area increased initially in both control and GA-treated plants but the increase was greater in the control plants. The doubling of apical area in control mature plants by 4 weeks after bud burst corresponds with the inception of flower initiation. In GA-treated plants, the dome area began to decrease slowly at about 4 weeks after bud burst. As indicated by the angle of divergence of the two uppermost leaf primordia, the phyllotaxis of treated plants had completed the change from mature spiral (2,3) to juvenile distichous (1,2) by 5 weeks after bud burst. By 4 weeks after bud burst the phyllotaxis of the GA_3 treated plants had changed substantially but dome area was at its maximum or only slightly below maximum. The area of primordia-free apical dome in GA-treated shoots 24 weeks after bud burst was twice as large as in untreated, juvenile shoots even though the treated shoots displayed a preponderance of juvenile characteristics. The shape of the apical dome was round in GA-treated, mature plants with juvenile characteristics, and oval in the control, juvenile plants. In control, mature plants the angle of divergence was close to 135 degrees and there was a slight reduction when the plants began to initiate flowers at the fourth week. In GA-treated mature plants the angle increased progressively from 135 to 180 degrees at the 5th week.

Under long (16 h) days in a greenhouse, apices of plants treated with 50 µg GA_3 were sampled 2 weeks after bud burst and showed macroscopic increases in internode elongation. As expected from work with other species, GA_3 increased cell division activity in the PRM. This was evident from the formation of a narrow column of very long pith cell files in the central area of the pith, some of which extended upwards to the site of the PRM initials. Adjacent pith and cortex tissues had a configuration similar to those in control shoots. In addition to changes in PRM activity, GA_3 treatment altered the configuration of cell layers in apical dome such that the random orientation of cells in the corpus region was replaced with a horizontal stratification of three or four cell layers parallel to the two layers of the tunica. Apical dome size in GA_3-treated plants appeared to be as large or larger than in control plants although this parameter was not measured. Horizontal stratification of cells in the apical dome may be related to the maintenance of dome size in treated shoots or to changes in phyllotaxis which are occurring at this time in GA_3-treated plants.

Discussion and conclusions

Substantial differences between the juvenile and mature forms of *H. helix* for apical and sub-apical meristematic activities were related to differences in rates of leaf (node and internode) initiation and emergence and also rates of internode extension. Further consideration of these differences enabled a morphogenetic analysis of GA_3-induced changes in phyllotaxis.

An increase in the area of the apical dome in GA_3-treated mature shoots was observed together with a change in phyllotaxis from a spiral to a lower order, distichous arrangement. Apical dome area of untreated plants also increased during the same period but no change in phyllotaxis occurred. These results are in marked contrast to observations on *Xanthium* (Maksymowych *et al.*, 1976) where GA_3 caused dome size to increase during a change to a higher-order phyllotaxis rather than a lower order as in *Hedera*. Area of apices on GA-treated mature *Hedera* shoots showing distichous phyllotaxis is about the same as those from bursting buds on control mature plants and twice the area of apices from control juvenile shoots, even 24 weeks after GA_3 treatment. These results indicate that the reduced area observed in fully juvenile plants follows rather than precedes changes from higher order (2,3) to lower order (1,2) phyllotaxis in GA₃ treated mature *Hedera* plants.

In *Chrysanthemum*, triiodbenzoic acid (TIBA) causes a similar change from higher-order spiral to lower-order distichous phyllotaxis (Schwabe, 1971). In this case, no change in area or volume of the apical dome was reported as a result of TIBA treatment. There was, however, a change in the shape of the apex as reflected by a decrease in the apical angle, a narrowing of the incipient stem below the primordia free apical dome and a greater vertical separation of the primordial insertions. Concomitant with the increased vertical spacing of primordia, the divergence angle of the younger primordia increased to give the distichous arrangement. It was concluded that increased vertical spacing seemed to be the important factor involved in TIBA-induced phyllotactic changes in *Chrysanthemum*.

In *Hedera*, greater subapical meristem activity in juvenile plants and the observed influence of GA₃ on increasing subapical meristem activity and internode length in mature shoots suggests that vertical spacing may be important in GA₃-induced phyllotactic changes. However, treatment of juvenile *Hedera* shoots with growth retardants shortens internodes but apparently has no effect on phyllotaxis (Clark and Hackett, 1981) and GA₃ also has marked effects on the configuration of tissues in the apical dome itself in *Hedera*. These latter effects are not consistent with vertical spacing of primordia having a major role in regulating phyllotaxis.

References

CLARK, J. and HACKETT, W.P. (1981). Interaction of ancymidol and benzyladenine in control of growth of juvenile *Hedera helix*. *Physiologia Plantarum*, **53**, 483–486

CORDERO, R.E., MURRAY, J.R. and HACKETT, W.P. (1985). Plastochron indices for juvenile and mature forms of *Hedera helix*. L. *American Journal of Botany*, **72**, 324–327

MAKSYMOWYCH, R., CORDERO, R.E. and ERICKSON, R.O. (1976). Long-term developmental changes in *Xanthium* induced by gibberellic acid. *American Journal of Botany*, **63**, 1047–1053

MAKSYMOWYCH, R. and ERICKSON, R.O. (1977). Phyllotaxtic change induced by gibberellic acid in *Xanthium* shoot apices. *American Journal of Botany*, **64**, 33–44

POLITO, V.S. and CHANG, Y-C. (1984). Quantitative nuclear cytology of English Ivy (*Hedera helix* L.) *Plant Science Letters*, **34**, 369–377

ROBBINS, W.J. (1957). Gibberellic acid and the reversal of adult *Hedera* to a juvenile state. *American Journal of Botany*, **44**, 743–746

ROGLER, C.E. and HACKETT, W.P. (1975). Phase change in *Hedera helix*: induction of the mature to juvenile phase change by gibberellin A₃. *Physiologia Plantarum*, **34**, 141–147

SCHWABE, W.W. (1971). Chemical modification of phyllotaxis and its implications. In *Control Mechanisms of Growth and Differentiation* (D.D. Davies and M. Balls, Eds), pp. 301–322, New York, Academic Press

STEIN, O.L. and FOSKET, E.B. (1969). Comparative developmental anatomy of shoots of juvenile and adult *Hedera helix*. *American Journal of Botany*, **56**, 546–551

7

CLONAL ANALYSIS OF MERISTEM DEVELOPMENT

D.E. JEGLA
Department of Biology, Kenyon College, Gambier, Ohio, USA

I.M. SUSSEX
Department of Biology, Yale University, New Haven, Connecticut, USA

Introduction

One of the fundamental questions in plant development is 'how does the meristem make the plant?' How does the meristem effect the juvenile to adult and the vegetative to reproductive phase changes? A number of different hypotheses have been proposed. At one extreme, morphogenetic signals from maturing parts of the plant are thought to instruct the apical meristem. One example, from photoperiodic studies, is that a signal, as yet unidentified, generated in the leaf in response to appropriate photoperiodic conditions, initiates the change from vegetative to reproductive development in the cells of the apical meristem (e.g. Heslop-Harrison, 1964). At the other extreme, the apical meristem has been considered to be self-determining (or self-regulating), responding to signals that arise within itself (Sussex, 1964).

Within either of these hypotheses there is the further question of whether differential function is partitioned in the apical meristem. Are there subpopulations of cells within the meristem that are active only during one or another developmental phase? It has been postulated, for example, that the summital cells of developing shoot apices form a reproductive meristem that begins to function only at the beginning of reproductive development (Steeves and Sussex, 1972). According to this idea, cells at the periphery of the meristem are the sole contributors to vegetative organs. Cell lineages contributing to vegetative and reproductive development are essentially separate. An extreme example of this is the méristème d'attente/anneau initial hypothesis of apical organization originally proposed by Buvat (1952, 1955). On the other hand, it has been postulated that the cells at the periphery of the meristem are constantly replenished by divisions in the more summital cells. In this case, all cells of the meristem are potential contributors to vegetative development. Vegetative and reproductive parts do not derive from separate cell lineages (Sussex and Steeves, 1967).

Clearly, up to a point, at least in the development of the embryo, a single stem-cell population gives rise to the entire shoot. The important question, then, is at what time in the ontogeny of the meristem do the cell lines that ultimately give rise exclusively to the reproductive portions of the shoot diverge from those that give rise to the vegetative portions of the shoot? Does this occur during embryogeny, such that the meristem of the mature embryo already contains a subpopulation of cells that will give rise exclusively to the floral parts? Does such a divergence occur at some time during early vegetative growth of the shoot? Or does it occur only at the end of vegetative development?

The conventional approach of studying the distribution of mitotic activity within the meristem has not been able to provide unequivocal evidence to answer this question. What is required to solve this problem is a way in which cells can be marked and their derivative cells identified at subsequent stages of development. Clonal analysis is such a method. In clonal analysis cells are mutagenized to produce distinct phenotypic markers such as pigment deficiencies that can be observed in the progeny of the mutagenized cell. Mutant progeny of the original mutagenized cell form phenotypically distinct sectors of tissue in the organism. Thus the cell lineage of a single mutagenized cell can be traced in the developing organism. If at the time of mutagenesis there are distinct populations of cells in the meristem that give rise to the vegetative and reproductive portions of the shoot, then there should be no sectors in the mature shoot that extend from the vegetative into the reproductive portions of the shoot. By mutagenizing plants at different times in development it is possible to establish when subpopulations of cells become distinct. We have used clonal analysis to analyse the development of the *Helianthus* shoot.

Helianthus

The question of when in the ontogeny of the shoot apical meristem the separation occurs of a subpopulation of cells that will give rise exclusively to the floral parts is of particular interest in such plants as sunflower (*Helianthus annuus*), which are considered day-neutral because the transition from the vegetative phase to the reproductive phase of development is not related to any obvious environmental cue. The sunflower terminal meristem initiates a predictable number of leaves and then becomes reproductive. The phase change appears to be internally controlled. Environmental influence on the amount of vegetative growth (number of vegetative nodes) produced by the apical meristem before conversion to a reproductive meristem in sunflower is relatively small (Jegla, 1985). In addition, much detailed information is available on the structure and function of the sunflower meristem (Steeves *et al.*, 1969; Langenauer and Davis, 1973; Langenauer, Davis and Webster, 1974; Langenauer, Atsmon and Arzee, 1975; Davis and Steeves, 1977; Davis, Rennie and Steeves, 1979; Sawhney, Rennie and Steeves, 1981; Marc and Palmer, 1982 and 1984; Jegla, 1985). In our study we used *H. annuus* cv. Peredovic, the cultivar studied in many of the investigations listed above. As Peredovic is an unbranched cultivar, the entire shoot is elaborated by the activity of a single terminal meristem.

In our study of sunflower development mutagenesis was accomplished by irradiating dry seeds with a ^{60}Co source. Seeds were exposed to a total of 20–30 Krad irradiation from a source delivering 200–240 rads per minute. Seeds were then planted in the field and the developing plants observed for mutant sectors. Of 1200 irradiated seeds 142 produced plants bearing sectors that were used in the analysis. A total of 151 sectors were analysed in these 142 plants. Only sectors that appeared to be morphologically normal and those extending for more than one node were included in the analysis. Mutant sectors in the epidermal layer were glabrous and those in the sub-epidermal layers were pigment deficient or albino (*Figure 7.1*). Epidermal sectors (derived from mutations in the L1 layer of the embryo meristem) were visible in the stem as well as in the leaves. Pigment-deficient and albino sectors (derived from mutations in the L2 and L3 layers of the embryo meristem) were clearly visible in the leaves but only occasionally visible in the stem. Of sectors limited to the vegetative portion of the shoot, those that were visible in the stem as well as in the leaves all originated at a node and terminated in a leaf.

Figure 7.1 A representative pigment-deficient sector extending through the vegetative leaves into the involucral bracts of a *Helianthus annuus* shoot grown from irradiated seed.

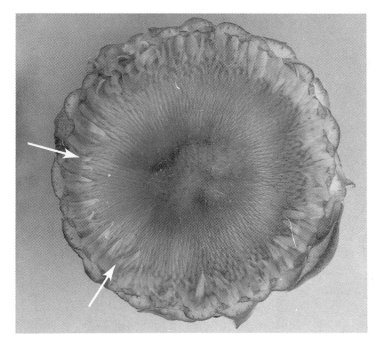

Figure 7.2 Inflorescence of *H. annuus* with pigment-deficient sector extending through the floret bracts to the centre of the inflorescence. Arrows point to edges of sector at rim of inflorescence. Same plant as pictured in *Figure 7.1*.

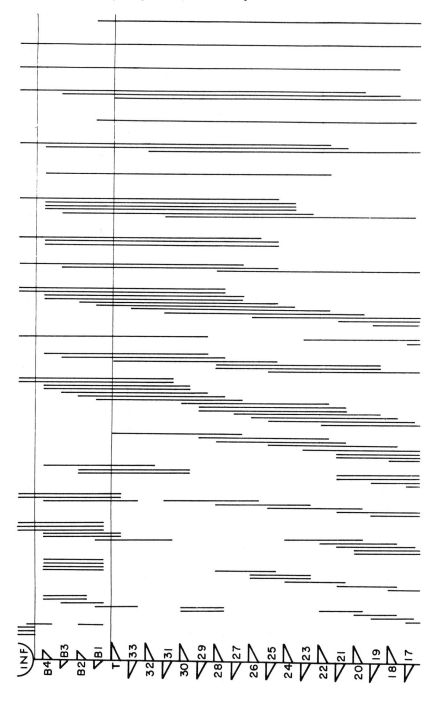

Figure 7.3   Distribution of mutant sectors in the upper half of the *Helianthus* shoot (142 plants). Each line represents one sector from node of origin to node of termination. Some of the sectors shown here originate below node 17. Sectors grouped from left to right by extent in number of nodes; 17–33, vegetative leaves; T, transitional leaf; B1–B4, involucral bracts; INF, inflorescence.

Table 7.1 POSITION OF TERMINATION (BY NUMBER AND PERCENT) OF MUTANT SECTORS ORIGINATING AT DIFFERENT LEVELS IN THE *HELIANTHUS* SHOOT (151 SECTORS IN 142 PLANTS)

	Termination of sectors							
	Vegetative leaves				Involucral bracts		Inflorescence	
	Lower half		Upper half					
Origin of sectors	No.	(%)	No.	(%)	No.	(%)	No.	(%)
Lower half vegetative leaves	35	(57)	24	(39)	1	(2)	1	(2)
Upper half vegetative leaves	—	—	32	(43)	30	(40)	13	(17)
Involucral bracts	—	—	—	—	8	(67)	4	(33)
Inflorescence	—	—	—	—	—	—	3	(100)

One hundred and one of the 151 sectors analysed affected at least one of the vegetative leaves in the upper half of the shoot. Fourteen percent of those sectors including vegetative leaves in the upper half of the shoot (17% of sectors originating in the vegetative leaves of the upper half of the shoot) extended acropetally through the involucral bracts into the inflorescence where they were visible in the floret bracts (*Figure 7.3, Table 7.1*). Most of these sectors extended to the region of the inflorescence centre (*Figures 7.1* and *7.2*). Clearly there has not yet been a clonal separation of reproductive from vegetative cell lines in the dry-seed embryo meristem of the sunflower. The question arises, then, of when in the ontogeny of the sunflower meristem such a separation occurs. Experiments are now under way to irradiate the meristems of seedlings of increasing age. Results from these experiments will tell us the latest time in which no separation of vegetative and reproductive cell lines occurs.

There is some degree of variation in the developmental stage of the embryo in the dry seeds of sunflower. While the embryos of virtually all seeds contain well-developed primordia of leaves one and two, the presence of primordia of leaves three and four is variable. While the latter are present in most seeds, they are absent in a significant number of seeds. The number of cells across the diameter of the meristem also is frequently one or two fewer in embryos lacking the third and fourth leaf primordia. It may be that shoots with very long sectors extending through many vegetative nodes into the inflorescence have developed from seeds with fewer cells in the embryonic meristem. Shoots with sectors that terminate before the inflorescence, on the other hand, may have derived from seeds in which the meristem cells had undergone additional cell division and established an additional independent lineage before becoming arrested. If this is indeed the case, then one would expect the divergence of vegetative and reproductive cell lines to occur very early in seedling development of the sunflower cultivar we are analysing.

Zea mays

The development of the maize shoot has been analysed extensively using clonal analysis by Coe and Neuffer (1978) and Johri and Coe (1982, 1983). The independence of cell lineages which contribute to successive portions of the developing shoot is more defined in the maize embryo meristem than it is in sunflower. There is a clear separation of lineages that contribute to the terminal inflorescence or tassel (male reproductive structure) and those that give rise to the vegetative portion of the plant. Mutant sectors virtually never cross from the upper vegetative portion of the plant into the tassel; vegetative and tassel sectors remain distinct. The very rare exceptions to this are considered by the investigators conceivably to be due to replacement of irradiation-killed summital cells by cells from lower on the apical dome (Johri and Coe, 1983). Thus it appears that in maize there already is established in the dry-seed embryo meristem a subpopulation of cells that will give rise exclusively to the terminal inflorescence.

Other dicotyledons

A similar analysis of five other dicotyledon species grown from chemically mutagenized seeds (*Nicotiana tabacum, N. glauca, Petunia hybrida, Linum grandiflorum,* and *Vicia faba*) by Dulieu (1969, 1970) showed that separation of reproductive from vegetative cell lines has not occurred in the dry-seed embryos of these species. A significant percentage of the sectors that originate above the first few nodes in the dicot species described by Dulieu eventually widen to encompass the entire summit of the shoot. Moreover, the totality of sectors is expressed well before the end of vegetative development in these species. This is most notable in the two *Nicotiana* species in which 50% of the sectors ultimately encompass the summit of the shoot and 83% (*N. tabacum*) to 98% (*N. glutinosa*) originate before the 6th node (Dulieu, 1969). Thus in the tobacco species a large portion of the vegetative shoot is derived from the same subpopulation of cells in the embryonic meristem from which the terminal flower derives. It appears, therefore, that a separate cell population that will give rise exclusively to the terminal reproductive portion is further from being established in these tobacco species than it is in sunflower. Analysis of later stages to determine when a cell population that will give rise exclusively to the floral parts is established was not reported.

Summary and discussion

The clonal separation of a subpopulation of cells that gives rise exclusively to floral parts of the shoot clearly does not occur at the same time in the ontogeny of different species of angiosperms. In the sunflower, *Helianthus annuus* cv. Peredovic, a dicotyledon, mutant sectors in plants grown from irradiated seed extend from the upper vegetative portion of the shoot into the inflorescence with significant frequency. Although a much higher percentage of sectors terminate before the inflorescence and a small number originate in the inflorescence or in the involucral bracts, it is clear that there is not yet a clonal separation of cell lines from which vegetative and reproductive portions of the shoot will derive in the mature embryo meristem. In the monocotyledon maize, on the other hand, such a separation is apparent by the time the embryo becomes arrested in the seed. When dry seeds are irradiated, mutant clones virtually never cross from the vegetative portion of the plant into the terminal inflorescence. Other dicotyledonous species studied are similar to sunflower in that the separation has not yet occurred in the embryo meristem. However, there are some notable differences between the other dicotyledonous species and sunflower, differences that are most marked in the two tobacco species investigated. In the tobacco species, for example, as high as 50% of the mutant sectors crossed from the vegetative shoot into the terminal flower. In addition, most sectors were very long, originating before the 6th node, and many eventually widened to encompass the entire summit of the shoot. Sectors in sunflower cross from the vegetative portion of the plant into the terminal reproductive portion with considerably less frequency, they continue to originate up to the inflorescence, and they never encompass the entire diameter of the shoot. Thus it appears that the independence of cell lineages that contribute to vegetative and reproductive portions of the shoot may be more defined in the sunflower embryo meristem than they are in the tobacco embryo meristem. However, they are clearly less defined in sunflower than they are in maize. The other dicotyledonous species studied appear to be intermediate between tobacco and sunflower in this respect. The next obvious step in the investigation of this problem must be to determine the latest time in which a lack of separation between vegetative and reproductive cell lines occurs in the terminal meristem of some of the dicotyledonous species. This is now in progress.

Acknowledgements

The cell lineage analysis of *Helianthus* was supported by two summer grants (No. IN-31-W in 1983 and No. IN-31-X in 1984) from the American Cancer Society.

References

BUVAT, R. (1952). Structure, évolution et fonctionnement du méristème apical de quelques Dicotylédones. *Annales Scientifique Naturelle Botaniques II Series*, **13**, 199–300

BUVAT, R. (1955). Le méristème apical de la tige. *Annales Biologie*, **31**, 595–656

COE, E.H., Jr. and NEUFFER, M.G. (1978). Embryo cells and their destinies in the corn plant. In *The Clonal Basis of Development* (S. Subtelny and I. Sussex, Eds), pp. 113–129. New York, Academic Press

DAVIS, E.L. and STEEVES, T.A. (1977). Experimental studies on the shoot apex of *Helianthus annuus*: the effect of surgical bisection on quiescent cells in the apex. *Canadian Journal of Botany*, **55**, 606–614

DAVIS, E.L., RENNIE, P. and STEEVES, T.A. (1979). Further analytical and experimental studies on the shoot apex of *Helianthus annuus*: variable activity in the central zone. *Canadian Journal of Botany*, **57**, 971–980

DULIEU, H. (1969). Mutations somatiques chlorophylliennes induites et ontogénie caulinaire. *Bulletin Scientifique Bourgogne*, **XXVI**, 1–84

DULIEU, H. (1970). Les mutations somatiques induites et l'ontogénie de la pouisse feuillée. *Annales Amélioration Plantes*, **20**, 27–44

HESLOP-HARRISON, J. (1964). Sex expression in flowering plants. *Brookhaven Symposiums on Biology*, **16**, 109–125

JEGLA, D.E. (1985). *Organization and Regulation in the Apical Meristem of the Sunflower, Helianthus annuus* L. Ph.D. Dissertation, Yale University

JOHRI, M.M. and COE, E.H. Jr. (1982). Genetic approaches to meristem organization. In *Maize for Biological Research* (W.F. Sheridan, Ed.), pp. 301–310. Grand Forks, ND, University Press

JOHRI, M.M. and COE, E.H. Jr. (1983). Clonal analysis of corn plant development. I. The development of the tassel and the ear shoot, *Developmental Biology*, **97**, 154–172

LANGENAUER, H.D. and DAVIS, E.L. (1973). *Helianthus annuus* responses to acute x-irradiation. I. Damage and recovery in the vegetative apex and effects on development. *Botanical Gazette*, **134**, 303–313

LANGENAUER, H.D., DAVIS, E.L. and WEBSTER, P.L. (1974). Quiescent cell populations in the apical meristems of *Helianthus annuus*. *Canadian Journal of Botany*, **52**, 2195–2201

LANGENAUER, H.D., ATSMON, D. and ARZEE T. (1975). Effects of gibberellic acid on DNA synthesis and histology in the shoot apex of *Helianthus annuus* during the transition to flowering. *Canadian Journal of Botany*, **53**, 2650–2659

MARC, J. and PALMER, J.H. (1982). Changes in mitotic activity and cell size in the apical meristem of *Helianthus annuus* L. during the transition to flowering. *American Journal of Botany*, **69**, 768–775

MARC, J. and PALMER, J.H. (1984). Variation in cell-cycle time and nuclear DNA content in the apical meristem of *Helianthus annuus* L. during the transition to flowering. *American Journal of Botany*, **71**, 588–595

SAWHNEY, V.K., RENNIE, P.J. and STEEVES, T.A. (1981). The ultrastructure of the central zone cells of the shoot apex of *Helianthus annuus*. *Canadian Journal of Botany*, **59**, 2009–2015

STEEVES, T.A., HICKS, M.A., NAYLOR, J.M. and RENNIE, P. (1969). Analytical studies on the shoot apex of *Helianthus annuus*. *Canadian Journal of Botany*, **47**, 1367–1375

STEEVES, T.A. and SUSSEX, I.M. (1972). *Patterns in Plant Development*. New Jersey, Prentice Hall

SUSSEX, I.M. (1964). The permanence of meristems: developmental organizers or reactors to external stimuli? *Brookhaven Symposiums on Biology*, **16**, 1–12

SUSSEX, I.M. and STEEVES, T.A. (1967). Apical meristems and the concept of promeristem. *Phytomorphology*, **17**, 287–291

8

FLORAL DETERMINATION: A CRITICAL PROCESS IN MERISTEM ONTOGENY

C.N. McDANIEL, S.R. SINGER,* J.S. GEBHARDT and K.A. DENNIN†
Plant Science Group, Department of Biology, Rensselaer Polytechnic Institute, Troy, NY, USA

Introduction

Flowering is a developmental process which depends on the ontogeny of the plant. The initiation of a flower by a shoot apical meristem therefore results from a sequence of events which occur in the various tissues and organs of the plant including the shoot apical meristems. Thus the developmental history of the various organs and tissues is important in the developmental response of a plant. Inherent in this view is the assumption that cells or groups of cells can exist in unique developmental states. Numerous reports in the literature indicate that this assumption is valid (McDaniel, 1984). For example, some cell cultures form embryos while others do not, regardless of the culture conditions. This observation indicates that some cells are in a developmental state which permits them to proceed along the developmental pathway of embryogenesis (Christianson, 1985).

This chapter focuses on the initiation of a floral meristem in the genus *Nicotiana*. Using the classic developmental concepts of induction, competence and determination (McDaniel, 1984; Slack, 1983), research efforts are aimed at identifying the developmental events which occur in the plant prior to the initiation of floral structures. Induction occurs when a developmental signal acts on competent cells to bring about a specific developmental response. Competence is the capacity of cells to respond in a specific way to a developmental signal. Determined cells exhibit the same developmental fate *in situ*, in isolation, and when grafted to a new position on the organism. These terms are conceptual and not mechanistic in nature. That is, stating that cells are competent or determined implies nothing about the specific mechanisms in arriving at or maintaining these developmental states. Competence and determination are operationally defined and very little is known about their molecular basis; that is, they exist in what might be considered a developmental 'black box' (*Figure 8.1*). It is this 'black box' which developmental biologists are seeking to understand.

Most research focuses on expression, and it is in this area that the powerful tools of molecular biology are being applied with considerable success. The research considered here concerns the earlier developmental events of competence and determi-

*Current address: Department of Biology, Carleton College, Northfield, MN, 55057, USA.
†Current address: Albany Medical School, 47 New Scotland Avenue, Albany, NY, 12208, USA

DEVELOPMENTAL "BLACK BOX"

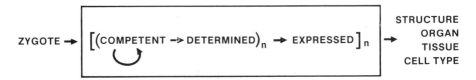

Figure 8.1 Developmental 'black box'. *See* text for explanation.

nation. As *Figure 8.1* indicates, cells must exhibit competence to respond to some signal or they will never change from their initial state. Cells may cycle through several states of competence but eventually they respond to a signal and become determined for some future developmental fate. Ultimately the developmental fate as established by the sequence(s) of competence-determination events is expressed. Even when one developmental fate has been expressed, the whole process may be reiterated.

This developmental 'black box' becomes more than an abstraction when meristem ontogeny is considered. Christianson and Warnick (1983, 1984, 1985) have shown that callus cells formed from *Convolvulus arvensis* leaf explants are initially incompetent to be induced to form shoot apical meristems. After a period in culture, they gain competence and can be induced by the appropriate medium to form shoots. Induction leads to cells which are determined to form shoot apical meristems and this determined state can be expressed on the inductive medium as well as on other media. The result of this sequence of developmental processes is a vegetative, shoot apical meristem. The meristem cells are now in a stable developmental state, the vegetative state. The whole sequence of processes as depicted in the developmental 'black box' will be reiterated when a vegetative apical meristem becomes florally determined and expresses this state by forming a flower (McDaniel, 1978; Dennin and McDaniel, 1985; Singer and McDaniel, 1986).

In principle it should be possible experimentally to separate competence, determination, and expression. In practice, this is possible only if these developmental states are temporally distinct in large enough units of time to permit experimental separation and if something is known about the inductive signal(s). In most systems it has not been possible to distinguish between competence and determination. As a result an operational definition is usually employed to define what is being studied. Competence is being studied if a signal is applied and the outcome is evaluated, while determination is being studied if the developmental fate *in situ*, and in one or more different environments, is measured. Therefore, whether a tissue is considered to be competent or determined depends upon the operation used to assess its developmental status.

In the studies on flowering in *Nicotiana* described here, the number, sources, and time of action for all of the signals involved are not known. It appears that inhibitors and/or stimulators are produced by the leaves (Lang, Chailakhyan and Frolova, 1977) and that signals may also emanate from the roots (Dennin and McDaniel, 1985; McDaniel, 1980). Hence floral determination is studied because the operational definition can be easily applied. However, competence and determination have not yet been separated in this system.

Floral determination in axillary bud meristems

Nicotiana tabacum cv. Wisconsin 38 and *N. silvestris* exhibit strong apical dominance. When the terminal flower opens (the first flower to open), none of the axillary buds below the inflorescence have grown out. On *N. tabacum* the axillary buds are arrested after producing from 6 to 9 leaf primordia while those of *N. silvestris* produce from 6 to 11 primordia prior to ceasing growth. The developmental fate of axillary buds *in situ* is measured by decapitating the plant above the bud in question, permitting the bud to mature, and counting the number of nodes produced below the terminal flower. The developmental fate in isolation is measured by removing the bud from the plant, allowing it to form roots, permitting it to mature, and counting the number of nodes produced below the terminal flower. The developmental fate at another location on the plant is established by grafting the bud to the base of the main axis, decapitating above the grafted bud, allowing it to mature, and counting the number of nodes produced below the terminal flower.

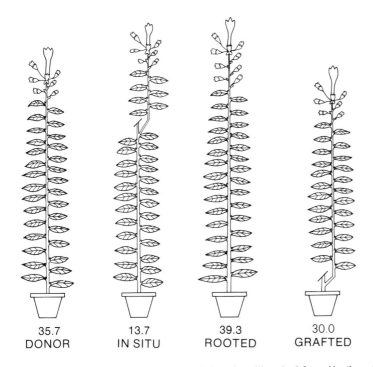

| 35.7 | 13.7 | 39.3 | 30.0 |
| DONOR | IN SITU | ROOTED | GRAFTED |

Figure 8.2 Developmental fate of the sixth-node axillary bud from *N. silvestris*. Plants were grown under inductive conditions. When the first flower opened, the developmental fate of axillary buds was measured *in situ* by decapitation, in isolation by rooting, and at a new place on the plant by grafting. For each manipulation the number of nodes present below the terminal flower of the bud-derived plant or shoot is given below the pot.

In *N. tabacum*, axillary buds exhibit one or two patterns of development (McDaniel, 1978). A rooted or grafted axillary bud either has the same developmental fate (i.e. produces the same number of nodes below the terminal flower) as *in situ* buds from similar positions on the main axis, or the bud has a developmental fate representative of its new environment (i.e. rooted buds produce a number of nodes similar to that of seed-derived plants and grafted buds produce a number of nodes similar to that of buds located near the graft site). Bud meristems that have the same developmental fate as *in situ* buds when they are rooted or grafted are therefore determined for that developmental fate. Since that fate is the production of a limited number of nodes and a terminal flower, these meristems can be considered to be determined for floral development. Determined buds have from 13 to 22 nodes below their terminal flowers. Since they have about nine nodes at the time of rooting or grafting, approximately 4–13 additional nodes are produced before the formation of the terminal flower.

Axillary buds of *N. silvestris*, when assayed in a similar way, also exhibit floral determination (Dennin and McDaniel, 1985; Dennin, 1985). As was observed for *N. tabacum*, only the uppermost axillary buds are florally determined. When rooted or grafted, buds that are not florally determined grow according to their new environments (*Figure 8.2*). Those that are florally determined produce a number of nodes below the terminal flower which is approximately the same number as they would have produced *in situ* (*Figure 8.3*). Although floral determination in

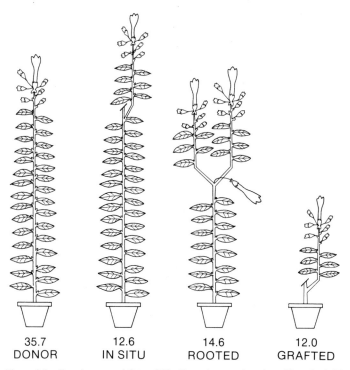

| 35.7 | 12.6 | 14.6 | 12.0 |
| DONOR | IN SITU | ROOTED | GRAFTED |

Figure 8.3 Developmental fate of *N. silvestris* second-node axillary bud. For details *see* legend to *Figure 8.2*.

axillary buds of *N. tabacum* and *N. silvestris* is similar in several respects, there is one significant difference. Almost all rooted, determined axillary buds of *N. silvestris* produce abnormal inflorescences where no floral cymes are present and in their place one or two vegetative shoots form. The inflorescences produced by determined axillary buds of *N. tabacum* often have fewer floral cymes than those of seed-derived plants but in other respects more than 95% are normal. Thus, in *N. silvestris* the normal developmental fate of the cells of the florally determined meristem has been altered by the rooting process or the presence of roots near the bud meristem such that there are two developmentally unique populations of cells in these determined meristems (*Figure 8.4*). One population is stably determined for floral development and will give rise to the terminal flower while neighbouring cells are either not stably determined or not determined for floral development and give rise to vegetative shoots.

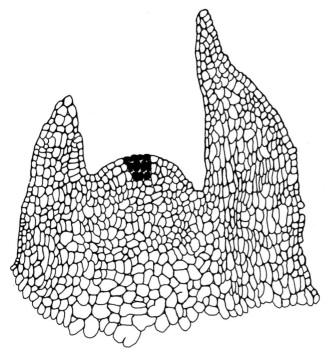

Figure 8.4   Two populations of cells in a determined axillary bud of *N. silvestris*. This is a tracing of a median longitudinal section of a third axillary bud (480 ×). Shaded cells are stably determined for floral development and will ultimately form the terminal flower. The number and positions of determined cells was arbitrarily selected. Other cells are not stably determined and will form the vegetative structures surrounding the terminal flower.

Floral determination in a growing meristem

As discussed above, developmentally arrested meristems can exist in two distinct developmental states: a vegetative state or a florally determined state. Growing meristems of *N. tabacum* also become florally determined. A population of *N. tabacum* plants at anthesis of the terminal flower was decapitated just above the tenth node axillary bud. On the day of decapitation, and every third day after decapitation, several of the buds or growing shoots were removed from the main axis and rooted. The total number of nodes below the terminal flower on the plants derived from these rooted buds was counted. Two populations of plants were observed (*Figure 8.5*). One population grew like seed-derived plants while the other produced a number of nodes similar to that of *in situ* tenth buds which matured on the main axis without being rooted. At the time when floral determination was first observed, the terminal flower had not formed.

The growing terminal meristem of a seed-derived *N. tabacum* plant exhibits a pattern of development similar to that of a growing axillary bud meristem (McDaniel *et al.*, 1985; Singer and McDaniel, 1986). Two large populations of field-grown plants were employed, one in the summer of 1984 and the other in the summer of 1985. Since a population of *N. tabacum* plants grown under the same environmental conditions produces a very uniform number of nodes (Seltmann, 1974; Thomas *et al.*, 1975), we arbitrarily employed the number of leaves equal to or greater than 3 cm (1985 plants) or 15 cm (1984 plants) in length as a measure of the age of the plant. Shoot tips were rooted or fixed for histological examination at various ages. A terminal meristem was florally determined if after rooting it produced the same number of nodes it would have produced had it remained *in situ*. In the 1984 population of plants employing 15 cm leaves, floral determination occurred between ages 10 and 12, while in the 1985 population of plants employing 3 cm leaves, floral determination occurred between ages 20 and 22. Histological analysis of meristems from plants at these ages indicated

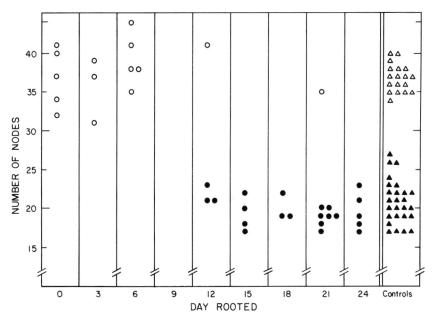

Figure 8.5 Floral determination in growing tenth-node axillary bud. The tenth-node axillary bud was not florally determined at the time of developmental arrest. Buds were forced to grow out by decapitation of the main shoot. At the time of decapitation, and at 3-day intervals, buds were excised and rooted. The number of nodes produced below the terminal flower is shown. Open circles (○) represent buds not florally determined at the time of excision and solid circles (●) represent buds determined for floral development at the time of excision. Open triangles (△) represent seed-derived plants and solid triangles (▲) represent tenth-node buds left *in situ*.

that in both populations about four nodes were produced after the meristems became florally determined. However, because of different weather conditions in the two years, the two populations of plants produced different numbers of nodes before forming the terminal flower. The 1984 control plants produced a total of 37.6 ± 1.8 (SD) nodes below the terminal flower while the 1985 population produced 41.6 ± 1.1 (SD) nodes. This observation indicated that the number of nodes produced by the terminal meristem before floral determination can be influenced by environmental conditions, but the number produced after floral determination is constant.

Determination in internode tissues

In day neutral tobacco, tissues from the upper portion of flowering plants will form *de novo* floral shoots *in situ* and in culture (Aghion-Prat, 1965a, b; Konstantinova *et al.*, 1969). At anthesis of the terminal flower, tissues from the inflorescence and from internodes many nodes below the inflorescence will form floral shoots in culture (*Figure 8.6*). The boundary between tissues with and without the capacity to form *de novo* floral shoots in culture is many nodes below the inflorescence but is located

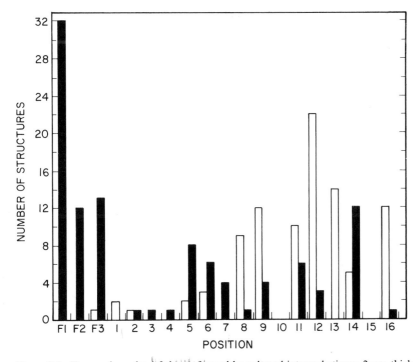

Figure 8.6 Type and number of shoots formed by cultured internode tissue; 2 mm thick slices of internodes were taken from the position indicated on a single *N. tabacum* plant at anthesis of the first flower. These were then cultured on a medium which contained no hormones (Linsmaier and Skoog, 1965). After 6 weeks, the number and type of shoots produced were recorded. Solid bars represent floral shoots and open bars represent vegetative shoots. F1, F2, F3 represent internodes in the inflorescence, while 1, 2, 3, etc. represent internodes from below the inflorescence. Internodes numbered basipetally.

above the base of the plant (McDaniel *et al.*, 1985; Singer, 1985). Although the tissues from the inflorescence often produce single flower buds and the tissues from below the inflorescence usually produce floral shoots with several nodes, the number of nodes produced by a *de novo* floral shoot is not consistently correlated with the position of the source tissue on the main axis. For example, on one plant of *N. tabacum* cv. Wisconsin 38, cultured internodes from the inflorescence produced floral shoots with 3.1 ± 1.2 (n = 22, range = 1–5) nodes; while, segments from internodes one to 17 produced floral shoots with 3.9 ± 0.6 (n = 15, range = 3–5) nodes. For a few plants there was a statistically significant correlation between the position of the source tissue and the number of nodes on floral shoots. Segments from internodes from the inflorescence of the plant represented in *Figure 8.6* produced floral shoots with 1.4 ± 0.7 (n = 54, range = 0–3) nodes, while floral shoots on segments from internodes one to 16 produced 3.7 ± 1.1 (n = 49, range = 1–7) nodes.

During the ontogeny of a plant the time when internode tissues gain the capacity to form *de novo* floral shoots in culture has been established (Singer, 1985; Singer and McDaniel, 1987). In the 1985 population of field-grown plants discussed above, internode tissues were cultured at various ages. At age 21 tissues at the 14th internode from the base of the plant that initially produced only vegetative structures gained the capacity to form floral shoots in culture. Tissues from above internode 14 only produced vegetative shoots in culture at age 21. As plants matured, tissues from above internode 14 gained the capacity to produce floral shoots. These observations established that tissues that could initially only form vegetative structures in culture changed their developmental state as a function of whole-plant ontogeny and progressed to a new developmental state, floral determination. At the time when tissues from internode 14 first gained the capacity to form *de novo* floral shoots in cultures, the terminal meristem became determined for floral development (Singer and McDaniel, 1986).

Discussion

The number of nodes produced by a terminal meristem before the formation of a terminal flower is precisely regulated (Seltmann, 1974; Thomas *et al.*, 1975). Although it is not clear how the plant employs nodes as a means of establishing when the terminal meristem is to make a flower, the parameter of node number is useful in the evaluation of growth patterns.

An axillary or terminal bud of tobacco exhibits one of two distinct patterns of growth when it is removed from its position *in situ*: either it produces a number of nodes representative of its new environment or it produces the same number it would have produced *in situ*. These results indicate that developmentally the bud is in one of two relatively stable states. It is either programmed for the production of leaves, internodes and associated tissues (vegetative state) or it is programmed for the production of a flower after producing a limited number of nodes (florally determined state). Since it is the meristem that produces the leaves or the flower, it is reasonable to assume that it is the meristem that exists in one of these two states.

It is clear that floral determination is a relatively stable state in *N. tabacum* since it is not usually disrupted by the manipulations involved in rooting and grafting. However, floral determination does exhibit different degrees of stability in different species. This is seen when *N. silvestris* and *N. tabacum* are compared. In *N. tabacum* normal inflorescences are formed by almost all rooted, florally determined, axillary buds. However, when florally determined axillary buds of *N. silvestris* are rooted, most of the meristems produce abnormal inflorescences indicating that under these circumstances only a subpopulation of cells in the meristem is stably determined for floral development. This instability of floral determination in *N. silvestris* is also apparent at the tissue level since tissues from the inflorescence do not form *de novo* floral shoots in culture (Aghion-Prat, 1965a; Bridgen and Veilleux, 1985; Chailak-hyan *et al.*, 1974). In contrast tissues from flowering *N. tabacum* do form *de novo* floral shoots in culture reflecting stable floral determination in this species. However, it is not a permanent state and can be reversed by various treatments.

It has been demonstrated in work from several laboratories that the hormonal composition of the culture medium can change the type of morphogenesis that is observed (Tran Thanh Van, Dien and Chlyah, 1974; Hillson and LaMotte, 1977; Wardell and Skoog, 1969). Tissues from the inflorescence which produce close to 100% floral shoots on a medium containing auxin $10^{-6}\,mol\,l^{-1}$ and cytokinin $10^{-6}\,mol\,l^{-1}$ will produce only vegetative shoots on a medium containing auxin $10^{-6}\,mol\,l^{-1}$ and cytokinin $10^{-5}\,mol\,l^{-1}$ (Tran Thanh Van, Dien and Chlyah, 1974). No culture medium is known that will enable tissues from a vegetative plant to produce floral shoots. Hormones do not therefore appear to bring about the state of floral determination, but they may either stabilize the state and permit it to be expressed or destabilize the state of floral determination and permit the expression of some other developmental state. Recently, oligosaccharins isolated from plant cell walls have been shown to mimic the actions of the plant hormones (Tran Thanh Van *et al.*, 1985) but the relationship between hormones and oligosaccharins is not known. Whether they are important in bringing about floral determination will not be known until vegetative tissue is shown to become florally determined under their influence.

Investigation of temporal and spatial aspects of floral determination in internode tissues shows that the first internode tissues to be florally determined are located about 24 nodes below the terminal meristem (Singer and McDaniel, 1987). Internode tissues above this point do not become florally determined or at least not stably determined until several days later. At about the same time that the first internode tissues are becoming florally determined, the terminal meristem is becoming florally determined (Singer and McDaniel, 1986). By the time the terminal inflorescence is expanding, all the internode tissues above the initial site of floral determination are florally determined. The fact that floral determination occurs at two distinct, well-separated locations prior to the formation of floral organs has several implications for the mechanisms involved in floral regulation. First, floral determination in internode tissues is not a result of a signal emanating from developing flowers or the inflorescence.

Second, the physical parameters of the meristem may be important in the actual formation of the flower but they cannot explain floral determination in internode tissues many nodes below the terminal meristem. Third, the fact that cells at a considerable distance from the terminal meristem undergo floral determination at the same time as the meristem itself undergoes floral determination indicates that deprivation of nutrients is not a means of regulating floral development here. That is, it is difficult to imagine a mechanism for directing nutrients to these two locations while maintaining inadequate nutrition at all the areas in between. Thus the nutrient diversion hypothesis (Sachs and Hackett, 1977; Sachs *et al.*, 1978) as an explanation for regulating flowering in *N. tabacum* does not appear tenable.

Floral determination in dayneutral tobacco can be described as an inductive process (McDaniel, 1984; Slack, 1983). That is, a systemic signal acts on competent cells and meristems to bring about a new developmental state, floral determination.

This process in day-neutral tobacco is similar to that described for photoperiodic tobacco (Hopkinson and Hannam, 1969; Waterkeyn, Martens, and Nitsch, 1965).

Acknowledgement

This work was supported in part by grants from the National Science Foundation (DCB84-09708) and the United States Department of Agriculture (84-CRCR-1-1490) to CNM and a National Science Foundation graduate fellowship to SRS.

Conclusion

Significant progress has been made in describing the flowering process in *Nicotiana* by considering flowering to be a developmental process. Groups of cells in shoot apical meristems have been shown to exist in a unique developmental state, floral determination. This state is reversible and its stability is a function of the genotype. Temporal and spatial analysis of floral determination in internode tissues and shoot apical meristems demonstrated that floral determination occurs synchronously at distinct locations. This observation brings into serious question several mechanisms which have been implicated in the regulation of flowering. Although the developmental approach to the flowering process will continue to be fruitful, it is clear that there are limitations to what can be learned from developmental physiology alone. Significant advances will be made when the developmental approach can be augmented with the powerful tools of genetics and molecular biology.

References

AGHION-PRAT, D. (1965a). Floral meristem-organizing gradient in tobacco stems. *Nature (London)*, **207**, 1211

AGHION-PRAT, D. (1965b). Néoformation de fleurs *in vitro* chez *Nicotiana tabacum* L. *Physiologie Végétale*, **3**, 229–303

BRIDGEN, M.P. and VEILLEUX, R.E. (1985). Studies of *de novo* flower initiation from thin cell layers of tobacco. *Journal of the American Society of Horticultural Science*, **110**, 233–236

CHAILAKHYAN, M.K., ADSENOVO, N.P., KONSTANTINOVA, T.N. and BAVRINA, T.V. (1974). Use of tobacco stem calluses for the investigation of some regularities of plant flowering. *Phytomorphology*, **24**, 86–96

CHRISTIANSON, M.L. (1985). An embryogenic culture of soybean: Towards a general theory of somatic embryogenesis. In *Tissue Culture in Forestry and Agriculture* (R.R. Henke, K.W. Hughes, M.P. Constantin and A. Hollaender, Eds), pp. 83–103. New York, Plenum

CHRISTIANSON, M.L. and WARNICK, D.A. (1983). Competence and determination in the process of *in vitro* shoot organogenesis. *Developmental Biology*, **95**, 288–293

CHRISTIANSON, M.L. and WARNICK, D.A. (1984). Phenocritical times in the process of *in vitro* shoot organogenesis. *Developmental Biology*, **101**, 382–390

CHRISTIANSON, M.L. and WARNICK, D.A. (1985). Temporal requirement for phytohormone balance in the control of organogenesis *in vitro*. *Developmental Biology*, **112**, 494–497

DENNIN, K.A. (1985). *Determination for Floral Development in Photoperiodic Tobacco*. M.Sc. Thesis. Troy, New York, Rensselaer Polytechnic Institute

DENNIN, K.A. and MCDANIEL, C.N. (1985). Floral determination in axillary buds of *Nicotiana silvestris*. *Developmental Biology*, **112**, 377–382

HILLSON, T.D. and LAMOTTE, C.E. (1977). *In vitro* formation and development of floral buds on tobacco stem explants. *Plant Physiology*, **60**, 881–884

HOPKINSON, J.M. and HANNAM, R.V. (1969). Flowering in tobacco: the course of floral induction under controlled conditions and in the field. *Australian Journal of Agricultural Research*, **20**, 279–290

KONSTANTINOVA, T.N., AKSENOVA, N.P., BAVRINA, T.V. and CHAILAKHYAN, M.K. (1969). On the ability of tobacco stem calluses to form vegetative and generative buds in culture *in vitro*. *Dokladie Akademie Nauk SSSR*, **187**, 466–469

LANG, A., CHAILAKHYAN, M.K. and FROLOVA, I.A. (1977). Promotion and inhibition of flower formation in a dayneutral plant in grafts with a short-day plant and a long-day plant. *Proceedings of the National Academy of Science of the USA*, **74**, 2412–2416

LINSMAIER, E.M. and SKOOG, F. (1965). Organic growth factor requirements of tobacco tissue cultures. *Physiologia Plantarum*, **18**, 100–127

McDANIEL, C.N. (1978). Determination for growth pattern in axillary buds of *Nicotiana tabacum* L. *Developmental Biology*, **66**, 250–255

McDANIEL, C.N. (1980). Influence of leaves and roots on meristem development in *Nicotiana tabacum* L. cv. Wisconsin 38. *Planta*, **148**, 462–467

McDANIEL, C.N. (1984). Competence, determination and induction in plant development. In *Pattern Formation: A Primer in Developmental Biology* (G. Malacinski, Ed.), pp. 393–412. New York, Macmillan

McDANIEL, C.N., SINGER, S.R., DENNIN, K.A. and GEBHARDT, J.S. (1985). Floral determination: timing, stability, and root influence. In *Plant Genetics* (M. Freeling, Ed.), pp. 73–87. New York, Alan R. Liss

SACHS, R.M. and HACKETT, W.P. (1977). Chemical control of flowering. *Acta Horticultura*, **68**, 28–49

SACHS, R.M., HACKETT, W.P., RAMINA, A. and MALOOF, C. (1978). Photosynthesic assimilation and nutrient diversion as controlling factors in flower initiation in *Bougainvillea* (San Diego Red) and *Nicotiana tabacum* cv. Wis. 38. In *Photosynthesis and Plant Development* (R. Marcelle, H. Clijsters and M. Van Pouchke, Eds), pp. 95–101. The Hague, Junk

SELTMANN, H. (1974). Effect of light periods and temperature on plant form of *Nicotiana tabacum* cv. Hicks. *Botanical Gazette*, **136**, 196–200

SINGER, S.R. (1985). *Spatial and Temporal Aspects of Floral Determination in* Nicotiana tabacum *L*. Ph.D. Thesis. Troy, New York, Rensselaer Polytechnic Institute

SINGER, S.R. and McDANIEL, C.N. (1986). Floral determination in the terminal and axillary meristems of *Nicotiana tabacum* L. *Developmental Biology* (in press)

SINGER, S.R. and McDANIEL, C.N. (1987). Floral determination in internode tissues of dayneutral tobacco first occurs many nodes below the apex (Submitted for publication)

SLACK, J.M.V. (1983). *From Egg to Embryo, Determinative Events in Early Development*. London, Cambridge University Press

THOMAS, J.F., ANDERSON, C.E., RAPER, C.D. and DOWNS, R.J. (1975). Time of floral initiation in tobacco as a function of temperature and photoperiod. *Canadian Journal of Botany*, **53**, 1400–1410

TRAN THANH VAN, M., DIEN, N.T. and CHLYAH, A. (1974). Regulation of organogenesis in small explants of superficial tissue of *Nicotiana tabacum* L. *Planta*, **119**, 149–159

TRAN THANH VAN, K., TOUBART, P., COUSSON, A., DARVILL, A.G., GOLLIN, D.J., CHELF, P. and ALBERSHEIM, P. (1985). Manipulation of morphogenetic pathways of tobacco explants by oligosaccharins. *Nature (London)*, **314**, 615–617

WARDELL, W.L. and SKOOG, F. (1969). Flower formation in excised tobacco stem segments: I. Methodology and effects of plant hormones. *Plant Physiology*, **44**, 1402–1406

WATERKEYN, L., MARTENS, P. and NITSCH, J.P. (1965). The induction of flowering in *Nicotiana*. I. Morphological development of the apex. *American Journal of Botany*, **52**, 264–270

IV

Vernalization

9

VERNALIZATION—ENVIRONMENTAL AND GENETIC REGULATION

K. NAPP-ZINN
Botanisches Institut der Universitat zu Köln, West Germany

The term 'vernalization' has at least two different meanings: on the one hand it is a cold treatment that induces or at least promotes flowering, and on the other it is the biochemical processes which occur during cold conditions allowing the development of the so-called 'internal conditions' (Klebs, 1903) that lead to ripeness-to-flower.

In the present context 'vernalization' is taken in the second sense. The development of the 'internal conditions' is governed by two groups of factors: genetic, which determine the type of the processes concerned; and environmental, which have primarily quantitative effects. As the roles of certain environmental factors in vernalization, particularly photoperiod and light intensity, were summarized recently (Napp-Zinn, 1984), this chapter will predominantly consider genetic aspects, and only towards the end will the behaviour of different genotypes under the influence of external factors be taken into account.

The roles of genetic factors in vernalization may be studied by two different approaches. The easier way is to expose plants to favourable conditions for flowering in terms of day-length, irrigation, soil, etc. but without chilling or with incomplete vernalization and then measure the flowering effects of certain genes. The more complicated but eventually more conclusive approach is to study the influence of monogenic differences between otherwise isogenic lines on those aspects of plant metabolism where changes may be correlated to the transition from the vegetative to the reproductive phase. These include the metabolism of nucleic acids, amino acids and plant hormones. Until now most research on vernalization has been of the first type. This will become evident in the first part of this chapter which will trace the analysis of so-called vernalization genes in the three plants most frequently used in this kind of research: *Triticum, Pisum* and *Arabidopsis*.

Conventional analysis of vernalization genes

TRITICUM

Excluded topics

Details of the localization of several vernalization genes on certain chromosomes will not be considered here as Law and his group have published much of this recently and this is readily available (Law, 1966; Law, Worland and Giorgi, 1976; Snape, Law and

Worland, 1976; Calahan and Law, 1979; Law, Worland and Young, 1980). Other important reviews have been written by Halloran (1976) and Major and Whelan (1985).

The so-called transformation of winter to summer wheats (and vice versa) will not be considered here as this seems to be more a historical problem of Marxism–Leninism than of biology. Stubbe (1955) has shown that the apparent transformational successes of Lysenko, Avakyan and others were due to experimentation with impure lines from which certain genotypes had been selected (for details *see* Napp-Zinn, 1961). More recently, transformations claimed by Rajki (1978) and Gulyaev, Berezkin and Magurov (1972) were disproved by Dionigi (1973) and Qualset and Peterson (1978).

Modes of segregation—numbers of genes involved

Wheat is a hexaploid, and therefore not a very convenient object for genetic analysis. At present the vernalization genetics of wheat are dominated by the nomenclature of Pugsley (1971, 1972) which supposes that there are four loci (*Vrn-1* to *Vrn-4*). The presence of the dominant allele at any one locus would cause the plant to become a summer annual. Many segregation data fit this hypothesis. Kyzlasov (1975) made 22 pairs of reciprocal crosses of 16 cultivars; in the F_1, the winter form was always recessive, and the F_2 segregation corresponded in general to a 3 summer:1 winter annual or a 15 summer:1 winter annual ratio, although in many cases the number of homozygous recessives was smaller than expected. In six of the back crosses of the F_1 generation with the recessive parent, the recessive appeared in only 25% of the plants, suggesting the involvement of two genes (Gulyaev and Kyzlasov, 1975). In the F_6 generation of crosses of day-neutral summer and winter wheats, Gotoh (1977) obtained 15 non-segregating lines which differed from each other with regard to the number of days before unfolding of the flag leaf; showing that genes of at least four loci were involved (cf. Gotoh, 1979a, b).

It seems, however, that Pugsley and several other workers were not aware of the older literature in this field. Tschermak (1923) reported a segregation of 3 winter:1 summer annual, and Cooper (1923) mentioned a 13 summer:3 winter wheat ratio. Such ratios would necessitate the presence of a further (fifth) gene *with the winter type dominant*. Only recently have findings which deviate from Pugsley's scheme gained new importance: Lbova and Chernyi (1980) report a F_2 segregation ratio of 57 early:7 late; Gotoh (1980) suddenly needs two 'new' genes (whose 'allelic relation ... to the *Vrn* genes is a matter for future investigation') in order to explain varietal differences in vernalization requirements, and Roberts and MacDonald (1984) postulate at least four alleles at the *Vrn-1* locus.

Cytoplasmic inheritance

For a long time research on extranuclear heredity seemed to be a privilege of German geneticists (Harwood, 1987), and vernalization requirements transmitted by cytoplasm were only known for *Epilobium* (Michaelis, 1939). There are now also at least two reports on cytoplasm-controlled cold requirements in wheat: Law, Worland and Young (1980) studied the dates of ear emergence of four nuclear genotypes in relation to the cytoplasms of *Triticum vulgare* and *Aegilops ovata*, respectively. *Aegilops* cytoplasm delayed ear emergence by 2–30 days (depending on genotype and degree of vernalization). Ward, Heyne and Paulsen (1983) arrived at a similar conclusion after transferring the genomes of certain *Triticum vulgare* cultivars into *Triticum Timophee-vii*.

PISUM

Successful genetic analysis of flowering in the garden pea dates back to Tschermak (1910), one of the rediscoverers of Mendel's rules who reported on the bifactorial control of flowering age, as subsequently did Wellensiek (1925). Almost half a century later Wellensiek (1969, 1973) induced two early flowering mutants with a reduced vernalization requirement in a late flowering pea strain by means of neutron irradiation. In Wellensiek's late strain and the intermediate mutant, the effects of 5 weeks at 5 °C, as measured by flowering time and nodes below the first flower, were only apparent under short photoperiods. A similar relation between vernalization and day-length was also evident in some of Murfet's experiments (1977a, b; 1979).

Before this work, more than 20 symbols for genes controlling flowering of pea could be seen in the literature. By studying crosses between 25 pea lines Murfet and his co-workers recognized that all segregations could be attributed to only four loci: at two of these, the dominant allele (*Lf* or *Sn*, respectively) rendered the plant a late flowering, vernalizable quantitative LDP (Murfet and Reid, 1974). The dominant allele of a third gene, *E*, is epistatic to *Sn* and annuls its delaying effect. *Lf*, however, is epistatic to *E*, and *Lf E Sn hr* is a late flowering, vernalizable quantitative LDP.

A number of alleles have become known at the *Lf* locus for the minimum number of nodes to be formed below the first flower: 5 with *lf*ᵃ, 8 with *lf*, 11 with *Lf*, and 15 with *Lf*ᵈ (Murfet, 1975). Wellensiek's mutant genes mentioned above were shown to be alleles at the *Lf* locus.

Recently two further flowering genes have been found in *Pisum*: *veg* (Gottschalk, 1979) keeps the plant vegetative in the homozygous condition (*veg veg*); flowering then cannot even be induced by vernalization (4 weeks at 5 °C; Reid and Murfet, 1984). In the case of a sixth gene, the recessive allele (*dne*) in the homozygous state makes *Sn* plants day-neutral and reduces their vernalization response practically to zero (King and Murfet, 1985).

ARABIDOPSIS

Most of the genes that cause a certain degree of vernalizability in *Arabidopsis* were discovered in mutation experiments. In at least three of Röbbelen's (1957) chloroplast mutants, flower initiation could be accelerated by cold (Napp-Zinn, 1964). McKelvie (1962) obtained six different late flowering vernalizable mutants, five of which were recessive: *f-1* to *f-5*, three of which could be localized on *different* chromosomes (with the aid of marker genes) and only one dominant (*F*). Van der Veen (1965) and Hussein and van der Veen (1965, 1968) report on 12 further mutants with various vernalization requirements (three dominant, one incompletely dominant, and eight recessive). Větřilová (1973) and Relichová (1976) report four further (incompletely dominant) late-flowering vernalizable mutants. This results in a total of approximately 24 genes, some of which, however, may be identical.

Population genetics and gene geography

These aspects of vernalization genes have been followed in *Arabidopsis* firstly by the genetic study of individual populations (Napp-Zinn; e.g. 1961, 1964, 1976). It was shown that many wild populations of *Arabidopsis thaliana* are mixtures of several genotypes as far as vernalization genes are concerned. This holds true for Röbbelen's local strain Antwerpen, and for populations from St. Blasien (Black Forest), Amorbach (Odenwald), Altenahr, Schalkenmehren (Eifel) and Genoble (France) as well (cf. Cetl, Dobrovolná and Effmertová (1965) and Perinová and Cetl (1983), for Moravian populations). As most of these populations are also genetically hetero-geneous with regard to germination, the combination of these two mechanisms is probably a strategy for survival under marginal conditions.

The second line of research uses comparisons and hybridization of selection lines from different local populations or 'races' with each other and with some standard lines, e.g. mutant lines and other lines with a monogenic vernalization requirement. This approach started with the genetic comparison of the winter annual race Stockholm (*St*) with the summer annual race Limburg-5 (*Li-5*). The discovery of one (stronger) dominant and one (weaker) recessive vernalization gene (*Fri* and *kry*), the former epistatic over the latter, accounted for only a part of the great vernalization requirement of *St* (Napp-Zinn, 1957). Whether backcross analysis (Napp-Zinn, 1962) favoured four, five or even more vernalization genes depended on the statistical criteria chosen. Since then sporadic experimentation in this field has concentrated on the detection of the two, three, or more genes which had not been isolated before. From the most recent results it appears that *Fri* is the only dominant vernalization gene in the race *St*, while all the others are recessive. *kry* appears hypostatic with regard to *Fri* and the remainder appear additive. All the natural winter annual and *late* summer annual populations tested so far (Zurich, Grenoble and Altenahr) contained the same vernalization gene *Fri* as the race Stockholm. Van der Veen (1965) however obtained an F_2 segregation from a cross Dijon × Limburg-2 that suggested *two dominant* vernalization genes. None of the vernalization genes of *St* or other wild races or populations have yet proved identical with any of McKelvie's experimentally induced vernalization gene mutants.

There is also the problem of correlation between vernalization requirement and ecological factors. According to Cetl, Dobrovalná and Effmertová (1965), winter annual *Arabidopsis* populations are limited to the warm and dry lowland in Moravia. At a similar location, Eberbach monastery (near Wiesbaden, Rhineland), however, *Arabidopsis* populations are strictly early summer annual, the 'cold and wet highland' population of Schalkenmehren (in the Eifel mountains) is pronouncedly winter annual. The regions of Grenoble and Cologne have essentially the same climates (annual precipitation 900 and 760 mm respectively, distributed all over the year, average temperatures of +1 °C in January and 19 °C in July), but quite contrasting *Arabidopsis* populations, predominantly winter annual at Grenoble, and early summer annual at Cologne. At Limburg/Lahn, where many summer annual *Arabidopsis* strains originated, a population has been found with almost exclusively winter annual descendants (Napp-Zinn, 1976).

Similar contradictions have been found with regard to cereals in primitive agricultural civilizations. In Nepal, for example, the vernalization requirement of local wheat cultivars increases with altitude, while that of barley strains does not show any correlation with altitude (Witcombe and Rao, 1976; Rao and Witcombe, 1977).

Gene physiology

THEORETICAL CONCLUSIONS FROM DOMINANCE

Vernalization requirements may be caused by dominant alleles, as in *Pisum* or by recessive alleles, as in *Triticum* (cf. Stankov, 1972) and *Arabidopsis*.

Dominant alleles are thought to cause the formation of a substance that is not formed when only the recessive alleles are present. This means that a dominant allele provoking a vernalization requirement would presumably be engaged in the synthesis of a flower inhibitor. It seems that in *Pisum*, the dominant gene *Sn* is involved in the production of a graft-transmissible inhibitor in the shoot and cotyledons under SD. The gene *E* lowers the production of the inhibitor by the cotyledons and *Lf* increases the threshold ratio of flower promoter to flower inhibitor necessary at the apex to cause flowering. Gene *Hr* acts in the leaves to delay the phasing out of *Sn* activity with age. Vernalization appears to influence flowering in *Pisum* by repression of *Sn* activity by low temperature (Murfet, 1979; Proebsting, 1984). *Hyoscyamus niger*, however, behaves differently. Although only a dominant allele is responsible for the vernalization requirement, a flower stimulus and not a flower inhibitor seems to be transmitted by grafting.

Contrastingly, in plants where a recessive allele causes the cold requirement, a flower promoter may not be formed that would be synthesized in the presence of the dominant allele.

IS VERNALIN A GIBBERELLIN?

The hypothetical end-product of the vernalization process, Vernalin, has often been thought to be a gibberellin but there are many arguments against this (Napp-Zinn, 1965). The chilling requirement of wheat like many other grasses has not been replaced by gibberellin treatments. Similarly, with various vernalizable *Pisum* genotypes, Wellensiek (1973) found no clear promotive effect of gibberellin. In some cases GA_3 lowered, but in most cases it increased the number of nodes below the first flower.

In *Arabidopsis*, on the other hand, practically all vernalization requiring genotypes, whether their cold requirements depend on dominant or recessive genes, respond to treatment with any gibberellin from GA_1 to GA_9 by an acceleration of flowering (Napp-Zinn, 1963). The level of endogenous gibberellin-like substances, however, parallels ripeness-to-flower, at least in the winter annual strain Stockholm (Bose, 1974).

GENES FOR VERNALIZATION AND DAY-LENGTH REQUIREMENTS

Vernalization and LD requirements are transmitted by strictly separated genes in wheat (Keim, Welsh and McConnel, 1973; Syme, 1973; Scarth and Law, 1983); *Ppd-1* on chromosome 2D, *Ppd-2* on 2B; insensitivity dominant, LD requirement recessive. In *Pisum*, however, the dominant alleles of the same two genes, *Lf* and *Sn*, are responsible for both vernalization and LD requirement. In *Arabidopsis* the genetic bases of LD requirement have not yet been studied in detail.

DIFFERENT VERNALIZATION GENES—DIFFERENT VERNALIZATION BEHAVIOUR

Influence of vernalization genes on age/effect relations in Arabidopsis

In *Arabidopsis thaliana* the effect of a given vernalization treatment (40 days at + 2 °C) varies with the age of the plant at the beginning of the cold treatment and with the genotype: the winter annual race Stockholm (whose cold requirement is based on at least four loci), the line H53 (*Fri Fri kry kry*), and McKelvie's mutant *F* show a phase of reduced vernalizability whether vernalization takes place in the light or in the darkness. The lines H51 (*Fri Fri*+ ^{kry} + ^{kry}) H36 and H43 (both + ^{Fry} + ^{Fry} *kry kry*), however, pass through a phase of reduced vernalizability only with regard to vernalization in darkness, not in the light (Napp-Zinn, 1960).

Different reaction types in wheat

Four near-isogenic lines (differing in *vrn-1* to *vrn-4*) have been examined by Salisbury, Berry and Halloran (1979), Berry, Salisbury and Halloran (1980), and Flood and Halloran (1984) and shown to react in different ways to various tractions of a given cold treatment. After 0–11 weeks of vernalization at 4 °C, the line with the *vrn-1* gene showed a cumulative response, those with *vrn-3* and *vrn-4* showed all-or-nothing responses, while *vrn-2* intensified these reactions. Flood and Halloran (1983) found Chinese Spring/Thatcher substitution lines of chromosomes 3B, 5B and 7B similar to Chinese Spring after certain periods of vernalization, and earlier than Chinese Spring after others.

ROLES OF VERNALIZATION GENES IN METABOLISM

The preceding observations lead to the question, 'which steps in which biosynthetic sequences are catalysed by vernalization genes?' There is very little conclusive information to help answer this. De Silva (1978) compared two isogenic lines of wheat (cv. Triple Dirk) which only differed with regard to the *Vrn-1/vrn-1* gene. After 5–6 weeks of vernalization, the recessive winter form *increased* the rate of (^{32}P-)ortho-phosphate incorporation into phospholipids while the dominant summer form showed a 75% *decrease* in ^{32}P-incorporation. At the same time (^{14}C-)acetate incorpo-ration into fatty acids increased in the winter form more than in the summer form. These findings support the idea that the *vrn-1* gene stimulates the synthesis of unsaturated membrane phospholipids during vernalization.

With many observations of this type it is not clear whether metabolic changes during the cold treatment are really causal to the flowering effect or merely unspecific effects of cold. Despite this, such experiments are not only worthwhile, but really indispensable for a better metabolic understanding of the vernalization process.

References

BERRY, G.J., SALISBURY, P.A. and HALLORAN, G.M. (1980). Expression of vernalization genes in near-isogenic wheat lines: Duration of vernalization period. *Annals of Botany, New Series*, **46**, 235–241

BOSE, K.K. (1974). *Untersuchungen an Arabidopsis Thaliana* (L.) Heynh. *über kinetische und biochemische Aspekte der Vernalisation*. Dissertation, Universität Köln

CALAHAN, C. and LAW, C.N. (1979). The genetical control of cold resistance and vernalization requirement in wheat (*Triticum aestivum*). *Heredity*, **42**, 125–132

CETL, I., DOBROVOLNÁ, J. and EFFMERTOVÁ, E. (1965). Distribution of spring and winter types in the local populations of *Arabidopsis thaliana* (L). Heynh. from various localities in western Moravia. *Arabidopsis Information Service*, **2**, 3

COOPER, H.P. (1923). Inheritance of the spring and winter growing habit in crosses between typical spring and winter wheats. *Journal of the American Society of Agronomy*, **15**, 15–24

DIONIGI, A. (1973). Informazioni sulla 'trasformazione Rajki' di frumenti primaverili in autumnali (il crepusculo della 'linea pura'). *Genetica Agraria*, **27**, 332–344

FLOOD, R.G. and HALLORAN, G.M. (1983). The influence of certain chromosomes of the hexaploid wheat cultivar Thatcher on time to ear emergence in Chinese Spring. *Euphytica*, **32**, 121–124

FLOOD, R.G. and HALLORAN, G.M. (1984). The nature and duration of gene action for vernalization response in wheat. *Annals of Botany, New Series*, **53**, 363–368

GOTOH, T. (1977). Intermediate growth habit wheat lines developed from a cross between spring and winter types. *Japanese Journal of Breeding*, **27**, 98–104

GOTOH, T. (1979a). Genetic studies on growth habit of some important spring wheat cultivars in Japan, with special reference to the identification of the spring genes involved. *Japanese Journal of Breeding*, **29**, 133–145

GOTOH, T. (1979b). Factors determining varietal differences of heading behavior of wheats. *Japanese Agricultural Research Quarterly*, **13**, 222–225

GOTOH, T. (1980). Gene analysis of the degree of vernalization requirement in winter wheat. *Japanese Journal of Breeding*, **30**, 1–10

GOTTSCHALK, W. (1979). A *Pisum* gene preventing transition from vegetative to reproductive stage. *Pisum Newsletter*, **11**, 10

GULYAEV, G.V., BEREZKIN, A.N. and MAGUROV, P.F. (1972). (Genetic adaptation of a variety to various growth conditions.) *Genetika*, **8**, No. 12, 82–85

GULYAEV, G.V. and KYZLASOV, V.G. (1975). (Inheritance of growth characteristics by winter and spring wheat hybrids.) *Sel'skokhozyajstvennyj Biologiya*, **10**, 729–735

HALLORAN, G.M. (1976). Genes for vernalization response in homoeologous group 5 of *Triticum aestivum*. *Canadian Journal of Genetics and Cytology*, **18**, 211–216

HARWOOD, J. (1987). Ideas of plasmatic heredity by German botanists 1920–1950. *Berichte der Deutschen Botanischen Gesellschaft*, **100**

HUSSEIN, H.A.S. and VAN DER VEEN, J.H. (1965). Induced mutations for flowering time. *Arabidopsis Information Service*, **2**, 6

HUSSEIN, H.A.S. and VAN DER VEEN, J.H. (1968). Genotypic analysis of induced mutations for flowering time and leaf number in *Arabidopsis thaliana*. *Arabidopsis Information Service*, **5**, 30

KEIM, D.L., WELSH, J.R. and MCCONNELL, R.L. (1973). Inheritance of photoperiodic heading response in winter and spring cultivars of bread wheat. *Canadian Journal of Plant Science*, **53**, 247–250

KING, W.M. and MURFET, I.C. (1985). Flowering in *Pisum*: A sixth locus, *Dne*. *Annals of Botany, New Series*, **56**, 835–846

KLEBS, G. (1903). *Willkürliche Entwicklungsänderungen bei Pflanzen. Ein Beitrag zur Physiologie der Entwicklung.* Jena, G. Fischer

KYZLASOV, V.G. (1975). (Segregation by spring–wheat characters and wintering of reciprocal hybrids of winter and spring wheats.) *Tsitologiya i Genetika*, **9**, 324–328

LAW, C.N. (1966). The location of genetic factors affecting a quantitative character in wheat. *Genetics*, **53**, 487–498

LAW, C.N. (1979). Genetical techniques available in wheat and their use in studying flowering. *Colloques Internationaux du CNRS*, **285** (La Physiologie de la Floraison), 215–216

LAW, C.N., WORLAND, A.J. and GIORGI, B. (1976). The genetic control of ear-emergence time by chromosomes 5A and 5D of wheat. *Heredity*, **36**, 49–58

LAW, C.N., WORLAND, A.J. and YOUNG, C.F. (1980). Developmental studies in wheat using whole chromosome substitution lines. *Proceedings of the XIV International Congress of Genetics*, Moscow, pp. 282–294

LBOVA, M.I. and CHERNYI, I.V. (1980). (Monosomic analysis of some characters of a radiation cultivar of spring wheat Novosibirskaya 67 and its initial form. II. Determination of genes controlling the growth habit.) *Genetika*, **16**, 485–492

McKELVIE, A.D. (1962). A list of mutant genes in *Arabidopsis thaliana* (L.) Heynh. *Radiation Botany*, **1**, 233–241

MAJOR, D.J. and WHELAN, E.D.P. (1985). Vernalization and photoperiod response characteristics of a reciprocal substitution series of Rescue and Cadet hard red spring wheat. *Canadian Journal of Plant Science*, **65**, 33–40

MICHAELIS, P. (1939). Keimstimmung und Plasmavererbung bei Epilobium. *Jahrbücher für wissenschaftliche Botanik*, **88**, 69–88

MURFET, I.C. (1975). Flowering in *Pisum*: Multiple alleles at the *If* locus. *Heredity*, **35**, 85–98

MURFET, I.C. (1977a). The physiological genetics of flowering. In *The Physiology of the Garden Pea* (J. F. Sutcliffe and J. S. Pate, Eds), pp. 385–430. London, Academic Press

MURFET, I.C. (1977b). Environmental interaction and the genetics of flowering. *Annual Review of Plant Physiology*, **28**, 253–278

MURFET, I.C. (1979). The physiological genetics of flowering in the garden pea. *Colloques internationaux du CNRS*, **285** (La Physiologie de la Floraison), 212–214

MURFET, I.C. and REID, J.B. (1974). Flowering in *Pisum*: The influence of photoperiod and vernalising temperatures on the expression of genes *Lf* and *Sn*. *Zeitschrift für Pflanzenphysiologie*, **71**, 323–331

NAPP-ZINN, K. (1957). Untersuchungen zur Genetik des Kältebedürfnisses bei *Arabidopsis thaliana*. *Zeitschrift für induktive Abstammungs- und Vererbungslehre*, **88**, 253–285

NAPP-ZINN, K. (1960). Vernalisation, Licht und Alter bei *Arabidopsis thaliana* (L.) Heynh. I. Licht und Dunkelheit während Kälte- und Wärmebehandlung. *Planta*, **54**, 409–444

NAPP-ZINN, K. (1961). Vernalisation und verwandte Erscheinungen. In *Handbuch der Pflanzenphysiologie* (W. Ruhland, Ed.), Vol. **16**, pp. 24–75. Berlin, Springer

NAPP-ZINN, K. (1962). Über die genetischen Grundlagen des Vernalisationsbedürfnisses bei *Arabidopsis thaliana*. I. Die Zahl der beteiligten Faktoren. *Zeitschrift für Vererbungslehre*, **93**, 154–163

NAPP-ZINN, K. (1963). Über den Einfluss von Genen und Gibberellinen auf die

Blütenbildung von *Arabidopsis thaliana*. *Berichte der deutschen botanischen Gesellschaft*, **76**, 77–89

NAPP-ZINN, K. (1964). Über genetische und entwicklungsphysiologische Grundlagen jahreszeitlicher Aspekte von Pflanzengesellschaften. In *Beiträge zur Phytologie* (K. Kreeb, ed.), pp. 33–49. Stuttgart, E. Ulmer

NAPP-ZINN, K. (1965). Physiologische Aspekte der Blütenbildung. *Scientia*, **100**, 135–141. Also in French: Aspects physiologiques de la mise à fleurs. *Scientia*, **100**, Supplement, 66–71

NAPP-ZINN, K. (1976). Population genetical and gene geographical aspects of germination and flowering in *Arabidopsis thaliana*. *Arabidopsis Information Service*, Vol. **13** (Proceedings of the 2nd international Symposium on Arabidopsis Research), pp. 30–33

NAPP-ZINN, K. (1984). Light and vernalization. In *Light and the Flowering Process* (D. Vince-Prue, B. Thomas and K. E. Cockshull, Eds), pp. 75–88. London, Academic Press

PERINOVÁ, B. and CETL, I. (1983). Internal differentiation of natural populations of *Arabidopsis thaliana* (L.) Heynh. in the genetic system of flowering time. *Arabidopsis Information Service*, **20**, 63–71

PROEBSTING, W.M. (1984). Genetic regulation of flowering in grafts on *Pisum sativum* L. *Plant Physiology*, **75**, 634–638

PUGSLEY, A.T. (1971). A genetic analysis of the spring–winter habit of growth in wheat. *Australian Journal of Agricultural Research*, **22**, 21–31

PUGSLEY, A.T. (1972). Additional genes inhibiting winter habit in wheat. *Euphytica*, **21**, 547–552

QUALSET, C.O. and PETERSON, M.L. (1978). Polymorphism for vernalization requirement in a winter oat cultivar. *Crop Science*, **18**, 311–315

RAJKI, S. (1978). Hybridisation in wheat breeding. *Acta Agronomica Academiae Scientiarum Hungaricae*, **27**, 207–213

RAO, A.R. and WITCOMBE, J.R. (1977). Genetic adaptation for vernalization requirement in Nepalese wheat and barley. *Annals of Applied Biology*, **85**, 121–130

REID, J.B. and MURFET, I.C. (1984). Flowering in *Pisum*: A fifth locus, *Veg. Annals of Botany, New Series*, **53**, 369–382

RELICHOVÁ, J. (1976). Some new mutants. *Arabidopsis Information Service*, Vol. **13** (Proceedings of the 2nd international Symposium on Arabidopsis Research), pp. 25–28

RÖBBELEN, G. (1957). Untersuchungen an strahleninduzierten Blattfarbmutanten von *Arabidopsis thaliana* (L.) Heynh. *Zeitschrift für induktive Abstammungs- und Vererbungslehre*, **88**, 189–252

ROBERTS, D.W.A. and MACDONALD, M.D. (1984). Evidence for the multiplicity of alleles at Vrn_1, the winter–spring habit locus in common wheat. *Canadian Journal of Genetics and Cytology*, **26**, 191–193

SALISBURY, P.A., BERRY, G.J. and HALLORAN, G.M. (1979). Expression of vernalization genes in near-isogenic wheat (*Triticum aestivum*) lines: Methods of vernalization. *Canadian Journal of Genetics and Cytology*, **21**, 429–434

SCARTH, R. and LAW, C.N. (1983). The location of the photoperiod gene, *Ppd2*, and an additional genetic factor for ear-emergence time on chromosome 2B of wheat. *Heredity*, **51**, 607–619

SILVA, N.S. DE (1978). Phospholipid and fatty acid metabolism in relation to hardiness and vernalization in wheat during low temperature adaptation to growth. *Zeitschrift für Pflanzenphysiologie*, **86**, 313–322

SNAPE, J.W., LAW, C.N. and WORLAND, A.J. (1976). Chromosome variation for loci controlling ear emergence time on chromosome 5A of wheat. *Heredity*, **37**, 335–340

STANKOV, I.K. (1972). (Study of F$_1$ hybrids between *Triticum sphaerococcum* Perc. and the species *T. durum* Desf. and *T. dicoccum* Schrank.) *Genetika i Selektsiya*, **25**, 199–210

STUBBE, H. (1955). Über die Umwandlung von Winterweizen in Sommerweizen. *Züchter*, **25**, 321–330

SYME, J.R. (1973). Quantitative control of flowering time in wheat cultivars by vernalization and photoperiod sensitivities. *Australian Journal of Agricultural Research*, **24**, 657–665

TSCHERMAK, E.v. (1910). Über die Vererbung der Blütezeit bei Erbsen. *Verhandlungen des naturforschenden Vereins zu Brünn*, **49**, 169–191

TSCHERMAK, E.v. (1923). Bastardierung. In *Handbuch der Landwirtschaftlichen Pflanzenzüchtung* (C. Fruwirth, Ed.), 4th edn., Vol. **4**, pp. 309–326

VAN DER VEEN. J.H. (1965). Genes for late flowering in *Arabidopsis thaliana*. In *Arabidopsis Research* (Report of an international Symposium held at the University of Göttingen), pp. 62–69. Göttingen: Arabidopsis Information Service

VĚTŘILOVÁ, M. (1973). Genetic and physiological analysis of induced late mutants of *Arabidopsis thaliana* (L.) Heynh. *Biologia Plantarum*, **15**, 391–397

WARD, R.W., HEYNE, E.G. and PAULSEN, G.M. (1983). Responses of alloplasmic (cytoplasm = *Triticum timopheevii*) and euplasmic wheats (*Triticum aestivum*) to photoperiod and vernalization. *Theoretical and Applied Genetics*, **66**, 61–66

WELLENSIEK, S.J. (1925). Genetic monograph on *Pisum*. *Bibliographia Genetica*, **2**, 343–476

WELLENSIEK, S.J. (1969). The physiological effects of flower forming genes in peas. *Zeitschrift für Pflanzenphysiologie*, **60**, 388–402

WELLENSIEK, S.J. (1973). Effects of vernalization and gibberellic acid on flower bud formation in different genotypes of pea under different photoperiods. *Scientia Horticulturae*, **1**, 177–192

WITCOMBE, J.R. and RAO, A.R. (1976). The genecology of wheat in a Nepalese centre of diversity. *Journal of Applied Ecology*, **13**, 915–924

10

CURD INITIATION IN THE CAULIFLOWER (*BRASSICA OLERACEA* VAR. BOTRYTIS L.)

J.G. ATHERTON, D.J. HAND and C.A. WILLIAMS
Department of Agriculture and Horticulture, University of Nottingham, Loughborough, UK

Introduction

Cauliflowers are not only an important vegetable crop but also most convenient subjects for studies on the physiology of vernalization. The commercial product is a large, immature inflorescence, usually called a curd, which is formed at the tip of the stem after a period of vegetative growth. The vegetative period comprises a juvenile phase during which the plant is unable to initiate a curd and a mature phase when it can. The duration of juvenility is determined primarily by growth rate and genotype whilst the duration of vegetative development after juvenility is determined by these same factors and also by a quantitative vernalization response in most cauliflower cultivars. A range of cultivars is available to growers in the UK that will provide continuous production of curds throughout the year. In this chapter, curd initiation will be examined in cauliflower cultivars that belong to the early summer group.

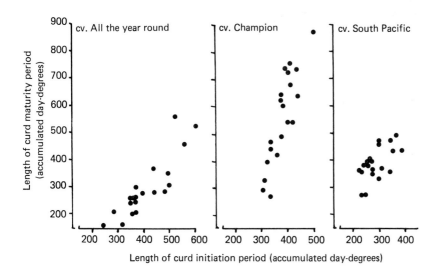

Figure 10.1 Relationships between curd initiation and curd maturity periods in three cauliflower cultivars (after Salter, 1969).

(*a*)

(*b*)

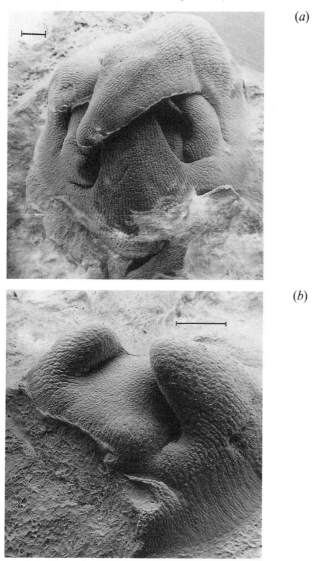

Figure 10.2   Scanning electron micrographs of shoot tips excised from mature cauliflower plants during vegetative growth: (*a*) Young leaves clustered around the apical dome (bar = 100 μm). (*b*) Apical dome and youngest leaf primordia (bar = 100 μm).

These form marketable curds in the fields between June and August, following transplanting during March. Chilling, rather than increasing photoperiod, is known to be their major environmental stimulus for curd initiation (Sadik, 1967).

Variability and unpredictability of curd initiation in the crop can cause major commercial problems. If transplants have curds initiated prior to establishment in the field, those curds are unlikely to grow to a marketable size. It is therefore necessary to keep transplants in a juvenile state during propagation. Growing at low temperatures (0–10 °C) in small modules and limiting inorganic nitrogen supplied from fertilizers can be used for this purpose. Curd maturity in the field often extends over a 2–6 week period which precludes once-over mechanical harvesting. Salter (1969) showed that the length of the curd maturity period was strongly correlated with the time over which the plants initiated curds (*Figure 10.1*). If initiation could be synchronized, uniformity in curd maturity would be expected. Temperature and inorganic nitrogen nutrition are two principal factors that affect the timing of curd initiation. These will be examined here together with possible mechanisms for their action.

The chilling stimulus for accelerating curd initiation in cauliflower is almost certainly perceived by the shoot tip, as it is in other brassicas (Ito, Saito and Hatayamo, 1966). The cauliflower is a short, caulescent plant with shoot tips comprising young leaves and leaf primordia situated around the apical dome and separated by expanding internodes (*Figure 10.2*). Relative to most other plants, the shoot tip components of the cauliflower are large, and easy to detach, measure and analyse for changes during vernalization. Attention is given in this chapter to changes in growth and dry matter distribution, particularly for carbohydrates, as these appear to have a regulatory role in flower initiation in other plants (Bodson and Bernier, 1985).

Temperature and curd initiation

The summer cauliflower will initiate a curd following growth under a wide range of conditions provided that it has reached a certain critical size. Apart from a few exceptions (Friend, 1985), these cultivars cannot be vernalized as ripe seeds. Shoot sizes at curd initiation in cvs Perfection and White Fox after growth at various constant temperatures are shown in *Table 10.1*. Curds were initiated on smaller plants at an earlier stage of development after they had experienced temperatures of 5 °C or 10 °C for 4 weeks. A clear, quantitative vernalization response to chilling was found in both cultivars with the more marked effect evident in the earlier cultivar, Perfection. This cultivar was used in all subsequent experiments described in this chapter.

Cardinal temperatures for vernalization were estimated by timing curd initiation in plants that had firstly been grown at a range of constant temperatures in growth chambers after the end of juvenility and then transferred back to a glasshouse controlled to give a mean daily temperature of 20 °C. Time of curd initiation was

Table 10.1 SHOOT SIZE AT CURD INITIATION IN CAULIFLOWER cvs 'PERFECTION' AND 'WHITE FOX' GROWN AT A RANGE OF TEMPERATURES FOR 4 WEEKS FOLLOWING COMPLETION OF A JUVENILE PHASE OF GROWTH (I.E. AFTER 19 LEAVES HAD INITIATED) (EACH VALUE IS A MEAN OF NINE.)

| Temperature (°C) | Shoot size at curd initiation | | | | | |
| | Leaf number | | Shoot fresh weight (g) | | Shoot dry weight (g) | |
	Perfection	White Fox	Perfection	White Fox	Perfection	White Fox
0	35	48	100	131	8.7	13.1
5	19	26	102	142	6.7	13.9
10	21	20	135	145	7.6	12.0
18	29	30	121	110	9.8	12.1
20	42	41	154	132	10.6	13.6
25	58	42	228	167	20.1	16.5

measured in terms of the number of leaves initiated before the curd. The reciprocal of this parameter indicates the rate of progress to curd initiation (*see* Chapter 2). The optimum temperature for vernalization was found to be 5.5 °C, and the maximum and minimum were 24.5 °C and -1.3 °C respectively (*Figure 10.3*). Similar, but more variable, responses to temperature were found when rate of progress to curd initiation was measured as reciprocals of either shoot weight at curd initiation or days to curd visibility. For practical purposes, temperatures outside the range 0–22 °C may be considered inhibitory to curd initiation in young, mature plants of this cultivar.

Promotion of curd initiation by chilling was associated with an overall reduction in growth relative to controls. When shoot tips comprising similar numbers of leaves were compared, however, the dry weights of those taken from chilled plants were significantly heavier ($p = 0.001$) (*Table 10.2*). This is consistent with previous findings of Sadik and Ozbun (1968) that showed carbohydrates to accumulate in the shoot tips of cauliflower during chilling. As chilling continued beyond 3 days, however, there was no significant change in total dry weight of the shoot tips. In view of the promotion of

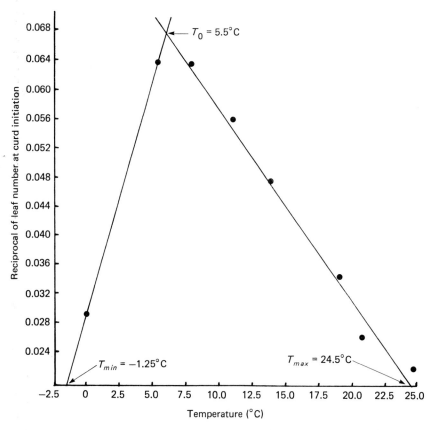

Figure 10.3 Effects of constant temperature on the rate of curd initiation in cauliflower cv. Perfection measured as the reciprocal of total leaf number at curd initiation. Temperature treatments began when plants had initiated 14 leaves and continued for 4 weeks.

Table 10.2   DRY WEIGHTS OF SHOOT TIPS EXCISED FROM PLANTS GROWN AT 20°C
AND 5°C IN GROWTH ROOMS. EACH SHOOT TIP COMPRISED FIVE LEAF PRIMORDIA
AND THE APICAL DOME. TEMPERATURE TREATMENTS BEGAN WHEN PLANTS HAD
INITIATED 19 LEAVES. (EACH VALUE IS A MEAN OF FIVE.)

Temperature (°C)	Weight of shoot tip (µg), days after start of treatment		
	3	*10*	*17*
5	192	180	204
20	120	105	120

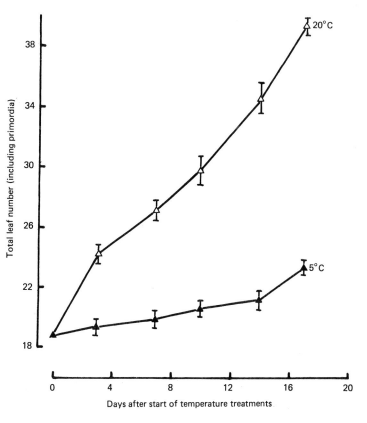

Figure 10.4   Leaf initiation in plants grown at 20°C and 5°C in growth rooms.
Treatments began at the 19 leaf stage. (Each value is a mean of 25. Bars give SE.)

curd initiation in cv. Perfection requiring at least 10–14 days chilling, it was apparent that simple accumulation of dry matter in the shoot tip alone could not explain the vernalization effect.

Analysis of growth in the components of the shoot tip during chilling enabled a better insight into the vernalization effect. As soon as the plants were chilled, leaf initiation at the shoot apex virtually stopped (*Figure 10.4*). There is evidence with other plants that the suppression of leaf development may be a critical event in the vernalization process. For example, many of the alternative treatments to chilling that will promote flowering under non-inductive conditions also inhibit leaf development (Evans, 1971). In the cauliflowers examined here, growth and dry matter

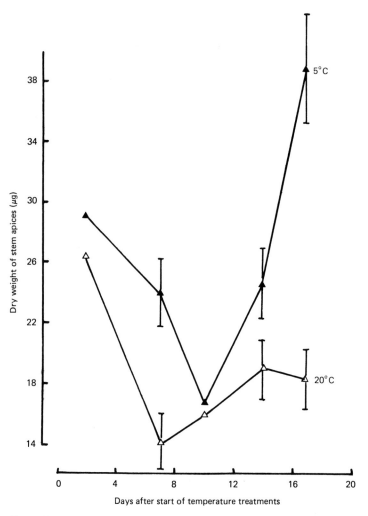

Figure 10.5 Changes in the dry weight of apical domes excised from plants grown at 20°C and at 5°C in growth rooms after initiating 19 leaves under glasshouse conditions. Each dome was taken to be the tissue area above the youngest leaf primordium. (Each value is a mean of five. Bars give SE.)

accumulation in existing leaf primordia continued for about 4 days during chilling. As no new leaves or internodes were initiated and shoot extension ceased, positionally similar (but ontogenetically different) leaf primordia at equivalent distances below the apical dome were larger in the chilled plants. Various speculations could be made regarding the proximity of these large leaf primordia to the apical dome and their effects on curd initiation.

Careful dissection of cauliflower shoot tips permits excision of the apical dome and measurement of dry weight and volume. Rapid accumulation of dry matter in the apical dome began after about 10 days chilling (*Figure 10.5*). This occurred before any curd initials were apparent and before the apical dome started to enlarge (*Figure 10.6*). The time of dry weight increase in the dome appeared to coincide with the minimum duration of chilling necessary to promote curd initiation in these plants. It was possible, therefore, that chilling acted in vernalization to suppress leaf initiation and leaf growth, which consequently allowed increased availability of dry matter to the apical dome, thereby permitting its development to curd initiation. Further work is now in progress to see whether similar changes occur during chilling in cauliflowers that are not subsequently accelerated in their progress to curd initiation, including juvenile plants and unresponsive cultivars.

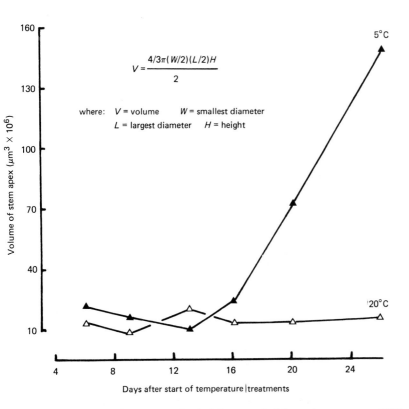

Figure 10.6 Changes in the volume of apical domes excised from plants grown at 20°C and 5°C in growth rooms. Domes and plant treatments were the same as described for *Figure 10.5*. (Each value is a mean of five.)

A sharp decline in the dry matter contents of the apical domes was measured at the start of temperature treatments. This was due to plants being transferred from high natural irradiance in a glasshouse to relative shade (c.60 W m^{-2}) in growth rooms. This observation implied that the absolute dry matter content of the apical dome is probably less critical for progress to curd initiation than its competitive sink activity relative to surrounding tissues. Effects of irradiance level on dry matter distribution in the shoot tip and on curd initiation are currently under examination.

Nitrogen and curd initiation

Withholding inorganic nitrogen fertilizers from cauliflower plants will restrict their growth in terms of leaf area and shoot size, an apparently similar restriction to that imposed by low temperature. This effect is used deliberately in the commercial production of transplants to hold the plants at a particular stage of development until field conditions are suitable for planting (Hiron, unpublished observations). Nitrogen starvation was used here as an experimental probe to test apparent correlations between leaf development, dry matter distribution and curd initiation that had been found in the low-temperature studies described above.

Under warm, non-promotive temperature conditions, nitrogen starvation markedly delayed curd initiation in terms both of time and of number of leaves produced before the curd (*Figure 10.7(a)*). This occurred despite achieving a considerable depression in leaf growth. Accumulation of dry matter in the whole shoot was also reduced by nitrogen starvation (*Figure 10.7(b)*). Nitrogen starvation of plants during low-temperature vernalization, however, had no inhibitory effect on curd initiation despite reducing both shoot weight and leaf area (*Table 10.3*). The rate of leaf initiation was unaffected by nitrogen in these experiments but vegetative growth and development continued longer as a result of nitrogen starvation under warm conditions.

Nitrogen deprivation has also been shown to delay flower initiation in other vernalizable plants either when grown under non-vernalizing conditions or where they had been partially vernalized, for example, winter rye (Gott *et al.*, 1955). Similarly nitrogen deficiency only delayed flower initiation in photoperiodically sensitive plants such as glasshouse carnation (Blake and Harris, 1960) and soyabean (Scully *et al.*, 1945) when they were grown under non-inductive conditions. Blake and Harris (1960) speculated that nitrogen deficiency probably reduced levels of metabolites at the stem apex to a point where floral initiation was delayed but leaf initiation could continue. Observations here with cauliflower are consistent with that view. *Table 10.4* shows that dry matter contents of the apical dome and young leaves were generally reduced by nitrogen starvation. This effect was not apparent in plants that had been chilled. Evidence of less dry matter being required to support leaf initiation than to permit curd initiation at the stem apex is given in *Figure 10.8*. In plants grown at non-inductive temperatures (c.20 °C), curds were initiated after about 33 leaves had formed provided that their dry weight was in excess of about 5 g. Where plants had accumulated less dry matter than this, many more leaves were initiated before the curd. No such pattern was evident for plants that had been vernalized. In chilled plants where leaf initiation is suppressed, it is probably the consequent diversion of dry matter to the apical dome, rather than the more general increase in dry matter availability to the shoot tip, that permits curd initiation.

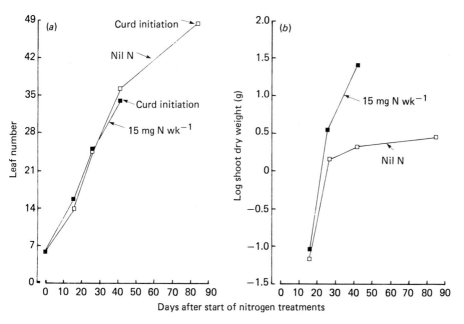

Figure 10.7 Effects of inorganic nitrogen fertilizer supply on (a) leaf initiation and (b) shoot dry weight in cauliflower cv. Perfection grown at a mean temperature of 20°C in the glasshouse. Treatments began on 30 May 1984 when seedlings were transferred to composts containing no nitrogenous base fertilizer. (Each value is a mean of 12.)

Table 10.3 LEAF DEVELOPMENT AT THE TIME OF CURD INITIATION IN CAULIFLOWER cv. PERFECTION, FED WITH NITROGEN AT DIFFERENT RATES AND GROWN IN EITHER WARM (20°C, MEAN) OR CHILLING (5°C) CONDITIONS FOR 4 WEEKS. NITROGEN TREATMENTS BEGAN WHEN PLANTS HAD INITIATED 5 LEAVES. TEMPERATURE TREATMENTS BEGAN WHEN PLANTS HAD INITIATED 14 LEAVES. (EACH VALUE IS A MEAN OF NINE.)

	Temperature:	20°C		5°C	
	Nitrogen (mg N week^{-1}):	0	15	0	15
Leaf number		48	33	29	31
Leaf area (cm^2)		139	490	146	448

Table 10.4 DRY MATTER DISTRIBUTION IN THE SHOOT TIPS OF PLANTS GROWN AT 20°C WITH AND WITHOUT SUPPLIED NITROGEN. SHOOT TIPS COMPRISED FIVE LEAF PRIMORDIA AND THE STEM APEX. MEASUREMENTS WERE MADE WHEN PLANTS HAD INITIATED 27–29 LEAVES. (EACH VALUE IS A MEAN OF FIVE.)

	Dry weights of leaves and stem apex (μg)					
	Decreasing leaf age					
Nitrogen supplied (mg N week^{-1}):	1	2	3	4	5	Apex
0	66	31	15	6	7	17
15	46	28	21	19	12	24

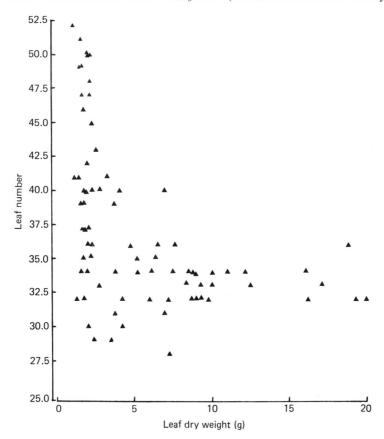

Figure 10.8   Leaf number and dry weight at curd initiation in cauliflower cv. Perfection grown at a range of nitrogen fertilizer rates under warm (mean 20°C) conditions in a glasshouse, starting May 1985.

A regulatory role for carbohydrates?

The changes in distribution of dry matter within the shoot tip described above can be taken substantially to reflect changes in carbohydrate distribution. Carbohydrates have long been known to have an important role in vernalization: their levels are known to increase in whole shoot tips of cauliflower and other plants during vernalization (Sadik and Ozbun, 1968; Fontes and Ozbun, 1972) and in onions, differences in levels of carbohydrates there correlate well with the degree of flower initiation obtained (Brewster, 1985). Furthermore, vernalization may only proceed in isolated buds or embryos when an external supply of sugars is provided (Purvis, 1944; Tashima, 1957; Kruzhilin and Schvedskaya, 1958). Feeding sugars to shoot tips cultured *in vitro* has also been shown, at least with photoperiodically sensitive plants, to reduce the requirement for an external flowering stimulus (Cumming, 1967; Friend *et al.*, 1984).

Preliminary investigations here with cauliflower have shown that sucrose applications to the shoot tip of intact plants can partially replace the low-temperature stimulus for curd initiation. Sucrose solutions were supplied four times at intervals of 5 days to the young leaves and vicinity of the apical dome using a fine hypodermic syringe. The plants had 22 leaves initiated at the start of the sucrose treatments and were grown at non-promotive temperatures (c.20 °C) in the glasshouse throughout. Curds initiated in the sucrose treatments after 37 leaves as compared with 46 leaves in plants supplied with water and 47 leaves in plants supplied with mannitol solutions made up to give equivalent osmotic potentials to the sucrose solutions (*Figure 10.9*). The sucrose effect was apparent at low concentrations (50–100 mol l^{-1}). Attempts to produce the same promotive effect failed when sucrose was fed through cut leaf blades lower down the plant.

There can be little doubt that events leading to curd initiation in cauliflower include preferential distribution of carbohydrate to the apical dome at the expense of the young leaves, leaf primordia and adjacent stem tissues. Similar changes have been associated with flower formation in *Pinus radiata* (Ross *et al.*, 1984) and are predicted

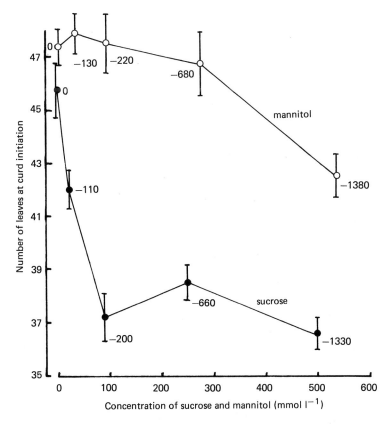

Figure 10.9 Leaf number at curd initiation in cauliflower plants that had been fed with sucrose or mannitol solutions via the shoot tip while growing at about 20°C under natural day-length conditions in the glasshouse. Osmotic potentials (kPa) are shown for each treatment. Each plant received four applications at intervals of 5 days. Treatments began on 12 September 1985 when plants had initiated 22 leaves. (Each value is a mean of 10; bars give SE.)

to occur in *Sinapis alba* during floral evocation (*see* Chapter 24). Various questions remain, however, regarding the role of carbohydrates during vernalization, particularly whether their role is direct or indirect. As Sachs considers these and other questions in detail in Chapter 23, it will suffice to say here that carbohydrate distribution between competing sinks will be determined by the abilities of those sinks to take up and use the carbohydrate. Such abilities will depend on enzyme activity which in turn can be governed by hormone action. It may be that changes in carbohydrate distribution are a consequence of changes in these factors rather than a cause of curd initiation. Whilst further study is required to examine this point, it should be noted that there is also increasing evidence of a regulatory role for carbohydrates in floral evocation, more subtle than that of a respiratory substrate or an osmotic solute (Cousson and Tran Than Van, 1983; Bodson and Outlaw, 1985).

Conclusions

Correlations between leaf development and progress of the apical dome to curd initiation were shown using growth analysis procedures on whole shoots and shoot tips of cauliflowers during their post-juvenile vegetative growth phase. Low temperatures allowed small plants to initiate curds apparently through suppressing leaf initiation thereby allowing the apical dome preference in the distribution of carbohydrates within the shoot tip. The accumulation of carbohydrate in the dome preceded any morphological change there and was coincident with the minimum duration of chilling required for vernalization to occur. Sucrose solutions supplied to shoot tips on intact plants substituted partially for the low-temperature effect, suggesting a direct regulatory role for carbohydrates in vernalization. This does not preclude a role for growth substances in the vernalization process (*see* Chapter 23).

Timing and stage of plant development for curd initiation are important to the commercial producer of cauliflower transplants. Ideally the transplant should be vegetative prior to planting in the field. Results presented in this chapter showed how temperature and nitrogen supply may be adjusted to ensure that the plants stay in a vegetative state. Whilst many more interactions between nitrogen levels, temperatures and cultivars need to be examined before a 'blueprint' for production can be made, the guidelines are quite clear.

Acknowledgements

We thank Mr T. Lord for assistance with many of the experiments and Dr R.W.P. Hiron for useful discussions. Financial support from the Agricultural and Food Research Council, the Science and Engineering Research Council and the Ministry of Agriculture, Fisheries and Food is gratefully acknowledged. Assistance from the Wolfson Institute of Interfacial Technology with scanning electron microscopy was much appreciated.

References

BLAKE, J. and HARRIS, G.P. (1960). Effects of nitrogen nutrition on flowering in carnation. *Annals of Botany*, **24**, 247–257

BODSON, M. and BERNIER, G. (1985). Is flowering controlled by assimilate level? *Physiologie Végétale*, **23**, 491–501

BODSON, M. and OUTLAW, W.H. Jr. (1985). Elevation in the sucrose content of the shoot apical meristem of *Sinapis* at floral evocation. *Plant Physiology*, **79**, 420–424

BREWSTER, J.L. (1985). The influence of seedling size and carbohydrate status and of photon flux density during vernalization on inflorescence initiation in onion (*Allium cepa* L.). *Annals of Botany*, **55**, 403–414

COUSSON, A. and TRAN THAN VAN, K. (1983). Light- and sugar mediated control of direct *de novo* flower differentiation from tobacco thin cell layers. *Plant Physiology*, **72**, 33–36

CUMMING, B.G. (1967). Circadian rhythmic flowering responses in *Chenopodium rubrum*: effects of glucose and sucrose. *Canadian Journal of Botany*, **45**, 2173–2193

EVANS, L.T. (1971). Flower induction and the florigen concept. *Annual Review of Plant Physiology*, **22**, 365–394

FONTES, M.R. and OZBUN, J.L. (1972). Relationship between carbohydrate level and flower initiation in broccoli. *Journal of the American Society of Horticultural Science*, **97**, 346–348

FRIEND, D.J.C. (1985). *Brassica*. In *Handbook of Flowering*, (A.H. Halevy, Ed.), pp. 48–77. Boca Raton, Florida, CRC Press

FRIEND, D.J.C., BODSON, M. and BERNIER, G. (1984). Promotion of flowering in *Brassica campestris* L. cv Ceres by sucrose. *Plant Physiology*, **75**, 1085–1089

GOTT, M.B., GREGORY, F.G. and PURVIS, O.N. (1955). Studies in vernalization of cereals. XIII. Photoperiodic control of stages in flowering between initiation and ear formation in vernalized and unvernalized Petkus Winter Rye. *Annals of Botany*, **19**, 87–126

ITO, H., SAITO, T. and HATAYAMO, T. (1966). Time and temperature factors for the flower formation in cabbage. II. The site of vernalization and the nature of vernalization sensitivity. *Tohoku Journal of Agricultural Research*, **17**, 1–15

KRUZHILIN, A.S. and SCHVEDSKAYA, Z.M. (1958). The vernalization of isolated buds of biennials in sugar solutions. *Dokl. Bot. Sci., Sect.*, **121**, 208–211 (Translated from Dokl. Akad. Nauk. SSSR. 121, 561–564).

PURVIS, O.N. (1944). studies in vernalization of cereals. III. The role of carbohydrate and nitrogen supply in the vernalization of excised embryos of Petkus winter rye. *Annals of Botany*, **8**, 285–314

ROSS, S.D., BOLLMAN, M.P., PHARIS, R. and SWEET, G.B. (1984). Gibberellin $A_{4/7}$ and the promotion of flowering in *Pinus radiata*: effects on partitioning of photoassimilate within the bud during primordia initiation. *Plant Physiology*, **76**, 326–330

SADIK, S. (1967). Factors involved in curd and flower formation in cauliflower. *Proceedings of the American Society of Horticultural Science*, **90**, 252–259

SADIK, S. and OZBUN, J.L. (1968). The association of carbohydrate changes in the shoot tip of cauliflower with flowering. *Plant Physiology*, **43**, 1696–1698

SALTER, P.J. (1969). Studies on crop maturity in cauliflower. 1. Relationship between the times of curd initiation and curd maturity of plants within a cauliflower crop. *Journal of Horticultural Science*, **44**, 129–140

SCULLY, N.J., PARKER, N.W. and BORTHWICK, H.A. (1945). Relationship of photoperiod and nitrogen nutrition to initiation of flower primordia in soybean varieties. *Botanical Gazette*, **107**, 218–231

TASHIMA, Y. (1957). Physiologie der Blütenbildung von *Raphanus sativus* mit besonderer Rücksicht auf die Vernalisation. *Mem. Faculty of Agriculture of Kagoshima University*, **3**, 25–38

11

CHARACTERS RELATED TO THE VERNALIZATION REQUIREMENT OF SUGAR BEET

K. LEXANDER
Hilleshög Research AB, Sweden

Introduction

The biennial sugar beet requires a period of low temperature followed by long days to bolt and flower (Lexander, 1980a, 1985). However, marked variability in vernalization requirement is found among sugar beet genotypes, and little is known about the physiological basis of this variation. By comparing the physiological characteristics of a wide variety of genotypes with their bolting percentage in the field, a greater knowledge of the causes of variation and the physiology of vernalization can be gained.

Plant material

The sugar beet examined here was diploid and consisted of inbred lines, single hybrids, three-way hybrids or open-pollinated populations. Individual seed-lots are referred to here as genotypes, regardless of whether they are genetically uniform. For all the genotypes examined in any one experiment, the bolting percentages originate from the same field trial. Trials were carried out in England, France, Holland or Sweden.

Experimental results

GROWTH

Stem growth after gibberellin treatment

Since gibberellins are probably involved in vernalization (Pharis and King, 1985), the response of different genotypes to applied GA_3 was examined.

The plants were grown in a greenhouse either in vermiculite watered with a nutrient solution or in fertilized soil. The temperature varied but was never below 15 °C. Continuous illumination or 18 h days were provided by extending natural daylight with artificial illumination from mercury lamps or metal halogen lamps, and incandescent bulbs. Aqueous solutions of GA_3 with 0.05% 'Tween' were supplied to

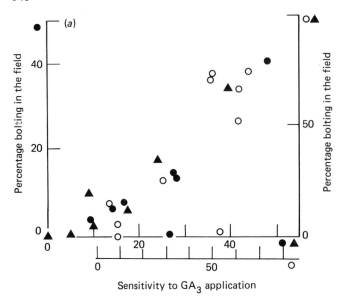

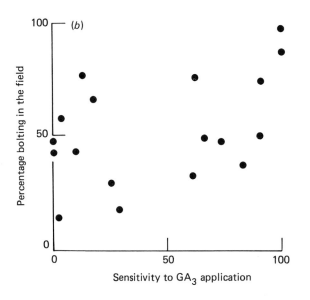

Figure 11.1   Comparison of the gibberellin sensitivity of young plants in a greenhouse and the bolting percentage of adult plants in the field. Gibberellin sensitivity is measured as the percentage of plants with the stem length exceeding a minimum value after GA$_3$ treatment. (*a*) Hybrids; ● ▲ ○: three different sets of genotypes in separate experiments and field trials. ●, 3 × 12.5 µg GA$_3$ per plant; stem length > 110 mm, ▲, 4 × 12.5 µg GA$_3$ per plant; stem length > 100 mm, ○, 4 × 12.5 µg GA$_3$ per plant; stem length > 125 mm or > 250 mm (different experiments). (*b*) Inbred lines. 3 × 12.5 µg GA$_3$ per plant; stem length > 55 mm or > 75 mm (different experiments).

the plants as drops between the cotyledons, either once, 2–3 weeks after sowing, or repeatedly, at intervals of a few days. 5–10 weeks after the last GA_3 application, entire stem length was measured, and the percentage of plants whose stem length exceeded a certain minimum value was calculated.

For hybrid plants, the percentage of stems that were longer than a minimum value after GA_3 treatment was positively correlated with the bolting percentage (*Figure 11.1(a)*). Some exceptions were found, however, which did not bolt easily in the field but showed a marked reaction to GA_3. For inbred lines, no clear correlation was obtained (*Figure 11.1(b)*). When increasing amounts of GA_3 were applied, bolting-susceptible genotypes reacted differently to bolting-resistant types by showing a much greater shoot extension response (*Figure 11.2*). With increasing amounts of GA_3, some bolting-susceptible genotypes show an increasing percentage of plants producing flowers (Lexander, 1985), whereas in most cases only stem elongation is induced.

Thus the magnitude of the stem elongation response to GA_3 is often related to the bolting susceptibility. However, the inbred lines and the non-bolting, but gibberellin-sensitive exceptions show that other factors can interfere with this relationship.

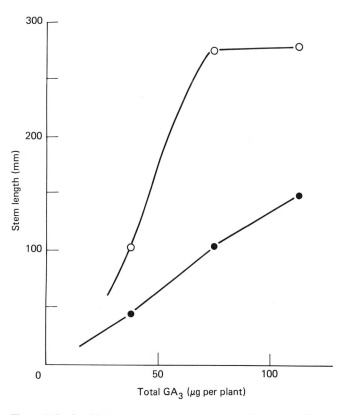

Figure 11.2 Sensitivity to increasing amounts of applied gibberellic acid: comparison of a bolting-susceptible genotype and a bolting-resistant one. GA_3 was given to each plant as three, six or nine applications of 12.5 μg. Stem length was measured 60 days after sowing. Means of two experiments are presented. Bolting susceptible genotype (○) gave 68% bolting in a field trial. Bolting resistant genotype (●) gave no bolting in the same trial.

150

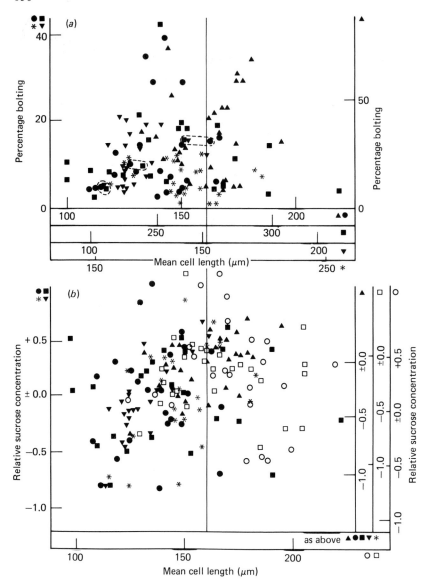

Figure 11.3 Cell length in the epidermis from hypocotyls of young plants compared with (a) the bolting percentage and (b) the sucrose concentration of adult plants in the field. (a) Each symbol represents one set of genotypes, which were examined together in one experiment. For three of these sets (● ■ ▼), three common genotypes were included in each experiment, and the horizontal scales are adjusted to make the values of these coincide (shown by dotted lines in the figure). For the two other sets of genotypes (* ▲), the scales are adjusted to make the pattern of these sets agree with the pattern of the other sets of both (a) and (b). (The differences in cell length ranges among the experiments are due to different greenhouse conditions for the separate experiments.) (b) The sucrose concentrations of adult roots in the field are expressed as relative values (e.g. +0.5 implies a sucrose concentration 0.5% higher than that of a standard genotype included in the field trial.)

Hypocotyl growth without gibberellin treatment

Since stem growth produced after the application of gibberellic acid is often related to bolting susceptibility, the possibility that differences in the growth of young plants without any GA_3 treatment might be related to bolting susceptibility was also examined. Two weeks after sowing, the mean cell length of the hypocotyl epidermis was measured in a range of genotypes by counting the number of cells in a 5 mm row.

The distribution of values seen when the cell length of young hypocotyls is plotted against bolting percentages in the field may be interpreted as a two-peaked curve (*Figure 11.3(a)*). The highest bolting percentages appear to correspond with two specific cell length ranges. When cell length in young plants is compared with the sugar concentration of adult roots (*Figure 11.3(b)*), the highest sugar concentrations are found for the cell length range corresponding to low bolting percentages (cf. *Figure 11.3(a)*). When the sucrose concentration is plotted against the bolting percentage, the highest bolting is associated with a particular, fairly high sucrose concentration (*Figure 11.4*). This would be consistent with the view that the highest bolting values correspond to high, but not the highest sugar concentrations. The associations are shown more clearly in a model which is based on data from these experiments and from elsewhere (*Figure 11.5*).

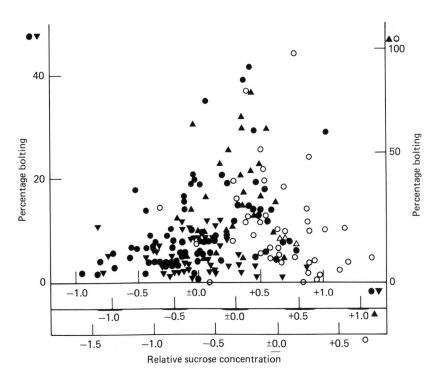

Figure 11.4   Sucrose concentration in adult sugar beet roots grown in the field compared with their bolting percentage.

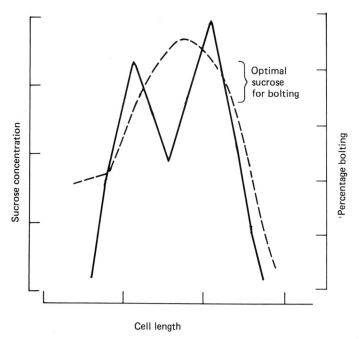

Figure 11.5 Possible associations between sucrose level, (---) cell length and susceptibility to bolting (—) in sugar beet.

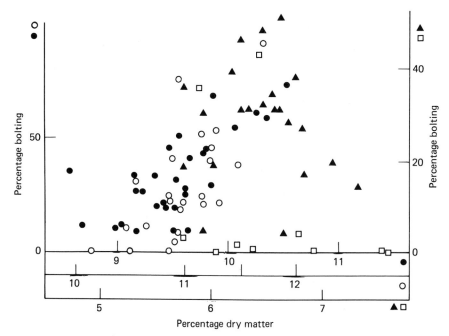

Figure 11.6 Dry matter percentage of young hypocotyls and roots compared with the bolting percentage in the field. The different dry matter ranges in these experiments are due to differences in the greenhouse conditions. The scales are adjusted to show the general pattern of the results. The dry matter percentage of hypocotyls + roots (▲ □ ○) or hypocotyls (●). Four sets of genotypes (▲ □ ○ ●), each set comprising one experiment and one field trial.

DRY MATTER CONTENT

The dry matter percentage of the hypocotyl, or hypocotyl plus taproot, was also determined for seedlings. Increasing bolting can be related to increasing dry matter percentage in hypocotyls and roots (*Figure 11.6*). One set of genotypes was found, however, where the highest dry matter values were accompanied by decreasing bolting. Consequently, it is suggested that there is an optimal specific dry matter content for bolting. If, however, other requirements are not fulfilled, bolting will not occur.

These measurements of growth and dry matter content of young, untreated plants, grown at non-vernalizing temperatures, showed that bolting susceptibility can be related to growth characteristics even before vernalizing conditions are experienced.

PROTEIN SULPHYDRYLS

Growth can involve changes in the state of protein sulphydryls (literature cited by Svensson, 1971). Such changes can also occur as a result of plants experiencing low temperature (Levitt, 1972). Sulphydryl parameters were therefore compared here with bolting susceptibility in sugar beet. Part of this investigation has been published elsewhere (Lexander, 1975) and will be described only briefly here.

In some cases, seeds were analysed. In other experiments, fully expanded leaves (0.5–1 g) were examined. The latter were taken from young plants grown in a greenhouse or in a growth room at 25 °C under continuous illumination. The seeds of the leaves were analysed for sulphydryls (and disulphides reduced by sulphite) using amperometric titration with silver ions in a buffer at low temperature under nitrogen. The ratio of sulphydryls titrated in the absence of urea to those titrated in the presence of urea (4.3 mol l^{-1}) ((-SH + -S-)$_{-urea}$/(-SH + -S-)$_{+urea}$; the -SH ratio)) was also determined. This is an expression of the accessibility of sulphydryls (and disulphides) in the native protein configuration compared with accessibility in proteins unfolded by urea.

With both leaf homogenates and protein precipitates from leaves, negative correlations were obtained between the bolting percentage in the field and (−SH + −S−) titrated in the presence of urea (*Figure 11.7*). Positive correlations were found between the bolting percentage in the field and the −SH ratio (*Figure 11.8*). The same relationship was also found for protein precipitates from ungerminated seeds (*Figure 11.9* ● ■). About 140 genotypes have now been tested and shown to conform to this pattern.

With seeds produced in the hot summer of 1976, however, no positive correlation between the bolting precentage and the −SH ratio was obtained. When seed was imbibed and kept at 4 °C for 31 days, dried and then analysed, the −SH ratio of the bolting-susceptible genotypes was found to have increased as a result of the cold treatment, whereas that of the bolting-resistant genotypes changed only slightly or not at all (*Figure 11.9* ○ □). The effect of low temperature on the −SH ratio of seeds during development was studied by producing seeds in growth rooms at different temperatures. Seeds harvested from mother-plants growing at low temperatures (12 °C/4 °C, day/night) had a higher −SH ratio and subsequently gave rise to plants with higher bolting susceptibility than did seeds produced at high temperatures (25 °C/18 °C) (Lexander, 1975).

The proteins examined here probably originate in cell membranes. They are found in the pellet after centrifugation at 50 000 g for 1 h at 4 °C. Polyacrylamide gel electrophoresis of protein precipitates in the presence of sodium dodecyl sulphate and

154

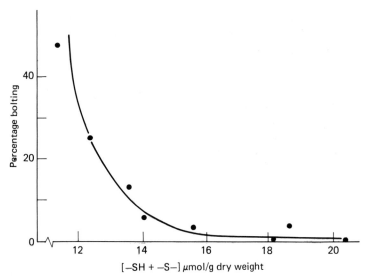

Figure 11.7 Bolting percentage and $(-SH + -S-)$ as μmol (g dry weight)$^{-1}$ titratable in the presence of urea, in homogenates of dried leaves.
(Values not corrected for $-SH$ present before sulphitolysis. Each point represents one sugar beet variety.) (Reproduced from Lexander (1975), by kind permission of publishers.)

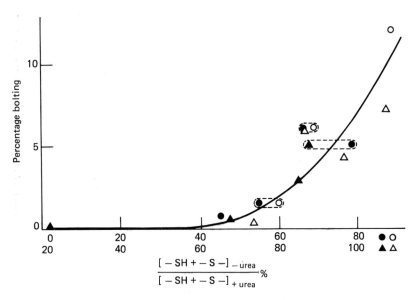

Figure 11.8 Bolting percentage and the ratio of $(-SH + -S-)$ titratable in the absence of urea to $(-SH + -S-)$ titratable in the presence of urea. Protein precipitates from leaves. Two series of varieties were analysed (● ○ and ▲ △). Within each series two experiments (filled and open symbols). Two points within a broken line depict one and the same variety. (Values not corrected for $-SH$ present before sulphitolysis.) (Reproduced from Lexander (1975), by kind permission of publishers.)

mercaptoethanol resulted in four main protein bands. An earlier report (Lexander, 1975) claimed that the ratio of the protein in band III to that in band I was negatively correlated with bolting. When more genotypes were tested, however, this relationship was not clearly maintained. This may be due to the $-SH$ ratio plotted against protein III: protein I giving two regression lines (*Figure 11.10*).

The results of the sulphydryl investigation show that membrane proteins are involved in regulating bolting susceptibility. Either their conformation *per se*, as reflected in the accessibility of sulphydryls to silver ions, or the number of reactive sulphydryls, or both, seem to determine bolting susceptibility. A few exceptions have been found, however, which do not bolt despite seemingly suitable sulphydryl accessibility.

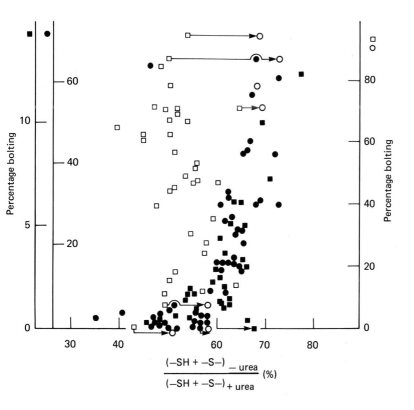

Figure 11.9 Bolting percentage and the ratio of ($-SH + -S-$) titratable in the absence of urea to ($-SH + -S-$) titratable in the presence of urea. Protein precipitates from seeds. □ ○ represent seeds produced in 1976 and ● ■ represent seeds produced in other years. ○ represents the seeds that were cold-treated before the analysis, as described in the text. Each arrow shows the effect of cold treatment on the SH ratio of the genotype in question. Each set of genotypes was tested in a separate bolting trial. (Values not corrected for $-SH$ present before sulphitolysis. Each point represents one genotype.) (After Lexander (1975, 1980b), by kind permission of publishers.)

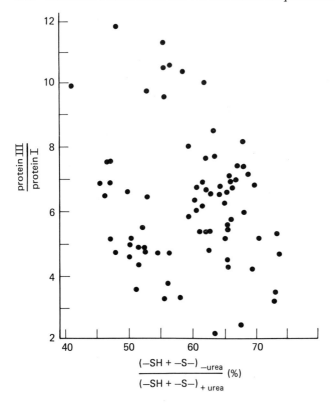

Figure 11.10   The ratio of $(-SH + -S-)$ titratable in the absence of urea to $(-SH + -S-)$ titratable in the presence of urea compared with the ratio between two proteins precipitated from seeds. Each point represents one genotype examined both for the '$-SH$ ratio' and for the 'Protein ratio', as described in the text.

Discussion

While these investigations do not elucidate mechanisms in the apex at the transition to the generative state, they do demonstrate that characteristics of the entire plant before it is induced to flower may determine its bolting susceptibility.

The conformation of membrane proteins has connections with bolting. If the accessibility of sulphydryls and disulphides in the native protein is high compared with accessibility in the unfolded protein, bolting susceptibility is generally high. Whether the number of easily reacting sulphydryls in membranes or the protein conformation is the most important factor is not clear. Seed lots produced in the hot year of 1976 did not give a positive correlation between the $-SH$ ratio and the bolting percentage. The reason may be that in most other years the immature seeds experience some cold which influences the membrane conformation whilst in 1976, they did not.

Another possibility is that high temperature during seed maturation depressed the $-SH$ ratio, which was restored by the cold treatment. Low temperature caused membrane conformation changes in experiments described here. If seeds are normally affected in this way during development, many of the characteristics described here would be due to a partial bolting induction. The physiological differences among genotypes may therefore reflect differences in sensitivity to bolting-inducing conditions. It is important to note that these differences between genotypes were found before full induction to flower.

Whichever explanation is true, membrane conformation and bolting are affected by temperature. Effects of low temperature on the sulphydryl state and on the conformation of membrane proteins have also been found for thylakoids of rye during cold acclimation (Griffith *et al.*, 1982). Hypothetically, a certain conformation is needed for the reactions leading to the bolting. If the state of the membranes is such that low temperature easily causes a suitable conformation, bolting susceptibility is high. If membrane properties are of crucial importance for bolting induction, it is not surprising that so many physiological characteristics are correlated with the bolting tendency, or that preparations from the entire plants can show relationships.

After vernalization, the endogenous concentration of gibberellins in sugar beet increases (Radley, 1975). Sensitivity to such compounds may determine whether bolting will occur. This sensitivity is a characteristic of the plant before it has experienced vernalizing conditions. It has been suggested that sensitivity to hormones is influenced by membrane properties (Starling *et al.*, 1984). The sensitivity of wheat to gibberellin is increased by low temperature, and this is attributed to an increase in hormone receptor sites (Singh and Paleg, 1985). Hypothetically, some beet genotypes are highly sensitive to gibberellin even before a cold period, whereas others attain high sensitivity when experiencing low temperature. The degree of sensitivity may be a function of the state of the cell membranes.

High bolting susceptibility was found for genotypes with cells of two particular lengths. Cell size is correlated with the sucrose concentration in adult beet. This relationship is non-linear and is described by an optimal curve (Milford, 1973 and *Figure 11.3(b)*). The optimal cell lengths for bolting found here both corresponded to the same sucrose concentration, which was not the highest concentration examined. In addition, plotting sucrose concentration against bolting percentage confirms that an optimal sucrose concentration exists for bolting (*Figure 11.4*). This agrees with the suggestion (Bodson and Bernier, 1985) that sugar can be limiting for the flower induction and that an optical sugar concentration is probable. It is also known that sucrose utilization accompanies flower induction in sugar beet (Schmid, 1974). The correlation between dry matter percentage of young, vegetative hypocotyls and roots, and the bolting percentage further supports the importance of assimilate level for bolting.

Exceptions were found for all the plant characters related to bolting. This was presumably because although the character in question was optimal for bolting, the requirements for one or more additional characteristics were not fulfilled. Several genes must therefore take part in the regulation of bolting susceptibility in biennial sugar beets (Zinecker and Prinzler, 1979). Relationships between the characteristics of non-induced plants and bolting susceptibility imply that some of these genes are active before bolting-inducing conditions occur. Whether others exist that are active only when such conditions are experienced is not known.

This investigation has shown that the factors involved in regulating bolting susceptibility are interrelated in a complex way. Misinterpretations are easily made if only a small number of genotypes are investigated.

Acknowledgements

I am deeply indebted to the plant breeders at Hilleshög AB, who provided the seed material and the field trial results. Thanks are also due to the laboratory assistants, who did much of the analytical work.

References

BODSON, M. and BERNIER, G. (1985). Is flowering controlled by the assimilate level? *Physiologie Végétale*, **23**, 491–501

GRIFFITH, M., BROWN, G.N. and HUNER, N.P.A. (1982). Structural changes in thylakoid proteins during cold acclimation and freezing of winter rye (*Secale cereale* L. cv. Puma). *Plant Physiology*, **70**, 418–423

LEVITT, J. (1972). Molecular basis of freezing injury and tolerance. In *Responses of Plants to Environmental Stresses*, pp. 188–228. London, Academic Press

LEXANDER, K. (1975). Bolting susceptibility of sugar beet (*Beta vulgaris*) in relation to sulfydryls and disulfides and to protein composition of membranes. *Physiologia Plantarum*, **33**, 142–150

LEXANDER, K. (1980a). Present knowledge of sugar beet bolting mechanisms. In *Proceedings of the 43rd Winter Congress of the International Institute of Sugar Beet Research*, pp. 245–258. Brussels, Institut International de Recherches Betteravières

LEXANDER, K. (1980b). Seed composition in connection with germination and bolting of *Beta vulgaris* L. (sugar beet). In *Seed Production* (P.D. Hebblethwaite, Ed.), pp. 271–291. London, Butterworths

LEXANDER, K. (1985). Beta vulgaris, Beet crops (Sugar, Forage, Vegetable). In *CRC Handbook of Flowering* (Abraham H. Halevy, Ed.), pp. 24–32. Boca Raton, Florida, CRC Press

MILFORD, G.F.J. (1973). The growth and development of the storage root of sugar beet. *Annals of Applied Biology*, **75**, 427–438

PHARIS, R.P. and KING, R.W. (1985). Gibberellins and reproductive development in seed plants. *Annual Review of Plant Physiology*, **36**, 517–568

RADLEY, M.E. (1975). Sugar beet. Growth substances and bolting. In *Report for 1974, Rothamsted Experimental Station* (C.P. Whittingham, Ed.), Part I, p. 35, Harpenden, England

SCHMID, M.G. (1974). Stoffwechselphysiologische Untersuchungen an vernalisierten und nicht vernalisierten Zuckerrüben. I. Enzymaktivitäten, Kohlenhydrate und Stickstoffhaltige Verbindungen im Epikotyl, Hypokotyl und Wurzelteil von vegetativen und blühinduzierten Zuckerrüben. *Angewandte Botanik*, **48**, 221–237

SINGH, S.P. and PALEG. L.G. (1985). Low-temperature induced GA_3 sensitivity of wheat. III. Comparison of low temperature effects on α-amylase production by aleurone tissue of dwarf and tall wheat. *Australian Journal of Plant Physiology*, **12**, 269–275

STARLING, R.J., JONES, A.M. and TREWAVAS, A.J. (1984). Binding sites for plant hormones and their possible roles in determining tissue sensitivity. *What's New in Plant Physiology*, **15**, 37–40

SVENSSON, S.-B. (1971). The effect of coumarin on root growth and root histology. *Physiologia Plantarum*, **24**, 446–470

ZINECKER, M. and PRINZLER, D. (1979). Ergebnisse der Züchtung auf Schossresistenz bei monokarpen Zuckerrüben. *Archiv für Züchtungsforschung, Berlin*, **9**, 299–310

12

VERNALIZATION IN WHEAT

J. KREKULE
Institute of Experimental Botany, Czechoslovak
Academy of Sciences, Prague, Czechoslovakia

Introduction

Most of the recent work on vernalization in wheat is agronomic and emphasizes it effects on time from sowing to harvest and on yield components (Syme, 1973; Wall and Cartwright, 1974; Halloran and Pennell, 1982; Pennell and Halloran, 1984). This approach necessarily considers the interaction of vernalization with growth processes and the photoperiodic control of development rather than vernalization alone. Whilst ecological aspects of vernalization are of interest, only limited generalizations can be made from them because of difficulties in summarizing the results obtained from a wide range of tests on different varieties in various environments.

The greatest advances in understanding vernalization in wheat have been made in explaining its genetic background. Berry, Salisbury and Halloran (1980) have interpreted the genetic factors involved in qualitative and quantitative vernalization responses and Pugsley (1983) has proposed a classification of vernalization requirements based on genotypic character. Physiological investigation of vernalization is made particularly difficult by the lack of direct markers of the vernalized state. Progress in this field had thus been slow and marked by an accumulation of phenomena, rather than by new concepts. Many studies on vernalization in wheat were inspired by Lysenko's theory of phasic development, as winter cereals fit its postulates *sensu stricto*. Although this theory has failed to achieve general validity, it did help provide new information on the physiology and ecology of vernalization published previously in Eastern Europe. One of the aims of this chapter is to make this information more generally available. New ideas on the physiology of vernalization, gained from studies on *Cichorium* (Joseph *et al.*, 1985) have yet to be examined using wheat.

The aim of this chapter is to review the adaptive roles of wheat vernalization and to describe and classify light and darkness effects in modifying or replacing cold requirement. The effect of cold treatment in decreasing photoperiodic requirements is also considered. Particular attention is given to those problems in the physiology of vernalization which appear most critical to future progress in understanding this phenomenon.

Adaptive traits in vernalization of wheat

Wheat is characterized by marked variability in its vernalization pattern. This is related to its world-wide distribution and reflected in differences in sensitivity to vernalization, associated with the geographical origin of the varieties and season of their cultivation (e.g. Hunt, 1979; Hoogendoorn, 1985). A most comprehensive evaluation of vernalization patterns of world winter wheat has been made by Razumov and his co-workers in the USSR. They regard vernalization as an adaptive process that decreases the risks of winter in temperate zones by preventing transition to the reproductive phase. Cereal plants in a vernalized state were also assumed to have low winter hardiness.

Razumov (1961) found that vernalization was weakly expressed or absent in wheat from subtropical areas such as the Arabian Peninsula, Ethiopia, India and Morocco. Notable exceptions were from high altitudes, such as the mountain regions of Ethiopia or Turkey, which required 14 days vernalization. Marked vernalization requirements were seen also in varieties from environments where no risks of low temperature related injury existed, such as Egypt. It was speculated that this was attributable to cultivation there during the coldest season of the year or to the origin of the variety being from colder areas. Halloran (1967) suggested that the vernalization requirement in some spring wheat varieties serves no adaptive purpose under present cultural practices. These requirements may represent a phylogenetically older part of the genome as the ancestral form of wheat is postulated to be a winter type (Kihara, 1958).

Surprisingly, the most marked vernalization requirement both in terms of treatment duration and its enhancing effect on reproductive development was found in varieties from the Netherlands, Scandinavia and the Baltic, areas with relatively mild winters. This pattern in vernalization was considered adaptive for periods in crop growth with average temperatures between 0 °C and + 10 °C (Razumov, 1961) ensuring that vernalization is not finished before the onset of sub-zero temperatures after autumn sowing. Moving eastwards in Euroasia, this period shortens, as does the vernalization response. Under the continental climate, the earlier onset of frost was matched by the ability of winter wheat to accomplish vernalization at temperatures as low as − 4 °C. Differences in rates of vernalization at 2 °C compared with 6 °C were observed in wheat varieties from southern USSR but were absent in those from northern areas again reflecting adaption.

Gradients of vernalization response, in terms of vernalization duration and shifts in vernalizing temperatures, have been found along longitudinal and latitudinal axes. However, it should be noted that most of the tested varieties were of local origin and have been selected for their high stability of yield. Such 'regional features' of vernalization tend to disappear as new, highly synthetic genotypes occur, which are selected for high yield performance. This is shown by the changing pattern of vernalization in Czechoslovak winter wheat within the last 40 years (Petr, 1984) (*Figure 12.1*). The geographical and climatical diversity of this country was formerly reflected by a wide range of vernalization requirements. During the 1950s and early 1960s varieties of an alternative and semi-winter character with a low vernalization response (less than 30 days of vernalization) were used. These varieties were replaced in the late 1960s by genotypes with a rather uniform vernalization pattern, mostly derived from Russian and German cultivars and requiring long-term vernalization.

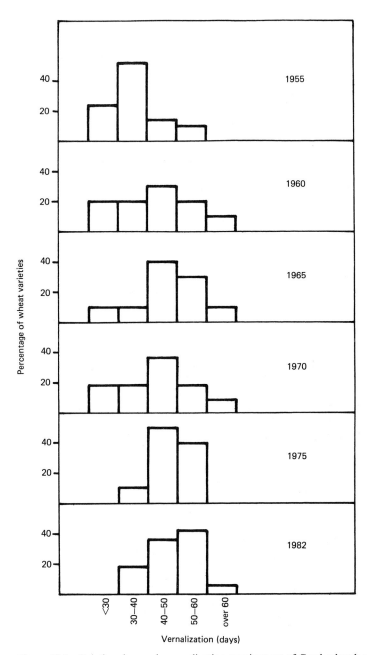

Figure 12.1 Relative changes in vernalization requirement of Czechoslovak winter wheat. Vernalization requirement is expressed as optimum duration of chilling treatment. The relative changes in distribution of varieties into classes of chilling treatment (abscissa) are given for the period 1955–1982. Modified after Petr (1984).

Light and photoperiodic effects in vernalization of wheat

Neither the time when vernalization finishes nor the exact temperature limits for vernalization are known for winter wheat at present. Whether light acts through modifying the vernalization process or as an alternative control mechanism is also unknown. Multiple sites for light effects are supposed and it is important to differentiate the categories of light action (*see* Napp-Zinn, 1984).

(A) EFFECT OF LIGHT AT OPTIMUM VERNALIZATION TEMPERATURES

Long days enhance vernalization in seedlings of wheat that are growing at optimum vernalization temperatures (Razumov, 1957; Markowski, 1959; Pogna, 1979). However, Hartmann (1968) did not find any difference between LD and SD when winter wheat varieties were vernalized for optimal times. Short days were slightly better at threshold vernalization level. Beneficial effects of LD have been confirmed by Krekule (1961b) and interpreted in terms of higher photosynthetic efficiency of long (16 h) days as compared with short (8 h) days. At a relatively low illuminance level (about 2000 lx), the vernalization of plants chilled under the short-day regimen was inhibited compared with those chilled in long days. With increasing light intensity, these differences practically disappeared. Vernalization did not take place in dark unless 2% sucrose was added to the cultivation medium. There were no apparent differences in the growth rate of shoots between LD and SD plants under higher illuminance conditions, although more sugars accumulated per gram of fresh weight in leaves of LD plants. These data are consistent with the view that a certain minimum level of assimilate is necessary for vernalization of cereals to take place.

(B) SUBSTITUTION OF SHORT DAYS FOR LOW TEMPERATURE

The ability of short days to substitute for vernalization or to enhance its effects has been known in winter wheat since the early 1930s (McKinney and Sando, 1933). Short days seem to be additive to suboptimal vernalization but are usually inhibitory to fully vernalized material (*Figure 12.2*). Two questions arise in relation to these effects: is the short-day effect independent of vernalization and to what extent is it of general occurrence? Razumov (1966) found the optimum temperatures for short-day action to range from 13° to 18 °C, within vernalization limits. No short-day effects were apparent at higher temperatures. However, using Japanese winter wheat varieties Norin 27 and 8, Limar (1975) reported that short-days completely replace the low temperature requirement for flowering. Similar effects have been observed with other winter-type grass species as *Lolium* (Cooper, 1960). Short-day treatments were found to be equally effective whether administered before (Razumov, 1961) or after chilling (Krekule, 1961b).

There is mounting evidence of varietal differences for the short-day effect. This effect is most marked in those varieties that have a prostrate habit of growth and where short-days inhibit leaf blade growth (Krekule, 1964; *Table 12.1*). The importance of changing the growth pattern in order to induce short-day vernalization was also seen in experiments where applied GA_3 delayed vernalization. This treatment largely removed leaf growth inhibition during short days and at the same time lessened the promotive effect of short days on vernalization (Krekule, 1962). It was

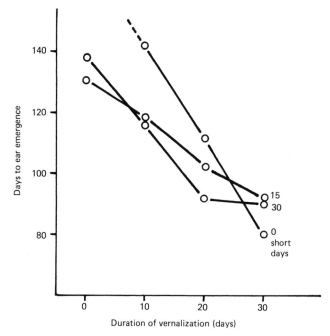

Figure 12.2 Promotive effect of short days in vernalization of winter wheat. Caryopses of winter wheat (*Triticum aestivum* L., var. Hodonínská holice) have been vernalized for different periods. The seedlings were grown after chilling treatment in short 8 h days under field conditions (natural long days of 14–15½ h were shortened using light-proof boxes). Non-vernalized plants under long days did not reach the double-ridge stage (after Krekulé, 1961).

Table 12.1 SHORT-DAY EFFECTS ON GROWTH AND VERNALIZATION IN WHEAT (*Triticum aestivum* L.). SPROUTED CARYOPSES WERE CHILLED AT 2–3°C AND THEN SOWN OUTDOORS IN LATE MAY (PRAGUE). THE NATURAL LONG DAY (14.5–16h) WAS SHORTENED TO 8h IN SHORT-DAY PLOTS. THE GROWTH DATA REFER TO PLANTS AT THE END OF SHORT-DAY TREATMENT

Variety	Duration of chilling (days)	Number of short days	Days to ear emergence	Mean ($\pm SD$) dry weight (g)	Mean ($\pm SD$) length of 4th leaf blade	Growth habit
Chlumecka 12	10	0	68	0.46 ± 0.032**	206 ± 7.2**	Erect
	40	0	58	0.42 ± 0.025	203 ± 7.1	Erect
	10	30	72	0.35 ± 0.081	144 ± 8.1**	Prostrate
Fanal	20	0	—	0.48 ± 0.034*	185 ± 7.4**	Erect
	40	0	80	0.40 ± 0.026	178 ± 8.2	Erect
	20	30	115	0.36 ± 0.029*	124 ± 6.5**	Prostrate
San Pastore	20	0	95	0.42 ± 0.056	202 ± 9.1	Erect
	40	0	54	0.44 ± 0.048	197 ± 8.4	Erect
	20	30	115	0.40 ± 0.081	210 ± 11.2	Erect

After Krekule (1964) and unpublished results.
Significant differences: * $P < 0.05$; ** $P < 0.01$; only treatments exposed to identical durations of chilling have been compared.

speculated that a higher sugar content might be important for stimulating vernalization (Krekule, 1961b). Limar (1975) found a markedly higher content of chlorophyll in leaves exposed to short-day regimens. However, direct evidence that assimilate accumulation is necessary in vernalization for any purpose other than its role in energy provision appears lacking.

Short-day effects that are either additive to low temperature or substituting for it should be distinguished from the flower inducing effect of prolonged dark periods. Adachi, Inouye and Ito (1970) and Kim, Furuya and Inouye (1978) found that 30 days of continuous darkness at 25 °C brought about flowering in winter barley. Using varieties which differed in response to short day, it was found that the 'dark effect' and 'short-day vernalization' were unrelated phenomena. Varieties which were unresponsive to short days were enhanced in their flowering by prolonged darkness. These experiments were performed in aseptic cultures and at least 1% sucrose in medium was essential for flowering in darkness. Although flowering in spring wheat in complete darkness has been reported (Sugino, 1975) the 'dark effect' there has not been investigated. It would be of interest to screen winter wheat varieties also for the existence of a 'dark effect'.

(C) SUBSTITUTION OF HIGH IRRADIANCE FOR LOW TEMPERATURE

Fedorov (1960) reported that unchilled winter wheat varieties such as Ukrayinka with an obligatory requirement for vernalization may reach anthesis following exposure to high levels of irradiance (about $350\,000\,\text{erg}\,\text{cm}^{-2}\,\text{s}^{-1}$, incandescent light) when grown at temperatures of 20 °C. This phenomenon has not yet been fully investigated. During the summer under field conditions winter wheat does not develop beyond the vegetative phase although the irradiance level then may be similar to that used in Fedorov's experiments. In other species of *Graminae*, such as *Festuca arundinacea*, continuous illumination at 27 °C was found to replace the low-temperature requirement (Blondon, 1972). Some clones were responsive only to higher irradiance level (at least $76\,000\,\text{erg}\,\text{cm}^{-2}\,\text{s}^{-1}$) whereas in one case $25\,600\,\text{erg}\,\text{cm}^{-2}\,\text{s}^{-1}$ was sufficient. It still remains to be seen whether it is continuous illumination (i.e. 24th photoperiod) or the irradiance level *per se* that is important in eliciting this effect in wheat.

Long-days (photoperiod duration of more than 17 h) may replace the vernalization requirement in winter-rye (Jewiss, Gregory and Purvis, 1959). The hours of high irradiance appear here to represent the determining factor for flowering. However, the possibility remains that disturbance of diurnal photoperiodicity by continuous illumination or by continuous darkness triggers flower initiation that otherwise remains suppressed.

(D) LOW-TEMPERATURE EFFECTS ON FLOWER INITIATION IN SHORT DAYS

Prolonged low-temperature treatment for at least 40 days will markedly promote flower initiation of some wheat varieties under short (8 h) days which are otherwise strongly inhibitory. Most of these varieties belong to groups which, under long day conditions, have practically no vernalization requirement. The inhibitory effect of short days (critical photoperiod > 12 h) prevents their initiating flowers when sown in autumn (Petr, 1960). These so-called 'alternative varieties' from Central Europe are distinguished by their marked winter hardiness (Petr, 1960). Similarly, the so-called semi-winter varieties with short vernalization requirement of about 20 days, such as former Czech varieties Chlumecka 12 and Dobrovicka 14, belong to this group. Again, the barrier for transition to the reproductive phase depends on the short-day response and may be cancelled by prolonged low-temperatures (Petr, 1984).

It is difficult to decide whether low-temperature removal of the short-day inhibition is identical with vernalization. In semi-winter wheat, the duration of vernalization under long days that enhances development under high temperatures is different from that which ensures development under short days. Although this rather suggests two distinct mechanisms, until the physiology of vernalization is better understood, such a distinction remains rather speculative. An identical pattern of behaviour with respect to low-temperature effects was found also for winter barley (Mokhtare and Limberg, 1977) and in some forage crops (Federov, 1975). Moreover, Babenko, Biryukov and Komarova (1971) reported that in winter wheat, the critical photoperiod became shorter after long chilling treatments which lasted for 100–120 days.

Light effects in vernalization of wheat are confusing because of its high ecotypical variability. On the one hand, there are certainly cases where developmental effects of temperature and light are independent (Flood and Halloran, 1984); on the other, different sites and types of interaction have been identified. Any effort towards understanding the physiology of light effects should attempt to distinguish firstly between photoperiodic and photosynthetic effects and secondly between those light actions mediated by a modification of the vernalization process, and those that are independent of it.

Vernalization during embryogenesis

The vernalization requirement may be fulfilled in wheat and in other cereals while the kernels are still developing in the ear. This phenomenon has been described in a monograph by Aghinyan (1958). Two main characteristics were found. Firstly the vernalization requirement changed during ear development, being lowest during the early stages of embryogenesis and grain filling (*Table 12.2*). Secondly, the most

Table 12.2 VERNALIZATION DURING EMBRYOGENESIS IN WHEAT (*Triticum aestivum* L. cv Krasnodarka): PERCENTAGE OF CHILLED PLANTS THAT DEVELOPED EARS. WHOLE PLANTS WERE TRANSFERRED FROM THE FIELD TO REFRIGERATED GROWTH ROOMS (1–3°C) AT INTERVALS FOLLOWING ANTHESIS. THESE WERE THEN CHILLED FOR 0–60 DAYS, DRIED AT ROOM TEMPERATURE AND STORED UNTIL SOWING IN THE FIELD IN THE FOLLOWING SPRING. EACH VALUE IS A MEAN OF 30 SAMPLES.

Transfer stage	*Weight of*	*Duration of chilling (days)*						
(days after anthesis)	*1000 grains (g)*	*0*	*10*	*20*	*30*	*40*	*50*	*60*
4	1.7	0	0	80	100	100	100	100
6	2.8	0	0	0	100	100	100	100
10	4.8	0	0	0	68	100	100	100
13	7.3	0	0	0	33	70	86	100
17	16.5	0	0	0	0	0	45	78
25	26.7	0	0	0	0	0	0	45

After Aghinyan (1958).

responsive period to vernalization was 10–12 days after fertilization when differentiation of the embryo was in complete and starch synthesis in plastids had not yet started. Under these conditions the vernalization required 10–20 days chilling instead of 40 days later on. Hoogendoorn (1984) found vernalization of kernels on growing plants to advance flower initiation more than vernalization of mature kernels.

During the earliest stages of development, an embryo may not possess any vernalization requirement. This requirement may gradually build up with time during endosperm development and the endosperm itself may cause the embryo to develop a low-temperature requirement. Cases of reversion in morphogenetic capabilities are commonly seen as a result of developmental change elsewhere in the plant (Nozeran, 1984). The low requirement for vernalization during embryogenesis merits careful physiological investigation. Changes in the methylation of nuclear DNA and other molecular changes may be involved in order to acquire and maintain the vernalized state.

Metabolic changes during vernalization

Interpretation of metabolic changes during vernalization is controversial and attention here will be concentrated on a few examples which appear important either because of their close relation to the expression of vernalization genes or because of their specificity. Using two isogenic lines of winter and spring wheat, de Silva (1978) was able to demonstrate a four-fold increase in unsaturated membrane, phospholipid synthesis after 30–40 days chilling in the winter genotype. This result is consistent with the data on the changes in hybridizable RNA, where new populations appeared only between 30 and 50 days of cold treatment (Ishikawa and Tateyma, 1977). There are some other reports which also indicate that changes in fatty acids are related to vernalization rather than to unspecific cold effect (*see* Chapter 11; and Lebedeva and Cheltsova, 1985).

Three distinct phases have been characterized in winter wheat vernalization by using metabolic inhibitors with different spectra of activity. These include inhibitors of respiration and oxidative phosphorylation, nucleic acid and protein antimetabolites and inhibitors of their synthesis (Krekule, 1961a; Tan *et al.*, 1981). Profound differences were found in the rate of RNA synthesis in coleoptiles of spring and winter types of wheat at devernalization temperatures (Páldi and Dévay, 1977).

Attempts to characterize vernalization in wheat by the states of phytohormones have failed. The observed changes seem to reflect growth changes and non-specific cold effects rather than developmental changes. Some promotive effects of gibberellins were observed at threshold level of chilling treatment (Suge and Yamada, 1965).

In general, although vernalization is an important tool for the manipulation of the vegetative duration of growth and hence the yield, its physiological nature remains obscure.

References

ADACHI, K.J., INOUYE, J. and ITO, K. (1970). Flower initiation in total darkness in long-day plant *Hordeum vulgare* L. var. nudum Hook f. winter naked barley. *Journal of the Faculty of Agriculture, Kyushu University*, **16**, 77–84

AGHINYAN, A.A. (1958). *On the Nature of Vernalization and on Variability of Plants* (in Russian). Izdatelstvo Glavnogo Upravleniya Selkhoz. Nauki MSKh Armiyanskoy SSR, Erevan

BABENKO, V.I., BIRYUKOV, S.V. and KOMAROVA, V.P. (1971). Effect of prolonged vernalization on seed ribonuclease activity and photoperiodic reaction in winter wheat (in Russian). *Fiziologia Rastenyi*, **18**, 932–940

BERRY, G.J., SALISBURY, P.A. and HALLORAN, G.M. (1980). Expression of vernalization genes in near-isogenic wheat lines: duration of vernalization period. *Annals of Botany*, **46**, 235–240

BLONDON, F. (1972). Action de différentes intensités d'éclairement en jours continus, à diverses températures sur le processus préparatoire à la floraison chez un clone de Festuca arundinacea Schreb. *Comptes Rendus des séances de l'Académie des Sciences Paris*, **274**, 218–221

COOPER, J.P. (1960). Short-day and low-temperature induction in *Lolium*. *Annals of Botany*, **24**, 232–246

DE SILVA, N.S. (1978). Phospho-lipid and fatty-acid metabolism in relation to hardiness and vernalization in wheat during low temperature adaptation to growth. *Zeitschrift für Pflanzenphysiologie*, **86**, 313–322

FEDOROV, A.K. (1960). Earing of winter cereals under conditions of relatively high temperature (in Russian). *Fiziologia Rastenyi*, **7**, 686–694

FEDOROV. A.K. (1975). *What is Known about Plants of Alternative Character* (in Russian). Moscow, Moskovskyi rabotschyi

FLOOD, R.G. and HALLORAN, G.M. (1984). The association of vernalization and photoperiod response in wheat. *Cereal Research Communications*, **12**, 5–11

HALLORAN, G.M. (1967). Gene dosage and vernalization response in homologous group 5 of *Triticum aestivum*. *Genetics*, **57**, 401–407

HALLORAN, G.M. and PENNELL, A.L. (1982). Duration and rate of development phases in wheat in two environments. *Annals of Botany*, **49**, 115–121

HARTMANN, W. (1968). Untersuchungen zur Kurztagswirkung auf kaltbedürftige Pflanzen. 1. Mitteilung. Kurztagwirkung auf Winter-weizensorten. *Flora Abteilung A*, **159**, 35–39

HOOGENDOORN, J. (1984). A comparison of different vernalization techniques in wheat *Triticum aestivum*. *Journal of Plant Physiology*, **116**, 11–20

HOOGENDOORN, J. (1985). The physiology of variation in the time of ear emergence among wheat varieties from different regions of the world. *Euphytica*, **34**, 559–571

HUNT, L.A. (1979). Photoperiodic responses of winter wheats from different climatic regions. *Journal of Plant Breeding*, **82**, 70–80

ISHIKAWA, K. and TATEYMA, M. (1977). Changes in hybridizable RNA in winter wheat embryos during germination and vernalization. *Plant and Cell Physiology*, **18**, 875–882

JEWISS, O.R., GREGORY, T.G. and PURVIS, O.N. (1959). The effect of very long days on the flowering of winter rye. *Journal of Linnéan Society, London*, **56**, 251–253

JOSEPH, C., BILLAT, J., SOUDAIN, P. and COME, D. (1985). The effect of cold, anoxia and ethylene on the flowering ability of buds of *Cichorium intybus*. *Physiologia Plantarum*, **65**, 146–160

KIHARA, H. (1958). Morphological and physiological variation among *Aegilopsis squarrosa* strains collected in Pakistan, Afghanistan and Iran. *Preslia*, **30**, 241–251

KIM, E.H., FURUYA, T. and INOUYE, J. (1978). Floral induction by dark pre-treatment in non-vernalized winter barley. *Journal of the Faculty of Agriculture, Kyushu University*, **22**, 119–124

KREKULE, J. (1961a). Application of some inhibitors in studying the physiology of vernalization. *Biologia Plantarum*, **3**, 107–114

KREKULE, J. (1961b). The effect of photoperiodic regime on vernalization of winter wheat. *Biologia Plantarum*, **3**, 180–191

KREKULE, J. (1962). Die hemmende Wirkung der Gibberellinšaure-Behandlung bei der Jarowisation der Winterweizen im Kurztag. *Die Naturwissenschaften*, **49**, 164–165

KREKULE, J. (1964). Varietal differences in replacing vernalization by a short day in winter wheat (in Russian). *Biologia Plantarum*, **6**, 299–305

LEBEDEVA, N.I. and CHELTSOVA, L.P. (1985). Effect of low temperature on the content of lipid fatty-acids in mitochondria of wheat seedlings varying in temperature resistance and length of vernalization (in Russian). *Selskokhozyaystvennaya Biologia*, **1**, 51–56

LIMAR, P.S. (1975). Physiological peculiarities of Japanese wheat of the group Norin (in Russian). *Bulleten Vsesoyuznogo Ordena Lenina i Ordena Druzhby Narodov Instituta Rastenyievodstva N.I. Vavilova*, **56**, 64–67

McKINNEY, H.H. and SANDO, W.S. (1933). Earliness and seasonal growth habit in wheat as influenced by temperature and photoperiodism. *Journal of Heredity*, **34**, 169–179

MARKOWSKI, A. (1959). The influence of light on the vernalization of winter wheat. Studies on the development of wheat. Part IV (in Polish). *Roczniki Nauk Rolniczych*, **79-A**, 689–731

MOKHTARE, F. and LIMBERG, P. (1977). On the winter spring type of Iranian barley cultivars reaction to vernalization by day length and light intensity. *Zeitschrift für Acker- und Pflanzenbau*, **145**, 85–102

NAPP-ZINN, K. (1984). Light and vernalization. In *Light and The Flowering Process* (D. Vince-Prue, B. Thomas, K.E. Cockshull, Eds), London, Academic Press

NOZERAN, R. (1984). Integration of organismal development. In *Positional Controls in Plant Development* (P.W. Barlow and D.J. Carr, Eds), Cambridge University Press

PÁLDI, E. and DÉVAY, M. (1977). Ribosomal RNA synthesis in spring and winter wheat varieties at temperatures active for vernalization and at neutral and devernalization temperatures. *Biochemie und Physiologie der Pflanzen*, **171**, 249–259

PENNELL, A.L. and HALLORAN, G.M. (1984). Influence of time of sowing, photoperiod, and temperature on supernumerary spikelet expression in wheat (Triticum). *Canadian Journal of Botany*, **62**, 1687–1692

PETR, J. (1960). Biology of Czech alternatives (in Czech). I. *Sborník Rostlinná Výroba*, **6**, 1473–1500

PETR, J. (1984). *Developmental Character of Winter Cereals as Related to Formation of Yield Components and their manipulation by PGR* (in Czech). Report on Research Project VI-4-10/6-3. Prague, University of Agriculture

POGNA, N.E. (1979). Interaction of kinetin and day length on vernalization of winter wheat. *Cereal Research Communications*, **7**, 175–181

PUGSLEY, A.T. (1983). The impact of plant physiology on Australian wheat breeding. *Euphytica*, **32**, 743–748

RAZUMOV, V.I. (1957). The progress of investigations on the theory of phasic development (in Russian). *Agrobiologiya*, **5**, 89–100

RAZUMOV, V.I. (1961). *Environment and Plant Development* (in Russian). Leningrad, Izdatelstvo Selkhoz. Literaturi, Zhurnalov i Plakatov

RAZUMOV, V.I. (1966). Effect of day length on plant vernalization. In *Differentiation oj*

Apical Meristems and Some Problems of Ecological Regulation of Development of Plants. Proceedings on the Symposium Praha-Nitra 1964. Academia Praha

SUGE, H. and YAMADA, N. (1965). Flower-promoting effect of gibberellin in winter wheat and barley. *Plant and Cell Physiology*, **6**, 147–160

SUGINO, M. (1975). Flower initiation of the spring wheat in total darkness. *The Botanical Magazine Tokyo*, **70**, 369–375

SYME, J.R. (1973). Quantitative control of flowering time in wheat cultivars by vernalization and photoperiod sensitivity. *Australian Journal of Agricultural Research*, **24**, 657–665

TAN, K.H., WANG, W.H., HE, H.W. and LI, S.Q. (1981). Effect of metabolic inhibitors on the vernalization process in winter wheat. *Acta Botanica Sinica*, **23**, 371–376

WALL, P.C. and CARTWRIGHT, P.M. (1974). Effect of photoperiod, temperature and vernalization on the phenology and spikelet numbers of spring wheats. *Annals of Applied Biology*, **76**, 299–309

13

VERNALIZATION IN THE ONION—A QUANTITATIVE APPROACH

J.L. BREWSTER
National Vegetable Research Station, Wellesbourne, Warwick, UK

Introduction

Historically the study of vernalization processes in onions began with applied research directed towards the control of flowering in onions grown from bulbs. A considerable amount of work was done between 1920 and 1960 to determine the effects of temperature on the development of inflorescences within bulbs. More recently research effort has gone towards understanding the control of inflorescence initiation and development in growing seedlings. This has been stimulated by the need to understand and prevent bolting in seed-sown overwintered crops, and also by the need to induce flowering and seed production within 12 months for planting breeding programmes. To achieve the latter, flowers must be induced in growing plants without going through the bulb stage (van Kampen, 1970).

In this chapter the effects of environment and internal factors on inflorescence initiation are reviewed. The main emphasis is on vernalization in growing seedlings but data from bulbs are also reviewed to show the similarities and differences between the two systems. The available data are presented in a form from which mathematical functions relating vernalization rate to environmental variables can be derived. Some of these functions have been combined into a mathematical model for inflorescence initiation in growing seedlings. This aims to summarize and integrate our knowledge of the processes involved and to enable prediction of inflorescence development in the field or glasshouse.

Environmental influences

TEMPERATURE

Growing seedlings

Brewster (1983) reported that the times required for inflorescence initiation were minimal and very similar, when seedlings were maintained at 9 or 12 °C for both an overwintered and a spring-sown cultivar, but more time was required at 6 °C. Leaf initiation rate was constant at a given temperature hence the leaf number at which an inflorescence was initiated gave an estimate of its time of initiation. Using this

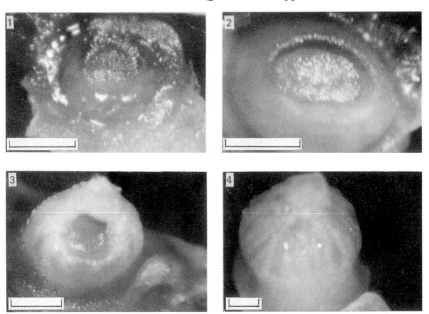

Figure 13.1 Stages in inflorescence development at the onion shoot apex. (1) A Vegetative apex initiating leaves alternately on each side of the apex. (2) Early inflorescence showing elongation and doming of apex. (3) The spathe begins to develop and cover the apical dome. (4) The ridged spathe completely covers the apical dome. Bars = 0.5 mm.

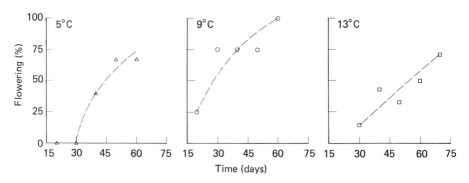

Figure 13.2 Percentage flowering in onion cv. Sapporoki on return to 20°C after various times at vernalizing temperatures (x axis). Data of Shishido and Saito (1975).

information, estimates were made of mean rate of development of the inflorescence through various stages after initiation (*Figure 13.1*).

Shishido and Saito (1975) exposed seedlings of an overwintered and a spring-sown cultivar to a range of temperatures for various periods and then transferred the plants to non-vernalizing temperatures and scored subsequent flowering. From their data it is possible to get an approximate estimate of time required for 50% of the plants to initiate at each temperature (*Figure 13.2*). These times are minimal at 9 °C and longer at lower or higher temperatures.

The reciprocal of this time has been used to calculate a 'rate of vernalization' at each temperature. These rates were scaled relative to the fastest rate for a particular cultivar in a particular experiment, which was given a value of unity. Using this scaling it was possible to derive a function relating vernalization rate to temperature using the combined data from several cultivars and from different experimental methods. *Figure 13.3* shows the relationship of relative vernalization rate to temperature in European and Japanese onion cultivars.

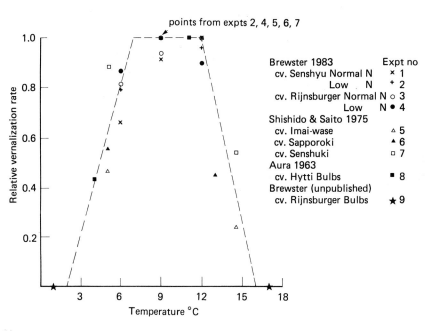

Figure 13.3 Relative rate of vernalization *vs.* temperature of Japanese and European onion cvs. Based on data listed in the key.

Bulbs

Numerous reports have shown that storage of bulbs in the range of temperatures 5–15 °C stimulates subsequent inflorescence development whilst lower or higher temperatures reduce it (Rabinowitch, 1985). Periodic dissection of bulbs stored at different temperatures showed that inflorescences in European and American cultivars are initiated most rapidly around 9–12 °C, are slower to form at 4–5 °C and fail to form at 1 °C or 17 °C (Boswell, 1924; Heath and Mathur, 1944; Hartsema, 1947; Aura, 1963). Thus the optimum temperatures are similar in bulbs and in seedlings. It should be noted, though, that in some tropical cultivars flowering was much better after bulb storage at 20 °C than at 10 °C (Uzo, 1983). Also, Kruzhilin and Shvedskaya (1962) reported that cultivars from the northern USSR had a temperature optimum of 3–4 °C, whereas for those from the south if was 9–10 °C. Thus cultivars seem to differ somewhat in their optimal temperature requirements depending on the locality to which they are adapted.

PHOTOPERIOD

In growing seedlings, long photoperiods accelerate inflorescence initiation (Brewster, 1983; Shishido and Saito, 1975). The data of Brewster (1983) in *Figure 13.4* and comparisons of responses of the overwintered cv. Senshyu with cv. Rawska, another spring-sown cultivar (Brewster, unpublished observations), indicate that the influence of photoperiod is stronger in spring-sown cultivars.

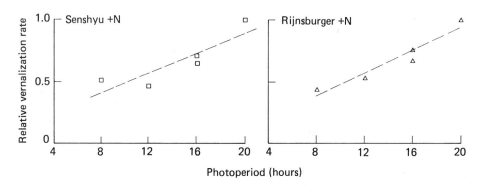

Figure 13.4   Influence of photoperiod on vernalization rate at 9°C. Derived from data of Brewster (1983).

NITROGEN NUTRITION

In growing seedlings a low nitrogen status favours inflorescence initiation (Shishido and Saito, 1976; Brewster, 1983). The most dramatic effect of low nitrogen was virtually to eliminate the long-photoperiod requirement for inflorescence initiation in the spring-sown cv. Rijnsburger. However, under long photoperiods low nitrogen causes only a slight acceleration in inflorescence initiation (Brewster, 1983).

PHOTON FLUX DENSITY (PFD)

Inflorescence initiation in seedlings appears insensitive to the PFD during vernalization (Brewster, 1985). Only in seedlings raised in low PFD did a lower PFD during vernalization have a delaying effect on inflorescence initiation. In contrast, low PFD during plant raising prior to vernalization does slow inflorescence initiation upon transfer to vernalizing temperatures compared with high PFDs during initial raising (Brewster, 1985).

Internal factors

PLANT SIZE

Growing seedlings

By transferring seedlings to inductive conditions at a series of known weights and leaf numbers and scoring inflorescence initiation after 77 days at 9 °C, it was shown that seedlings of the spring-sown cv. Rijnsburger with a shoot dry weight over 0.06 g can initiate inflorescences, whereas the autumn sown cv. Senshyu semi-globe yellow had to be 0.45 g or more in dry weight (Brewster, 1985). These critical weights were those at which 50% of plants would initiate as estimated by probit analysis. The data indicated a sharp increase from no initiation in plants just below the critical weight to maximal initiation in plants just above the critical weight. Shishido and Saito (1976) found a similar contrast in critical size between an autumn and spring-sown cv. They estimated that the spring sown cv. Sapporoki could start vernalizing if the maximal sheath diameter was more than 3.3 mm, whereas the autumn-sown cv. Senshuki had to be more than 6 mm in diameter.

These critical weights corresponded to approximately seven leaves initiated for Rijnsburger and 10 for Senshyu. During the vernalizing treatment a further 2.7 leaves were initiated, on average, before the inflorescence initial was differentiated at the apex. Thus the minimum number of leaves up to a visible inflorescence initial were approximately 10 and 13 leaves for the two cultivars, respectively. In other work the minimum total number of leaves initiated before the apex can form an inflorescence has been estimated in both growing plants and bulbs to be in the range 10–14 depending on cultivar (Rabinowitch, 1985). However, where growing seedlings are considered, the critical leaf number above which vernalization can start is 2–3 less than the minimum number of leaves up to the differentiated apex, since it takes a finite time (about 40 days minimum in cv. Rijnsburger) for the apex to differentiate into an inflorescence. Prior to any observable morphological change at the apex leaf initials continue to be produced at about one every 2 weeks at 9 °C (Brewster, 1983).

Bulbs

Heath *et al.* (1947) concluded that sets (small bulbs) of the spring-sown cv. Ailsa Craig of 4–7 g fresh weight can initiate flowers but that lighter ones cannot. Therefore it seems that 4 g fresh weight is an approximate lower weight limit for inflorescence initiation in stored bulbs. However, unlike the sharp transition from zero to maximal inflorescence initiation rate found in seedlings, the rate of inflorescence initiation increases with bulb size over quite a wide range (Thompson and Smith, 1938; Aura, 1963; Shishido and Saito, 1977). *Figure 13.5* (derived from the data of Shishido and Saito, 1977) shows the relationship between bulb weight and initiation rate for two cultivars. The graph indicates that the spring-sown cv. Sapporoki reached its half maximal vernalization rate at approximately 14 g fresh weight whereas the autumn-sown Senshuki needed to be about 28 g. As with seedlings, the critical weight for vernalization was higher in the autumn-sown cultivar. It appears that a higher bulb weight than seedling weight is necessary before vernalization can begin. A bulb of 4 g fresh weight would have a dry weight of 0.40–0.48 g (assuming 10–12% dry matter), 7–8 times heavier than the 0.06 g critical dry weight for a Rijnsburger seedling.

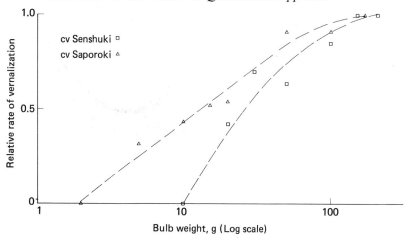

Figure 13.5 Influence of bulb fresh weight (log scale) on relative rate of vernalization. Derived from data of Shishido and Saito (1977).

BIOCHEMICAL FACTORS

Low internal levels of non-structural carbohydrates correlate with delayed inflorescence initiation (Shishido and Saito, 1975, 1977; Brewster, 1985). These have been achieved by raising plants in conditions of low PFD and high temperature prior to vernalization (Brewster, 1985) and by defoliation (Shishido and Saito, 1977). It is possible that the influence of low nitrogen on vernalization may be via carbohydrate status since reductions in nitrogen supply to the roots increase the internal non-structural carbohydrate levels (Shishido and Saito, 1976; Brewster, 1985). Carbohydrate concentrations appear to be important in floral evocation in a number of species (Bodson, 1977; Bernier, Kinet and Sachs, 1981).

Shishido and Saito (1984) reported that injection with 20, 100 or 500 ppm GA_3 solutions into leaves just prior to exposure to a 9 °C vernalizing treatment, shortened the minimum time for inflorescence induction in small seedlings but that there was less effect in larger seedlings. In stored bulbs, a rise in the levels of gibberellin-like substances was detected in extracts from apical tissue made just before visible floral initiation (Thomas, 1969; Isenberg *et al.*, 1974). Kampen and Wiebosch (1970) reported an increase in percentage flowering when bulbs were soaked in 300 ppm GA_3.

Modelling inflorescence development in seedlings in the field

Some of the information outlined above has been combined in a model to simulate inflorescence initiation in field conditions. The model utilizes meteorological data to predict when inflorescences reach stage 4 (*see Figure 13.1*). It has been tested using data from overwintered crops of cv. Senshyu Semi-globe Yellow at Wellesbourne.

Three consecutive phases of development are modelled:

1. Growth from sowing to the critical size for vernalization.
2. Vernalization i.e. development from stage 1 to the start of inflorescence initiation at the apex.

3. Further inflorescence development to stage 4 (*see Figure 13.1*).

The effects of time, temperature, photoperiod and plant size are incorporated in the model but not those of nitrogen, PFD and biochemical factors.

In outline, the growth in shoot dry weight from seedling emergence is predicted using accumulated thermal time (day-degrees between 6 and 20 °C). The date on which the shoot reaches 0.45 g dry weight is calculated. At this stage the plants can begin to vernalize. The rate of vernalization at a given temperature is modelled by the function shown in *Figure 13.3*, assuming that the maximum rate of progress from a vegetative apex to the start of inflorescence differentiation (hereafter termed 'inflorescence initiation') under a 16 h photoperiod is 0.01681 d^{-1} (0.01681 = 1/days to initiation; *see* model specification below). Daily temperatures are assumed to follow a sine curve between the maximum and minimum. The net vernalization rate for each day is calculated as the function in *Figure 13.3* integrated over the daily temperature course. The net rate for a day is then adjusted for the photoperiod effect using the function for cv. Senshyu in *Figure 13.4*. Daily increments of vernalization are accumulated until a value of unity is reached, this is the predicted date of inflorescence initiation. Accumulated day-degrees above 0 °C from this time onwards are used to predict when stage 4 inflorescences are produced.

MODEL SPECIFICATION

The sequence of growth and development is modelled thus:

1. Seedling emergence is assumed to be 10 days after sowing. Experience has shown this to occur for summer sown crops if irrigation is applied to the seedbed (Brewster, Salter and Darby, 1977).

2. Growth in shoot dry weight from emergence is given by:

$$\log_e W = -6.086 + 0.01114 DD \qquad (13.1)$$

where W = shoot dry weight (g), DD = accumulated day-degrees between 6 and 20 °C. This equation has been shown to describe the growth of overwintered onions less than 1 g shoot dry weight (Brewster, Salter and Darby, 1977). Daily increments in thermal time (DD) were calculated from daily maximum and minimum temperatures using the standard meteorological office approximations (Meteorological Office, 1946).

3. The date on which the shoot dry weight first exceeds 0.45 g, the 'critical size' for Senshyu, is calculated and the vernalization calculation is started from this date. Daily vernalization rate, $RV(t)$, at a 16 h photoperiod was calculated using the following function of temperature, t (°C):

$$RV(t) = \begin{cases} 0 \text{ for } t < 2 \\[2mm] \frac{k}{5}(t-2) \text{ for } 2 < t < 7 \\[2mm] k \text{ for } 7 < t < 12 \text{ where } k = 0.01680672 \\[2mm] k - \frac{k}{4}(t-12) \text{ for } 12 < t < 16 \\[2mm] 0 \text{ for } 16 < t \end{cases} \qquad (13.2)$$

This function was derived as a series of linear approximations to the data in *Figure 13.3*. Cv. Senshyu took, on average, 59.5 days to inflorescence initiation at 9 °C under 16 h photoperiods (Brewster, 1983): the value of k is the reciprocal of this.

Daily temperatures were assumed to follow a sinusoidal daily course represented as:

$$t = f(h) = t_m + t_a \sin \left\{ \frac{\pi}{12}(h - h_x + 6) \right\}$$

where $t =$ temperature, $h =$ time (hours), $t_m =$ mean temperature, $t_a =$ temperature amplitude, $h_x =$ time of maximum temperature.

The daily increment in vernalization is the mean value of $RV(t)$ over 24 hours (RV_{mean}), given by:

$$RV_{mean} = \frac{1}{24} \int_0^{24} RV(t)dh = \frac{1}{24} \int_0^{24} RV(f(h)) \, dh$$

It can be shown that this reduces to:

$$RV_{mean} =$$

$$k \left\{ \left[\left[\frac{t_m - 2}{5} \right] \left[\begin{array}{c} \text{Proportion} \\ \text{of day} \\ \text{above 2 °C} \end{array} - \begin{array}{c} \text{Proportion} \\ \text{of day} \\ \text{above 7 °C} \end{array} \right] + \left[\begin{array}{c} \text{Proportion} \\ \text{of day} \\ \text{above 7 °C} \end{array} - \begin{array}{c} \text{Proportion} \\ \text{of day} \\ \text{above 12 °C} \end{array} \right] \right] + \right.$$

$$\left. \left[\frac{(16 - t_m)}{4} \right] \left[\begin{array}{c} \text{Proportion} \\ \text{of day} \\ \text{above 12 °C} \end{array} - \begin{array}{c} \text{Proportion} \\ \text{of day} \\ \text{above 16 °C} \end{array} \right] \right\} \qquad (13.3)$$

The proportion of the day above $t = 1$ if the minimum temp $> t$
$= 0$ if the maximum temp $< t$

$$= \frac{1}{2} - \frac{1}{\pi} \sin^{-1} \left[\frac{t - t_m}{t_a} \right] \text{ if minimum} < t < \text{maximum } t$$

To correct RV_{mean} for photoperiods other than 16 h, the daily photoperiod was calculated as:

$$PP = 13.604 + 4.5298 \sin (2\pi (D - 80.75)/365) \qquad (13.4)$$

where D is the Julian date. This equation was derived by fitting a sine curve for the duration of sunrise to the sunset plus twice the civil twilight at 52.5 N from tabulations for 4-day intervals throughout the year (List, 1951).

The RV_{mean} calculated using (Equation 13.3) is corrected for photoperiod by:

$$RV'_{mean} = RV_{mean} (0.1285 + 0.0545 \, PP) \qquad (13.5)$$

where $RV'_{mean} =$ mean daily vernalization rate. Equation 13.5 is illustrated in *Figure 13.4*.

4. Values of RV'_{mean} are summed and the date on which $\Sigma RV'_{mean}$ first exceeds unity is calculated. This is termed the date of inflorescence initiation and should predict the mean date at which the shoot apex ceases leaf initiation and starts to differentiate into an inflorescence.

5. Development rate from inflorescence initiation to stage 4 (*see Figure 13.1*), RD, was modelled as:

$$RD = 0.00287\ D_0 \qquad\qquad (13.5)$$

where, D_0 = accumulated day degrees above 0 °C. Equation 13.5 was based on data of Brewster (1983). Thermal time above 0 °C is accumulated and the date on which RD first exceeds unity is the predicted mean date of inflorescences reaching stage (4).

It would have been desirable to model inflorescence development rate from stage 4 onwards, but the available data was too variable to model this satisfactorily. It is known that at this stage inflorescence growth rate increases with the temperature in the range 6–12 °C, and with photoperiod at 9 °C (Brewster, 1983). Also the final stages of development can be curtailed by bulbing which can 'compete' with inflorescence development and suppress it if high temperatures accompany long photoperiods (Heath and Holdsworth, 1948; van Kampen, 1970).

COMPARISONS OF MODEL PREDICTIONS WITH FIELD DATA

Dissections and examination of plants for inflorescence initials have been done on small samples of plants in three seasons. These show that inflorescence initials, where they occurred, were first seen around the time that the model predicted the occurrence of inflorescence initiation (*Table 13.1*).

Much more data were available on the final percentage of plants flowering in field trials. Results from 42 sowings of cv. Senshyu Semi-globe Yellow made at Welles-

Table 13.1 PREDICTED AND OBSERVED DATES OF INFLORESCENCE INITIATION IN OVERWINTERED ONION CROPS

Season	Sowing date	Date of inflorescence initiation predicted by the model	Date when inflorescences first seen	Date when 25% of plants contained an inflorescence	Final bolting (%)
1973/74	2 Aug	4 Feb	14 Jan	14 Jan	86
	15 Aug	5 Apr	4 Feb	(Data too variable)	1
	29 Aug	5 Jun	Not seen	Not reached	3
1973/74	15 Aug	6 May	Not seen	Not reached	3
1977/78	2 Aug	20 Mar	16 Mar	5 Mar	27
	9 Aug	26 Mar	27 Feb	21 Mar	22
	16 Aug	6 Apr	16 Mar	Not reached	14
	23 Aug	27 Apr	16 Mar	Not reached	6

Note: bulbing commences mid to late April therefore initials predicted after that date are unlikely to develop and be seen.

bourne covering every season between 1973/74 and 1984/85 were available. There is a general tendency for the percentage flowering to decrease with later sowing, but there is considerable yearly variation in the percentage bolting from sowing on a given date (*Figure 13.6*). Part of this variation may be because differences in temperature from season to season affect the rate at which inflorescences can initiate. It is reasonable to assume that inflorescences must reach a certain stage of development before mid to late April, when bulbing begins, if they are to avoid suppression by developing bulbs and are to emerge to form visible 'bolters'. If this is correct, bolting should be related to the date at which inflorescences reach a given stage. Furthermore, if the time to reach a given stage of inflorescence development is normally distributed in the population, there should be a sigmoid relationship between percentage bolting in the population and the mean date of reaching a given stage. This implies a linear relationship between the probit of percentage bolting and the mean date of inflorescence initiation.

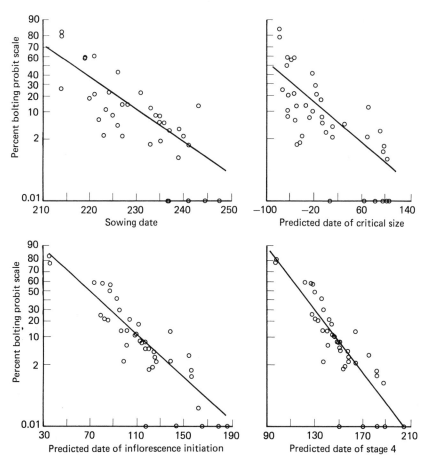

Figure 13.6 Percentage bolting of onion cv. Senshyu semi-globe Yellow in field plots from 42 sowings made between 1973 and 1984 *vs.* (*a*) sowing date, (*b*) predicted date of reaching 0.45 g shoot dry weight (critical size), (*c*) predicted date of inflorescence initiation, (*d*) predicted date of reaching a stage 4 inflorescence. The dates are expressed in Julian days. (The negative values in (*b*) apply to dates before 31 Dec.)

Figure 13.6 shows the relationships between percentage bolting plotted on a probit scale and the predicted dates of reaching the critical size to begin vernalization, inflorescence initiation and a stage 4 inflorescence. Fitting probit curves to the data assuming equal replication for all forty-two points resulted in mean residual deviance values of 126, 166, 61 and 56 for fits of sowing date, date of critical size, date of inflorescence initiation and date of stage (4) respectively. Clearly the date of reaching critical size was a less reliable predictor of bolting than simple sowing date but the residual deviance from fitting the date of stage 4 was only 44% that of fitting the sowing date alone, a highly significant improvement. The fitted lines are shown in *Figure 13.6* and the goodness of fit can be judged from the scatter about these lines.

For fitting the model, the only input data were the sowing dates and daily maximum and minimum air temperatures. Clearly the model can account for a considerable fraction of the scatter in percentage bolting but by no means all of it. The remaining discrepancies could be the result of effects not considered in the model which were different from sowing to sowing for example, pest, disease or weather damage to plants. Such influences would be difficult to incorporate in any model for field performance.

In addition important factors may have been overlooked. Plant nitrogen status affects the vernalization rate by decreasing its sensitivity to photoperiod (Brewster, 1983). In some field experiments with overwintered onions percentage bolting has been shown to increase as applied nitrogen decreased (Cleaver and Turner, 1975). It may be possible to simulate such effects using models for soil nitrogen status and plant nitrogen uptake and growth (Burns, 1980; Greenwood, Neeteson and Draycott, 1985). A further possibility is that some of the assumptions implicit in the model are erroneous. In particular the model assumes that the influences of temperature and photoperiod on vernalization rate are simply multiplicative (Equation 13.4). Data on the photoperiod effect at temperatures other than 9 °C are not available to test this. Also the model assumes that the effect of successive temperatures on vernalization rate are simply additive. Experiments to test whether vernalization at say 9 °C is equally rapid after a previous period at say 3 °C or at 16 °C have not been done with onions. Some early data with onion sets suggested that inflorescence initiation rate after a period at 0–1.5 °C was faster on return to 12.5 °C than in sets stored continuously at 12.5 °C (Heath and Mathur, 1944).

The model could be adapted to simulate bolting in spring-drilled crops using constants in Equations 13.3 and 13.5 appropriate to a spring-sown cultivar (Brewster, 1983). For this purpose a more elaborate predictor of emergence date would be necessary. For onion seeds in moist soil the reciprocal of the time from sowing to emergence is linearly related to the mean temperature between sowing and emergence (Finch-Savage, 1984). This relationship could be incorporated and used before Equation 13.1 is used to predict seedling growth. Equations 13.2 and 13.3 might be useful for predicting inflorescence initiation in bulbs stored in fluctuating temperatures if values of the constant k were known. More generally Equation 13.3 modified with appropriate constants might be useful for modelling vernalization in other crops growing in fluctuating temperatures provided that a relative vernalization rate varied with temperature in a similar way to onions (*Figure 13.3*).

Acknowledgements

I would like to thank Mr G. E. L. Morris for deriving Equation 13.3 and programming this model in GENSTAT, Mr B. D. Dowker for providing data on bolting in field trials between 1973 and 1985 and Miss H. A. Butler for technical assistance.

References

AURA, K. (1963). Studies on the vegetatively propagated onions cultivated in Finland with special reference to flowering and storage. *Annales Agriculturae Fenniae*, **2**, Supplement 5, 1–74

BERNIER, G., KINET, J.M. and SACHS, R.M. (1981). *The Physiology of Flowering*, Vol. II, 231 pp. Florida, CRC Press

BODSON, M. (1977). Changes in the carbohydrate content of the leaf and the apical bud in *Sinapis* during transition to flowering. *Planta*, **135**, 19–23

BOSWELL, V.R. (1924). Influence of the time of maturity of onions on the behaviour during storage, and the effect of storage temperature on subsequent vegetative and reproductive development. *Proceedings of the American Society for Horticultural Science*, **20**, 234–239

BREWSTER, J.L. (1983). Effects of photoperiod, nitrogen nutrition and temperature on inflorescence initiation and development in onion (*Allium cepa* L.) *Annals of Botany*, **51**, 429–440

BREWSTER, J.L. (1985). The influence of seedling size and carbohydrate status and of photon flux density during vernalization on inflorescence initiation in onion (*Allium cepa* L.). *Annals of Botany*, **55**, 403–414

BREWSTER, J.L., SALTER, P.J. and DARBY, R.J. (1977). Analysis of the growth and yield of overwintered onions. *Journal of Horticultural Science*, **52**, 335–346

BURNS, I.G. (1980). A simple model for predicting the effects of winter leaching or residual nitrate on the nitrogen fertilizer need in spring crops. *Journal of Soil Science*, **31**, 187–202

CLEAVER, T.J. and TURNER, M.K. (1975). *National Vegetable Research Station Annual Report for 1974*, p. 58

FINCH-SAVAGE, W.E. (1984). Effects of fluid drilling germinating onion seeds on seedling emergence and subsequent plant growth. *Journal of Agricultural Science, Cambridge*, **102**, 461–468

GREENWOOD, D.J., NEETESON, J.J. and DRAYCOTT, A. (1985). Response of potatoes to N fertilizer: Dynamic model. *Plant and Soil*, **85**, 185–203

HARTSEMA, A.M. (1947). De periodieke ontwikkeling van *Allium cepa* L. var. Zittaver Reisen. *Mededelingen van de Landbouwhoogeschool te Wageningen*, **48**, 265–300

HEATH, O.V.S. and HOLDSWORTH, M. (1948). Morphogenic factors as exemplified by the onion plant. In *Growth* (J. F. Danielli and R. Brown, Eds) *Society of Experimental Biology Symposium II*, pp. 326–350. Cambridge University Press

HEATH, O.V.S., HOLDSWORTH, M., TINCKER, M.A.H. and BROWN, F.C. (1947). Studies in the physiology of the onion plant. III. Further experiments on the effects of storage temperature and other factors on onions grown from sets. *Annals of Applied Biology*, **34**, 473–502

HEATH, O.V.S. and MATHUR, P.B. (1944). Studies in the physiology of the onion plant. II. Inflorescence initiation and development, and other changes in the internal morphology of onion sets, as influenced by temperature and daylength. *Annals of Applied Biology*, **31**, 173–186

ISENBERG, F.M.R., THOMAS, T.H., PENDERGRASS, M. and ABDEL-RHAMAN, M. (1974).

Hormone and histological differences between normal and maleic hydrazide treated onions stored over winter. *Acta Horticulturae*, **38**, 95–125

KAMPEN, J. VAN. (1970). (Shortening the breeding cycle in onion) *Medelingen Proefstation voor de Groenteteelt in de Vollegrond*, **51**, 72pp.

KAMPEN, J. VAN and WIEBOSCH, W.A. (1970). (Experiments with some growth regulators for seed production in onions). *Medelingen Proefstation voor de Groenteteelt in de Vollegrond*, **47**, 27pp.

KRUZHILIN, A.S. and SHVEDSKAYA, Z.M. (1962). (Peculiarities of the phasic of development and morphogenesis in onion.) *Fiziologiya Rasteni*, **9**, 466–475

LIST, R.J. (1951). *Smithsonian Meteorological Tables* (6th edn) Washington, USA, Smithsonian Institution

METEOROLOGICAL OFFICE (1946). *Tables for the Evaluation of Daily Values of Accumulated Temperature Above and Below 42°F for Daily Values of Maximum and Minimum Temperature.* Leaflet No. 10, London, Meteorological Office

RABINOWITCH, H.D. (1985). Onions and other edible alliums. In *Handbook of Flowering* (A. H. Halevy, Ed.), Vol. **1**, Boca Raton, Florida, CRC Press

SHISHIDO, Y. and SAITO, T. (1975). Studies on the flower bud formation in onion plants. I. Effects of temperature, photoperiod and light intensity on the low temperature induction of flower buds. *Journal of Japanese Society of Horticultural Science*, **44**, 122–130

SHISHIDO, Y. and SAITO, T. (1976). Studies on the flower bud formation in onion plants. II. Effects of physiological conditions on low temperature induction of flower bud on green plants. *Journal of Japanese Society for Horticultural Science*, **45**, 160–167

SHISHIDO, Y. and SAITO, T. (1977). Studies on the flower bud formation in onion plants. III. Effects of physiological conditions on the low temperature induction of flower buds in bulbs. *Journal of the Japanese Society for Horticultural Science*, **46**, 310–316

SHISHIDO, Y. and SAITO, T. (1984). Effects of plant growth regulators on low temperature induction of flower buds in onion plants. *Journal of Japanese Society for Horticultural Science*, **53**, 45–51

THOMAS, T.H. (1969). The role of growth substances in the regulation of onion bulb dormancy. *Journal of Experimental Botany*, **20**, 124–137

THOMPSON, H.C. and SMITH, O. (1938). Seedstalk and bulb development in the onion (*Allium cepa* L.). *Bulletin of the Cornell Agricultural Experimental Station*, No. **708**

UZO, J.O. (1983). Induction of biennial reproductive development in short day onion cultivars in a low latitude tropical environment. *Gartenbauwissenschaft*, **48**, 149–153

V

Photoperiodic Induction and Evocation to Flower

14

ENVIRONMENTAL AND GENETIC REGULATION OF PHOTOPERIODISM—A REVIEW

A.R. REES

Crop Science Division, Glasshouse Crops Research Institute, Littlehampton, UK

Introduction

The title of this review covers an enormous subject: there is already some information on thousands of species, although this number represents less than 2% of all flowering plants, with a major bias towards northern temperate ones. Of the species reported on, 80–85% show some photoperiodic behaviour, but even this estimate is biased because most of the work on photoperiodism is done on photoperiodically responsive plants.

Unfortunately the complexity of photoperiodic responses to environmental factors means that the information available for a given species, or group of species is far from complete, except in the case of model examples, or where there has been a major input to species of commercial importance. Further, intense effort has often been made on a single clone or cultivar, despite its behaviour being unique or non-representative of its close relatives. The range of experimentation has necessarily been limited: experiments commonly done at single temperatures or single light levels preclude a full investigation of the interaction of relevant environmental factors and the determination of optimum and critical values. Further, many studies fail to distinguish photoperiodic effects on floral initiation from those on subsequent development to anthesis.

There is such diversity in the flowering behaviour of plants that one is faced with a dilemma: the range and variety of response makes it difficult to find patterns or to make generalizations that have some meaning and predictive value. If this could be achieved, it would be at the expense of losing sight of the range of varietal response and its ecological significance (Evans, 1975).

The behaviour of plants in the wild is closely related to their environment, a view confirmed by studies of differences in behaviour of ecotypes, but there is little experimental information to quantify this relationship. The attributes that fit a species, variety or ecotype to its particular ecological niche are poorly understood. An ability to constrain a life cycle to a seasonal climate is clearly important, and photoperiodic control, not only of flowering, is a mechanism for achieving this, and so avoid climatic extremes of winter cold and summer drought. For crop plants the concept of the ideotype (Donald, 1960) attempts to fit plants to environments and maximize economic productivity, but it has been suggested that even for a single ecological niche, several ideotypes could be equally valid (Simmonds, 1979).

Adaptive significance of photoperiodic behaviour

It is axiomatic that within a species the possession of an attribute such as photoperiodic behaviour confers some competitive advantage over other species within the constraints of space (ecological niche, latitudinal limits) and of time (season of year). However, experimental ecology has not gone far to examine closely these advantages; we rely on observation and deduction. For an annual species the competitive advantage is expressed in seed number. It can be postulated that one strategy of a requirement for a delay in flowering is to build up a vegetative plant capable of supporting a large number of flowers and the complete development of the resultant seeds. Another strategy is that of the ephemeral plant with a short life cycle, a low seed production but several generations within each growing season giving a large annual seed number spread in time. For perennials the situation is more complex. Plant periodicity is closely coupled with the environment, the main signals being temperature and day-length.

In temperate climates such control, modified by rates of development under the fine tuning of ambient temperature, apparently works well. It is common to find that ecotypes collected at higher and higher latitudes require progressively longer days to induce flowering, a response related to the later start of the growing season. In the moist lowland tropics more subtle controls are required; near the equator seasonal differences in climate are minimal and the main environmental factors of temperature, water supply and light are close to constancy. For example, Singapore has an extremely uniform climate: the longest day is 10 minutes longer than the shortest and the mean monthly temperatures vary by only 2 °C. These fluctuations probably have no controlling effect on plant life (Holttum, 1953).

In the moist tropics, in any season some plants are in flower and some flower continuously. Indeed in this habitat there is probably the widest range of flowering behaviour from non-seasonal to very precisely seasonal, annual flowering, to synchronous flowering at intervals of several years to monocarpic gregarious flowering (Longman, 1985). A number of tropical plants have been shown to be sensitive to day-length; a number of shrub species are SD plants, although it cannot be assumed that most species are SD plants or DN plants, because a substantial minority are LD plants, and the SD plants are not necessarily qualitatively so (Longman, 1985). Despite the comparative constancy of environment, flowering in tropical forest trees is usually periodic, with fewer than 2% ever-flowering. Considering the forest as a whole, in some years there is more flowering than in others, in any month some plants will be flowering, and there are clear seasonal peaks of flowering even in uniform climates. For accurate timekeeping, photoperiodically responsive plants near the equator must be highly sensitive to small changes in day-length because of the very small day-to-day differences in day-length. Of the photoperiodic plants in the tropics, the predominance of SD plants may reflect the fact that high night temperatures generally inhibit flowering in LD plants (Evans, 1975). There are examples of species that flower only in the wet season and others that flower in the dry season, with some indication of an interaction of plant habit and habitat with flowering time. In general our knowledge of flowering behaviour within plant communities is poor, especially in relation to animals as pollinators, dispersal agents and as seed predators. Different strategies have been evolved to maximise seed production, dispersal and survival.

A narrow photoperiodic response within an ecotype can ensure accuracy of timing of flowering and the synchrony of flowering within the population which is essential for outbreeding species. The timing (calendar-related) synchrony is less important in the tropics than in higher latitudes. In the far north, the short summer imposes a growth/flowering/seeding 'window' within which plant activity occurs, but in the moist tropics synchrony can be more important than the seasonal timing of flowering. It is clearly advantageous if all the plants in the area flower together, especially if the plants are not abundant, and it helps to counteract seed predation if the seeds or fruits ripen together. Therefore, because of the small amplitude in day-length and a lesser requirement for precise timing (in the calendar sense) of flowering, in the wet tropics, it is not surprising that photoperiodic plants are not as common as in the temperate zones.

In addition to the broad latitudinal differences that affect day-length, seasonality and temperature there are also differences of habitat caused by altitude and by climatic factors such as availability of water, which have profound influences on plant communities. An extreme habitat is the desert. In the major desert areas of the world, there is found a range of strategies to preserve flexibility of flowering response to relate to the dominant environmental factor, rainfall, which varies in amount, and in its spatial and temporal distribution. The adaptation encountered depends on life form and has been summarized by Evenari and Gutterman (1985). All desert annuals are facultative photoperiodic plants which enables them to complete their life cycle in one year in an unstable environment, and thereby survive. They are of two kinds: summer annuals which are generally quantitative SD plants with a thermoperiodic requirement, and winter annuals which are quantitative LD plants. Perennials can avoid the need to flower every year; some are DN plants which can flower whenever conditions are favourable, whilst others are either SD plants or DN plants, often with separate controls for flower initiation and for subsequent development to anthesis.

Photoperiodic response

Several reviewers have looked for patterns of photoperiodic behaviour related to groups, genera, species, life forms and within species across different latitudes. Some have been successful. It has been stated that there is no simple relationship between plant classification and flowering response type: Salisbury (1963) cites the Compositae as a family where all major response types are known to occur. Further, the same response type can be found in widely unrelated families. In deciduous fruit trees of the Rosaceae, there is no constancy of photoperiodic behaviour even within the same species (Gur, 1985). In other cases general associations between taxonomic groupings and photoperiodic behaviour do occur. For 16 grain legume species, Summerfield and Roberts (1985a) indicate that the Vicieae, Cicereae and Genisteae are DN plants or LD plants, whilst the Phaseoleae are DN plants or SD plants. Similarly there appears to be a link with some life forms; many geophytes are DN plants whilst annuals tend to be quantitatively photoperiodic (Evenari and Gutterman, 1985).

Cumming (1969) determined the photoperiodic responses of 33 species of *Chenopodium*; 25 were SD plants and 8 were LD plants. *Fragaria vesca* is relatively insensitive to photoperiod, whilst *F. virginiana* is highly sensitive (Guttridge, 1969). All *Amaranthus* species examined are qualitative or quantitative SD plants (Kigel and Rubin, 1985). For *Avena* species, quantitative LD plants, there appears to be a relationship between geographical origin with those from the northerly latitudes showing the greatest response to day-length (Shands and Cisar, 1985).

Within a species, cultivars often display a wide range of quantitative response, as seen in *Antirrhinum majus* (Cockshull, 1985a), described as a typical quantitative LD plant, capable of flowering in short days but flowering earlier and at a lower leaf number in long days. Some cultivars are almost unaffected by day-length, particularly the late flowering ones, and there is near-continuous variation among cultivars in the magnitude of their response to long days. The selection of cultivars for different latitudes has led to a wide range of sensitivities; some cultivars of soybean at the northern end of the species range can be successfully grown only within an 80 km band of latitude (Hamner, 1969).

Individual species show a remarkable diversity of response over a wide range of latitude, also modified by climate. Evans (1975) describes the range of behaviour shown by kangaroo grass (*Themeda australis*) in Australia: the northern tropical populations are strictly SD plants which flower at the end of the monsoon; those from middle-latitude coastal areas are intermediate day plants, whilst further south the populations are mostly LD plants (often qualitative) which flower at the end of the winter/spring rainfall period. Populations in the dry centre of Australia are DN plants, whose flowering response is to the occasional, seasonally unpredictable rainfall. This species is claimed to be the first known to contain SD, LD and DN races, and is thought to have entered Australia from the tropics.

In a collection of *Chenopodium rubrum* ecotypes, Cumming (1969) found the most extreme short-day response in his most southerly material (39 °N) and that the sensitivity of the flowering response decreased with increase in original latitude (to 63 °N). The most northerly ecotypes can flower in a wide range of photoperiods and tend towards being quantitative SD plants. Conversely the more southerly ecotypes flower in a narrow range of daily dark periods and tend to be qualitative SD plants.

Environmental factors

LIGHT

Photoperiodism by definition is a response to change in the length of day, or more accurately night, which is an accurate measure of time, and hence of season, at all latitudes. It is worth a reminder that in nature day-to-day changes in day-length are not constant throughout the year, and differ markedly at a given time of year with latitude. Further, change in day-length occurs progressively: in nature there are no night-breaks nor a small number of inductive cycles, followed by a return to non-inductive conditions: conditions frequently employed in experimental investigations.

Light has several components in the photoperiod context: irradiance, duration and spectral effects, also with a time element in the sense of the duration and number of cycles required to produce a response and in the sense of interaction with stage of plant development i.e. whether the plant is competent to respond to an imposed inductive day-length by flower initiation or by post-initiation development to anthesis.

Irradiance

A short-day can be effectively extended by artificial light or by a night-break treatment. In natural days, what demarcates 'light' and 'dark'? Experiments have shown that inhibition of flowering in *Xanthium* by a light-break in the middle of a long dark period could occur at light levels that had little or no effect at the beginning of the dark period (Salisbury, 1981). Further, the transition from day to night takes only 6–12 minutes. To delay the initiation of dark measurement, irradiance levels (400–800 nm) of about 18–90 mW m^{-2} are required, whereas inhibition during the middle 2 h of the 16 h dark period requires only 2–18 mW m^{-2}. These levels are well above the light from a full moon (about 0.9 mW m^{-2}, 400–800 nm).

In *Pharbitis*, photoperception was measured (Vince-Prue and Lumsden, 1985) in an experiment where irradiance was decreased in steps before transferring the plants to darkness. Maximum sensitivity occurred after 8–9 h, and 'dark' timing appeared to begin when the irradiance in white light was lowered to 2 W m^{-2}.

The differences between these estimated irradiance thresholds can probably be accounted for by spectral effects, differences between species and the difficulties of this kind of experimentation.

More recently, Summerfield and Roberts (*see* Chapter 15) suggested that for grain legumes, with a photoperiodic requirement for post-initiation development to flowering, differences in irradiance sensitivity are minimal, a situation that may hold for other plant groups too. Sensitivity, i.e. the relative flowering response per unit difference in photoperiod, may well be more important than differences in threshold light.

In some instances high light must precede the dark period before flowering of SD plants is induced. This seems particularly true for very short or low-irradiance photoperiods. It is likely that there is a photosynthetic component to this requirement, but it has also been suggested that the high-light dependence is not merely one of plant carbohydrate status. There is some evidence that some primary products of the light period (probably photosynthetic ones) are required, and there have been examples of substitution of sucrose for the absence of high irradiance light (Cockshull, 1984). In commercial horticultural practice it is well known that the quantity of radiant energy received in the daily light period measured as a daily integral strongly influences the response of chrysanthemum to inductive long night, and that poor light delays flowering, especially in the early stages of receptacle and floret initiation (Cockshull, 1972).

Duration

Critical day-length is defined as the day-length below which the flowering of SD plants occurs, or above which the flowering of LD plants occurs. There is still some ambiguity about the variation in response in the population. Critical day-lengths range from about 9–16 h for a range of LD plants and SD plants (Vince-Prue, 1975). However, as many other factors affect the critical day-length—including plant age, cultivar, temperature and irradiance—the critical day-length as a concept has limitations although it is a useful practical guide.

The number of inductive cycles is another time/light interaction. Several species respond to a single cycle, e.g. *Anagallis, Pharbitis, Sinapis, Xanthium*, whilst others require several weeks (*Fragaria vesca*; Guttridge, 1969). In many cases there are quantitative effects of increasing cycle number on the rate of development to anthesis in terminally flowering plants, or on the numbers of flowers produced—the classic demonstration of this being for *Kalanchoe* where the dichasium becomes more branched with an exponential increase from one to several hundred flowers over a cycle number of 2–14 (Schwabe, 1969). In the SLD plant *Bryophyllum daigremontia-*

num at least 60 long days are required followed by about 15 short days to ensure flowering (Zeevaart, 1969b). Effective cycle numbers differ between species, varieties and strains, and have been reported to be affected by plant age (older plants being more responsive), temperature, the day-length used and the irradiance during the light period. Not surprisingly, no data exist that investigate fully the interactions involved with all these variables even for one cultivar. The data of Friend (1969) for *Brassica campestris* illustrate the formidable experimental complexity. In response to one inductive day given for different durations (8–23 h) to seedlings aged 2–5 days at two temperatures (25 and 30 °C), more plants flowered after treatment at 25 than at 30 °C, the response was greater the older the seedlings, and there were both qualitative and quantitative responses to the duration of the light period.

Some plants are capable of responding to small differences in day-length. Indeed the possession of a response would otherwise be of little value to plants growing near the equator where seasonal variation in day-length is minimal. Reports exist of responses to ten-minute differences having an effect on flowering of tropical SD plants, although the response may require many cycles (Njoku, 1958).

Spectral aspects

Consideration of spectral aspects falls into two areas; those due to spectral composition of artificial lights and those occurring naturally, including spectral changes caused by filtering effects of other vegetation or to changes in the optical path length at the ends of the day.

In practice it has been found that, in general, red light (600–700 nm wavelength) is the most suitable for use as a night break, whilst LD plants respond best to a mixture of red and far-red light (700–800 nm). Prevention of flowering of many SD plants can be best achieved by a day-length extension of red light. Tungsten-filament lamps, rich in red and far-red wavelengths, are suitable for day-length extension and for night-break lighting although the efficacy of the red radiation is partly reduced by the far-red. The better spectral characteristics of fluorescent and mercury-fluorescent lamps are offset by their higher installation costs, so that in commercial practice the light source most commonly used is the tungsten-filament lamp.

In natural twilight there is a decrease in the red:far-red ratio (660:730 nm) as official sunset is approached or even before sunset under cloudy conditions (Salisbury, 1981). This has important possibilities as light quality just before darkness affects flowering, red light being promotive in the SD plant *Pharbitis*, whilst far-red is promotive in Wintex barley (a LD plant). Moonlight is spectrally similar to that of light just after sunset.

TEMPERATURE INTERACTIONS

Photoperiodic response cannot be considered in isolation from temperature, because it is rare to find a plant in which day-length response is wholly independent of temperature, and many plants that are day neutral at one temperature are sensitive to day-length at another.

Whilst vernalization is dealt with elsewhere in detail, it is worth commenting on interactive effects, as opposed to the qualitative situation where, in the absence of prior low-temperature treatment, no flowering can occur irrespective of photoperiodic treatment. Quantitative responses appear as a reduction in the number of inductive photoperiods required to secure initiation following vernalization, or a similar effect on duration of the photoperiod implying that the apex has proceeded some way towards the flowering state, and requires less further photoperiodic stimulation. In contrast, chilling of established strawberry plants can inhibit subsequent flower induction, a phenomenon likened to a low-temperature dormancy breaking in woody plants, and promote vegetative growth (Guttridge, 1969).

In general higher temperatures accelerate anthesis in plants grown in inductive daylengths but there can be a complete suppression of flowering at low temperature (below 8 °C in *Kalanchoe*; Schwabe, 1969) or a decreased response at high temperture (above 30 °C in *Kalanchoe*; Schwabe, 1969). For *Perilla*, no flowers are produced at 0–10 °C; flower buds occur after 17 days at 20–22 °C but only after 37 days at 30–35 °C, all temperatures being during the dark period (Zeevaart, 1969a). Examples are common of the need for more inductive cycles for effective flower initiation at lower temperatures, or for a longer dark period for induction of flowering where a single dark period is inductive. However, few responses are as dramatic as with *Silene* (Wellensiek, 1969) where the mean number of long-day cycles needed to induce flowering was shown to fall regularly from 30 to 1 after increasing temperature in 3 °C steps from 9 to 24 °C. At 32 °C, flowering occurred in short days.

An interesting effect of temperature has been demonstrated by Cumming (1969) with an ecotype of *Chenopodium rubrum*. Earliest flowering occurred at intermediate photoperiods when the plants were grown at constant temperatures of 15 or 20 °C. But at 25 °C earliest initiation occurred at both 12 and 24 hour photoperiods giving a bimodal response termed 'ambiphotoperiodism'. At 30 °C, earliest floral initiation occurred in continuous light.

The photo-thermal response of cowpea, *Vigna unguiculata*, has been elegantly described by Summerfield and Roberts (1985b), based on factorial experiments examining 12 photoperiod/night temperature combinations on progress to flowering. Some cultivars are unresponsive to photoperiod but respond linearly to mean daily temperature. Other cultivars are quantitative SD plants, with a response linearly relating photoperiod to the reciprocal of time to flowering. The interaction of these two equations is seen in photoperiodically sensitive cultivars as two intersecting response surfaces, flowering being determined by whichever equation calls for the greatest delay. This scheme allows the definition of the critical photoperiod as the one, in any temperature regimen, above which flowering is either delayed (quantitative) or prevented (qualitative response); it is not constant, but varies with temperature, more so if sensitivity to photoperiod is low.

Resolving the complexity of the temperature/photoperiod interaction of different cultivars illustrated by this work is a major step forward in understanding plant responses, yet the work involved in determining such information for other photoperiodic crop plants is daunting.

OTHER INTERACTIONS

Under some conditions photoperiodic responses can be qualitatively changed: some LD plants will flower in complete darkness, some SD ones in continuous light (in some cases only if the intensity is not too high, or if the temperature sufficiently low, or high). Many SD plants can flower in long days and low temperature. There is a suggestion that there may be an equivalence, in SD plants, of lower temperatures and long dark periods comparable with that in plants which respond to vernalization, where short days may substitute for the low temperature (Evans, 1965). Indeed the selection of a specific growing temperature can either remove a photoperiodic requirement or alter the requirement qualitatively as shown by Wellensiek (1969) for *Silene*. Here, long days, short days at either high or low temperatures, or growth regulator application all lead to flowering; induction can occur after four distinct treatments.

Juvenility, the period early in the plant's life when it cannot respond to various stimuli by flowering, has long been recognized. The length of the juvenile period varies with species, is commonly many years in trees, and can also vary significantly between cultivars. In late varietes of *Pisum*, the juvenile state can last up to 50 nodes, can be shortened by vernalization, and have interactions with day-length, with earlier flowering being promoted in short days but not in long days (Haupt, 1969).

Flower development from initiation to anthesis frequently has different or more stringent requirements than for initiation. In coffee, the initiation of flowers is under photoperiodic control but their anthesis depends on rain or the temperature drop associated with rain. For chrysanthemum, treatments that fail to completely inhibit flower initiation, when continued, do not permit further flower development. At a night length greater than about 10.5 h, flowers are initiated most rapidly. However, a night length of 11.5 h is required to allow these flowers to develop to anthesis.

Flowering responses to environmental factors are highly complex with interactions between plant age and stage of development, with growing temperatures and several aspects of the light climate, on flower initiation and on subsequent development to anthesis. There are qualitative and quantitative reponses, several photoperiodic response types, and the flowering responses are modified by the plant's morphology, branching habit, etc. Salisbury (1963) suggested that there were nearly 800 possible response types if all the subdivisions of day-length responses, the degree of day-length control and interactions with temperature are included. Examples of fewer than 10% of these have, however, been identified as yet. It is only because of major inputs on selected crops over years usually by numbers of researchers that progress has been made in the understanding of the behaviour of a few plants or groups of plants.

SOME EXAMPLES

In protected horticulture, opportunities are exploited to control closely the production, timing and quality of flowers, or to prevent flowering, by environmental manipulation. Detailed schedules have been developed for individual cultivars or cultivar groups and are followed by growers, where day/night temperatures, photoperiod and supplementary lighting are modified according to time of year, latitude and stage of development of the crop. Such detailed information is difficult to summarize adequately, but two examples are quoted.

Chrysanthemum

Thousands of cultivars of this popular cut flower and pot plant have been developed with a wide range of form, colour, and flowering behaviour, and flowers are available all year round (AYR). Autumn- and winter-flowering types are SD plants and include the cultivars used for AYR production in heated greenhouses. These are classified into response groups which require between 6 and 15 weeks at 16 °C under autumn conditions from the first inductive short days and harvesting. The summer flowering types, frequently regarded as DN plants, but more recently shown to be quantitative SD plants, have been less exploited commercially. The range of response types is sufficiently wide to achieve year-round flowering in Japan by manipulation of planting time, of location and the use of simple protection at certain times of year. In most other countries, AYR production involves short-day cultivars which have lost their vernalization requirement or do not exhibit it when grown from vegetative stock plants; these normally flower in the autumn.

Stock plants are kept vegetative by long-day, night-break or intermittent lighting treatments and information is available on appropriate lamps, and on the duration, timing and quantity of light required to achieve this in the most effective and efficient manner. The inhibition of flowering is a quantitative response, with more pronounced inhibition as the duration or the flux density of the light during the night-break increases. Flower initiation eventually occurs in all cultivars when grown in long days, and a measure of the tendency of a cultivar to flower in long days is given by the number of leaves produced (a range of 20–94 under UK conditions for 86 cultivars), and by the duration of the vegetative period in long days (21–121 days). Initiation is therefore a quantitative response to short days. Cuttings taken from the stock plants are rooted and grown in long days to allow sufficient internodes to extend before flowers are initiated by short-day treatment using natural day-lengths in the winter and using blackouts in the summer drawn over the plants to shorten the natural day.

Night-break lighting is widely used as a means of keeping plants vegetative during the short-day winter period. This inhibition is quantitative, depending on the light integral, but is dependent on cultivar. The effectiveness of the night break is also dependent on the time it is applied, being most effective in the middle of the dark period. In commercial practice, 4 or 5 h night-breaks are placed around midnight to divide the night into equal parts. Cyclic lighting uses several short light periods distributed over a 4 h period in the middle of the night and can be financially worthwhile; commonly used cycles are 1 min in 5 min, 6 in 30, 10 in 30 and 15 in 30.

The optimum number of short days is 7–8 for most rapid flower initiation at the terminal apical meristem; with increase in the number of short days, more axillary meristems become committed to flower initiation. The minimum effective number of short days is about three, but this is a quantitative response as a single day can initiate a terminal flower, and the number increases greatly as the daily light integral declines. The duration of the light period also has a quantitative effect on initiation; there is no inhibition by day-lengths below about 9 h duration and maximum inhibition by periods longer than about 18 h, with a quantitative response between, i.e. there is no critical day-length. In general the higher the response group number the shorter the maximum day-length at which rapid flower initiation can still occur. The effects of day-length on flower development from initiation to anthesis is complex; although some early flowering cultivars can reach anthesis in continuous light, most develop most rapidly in short days. Late-flowering cultivars fail to develop normal flowers in long days, and the inhibitory effect of long days depends on time of treatment. Under natural low-light conditions, flowering is delayed, an effect confirmed in experiments using artificial light.

The high light requirement (c. $125\,\mathrm{J\,cm^{-2}\,day^{-1}}$) is particularly important for the first 2 weeks of the inductive short-day treatment, to prevent undue delay. After the first 2 weeks, low light ($30\text{–}60\,\mathrm{J\,cm^{-2}\,day^{-1}}$) delays receptacle initiation in lateral branches and also the rate of floret initiation. Once floret initiation is complete, the rate of subsequent development is unaffected by low light.

There are complex effects of temperature on chrysanthemum flowering classified by responses to temperature during the long-day period on the plants' subsequent flowering behaviour in short days, and also on responses to temperature in short days. Most cultivars used today for AYR flowering would be classed as thermozero; i.e. they can flower over a wide range of temperatures, with no carry-over of temperature treatments given during the long-day period. But in summer-flowering cultivars, temperature has a greater effect on flower initiation and subsequent development than day-length. Effects of temperature on flower initiation and development have been studied in the chrysanthemum, using day-lit controlled environment cabinets (Cockshull *et al.*, 1981). Flower initiation and the early stages of flower development of many cultivars are highly correlated with average temperatures, irrespective of whether this is achieved by day:night combinations of 20:10, 15:15 or 10:20 °C using 12 h day and night periods. These observations have some bearing on considerations of photoperiodic mechanisms; night temperatures are considered to have an effect on the synthesis of flower-forming compounds in some SD plants.

This information on chrysanthemum summarized above for UK conditions relies heavily on work by Cockshull (1972; 1985a, b) to which the reader is referred for further details. American data are given by Kofranek (1980).

Easter lily

A different commercial problem faces the Easter lily forcer, who is marketing a flowering pot plant for a specific but annually variable date. The plant has a vernalization requirement at 1.5–7 °C of 6 weeks, which results in rapid, uniform shoot emergence and subsequent rapid and uniform flowering. The vernalization can be at least partly satisfied in the field before the bulbs are lifted and can introduce unwanted season-to-season variability in subsequent behaviour. A long-day treatment can substitute for, or saturate, the effect of cold on a week-for-week basis, and is used as an insurance that the plants will grow rapidly. This is achieved commercially using a 4 h night break, or cyclic lighting. Above 21 °C devernalization occurs, and, interestingly, long-day treatment is also ineffective. In its natural habitat, the Liu-chiu (Ryukus) islands (27 °N), the plants respond to photoperiod, because ambient temperatures normally exceed 21 °C (Rees, 1985; Wilkins, 1980).

Genetics of photoperiodism

In practice, there is still remarkable ignorance of the genetics of the day-length response and its evolutionary history (Simmonds, 1979). Past advances have been achieved by selection of material highly adapted and therefore successful in a certain situation or by producing new strains and cultivars and selecting from these, i.e. a range of genotypes has been exposed to selection pressure directly by the environment or by man in a given environment, and the most successful material preserved.

Most plants are outbreeders, so that populations are variable, evolutionarily flexible and throw up favourable recombinants. Man selects and retains the valuable and desirable characteristics for his crop plants. In some cases flowering is not required because the energy used for flowering is more effective if diverted to the desired vegetative parts. Non-flowering mutants can be selected and propagated or clones used which do not flower in the required latitudes. Sugar-cane clones originating near the equator can be used successfully in higher latitudes (Moore, 1985). Fibre production in jute is adversely affected if plants flower; and for use in latitudes with inductive day-lengths, breeders have produced cultivars that do not flower in the day-lengths of those latitudes (Simmonds, 1979). Many salad crops produce vegetative commercial end-products—lettuce, endive, celery—where flowering is not required. Lettuce is an LD plant, with a critical day-length of about 14 h. Glasshouse cultivars have been developed for winter growing under glass in the UK; these are unsuitable for summer growing, because they flower rapidly. Lettuces have also been bred for growing in the summer under glass or plastic cover, so that year-round production schedules are now possible. These types, although still LD plants, tend towards being day neutral, and mature to the harvesting stage within 7 weeks of sowing without 'bolting' (Smith, 1983). To lengthen the growing season of sugar beet, selection against 'bolting' has been achieved by adjusting the photoperiod/vernalization requirement, allowing earlier sowing.

Modifications in photoperiodic response can be major ones, allowing a species to be grown in other latitudes, or they may be more subtle, extending an existing range north or south, or providing a range of cultivars selected so that flowering fits in with some climatic variable. Such approaches have led to varieties grouped into maturity classes adapted to different latitudes, like the ten classes of soybean grown from Canada south to the Gulf Coast of the USA (Hamner, 1969). Another example is the range of West African genotypes of sorghum whose flowering has been selected to coincide with the average date of the end of the rainy season (itself determined by latitude) so that grain loss by insect and fungal attack is minimized by dry conditions (Murfet, 1977). The selection pressures of climate, and the consequences of the failure of one plant to flower with its fellows are strong; in the former progeny are few, in the latter there could be none.

In contrast to these examples of selecting plants to fit closely a given aspect of the environment, in some cases there has been breeding to lose sensitivity to day-length so that plants can flower in many different latitudes. The well-known examples are the wheats of the 'green revolution', but other wheats also have insensitivity to day-length so that flowering time is not under close environmental control but depends on sowing date and rates of development, including the length of the juvenile period (Law and Scarth, 1984).

Although it has been suggested (Hillman, 1962) that genetic control of flowering is simple, judged by the ease with which early and late flowering cultivars have been produced in a wide range of crop plants, the existence of quantitative responses implies that the underlying genetic mechanism is complex. Simple genetic systems give qualitative variation. The range of photoperiodic responses in ecotypes and in varieties and strains of cultivated species implies polygenic control. For instance, Wellensiek (1969) selected *Silene* over two generations from a stain that flowered only after ten or more long-day cycles, producing a new strain that gave 90% flowers after only six cycles and another that would not flower even after twelve. It is important that a wide genetic base be retained to allow such selections to be made in crop plants; there are examples of introductions to 'new' countries of very restricted numbers of individual plants. However, in wild populations with apparent phenotypic uniformity there may be more genetic diversity than might be suspected because interaction between environment and the genotype masks gene expression (Murfet, 1977). For some hemp cultivars variation in time to flower between individuals is high under continuous light because this treatment exposes 'otherwise concealed genetic diversity' (Heslop-Harrison and Heslop-Harrison, 1969).

The presence or absence of a photoperiodic response as well as the response type and sensitivity are all under genetic control. However, there seems to be no clear pattern of genetic control; the requirement for short days, for example, might be determined by a recessive or dominant gene involving a single allelic gene pair, or control may be by one, two or several genes. Further, a response to a specific photoperiodic requirement for flowering can be easily acquired or lost. Deductions about geographic origins of species or families based upon their photoperiodic behaviour must therefore be treated cautiously. The colonization of adjacent geographical habitats probably requires less genetic change than a larger latitudinal move. The kind of adaptation shown by the sorghums described above could be achieved either by small changes in the background of polygenes or the substitution at major loci of mutant alleles differing only slightly from the original ones. For sorghum it has been achieved by selection for a major recessive mutant reducing the requirement for short days (Murfet, 1977).

SOME EXAMPLES

Pisum

As with environmental manipulation of flowering behaviour, the complexity of the genetical component of the behaviour of a given species can only be appreciated after considerable inputs by many workers over many years. One of the best understood species is *Pisum*, for which Murfet (1985) has provided a recent summary. Flowering can be measured in several ways: node of main stem which bears the flower initial, flowering time (days from sowing to first open flower), and time of flower initiation as determined by dissection. Each has its attraction depending on the practical or physiological importance of the measurement to the measurer. There are four fairly distinct phenotypic classes: day neutral, early-initiating, late (quantitative long-day) and late (approaching qualitative long-day). The differences between these classes are determined mainly by major genes, whilst those within classes are determined by major genes, minor genes and polygenic systems. The classes bear little relation to grower terms used to describe maturity date at a given location, e.g. 'second-early'. Six major gene loci have been identified (these are *Lf, E, Sn, Dne, Hr* and *Veg*) and three are concerned with photoperiodic response (*Sn, Dne* and *Hr*). The first two are concerned with induction and apparently result in a graft-transmissible floral inhibitor, whose output is blocked in continuous light and is decreased at low temperature. *Hr* magnifies the effect of the other two. Minor genes for flowering appear to be major genes for other characteristics such as internode length, and these and other genes affect flowering either directly or by modifying the expression of the major flowering genes to provide quantitative systems of response. The distinction drawn between major genes and polygenes may not be as great as implied above, the differences between them being only in the magnitude of their phenotypic effects.

The mutant *veg* completely prevents flower initiation irrespective of other genes present. The four alleles of *Lf* confer a minimum node number for floral initiation of 15, 11, 8 and 5 and operate at the shoot apex to determine the threshold level of flowering signal necessary for evocation. *E* is believed to operate in the cotyledons by reducing the inhibitory effect of the *Sn Dne* system. It determines the phenotypic class, causing early flowering in certain combinations, e.g. *E Sn Dne hr* belongs to the early initiating class.

Cestrum

Cestrum nocturnum is an LSD plant, and crosses with the DN plant *C. elegans* and *C. reflexum* (an LSD plant below 19 °C) made by Griesel (1966) suggest that there are at least two indepenent genes or gene groups responsible for flower initiation in *C. nocturnum*. Despite some quantitative differences a single dominant gene is considered to control the response to LSD. Evidence from the flowering response of the F1, F2 and back-crosses led to the conclusion that the long-day requirement is controlled by one or more recessive genes whose action is temperature dependent. At temperatures below 19 °C flowering of *C. nocturnum* is independent of day-length and occurs in long days with a temperature drop.

Discussion

It is not possible to attempt any synthesis of environmental and genetic regulation of photoperiodism because of the extreme complexity and volume of information, summarized by Murfet (1977): 'Flowering is the end-result of physiological processes, biochemical sequences, and gene action, with the whole system responding to the influence of environmental stimuli and the passage of time.'

Many years ago, Gregory (1936) raised the question of whether the transition to flowering should be regarded as a part of the normal sequence, thereby inverting the thinking on flower promotion to one of inhibition. This concept embodied a gradual move towards floral initiation, in contrast to the qualitative switching mechanism envisaged for plants which respond to a single inductive cycle. There is now a greater realization that there are quantitative aspects to flower initiation, and progress along the route to flowering can be enhanced by several factors which are known to interact, such as vernalization and plant age (including the duration of juvenility) even if the time elapsed is in a non-inductive day-length. In hemp, for instance, the effectiveness of a series of inductive cycles depends on the age of the plant; a young plant needs more cycles than an older one (Heslop-Harrison and Heslop-Harrison, 1969). The ultimate in this progression is of course the eventual flowering of a plant kept for a long time in non-inductive conditions, an event that is probably not observed as frequently as it might be because the experiment is not run for long enough. Support for a theory of progression towards flowering has been obtained from anatomical, histological and morphological observations, and Heslop-Harrison and Heslop-Harrison (1970) have suggested that photoperiod regulates the rate of progress towards flowering. The SD plant chrysanthemum, which eventually initiates flowers in long days, although flowering is accelerated by short days, fits this concept. So also does the range of response in antirrhinum which can flower in short days, but will flower earlier, and at lower nodes, in long days. Flowering in both examples can be regarded as a result of an autonomous induction in a non-inductive day-length enhanced by, or supplanted by, a photoperiodic induction in the flower-promoting day-length. Cockshull (1984) in an analysis of the flowering behaviour of four short-day plants suggests that all effects of light on induction in this group are quantitative responses to radiant energy. He postulates a mechanism integrating information on energy or photon flux density to produce a quantitative response.

Whilst an overview of the whole field of photoperiodic response is daunting because of its complexity and sheer volume, it is encouraging that in the few plants or plant groups that have been studied intensively, sufficient understanding has been achieved to allow successful commercial exploitation. Information on year-round growing schedules has been accumulated and assembled, and is continually being updated for use with new cultivars (many of which are selected on grounds other than their specific photoperiodic response) with new equipment such as lamps of different spectral quality, and with understanding of more efficient methods of illumination such as cyclic lighting to reduce the consumption of electricity and also selecting the time of night to use lighting to reduce the cost of the electricity consumed. This effectively horticultural approach of modifying the environment to control flowering of crops is in contrast to those in agricultural practice where the far smaller control of environment that is practicable has encouraged the adaptation of the genotype of the crop to suit the growing region. In general, attempts to control flowering in the field by artificial lights or searchlights have not proved economic for agricultural crops (Moore, 1985) but it has been used for some high-value flower crops. Much of this work has been done by empirical selection from the range of phenotypic behaviour exhibited—in the past selection by primitive man mimicked the selection pressures that occurred in the wild to produce ecotypes. The successful production of seed or fruit for human use would have the same value as that for the plant's survival. Mass selection is usually applied to material which it is thought has the capacity for adaptation, although in some cases there has been a conscious attempt to cross and back-cross with more unspecialized genotypes. There is a danger, however, that foreign stock may lack the capacity to adapt to critical environmental factors like day-length.

More recently such selection has adopted a more scientific basis with improved understanding of the inheritance of responses to day-length and temperature, in two directions: towards producing DN plants which can be grown in a wide range of climates and towards plants with specific day-length responses so that they can flower or be kept vegetative, as required in the given habitat. Such approaches, often using quite simple techniques such as screening genotypes using a light gradient in the field to observe photoperiodic behaviour as an aid to selecting parental material in a breeding programme, represents an advance over random crossing and selection.

Care must be exerted that progress along scientific and investigational lines does not depart too far from the more pragmatic approach of the environmental scientist and the breeder. Use of the terms 'short-day lettuce' means to the breeder and grower a plant that reaches a harvestable state in short days. It is not a short-day plant. Similarly some chrysanthemums are described as 'early flowering' in the sense of short life cycle, flowering early in the chrysanthemum season, i.e. in early autumn, not early in the calendar year.

With modern data handling systems it might also be possible to build up a photoperiodic behaviour data bank in the hope that data on individual cultivars could be rapidly retrieved and that some generalization or patterns could be identified. At a more basic level, there is a need for more experimental ecological work to ascertain and quantify the benefits to individual species of certain photoperiod behaviour as related to its ecological niche.

Finally, it is perhaps salutary that the simple pigeon-hole concept of plant response to day-length has, on further extensive investigation, proved to be immensely complex. But this is perhaps what we should expect if evolution and the survival of the fittest have biological meaning.

References

COCKSHULL, K.E. (1972). Photoperiodic control of flowering in the chrysanthemum. In *Crop Processes in Controlled Environments* (A.R. Rees, K.E. Cockshull, D.W. Hand and R.G. Hurd, Eds), pp. 235–250. London, Academic Press

COCKSHULL, K.E. (1984). The photoperiodic induction of flowering in short-day plants. In *Light and the Flowering Process* (D. Vince-Prue, B. Thomas and K.E. Cockshull, Eds), pp. 33–49. London, Academic Press

COCKSHULL, K.E. (1985a). *Antirrhinum majus*. In *Handbook of Flowering*, Vol. I (A.H. Halevy, Ed.), pp. 476–481. Boca Raton, Florida, CRC Press

COCKSHULL, K.E. (1985b). *Chrysanthemum morifolium* Ramat. In *Handbook of Flowering*, Vol. II (A.H. Halevy, Ed.), pp. 238–257. Boca Raton, Florida, CRC Press

COCKSHULL, K.E., HAND, D.W. and LANGTON, F.A. (1981). The effects of day and night temperature on flower initiation and development in chrysanthemum. *Acta Horticulturae*, **125**, 101–109

CUMMING, B.G. (1969). *Chenopodium rubrum* L. and related species. In *The Induction of Flowering* (L.T. Evans, Ed.), pp. 156–185. Melbourne, Macmillan

DONALD, C.M. (1960). The breeding of crop ideotypes. *Euphytica*, **17**, 385–403

EVANS, L.T. (1965). The nature of flower induction. In *The Induction of Flowering* (L.T. Evans, Ed.), pp. 455–480. Melbourne, Macmillan

EVANS, L.T. (1975). *Daylength and the Flowering of Plants*, Menlo Park, California, W.A. Benjamin

EVENARI, M. and GUTTERMAN, Y. (1985). Desert plants. In *Handbook of Flowering*, Vol. I (A.H. Halevy, Ed.), pp. 41–59. Boca Raton, Florida, CRC Press

FRIEND, D.J.C. (1969). *Brassica campestris* L. In *Induction of Flowering* (L.T. Evans, Ed.), pp. 364–375. Melbourne, Macmillan

GREGORY, F.G. (1936). The effect of the length of day on the flowering of plants. *Scientific Horticulture*, **4**, 143–154

GRIESEL, W.O. (1966). Inheritance of factors affecting floral primordia initiation in *Cestrum*; hybrids of *C. elegans* and *C. nocturnum*. *Plant Physiology*, **41**, 111–114

GUR, A. (1985). Rosaceae—Deciduous fruit trees. In *Handbook of Flowering*, Vol. I (A.H. Halevy, Ed.), pp. 355–389. Boca Raton, Florida, CRC Press

GUTTRIDGE, C.G. (1969). *Fragaria*. In *The Induction of Flowering* (L.T. Evans, Ed.), pp. 247–267. Melbourne, Macmillan

HAMNER, K.C. (1969). *Glycine max* (L.) Merrill. In *The Induction of Flowering* (L.T. Evans, Ed.), pp. 62–89. Melbourne, Macmillan

HAUPT, W. (1969). *Pisum sativum* L. In *The Induction of Flowering* (L.T. Evans, Ed.), pp. 393–408. Melbourne, Macmillan

HESLOP-HARRISON, J. and HESLOP-HARRISON, Y. (1969). *Cannabis sativa* L. In *The Induction of Flowering* (L.T. Evans, Ed.), pp. 205–226. Melbourne, Macmillan

HESLOP-HARRISON, J. and HESLOP-HARRISON, Y. (1970). The state of the apex and the response to induction in *Cannabis sativa*. In *Cellular and Molecular Aspects of Floral Induction* (G. Bernier, Ed.), pp. 3–26. London, Longman

HILLMAN, W.S. (1962). *The Physiology of Flowering*, New York, Holt, Rinehart & Winston

HOLTTUM, R.E. (1953). Evolutionary trends in an equatorial climate. *Symposia of the Society for Experimental Biology*, **7**, 159–173

KIGEL, J. and RUBIN, B. (1985). *Amaranthus*. In *Handbook of Flowering*, Vol. I (A.H. Halevy, Ed.), pp. 427–433. Boca Raton, Florida, CRC Press

KOFRANEK, A.M. (1980). Cut chrysanthemums. In *Introduction to Floriculture* (R.A. Larson, Ed.), pp. 3–45. New York, Academic Press

LAW, C.N. and SCARTH, R. (1984). Genetics and its potential for understanding the action of light in flowering. In *Light and the Flowering Process* (D. Vince-Prue, B. Thomas and K.E. Cockshull, Eds), pp. 193–209. London, Academic Press

LONGMAN, K.E. (1985). Tropical forest trees. In *Handbook of Flowering*, Vol. I (A.H. Halevy, Ed.), pp. 23–39. Boca Raton, Florida, CRC Press

MOORE, P.H. (1985). *Saccharum*. In *Handbook of Flowering*, Vol. I (A.H. Halevy, Ed.), pp. 243–262. Boca Raton, Florida, CRC Press

MURFET, I.C. (1977). Environmental interaction and the genetics of flowering. *Annual Review of Plant Physiology*, **28**, 253–278

MURFET, I.C. (1985). *Pisum sativum*. In *Handbook of Flowering*, Vol. IV (A.H. Halevy, Ed.), pp. 97–126. Boca Raton, Florida, CRC Press

NJOKU, E. (1958). The photoperiodic response of some Nigerian plants. *Journal of the West African Science Association*, **4**, 99–111

REES, A.R. (1985). *Lilium*. In *Handbook of Flowering*, Vol. I (A.H. Halevy, Ed.), pp. 288–293. Boca Raton, Florida, CRC Press

SALISBURY, F.B. (1963). *The Flowering Process*. Oxford, Pergamon

SALISBURY, F.B. (1981). Twilight effect: initiating dark measurement in photoperiodism of *Xanthium*. *Plant Physiology*, **67**, 1230–1238

SCHWABE, W.W. (1969). *Kalanchoe blossfeldiana* Poellniz. In *The Induction of Flowering* (L.T. Evans, Ed.), pp. 226–246. Melbourne, Macmillan

SHANDS, H.L. and CISAR, G.L. (1985). *Avena*. In *Handbook of Flowering*, Vol. I (A.H. Halevy, Ed.), pp. 523–535. Boca Raton, Florida, CRC Press

SIMMONDS, N.W. (1979). *Principles of Crop Improvement*. London, Longmans

SMITH, J.M. (1983). Lettuce breeding. Cultivars for summer production under protection. *Report of the Glasshouse Crops Research Institute for 1982*, pp. 77–79

SUMMERFIELD, R.J. and ROBERTS, E.J. (1985a). Grain legume species of significant importance in world agriculture. In *Handbook of Flowering*, Vol. I (A.H. Halevy, Ed.), pp. 61–73. Boca Raton, Florida, CRC Press

SUMMERFIELD, R.J. and ROBERTS, E.J. (1985b). *Vigna unguiculata*. In *Handbook of Flowering*, Vol. I (A.H. Halevy, Ed.), pp. 171–184. Boca Raton, Florida, CRC Press

VINCE-PRUE, D. (1975). *Photoperiodism in Plants*. London, McGraw-Hill

VINCE-PRUE, D. and LUMSDEN, P.J. (1985). Photoperiodism: time measurement and photoperception. *Report of the Glasshouse Crops Research Institute for 1984*, pp. 35–47

WELLENSIEK, S.J. (1969). *Silene armeria* L. In *The Induction of Flowering* (L. T. Evans, Ed.), pp. 350–363. Melbourne, Macmillan

WILKINS, H.F. (1980). Easter lilies. In *Introduction to Floriculture* (R.A. Larson, Ed.),. pp. 327–352. New York, Academic Press

ZEEVAART, J.A.D. (1969a). *Perilla*. In *The Induction of Flowering* (L.T. Evans, Ed.), pp. 116–155. Melbourne, Macmillan

ZEEVAART, J.A.D. (1969b). *Bryophyllum*. In *The Induction of Flowering* (L.T. Evans, Ed.), pp. 435–456. Melbourne, Macmillan

15

EFFECTS OF ILLUMINANCE ON FLOWERING IN LONG- AND SHORT-DAY GRAIN LEGUMES: A REAPPRAISAL AND UNIFYING MODEL

R.J. SUMMERFIELD and E.H. ROBERTS
University of Reading, Department of Agriculture, Plant Environment Laboratory, Reading, UK

Introduction

Growing seasons, during which environmental conditions favour the accumulation of dry-matter in a crop as a whole, are determined by climate. Crop development must be such that its growth cycle can fit into those constraints imposed by, for example, extremely cold or warm temperatures and the seasonal availability of water (Bunting, 1975). With grain legumes, timely flowering of both the botanically indeterminate forms (the most common growth habit) and those that are determinate has important consequences for both relative yield and date of harvest (Summerfield and Wien, 1980). Responses to two environmental factors—photoperiod and mean temperature—modulate rates of progress towards flowering in the short-day legumes; and together with responses to vernalization the same factors dictate the climatic domains to which long-day legumes are best adapted (Summerfield and Roberts, 1985a). Relative responsiveness to each of this trio of factors is strongly correlated with taxonomic grouping and with climatic conditions prevalent in the various regions wherein the legumes have their origin (*Table 15.1*).

Flowering of the grain legumes is, in general, notoriously sensitive to photothermal conditions so that the durations of the pre-flowering periods vary enormously between genotypes depending on location and date of planting. Breeders of grain legumes are seeking to exploit this plasticity not only in releasing to farmers genotypes well-adapted to particular environmental niches but also to help in their crossing programmes—e.g., by manipulating dates of sowing or by extending natural day-lengths with artificial lights to promote synchronous flowering of exotic and local germplasm (e.g. Sethi *et al.*, 1981; Goldsworthy, 1982; Summerfield and Roberts, 1985a). This chapter will consider just one aspect of photoperiodism—that of responsiveness to dim light at dawn and dusk. The implications of the conclusions from this work for the interpretation of photoperiodic responses in natural environments and for the conduct of breeding programmes is then discussed.

Species of grain legume examined

Table 15.1 summarizes the photo-thermal and vernalization responses of flowering in the principal grain legume crops. Two species from each of the two obvious major groups, short-day species unresponsive to vernalization and long-day species sensitive

Table 15.1 PHOTO-THERMAL RESPONSES OF THE MAJOR SPECIES OF GRAIN LEGUMES IN RELATION TO THEIR CENTRES AND LATITUDES OF ORIGIN (COMPILED FROM SMARTT AND HYMOWITZ (1985) AND NUMEROUS OTHER SOURCES)

Species	Centre and latitude of origin	Photoperiodic response†					Vernalization response†		Flowering sooner in response to warmer air temperature‡			
		Short day		DN	Long day				By day	By night	Mean	Constant
		O	Q		O	Q	O	Q				
Pisum sativum	Asia/Mediterranean 30–45°N			*		*		*		*	*	*
Glycine max	NE China 34–40°N		*	*					*	*	*	*
Cicer arietinum	Caucasus and/or Asia Minor 30–45°N			*		*		*	*	*	*	*
Lens culinaris	E Mediterranean/ W Iran 30–40°N			*		*		*			*	*
Lupinus (European spp.)	Mediterranean 30–45°N			*		*		*			*	
Vicia faba	E Mediterranean/ Turkey 30—40°N			*		*		*			*	*
Arachis hypogaea	S Bolivia/ N Argentina 20–25°S			*							*	*
Phaseolus lunatus	Mexico/Guatemala and Peru? 15–25°N		*	*					*	*	*	*
Phaseolus vulgaris	5–15°S?		*	*					*	*	*	*
Vigna mungo/radiata	India 10–25°N	*		*						*		*
Vigna unguiculata	Africa/India 10–25°N	*		*						*	*	*
Cajanus cajan	India 10–25°N	*		*							*	
Psophocarpus tetragonolobus	Papua New Guinea? 4–10°S	*		*							*	

† O and Q denote obligate and quantitative responses, respectively; DN denotes 'day-length-neutral' (short days usually 12 h duration, or less, and long days usually 14–16 h, or longer; day-length neutral rating based on responses in photoperiods from 4–24 h duration in different experiments).
‡ Where day–night temperatures have not been combined factorially it is possible only to describe flowering responses in terms of a range of weighted mean temperatures of the diurnal fluctuations investigated. Constant temperatures refer to studies without a diurnally changing thermal regime.

to vernalization are to be considered here. *Glycine max* (soyabean) and *Phaseolus vulgaris* (common bean) represent the first group, and *Cicer arietinum* (chickpea) and *Lens culinaris* (lentil) represent the second.

SOYABEAN (*GLYCINE MAX*)

Though primarily a crop of temperate regions and intermediate elevations in the tropics, soyabeans are now cultivated in a remarkably diverse range of climates: from the equator to latitudes 55 °N or S and at altitudes that range from below sea level to about 2000 m (Whigham, 1983). The timing of developmental events, particularly the initiation of floral primordia and their subsequent expansion into open flowers, differs markedly throughout this wide range of environments depending on the genotype grown and the date on which it is planted. Flowers may appear as early as 25 days after sowing or not until after 50–60 days, or much later (Carlson, 1973).

Soyabeans are one of the classical short-day plants (SDP); some genotypes respond as quantitative SDP, others as qualitative SDP. Vast amounts of research data have been published on the photoperiodic regulation of flower initiation in soyabeans, and several reviews of this topic have appeared during the past 50 years (*see* Summerfield and Roberts, 1985b; Hume *et al.*, 1985).

COMMON BEAN (*PHASEOLUS VULGARIS*)

Common beans are the most widely grown of the four species of *Phaseolus* which are prominent as cultivated food crops in the Old and New World (Laing *et al.*, 1983). Indeterminate, prostrate or semi-climbing, heavily branched forms (land-races exploited in subsistence cultivation at sparse densities and usually involving inter-cropping with maize in the warmer regions) are most common in the major germplasm collections. At the other extreme, determinate, erect forms with few branches are cultivated as sole crops in temperate regions, notably in the USA and Europe (Evans, 1980; Adams *et al.*, 1985). Indeterminate, ancestral forms are often strongly responsive to photoperiod and react in a manner typical of quantitative SDP; those cultivars developed in temperate zones can be far less sensitive (Summerfield and Roberts, 1985c). Genotypes may come into flower after fewer than 30 days from sowing or not until at least 20–30 days later—depending on where and when they are grown.

CHICKPEA (*CICER ARIETINUM*)

Chickpeas are cultivated almost exclusively on residual soil moisture during the post-rainy seasons of subtropical winters, or during the spring and summer months in the northern hemisphere (Smithson *et al.*, 1985). There are two different 'types' with, perhaps, different centres of evolution and diversity (Ramanujam, 1976), which are grown in, and recognized to be best-adapted to, different regions. The so-called 'desi' types constitute about 80% of world production and are confined to the Indian subcontinent, Ethiopia, Mexico and Iran. They have relatively small, angular seeds, a short, sometimes prostrate habit, and small leaflets on anthocyanin-pigmented stems. In contrast, the 'kabuli' (or garbanzo) types account entirely for the crops of

Afghanistan through West Asia to Northern Africa, Southern Europe and the Americas. These types have relatively large, rounded seeds, a relatively tall and upright habit, and large leaflets on stems seldom pigmented with anthocyanins.

Many genotypes, and perhaps the kabuli types especially, are responsive to vernalization; some may have a juvenile phase and the majority respond to photoperiod in a manner typical of quantitative long-day plants (LDP)—so that crops may come into flower approximately 30–70 days from sowing in different regions and growing seasons (Summerfield and Roberts, 1985d).

LENTIL (*LENS CULINARIS*)

Lentils were one of the first grain legume crops to be domesticated—in the Fertile Crescent of West Asia—and had been widely disseminated throughout the Mediterranean region, Asia and Europe by the Bronze age (Cubero, 1981). As in chickpea, has proved useful for breeders and others to divide lentil germplasm into two groups based on seed size and various morphological characters. The so-called *macrosperma* types—relatively tall, with large seeds and leaflets, and vegetative structures seldom pigmented with anthocyanins—are found mainly in the Mediterranean region and New World; whereas the *microsperma* types—shorter, with smaller seeds and leaflets, and commonly with pigmented stems—predominate in the Indian subcontinent and the Near East.

The crop is normally sown after autumn rains in the Mediterranean region, or after monsoon rains in India and Pakistan; it is confined to higher elevations in Ethiopia and Mexico and is grown during the springtime months in Iran and Turkey (Summerfield *et al.*, 1982). Many lentil genotypes are responsive to vernalization; a juvenile phase is suspected in others, and most are quantitative LDP (Summerfield *et al.*, 1985a). Inappropriate photoperiod response has limited the introduction of Mediterranean accessions into India—where most of the world's lentils are grown—thus restricting the genetic base (and so the rate of progress by breeding) of material cultivated in that country (Erskine and Hawtin, 1983). As in those legumes responding to photoperiod as SDP, a relaxation of the photoperiodic modulation of flowering in lentil is seen to represent one component of broadening the latitudinal adaptation of the crop—as, for example, in the movement of *Phaseolus* spp. to Europe from the Americas (Evans, 1976).

Responsiveness to dim light

In photoperiodism, a plant must discriminate between day and night, measure the duration of one or both, and in response control some process such as flowering (Salisbury, 1981). In natural environments, the transition to and from darkness is not abrupt, but occurs through a gradually changing irradiance during twilight. Hughes *et al.* (1984) and also Lumsden and Vince-Prue (1984) have considered this problem recently and have concluded that the demarcation between day and night, as perceived by plants, is most likely to be signalled by a particular value of irradiance rather than by a change in spectral quality.

At what point do plants begin to respond to darkness or to light at dawn? Vince-Prue (1975) has considered these questions for plants in general; she concluded that little is known about the significance of responsiveness to dim light, in crops or naturalized floras, and especially in LDP. But, in three of the four species of grain legumes considered here, previous researchers have concluded that genotypes within species differ in their sensitivity to small values of illuminance such as those which prevail during twilight, and that these differences could be significant components of the adaptation of each species to contrasting geographical locations, as for example in soyabean (Borthwick and Parker, 1938; Yoshida, 1952; Takimoto and Ikeda, 1961; Major and Johnson, 1974); in common bean (Duarte, 1976); and in chickpea (ICRISAT, 1981; Sethi *et al.*, 1981).

Perspective

The work described here involves the interpretation of several experiments in which plants were subjected to natural short-days which were extended to long-days of at least 16 h by illumination provided by tungsten incandescent lamps. In each case, different plants were subjected to different values of illumination by growing them at different distances from the lamps along an illuminance gradient.

The work we discuss was carried out in different locations and in the field or in artificial climates, but in all cases the flowering responses of different genotypes within species were related to the illuminance of the artificial lighting used. Although measures of illuminance (in lux) weight the energy flux at different wavelengths according to the sensitivity of the human retina with maximum weighting as 555 nm, this does not present problems when plants are subjected to lamps of similar spectral emission characteristics—as they were in the comparisons made here. And so, even if the supplementary illumination had been measured as irradiance (in W m^{-2}), in which there is no weighting, similar conclusions would have been drawn.

Since we are dealing with photochemical reactions, it could be argued that the most appropriate measure of supplementary light would have been photon fluence rate (mol m^{-2} s^{-1}). Then, comparisons between different qualities of radiation, say between an artificial light source and natural daylight, would be valid in quantum terms. Such comparisons, however, can only be related quantitatively to a physiological reaction providing that three other pieces of information are available:

1. The photon spectral distribution (PSD) of the lamp.
2. The PSD of daylight.
3. The photon action spectrum of the physiological reaction under investigation, in this case the photoperiodic flowering response.

The first piece of information can be obtained easily; the second can be measured but is highly variable within the period of twilight (Hughes *et al.*, 1984)—i.e. at the time crucial in the present consideration; and the third piece of information is not yet available. Although it seems certain that phytochrome is involved in the photoperiodic flowering response, its role is not clear; there is evidence too that additional pigments may also play a part and yet others, such as chlorophyll, probably interfere with absorption by the active pigment(s) and therefore with the action spectrum (e.g. Hughes *et al.*, 1984; Vince-Prue, 1983a).

It follows from these arguments that when experiments are carried out in which physiological effects of different irradiance values or photon fluence rates of artificial light are compared, there is no way of translating these values precisely into equivalent values of natural daylight, and especially during twilight when there are rapid changes in spectral quality. In spite of this frustrating difficulty, it seems unlikely that large errors will be a penalty of using data obtained from experiments involving artificial light to estimate day-length in the field as perceived by plants. This is because although considerable changes in PSD occur during twilight, changes in log photon fluence rates also occur rapidly (*see Figure 15.8*); and although changes in fluence rate at different wavelengths are not necessarily synchronized, they are never far out-of-phase (Hughes *et al.*, 1984). Whatever measure of radiation is used for artificial light (illuminance, irradiance or photon fluence rate), none is ideal for concluding the day-length perceived by plants in the field. On the other hand, whichever measure of radiation is used, the errors are likely to be small because of the rapid changes at all wavelengths during twilight and because any lack of synchrony in these changes is small. For these reasons, and since the results of all authors we consider here were all measured in lux or foot candles, we will, for the most part, discuss the data in terms of illuminance.

Illuminance gradients

Irrespective of the species involved, genotypes have been evaluated by growing them at increasing distances from a row of lights along an illuminance gradient. Their times to flowering (days from sowing or emergence; f) have then been related to illuminance. Major and Johnson (1974), for example, used a row of 150 W incandescent floodlights suspended 1.5 m above their plots to create a gradient from 100 to 2 lux to test ten genotypes of soyabean of contrasting maturity. The lamps remained lit throughout their investigation (i.e. a photoperiod of 24 h). Quartets of brighter (300 W) incandescent lamps, suspended 3 m above the ground, were employed by Duarte (1976) to give a similar illuminance range (from about 90 to under 1 lux) for 18 h in each diurnal cycle. She evaluated 278 common bean genotypes of contrasting growth habit and recognized as either 'temperate' or 'tropical' in their adaptation. With chickpea, researchers in India (ICRISAT, 1981) suspended two 1000 W incandescent bulbs at 1.5 m above the ground to test the responses of four genotypes—early, medium and late-flowering at Hyderabad (17 °N)—along a gradient from 270 to under 1 lux applied as a 24 h photoperiod. Summerfield *et al.* (1984) created an illuminance gradient in a glasshouse by suspending two 300 W incandescent bulbs 1 m above a growing bench. They evaluated the responses of six genotypes of lentil of diverse origin at illuminance values from 2000 to under 40 lux, the lamps being lit for 16 h during each diurnal cycle. In each of these four investigations, as expected, illuminance decreased geometrically as distance from the light source increased, as predicted by the Inverse Square Law: Illuminance (I) is inversely proportional to the square of the distance (d) from a point source of light with radiant emittance E (Bickford and Dunn, 1972):

$$I = E/d^2 \tag{15.1}$$

Algebraic manipulation of Equation 15.1 gives:

$$1/I^{0.5} = d/E^{0.5} \tag{15.2}$$

As a typical example, we show in *Figure 15.1* our recalculations involving the data of Duarte (1976).

Experiments in which short-days in natural daylight have been extended to long days using tungsten incandescent lights, and with plants grown along an illuminance gradient from those lights, have prompted conclusions such as 'there was no apparent

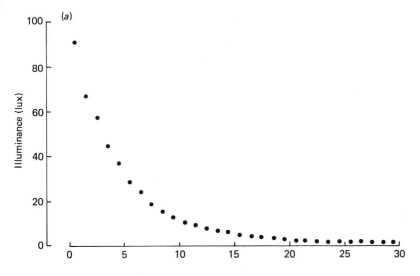

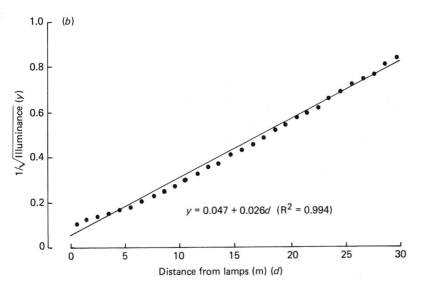

Figure 15.1 (*a*) Relation between illuminance (lux) and distance (*m*) from a series of quartets of 300 W incandescent bulbs spaced 7 m apart and 3 m above the ground; and (*b*) the same data replotted to show the relation between 1/√illuminance and distance from the lights (calculated from Duarte, 1976; each point is the mean of 14 values across the plots at each distance from the lamps, i.e. seven values with the photocell orientated horizontally and seven values with it held vertically).

threshold light intensity for delaying flowering [of soyabeans] ... sensitivity [to illuminance] appeared to be greater for the adapted cultivars than for the unadapted ones' (Major and Johnson, 1974); 'sensitivity of the [chickpea] cultivars to decreasing light intensity seemed to be related to their duration to flower in natural [short] day-lengths .... The critical light intensity thus seems to be higher for cultivars of late duration than for early cultivars' (ICRISAT, 1981); and 'most of the sensitive lines [to photoperiod] evaluated showed a response only above 14 lux ... [but some common beans] may be responsive to light intensities less than 14 lux, showing a continuous decrease in days to flowering out to 26 m [about 1.5 lux] from the lamps' (Duarte, 1976). Notwithstanding these original interpretations, an alternative explanation is considered below which might serve as a basis for a unifying model for these three species, and also for lentils. It is suggested that the differences in times to flowering observed along the gradients are not due to differences in sensitivity to irradiance or photon fluence rate, but are an inevitable consequence of differences in photoperiod sensitivity (i.e. relative differences in time to flower in two contrasting photoperiods).

Illuminance and photoperiodic responsiveness

Although the convenient linear relation between the square root of the inverse of illuminance and distance from the lamps (*Figure 15.1(b)*) has been used elsewhere in studies with grain legumes (e.g. Major and Johnson, 1974), there is no reason why photoperiodic phenomena should be related to the inverse square of illuminance or irradiance. With photochemical reactions (e.g. the exposure of film in a camera) and in photobiological processes (e.g. photoperiodism and photomorphogenesis), responses commonly seem to relate simply to the logarithm of irradiance or logarithm of photon fluence rate, and certainly such a relation is more plausible biologically (Withrow, 1959).

In both SD and LD grain legumes it is now known that day-length is related more simply to their rate of progress towards flowering ($1/f$) than to time to flowering (f), since in the former case the relation is linear (e.g. Hadley *et al.*, 1983 for soyabean and common bean; Roberts *et al.*, 1985 for chickpea; and Summerfield *et al.*, 1985b for lentil). Thus it seems sensible to express data in these terms and so investigate relations between $1/f$ and log illuminance, in order to expose any effects of illuminance on flowering in the clearest way.

We now consider the relations between log illuminance and rates of progress towards flowering which might be predicted when plants differing inherently in their photoperiod sensitivity are grown in experiments in which short natural day-lengths are extended by light of different illuminance. *Figure 15.2(a)* shows the responses predicted for quantitative LDP and quantitative SDP which, for simplicity, are assumed to have the same threshold (I_T) and saturation (I_S) illuminance values, respectively. In quantitative LDP the rate of progress towards flowering will be increased when relatively short natural days are extended by artificial illumination. Conversely, in quantitative SDP, the rate of progress towards flowering will be decreased when relatively short natural days are extended. The illuminance needed to saturate the photoperiodic response (I_S) can be defined in this type of experiment as: 'that illuminance above which there is no significant decrease (in LDP) or increase (in SDP) in the time taken to flower'. The threshold illuminance (I_T) we consider to be 'that illuminance below which there is no further significant delay (in LDP) or hastening (in SDP) in time to flowering'.

For species endowed with an obligate response to photoperiod (*Figure 15.2(b)*), providing the artificial light extends the natural day-length beyond the critical photoperiod, once saturation illuminance has been reached flowering will be delayed indefinitely in SDP ($1/f = 0$), whereas in LDP time to flowering will be after an irreducible minimum time ($1/f = a$ maximum but finite value). Conversely, below the threshold illuminance, the flowering of an obligate LDP will be delayed indefinitely ($1/$

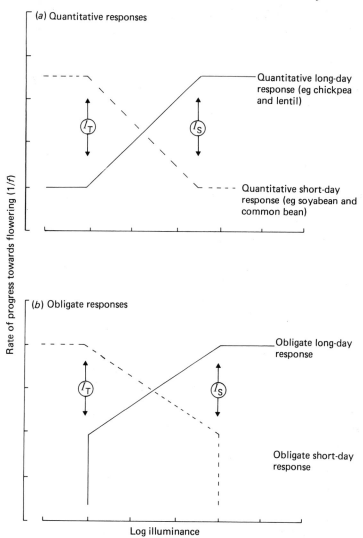

Figure 15.2   Schematic representations to illustrate the relations between log illuminance and rates of progress towards flowering ($1/f$) predicted for (*a*) quantitative long- (———) or short-day (– – –) species; and (*b*) obligate long-(———) or short- (– – –) day species in experiments in which relatively short days are extended by supplementary illumination of various illuminance values. I_T and I_S denote threshold and saturation illuminance values, respectively (*see* text). (Reproduced from Summerfield *et al.* (1984) by kind permission of authors and publishers.)

$f = 0$); whereas in SDP (and assuming the natural photoperiod is shorter than the critical value) flowers will first appear after an irreducible minimum duration ($1/f = a$ maximum but finite value).

Thus, these relations predict a change in slope for both SDP and LDP at saturation illuminance; in SDP the direction of such changes will depend on whether the genotype has a quantitative or obligate response, but it will always be in the same direction for both obligate and quantitative LDP. The converse applies at the threshold illuminance.

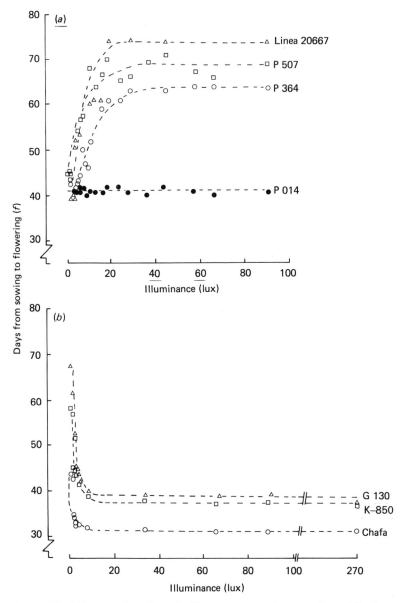

Figure 15.3 (*a*) Days to flowering (*f*) of four genotypes of common bean defined as insensitive (PO14; ●); or slightly (P364; ○), moderately (P507; □) or acutely (Linea 20667; △) sensitive to photoperiod when grown along an illuminance gradient (calculated from data in Duarte, 1976). (*b*) As in (*a*) for three genotypes of chickpea relatively early (Chafa; ○), medium (K-850; □) or late (G130; △) flowering at Hyderabad (17°N), India (calculated from data in ICRISAT, 1981). All broken lines have been fitted by eye to illustrate trends.

Model appraisal

The model illustrated in *Figure 15.2(a)* has been validated elsewhere for lentil (Summerfield *et al.*, 1984) and soyabean (Summerfield *et al.*, 1985c). It can now be evaluated further using data for common bean (Duarte, 1976) and chickpea (ICRI-SAT, 1981). Replots of the original data, where *f* was related to illuminance, are shown in *Figure 15.3* for each of four genotypes of common bean (*Figure 15.3(a)*) and three genotypes of chickpea (*Figure 15.3(b)*) selected, in both cases, to illustrate the responses of materials defined as relatively insensitive or sensitive to photoperiod. Then *Figure 15.4* shows the responses of these seven genotypes in terms of their

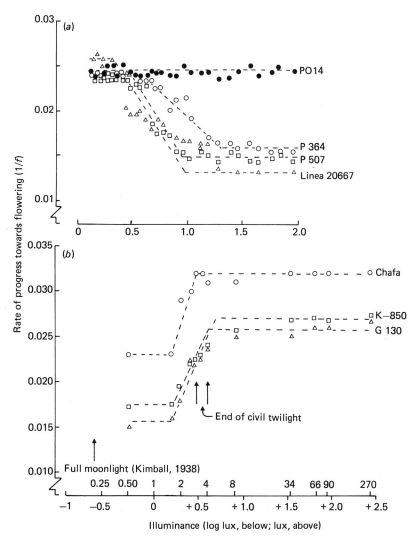

Figure 15.4 Replots of data shown in *Figure 15.3(a)* to expose the relations between rates of progress towards flowering (1/*f*) and log illuminance for four genotypes of common bean. (*b*) As in (*a*) for three genotypes of chickpea (*Figure 15.3(b)*). All broken lines have been fitted by eye; symbols as in *Figures 15.3(a)* and *15.3(b)*, respectively.

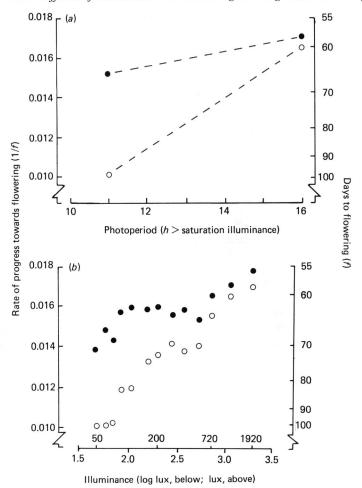

Figure 15.5   Relations between (*a*) photoperiod (*h* > saturation illuminance) and rate of progress towards flowering (1/*f*) for quantitative long-day lentil cultivars acutely (cv. Laird; ○) or slightly (cv. Precoz; ●) sensitive to day-length. (*b*) Log illuminance provided by supplementary lights extending natural days of 10–12 h to 16 h and rate of progress towards flowering (1/*f*) for lentil genotypes differing in photoperiod sensitivity (○, mean values for the more-sensitive genotypes cvs Laird, Tekoa, Chilean '78 and Brewer; ●, means for less sensitive genotypes cv. Precoz and accession LC 800 028). Data in (*a*) are from Summerfield *et al.* (1985b). (*b*) Reproduced from Summerfield *et al.* (1984), by kind permission of authors and publishers.

respective rates of progress towards flowering (1/*f*) at different values of log illuminance.

The general trends illustrated in *Figure 15.4* (as suggested by the broken lines) are strikingly similar to those predicted in *Figure 15.2* for both quantitative SDP and quantitative LDP. The threshold or saturation illuminance values for these species, or for soyabeans or lentils, cannot be determined unequivocally from the data available—but can be estimated as shown in *Table 15.2*.

Threshold illuminance values for the inhibition or promotion of flowering in short- and long-day species, respectively, vary widely (by two or three orders of magnitude), although between approximately 1 and 50 lux from tungsten-filament lamps is sufficient to counteract the effect of darkness in many species (Vince-Prue, 1975). Clearly, further work is required to determine these points more accurately in each of the species of grain legume considered here.

Table 15.2 ESTIMATES OF THE THRESHOLD (I_T) AND SATURATION (I_s) RANGES OF ILLUMINANCE (lux) PROVIDED BY TUNGSTEN INCANDESCENT LAMPS FOR PHOTOPERIODIC PERCEPTION IN EACH OF FOUR SPECIES OF GRAIN LEGUMES

Species of legume	*Estimated illuminance range*		*Source of information*
	I_T	I_s	
Soyabean	1–2	>20	Original data of Major and Johnson (1974) re-evaluated by Summerfield *et al.* (1984, 1985c)
Common bean	2–4	10–20	Original data of Duarte (1976) re-evaluated here (*Figures 15.3(a)* and *15.4(a)*)
Chickpea	1–2	3–8	Original data of ICRISAT (1981) re-evaluated here (*Figures 15.3(b)* and *15.4(b)*)
Lentil	60–70	720–1150	Summerfield *et al.* (1984)

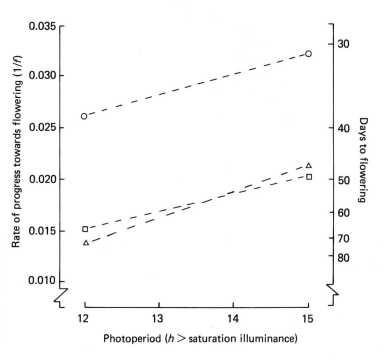

Figure 15.6 Relations between photoperiod (*h* > saturation illuminance) and rate of progress towards flowering (1/*f*) for three chickpea genotypes of different field maturity (ICRISAT, 1981) and sensitivity to photoperiod (Roberts *et al.*, 1985). Genotypes and symbols as in *Figures 15.3(b)* and *15.4(b)*.

Figures 15.4–15.7 taken together, consider the implications of the flowering responses of genotypes with different sensitivity to photoperiod but similar sensitivity to illuminance for both threshold and saturation values when grown along an illuminance gradient. This exercise leads to a simple hypothesis which explains the seemingly different responses to different illuminance values of lentils, chickpeas and soyabeans. Sufficient data are not yet available to allow an evaluation of this explanation for common beans.

Figure 15.5(a) shows typical times taken to flower for two quantitative LD lentil cultivars that differ in relative photoperiod sensitivity (the delay in time to flower in short-days is greater in one cultivar than the other), when grown in the same thermal regimen and when the illuminance during the photoperiod is greater than I_S (as, for example, in experiments in growth cabinets when darkness usually changes abruptly to maximum irradiance and *vice versa*). The more sensitive response ($\bigcirc$) is typical of that shown by cvs Laird, Tekoa and Chilean '78, while the less sensitive response ($\bullet$) typifies that of cv. Precoz and accession LC 800 028 (Summerfield *et al.*, 1985b). Whilst all genotypes came into flower after more-or-less the same time in 16 h days, those which are more sensitive to photoperiod flowered much later in shorter days.

If genotypes with sensitivity to photoperiod such as those shown in *Figure 15.5(a)* are grown along an illuminance gradient which extends natural short-days to long-days, and all of them have similar threshold and similar saturation illuminance values, it is inevitable that the relations between the illuminance of artifical light and days to flowering will be different: cultivars less sensitive to photoperiod will have the smaller gradients when the rate of progress towards flowering, $1/f$ (since the relation will then be linear), is plotted as a function of illuminance. *Figure 15.5(b)* confirms this relation for the six genotypes investigated hitherto (Summerfield *et al.*, 1984).

Figure 15.6 shows the time taken for three chickpea genotypes of different relative maturity in the field (well known and extensively used by researchers at ICRISAT) to come into flower in different photo-thermal regimens (Roberts *et al.*, 1985). When cultivars differing in this way are grown along an illuminance gradient of lighting used to extend a short-day (of about 12 h) to a long-day (24 h) (ICRISAT, 1981), and if all of them have similar respective threshold and saturation illuminance values, and since the gradients in *Figure 15.6* are similar, it would be expected that the gradients with respect to illuminance between threshold and saturation values would also be similar. This is shown to be the case in *Figure 15.4(b)*.

Finally, *Figure 15.7(a)* shows the times taken for soyabean genotypes of different USA Maturity Groups (MG) to flower when sown in May in Columbia, Missouri (39 °N), where natural day-lengths were close to 15 h 30 min (Francis, 1972), and when grown in 24 h days in the same location using artificial light of illuminance 20 lux (data calculated from Major and Johnson, 1974). Cultivars recognized as 'adapted' to the region (MG II–IV) are more sensitive to photoperiod than those from further north (MG I) or south (MG V). As with lentils and chickpeas it is once again inevitable that the most photoperiod-sensitive cultivars will also appear more sensitive to differences in illuminance when evaluated along an illuminance gradient, as *Figure 15.7(b)* confirms.

In summary, we suggest that our alternative model of the relation between illuminance and time to flowering in both quantitative long-day and quantitative short-day grain legumes (*Figure 15.2(a)*) provides a conceptually simpler and more plausible explanation of data previously interpreted in terms of differences in responsiveness to dim light. We suggest that within-species differences in sensitivity to illuminance, in terms of both threshold and saturation values, are probably smal

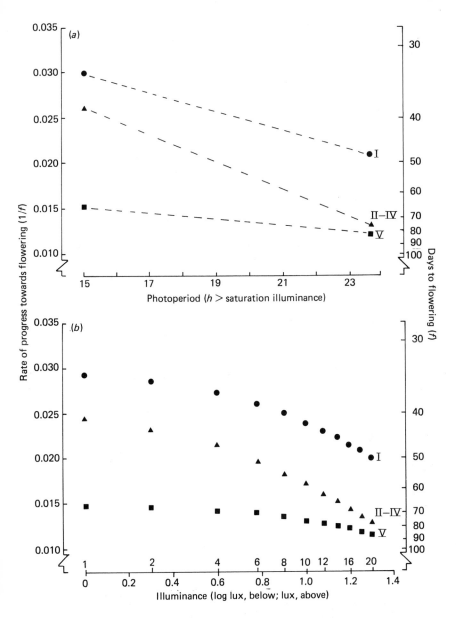

Figure 15.7 Relations between (*a*) photoperiod (*h* > saturation illuminance) and rate of progress towards flowering (1/*f*) for soyabean cultivars of different Maturity Groups; and (*b*) log illuminance and rate of progress towards flowering (1/*f*) for the same groups of cultivars grown along an illuminance gradient which extended natural days of about 15 h 30 min duration to 24 h (both relations recalculated from Major and Johnson, 1974). The symbols ●, ▲ and ■ denote average responses of 2, 6 and 2 cultivars from USA Maturity Groups I, II-IV and V, respectively.

in relation to the rapid changes of illuminance that occur during twilight (*Figure 15.8*); and so the perception of day-length does not vary markedly between genotypes within those species of grain legume considered here. Differences in genotypic responses, then, are due almost entirely to differences in response to day-length itself.

The range of illuminance from threshold to saturation appears to be about one order of magnitude in each of the species considered here (*Table 15.2*), though possibly less in chickpea. It seems therefore that there is some vagueness in timing which typically extends over a period of about 30 minutes of twilight in temperate latitudes (*Figure 15.8(b)*). This apparent lack of precision in timing need not affect the photoperiodic response since it seems probable that plants will integrate illuminance with time throughout this period—in an analagous manner to the integration of photoperiodic extensions at different illuminance values between threshold and saturation which occurred in the experiments described earlier. The relations in *Figure 15.2*, supported by those in *Figures 15.4(b), 15.5(b)* and *15.7(b)*, show linear responses to log illuminance between threshold and saturation, and the relation between time and log illuminance during twilight is also known to be linear (Hughes *et al.*, 1984). Accordingly, the appropriate single illuminance value which integrates between the threshold and saturation values, and which could be taken to mark the beginning and end of the photoperiod, could be calculated as follows:

$$I_D = 10^{(\log I_S + \log I_T)/2} \tag{15.3}$$

where I_D is that illuminance value during twilight which marks the beginning and end of the photoperiod, I_S is the saturation illuminance and I_T is the threshold illuminance.

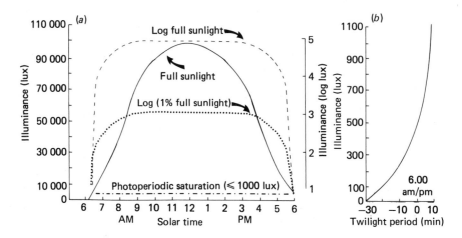

Figure 15.8 (*a*) Linear (——) and logarithmic (– – –) plots of sunlight illuminance on a horizontal surface for clear days at the spring and autumnal equinoxes typical of the mid latitudes; temporal trends in illuminance equivalent to 1% full sunlight (a heavily overcast sky), and the illuminance thought to more than saturate photoperiod responses in plants are also shown for comparison (. . . . and –·–·–, respectively). (*b*) Time course for twilight illuminance at dawn and dusk (0 = time of appearance/disappearance of edge of solar disc, respectively). (Both figures recalculated and redrawn, in part, from *A Kinetic Analysis of Photoperiodism: Photoperiodism and Related Phenomena in Plants and Animals* (R. B. Withrow, Ed.), Publication No. 55, American Association for the Advancement of Science (1959).)

However, before applying such estimations it is necessary to reiterate the difficulties in comparing illuminance values during twilight with the results from experiments using artificial light. Only approximate comparisons are possible because of insufficient information about the action spectra of photoperiodic responses. Nevertheless, in most species, including those discussed here, it is probable that the red wavelengths are most important, and in LDP far-red increases the effectiveness of red light (Vince-Prue, 1975). Considering this information, together with knowledge of the spectral energy distribution of incandescent tungsten lamps, which are rich in red and far-red (Bickford and Dunn, 1972), the spectral energy distribution of twilight (Hughes *et al.*, 1984), and the weighting of illuminance measurements centring on 555 nm, it seems probable that incandescent tungsten illumination is about twice as efficient as twilight with regard to photoperiodic phenomena when compared in terms of illuminance.

If this assertion is correct, to estimate illuminance values in natural environments which could be taken to mark the beginning and end of the photoperiod, I_D, the values shown in *Table 15.2* should first be doubled before Equation 15.3 is applied. Taking the mean I_S and I_T values for each species as a starting point, the calculated I_D values are: 11 lux for soyabean; 13 lux for common bean; 6 lux for chickpea and 490 lux for lentil.

In defining natural day-lengths it has been a common and convenient practice to assume that day-length includes civil twilight, which is defined to start in the morning and end in the evening when the true centre of the sun is 6° below the horizon (Kimball, 1938). Typically, this corresponds with an illuminance of 3 lux (Griffiths, 1976) or 4 lux (Vergara and Chang, 1976). A consideration of these values in conjunction with *Figure 15.8(b)* confirms that the inclusion of civil twilight in estimates of photoperiodic day-lengths seems to be justified for soyabean, common bean and chickpea. In the case of lentil, however, such a convention would appear to overestimate day-length. For an I_D value of 490 lux, examination of *Figure 15.8(b)* suggests that a reasonably accurate and convenient convention in lentil would be to consider that sunrise and sunset mark the beginning and end of the day. Whilst the much larger value of I_D for lentil (490 lux) compared with that for each of chickpea, soyabean and common bean (6–13 lux) may reflect a true difference between those species, the different durations of extended day-length used in the four original investigations (i.e. 16 h compared with 24, 24 and 18 h, respectively) may also have had important and confounding consequences. Since the threshold value of illuminance is often much smaller for night-break lighting than the critical values at dawn and dusk (Vince-Prue, 1975), the possibility remains that treatments which extend natural short-days to very long-days using artificial light will, in fact, have effects more compatible with those of night-break lighting rather than longer days *per se* (i.e. threshold illuminance values will be smaller than the critical values at dawn or dusk). This possibility has yet to be tested.

Even though threshold and saturation illuminance values for photoperiodic responses in these four species of grain legume typically differ by about an order of magnitude (*Table 15.2*), it has been argued earlier that this need not seriously affect the precision with which day-length is perceived by the plant. Another way in which the precision of perception might be affected is by weather-induced variations in illuminance during twilight (Salisbury, 1963). However, Hughes *et al.* (1984) have shown that in central England cloudiness has comparatively little effect on photon fluence rate and that the timing of day-length to a given rate is unlikely to be affected by weather conditions by more than about 10 minutes. Ten minute differences in photoperiod can have considerable effects on flowering—at least in tropical SDP

(Njoku, 1958; Roberts and Carpenter, 1962)—but in most crop species maximum photoperiodic response requires several cycles. In lentil, for example, it has recently been shown in three genotypes of diverse origin that, once the plants have become sensitive to photoperiod, then between 12 and 20 cycles of 16h days (which are strongly inductive photoperiods) are required to induce flowering (Roberts *et al.*, 1986). Furthermore, the inductiveness of successive cycles of different durations appear to be integrated in a simple manner. The effect of an occasional cloudy morning or evening will therefore be minimized because of this integration of cycle-duration over a number of cycles.

A comparative investigation, with species and genotypes known to differ in their sensitivity to photoperiod, and including illuminance values extending beyond the ranges used previously (*Figures 15.3–15.5* and *15.7*) might well prove definitive, and we plan such a study on a wide range of grain legumes in the near future. It is important that subsequent studies are designed to include natural day-length controls (and, perhaps, even abrupt transitions from light into complete darkness) in order to identify threshold illuminance values more precisely. Ideally, experiments should also be designed to differentiate between threshold and saturation irradiance values separately at dawn and dusk, since there is some evidence that these may be different (Vince-Prue, 1981; 1983a). It would also be desirable to include both obligate long- and short-day genotypes of appropriate species (in order to see if their response conforms to the model proposed in *Figure 15.2(b)*), providing that such genotypes had been identified reliably beforehand. Then again, if the extremes of illuminance are extended, as we suggest, it will be important to separate photoperiodic from photosynthetic effects at locations close to the lamps since photoperiodic induction in long-day plants may involve photosynthetic effects too (Vince-Prue, 1983b).

Practical implications

There are important practical implications of the responses described earlier for artificial manipulations of photoperiod either in controlled environments or in the field. It is well known that breeding programmes can be accelerated if generation times can be shortened (for chickpeas *see* Sethi *et al.*, 1981). Equally well known is the fact that natural short photoperiods can be extended by suspending incandescent lamps above the crop so that day-lengths characteristic of a range of latitudes can be imposed at a single location (Summerfield *et al.*, 1979). Obviously, such lighting schemes should be designed so that plot areas are illuminated as uniformly as possible. Although complete uniformity is difficult to achieve in practice, what is now clear is that variations in illuminance of day extension light should not affect the results of trials designed to investigate the relative sensitivity of genotypes to photoperiod *per se* providing the minimum illuminance is greater than the saturation value.

Alternatively, breeders may wish their parental lines to flower sequentially when planted on the same date in one location in order to spread the burden of effecting crosses and to facilitate crosses between early and late flowering parents. This is likely to be especially important in a crop like lentils where earlier-formed flowers are known to be far more suitable for successful crosses than those appearing later—for physiological reasons as well as climatological trends such as progressively hotter and drier air (Mera and Erskine, 1982; Summerfield *et al.*, 1985a). Seeding plants along an illuminance gradient may be one way to improve the flexibility, and so the efficiency, of such breeding programmes.

Acknowledgements

We thank the Overseas Development Administration of the UK Foreign and Commonwealth Office, the USDA-ARS (Western Region) and the Washington and Idaho Dry Pea and Lentil Commissions for their generous financial support. The constructive comments of our colleagues at ICARDA, Syria and at ICRISAT, India, and the engineering, technical and secretarial assistance of Messrs D. Dickinson, A.C. Richardson, K. Chivers, S. Gill, M. Craig, R.W. Short, Miss C. Chadwick, Mrs E. Waldher and Mrs. J. Allison are gratefully acknowledged.

References

ADAMS, M.W., COYNE, D.P., DAVIS, J.H.C., GRAHAM, P.H. and FRANCIS, C.A. (1985). Common bean (*Phaseolus vulgaris* L.). In *Grain Legume Crops* (R.J. Summerfield and E.H. Roberts, Eds), pp. 433–474. London, Collins

BICKFORD, E.D. and DUNN, S. (1972). *Lighting for Plant Growth*. Kent, Ohio, The Kent State University Press

BORTHWICK, H.A. and PARKER, M.W. (1938). Photoperiodic perception in Biloxi soybeans. *Botanical Gazette*, **100**, 374–387

BUNTING, A.H. (1975). Time, phenology and the yield of crops. *Weather*, **30**, 312–325

CARLSON, J.B. (1973). Morphology. In *Soybeans: Improvement, Production and Uses* (B.E. Caldwell, Ed.), pp. 17–95. Madison, Wisconsin, American Society of Agronomy

CUBERO, J.I. (1981). Origin, taxonomy and domestication. In *Lentils* (C. Webb and G.C. Hawtin, Eds), pp. 15–38. Farnham Royal, Commonwealth Agricultural Bureaux

DUARTE, M.T.M. (1976). Screening for photoperiod response in dry beans (*Phaseolus vulgaris* L.). *Centro Internacional de Agricultura Tropical (CIAT) Research Report*, pp. 92. Cali, Colombia

ERSKINE, W. and HAWTIN, G.C. (1983). Pre-breeding in faba beans and lentils. *Genetika*, **15**, 287–294

EVANS, A.M. (1976). Beans. In *Evolution of Crop Plants* (N.W. Simmonds, Ed.), pp. 168–172. London, Longman

EVANS, A.M. (1980). Structure, variation, evolution and classification in *Phaseolus*. In *Advances in Legume Science* (R.J. Summerfield and A.H. Bunting, Eds), pp. 337–348, London, HMSO

FRANCIS, C.A. (1972). *Natural Daylengths for Photoperiod-Sensitive Plants*. Centro Internacional de Agricultura Tropical Technical Bulletin No. 2, pp. 32, Cali, Colombia

GOLDSWORTHY, P.R. (1982). Objectives and achievements in the improvement of grain legumes. *Proceedings of the Nutrition Society*, **41**, 27–39

GRIFFITHS, J.F. (1976). Sunrise, Sunset. *Weather*, **31**, 427–429

HADLEY, P., SUMMERFIELD, R.J. and ROBERTS, E.H. (1983). Effects of temperature and photoperiod on reproductive development of selected grain legume crops. In *Temperate Legumes: Physiology, Genetics and Nodulation* (D. Gareth Jones and D.R. Davies, Eds), pp. 19–41. London, Pitmans

HUGHES, J.E., MORGAN, D.C., LAMBTON, P.A., BLACK, C.R. and SMITH, H. (1984). Photoperiodic time signals during twilight. *Plant, Cell and Environment*, **7**, 269–277

HUME, D.J., SHANMUGASUNDARAM, S. and BEVERSDORF, W.D. (1985). Soyabean (*Gly-*

cine max (L.) Merrill). In *Grain Legume Crops* (R.J. Summerfield and E.H. Roberts, Eds), pp. 391–432. London, Collins

ICRISAT (1981). Chickpea physiology. In *ICRISAT Annual Report 1979/80*, pp. 79–81. Patancheru, India, ICRISAT

KIMBALL, H.H. (1938). Duration and intensity of twilight. *Monthly Weather Review*, **66**, 279–286

LAING, D.R., KRETCHMER, P.J., ZULUAGA, S. and JONES, P.G. (1983). Field Bean. In *Potential Productivity of Field Crops Under Different Environments* (S. Yoshida, Ed.), pp. 228–248. Manila, Philippines, IRRI

LUMSDEN, P.J. and VINCE-PRUE, D. (1984). The perception of dusk signals in photoperiodic time measurement. *Physiologia Plantarum*, **60**, 427–432

MAJOR, D.J. and JOHNSON, D.R. (1974). Effects of light intensity on development of field-grown soybeans. *Crop Science*, **14**, 839–841

MERA, M.K. and ERSKINE, W. (1982). Crossing techniques for lentil under field conditions. *Lens*, **9**, 11–15

NJOKU, E. (1958). The photoperiodic response of some Nigerian plants. *Journal of the West African Science Association*, **4**, 99–111

RAMANUJAM, S. (1976). Chickpea (*Cicer arietinum*) Leguminosae—Papilonate. In *Evolution of Crop Plants* (N.W. Simmonds, Ed.), pp. 157–159. London, Longman

ROBERTS, E.H. and CARPENTER, A.J. (1962). Flowering response of rice to different photoperiods of uniform daily amounts of light radiation. *Nature (London)*, **196**, 1077–1078

ROBERTS, E.H., HADLEY, P. and SUMMERFIELD, R.J. (1985). Effects of temperature and photoperiod on flowering in chickpeas (*Cicer arietinum*). *Annals of Botany*, **55**, 881–892

ROBERTS, E.H., SUMMERFIELD, R.J., MUEHLBAUER, F.J. and SHORT, R.W. (1986). Flowering in lentil (*Lens culinaris* Medic.); The duration of the photoperiodic inductive phase as a function of accumulated day-length above the critical photoperiod. *Annals of Botany*, **58**, 235–248

SALISBURY, F.B. (1963). *The Flowering Process*. New York, Pergamon Press

SALISBURY, F.B. (1981). Responses to photoperiod. In *Physiological Plant Ecology, Volume 1, Responses to the Physical Environment* (O.L. Lange, P.S. Nobel, C.B. Osmond and H. Ziegler, Eds), pp. 135–168. New York, Springer-Verlag

SETHI, S.C., BYTH, D.E., GOWDA, C.L.L. and GREEN, J.M. (1981). Photoperiodic response and accelerated generation turn-over in chickpea. *Field Crops Research*, **4**, 215–225

SMARTT, J. and HYMOWITZ, T. (1985). Domestication and evolution of grain legumes. In *Grain Legume Crops* (R.J. Summerfield and E.H. Roberts, Eds), pp. 37–72. London, Collins

SMITHSON, J.B., THOMPSON, J.A. and SUMMERFIELD, R.J. (1985). Chickpea (*Cicer arietinum* L.). In *Grain Legume Crops* (R.J. Summerfield and E.H. Roberts, Eds), pp. 312–390. London, Collins

SUMMERFIELD, R.J. and ROBERTS, E.H. (1985a). Grain legume species of significant importance in world agriculture. In *A Handbook of Flowering* (A.H. Halevy, Ed.), pp. 61–73. Boca Raton, Florida, CRC Press

SUMMERFIELD, R.J. and ROBERTS, E.H. (1985b). *Glycine max*. In *A Handbook of Flowering* (A.H. Halevy, Ed.), pp. 100–117. Boca Raton, Florida, CRC Press

SUMMERFIELD, R.J. and ROBERTS, E.H. (1985c). *Phaseolus vulgaris*. In *A Handbook of Flowering* (A.H. Halevy, Ed.), pp. 139–148. Boca Raton, Florida, CRC Press

SUMMERFIELD, R.J. and ROBERTS, E.H., (1985d). *Cicer arietinum*. In *A Handbook of Flowering* (A.H. Halevy, Ed.), pp. 92–99. Boca Raton, Florida, CRC Press

SUMMERFIELD, R.J. and WIEN, H.C. (1980). Effects of photoperiod and air temperature on growth and yield of economic legumes. In *Advances in Legume Science* (R.J. Summerfield and A.H. Bunting, Eds), pp. 17–35. London, HMSO

SUMMERFIELD, R.J., MINCHIN, F.R. and WIEN, H.C. (1979). Screening for environmental adaptability in soyabean and cowpea: an improved strategy. *World Crops*, **31**, 21–23

SUMMERFIELD, R.J., MUEHLBAUER, F.J. and SHORT, R.W. (1982). Description and culture of lentils. *United States Dept Agriculture Production Research Report* No. 181, pp. 22

SUMMERFIELD, R.J., MUEHLBAUER, F.J. and ROBERTS, E.H. (1984). Controlled environments as an adjunct to field research on lentils (*Lens culinaris*). III. Photoperiodic lighting and consequences for flowering. *Experimental Agriculture*, **20**, 1–18

SUMMERFIELD, R.J., MUEHLBAUER, F.J. and ROBERTS, E.H. (1985a). *Lens culinaris*. In *A Handbook of Flowering* (A.H. Halevy, Ed.), pp. 118–124. Boca Raton, Florida, CRC Press

SUMMERFIELD, R.J., ROBERTS, E.H., ERSKINE, W. and ELLIS, R.H. (1985b). Effects of temperature and photoperiod on flowering in lentils (*Lens culinaris*). *Annals of Botany*, **56**, 659–671

SUMMERFIELD, R.J., SHANMUGASUNDARAM, S., ROBERTS, E.H. and HADLEY, P. (1985c). Adaptation of soybeans to photo-thermal environments and implications for screening germplasm. In *Soybean in Tropical and Subtropical Cropping Systems* (S. Shanmugasundaram and E.W. Sulzberger, Eds), pp. 333–352. Shanhua, Taiwan, AVRDC

TAKIMOTO, A. and IKEDA, K. (1961). Effect of twilight on photoperiodic induction in some short day plants. *Plant and Cell Physiology*, **2**, 213–229

VERGARA, B.S. and CHANG, T.T. (1976). *The Flowering Responses of the Rice Plant to Photoperiod*. Manila, Philippines, IRRI

VINCE-PRUE, D. (1975). *Photoperiodism in Plants*. London, McGraw-Hill

VINCE-PRUE, D. (1981). Daylight and photoperiodism. In *Plants and the Daylight Spectrum* (H. Smith, Ed.), pp. 223–242. London, Academic Press

VINCE-PRUE, D. (1983a). The perception of light–dark transitions. *Philosophical Transactions of the Royal Society, London, Series B.*, **303**, 523–536

VINCE-PRUE, D. (1983b). Photoperiodic control of plant reproduction. In *Strategies of Plant Reproduction* (W. Meudt, Ed.), pp. 73–98. St Albans, Granada Publishing

WHIGHAM, D.K. (1983). Soybean. In *Potential Productivity of Field Crops under Different Environments* (S. Yoshida, Ed.), pp. 205–226. Manila, Philippines, IRRI

WITHROW, R.B. (1959). A kinetic analysis of photoperiodism. In *Photoperiodism* (R.B. Withrow, Ed.), pp. 439–447. Washington, American Association for the Advancement of Science

YOSHIDA, S. (1952). Photoperiodic responses in soybean plants under long-day conditions with supplemental illumination of different intensities at night. *Proceedings of the Crop Science Society of Japan*, **21**, 127–128

16

THE GENETIC CONTROL OF DAY-LENGTH RESPONSE IN WHEAT

C.N. Law
Plant Breeding Institute, Cambridge, UK

Introduction

A comprehensive picture of the genetic control of day-length response in wheat is not yet available. Despite the ready access to a wide range of specially constructed genetic stocks in wheat, it is by no means certain that all the genes for day-length response have been identified and their chromosomal locations determined. Also, the description of the activities of those genes that have been identified has only just commenced (Scarth, Kirby and Law, 1985).

Conventional genetic analyses have provided a model based upon two dominant loci, *Ppd1* and *Ppd2*, for day-length insensitivity, with multiple alleles at both loci (Pugsley, 1966; Keim, Welsh and McConnell, 1973; Klaimi and Qualset, 1973). These findings have largely been confirmed from the applications of cytogenetic techniques and two homoeologous chromosomes 2D and 2B, suggested as carrying the genes *Ppd1* and *Ppd2* respectively, have been identified (Welsh *et al.*, 1973; Law, Sutka and Worland, 1978). Subsequent work has shown that these chromosomes do indeed carry single major genes affecting day-length response (Scarth and Law, 1983; Worland and Law, 1986). Chromosomes 2A, 3D, 4B, 6B and all the chromosomes of homoeologous group 1 have also been mentioned as having some influence on the response to day-length (Morrison, 1961; Kuspira and Unrau, 1957; Halloran and Boydell, 1967; Law and Scarth, 1984). Often these affects are ascribed to the action of modifiers but it is very likely that major genes are also involved.

In this chapter, the results of recent experiments into the genetics of day-length response using newly developed cytogenetic material are presented as well as work to describe the developmental events controlled by already identified major genes for day-length. The consequences that some of these genes have had and continue to have for the adaptation of wheat and their influence on characters of interest to the breeder are also considered.

Genetic analysis in wheat

In wheat, the identification of genes and their assignment to positions on chromosomes is aided to a great extent by specially developed cytogenetic stocks. These are of two types. Firstly, those where individual chromosomes have been lost or increased in dosage. These stocks are referred to as aneuploids and exist for each of the 21 different chromosomes of the hexaploid wheat, *Triticum aestivum* $(2n = 6x = 42)$ (Sears, 1954). Second, individual chromosomes have been transferred from one variety or related species and substituted for a homologous or closely related chromosome in a recipient variety. These substitution lines can be produced for each chromosome in turn so that 21 different lines can be produced between a recipient and donor variety. Several substitution sets covering a range of different varieties and related species have been produced.

The aneuploid lines permit an assessment of the effects of whole chromosomes. The substitution lines, on the other hand, reflect allelic differences between the substituted chromosome and its homologue in the recipient. They can therefore be used to identify individual genes and to determine their position on the chromosome map. The analytical resolution of the substitution line approach is increased greatly over more conventional genetic analyses because studies are carried out on material where the genetic background is held constant and segregation is confined to one chromosome only.

The use of aneuploids and substitution lines has developed over the years and well-tried and documented methods are available for analysing quantitative as well as qualitative characters (Law and Worland, 1973; Law, Snape and Worland, 1983). The application of some of these methods to the analysis of the genetics of day-length response provides the basis of much of the work described in this chapter.

The study of the Cappelle–Besostaya I chromosome substitution lines

Two varieties, Cappelle-Desprez and Besostaya I, were chosen to study the genetical control of day-length response as well as a range of other important characters. Cappelle-Desprez was bred in France in 1950 and was grown extensively throughout Western Europe for about 15 years. It is a winter wheat, responsive to vernalization and day-length. The second variety, Besostaya I, was bred in the USSR by the famous Russian wheat breeder, Lukyanenko, and was for many years the most widely grown winter wheat in the world. It is responsive to vernalization, although not to the same degree as Cappelle-Desprez, and is day-length insensitive.

The chromosome substitution lines were developed at the Plant Breeding Institute (PBI), Cambridge using Cappelle-Desprez as the recipient and Besostaya I as the donor parent. Twenty of the twenty-one possible single chromosome substitution lines, in which individual chromosomes of Cappelle-Desprez are replaced by their homologues from Besostaya I, have been produced. The remaining substitution line for the $5B^L$–$7B^L$ translocated chromosome is still being developed. The established substitution lines were grown in replicated field experiments in 1983, 1984 and 1985 and days to ear emergence recorded.

The results of the field experiments averaged over the three years and using the line × year interaction as error are summarized in *Table 16.1*. The lines were sown during the winter so that low temperatures would be anticipated to reduce differences due to genes influencing vernalization requirement. The effect of the short-days of winter and early spring, on the other hand, would be expected to accentuate the differences due to day-length genes. Alleles for insensitivity to day-length would confer earliness compared with alleles for sensitivity.

The relative insensitivity of Besostaya I compared with Cappelle-Desprez was evident in the field experiment, Besostaya I being on average 7 days earlier. Amongst

Table 16.1   AVERAGE DAYS TO EAR EMERGENCE FROM ARBITRARY DATES IN EACH OF THE YEARS 1983, 1984 AND 1985 OF SINGLE CHROMOSOME SUBSTITUTION LINES OF BESOSTAYA I INTO CAPPELLE-DESPREZ GROWN UNDER FIELD CONDITIONS FROM A WINTER SOWING

Chromosome	Average days to ear emergence	Difference from Cappelle-Desprez	Difference from Besostaya I
1A	10.44	+1.77*	+8.71**
1B	7.68	−0.99	+5.95**
1D	6.60	−2.07*	+4.87**
2A	8.21	−0.46	+6.48**
2B	8.09	−0.58	+6.36**
2D	5.47	−3.20**	+3.74*
3A	9.99	+1.32	+8.26***
3B	9.13	+0.46	+7.40**
3D	7.62	−1.05	+5.89***
4A	8.33	−0.34	+6.60***
4B	9.83	+1.16	+8.10***
4D	9.36	+0.69	+7.63**
5A	6.87	−1.80*	+5.14***
5D	9.79	+1.06	+8.06***
6A	8.92	+0.28	+7.19***
6B	9.80	+1.13	+8.07***
6D	2.30	−6.37***	+0.57
7A	9.77	+1.10	+8.04***
5B^S–7B^S	6.33	−2.34*	+4.60**
7D	8.52	−0.15	+6.79
Besostaya I	1.73	−6.94***	
Cappelle-Desprez	8.67		+6.94***

* P = 0.05–0.01; ** P = 0.01–0.001; *** P < 0.001.

the substitution lines, there were several that were significantly earlier than Cappelle-Desprez, but only two lines carrying chromosome 2D and 6D of Besostaya I respectively were indistinguishable or similar to Besostaya I. The other substitution lines, 1A, 1D, 5A and 5B^S–7B^S were only marginally earlier than Cappelle-Desprez. Chromosome 5A is known to be the location of the gene, *Vrnl*, for vernalization requirement (Law, Worland and Giorgi, 1976); the short-arm of 7B is also the site of *Vrn5* (Law, 1967); chromosomes 1A and 1D have been suggested as carrying genes sensitive both to vernalization and to day-length (Law and Scarth, 1984). The most likely explanation for these relatively small effects is therefore that they are due to *Vrn* genes, whose differences have not been entirely removed by the vernalizing temperatures experienced in these experiments. The effects of 2D and 6D are however, different. The striking effect of 2D is almost certainly due to the day-length gene, *Ppdl* previously located on this chromosome (Welsh *et al.*, 1973), but the major effect of 6D is new and there are no previous reports of this chromosome carrying either *Ppd* or *Vrn* genes.

As is evident from this experiment, it is not always easy to assign observed effects as being due to *Ppd* or *Vrn* genes, even though such 'winter-sown' experiments accentuate differences owing to day-length sensitive genes compared with those influencing vernalization requirement. However, a third category of gene, influencing development, independently of day-length and vernalization may confuse the analysis of such data even more. The presence or such genes on chromosomes 3A, 4B, 4D and 6B has recently been inferred by Hoogendoorn (1985) and a similar factor was located on the long-arm of chromosome 2B by Scarth and Law (1983). In the experiments described, it is not possible to distinguish such genes from those which are responsive to day-length and/or vernalization; the 6D chromosome effect cannot therefore be classified. An experiment using controlled short- and long-day treatments is required.

Such an experiment was carried out in 1985 with the Cappelle-Desprez/Besostaya I substitution lines in a specially constructed glasshouse, containing an automated trolley system which allowed the plants to be given long and short-day-lengths throughout their life-cycle. Before being placed in the glasshouse, all the plants were given 4 weeks of low temperature (5–8 °C) to satisfy partially the vernalization requirements of the recipient and donor varieties. The results for both day-lengths are presented in *Table 16.2* along with estimates of the interaction between the effect of day-length and the effect of substituting Besostaya I chromosomes into Cappelle-Desprez.

Under long-days the substitution lines for chromosomes 5A, 6A and 6D were significantly earlier and lines for 1A, 3A and 3D later than Cappelle-Desprez. Under

Table 16.2 TIME TO EAR EMERGENCE IN DAYS FOR THE CHROMOSOME SUBSTITUTION LINES OF BESOSTAYA I INTO CAPPELLE-DESPREZ, BESOSTAYA I AND CAPPELLE-DESPREZ GROWN UNDER SHORT AND LONG DAY-LENGTHS. THE SHORT DAY-LENGTH CONSISTED OF 8 H NATURAL DAYLIGHT AND THE LONG DAY-LENGTH, 8 H NATURAL DAYLIGHT + 16 H LOW-INTENSITY INCANDESCENT LIGHTING

Chromosome	Short days	Long days	Difference from Cappelle-Desprez		g
			Short days	Long days	
1A	149.8	137.3	+ 1.8	+ 10.6*	− 8.8*
1B	147.5	118.5	− 0.5	− 8.2	− 7.7
1D	144.7	119.1	− 3.3*	− 7.6	− 4.2
2A	146.9	127.1	− 1.1	+ 0.4	+ 1.6
2B	146.3	125.4	− 1.7	− 1.3	+ 0.4
2D	131.5	122.2	− 16.5***	− 4.5	+ 12.0***
3A	149.5	137.5	+ 1.5	+ 10.8*	− 9.3*
3B	146.7	132.7	− 1.3	+ 6.0	− 7.3
3D	147.7	137.8	− 0.3	+ 11.1*	− 11.4*
4A	147.7	129.8	− 0.3	+ 3.1	− 3.5
4B	147.7	129.8	− 0.3	+ 3.1	− 3.4
4D	148.0	125.3	0.0	− 1.4	+ 1.3
5A	145.7	108.3	− 2.3	− 18.4**	− 16.0***
5D	149.8	131.3	+ 1.8	+ 4.6	− 2.9
6A	148.5	112.7	+ 0.5	− 14.0*	− 14.5***
6B	148.0	130.0	0.0	+ 3.3	− 3.3
6D	129.8	111.3	− 18.2***	− 15.4**	+ 2.8
7A	152.0	134.0	+ 4.0*	+ 7.3	− 3.3
5B^s–7B^s	145.4	119.6	− 2.6	− 7.1	− 4.6
7D	147.0	132.0	− 0.3	+ 5.3	− 5.7
Besostaya I	131.2	120.8	− 16.8***	− 5.8	+ 11.0**
Cappelle-Desprez	148.0	126.7			

Note: The g or interaction estimates were calculated from the comparison of Cappelle-Desprez with each substitution line under short days and long days using the formula, Cappelle-Desprez (short days) − Cappelle-Desprez (long days) − substitution line (short days) + substitution line (long days). This comparison gives an estimate of the interaction between the effect of the substituted chromosome and the effect of the day-length treatment on ear-emergence time.
* P = 0.05–0.01; ** P = 0.01–0.001; *** P < 0.001.

short-days, the major effects were confined to the lines for chromosome 2D and 6D. However, the interaction estimates are the most interesting and significant positive estimates were obtained for the 2D substitution line and Besostaya I. This reflects the expected day-length interaction for Besostaya I compared with Cappelle-Desprez and the activities of the *Ppd1* gene on chromosome 2D. The other significant interaction estimates, on the other hand, are all negative to give greater differences under long-days than short-days. This is difficult to explain in terms of genes for day-length where long-day variation should be minimal. A possible explanation might be the short-day treatment acting as a substitute for vernalization. This has some support, since the largest negative interaction was found for the 5A substitution line which in the previous experiment also reduced the time to ear-emergence and is the known location of *Vrn1*. Similar correlations between the two experiments occur for chromosome 1A as well as chromosomes 3A and $5B^S$–$7B^S$ which although not significantly different from Cappelle-Desprez in the second experiment give differences in the same direction. The major effect of chromosome 6A in the second experiment is not, however, evident in the earlier experiment. At the moment, there is no explanation for this discrepancy.

The most striking outcome of the second experiment is the effect of chromosome 6D, the substitution line being early in both long and short-days and the interaction insignificant. The effect of 6D cannot therefore be ascribed to a day-length interaction, nor as a response to vernalization and must therefore be considered as a 'developmental rate' effect. This is a major chromosomal effect which extends as *Table 16.3* shows to leaf and spikelet primordia, both being reduced in the substitution line compared with Cappelle-Desprez. The effect of chromosome 6D is larger than that reported by Scarth and Law (1983) for the factor on chromosome 2B and the chromosomal differences ascribable to earliness *per se* by Hoogendoorn (1985). As might be expected from its major effect on spikelet primordia, the 6D substitution line has consistently produced lower yields than Cappelle-Desprez in large-scale yield trials at Cambridge (13% lower in 1984 and 12% in 1985). If this chromosome were to act in a similar manner in Besostaya I itself and in other varietal backgrounds then a similar yield penalty might also be expected although as is indicated later, environmental interactions may change and indeed, reverse the effect.

Table 16.3 NUMBER OF LEAVES AND SPIKELETS PRODUCED BY CAPPELLE-DESPREZ (BESOSTAYA I 6D), CAPPELLE-DESPREZ (BESOSTAYA I 2D), BESOSTAYA I AND CAPPELLE-DESPREZ GROWN UNDER SHORT AND LONG DAYS. SHORT DAYS = 8 H NATURAL DAYLIGHT. LONG DAYS = 8 H NATURAL DAYLIGHT + 16 H INCANDESCENT LIGHT

Genotype	Leaf No.			Spikelet No.		
	Short days	Long days	g	Short days	Long days	g
Cappelle-Desprez (Besostaya I 6D)	11.7	10.3	+0.67	22.7	20.3	+0.70
Cappelle-Desprez (Besostaya I 2D)	11.8	11.3	+1.50**	24.0	23.0	+2.10*
Besostaya I	11.3	11.9	+2.55***	21.5	20.5	+2.10*
Cappelle-Desprez	13.0	11.0		25.9	22.8	

Note: The g estimates were calculated following the procedure described at the foot of *Table 16.2*.
* P = 0.05–0.01; ** P = 0.01–0.001; *** P < 0.001.

The origins of Besostaya I chromosomes

Besostaya I originated from a cross between Skorospelka-3 and Lutescens 17; Skorospelka-3 can be traced back to an Italian source, the variety Ardito. This was produced by the famous Italian wheat breeder, Nazarino Strampelli who used earliness as a major objective in all his breeding programmes. It seems likely that the earliness that Strampelli was seeking was in fact a day-length insensitivity which allowed Italian winter wheats to develop early on in the year so as to avoid the high temperatures in May and June; it also seems likely that this earliness was obtained along with important genes for semi-dwarfism from a Japanese wheat, Akakomugi (Law, 1983). It is therefore possible that the day-length insensitivity of Besostaya I may have originated from this source. Evidence supporting this comes from the study of the Strampelli wheat Mara which is early and is also related to Ardito. Chromosome substitutions of Mara into Cappelle-Desprez have shown that Cappelle-Desprez (Mara 2D) is also day-length insensitive relative to Cappelle-Desprez (Worland and Law, 1986). Cappelle-Desprez (Mara 2D) was also grown in the day-length experiment just described and the ear-emergence times, under short- and long-days were identical with those observed for Cappelle-Desprez (Besostaya I 2D) suggesting that they are genetically the same.

The origin of the 6D chromosome of Besostaya I is, however, not as clear. Cappelle-Desprez (Mara 6D) is not an 'early' line and it is therefore possible that the 6D effect of Besostaya I originated from a totally different source, possibly through Lutescens 17 and other Russian wheats which presumably also had had a history of being selected for earliness. If this should prove to be so, then two major breeding programmes, the one in Italy and the other in the USSR, achieved their objective of earliness but by different genetic and possibly physiological routes.

The genetic analysis of chromosome 2D

Although the analysis of the Cappelle-Desprez/Besostaya I substitution lines revealed only chromosome 2D as controlling a day-length response, it is still necessary to show that this is due to *Ppd1* and not to other genes. At the moment this cannot be done for Besostaya I 2D. Homozygous recombinant lines, however, exist from the cross of Cappelle-Desprez with Cappelle-Desprez (Mara 2D), the substitution line identical phenotypically with Cappelle-Desprez (Besostaya I 2D). Such lines reflect only the genetic differences between the 2D chromosomes of Cappelle-Desprez and Mara (or Besostaya I), because all the other chromosomes are constant. Ninety homozygous recombinant lines were grown in a replicated trial from a winter-sowing to provide short-day conditions and days to ear-emergence scored. Two distinct classes of equal size were observed, indicating that a single gene, presumably *Ppd1*, was responsible for all the variation in ear-emergence time (Worland and Law, 1986). It would seem reasonable to conclude therefore that the *Ppd1* allele present on Mara 2D is found also on Besostaya I 2D and that the differences in time to ear-emergence between these chromosomes and their homologue in Cappelle-Desprez is due to this gene alone.

Additional genes affecting other characters of interest in breeding were also identified in this study and their location on the genetic map determined. This gives the relative position of *Ppd1* to other genes on 2D, and, as *Figure 16.1* shows, permits a comparison between the genetic maps of the related 2B and 2D chromosomes. From this it is apparent that *Ppd1* and *Ppd2* occupy similar positions on the two chromosomes indicating that they are probably related genes.

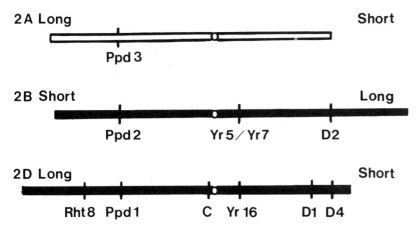

Figure 16.1 Genetic maps for chromosomes 2A, 2B and 2D of wheat showing the locations of day-length sensitive genes (*Ppd*), *Rht8* for semi-dwarfism, genes for yellow-rust resistance (*Yr*), genes for hybrid dwarfism (D), and a gene for Compactoid spike (C). The genetic map of chromosome 2A is conjectural.

The influence of *Ppd1* on development

Two separate studies of the effect of *Ppd1* on spike development have been made. Scarth, Kirby and Law (1985) described the different growth and development of the shoot apex of the variety Chinese Spring (day-length sensitive) and the substitution line in which chromosome 2D of the Mexican variety, Ciano 67 (day-length insensitive) replaced its homologue in Chinese Spring. This study was carried out in a controlled environment under conditions of 8 h day-lengths throughout the experiment. In the second study, the Cappelle-Desprez (Mara 2D) homozygous recombinant lines were grown as winter wheats in the field in 1984. The results of the first experiment are summarized in *Table 16.4* and indicate that the substitution of the Ciano 67 2D chromosome, carrying the insensitive *Ppd1* allele, into Chinese Spring had no effect on the time of spikelet initiation or the rate of initiation, but produced fewer spikelets than Chinese Spring. This difference in spikelet number accounted for the earlier emergence of Chinese Spring (Ciano 67 2D) but in addition, the rate of growth of the spikes following the formation of terminal spikelets was much greater than in Chinese Spring.

Table 16.4 NUMBER OF LEAVES AND SPIKELETS AND RATES OF SPIKELET INITIATION IN CHINESE SPRING AND CHINESE SPRING (CIANO 67 2D) GROWN UNDER AN 8 H DAY-LENGTH IN A CONTROLLED ENVIRONMENT ROOM (SCARTH, LAW AND KIRBY, 1985)

Genotype	No. of leaves	No. of spikelets	Spikelets initiated (d^{d-1})
Chinese Spring (*ppd1*)	9.0	28.4	0.89 ± 0.03
Chinese Spring (Ciano 67 2D) (*Ppd1*)	9.0	25.7	1.04 ± 0.04

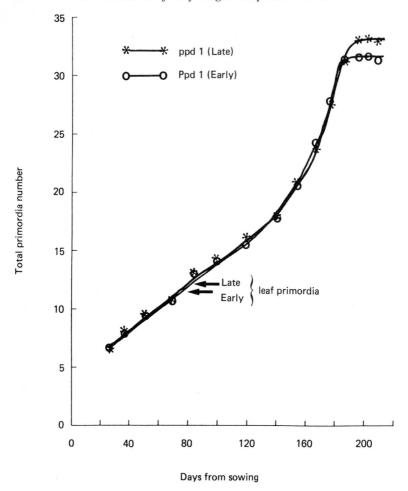

Figure 16.2   Number of primordia plotted against time for the average of the four *Ppd1* and the four *ppd1* lines derived from the cross of Cappelle-Desprez with Cappelle-Desprez (Mara 2D).

   A similar result emerged from the study of the Cappelle-Desprez (Mara 2D) recombinant lines in the field. Altogether eight lines were sampled, four homozygous for *Ppd1* from Mara and four for *ppd1* from Cappelle-Desprez. These eight lines had previously been classified for the genes such as *Rht8* for dwarfism described in *Figure 16.1*, and it was therefore possible to determine the contributions that such genes might make to ear-development, independent of *Ppd1*. As *Figure 16.2* shows, spikelet primordia developed at the same rate among all the eight lines but stopped producing primordia for the four *Ppd1* lines approximately 8–10 days before the *ppd1* lines. This resulted in fewer primordia (average 1.6) for the earlier developing lines. The similarities between the eight lines other than the *Ppd1–ppd1* effects indicated that the other genes that separate the eight lines had no effect on spikelet development.
   These results are similar to those reported by Scarth and Law (1983) for *Ppd2*, the locus on chromosome 2B, indicating that *Ppd1* and *Ppd2* are functionally identical.

They are also located at comparable positions on the genetic maps of the two chromosomes (*Figure 16.1*). This strongly suggests that they are the same genes, duplicated as a consequence of the polyploid nature of wheat. These genes for day-length therefore influence the duration rather than the rate of spikelet initiation in response to different day-lengths, but thereafter appear to effect the rate of growth and development of the spikelets (Scarth, Kirby and Law, 1985). The timing of final spike initiation appears to trigger other developmental stages, for example, stem elongation which occurs earlier in all lines carrying the insensitive allele of *Ppd1*.

Adaptive role of *Ppd* genes

So far, the study of the behaviour of the *Ppd* genes has been confined to experiments in controlled environments or in the field at Cambridge. In a series of experiments carried out in ten different countries, the time to ear-emergence was recorded for the variety Chinese Spring and two chromosome substitution lines in this variety. The

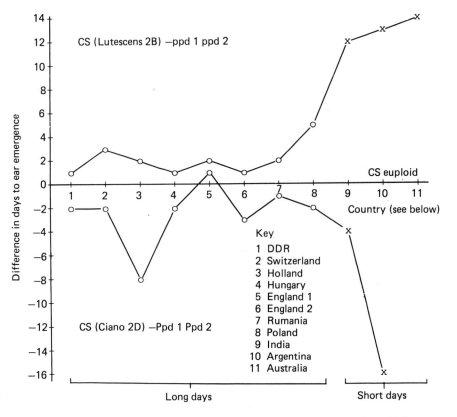

Figure 16.3 Differences in days to ear-emergence from Chinese Spring (*ppd1 Ppd2*) for the two substitution lines, Chinese Spring (Lutescens 2B) (*ppd1 ppd2*) and Chinese Spring (Ciano 67 2D) (*Ppd1 Ppd2*) when grown in ten different countries either under long-day or short-day conditions. England 1 and 2 refer to two different spring sowing dates.
1 = East Germany; 2 = Switzerland; 3 = Netherlands; 4 = Hungary; 5 = England 1; 6 = England 2; 7 = Rumania; 8 = Poland; 9 = India; 10 = Argentina; 11 = Australia.

two lines, Chinese Spring (Lutescens 62 2B) and Chinese Spring (Ciano 67 2D) differ from Chinese Spring, the former carrying the more sensitive allele, *ppd2* on chromosome 2B, the latter, the more insensitive allele *Ppd1* on 2D. The results of these experiments are described in *Figure 16.3*. The largest allelic differences were observed in India, Argentina and Australia, all countries where wheat is grown during the winter months when temperatures are suitable for wheat growing, but day-lengths are short. Insensitive *Ppd* genes are therefore important to the wheats of these countries if they are to mature early and avoid the damaging high temperatures of summer. Chinese Spring (Ciano 67 2D) was thus very early compared with Chinese Spring in these countries, whereas Chinese Spring (Lutescens 62 2B) was later. For the European countries, the differences between the two lines were small. This reflects the influence of the long-day growing conditions since in all these countries, the lines were spring sown.

The important adaptive nature of the *Ppd* genes is very evident from the results of these experiments. Almost certainly particular *Ppd* genes have had a decisive effect on the spread of wheat throughout the world. As has been mentioned, the Italian wheats probably obtained their *Ppd1* insensitivity from the Japanese source, Akakomugi, and this has been used widely by breeders in Mediterranean countries and further afield, for example, Besostaya I in the USSR.

It is not certain whether the extremely potent chromosome 2D effect of Mexican wheats as shown in the behaviour of Chinese Spring (Ciano 67 2D) is due to the same *Ppd1* allele. Mediterranean wheats were used by Norman Borlaug in the early days at the International Maize and Wheat Improvement Centre, CIMMYT, Mexico and this allele could therefore have been transferred to the important semi-dwarf wheats of the 'green revolution' which proved so adaptable—undoubtedly because of their day-length insensitivity. However, comparisons between the substitution lines Cappelle-Desprez (Mara 2D), Cappelle-Desprez (Besostaya I 2D) and Cappelle-Desprez (Ciano 67 2D) grown under short-day conditions at the PBI, Cambridge, indicate the latter line to be much earlier than the other two. Although this may signify the presence of a second locus, it equally could mean that a different *Ppd1* allele was involved and therefore a different source was used in the breeding of Mexican wheats.

Likewise it was once thought that the day-length insensitivities of Australian wheats originated from Indian wheats and that this insensitivity could be linked to the gene *Ppd2* on chromosome 2B. This was based upon the observation that the Australian wheat variety Spica, carries this gene (Scarth, 1983; Hoogendoorn, 1985). However, recent studies at the PBI, Cambridge (Islam, unpublished observations) suggest that indigenous Indian wheats carry a gene or genes for insensitivity on chromosome 2A (probably the previously identified homoeoallele, *Ppd3* (Law, Sutka and Worland, 1978)) and not 2B. Clearly, much more work needs to be done if the history of the *Ppd* genes and their influence on wheat breeding is to be understood.

Interaction of genes for day-length with those for vernalization

One of the advantages of the precisely defined genetic stocks available in wheat is that it is possible through simple crossing designs to test for the presence of interaction between different genes and also whether such interactions in their turn interact with different environments. These methods are now well established in wheat cytogenetics and lead to estimates of the various parameters describing additive genetic effects, dominance, non-allelic interaction and so on (Mather and Jinks, 1971).

This approach was used by my colleague, Dr J.W. Snape, in collaboration with Dr R.A. McIntosh of the Plant Breeding Institute in Sydney, Australia to study the interaction between a gene (*Ppd2*) for day-length insensitivity and a gene (*Vrn3*) for vernalization requirement on time to ear-emergence in Cambridge, England and in Sydney, Australia. Two chromosome substitution lines of Chinese Spring were used, Chinese Spring (Cappelle-Desprez 5D) and Chinese Spring (Lutescens 2B). Chinese Spring obtains its reduced vernalization requirement from the gene *Vrn3* on chromosome 5D. Replacement of this chromosome by Cappelle-Desprez 5D which carries the less potent *vrn3* allele produces a substitution line with increased vernalization requirement. Chinese Spring (Lutescens 62 2B) as already described is more sensitive to day-length than Chinese Spring because of its less potent *ppd2* allele. These two substitution lines along with Chinese Spring were intercrossed to produce 21 genetically different families and these were grown in both Cambridge and Sydney. The environment of Australia provides short-days and, early on, cool vernalizing conditions whereas from a spring sowing in Cambridge, long-days and minimal vernalization conditions occur.

The results obtained from this joint experiment are given in *Table 16.5*; only the times to ear-emergence for Chinese Spring and the two substitution lines are indicated, but the estimates of the genetical parameters based upon the phenotypes of the means of all 21 families are included. It is clear from these estimates that the chromosome 5D effect due to *Vrn3* is greater in Cambridge than in Sydney, whereas the chromosome 2B effect due to *Ppd2* is greater in Sydney than in Cambridge. The long-day environment in Cambridge as expected therefore removes the effect of the day-length genes whereas its minimal vernalization environment has little influence on the difference between the *Vrn3* alleles. In Sydney, on the other hand, partial vernalization has taken place to give the smaller chromosome 5D estimate, but the

Table 16.5 DAYS TO EAR EMERGENCE FROM AN ARBITRARY DATE FOR CHINESE SPRING (*Vrn3 Vrn3 Ppd2 Ppd2*), CHINESE SPRING (CAPPELLE-DESPREZ 5D) (*vrn3 vrn3 Ppd2 Ppd2*), AND CHINESE SPRING (LUTESCENS 62 2B) (*Vrn3 Vrn3 ppd2 ppd2*) GROWN AT CAMBRIDGE, ENGLAND AND SYDNEY, AUSTRALIA. THE ESTIMATES OF THE GENETICAL PARAMETERS ARE BASED UPON THE MEANS OF 21 DIFFERENT FAMILIES DERIVED FROM CROSSING THE ABOVE THREE GENOTYPES

Genotype		Cambridge, England	Sydney, Australia
Chinese Spring		31.8	9.0
Chinese Spring (Cappelle-Desprez 5D)		54.1	19.0
Chinese Spring (Lutescens 62 2B)		29.7	22.8
Estimates of genetical parameters m (mid-point)		41.62***	21.09***
Additive chromosome effects	d_{5D}	11.44***	6.44***
	d_{2B}	−0.88	8.20***
Within chromosome interaction effects	h_{5D}	−8.19***	−2.46**
	h_{2B}	−0.65	−1.35
	$\chi^2[16]$	22.28	16.49
	P	0.13	0.42

** P = 0.01–0.001; *** P < 0.001.

short-day environment has little impact on the day-length difference. These main effects are therefore exactly predictable. However, the fitted models also indicate that apart from dominance, there is no evidence for any interaction between the *Ppd* and *Vrn* genes in their control of time to ear-emergence. The additive-dominance model is adequate to explain the observed variation. The two sets of genes therefore act independently on this complex character, suggesting perhaps that they may influence different component processes.

The effects of *Ppd* genes on characters other than time to ear-emergence

The identification of particular genes not only leads to a means of testing for interactions between genes, but it also allows a study of the effects of a gene on characters other than that used in its identification. The recognition of such pleiotropic effects could be valuable to the physiologist in understanding causal relationships and plant processes, and they are extremely important in crop breeding. So far, the effects of the *Ppd* genes have been described in terms of time to ear-emergence and primordia numbers. As mentioned on a number of occasions, this control of development is of paramount importance in adapting the wheat crop to growth in various parts of the world by enabling the crop to avoid adverse environmental conditions. However, it would be useful to quantify in yield terms this adaptive role and in so doing possibly uncover other effects of the *Ppd* genes on characters affecting wheat varietal performance.

The special genetic stocks, particularly near isogenic lines, enable such studies to be carried out and it is a major objective of the wheat genetical studies at PBI, Cambridge. In the case of the *Ppd* genes, the homozygous recombinant lines produced to analyse the genetic differences between the 2D chromosomes of Mara and Cappelle-Desprez are ideal for studying the pleiotropic effects of *Ppd1*. During 1984 these homozygous recombinant lines were grown as drilled trials in England at Cambridge, at Novi Sad in Yugoslavia, at Martonvasar in Hungary, and at Fundulea in Rumania. The lines had all been classified previously as homozygous for *Ppd1* or its allele as well as for the other major genes described in *Figure 16.1*. The combinations of genes between the lines were such that independent comparisons could be made for each of the major genes including *Ppd1*. The results of these trials are described in *Table 16.6* for *Ppd1* and its effects on time to ear-emergence, height and plot yields.

The differences in ear-emergence times are very similar in each of the four countries. However, the summation terms become progressively less the further south the trials are carried out. This indicates the earlier emergence dates in Mediterranean countries compared with England and possibly reflects the accelerating effect of higher temperatures and/or light intensities. The influence of the day-length gene, on the other hand, is constant—a consequence perhaps of the small differences in latitude between the four countries. For height, the difference between *Ppd1* and *ppd1* is significant and indicates a direct effect of this gene on this character. The earlier allele, as might be expected, gives shorter plants in all four environments. However, as the mean height of the plants becomes progressively shorter further south, the difference between the effects of the two alleles becomes larger. This is in fact a negative interaction between the genotype and the environment. The better the height

Table 15.6 COMPARISONS REPRESENTED AS THE SUM OF AND DIFFERENCE BETWEEN THE MEANS OF HOMOZYGOUS RECOMBINANT LINES CARRYING *Ppdl* AND THOSE CARRYING *ppdl* FOR THE CHARACTERS, TIME TO EAR EMERGENCE, FINAL PLANT HEIGHT AND MEAN PLOT YIELD. THE LINES WERE GROWN IN DRILLED FIELD TRIALS IN ENGLAND, HUNGARY, RUMANIA AND YUGOSLAVIA DURING THE SEASON 1984/85

	Ear-emergence (days)				Height (cm)				Yield (gm)			
	Ppdl	*ppdl*	*Sum*	*Difference*	*Ppdl*	*ppdl*	*Sum*	*Difference*	*Ppdl*	*ppdl*	*Sum*	*Difference*
England	9.2	14.8	24.0	−5.6	112.5	115.9	228.4	−3.4	4734	5237	9971	−503
Hungary	8.7	16.8	25.5	−8.1	98.3	102.5	200.8	−4.2	—	—	—	—
Rumania	8.7	13.0	21.7	−4.3	84.3	90.8	175.1	−6.5	4270	4163	8433	+107
Yugoslavia	4.5	9.5	14.0	−5.0	81.1	91.4	172.5	−10.3	3589	3220	6809	+369

producing environment, the smaller the *Ppd* effect on height whereas the converse holds for a poor height environment. It is difficult to explain this from the information available, but it may be associated with the onset of high temperatures and possibly droughted conditions in the more southerly countries. Such conditions are likely to arise at the time when the *Ppd* and *ppd* genotypes either have diverged or are beginning to diverge developmentally. High temperatures might be expected to have a stimulatory effect on stem elongation in the later emerging lines, for instance.

This type of explanation probably also accounts for the yield differences. In this case, a switch in yield occurs so that in England, the highest yielding environment, it is the *ppd* allele for lateness that produces the highest plant yields. In the poorer yielding environments of Yugoslavia and Rumania, on the other hand, it is the early *Ppd* lines that are the highest yielding; possibly because they escape the adverse effects on fertility and grain filling of high temperatures and droughted conditions.

Conclusions

The study of the Cappelle-Desprez/Besostaya I substitution lines has confirmed rather than extended the understanding of the genetics of day-length response in wheat. This need not mean that such genes are confined solely to the three chromosomes of homoeologous group 2. Other varietal sources need to be studied before an unequivocal statement about the numbers of genes can be made. The present studies have, however, revealed on chromosome 6D of Besostaya I a possible alternative genetic system for regulating development which apparently acts independently of day-length and vernalization. How this chromosome affects the performance of Besostaya I needs further study. As mentioned previously, the Cappelle-Desprez (Besostaya I 6D) substitution line gave reduced yields compared with Cappelle-Desprez in field trials in England. However, as the investigation with *Ppd1* has shown, positive effects on yield can be reversed with a change of environment and this may well be case with the effects of Besostaya I 6D. The interaction, if any, between the 6D effect and the activities of the *Ppd* genes also needs investigation using the methods described in this paper for day-length and vernalization genes. The developmental changes occurring between the two types of effect require studying to identify differences of form and structure as well as in their times of appearance. The aim of this work should be the evaluation of the contribution that these genetic effects can make to varietal performance under a range of conditions. This should lead to definitions of the optimal genotypes for particular environments which would be of value to wheat breeding.

Throughout this chapter, the emphasis has been on the analysis of genetic effects and the description of such effects in relation to breeding. This should not be the sole purpose of these studies. The results of these analyses and in particular the genetic stocks that emerge from it should be valuable to the physiologist and biochemist who are interested in plant processes. They also provide genetic 'targets' for the molecular biologist who is seeking to isolate and study genes that are of importance to agriculture. Indeed, as pointed out be Law and Scarth (1984), the molecular isolation and characterization of day-length genes may turn out to be the most effective way of describing the processes involved in the flowering of plants. However, before the isolation of such genes can be attempted, it is essential to identify the genes worthy of being isolated.

Acknowledgements

I acknowledge the help of the following in providing data presented in this chapter: Dr J. Sutka, Agricultural Research Institute, Martonvasar, Hungary; Dr G. Kleijer, Station Federale de Recherches Agronomiques de Changins, Nyon, Switzerland; Dr J. Bhowal, Indian Agricultural Research Institute, New Delhi, India; Dr A. Giura, Research Institute for Cereals and Industrial Crops, Fundulea, Rumania; Dr S. Petrovic, Institute of Field and Vegetable Crops, Novi Sad, Yugoslavia; Dr W. Lange, Foundation for Agricultural Plant Breeding, Wageningen, The Netherlands; Dr D. Mettin, Institute for Genetics and Plant Breeding, Gatersleben, DDR; Dr. R.A. McIntosh, Plant Breeding Institute, Sydney, Australia; E.Y. Suarez, Department of Genetics, University of Buenos Aires, Argentina; Dr D. Miazga, Institute of Plant Breeding, Lublin, Poland. I should also like to thank my colleagues Mr A.J. Worland, Miss B.P. Parker and Mr A. Krattiger who have helped carry out the experimental work and have assisted in the preparation of the manuscript.

References

HALLORAN, G.M. and BOYDELL, C.W. (1967). Wheat chromosomes with genes for photoperiodic response. *Canadian Journal of Genetic Cytology*, **9**, 394–398

HOOGENDOORN, J. (1985). A reciprocal F₁ monosomic analysis of the genetic control of time of ear-emergence, number of leaves and number of spikelets in wheat (*Triticum aestivum* L). *Euphytica*, **34**, 545–558

KEIM, D.L., WELSH, J.R. and MCCONNELL, R.L. (1973). Inheritance of photoperiodic heading response in winter and spring cultivars of bread wheat. *Canadian Journal of Plant Science*, **53**, 247–250

KLAIMI, Y.Y. and QUALSET, C.O. (1973). Genetics of heading time in wheat (*Triticum aestivum* L). I. The inheritance of photoperiodic response. *Genetics*, **74**, 139–156

KUSPIRA, J. and UNRAU, J. (1957). Genetic analysis of certain characters in common wheat using whole chromosome substitution lines. *Canadian Journal of Plant Science*, **37**, 300–326

LAW, C.N. (1967). The location of genetic factors controlling a number of quantitative characters in wheat. *Genetics*, **56**, 445–461

LAW, C.N. (1983). Prospects for directed genetic manipulation in wheat. *Genetics and Agriculture*, **37**, 115–132

LAW, C.N. and WORLAND, A.J. (1973). Aneuploidy in wheat and its uses in genetic analysis. In *Annual Report, Plant Breeding Institute, 1972*, pp. 25–65

LAW, C.N., WORLAND, A.J. and GIORGI, B. (1976). The genetic control of ear-emergence time by chromosomes 5A and 5D of wheat. *Heredity*, **36**, 49–58

LAW, C.N., SUTKA, J. and WORLAND, A.J. (1978). A genetic study of day-length response in wheat. *Heredity*, **41**, 185–191

LAW, C.N., SNAPE, J.W. and WORLAND, A.J. (1983). Chromosome manipulation and its exploitation in the genetics and breeding of wheat. *Stadler Symposium, University of Missouri, Columbia*, Vol. **15**, pp. 5–23

LAW, C.N. and SCARTH, R. (1984). Genetics and its potential for understanding the action of light in flowering. In *Light and The Flowering Process* (D. Vince-Prue, Ed.), pp. 193–209. London, Academic Press

MATHER, K. and JINKS, J.L. (1971). *Biometrical Genetics*. London, Chapman and Hall

MORRISON, J.W. (1961). The monosomic analysis of growth habit in winter wheat. *Zeitschrift Vererbhehre*, **91**, 141–151

PUGSLEY, A.T. (1966). The photoperiodic sensitivity of some spring wheats with special reference to the variety Thatcher. *Australian Journal of Agricultural Research*, **17**, 591–599

SCARTH, R. (1983). *The Genetics of the Day length Response in Wheat and its Effect on Development*. Ph.D. thesis, Cambridge University

SCARTH, R. and LAW, C.N. (1983). The location of the photoperiod gene, *Ppd2*, and an additional genetic factor for ear-emergence time on chromosome 2B of wheat. *Heredity*, **51**, 607–619

SCARTH, R. and LAW, C.N. (1984). The control of the day length response in wheat by the group 2 chromosomes. *Zeitschrift Pflanzenzüchtung.*, **92**, 140–150

SCARTH, R., KIRBY, E.J.M. and LAW, C.N. (1985). Effects of the photoperiod genes *Ppd1* and *Ppd2* on growth and development of the shoot apex in wheat. *Annals of Botany*, **55**, 357–359

SEARS, E.R. (1954). The aneuploids of common wheat. *Missouri Agricultural Experimental Station, Research Bulletin*, **572**, 1–58

WELSH, J.R., KEIM, D.L., PIRASTEH, B. and RICHARDS, R.D. (1973). Genetic control of photoperiod response in wheat. In *Proceedings of the 4th International Wheat Genetics Symposium*, pp. 879–884

WORLAND, A.J. and LAW, C.N. (1986). Genetic analysis of chromosome 2D of wheat. I. The location of genes affecting height, day length insensitivity, hybrid dwarfism and yellow-rust resistance. *Zeitschrift Pflanzenzüchtung*, **96**, 331–345

17

PHOTOPERIODIC PROCESSES: INDUCTION, TRANSLOCATION AND INITIATION

G.F. DEITZER
Smithsonian Environmental Research Center, Rockville, Maryland, USA

Introduction

This chapter will not attempt to provide an inclusive review of all aspects of flowering from induction in the leaf to evocation at the apex but rather, focus attention on a number of critical, unresolved questions that will be discussed in much greater detail in the subsequent chapters (18 to 22). Discussion will be further restricted to only a few well-characterized examples with no attempt to include a full compendium of all of the exceptions and ambiguities that exist in the literature. At the same time, every effort will be made to provide an accurate overview of current knowledge that will orient the reader to the complexities that will follow in succeeding chapters. It is precisely these complexities that must be brought into sharp focus and dealt with if we are ever to understand flowering at the physiological and biochemical level.

Photoperiodic processes are those processes that are determined or influenced by day-length. They have evolved as a means of detecting and responding to seasonal changes and serve the purpose of synchronizing and optimizing many metabolic and physiological parameters. Thus, part of the complexity arises from the fact that not all responses to day-length changes are directly related to flowering. They may, of course, be indirectly involved, and may even be an essential component, in the sequence of events from photoreception in the leaf to the ultimate transformation and development of the apex. It should also be noted that the flowering of many plants is not influenced by day-length. However, grafting experiments between different response types (Lang, 1965), including day-neutral varieties (Lang *et al.*, 1977; Lang, 1980), suggest the attractive hypothesis that all plants share a common pathway, or pathways (Bernier, 1984), to traverse this developmental sequence.

Some of the material in this chapter has been reviewed in greater detail previously by Bernier *et al.* (1981), Champagnat and Jacques (1979), Halevy (1985), Vince-Prue (1983, 1985) and Vince-Prue *et al.* (1984). New information is presented now on a genetic system of photoperiod mutants in barley and the photoperiodic regulation of photosynthesis and assimilate partitioning.

Induction

Flowering is not regulated by photoperiod in all plants and photoperiodism is the basis for the regulation of more than just flowering. The evolution of mechanisms to perceive the relative length of light and darkness in a daily cycle confers upon these organisms an adaptive advantage by optimizing their growth and development under specific environmental conditions. While this adaptive advantage allows wild species to occupy successfully well-defined geographical locations and ecological niches, it presents agriculture with the problem of reversing evolutionary trends in order to increase the range for the cultivation of crop species.

As a specific example, adapted cultivars of barley grown in eastern Montana, USA, produced a lower yield than the same cultivars (Betzes) grown in western Montana. Since these are relatively late-heading spring cultivars, they do well in the cooler mountains of the western part of the state but are unable to tolerate the summer heat and drought stress in the eastern part of the state. Growers were therefore interested in the production of a cultivar that would head earlier, before the summer became too hot and dry. A series of 10 isotypic lines were developed (Smail *et al.*, unpublished observations) by mutation with diethyl sulphate and backcross methodology to create a heading date series ranging over 10 days in 1-day increments (*Table 17.1*). Field analysis of heading dates in nine Montana environments revealed consistent differences among 9 of the 10 isotypes. The heading response of the earliest isotype (isotype-1) was not environmentally consistent as determined by stability regression analysis.

Table 17.1   PEDIGREE AND MEAN DAYS TO HEADING (DTH) FOR 10 ISOTYPES OF SHABET BARLEY WHEN GROWN FROM SPRING PLANTINGS IN OVER NINE ENVIRONMENTS (1981–1983) IN MONTANA, USA

Isotype	Pedigree	Description	Mean DTH
1	Compana dwarf (Des mutant M$_2$)/7*Betzes//2*Shabet	Early, normal stature	51.2 A†
2	Orange Lemma/*7 Betzes//2*Shabet	Early, normal lemma	53.7 A
3	Prior/*7 Betzes (Erbet)	Early	52.9 A
4	Orange Lemma/*7 Betzes//2*Shabet	Early, normal lemma	56.3 B
5	Des M$_2$ Shabet/*2 Shabet	Early	57.5 B
6	Des M$_2$ Shabet/*2 Shabet	Early	60.9 C
7	Des M$_2$ Shabet/*2 Shabet	Normal	62.5 CD
8	Shabet	Normal	62.8 CD
9	Des M$_2$ Shabet/*2 Shabet	Late	63.5 D
10	Erbet/*7 Shabet (Ershabet)	Early	52.9 A
		Pooled LSD =	2.96

* Similar letters denote non-significant mean differences according to LSD (P = 0.05).

Comparison of heading rates under 8-, 12- and 16-hour photoperiods revealed that isotype-1 expressed a photoperiod-insensitive heading response when grown under growth chamber conditions (*Figure 17.1*). Duncan's multiple range analysis of the isotype means (*Table 17.2*) established that:

1. Isotype-1 was significantly different from the other 9 isotypes under all three photoperiods.
2. Isotypes-2 through -10 were not significantly different under 8-hour photoperiods.
3. Three groups could be distinguished under 12-hour and five groups under 16-hour photoperiods. Although differences could be detected as early as 20 days from planting, all of the isotypes eventually reach the same growth stage.

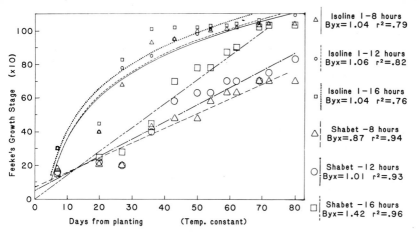

Figure 17.1 Comparison of photoperiod insensitive isotype 1 versus Shabet (isotype 8) barley Feeke's growth stage (× 10) development under 8-, 12- and 16-hour photoperiod treatments; r^2 values are all significant at $P = 0.01$.

Table 17.2 COMPARISON OF 10 MATURITY ISOTYPES OF SHABET BARLEY SAMPLED ON 10 DATES FOR FEEKE'S GROWTH STAGE WHEN GROWN UNDER 8-, 12-, AND 16-HOUR PHOTOPERIODS. NUMBER OF SIGNIFICANTLY DIFFERENT MEAN GROUPINGS OF FEEKE'S GROWTH STAGES* ACCORDING TO DUNCAN'S MULTIPLE RANGE TEST.

	Days from planting									
Photoperiod	7	20	27	36	43	50	59	62	69	72
8 hours	1	1	2	2	2	2	2	2	2	1
12 hours	1	2	2	2	3	3	3	4	2	1
16 hours	1	2	2	5	5	5	3	3	2	1

* *See Figure 17.1* for individual data points and regression comparison of each isotype over all sampling dates.

Since these results were based on Feeke's growth stages, which is a linearized developmental sequence based on growth of the main tiller (Large, 1954), differences may reflect changes in vegetative as well as floral development. Therefore, the specific promotion of floral stage by far-red light was examined using non-linear morphological changes of only the developing inflorescence by dissection of the apex in three isotypes and compared with the cultivar Wintex (Deitzer *et al.*, 1979). Under conditions where Wintex showed a promotion of more than 60% in floral stage and an increase of more than 30% in apex length, there was no significant difference in isotype-1 (*Table 17.3*). Isotype-8, the wild-type parental strain, was very similar to Wintex. Isotype-3 showed an intermediate response as it had using the Feeke's growth stages.

The far-red light promotion of flowering in Wintex barley is thought to be

Table 17.3 PROMOTION OF FLORAL INDUCTION IN THREE SHABET ISOTYPES AND
WINTEX BARLEY BY 72 h OF FAR-RED (FR) LIGHT ADDED TO DAYLIGHT
FLUORESCENT (DF) LIGHT

Variable	Treatment	Isotype			
		1	*3*	*8*	*Wintex*
Floral	DF	8.8 ± 0.1	4.5 ± 0.3	2.6 ± 0.4	2.5 ± 0.5
stage	DF + FR	9.2 ± 0.6	5.9 ± 0.3	4.4 ± 0.2	4.1 ± 0.1
	% increase	5	31	69	64
Spike	DF	5.0 ± 0.4	1.9 ± 0.1	1.2 ± 0.1	1.2 ± 0.1
length	DF + FR	5.27 ± 1.0	2.6 ± 0.2	1.8 ± 0.1	1.7 ± 0.1
(mm)	% increase	4	37	43	34
Dry	DF	1.1 ± 0.1	0.9 ± 0.1	0.7 ± 0.1	0.7 ± 0.1
weight	DF + FR	1.1 ± 0.2	1.0 ± 0.1	0.9 ± 0.1	0.8 ± 0.1
(g plant^{-1})	% increase	0	11	14	14

mediated by phytochrome in the leaf (Deitzer *et al.*, 1979) and so isotype-1 may represent a photoperiod mutant that lacks phytochrome control. The genetic control of photoperiod insensitivity in barley has been cited as being directed by as few as one recessive gene (Barham and Rasmusson, 1981; Dormling *et al.*, 1975; Fejer and Fedak, 1979; Takahashi and Yasuda, 1971). Thus while a great deal more work will be required to establish where in the sequence of phytochrome-mediated events this gene acts, the isogenic nature of this mutant suggests the possibility that there is at least one protein in the leaf whose synthesis is normally inhibited by high levels of P_{fr}. Addition of far-red light would decrease the level of this inhibition allowing expression of the gene that leads ultimately to the production of a floral stimulus. Alternatively, high levels of P_{fr} may promote the synthesis of a protein that is involved with the production of a flower-inhibiting substance and far-red would then reduce the level of this inhibitory substance. Isotype-1 may be defective in this gene, producing little or no inhibitor irrespective of the P_{fr} concentration.

The most extensively investigated genetic system for the photoperiodic regulation of flowering is that described for pea, *Pisum sativum* (Murfet, 1985). Six major loci have been identified that confer or modulate the ability to perceive and respond to day-length changes. Of these, two genes (*Sn* and *Dne*) acting together confer photoperiodic sensitivity. The end product of their interaction is a graft-transmissible floral inhibitor (Barber, 1959; Murfet, 1971; Murfet and Reid, 1973; Paton and Barber, 1955). Thus, if isotype-1 in barley is analogous to the recessive *sn dne* condition in pea, then the gene that is responsible for the production of a flower-inhibitory substance is not expressed or is not present. The evidence for, and possible mode of action of, floral inhibitors have been summarized recently by Schwabe (1984) and will not be discussed further here. However, since most of the evidence for both promoter and inhibitor indicate that they are mobile substances, acting at least over short distances, they will be considered again in the next section on translocation.

That phytochrome can act at the level of gene expression has long been suspected based on physiological experiments (Mohr, 1972) and has recently been demonstrated directly using molecular hybridization techniques (Gollmer and Apel, 1983; Stiekema *et al.*, 1983). Phytochrome (i.e. P_{fr}) has been shown in barley both to increase the level of translatable mRNA for the light-harvesting chlorophyll a/b protein (Apel, 1979) and to decrease the level of mRNA coding for the NADPH: protochlorophyllide oxidoreductase (Apel, 1981). P_{fr} could therefore influence the level of a flower-promoting substance within an individual cell by either activating a gene for the synthesis of an inhibitor or by repressing a gene for the synthesis of a promoter.

Whether the action of phytochrome is direct or indirect, however, is not known since phytochrome may influence the state of cellular membranes (Marme, 1977) that in turn could lead to changes in gene expression. A large amount of evidence has accumulated for a phytochrome involvement in the nyctinastic (night closure) leaflet movement in plants that have specialized organs (pulvini) allowing large and rapid movements to be produced by changes in turgor pressure (for review see Satter and Galston, 1981). These movements are based on massive fluxes of K^+, Cl^-, H^+ and other ions in the pulvinus at the base of the leaflet. Opening is caused when the cells in the ventral, extensor region of the pulvinus take up K^+, Cl^- and as a consequence, water, causing them to swell. At the same time the oppositely positioned flexor cells lose ions and water causing them to shrink. A model to explain the mechanism of how these ion movements occur has been proposed (Satter, 1979) which suggest that H^+ fluxes are coupled to, and energize, oppositely directed K^+ fluxes. The plasma membranes of both flexor and extensor cells contain an ATP dependent H^+-pump along with co-transport systems regulated by the resulting transmembrane pH gradient. The net H^+ fluxes, after being stimulated by light, continue to vary rhythmically. Phytochrome (P_{fr}) is able to reset this rhythm (Simon *et al.*, 1976) and the extent and direction of the phase shift is dependent on the time when a red light perturbation occurs. Thus, P_{fr} is assumed to interact directly with some aspect intimately associated with the clock mechanism and this interaction presumably takes place at or near the plasma membrane.

Phytochrome is also known to affect a number of physiological and developmental events in plants that depend on calcium (for review see Hepler and Wayne, 1985). P_{fr} has been shown to enhance net Ca^{2+} efflux from isolated mitochndria (Roux *et al.*, 1981) and net Ca^{2+} influx across the plasma membrane (Dreyer and Weisenseel, 1979). A recent model (Goto *et al.*, 1985) proposes that a self-sustaining circadian oscillator is initiated by a light-dependent mobilization of Ca^{2+} into the cytoplasm that then immediately activates a Ca^{2+}-calumodulin complex. As a second messenger, the Ca^{2+}-calmodulin may be involved in the molecular events that are the basis for the action of growth substances (Kelly, 1984; Dieter, 1984). It is also known to activate a number of enzymes such as protein kinases and phosphatases. Especially interesting in this discussion is the report of a Ca^{2+}-calmodulin activated phosphorylation of a H^+-ATPase in corn roots (Zocchi *et al.*, 1983) and the report of a requirement for Ca^{2+} during the inhibition of stomatal opening by abscisic acid (DeSilva *et al.*, 1985). Since both leaf movements and stomatal responses function through ion fluxes based presumably on H^+-pumps, there may be a common mechanism involving Ca^{2+} and calmodulin in the circadian time measuring system in plants.

As has been reported for leaf-movements (Satter *et al.*, 1981), there is an additional complication in understanding the ability of phytochrome to control the photoperiodic expression of flowering. In addition to direct effects on the levels of promoters and inhibitors, phytochrome also interacts with a circadian time-keeping mechanism that determines the sensitivity of the plant to light. The phase relationships for phytochrome-mediated promotion and inhibition both in long- and in short-day plants (for review *see* King, 1984) have been shown to be sensitive to entrainment by light. The dual nature of light has been demonstrated in barley (Deitzer *et al.*, 1982), *Xanthium*

(Papenfuss and Salisbury, 1967), *Chenopodium* (King and Cumming, 1972) and *Pharbitis* (Lumsden *et al.*, 1982). Both of these aspects appear to be mediated by phytochrome (Vince-Prue, 1985).

The effect of light on time measurement has been most extensively studied in *Pharbitis* (Lumsden *et al.*, 1982; Lumsden and Vince-Prue, 1984; King *et al.*, 1982) and will be discussed extensively in the next chapter. Suffice it to say here that a pulse of red light, given during what would otherwise be an inductive dark period, shows an alternation of inhibition and promotion of flowering depending on when the pulse is given. This alternation repeats with a periodicity of about 24 hours. The inhibitory phase is equivalent to the effect of red light given as a night-break and is the basis for that response. When the light period preceding an inductive dark period is greater than 6 hours, the inhibitory effect of red light always occurs 8–9 hours after the light is turned off. Thus the rhythm in sensitivity to red light is initiated by the transition to darkness and is the basis for both the critical night length and the night-break response.

Based on these results, it has been suggested that the two separate phytochrome responses are mediated by different pools of phytochrome (Vince-Prue, 1983; Takimoto and Saji, 1984). Evidence for the existence of two pools of phytochrome has been reported in light-grown tissue (Heim *et al.*, 1981). Using the herbicide Norflurazon to cause photobleaching of leaves (Jabben and Deitzer, 1978a), it was discovered that 98% of the phytochrome measurable in the etiolated seedling disappeared, with a half-life of less than 2 hours. The remaining 2% appeared, however, to be very stable and, when returned to darkness, the P_{fr} disappeared slowly enough for it to be detected as long as 24 hours later (Jabben and Deitzer, 1978b). The pool of phytochrome that predominates in the light has been termed 'stable' to differentiate it from the 'labile' pool that predominates in etiolated tissue (Jabben and Holmes, 1985). Recent evidence (Cordonnier, unpublished observations), obtained using monoclonal antibodies able to distinguish between phytochrome derived from dark- and light-grown tissue, indicates that the two pools may differ in primary structure and thus may arise as different gene products. The 'labile' pool of phytochrome is assumed to be responsible for the onset of timing being initiated when P_{fr} falls below a low threshold level. The 'stable' pool would then provide the P_{fr} required later in the dark period.

Another observation that may affect the detection of day-length by phytochrome is that the expression of the phytochrome gene(s) is inhibited by light and that this inhibition is mediated by phytochrome (Gottmann and Schäfer, 1982; Colbert *et al.*, 1985). Thus, since phytochrome is able to regulate its own synthesis, it is possible that the effect of far-red light on the rhythmic promotion of flowering in barley and *Lolium* (Deitzer *et al.*, 1979; Vince-Prue, 1983) is based on the reversal of the light-dependent inhibition of phytochrome mRNA synthesis. It has been shown that the addition of far-red to white light leads to an increase in P_{tot} (Smith, 1981). It is suggested that this increase in P_{tot} is restricted to the 'labile' pool of phytochrome which is normally synthesized only in the dark. Perhaps it is this pool of phytochrome that is responsible for the inhibitor production during darkness that is reversed by increasing day-lengths.

Several recent publications have described a number of promising approaches attempting to identify the photoperiodically regulated products of gene expression in the leaf. Qualitative changes in leaf proteins have been reported in *Pharbitis* using immunoprecipitation on Octerlony double-diffusion plates and immunoelectrophoresis following induction (Maeng, 1982). Also Warm (1984) has demonstrated differences in the products of *in vitro* translated mRNAs in *Hyoscyamus niger*. Unfortunately, since phytochrome and photoperiodism have been shown to regulate a multiplicity of responses unrelated to flowering (e.g. the synthesis of the chloroplast proteins cited above), there is currently no way to establish whether these changes are directly related to floral induction. Utilizing these techniques in combination with genetic approaches (Law and Scarth, 1984) may be the most expeditious means of finding at least one of the events leading to the production of a floral stimulus or translocatable inhibitor.

Translocation

Since a quantifiable response in the leaf is lacking, and the identity of the effector molecule(s) produced is unknown (Schwabe, 1984; Zeevaart, 1979, 1984), it is necessary to measure some change that takes place in apical or lateral meristems that are some distance removed from the site of induction. The preponderance of evidence supports the conclusion that the floral stimulus (both promoter and inhibitor) is carried passively between leaf and apex as part of the normal translocation stream in the phloem. Thus any perturbation of the assimilate translocating pathway should result in an interference with floral evocation. For example, a low-temperature treatment given to the stem section between an induced *Pharbitis* leaf and the apex inhibited both sugar translocation and flowering (Kavon and Zeevaart, 1979). Ogawa and King (1979) were also able to show that cytokinin inhibited the export of ^{14}C from cotyledons of *Pharbitis* to the same extent that it inhibited flowering.

Day-length directly influences the amount of carbohydrate that is exported from the leaf in a number of species by regulating the partitioning of newly fixed carbon between soluble sugars and starch (Chatterton and Silvius, 1979, 1980a, b). Starch levels in the leaves of plants grown under short-days are typically 2–3 times higher than in leaves kept in long-days. This increased accumulation of starch has been found to be the result of decreased translocation (Sicher *et al.*, 1982). Day-length extensions with dim white or far-red light, night-break, and shifted short-days all indicated that this response was truly photoperiodic and suggested that it was mediated by phytochrome (Britz *et al.*, 1985a). The rates of net photosynthesis, starch accumulation and total soluble carbohydrate accumulation were found to be based on a circadian rhythm when plants were transferred from continuous dim light or darkness to bright light for 6 hours (Britz *et al.*, 1985b). Shortening the light period by 8 hours resulted in a phase advance in the rhythms both of starch and of soluble-sugar accumulation but not in net photosynthesis (Britz, 1986). The extent of the phase shift was equivalent to the decrease in the photoperiod, strongly suggesting that they were synchronized to the light-off signal. Further, it appears that this regulation of photosynthate partitioning is not only restricted to the leaf but also continues to function in isolated chloroplasts (Robinson, 1984). Thus it appears that the rhythmic control of the translocation of sugar out of the leaf may be regulated by the same mechanism as the onset of time measurement for flowering in *Pharbitis* (Lumsden *et al.*, 1982).

Finally, the floral stimulus presumably must move along with a sugar gradient (Lee *et al.*, 1980) in the symplast to the veins in the leaf (Geiger, 1975). They are then transferred to the apoplast near the minor veins (Geiger, 1979). This unloading into the vascular free space is stimulated by potassium ions in sugar beet (Doman and Geiger, 1979), suggesting that there may be an active proton co-transport mechanism involved. Uptake into the sieve tubes from the vascular free space probably occurs through the phloem parenchyma and/or companion cells and is also an active carrier-mediated process. Transfer from the companion cells to the sieve tubes is symplastic (Gifford and Evans, 1981). The stimulation of unloading into the vascular free space by potassium ions is especially interesting given the rhythmic nature of the regulation of assimilate partitioning. Rhythmic changes in potassium ion movements are the basis for the circadian regulation of leaf movements (Satter and Galston, 1981), suggesting that a common membrane-mediated process could link the phytochrome interaction with all of these physiological events.

Initiation

The term initiation is fully synonomous with the more specific term evocation (Evans, 1971) and they will be used interchangeably here. Evocation is defined as the events that occur at the apex as a consequence of the arrival of the floral stimulus from the leaf, transforming it from an indeterminate to a determinate organ. As with the events in the leaf, changes in such environmental parameters as photoperiod or temperature may lead to a multiplicity of effects, not all of which are directly and causally related to floral morphogenesis. These events will be considered in detail in Chapters 23, 24 and 25 will therefore be mentioned only briefly here.

Early morphological changes that most physiologists use as indicators of evocation are:

1. The stimulation of precocious axillary bud growth.
2. Enlargement of the apex.
3. A change in the size, arrangement and rate of formation of primordia.
4. A change in internode length.
5. A change in the form of primordia development from leaf to bract (Lyndon and Francis, 1984).

Of these, only apex enlargement has been suggested to be the cause of evocation (Charles-Edwards *et al.*, 1979; Thornley and Cockshull, 1980). Cytological changes generally result in the loss of distinguishable patterns of zonation in the apical dome (Nougarède, 1967). These are accompanied by histochemical changes in the distribution of RNA, ribosome density and enzyme activity (Lin and Gifford, 1976; Jacqmard, 1978).

Of particular interest to this discussion (relative to the regulation of translocation at the source) is the finding that there are changes in the size and number of starch grains in the apex at the time of evocation (Bernier, 1971). Also, the recent elegant quantitative measurements of carbohydrate changes in apical cells (Bodson and Outlaw, 1985) suggest that carbohydrate changes may be the cause of the observed early increases in apical growth and rates of cell division. There is evidence that light can regulate the uptake of sugars by sink tissues such as apical meristems (Thaine *et al.*, 1959). Thus if the mechanism for phloem unloading at the apex is regulated by the same rhythmic phenomenon as that described above for phloem loading in the leaf, photoperiod could directly influence events at the apex. That is not to say that a floral stimulus can be produced by the apex but rather that light perceived by apical tissues could modify the responsiveness of the apex to the arrival of that stimulus (Gressel *et al.*, 1980).

References

APEL, K. (1979). Phytochrome-induced appearance of mRNA activity for the apoprotein of the light-harvesting chlorophyll a/b protein of barley (*Hordeum vulgare*). *European Journal of Biochemistry*, **97**, 183–188

APEL, K. (1981). Protochlorophllide holochrome of barley. Phytochrome-induced decrease in translatable mRNA coding for the NADPH: Protochlorophyllide oxidoreductase. *European Journal of Biochemistry*, **10**, 89–93

BARBER, H.N. (1959). Physiological genetics of Pisum II. The genetics of photoperiodism and vernalization. *Heredity*, **13**, 33–60

BARHAM, R.W. and RASMUSSON, D.C. (1981). Inheritance of photoperiod response in barley. *Crop Science*, **21**, 454–456

BERNIER, G. (1971). Structural and metabolic changes in the shoot apex in transition to flowering. *Canadian Journal of Botany*, **49**, 803–819

BERNIER, G. (1984). The factors controlling floral evocation: an overview. In *Light and the Flowering Process* (D. Vince-Prue, B. Thomas and K. Cockshull, Eds), pp. 277–294. London, Academic Press

BERNIER, G., KINET, J.M. and SACHS, R.M. (1981). *The Physiology of Flowering*, Vols I–III, Boca Raton, Fl, CRC Press

BODSON, M. and OUTLAW, W.H. (1985). Elevation in the sucrose content of the shoot apical meristem of *Sinapis alba* at floral evocation. *Plant Physiology*, **79**, 420–424

BRITZ, S.J. (1986). Role of circadian rhythms in Photoperiodic response of photosynthate partitioning in sorghum leaves. In *Phloem Transport* (R. Cronshaw *et al.*, Eds), pp. 527–534, New York, Alan R. Liss

BRITZ, S.J., HUNGERFORD, W.E. and LEE, D.R. (1985a). Photoperiodic regulation of photosynthate partitioning in leaves of *Digitaris decumbens* Stent. *Plant Physiology*, **78**, 710–714

BRITZ, S.J., HUNGERFORD, W.E. and LEE, D.R. (1985b). Photosynthate partitioning into *Digitaria decumbens* leaf starch varies rhythmically with respect to duration of prior incubation in continuous dim light. *Photochemistry and Photobiology*, **42**, 741–744

CHAMPAGNAT, P. and JACQUES, R. (1979). *La Physiologie de la Floraison*, Paris, CNRS

CHARLES-EDWARDS, D.A., COCKSHULL, K.E., HORRIDGE, J.S. and THORNLEY, J.H.M. (1979). A model of flowering in Chrysanthemum. *Annals of Botany*, **4**, 557–566

CHATTERTON, N.J. and SILVIUS, J.E. (1979). Photosynthate partitioning into starch in soybean leaves. I. Effects of photoperiod versus photosynthetic period duration. *Plant Physiology*, **64**, 749–753

CHATTERTON, N.J. and SILVIUS, J.E. (1980a). Photosynthate partitioning into leaf starch as affected by daily photosynthetic period duration in six species. *Physiologia Plantarum*, **49**, 141–144

CHATTERTON, N.J. and SILVIUS, J.E. (1980b). Acclimation of photosynthate partitioning and photosynthetic rates to changes in the length of daily photosynthetic period. *Annals of Botany*, **46**, 739–745

COLBERT, J.T., HERSHEY, H.P. and QUAIL, P.H. (1985). Phytochrome regulation of phytochrome mRNA abundance. *Plant Molecular Biology*, **5**, 91–101

DEITZER, G.F., HAYES, R. and JABBEN, M. (1979). Kinetics and time dependence of the effect of far-red light on the photoperiodic induction of flowering in Winter barley. *Plant Physiology*, **64**, 1015–1021

DEITZER, G.F., HAYES, R. and JABBEN, M. (1982). Phase shift in the circadian rhythm of floral promotion by far-red energy in *Hordeum vulgare* L. *Plant Physiology*, **69**, 597–601

DESILVA, D.L.R., COX, R.C., HETHERINGTON, A.M. and MANSFIELD, T.A. (1985). Suggested involvement of calcium and calmodulin in the responses of stomata to abscisic acid. *New Phytology*, **101**, 555–563

DIETER, P. (1984). Calmodulin and calmodulin-mediated processes in plants. *Plant Cell Environment*, **7**, 371–380

DOMAN, D.C. and GEIGER, D.R. (1979). Effect of exogenously supplied foliar potassium on phloem loading in *Beta vulgaris* L. *Plant Physiology*, **64**, 528–533

DORMLING, I., GUSTAFSSON, A. and EKMAN, G. (1975). Growth disorders and phenotype variability in phytotron-cultivated barley. *Hereditas*, **79**, 255–272

DREYER, E.M. and WEISENSEEL, M.H. (1979). Phytochrome mediated uptake of calcium in *Mougeotia* cells. *Planta*, **146**, 31–39

EVANS, L.T. (1971). Flower induction and the florigen concept. *Annual Review of Plant Physiology*, **22**, 365–394

FEJER, S.D. and FEDAK, G. (1979). Day-length sensitivity in spring barley. *Barley Genetic News*, **9**, 19–20

GEIGER, D.R. (1975). Phloem loading. In *Encyclopedia of Plant Physiology* (M.H. Zimmermann and J.A. Milburn, Eds), Vol. 17, pp. 395–431, Berlin, Springer Verlag

GEIGER, D.R. (1979). Control of partitioning and export of carbon in leaves of higher plants. *Botanical Gazette*, **140**, 241–248

GIFFORD, R.M. and EVANS, L.T. (1981). Photosynthesis, carbon partitioning and yield. *Annual Review of Plant Physiology*, **32**, 485–509

GOLLMER, I. and APEL, K. (1983). The phytochrome-controlled accumulation of mRNA sequences encoding the light-harvesting chlorophyll a/b protein of barley (*Hordeum vulgare* L.) *European Journal of Biochemistry*, **133**, 309–313

GOTO, K., LAVAL-MARTIN, D.L. and EDMUNDS, L.N. Jr. (1985). Biochemical modeling of an autonomously oscillatory circadian clock in *Euglena*. *Science*, **228**, 1284–1288

GOTTMANN, K. and SCHÄFER, E. (1982). *In vitro* synthesis of phytochrome apoprotein directed by mRNA from light- and dark-grown *Avena* seedlings. *Photochemistry and Photobiology*, **35**, 521–525

GRESSEL, J., ZILBERSTEIN, J.A., PORATH, D. and ARZEE, T. (1980). Demonstration with fiber illumination that *Pharbitis* plumules also perceive flowering photoinduction. In *Photoreceptors and Plant Development* (J. deGreef, Ed.), pp. 525–530, Antwerpen University Press

HALEVY, A.H. (1985). *Handbook of Flowering*, Vol. 1–4, Boca Raton, FL, CRC Press

HEIM, B., JABBEN, M. and SCHÄFER, E. (1981). Phytochrome destruction in dark- and light-grown *Amaranthus caudatus* seedlings. *Photochemistry and Photobiology*, **34**, 89–93

HEPLER, P.K. and WAYNE, R.O. (1985). Calcium and plant development. *Annual Review of Plant Physiology*, **36**, 397–439

JABBEN, M. and DEITZER, G.F. (1978a). A method for measuring phytochrome in plants grown in white light. *Photochemistry and Photobiology*, **27**, 799–802

JABBEN, M. and DEITZER, G.F. (1978b). Spectrophotometric phytochrome measurements in light-grown *Avena sativa* L. *Planta*, **143**, 309–313

JABBEN, M. and HOLMES, M.G. (1985). Phytochrome in light-grown plants in *Encyclopedia of Plant Physiology* (W. Shropshire, J. and H. Mohr, Eds), NS Vol. 16b, pp. 704–722. Berlin, Springer Verlag

JACQMARD, A. (1978). Histochemical localization of enzyme activity during floral evocation in the shoot apical meristem of *Sinapis alba*. *Protoplasma*, **94**, 315–324

KAVON, D.L. and ZEEVAART, J.A.D. (1979). Simultaneous inhibition of translocation of phtosynthate and of floral stimulus by localized low-temperature treatment in short-day *Pharbitis nil*. *Planta*, **144**, 201–204

KELLY, G.J. (1984). Calcium, calmodulin and the action of plant hormones. *Trends in Biochemical Science*, **97**, 4–5

KING, R.W. (1984). Light and photoperiodic timing. In *Light and The Flowering Process* (D. Vince-Prue, B. Thomas and K.E. Cockshull, Eds), pp. 91–106. London, Academic Press

KING, R.W. and CUMMING, B. (1972). Role of phytochrome in photoperiodic time measurement and its relation to rhythmic timekeeping in the control of flowering in *Chenopodium rubrum*. *Planta*, **108**, 39–57

KING, R.W., SCHÄFER, E., THOMAS, B. and VINCE-PRUE, D. (1982). Photoperiodism and rhythmic response to light. *Plant Cell and Environment*, **5**, 395–404

LANG, A. (1965). Physiology of flower initiation. In *Encyclopedia of Plant Physiology* (W. Ruhland, Ed.), Vol. XV/I, pp. 1380–1536. Berlin, Springer Verlag

LANG, A. (1980). Inhibition of flowering in long-day plants. In *Plant Growth Substances* (F. Skoog, Ed.), pp. 310–322. Berlin, Springer Verlag

LANG, A., CHAILAKHYAN, M. KH. and FROLOVA, I.A. (1977). Promotion and inhibition of flower formation in a day-neutral plant in grafts with a short-day plant and a long-day plant. *Proceedings of the National Academy of Science, USA*, **74**, 2412–2416

LARGE, E.C. (1954). Growth stages in cereals. Illustrations of the Feeke's scale. *Plant Pathology*, **3**, 128–129

LAW, C.N. and SCARTH, R. (1984). Genetics and its potential for understanding the action of light in flowering. In *Light and The Flowering Process* (D. Vince-Prue, B. Thomas and K. E. Cockshull, Eds), pp. 193–210. London, Academic Press

LEE, H.J., ASHLEY, D.A. and BROWN, R.H. (1980). Sucrose concentration gradients in wheat leaves. *Crop Science*, **20**, 95–99

LIN, J. and GIFFORD, E.M. (1976). The distribution of ribosomes in the vegetative and floral apices of *Adonis aestivalis*. *Canadian Journal of Botany*, **54**, 2478–2483

LUMSDEN, P., THOMAS, B. and VINCE-PRUE, D. (1982). Photoperiodic control of flowering in dark-grown seedlings of *Pharbitis nil* Choisy: The effect of skeleton and continuous light photoperiods. *Plant Physiology*, **70**, 277–282

LUMSDEN, P.J. and VINCE-PRUE, D. (1984). The perception of dusk signals in photoperiodic time measurement. *Physiologia Plantarum*, **60**, 427–432

LYNDON, R.F. and BATTEY, N.H. (1985). The growth of the shoot apical meristem during flower initiation. *Biologia Plantarum (Praha)*, **27**, 339–349

LYNDON, R.F. and FRANCIS, D. (1984). The response of the shoot apex to light-generated signals from leaves. In *Light and The Flowering Process* (D. Vince-Prue, B. Thomas and K.E. Cockshull, Eds), pp. 171–192. London, Academic Press

MAENG, J. (1982). Immunological analysis of proteins in the leaf of *Pharbitis nil* during photoinduction of flowering. *Korean Journal of Botany*, **25**, 169–174

MARMÉ, D. (1977). Phytochrome: Membranes as possible sites of primary action. *Annual Review of Plant Physiology*, **28**, 173–198

MOHR, H. (1972). *Lectures on Photomorphogenesis*. Berlin, Springer Verlag

MURFET, I.C. (1971). Flowering in *Pisum*: Reciprocal grafts between known genotypes. *Australian Journal of Biological Sciences*, **24**, 1089–1101

MURFET, I.C. (1985). *Pisum sativum*. In *Handbook of Flowering* (A.H. Halevy, Ed.), Vol. IV, pp. 97–126. Boca Raton, FL, CRC Press

MURFET, I.C. and REID, J.B. (1973). Flowering in *Pisum*: The influence of photoperiod and vernalizing temperatures on the expression of genes Lf and Sn. *Zeitschrift für Pflanzenphysiologie*, **71**, 323–331

NOUGAREDE, A. (1967). Experimental cytology of the shoot apical cells during vegetative growth and flowering. *International Review of Cytology*, **21**, 203–351

OGAWA, T. and KING, R.W. (1979). Indirect action of benzyladenine and other chemicals on flowering of *Pharbitis nil* Chois. *Plant Physiology*, **63**, 643–649

PAPENFUSS, H.D. and SALISBURY, F.B. (1967). Properties of clock resetting in flowering of *Xanthium*. *Plant Physiology*, **42**, 1562–1568

PATON, D.M. and BARBER, H.N. (1955). Physiological genetics of *Pisum*. I. Grafting experiments between early and late varieties. *Australian Journal of Biological Sciences*, **8**, 231–240

ROBINSON, J.M. (1984). Photosynthetic carbon metabolism in leaves and isolated chloroplasts from spinach plants grown under short and intermediate photosynthetic periods. *Plant Physiology*, **75**, 397–409

ROUX, S.J., MCENTIRE, K., SLOCUM, R., CEDEL, T.E. and HALE, C. II (1981). Phytochrome induces photoreversible calcium fluxes in a purified mitochondrial fraction from oats. *Proceedings of the National Academy of Science of the USA*, **78**, 283–287

SATTER, R.L. (1979). Leaf movements and tendril curling. In *Encyclopedia of Plant Physiology* (W. Haupt and M.E. Feinleib, Eds), Vol. 7, pp. 442–484. Berlin, Springer Verlag

SATTER, R.L. and GALSTON, A.W. (1981). Mechanisms of control of leaf movements. *Annual Review of Plant Physiology*, **32**, 83–110

SATTER, R.L., GUGGINO, S.E., LONERGAN, T.A. and GALSTON, A.W. (1981). The effects of blue and far-red light on rhythmic leaf movements in *Samanea* and *Albizzia*. *Plant Physiology*, **57**, 965–968

SCHWABE, W.W. (1984). Photoperiodic induction: Flower inhibiting substances. In *Light and the Flowering Process* (D. Vince-Prue, B. Thomas and K.E. Cockshull, Eds), pp. 143–156. London, Academic Press

SICHER, R.C., HARRIS, W.G., KREMER, D.F. and CHATTERTON, N.J. (1982). Effects of shortened day length upon translocation and starch accumulation by maize, wheat and pangola grass leaves. *Canadian Journal of Botany*, **60**, 1304–1309

SIMON, E., SATTER, R.L., and GALSTON, A.W. (1976). Circadian rhythmicity in excised *Samanea* pulvini. II. Resetting the clock by phytochrome conversion. *Plant Physiology*, **58**, 421–425

SMITH, H. (1981). Evidence that P_{fr} is not the active form of phytochrome in light-grown maize. *Nature (London)*, **293**, 163–165

STIEKEMA, W.J., WIMPEE, C.F., SILVERTHORNE, J. and TOBIN, E.M. (1983). Phytochrome control of the expression of two nuclear genes encoding for chloroplast proteins in *Lemna gibba* L. G3. *Plant Physiology*, **72**, 717–724

TAKIMOTO, A. and SAJI, H. (1984). A role of phytochrome in photoperiodic induction: two-phytochrome-pool theory. *Physiologia Plantarum*, **61**, 675–682

TAKAHASHI, R. and YASUDA, S. (1971). Genetics of earliness and growth habit in barley. In *Barley Genetics II* (R.A. Nilan, Ed.), pp. 388–408. Pullman, Washington State University Press

THAINE, R., OVENDEN, S.L. and TURNER, J.S. (1959). Translocation of labelled assimilates in the soybean. *Australian Journal of Biological Science*, **12**, 349–372

THORNLEY, J.H.M. and COCKSHULL, K.E. (1980). A catastrophe model for the switch from vegetative to reproductive growth in the shoot apex. *Annals of Botany*, **46**, 333–341

VINCE-PRUE, D. (1983). Photomorphogenesis and flowering. In *Encyclopedia of Plant Physiology* (W. Shropshire, Jr. and H. Mohr, Eds), Vol. 16b, pp. 457–490. Berlin, Springer Verlag

VINCE-PRUE, D. (1985). What do we know about the fundamental physiological causes and mechanisms in relation to flower induction and development? *Nordishe Jordbrugsforsheves Forening*, **22**, 16–35

VINCE-PRUE, D., THOMAS, B. and COCKSHULL, K.E. (Eds) (1984). *Light and the Flowering Process*. London, Academic Press

WARM, E. (1984). Changes in the composition of *in vitro*-translated leaf mRNA caused by photoperiodic flower induction of *Hyoscyamus niger*. *Physiologia Plantarum*, **61**, 344–350

ZEEVAART, J.A.D. (1984). Photoperiodic induction, floral stimulus and flower-promoting substances. In *Light and the Flowering Process* (D. Vince-Prue, B. Thomas and K.E. Cockshull, Eds), pp. 137–142. London, Academic Press

ZEEVAART, J.A.D. (1979). Perception, nature and complexity of transmitted signals. In *La Physiologie de la Floraison* (P. Champagnat and R. Jacques, Eds), pp. 59–90. Paris, CNRS

ZOCCHI, G., ROGERS, S.A. and HANSON, J.B. (1983). Inhibition of proton pumping in corn roots is associated with increased phosphorylation of membrane proteins. *Plant Science Letters*, **31**, 215–221

18

INDUCTIVE EVENTS IN THE LEAVES: TIME MEASUREMENT AND PHOTOPERCEPTION IN THE SHORT-DAY PLANT, *PHARBITIS NIL*

D. VINCE-PRUE
Glasshouse Crops Research Station, Littlehampton, UK

P.J. LUMSDEN
National Institute for Basic Biology, Okazaki, Japan

The photoperiodic induction of flowering takes place in the leaves under the control of a mechanism that is capable of measuring time. In seedlings of *Pharbitis nil*, induction occurs when a single period of darkness longer than a critical duration is interposed into continuous light, thus establishing that—in common with the majority of short-day plants (SDP)—elapsed time in darkness is the crucial timekeeping factor for floral induction. However, exposure to light is also an integral part of the overall mechanism. The aim of the work described here was to obtain a better understanding of the nature and functions of the light reactions involved in the photoperiodic induction of flowering.

Methods

The SDP *Pharbitis nil* (Japanese Morning Glory) cv Violet can be induced to flower by exposing plants to a single dark period following a photoperiod of several hours in white light, or even following a short pulse of light provided that this is accompanied by an application of the cytokinin, benzyladenine (Ogawa and King, 1979). In the experiments reported here, 3-day-old dark-grown seedlings were exposed to a single light period followed by a single dark period. During the light period, plants were sprayed with benzyladenine ($120\,\mu mol\,l^{-1}$ with 0.05% Tween 20 and 2% ethanol). After the experimental light–dark cycle, the plants were grown on in continuous light for a further 12 days, when the number of flower buds was determined.

The role of light in timekeeping

A characteristic feature of SDP is that flowering is prevented when a brief exposure to light is given at a particular time during an otherwise inductive dark period. The first approach used here to understanding the role of light in relation to timekeeping was to examine how the time of maximum sensitivity to such a night-break (NBmax) was related to the photoperiod. The duration of the single photoperiod was varied and followed with an inductive dark period of constant duration, interrupted by a 10-min night-break. Following a 10-min photoperiod, there was a rhythmic response to the time at which a night-break was given, with periods of inhibition occurring at about 24 h intervals. With longer photoperiods, the rhythm was gradually damped and, after 24 h, there was essentially only a single night-break response (*Figure 18.1*). For photoperiod durations up to 6 h, the first inhibition point occurred at about 15 h after the *beginning* of the light period but, with photoperiods longer than 6 h, the first NBmax always occurred at about 9 h after the *end* of the light period (*Figure 18.2(a)*). In both cases, a second NBmax occurred approximately 24 h after the first (Lumsden *et al.*, 1982).

Thus timing of sensitivity to a night-break in *Pharbitis* appears to be controlled by a circadian rhythm which is initiated (or re-set) by a light-on signal; this rhythm continues to run in light for about 6 h, with a light-sensitive phase occurring at about 15 h after the light-on signal (at circadian time (CT) = 15). However, the rhythm behaves as if it were suspended after about 6 h in continuous light, thereafter being released (at CT = 6) by the light-dark transition so that the time of maximum sensitivity to a night-break occurs about 9 h later (i.e. at CT = 15) irrespective of the photoperiod duration. At temperatures sufficient to sustain growth, the natural day-length is always longer than 6 h so that the flowering rhythm will be timed from the end of the photoperiod. Results similar to these have been obtained for *Xanthium strumarium*, another SDP flowering in response to a single photoinductive cycle (Papenfuss and Salisbury, 1967). The *Xanthium* results were obtained with previously light-grown plants showing that rhythm initiation (or re-setting) by a light-on signal and its subsequent suspension in continuous light are relevant to normal conditions of growth, as well as to dark-grown seedlings.

In *Pharbitis*, however, seedlings that had received a prior exposure to light did not respond in exactly the same manner as dark-grown seedlings. Following a single 24-h photoperiod, the major effect of a pulse of R light early in the subsequent dark period was to delay the phase of the light-off rhythm by between 1 and 3 h (cf. *Figure 18.5*).

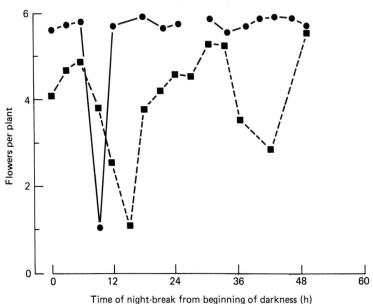

Figure 18.1   Flowering response of dark-grown seedlings to a 10-min R interruption of an inductive 48-h dark period following a single photoperiod of 24-h (●) or 10-min (■) duration. (Reproduced from Lumsden *et al.* (1982) and Lumsden (1984) by kind permission of publishers.)

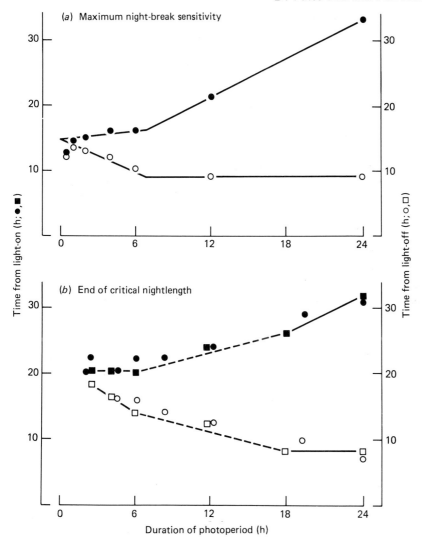

Figure 18.2 Times of (*a*) maximum sensitivity to a night-break or (*b*) the end of the critical dark period as a function of the duration of the preceding photoperiod. The points are plotted from the beginning (●, ■) and from the end (○, □) of the photoperiod. (Reproduced from Lumsden *et al.* (1982) and Lumsden (1984) by kind permission of publishers.)

At this time, therefore, a short exposure to light appeared primarily to interact with the existing 'light-off' rhythm set at the transition to darkness. After 6 h in darkness, it required exposure to light for about 2 h before a new rhythm was evident (Lumsden, unpublished observations).

Under natural conditions, the major determinant of flowering in SDP is the night-length and so it is important to establish whether this is timed in the same way as the night-break. In dark-grown *Pharbitis* seedlings, a 24 h periodicity in the response to the duration of darkness was seen after short photoperiods (Lumsden, 1984) confirming that a circadian rhythm underlies the measurement of the critical night-length. As with the night-break, the critical night-length appeared to be timed from light-on with photoperiods of up to about 6 h and to be a constant from light-off with longer photoperiods (*Figure 18.2(b)*). Similar results have been obtained by Saji *et al.* (1984). Despite the ambiguity with intermediate durations of photoperiod (*Figure 18.2(b)*), it seems a reasonable conclusion that the critical night-length depends on the same flowering rhythm as that which gives rise to the night-break response and is controlled by light in the same way.

These results show that a major function of the photoperiod is to set the phase of the circadian timer in such a way that, after several hours in continuous light, a light/dark transition releases the rhythm (or re-sets it) at a constant phase point. During darkness, the circadian timer established phases of sensitivity to light and the flowering response depends on whether the light-sensitive phase of the rhythm has been reached before the next exposure to light (dawn) occurs. This concept envisages that there are two different functions of light: to set the phase of the timekeeping rhythm and to interact with a particular phase of this rhythm to inhibit flowering in the classical night-break effect. Additionally, it has been found that the removal of the Pfr form of phytochrome early in the night can, under some conditions, also inhibit induction (Vince-Prue, 1983). From this brief summary, it is evident that light has 258 multiple actions in the photoperiodic control of flowering in the SDP *Pharbitis* and, therefore, the identity and functioning of the photoreceptor needs to be considered in each case.

The night-break response

The reversibility of a red (R) night-break (which would convert phytochrome to Pfr) by a brief exposure to far-red (FR) light (which would re-convert phytochrome to Pr) has established that phytochrome is the photoreceptor for the night-break response in a number of SDP, including *Pharbitis* (Fredericq, 1964). Although reversibility cannot be demonstrated under some conditions, because FR light is itself inhibitory to flowering when given at the time of NBmax (*Figure 18.3*), an action spectrum determined under such conditions has confirmed that the R night-break effect requires the photoconversion of Pr to Pfr (Saji *et al.*, 1983).

Since Pr→Pfr photoconversion is required, it is evident that the Pfr present at the end of the photoperiod is no longer present (or is no longer active) at the time of the night-break. This has led to the classical concept that the beginning of dark time measurement is coupled to the reduction of Pfr to a sub-threshold level, while the night-break inhibition requires the photoformation of Pfr. However, it is also evident from results of other experiments that Pfr is actually present and active at the time of the night-break, since its removal at this time by exposure to FR light can inhibit flowering (*Figure 18.3*).

Reversibility experiments have clearly established that flowering is restored by a subsequent exposure to R, except at the NBmax time, when R light is itself inhibitory (Saji *et al.*, 1983). Thus in recent years it has gradually become widely accepted that the classic model is inadequate and that the operation of the photoperiodic mechanism in SDP must involve either two different 'pools' of phytochrome or two different modes of action. The two-pool concept suggests that part of the total Pfr pool is stable in darkness and is required for floral initiation, while part is rapidly lost following transfer to darkness and is involved in the perception of the light/dark

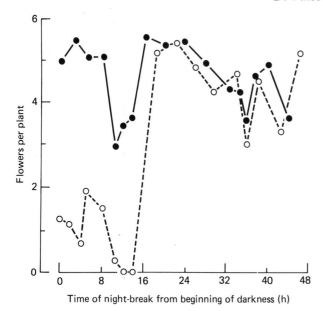

Figure 18.3 Flowering response of dark-grown seedlings to an interruption of an inductive 72-h dark period with either R (●) or FR (○) light. The interruption was given for 10 min in each case and the photoperiod duration was 4 h. (Reproduced from Lumsden (1984) by kind permission of publishers.)

transition and in the night-break effect. The physiological observations can also be accommodated by an alternative model with a single pool of phytochrome; it has been suggested, for example, that a Pfr-receptor complex dissociates in darkness leading to the end-of-day-signal, while the night-break establishes the formation of a new Pfr-receptor complex which inhibits flowering (Thomas and Vince-Prue, 1986). The persistent effect of Pfr in darkness could then be due to a stable Pfr-receptor complex. However, present evidence is insufficient to establish whether it is the kinetics of Pfr loss or the rate of dissociation of a Pfr-receptor complex that is important.

Control of the rhythm

The photoreceptor for the action of light in controlling the phase of the flowering rhythm has been far less studied than that for the night-break response. From the results already described, it is evident that the photocontrol of the rhythm involves at least three components: a light-on signal, a light-off signal and the apparent 'suspension' of the rhythm in continuous light.

Relatively little information is available on the nature of the light-on signal which initiates (or re-sets) the rhythm or on the photoreceptor involved in the action of continuous light to 'suspend' the rhythm. For dark-grown *Pharbitis* seedlings, a saturating pulse of R light is sufficient to act as a light-on signal and start the flowering rhythm (King *et al.*, 1982; and *Figure 18.1*). The possible involvement of phytochrome in the perception of this light-on signal has been examined by attempting to reverse the R light pulse with FR (Lumsden, 1984). The results were inconclusive, however, because of the Pfr requirement for flowering under these conditions. Despite the failure to show FR reversibility with respect to establishing the rhythm, the sensitivity to very short exposures of R light strongly suggests that phytochrome is the photoreceptor for the light-on signal.

Suspension of the rhythm is achieved in continuous white light after about 6 h. When plants were exposed to different coloured light for a single 24-h photoperiod (terminated with 10 min R to establish the same level of Pfr at the beginning of the dark period), the phase of the rhythm in the subsequent dark period was essentially the same after white, R, FR, or blue light, with NBmax occurring 8–9 h after the end of the photoperiod (Vince-Prue, 1981). Although FR, and, in particular, blue light gave less flowering and the NBmax time was more sharply defined after R or white light, the phasing (suspension) of the rhythm appeared to be just as effectively established in all treatments allowing no conclusion regarding the photoreceptor. It is clear, however, that the rhythm was not suspended by two pulses of R separated by 24h of darkness (Lumsden *et al.*, 1982) and so, if Pfr is the key factor, the maintenance of only about 3% Pfr/P is sufficient to effect suspension. The stable Pfr which has been shown to be present in the dark interval between the two R pulses for at least 12 h and to be required for flowering (Friend, 1975) is clearly not effective in suspending the rhythm.

Because the critical timekeeping feature in SDP is initiated by the light/dark transition at dusk, the nature of the light-off signal has received more attention than the other components of rhythm control. A number of earlier experiments established that an end-of-day exposure to FR, which would rapidly lower Pfr by photoconversion to Pr, had little effect on dark time-keeping in SDP, whether assessed by NBmax or critical night-length (Takimoto and Hamner, 1965; King and Cumming, 1972; Salisbury, 1981). More recently, we have carried out a very detailed examination of the effect of an end-of-day exposure to FR on the time of NBmax in *Pharbitis* and our results have also indicated that, at most, there is an acceleration of 30–40 min compared with plants transferred to darkness from R light (*Figure 18.4*). Thus, if the light/dark transition is sensed by a reduction in Pfr, this must involve a very rapidly lost pool. Earlier spectrophotometric measurements on bleached *Pharbitis* seedlings transferred to darkness from white fluorescent light are consistent with these results since they indicated the presence of Pfr which declined below the limit of detection within about 60 min, apparently by reversion to Pr (Vince-Prue *et al.*, 1978).

However, it is important to recognize that the existence of a pool of Pfr which is rapidly lost following transfer to darkness does not itself prove that the light-off signal is generated when a sub-threshold level of Pfr is achieved. Even the slight acceleration of timing following end-of-day FR could be explained by the more rapid dissociation of a Pfr-receptor complex in FR, as well as by the removal of Pfr. Consequently, the nature of the light-off signal is still open to question and experiments to distinguish between possible mechanisms (Thomas and Lumsden, 1984) remain to be carried out. The natural end-of-day signal is most probably a lowering of irradiance to a sub-threshold level during twilight (Salisbury, 1981; Lumsden and Vince-Prue, 1984).

In a subsequent series of experiments, plants were first exposed to 24 h white light in order to initiate and suspend the rhythm. This was followed by an extension treatment of 6 h in which the light conditions were varied. Thus in these experiments (Lumsden and Vince-Prue, 1984), the light-off signal was investigated in a different way, by attempting to determine what light input will prevent the release of the

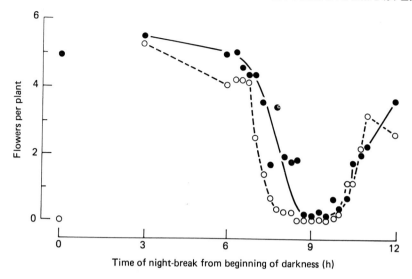

Figure 18.4 The effect of an end-of-day exposure to FR on the time of sensitivity to a 10-min R night-break. Plants were transferred to a 72-h dark period following 24-h white fluorescent light, 80 W m⁻² (●) or 24 h white light terminated by 5 min FR (○). Control plants (0) received no R night-break. (Reproduced from Lumsden and Vince-Prue (1984) by kind permission of publishers.)

'suspended' rhythm. A fully effective extension (equivalent to continuous light) would give NBmax 8–9 h after the end of the extension; a completely ineffective one (equivalent to darkness) would give NBmax 8–9 h after the end of the 24-h period in white light.

To investigate whether phytochrome is involved in the perception of continuous light, 5-min pulses of R were given at different frequencies during the 6-h extension. It was found that hourly pulses of R were just as effective as continuous light in delaying the time of NBmax. Less frequent pulses were less effective but resulted in some delay compared with darkness. The effectiveness of R pulses suggests that phytochrome is the photoreceptor for the effect of continuous light to prevent release of the rhythm. However, there was no evidence for FR reversibility of the R light pulses and so the latter cannot act simply by maintaining Pfr above some threshold value in the intervening dark periods. If Pfr is involved, coupling to the rhythm must be extremely rapid. When terminated with R, an extension with continuous FR (but not FR pulses) was equivalent to continuous R light (Thomas and Lumsden, 1984) indicating that the maintenance of even a low Pfr/P ratio prevented release of the rhythm.

In the absence of a terminal R, however, there was no clear light-off signal (Takimoto, 1967), although the interpretation of these results is complicated by the Pfr-requirement for flowering. Therefore, although continuous FR appears both to suspend the thythm (Vince-Prue, 1981) and to maintain it in suspension (Thomas and Lumsden, 1984), it is not yet clear whether a higher Pfr/P ratio is required for the generation of a light-off signal. This *zeitgeber* may be needed to 're-set' the rhythm to a particular CT at the onset of darkness rather than simply releasing it from a 'light-limit' cycle. To resolve this question, it would be necessary to carry out experiments under conditions where effects on phasing of the rhythm can be clearly distinguished from the effect of FR to depress the flowering response.

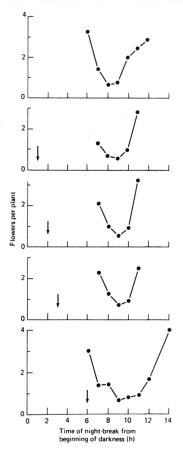

Figure 18.5   Effect of a 10 min R light interruption given at different times after the
onset of darkness (indicated by arrows) on the time of maximum sensitivity to a
night-break. Plants received a 24-h photoperiod followed by a 72-h inductive dark period,
with a 10-min R night-break given at different times as indicated on the abscissa.
(Reproduced from Lumsden *et al.* (1986) by kind permission of publishers.)

One problem with the day-extension pulse experiments is that, when given after 6 h
of darkness, even a single pulse of R seemed to delay the rhythm by 2–3 h, indicating
the possibility that the apparently continued 'suspension' of the rhythm might
actually be a consequence of repeated phase-shifting by the R pulses. This has now
been examined by giving a single pulse of R at different times after transfer to
darkness from continuous white light and determining the effect on the time of
NBmax. The results (*Figure 18.5*) show that a single pulse of R given after 1, 2 or 3 h
of darkness delays NBmax by about 1 h, whereas after 6 h in darkness the delay is
about 2–3 h. The behaviour of the rhythm in the earlier intermittent pulse treatments
can, therefore, be represented as in *Figure 18.6*, where the time of NBmax in each
treatment corresponds to circadian time (CT) = 14. Thus hourly pulses of light elicit a
phase shift (delay) of 1 h and so continually return the rhythm to CT6, the position it
is assumed to occupy during continuous white light. Pulses of light every 2 or 3 hours
also delay the rhythm but, because of the extra time in darkness, the rhythm is not

returned to the same position as in continuous light and so, after 6 h of such treatments, the phase of the rhythm is not delayed as much as by hourly pulses.

This demonstration that the effect of repeated pulses can be explained in terms of the effect of each pulse to phase-shift the 'released' rhythm casts doubt on the earlier interpretation that repeated pulses maintain the rhythm in 'suspension'. Therefore, it cannot be concluded on the basis of the pulse-extension experiments that phytochrome is the photoreceptor involved in preventing release of the rhythm. However, it is evident that 'suspension' and phase-shifting are characteristics of the response of the pacemaker to the input of light. The sensitivity of phase-shifting to a small input of R light strongly indicates that phytochrome is the photoreceptor in this case and it is arguable that, since the pacemaker is clearly accessible to the action of phytochrome,

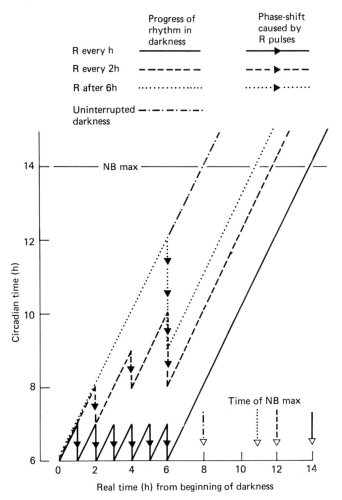

Figure 18.6 Theoretical behaviour of the photoperiodic response rhythm following R light pulses given at different frequencies during a 6-h extension following a 24-h photoperiod. The pulses are at hourly, 2-hourly and 6-hourly intervals and are shown in real time. The resulting shift of the rhythm is shown in terms of circadian time, where the end of the photoperiod corresponds with circadian time 6.

it is likely that all aspects of rhythm-phasing by light are dependent on this photoreceptor. However, this question is at present unresolved.

One consequence of the demonstration that the photoperiodic rhythm in *Pharbitis* is subject to phase-shifting is to raise questions about the action of the night-break. As outlined earlier, a commonly accepted hypothesis is that light has two different actions: phasing of the rhythm and the direct interaction with a light-sensitive or photoinducible phase of the rhythm in the night-break effect. However, it has also been proposed that light may only have one action, namely to affect the phase of the circadian rhythm. In this model, the night-break response in SDP results from the fact that, at certain times, the rhythm (or rhythms) is phase shifted in such a way as to inhibit floral induction. One approach to distinguish between the two hypotheses is to compare the sensitivities of the night-break response with that of phase-shifting on the assumption that, if the night-break effect is simply a consequence of rephasing, the two responses will have the same dose relationships. Experiments have been carried out at Okazaki, Japan to compare the relative sensitivites of the two responses at 6 and 8 h after the end of a 24-h photoperiod. The results (*Figure 18.7*) show that there are differences in the dose–response relationships, with the night-break showing increased sensitivity at 8 h, when the sensitivity of the phase-shifting response was reduced. A similar conclusion was reached from experiments carried out on seedlings given only a 10-min photoperiod as in *Figure 18.7* (Lee *et al.*, 1986). Thus for plants grown under different conditions and with different expressions of the photoperiodic rhythm there is evidence that the night-break inhibition can be distinguished from the

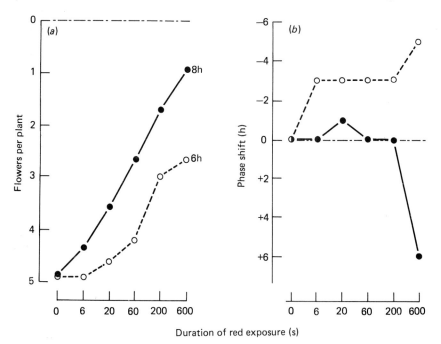

Figure 18.7 Dose-response curves for (*a*) the inhibition of flowering and (*b*) phase-shifting of the photoperiod rhythm at 6 h (○) and 8 h (●) after the beginning of a 72-h inductive dark period following a 24-h photoperiod. The phase-shifting response was assayed from the time of maximum sensitivity to a subsequent night-break. (Reproduced from Lumsden and Furuya (1986) by kind permission of authors and publishers.)

phase-shifting response in terms of differential sensitivity. It is therefore clear that, although the phase of the photoperiodic rhythm in *Pharbitis nil* can be shifted by a R pulse, the observed inhibition of flowering at NBmax must result from another action of light, most probably a direct interaction with the rhythm as proposed in Pittendrigh's 'External-Coincidence' model for photoperiodism (Pittendrigh, 1966).

The Pfr-requiring reaction

This reaction has been extensively studied but its role in the overall photoperiodic mechanism remains obscure. Action spectra and R-reversibility of the inhibition of flowering by end-of-day FR have established that Pfr is required for realization of the flowering reponse (Nakayama *et al.*, 1960). Experiments of the kind shown in *Figure 18.3* have shown that this effect is dependent on the presence of Pfr which is stable in darkness and may continue to promote flowering for many hours. However, as we have already discussed, the light-off signal and the night-break response seem to involve a different pool of phytochrome, or a different Pfr-receptor association. Surprisingly, it has never been established that the Pfr-requiring reaction takes place at the same site as the photoperiodic timekeeping reactions. For example, it has recently been observed that FR light can directly influence cell-cycle events in excised apical domes of *Silene coeli-rosa* (Ormrod, 1985) and such effects could be associated with the expression of flowering. Consequently, we have recently investigated the site of perception for the FR inhibition of flowering in *Pharbitis*, using optical fibres to deliver FR light to the apex or cotyledon. The results (*Figure 18.8*) have established for the first time that this FR effect is sensed primarily in the expanded cotyledon. Thus the perception of light for the Pfr-requiring reaction takes place in the same organ as for perception of the critical night-length and the two pools or actions of phytochrome which have been postulated to explain the physiological responses to R and FR light must, therefore, co-exist within the leaf, although not necessarily within the same cell.

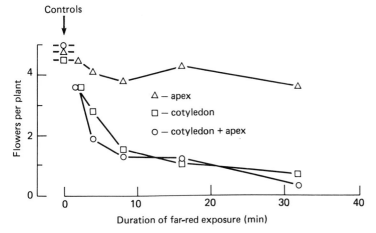

Figure 18.8   Site of perception of the Pfr-requiring reaction. Plants received various durations of FR light (λmax 729 nm; 0.13 W m^{-2}) delivered to the cotyledon, apex, or cotyledon plus apex using an optical fibre system. (Reproduced from Knapp *et al.* (1986) by kind permission of authors and publishers.)

The fact that, under some conditions, the Pfr-requirement for flowering continues well into the dark period has been a major consideration in the development of the two-pool/two-action hypotheses. However, continued action of Pfr during the dark period does not seem to be an essential feature of the photoperiodic mechanism in *Pharbitis nil*. After a photoperiod of <12 h, flowering was completely prevented when a FR exposure was given at least 16 h into the dark period but, when the light period was extended to 32 h, a terminal FR treatment did not inhibit flowering and the Pfr-requiring reaction must have been completed during the photoperiod itself (Lumsden, 1984). There is some evidence that the Pfr-requiring reaction is actually accomplished more rapidly in the light and also at higher irradiances (Vince-Prue, 1983). The significance of these observations is, however, not understood.

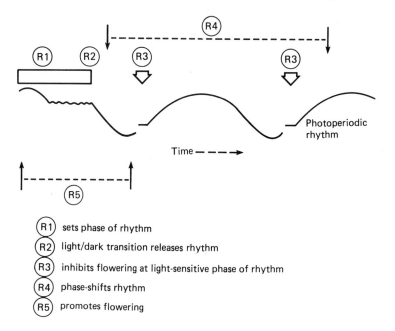

Figure 18.9   Schema showing multiple actions of light in the photoperiod control of flowering in the SDP, *Pharbitis nil.*

A model for the photoperiodic mechanism in *Pharbitis nil*

The various points discussed in this chapter are drawn together and presented in the form of a simple model for the operation of the photoperiodic mechanism in the cotyledons of *Pharbitis nil* (*Figure 18.9*). It comprises the initiation and 'suspension' (R1) of a circadian rhythm, which is released at the light/dark transition (R2) to free-run in darkness. Phases of sensitivity to light are established by the pacemaker and, at these times, light interacts with the rhythm to inhibit flowering (R3). Light also phase-shifts the rhythm (R4), the direction and magnitude of the phase-shift depending on when the light pulse is given. Finally, Pfr must be present in the cotyledons for many hours in order to achieve flowering (R5). Phytochrome is probably the only photoreceptor which inputs to the pacemaker to control the ryhthm and to interact with the rhythm at the light-sensitive phase. However, a large body of physiological evidence indicates that the multiple actions of phytochrome cannot be explained in terms of a single pool of phytochrome acting only as Pfr.

References

FREDERICQ, H. (1964). Conditions determining effects of far-red and red irradiations on flowering response of *Pharbitis nil. Plant Physiology*, **39**, 812–816

FRIEND, D.J.C. (1975). Light requirements for photoperiodic sensitivity in cotyledons of dark-grown *Pharbitis nil. Physiologia Plantarum*, **35**, 286–296

KING, R.W. and CUMMING, B. (1972). The role of phytochrome in photoperiodic time-measurement and its relation to rhythmic time-keeping in the control of flowering in *Chenopodium rubrum* L. *Planta*, **108**, 39–57

KING, R.W., SCHÄFER, E., THOMAS, B. and VINCE-PRUE, D. (1982). Photoperiodism and rhythmic response to light. *Plant, Cell and Environment*, **5**, 395–404

KNAPP, P.H., SAWHNEY, S., GRIMMET, M. and VINCE-PRUE, D. (1986). Site of perception of the far-red inhibition of flowering in *Pharbitis nil* Choisy. *Plant and Cell Physiology*, **27**, 1147–1152

LEE, H.S.J., VINCE-PRUE, D. and KENDRICK, R.E. (1986). Phase shifting effects in the photoperiodic rhythm of flowering in dark-grown seedlings of *Pharbitis nil* Chois. *Plant and Cell Physiology* (in press)

LUMSDEN, P.J. (1984). *Photoperiodic Control of Floral Induction in* Pharbitis nil. Ph.D. Thesis, University of Sussex

LUMSDEN, P.J. and FURUYA, M. (1986). Evidence for two actions of light in the photoperiodic induction of *Pharbitis nil. Plant and Cell Physiology*, **27** (in press)

LUMSDEN, P.J. and VINCE-PRUE, D. (1984). The perception of dusk signals in photoperiodic time-measurement. *Physiologia Plantarum*, **60**, 427–432

LUMSDEN, P.J., THOMAS, B. and VINCE-PRUE, D. (1982). Photoperiodic control of flowering in dark-grown seedlings of *Pharbitis nil* Choisy. The effect of skeleton and continuous light photoperiods. *Plant Physiology*, **70**, 277–282

LUMSDEN, P.J., VINCE-PRUE, D. and FURUYA, M. (1986). Phase-shifting of the photoperiodic flowering response rhythm in *Pharbitis nil* by red-light pulses. *Physiologia Plantarum*, **67**, 604–607

NAKAYAMA, S., BORTHWICK, H.A. and HENDRICKS, S.B. (1960). Failure of photoreversible control of flowering in *Pharbitis nil. Botanical Gazette*, **121**, 237–243

OGAWA, Y. and KING, R.W. (1979). Establishment of photoperiodic sensitivity by benzyladenine and a brief red irradiation in dark-grown seedlings of *Pharbitis nil* Chois. *Plant and Cell Physiology*, **20**, 115–122

ORMROD, J.C. (1985). *The effects of light on cell division in the shoot apical meristem of* Silene coeli-rosa [L.] *Godron in relation to the transition to floral growth*. Ph.D. Thesis, University of Wales

PAPENFUSS, H.D. and SALISBURY, F.B. (1967). Aspects of clock resetting in flowering of *Xanthium. Plant Physiology*, **42**, 1562–1568

PITTENDRIGH, C.S. (1966). The circadian oscillation in *Drosophila pseudoobscura*: a model for the circadian clock. *Zeitschrift für Pflanzenphysiologie*, **54**, 275–307

SAJI, H., VINCE-PRUE, D. and FURUYA, M. (1983). Studies on the photoreceptors for the promotion and inhibition of flowering in dark-grown seedlings of *Pharbitis nil* Choisy. *Plant and Cell Physiology*, **67**, 1183–1189

SAJI, H., FURUYA, M. and TAKIMOTO, A. (1984). Role of the photoperiod preceding a flower-inductive dark period in dark-grown seedlings of *Pharbitis nil* Choisy. *Plant and Cell Physiology*, **25**, 715–720

SALISBURY, F.B. (1981). Twilight effect: initiating dark time measurement in photo-periodism of *Xanthium*. *Plant Physiology*, **67**, 1230–1238

TAKIMOTO, A. (1967). Studies on the light affecting the initiation of endogenous rhythms concerned with photoperiodic responses in *Pharbitis nil*. *Botanical Magazine, Tokyo*, **80**, 241–247

TAKIMOTO, A. and HAMNER, K.C. (1965). Effect of far-red light and its interaction with red light in the photoperiodic response of *Pharbitis nil*. *Plant Physiology*, **40**, 859–864

THOMAS, B. and LUMSDEN, P.J. (1984). Photoreceptor action and photoperiodic induction in *Pharbitis nil*. In *Light and The Flowering Process* (D. Vince-Prue, B. Thomas and K.E. Cockshull, Eds), pp. 107–121. London, Academic Press

THOMAS, B. and VINCE-PRUE, D. (1986). Photoperiodic control of floral induction in short-day and long-day plants. In *Models in Plant Physiology/Biochemistry/ Technology* (D. Newman and K. Wilson, Eds), Boca Raton, Fl., CRC Press (In press)

VINCE-PRUE, D. (1981). Daylight and photoperiodism. In *Plants and the Daylight Spectrum* (H. Smith, Ed.), pp. 223–242. London, Academic Press

VINCE-PRUE, D. (1983). Photomorphogenesis and flowering. In *Encyclopedia of Plant Physiology, New Series* (W. Shropshire and H. Mohr, Eds), Vol. 16, Chapter 18, pp. 457–490.

VINCE-PRUE, D., KING, R.W. and QUAIL, P.H. (1978). Light requirement, phytochrome and photoperiodic induction of flowering of *Pharbitis nil* Chois. II. *Planta*, **141**, 9–14

19

PHOTOPERIODIC INDUCTION AND THE FLORAL STIMULUS IN *PERILLA*

J.A.D. ZEEVAART
MSU-DOE Plant Research Laboratory, Michigan State University, Michigan, USA

G.L. BOYER
Department of Chemistry, State University of New York, New York, USA

Introduction

Perilla is a short-day plant (SDP) which has been used extensively for demonstrating transmission of the floral stimulus from one induced partner (donor) to a vegetative receptor. Much of the early work was performed with a red-leafed species, *P. crispa* (for a review, see Zeevaart, 1969). More recently, a species with green leaves, *P. ocymoides*, has been studied (Allot-Deronne, 1983; for a review *see* Zeevaart, 1986). In the experiments described in this chapter photoperiodic induction and transmission of the floral stimulus were compared in green and red *Perilla*. The approach used to determine the chemical nature of the stimulus was to analyse phloem exudate rather than leaf extracts.

Materials and methods

Perilla crispa (Thunb.) Tanaka (red-leafed) and *Perilla ocymoides* L. (green-leafed) were grown in a greenhouse in which the natural day-length was extended with light from incandescent bulbs or fluorescent tubes to give a photoperiod of 20 h. For induction of flowering, plants were given short-day treatments which consisted of 8 h light and 16 h darkness at 23 °C. Leaf grafts were performed as before (Zeevaart, 1958). Grafted plants were kept in a growth chamber at 23 °C. A photoperiod of 20 h was maintained with 12 h of high-intensity light from fluorescent tubes and incandescent lamps (12.5 mW cm^{-2}), followed by an 8 h period of low-intensity light from the incandescent lamps only (3 mW cm^{-2}). The flowering quotient indicates the number of receptors with flower buds out of the total number of plants in a treatment. For analysis of phloem exudate the plants were grown under three different light regimes: short days (SD; 8 h light, 16 h darkness), long days (LD; 20 h light, 4 h darkness), and short days with interrupted night (NI; 8 h light, 16 h darkness, but with a 15-min light break in the middle of the dark period). EDTA-enhanced phloem exudate from detached leaves was obtained using the technique of King and Zeevaart (1974). Leaves were removed from the plants, recut under EDTA, and placed in darkness in beakers containing a 1–2 cm layer of K^{+}-EDTA 20 mmol l^{-1}, pH 7.0. After 1 h, the petioles were rinsed with distilled water to remove residual EDTA, and placed in beakers (up to 20 leaves per beaker) with distilled water overnight. As shown previously (King and Zeevaart, 1974), most of the carbohydrates were found

269

in the distilled water, so that the EDTA fraction was discarded. For dry weight determinations the exudate was lyophilized. Total carbohydrates were determined colorimetrically using the phenol–sulphuric acid method (Dubois *et al.*, 1956). Sugar composition was determined by gas chromatography of the trimethylsilyl ethers (Sweeley *et al.*, 1963), using a 180×0.2 cm glass column packed with 0.5% SP-2100 and a temperature program of 120 °C for 5 min, followed by a 5 °C min^{-1} rise to a final temperature of 310 °C. Protein concentration in the water fraction was determined by the method of Bradford (1976).

For further analysis the exudate was fractionated into neutral, basic, and acidic fractions according to Atkins and Canvin (1971). Organic acids were analysed as their trimethylsilyl derivatives (Stumpf and Burris, 1979), using a 3% SE-30 column $(0.2 \times 180\,\text{cm})$ which was temperature programmed from 85 °C to 185 °C. Amino acids were analysed with a Durrum D-500 physiological analyser (Moore and Stein, 1963).

Results

FLOWER FORMATION IN RED *PERILLA* WITHOUT ROOTS

It has been shown previously that detached leaves of red *Perilla* in the absence of any buds or roots can be induced, since such leaves can induce flower formation when grafted to vegetative receptors (Zeevaart, 1958). However, it remained to be demonstrated that the actual formation of flower primordia can also take place on shoots without roots. Leaves of red *Perilla* were therefore given SD treatment on long debudded stems placed in half-strength Hoagland's nutrient solution. To prevent root formation, the basal 1 cm sections of the stems were cut off every day. After 29 SD, the leaves were grafted either onto intact plants, or onto stems with two receptor shoots and no roots. In the latter treatment, a 1 cm piece was cut from the base of the stem every day until flower buds appeared on the receptor shoots.

As the results in *Table 19.1* show, leaves exposed to 29 SD in the absence of roots caused flower formation in receptor shoots on stems without roots. Shoots on stems without roots developed more slowly than those on intact plants, resulting in a slight delay in appearance of flower buds. However, it is clear from these results that in red *Perilla* both induction in the leaf and formation of flower primordia on the receptor shoots can take place in the absence of roots. A similar experiment with green *Perilla* was inconclusive, since the receptor buds on all plants without roots failed to grow out and died within 2 weeks after the stems had been detached from the root systems.

Table 19.1 INDUCTION OF RED *Perilla* LEAVES IN THE ABSENCE OF ROOTS AND BUDS, AND TRANSMISSION OF THE FLORAL STIMULUS TO RED RECEPTOR SHOOTS WITHOUT ROOTS*

Donor		*Receptor*	*Days until flower bud appearance*
SD	− Roots	− Roots	19.7
SD	− Roots	+ Roots	19.0
SD	+ Roots	− Roots	18.0
SD	+ Roots	+ Roots	14.0
LD	− Roots	− Roots	—
LD	+ Roots	− Roots	—

* Donor leaves received 29 SD. All receptors grafted with SD treated leaves produced flower buds; all receptors grafted with LD receptors remained vegetative.

RECIPROCAL GRAFTS BETWEEN GREEN AND RED *PERILLA*

For comparison of the floral stimuli in green and red *Perilla*, leaf grafts (30 cm²) were made in all four possible combinations. Green donor leaves caused rapid flower formation both in green and in red receptor shoots. Macroscopically visible flower buds appeared after 11–12 days, and the first flowers on the receptor shoots opened 20 days after grafting (*Table 19.2*). This compares with approximately 28 days needed from beginning of SD treatment until anthesis in both species. Receptor shoots on plants grafted with non-induced leaves remained vegetative (*Figure 19.1*). With red donor leaves flower buds appeared on red and green receptor shoots after 13 and 15 days, respectively, while anthesis did not start until 36 and 38 days after grafting (*Table 19.2*). It is obvious from these results that induced green *Perilla* leaves are considerably more effective donors than those from red plants. Apparently green *Perilla* produces more floral stimulus per unit leaf area than the red species.

Table 19.2 TRANSMISSION OF THE FLORAL STIMULUS IN RECIPROCAL GRAFTS BETWEEN GREEN AND RED *Perilla**

Donor leaves	Receptor shoots	Days until flower bud appearance	Days until anthesis
Green	Green	12.6	20.6
Green	Red	11.0	20.0
Red	Red	13.1	36.3
Red	Green	14.6	38.1

* Donor leaves were exposed to 25 SD. Eight grafts per treatment

Figure 19.1 Transmission of the floral stimulus from green *Perilla* donor leaves to green and red receptors, and absence of flowering when grafted with non-induced leaves. From left to right: induced/green, non-induced/green, induced/red, non-induced/red. Photographed 34 days after grafting.

Table 19.3   DURATION OF THE GRAFTING CONTACT NECESSARY BETWEEN GREEN DONOR LEAVES AND RED RECEPTOR STOCKS OF *Perilla* FOR TRANSMISSION OF THE FLORAL STIMULUS*

Grafting contact (days)	Flowering quotient	Days until flower bud appearance	Days until anthesis
2	0/10	—	—
3	0/10	—	—
4	0/10	—	—
5	2/10	23.0	—
6	6/10	21.7	—
7	8/10	18.9	—
8	4/4	12.0	35.8
10	4/4	11.5	33.5
12	4/4	12.3	30.0
—	4/4	10.3	21.3

* Donor leaves exposed to 27 SD.

Table 19.4   DURATION OF SD INDUCTION OF GREEN *Perilla* LEAVES AND TRANSMISSION OF THE FLORAL STIMULUS TO RED *Perilla* RECEPTORS

Number of SD	Flowering quotient		Days until flower bud appearance
	Donors	Receptors	
0	0/2	0/3	—
5	0/3	0/6	–
7	3/3	1/6	63.0
10	3/3	6/6	34.8
12	3/3	6/6	15.3
15	3/3	6/6	14.8
19	3/3	6/6	12.0
24	4/4	3/3	10.0

DURATION OF GRAFTING CONTACT

Considering the rapid flowering response in the graft combination green donor/red receptor, the minimal duration of grafting contact necessary for transmission of the floral stimulus was determined. In agreement with results obtained with red *Perilla* (Zeevaart, 1958), grafting contact had to be at least 7 days for appearance of flower buds on a high percentage of the receptor shoots (*Table 19.3*). It is also clear from the data in *Table 19.3* that the longer the contact between donor and receptor, the earlier flower buds appeared on the receptors and anthesis took place. This indicates that the floral stimulus is transmitted continuously from the donor to the receptor and suggests that the level of the stimulus at any given time is very low (*see* Discussion).

DURATION OF INDUCTION

Allot-Deronne (1983) reported that green donor leaves exposed to a subthreshold induction (3, 4, 5 SD) caused flowering in red receptors after 80–89 days. In our own experiments it was established that donor leaves can transmit the floral stimulus to receptor shoots only when the donor plants themselves can produce flower buds (*Table 19.4*). The discrepancy with the results of Allot-Deronne (1983) can be explained by assuming that the donor leaves given subthreshold induction gradually acquired the induced state under LD and thus could transmit the floral stimulus after 80 days (*see* below).

INDIRECT INDUCTION

In earlier work (Zeevaart, 1958), it was established that indirect induction does not occur in red *Perilla*, i.e. leaves on receptor shoots induced to flower by grafting cannot themselves function as donors. On the other hand, it has been reported that indirect induction is possible in green *Perilla* (Allot-Deronne, 1983). This question was therefore reinvestigated in both species with the following results.

1. Leaves taken from a flowering *green* receptor shoot induced flower formation in both green and red receptors, regardless of whether the original donor leaf was green or red (*Table 19.5*). However, control grafts, i.e. green 'donor' leaves taken from vegetative shoots (grafted with non-induced leaves) also caused flower formation, albeit considerably later than with leaves from flowering shoots (*Table 19.5*).
2. Leaves taken from flowering red receptor branches never caused flower formation in either red or green receptors (*Table 19.6*).

It would appear from these results that the floral stimulus is self-perpetuating in green, but not in red *Perilla*. However, since flower formation is ultimately (after 80–120 days) also observed after grafting with non-induced leaves, production of the floral stimulus without SD treatment can take place in old, non-induced leaves of the green species. Thus leaves of green *Perilla* slowly acquire the induced state under LD. On the other hand, in red *Perilla* exposure to a minimal number of inductive cycles is an absolute prerequisite for production of the floral stimulus. Thus, the red species is a qualitative SDP, whereas the green one shows a facultative SD response (Jacobs, 1982).

Table 19.5   INDIRECT INDUCTION IN GREEN *Perilla**

Donors in first grafts		Receptors in second grafts	Flowering quotient	Days until flower bud appearance
SD	green	Green	9/9	51.6
		Red	7/10	78.6
LD	green	Green	10/10	78.9
		Red	4/10	109.3
SD	red	Green	10/10	71.4
		Red	7/10	98.1
LD	red	Green	10/10	83.3
		Red	8/10	116.5

* Donor leaves in first grafts received 26 SD. Leaves on green receptor shoots of the first grafts were used as donor leaves in the second grafting. Second grafting was performed 20 or 23 days after first grafting.

Table 19.6 NO INDIRECT INDUCTION IN RED *Perilla**

Donors in first grafts	Receptors in second grafts	Flowering quotient	Days to flower bud appearance
SD green	Green	0/10	—
	Red	0/6	—
LD green	Green	0/10	—
	Red	0/6	—
SD red	Green	0/4	—
	Red	0/4	—
LD red	Green	0/4	—
	Red	0/4	—

* Donor leaves in first grafts received 26 SD. Leaves on red receptor shoots of the first grafts were used as donor leaves in the second grafting. Second grafting was performed 20 or 23 days after first grafting.

Analysis of phloem exudate

It is clear from the results presented above that transmission of the floral stimulus can be easily demonstrated in *Perilla*. Since the floral stimulus is translocated in the phloem (King and Zeevaart, 1973), EDTA-enhanced phloem exudate (King and Zeevaart, 1974) obtained from induced and vegetative *Perilla* plants was analysed for carbohydrates, organic acids, and amino acids.

CARBOHYDRATES

Over 80% of the dry weight of the exudate consisted of carbohydrates with protein present in only small amounts (less than 1% by weight). The bulk of the sugars consisted of raffinose (25%), stachyose (37%), and verbascose (19%). Sucrose was present as a minor constituent (5%), along with the monosaccharides glucose (9%) and galactose (6%).

The relative composition of the phloem carbohydrates did not change significantly with the different photoperiods, but the absolute amounts obtained were dependent on the photoperiodic conditions (*Table 19.7*). Exudates obtained from plants in SD contained almost twice as much carbohydrate as exudates from the corresponding plants in LD or NI conditions. Vegetative plants that were transferred to SD gradually increased their sugar content. Conversely, plants grown in SD and then returned to NI showed a gradual decline in the amount of carbohydrate present in the phloem exudate. This change in sugar level takes place independently of the ability of the leaves to induce flower formation, since *Perilla* leaves, once induced, remain induced after transfer back to non-inductive conditions (Zeevaart, 1958).

ACIDIC FRACTION

Composition of this fraction, as analysed by GLC, was essentially the same for exudate obtained from plants in SD, LD, or NI. Organic acids identified were: citric, lactic, malic, malonic, succinic, and tartaric acids. These organic acids have also been reported to be present in the phloem of other species (Ziegler, 1975).

Table 19.7 COMPARISON OF THE EDTA-ENHANCED PHLOEM EXUDATE OBTAINED FROM GREEN *Perilla* LEAVES UNDER THREE DIFFERENT PHOTOPERIODIC CONDITIONS*

Dry weight	SD	NI	LD
Mean (±SE) dry weight (mg)	17.8 ± 3.0	11.1 ± 1.0	9.6 ± 1.1
Mean (±SE) total carbohydrate (mg)	16.5 ± 0.5	8.5 ± 1.2	8.1 ± 1.3
% dry weight	92	77	84

* Three groups of 18 plants used in each treatment.

BASIC FRACTION

No differences were observed in fractions obtained from SD and NI plants. The major amino acids detected in the phloem exudate were aspartic acid (20%) and glutamine (40%), with lesser amounts of serine (5%), threonine (3%), and alanine (3%). A similar composition of the amino acids in phloem exudate has been reported for *Ricinus* (Hall and Baker, 1972), wheat (Simpson and Dalling, 1981), and barley (Tully and Hanson, 1979).

Discussion

The results of the interspecific grafts (*see Table 19.2*) demonstrate that leaves of green *Perilla* are more effective donors than those from red plants. Nevertheless, the grafting contact had to be at least 7 days for flower buds to appear on the receptors (*see Table 19.3*). With longer duration of the contact between donor and receptor, the flowering response increased considerably. This indicates that the floral stimulus is transmitted continuously from the donor leaves to the receptor buds and suggests that the level of stimulus is always very low. This may explain why no differences in the phloem exudates from vegetative and induced leaves were detected (assuming that the EDTA-enhanced exudate is representative of the sieve tube contents). Plant growth substances are known to be present in the phloem (Ziegler, 1975). In the EDTA-enhanced exudate from green *Perilla* we measured by gas chromatography with electron capture detector approximately 1 ng abscisic acid per mg dry weight exudate. As measured by the *d-5* maize bioassay, the gibberellin-like activity in the exudate was less than 1 ng (g dry weight^{-1}). If the flower-inducing material occurs in a similar concentration, it would not be detected by the methods employed. Another possible approach to isolate the floral stimulus is to test for flower-inducing activity in the exudate. However, we have been unable to obtain consistent results with this approach. Purse (1984) incorporated the entire exudate into the medium on which *Perilla* shoot tips were cultured, and also failed to obtain reproducible results. Thus the nature of the floral stimulus remains unknown.

Conclusions

The presence of the floral stimulus in *Perilla* is obvious from grafting experiments, but its chemical nature remains to be determined. The low levels and lack of a bioassay appear to be major reasons for the failure to isolate the active material. Clearly, identification of the floral stimulus remains a central theme in the physiology of flowering.

Green *Perilla* produces more floral stimulus per unit leaf area than the red species. Photoinduction is strictly localized in red *Perilla*, but indirect induction is possible in green *Perilla*. This, at least in part, is due to the less strict photoperiodic requirement of the green species.

Acknowledgement

This work was supported by the United States Department of Energy under Contract DE-AC02-76ER01338.

References

ALLOT-DERONNE, M. (1983). *Feuille et Induction Florale. Analyse sur une Plante-modèle: le* Perilla, pp. 1–170. Thèse de Doctorat d'État. Université de Paris VI

ATKINS, C.A. and CANVIN, D.T. (1971). Photosynthesis and CO_2 evolution by leaf discs: gas exchange, extraction, and ion-exchange fractionation of ^{14}C-labelled photosynthetic products. *Canadian Journal of Botany*, **49**, 1225–1234

BRADFORD, M.M. (1976). A rapid and sensitive method for the quantitation of microgram quantities of protein utilizing the principle of protein-dye binding. *Analytical Biochemistry*, **72**, 248–254

DUBOIS, M., GILES, K.A., HAMILTON, J.K., REBERS, P.A. and SMITH, F. (1956). Colorimetric method for the determination of sugars and related substances. *Analytical Chemistry*, **28**, 350–356

HALL, S.M. and BAKER, D.A. (1972). The chemical composition of *Ricinus* phloem exudate. *Planta*, **106**, 131–140

JACOBS, W.P. (1982). Comparison of photoperiodic sensitivity of green-leafed and red-leafed *Perilla*. *Plant Physiology*, **70**, 303–306

KING, R.W. and ZEEVAART, J.A.D. (1973). Floral stimulus movement in *Perilla* and flower inhibition caused by non-induced leaves. *Plant Physiology*, **51**, 727–738

KING, R.W. and ZEEVAART, J.A.D. (1974). Enhancement of phloem exudation from cut petioles by chelating agents. *Plant Physiology*, **53**, 96–103

MOORE, S. and STEIN, W.H. (1963). Chromatographic determination of amino acids by the use of automatic recording equipment. *Methods of Enzymology*, **6**, 819–831

PURSE, J.G. (1984). Phloem exudate of *Perilla crispa* and its effects on flowering of *P. crispa* shoot explants. *Journal of Experimental Botany*, **35**, 227–238

SIMPSON, R.J. and DALLING, M.J. (1981). Nitrogen redistribution during grain growth in wheat (*Triticum aestivum* L.) III. Enzymology and transport of amino acids from senescing flag leaves. *Planta*, **151**, 447–456

STUMPF, D.K. and BURRIS, R.H. (1979). A micromethod for the purification and quantification of organic acids of the tricarboxylic acid cycle in plant tissues. *Analytical Biochemistry*, **95**, 311–315

SWEELEY, C.C., BENTLEY, R., MAKITA, M. and WELLS, W.W. (1963). Gas-liquid chromatography of trimethylsilyl derivatives of sugars and related substances. *Journal of the American Chemical Society*, **85**, 2495–2507

TULLY, R.E. and HANSON, A.D. (1979). Amino acids translocated from turgid and water-stressed barley leaves. I. Phloem exudation studies. *Plant Physiology*, **64**, 460–466

ZEEVAART, J.A.D. (1958). Flower formation as studied by grafting. *Mededelingen Landbouwhogeschool Wageningen*, **58** (3), 1–88

ZEEVAART, J.A.D. (1969). *Perilla*. In *The Induction of Flowering. Some Case Histories* (L.T. Evans, Ed.), pp. 116–144. Melbourne, Macmillan

ZEEVAART, J.A.D. (1986). *Perilla*. In *CRC Handbook of Flowering* (A.H. Halevy, Ed.), Vol. **5**, pp. 239–252. Boca Raton, Fl. CRC Press

ZIEGLER, H. (1975). Nature of transported substances. In *Transport in Plants I. Phloem Transport* (M.H. Zimmermann and J.A. Milburn, Eds), *Encyclopedia of Plant Physiology*, pp. 59–100. New Series, Vol. 1. Berlin, Springer-Verlag

20

A NEW STRATEGY FOR THE IDENTIFICATION OF NATIVE PLANT PHOTOPERIODICALLY REGULATED FLOWERING SUBSTANCES

M.J. JAFFE
Biology Department, Wake Forest University, North Carolina, USA
K.A. BRIDLE
R.J. Reynolds Tobacco Company, Winston-Salem, North Carolina, USA
J. KOPCEWICZ
Plant Physiology Institute, Copernicus University, Torun, Poland

Introduction

Most plants do not flower randomly but are synchronized with climatic changes in such factors as thermoperiod or scotoperiod. In the latter case, photoperiod designation has historically been used (e.g. short day (SD) or long day (LD)), and this convention will be followed in this chapter. Rather than give an exhaustive survey of the literature (*see*, for example, Zeevaart, 1976), this section will concentrate on aspects of flowering directly related to photoperiodic control of floral induction via putative flowering substances. For convenience, the flowering process has been divided into several stages. For SDP these are outlined in *Table 20.1*.

Different ideas have been advanced over the years to explain the change from vegetative to floral growth. Garner and Allard (1920) proposed the term 'photoperiodism' as part of the concept that day-length could be perceived by plants and used to control seasonal flowering. Later, Borthwick and Hendricks (Borthwick *et al.*, 1952) showed that the perception of the photoperiod was dependent on absorption of light by the pigment phytochrome. Considering the many different types of plant responses (e.g. both facultative and obligate LD or SD plants, as well as day neutral types), it seems unlikely that a single mechanism will control all types of flowering. None the less, several 'universal' hypotheses have been advanced in the last 50 years. According to Lang (1952) two basically different approaches have been visualized in these hypotheses: inductive conditions promote flowering or non-inductive conditions inhibit it. The former idea implies that plants are incapable of flowering unless induced, the latter implies that all plants are capable of flowering but are suppressed by inhibitors produced during non-inductive conditions.

What might these promotors and inhibitors be? In 1882, Sachs proposed the idea of 'flower forming substances' as part of a scheme envisaging the generation of each organ to be under the control of its specific 'organ forming substance'. By using grafting experiments, Chailakhyan (1936) discovered that leaves from induced tobacco plants could be grafted to de-leafed uninduced plants, causing them to flower. He coined the term 'florigen' to represent the graft-transmissible principle. He suggested that florigen could be produced in leaves held under inductive conditions, then transported to the apex where it is involved in the initiation of floral growth (i.e. evocation). Today, this forms the basis for the hormonal or florigen hypothesis of flowering (Zeevaart, 1958). 'Inhibitor', hypotheses also have been advanced, starting from the early observations that flowers can be formed in plants of *Hyoscyamus*

Table 20.1   SEQUENCE OF EVENTS IN THE PHOTOPERIODIC CONTROL OF SHORT-DAY PLANTS

---

1. In the short-night (LD) the plant does not flower.
2. The phytochrome system in the leaf mediates the detection of one or more long nights (SD). This is the sensory act of flower induction.
3. One or more electrochemical and/or biochemical transductive steps occur in the leaf which mediate induction.
4. An integrating signal is sent from the induced leaf to lateral and/or terminal buds.
5. The signal is received by something in the bud causing the bud to change from vegetative to floral development. This is the primary act of evocation.
6. Differentiation of a flower occurs.
7. The mature flower opens (i.e., anthesis).

Table 20.2   ALTERNATIVE MODELS FOR THE PHOTOPERIODIC CONTROL OF FLOWERING IN SD PLANTS

---

1. In long days, one or more flowering inhibitors are produced in the leaf and travel to the bud (i.e., hormone action) to prevent evocation. In short days, the inhibitor(s) are not produced, or may be produced but not travel to the bud.
2. In long days, one or more flowering promoters are not produced or may be produced but not travel to the bud (i.e., hormone action) to cause evocation. In short days, one or more flowering promoters are produced and travel to the bud.
3. A combination of (1) and (2), above.
4. In long days, one or more flowering inhibitors are made in the leaf or travel to the leaf from elsewhere in the stem, but act only in the leaf. In short days, one or more flowering inhibitors disappear from the leaf.
5. A combination of (4) and (2), above.

Note: In either (2) or (4), above, the flowering promotor(s) might be organic molecular species or trophic factors such as increased nitrogen supply.

(LDP) and *Chenopodium amaranticolor* (SDP) kept in non-inductive conditions, by continually removing all leaves (Lang, 1952). Further, Withrow *et al.* (1943) reported that non-induced leaves positioned between induced leaves and the apex have an inhibitory effect in Spinach. An outline of the possible types of endogenous mediators of the photoperiodic control of flowering in SDP is shown in *Table 20.2*.

Of central importance in this study is the chemical regulation of reproductive initiation. Only naturally occurring substances that are photoperiodically controlled will be addressed here. In order to link causally any native substance to flowering, its quantitative dynamics must be known. Even so, the interactions of phytohormones can be so complex that causal relationships have not yet been determined (Moore, 1979). There are a number of problems that arise when trying to ascertain the kinetic relationships:

1. Extractions give a series of static pictures of a dynamic system and, not knowing the sequences and timing of physiological events, it may be difficult to interpret kinetic data.
2. Extraction destroys the *in vitro* compartmentation of substances and changes concentrations that may be of importance. It also sometimes brings a substance together with a degradative enzyme system, an event that might not occur in nature.
3. The method of extraction itself may produce artefacts (e.g. breakdown products of a significant compound), which themselves may interfere with a true interpretation.

Difficulties of extraction and the lack of resolution in older technology have rendered the few attempts to extract flowering promotors fairly unsuccessful. Further, the strategies employed were sometimes defective.

Often control extracts from non-induced organs were omitted, and bioassay plants were employed that were very different (but, perhaps easier to use) than the extracted plants. One of the first attempts by Hamner and Bonner (1938) produced variable results but stimulated Lincoln *et al.* (1960) to try to extract a 'floral initiating factor' from *Xanthium*. They extracted lyophilized SD induced leaves in methanol, and applied the extract in lanolin paste to leaves of uninduced plants. They used only lanolin paste as a control and failed to make extracts from uninduced plants for bioassay. Depending on early floral differentiation as the assay criterion, they did not let the plants go to flower production or to anthesis. They found that 50% of the extract-treated plant buds seemed to be floral, while none of the controls were. Roberts (1965) claimed to have extended their work to corn but did not publish his methods. Hodson and Hamner (1970) extended the earlier work including extracts of uninduced leaves in the experiment. Their acetone extracts produced flowering only in the presence of exogenous GA_3 on *Xanthium strumarium*, although on *Lemna*, GA_3 was not needed. More recently, a very creative study by Cleland and Ajami (1974) demonstrated that salicyclic acid extracted or obtained as aphid honeydew from *Xanthium* will cause flowering in *Lemna*. However, its content does not change owing to induction in *Xanthium* and its does not induce flowering in uninduced *Xanthium* plants.

More recently, Tran Thanh Van *et al.* (1985) using tobacco explant tissue cultures, found that certain unidentified oligosaccharins can induce flowering, whereas others can induce vegetative buds. While this work is obviously of great significance, the *in vitro* system required a pH of 3.8 to affect the developmental changes. It is unlikely that such a low pH would normally be found in plant cells *in vivo*.

Most of the attempts to extract flower promoting substances from plants seem to have been based on the assumption that if it is present, and if it is added to an uninduced plant, it should cause flowering. However, this assumption would not be true if the uninduced plant contained a flowering inhibitor that blocked the effect of the promotor. This problem seems to have been partially addressed in only two previous studies. Pryce (1972) found that gallic acid, extracted from leaves of non-flowering plants of *Kalanchoe blossfeldiana* inhibited flowering of induced plants. Although the gallic acid was also present in leaves of flowering *Kalanchoe*, it was suggested that it might exist in a different form. In an extension of this work, Schwabe (1984) claimed that the gallic acid was an artefact and that the real inhibitor was an unidentified compound. In another study (Aharoni *et al.*, 1985), extracts of induced or uninduced *Pharbitis* cotyledons which had been fed radioactively labelled acetate were chromatographed on TLC. A labelled spot present in the uninduced cotyledon disappeared upon induction. Further, this disappearance followed the same time course as floral induction. Thus a search for a photoperiodically controlled floral inhibitor in *Pharbitis* seems potentially fruitful.

Because of the failure of previous attempts using crude extracts to obtain flowering promotors or inhibitors a new approach has been adopted in our work.

General strategy

Uninduced and induced leaves or cotyledons are extracted for 1 hour in methanol or acetone. Both water and methylene chloride fractions are obtained from these extracts, and half of each fraction is TMS-derivatized. The samples are injected onto high-resolution gas chromatography (HRGC) columns within 6 hours after harvesting. It is considered vital that the samples should be chromatographed the same day as collected, to avoid potential lability and other processing or storage artefacts. The water fractions are run on a polar column while the methylene chloride fractions are run on a non-polar column. In all cases, ultra-high resolution wall-bonded capillary columns are used together with a universal detector.

When a chromatographic peak is seen to change qualitatively (i.e., appear *de novo* or disappear completely), it is flagged for further study. If it is derivatized, it must be de-derivatized. The peak is then analysed by HRGS-mass spectroscopy (HRGS-MS) for preliminary identification. The compound is obtained in the authentic form (by purchase or synthesis), analysed by HRGC-MS, and the identity of the unknown peak confirmed by comparison. If necessary, further confirmation of the structure can be obtained by NMR spectroscopy. After identification, plants of the same species are treated exogenously with the compound. Potential inhibitors are sprayed on photoperiodically induced plants to see if they will block flowering. Potential promotors are sprayed on uninduced defoliated plants to see if they will cause flowering.

This method has been used successfully to demonstrate one flowering inhibitor and also that there are at least two other possible candidate compounds. The advantages of this approach are shown in *Table 20.3*.

Table 20.3   THE DISAPPEARANCE OF BEHD AND THE INDUCTION OF FLOWERING DUE TO ONE OR TWO INDUCTIVE LONG NIGHTS (SD)

Number of inductive or non-inductive cycles	Treatment	BEHD	Flowering (%)
1	LD	1.5	0
	SD	0.4	95
2	LD	1.5	0
	SD	0.0	100

LD = Long day; SD = short day.

An inhibitor from short-day plants

The SDP *Pharbitis nil, Xanthium strumarium* and *Chenopodium rubrum* were used both for extraction and for spray-testing. The *Pharbitis* plants were grown under 8-hours light–8 hours dark–1 hour light–7 hours dark, short nights until they were 6 days old. They were transferred to a regimen where the night-break was left out for two nights to provide two inductive SD cycles. Control plants were kept in the LD regimen. *Xanthium* and *Chenopodium* plants were grown under 20 hour light–8 hour dark or continuous light regimens, respectively, until ready to be induced. *Xanthium* plants were given 2 SD when they were 35 days old. *Chenopodium* plants were given up to 5 SD when they were 21 days old. For these two species, the SD cycle was the same as for *Pharbitis*. Following the inductive SD cycle(s), the first to fourth penultimate leaves from *Xanthium* and *Chenopodium* or the *Pharbitis* cotyledons were extracted and processed.

Samples were obtained that exhibited a peak at a relative retention time (RRT) of 28.4 min from uninduced cotyledons of *Pharbitis* (*Figure 20.1*). Similar samples taken from cotyledons of induced plants lacked this peak (*Figure 20.1*). HRGC-MS suggested that the compound was a 2-hexanoic acid dioctyl ester. Chromatography of the three possible isomers, as well as mass spectroscopy confirmed that the unknown compound was *bis*(2-ethylhexyl)hexane dioate (BEHD).

The concentration of BEHD in non-induced *Pharbitis* cotyledons averaged 0.2 nmol (g fresh weight)$^{-1}$. In our hands, the 5-day-old plants needed 1 SD for partial, and 2 SD inductive cycles for complete flowering (*Table 20.3*). The decrease in the concentration of BEHD was inversely correlated with the increase in flowering (*Table 20.3*). Similar observations were made with the other two SDP. Whereas uninduced *Xanthium* leaves contained BEHD, the induced leaves had none. The concentration of BEHD was inversely related to the flowering of these plants. The

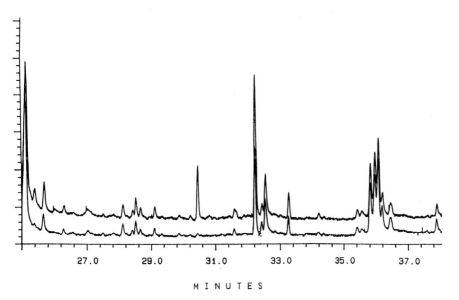

Figure 20.1 Computer reconstructions of chromatograms of induced (top) and uninduced (bottom) Pharbitis cotyledonary extracts. The BEHD peak appears at a RRT of 29.7 minutes.

Table 20.4 THE EFFECTS OF (0.1 mmol l^{-1}) BEHD SPRAYS TO RUN-OFF ON FLOWERING IN VARIOUS SPECIES OF PLANT

Plant type	Species	Flowering (% inhibition)
SDP	Chenopodium rubrum	34
	Impatiens balsamina	40
	Pharbitis nil	39
	Xanthium strumarium	72
LDP	Sinapis arvensis	100
	Chenopodium murale	100
	Tetragonia tetragonoides	50
	Angallis arvensis	40
DNP	Cucumis sativus	33
	Pisum sativum	40
	Phaseolus vulgaris	56
	Nicotiana tabacum	90

Chenopodium plants required five or more SD inductive cycles for optimum flowering. The decrease of BEHD was inversely related to the induction of flowering.

To be considered as a possible native flowering inhibitor, it is not enough to show that BEHD disappears from the plant upon floral induction. If it is applied exogenously it should inhibit flowering in photoperiodically induced plants. BEHD (0.1 mmol l^{-1}) was sprayed to run-off onto the whole plants in 30% acetone + 0.01% Tween-20. The control sprays lacked BEHD. The 3 SDP were grown under LD and spraying began 1 day before the first inductive cycle and continued, after the return to LD, daily, or on alternate days for 1 week after the end of induction. *Figure 20.2* shows the results with *Pharbitis*. Flowering at the buds at all nodes was inhibited. Similar or more pronounced results were obtained with *Xanthium* and *Chenopodium*. A DN variety of tobacco was grown in the greenhouse and sprayed for 4 days before the plants were ready to flower. All of the other species tested were grown at intervals in the greenhouse from early spring through fall, and were sprayed daily during the duration of each experiment. The experiments lasted from 37 days for *Pharbitis* to 76 days for *Impatiens*. Each experiment was replicated three times with an average of 20 plants per treatment. Exogenously applied BEHD, at 0.1 mmol l^{-1}, has pronounced flowering inhibitory activity on 5 SDP, 4 LDP and 3 DNP (*Table 20.4*). It is important to note that BEHD only inhibited flowering completely in certain cases.

Does BEHD act in the leaf during induction or in the bud during evocation? When different parts of the plant are assayed for BEHD, it is found everywhere, with the highest concentration in the bud. However, it only disappears in the leaf following induction. When BEHD was applied only to the leaf or only to the bud, flowering was inhibited only when BEHD was applied to the leaf. Thus, it seems that BEHD acts in the leaf during induction.

Kinetic studies of the BEHD effect show there is inhibition of flowering even if the BEHD is applied only during the SD inductive cycles. Long-term treatment with the

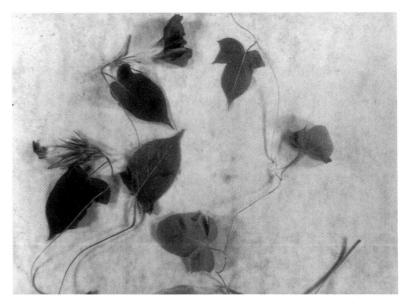

Figure 20.2   The effect of BEHD 0.1 mmol l^{-1} sprayed to run-off on *Pharbitis nil*. The plant on the left was sprayed with a control solution. The plant on the right was sprayed with BEHD.

inhibitor is not necessary. When the time course of the disappearance of BEHD was monitored, it was found that the decrease occurred at the very end of the long night. In this respect, it corresponded very closely to the decrease of ATP in the buds shown recently by Thigpen and Sachs (1985).

In addition to the inhibition of flowering, exogenous BEHD promoted vegetative growth in several species. The plants grew more and produced larger, darker green leaves than did those sprayed with the control solution. BEHD may be part of the native mechanism that keeps the plant vegetative. If this is so, it might be part of the balance of regulators that can shift the plant toward flowering or toward vegetative growth. BEHD meets both of the criteria to make it a successful candidate for a photoperiodically controlled native flowering substance. It disappears due to induction in at least three different short day plants, and when exogenously applied to those same plants (as well as others) otherwise capable of flowering, it displays floral inhibitory activity.

Table 20.5 WORKING HYPOTHESIS FOR THE PROPOSED BEHD-MEDIATED PHOTOPERIODIC ACTION IN SHORT-DAY PLANTS

1. In the leaf, phytochrome detects the extent of the long night by the release from the plasma membrane of bound phytochrome only at the end of the long night.
2. As the result of one or more transduction steps, BEHD in the leaf disappears at the end of the long night. When the daylight begins again, BEHD reappears. It is this transient disappearance of BEHD that triggers induction.
3. The disappearance of BEHD at the end of the long night sets off a process which results in the translocation of a flower promoting principal (FPP) from the induced leaf to the bud.
4. The FPP reaches its target in the bud. This target may be a receptor of some sort for the FPP molecule. When the FPP reaches its target, evocation results.

Figure 20.3 shows the type of time course of the decrease and disappearance of BEHD to be found in *Pharbitis* during short and long nights. It seems that the disappearance of BEHD at the end of the long night acts as a trigger which probably causes some flower promoting principal (FPP) to travel from the leaf to the bud and convert it from a vegetative to a flowering bud (i.e. evocation) (*see Table 20.5*). If these kinetics are correct, it is very important to look for the disappearance of an inhibitor at the correct time. This may explain the failure of other laboratories to detect photoperiodically induced inhibitors.

It is interesting to speculate about the nature of the FPP mechanism. The FPP may be a trophic factor, such as an increase in nitrogen, or it may be a hormone, travelling from the leaf to the bud. The grafting experiments mentioned in the introduction reinforce this suggestion. However, there are two possible ways the BEHD may mediate induction in the leaf (*see Table 20.5*). First, FPP may be synthesized only after the disappearance of BEHD. This might also require the *de novo* synthesis of new biosynthetic enzymes, and account for Suge's (1972) observation that a FPP does not leave the leaf until 4–6 hours after the end of the long night. Preliminary experiments involving the carefully timed application of inhibitors of RNA and protein synthesis suggest that the synthesis of new enzymes may be required for flowering after the disappearance of BEHD.

The second possible mode of action of BEHD involves the release of an FPP that is already present in the leaf before induction. If this is the case, it will be impossible to demonstrate the *de novo* appearance of a chromatographic peak in the leaf following

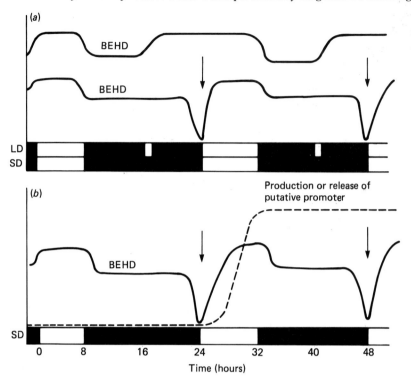

Figure 20.3 Working hypothesis for the role(s) of the flowering inhibitor BEHD, and a putative promoter in short-day plants. The curves in solid lines are taken from available data. The curve in dotted line is speculative. In this hypothesis, the BEHD titre decreases slightly after dark, but only disappears near the end of a long night (A). The disappearance of BEHD (arrows), acts as a trigger, causing the release of a previously sequestered promoter or the synthesis and subsequent release of the promoter. The promoter then travels to the bud to cause evocation. NOTE that the two BEHD curves in 'a' start at the same titre.

induction. However, its appearance should be demonstrable in the petiole. Experiments are now in progress to test this hypothesis.

The involvement of the natural flowering inhibitor BEHD in short-day photoperiodic induction in *Pharbitis nil* has been clearly demonstrated. However, although it also regulates flowering in two other SDP, it is important to caution that it is not necessarily part of a universal mechanism for controlling flowering. It is just as possible that other photoperiodically regulated native flowering inhibitors will be found in other plants, and that one or more such flowering promoters will also be found.

References

AHARONI, M., GOLDSCHMIDT, E.E. and HALVEY, A. (1985). Changes in metabolites of Acetate-1-C following floral induction of *Pharbitis nil* plants. *Journal of Plant Physiology*, **120**, 145–152

BORTHWICK, H.A., HENDRICKS, A.B., PARKER, M.W., TOOLE, E.H. and TOOLE, V.K. (1952). A reversible photoreaction controlling seed germination. *Proceedings of The National Academy of Science of The USA*, **38**, 662–666

CHAILAKHYAN, M.K. (1936). On the mechanism of the photoperiodic reaction. *C.R. Dolk. Acad. Sci. USSR*, **10**, 89–93

CLELAND, C.F. and AJAMI, A. (1974). Identification of the flower-inducing factor isolated from aphid honeydew as being salicyclic acid. *Plant Physiology*, **54**, 904–906

GARNER, W.W. and ALLARD, H.A. (1920). Effect of length of day on plant growth. *Journal of Agricultural Research*, **18**, 553–606

HAMNER, K.C. and BONNER, J. (1938). Photoperiodism in relation to hormones as factors in floral initiation. *Botanical Gazette*, **100**, 388–431

HODSON, H.K. and HAMNER, K.C (1970). Floral inducing extact from *Xanthium*. *Science*, **167**, 384–385

LANG, A. (1952). Physiology of flowering. *Annual Review of Plant Physiology*, **3**, 265–306

LINCOLN, R.G., MAYFIELD, D.L. and CUNNINGHAM, A. (1960). Preparation of a floral initiating extract from *Xanthium*. *Science*, **133**, 55–56

MOORE, T.C. (1979). *Biochemistry and Physiology of Plant Hormones*, New York, Springer-Verlag

PRYCE, R.J. (1972). Gallic acid as a natural inhibitor of flowering in *Kalanchoe blossieldiana*. *Phytochemistry*, **11**, 1911–1918

ROBERTS, R.H. (1965). Sex hormone in plants. (abstract). *Plant Physiology*, **40**, xlv–xlvi

SACHS, J. (1882). Stoff und Form der Pflanzenorgane. *Arb. Bot. Inst. Würzburg*, **2**, 452–488

SCHWABE, W.W. (1984). Photoperiodic induction—flower inhibiting substances. In *Light and the Flowering Process* (D. Vince-Prue, B. Thomas and K.E. Cockshull, Eds), New York, Academic Press

SUGE, H. (1972). Inhibition of photoperiodic floral induction in *Pharbitis nil* by ethylene. *Plant and Cell Physiology*, **13**, 1031–1038

THIGPEN, S.P. and SACHS, R.M. (1985). Changes in ATP in relation to floral induction and initiation in *Pharbitis nil*. *Physiologia Plantarum*, **65**, 156–162

TRAN THANH VAN, K., TOUBART, P., COUSSON, A., DARVILL, A.G., GOLIN, D.J., CHELF, P. and ALBERSHEIM, P. (1985). Manipulation of the morphogenetic pathways of tobacco explants by oligosaccharins. *Nature (London)*, **314**, 615–617

WITHROW, A., WITHROW, R.T. and BIEBLE, J.P. (1943). Inhibiting influence of the leaves on the photoperiodic response of Nobel Spinach. *Plant Physiology*, **18**, 294–298

ZEEVAART, J.A.D. (1958). Flower formation as studied by grafting. *Meded. Landbouwhogesch. Wageningen*, **58**

ZEEVAART, J.A.D. (1976). Physiology of flower formation. *Annual Review of Plant Physiology*, **27**, 321–348

21

EFFECTS OF LIGHT ON CELL DIVISION IN THE SHOOT MERISTEM DURING FLORAL EVOCATION

D. FRANCIS
Department of Plant Science, University College, Cardiff, UK

Introduction

The events of floral evocation, which commit the shoot apex to a floral mode of growth (Evans, 1971), have been reviewed recently (Lyndon and Francis, 1984; Francis and Lyndon, 1985). The intention of the present paper is not to duplicate these reviews but to develop two themes on light and the flowering process in the target tissue, the shoot meristem. The first concerns the events of evocation in relation to the arrival of a multicomponent floral stimulus. The second will propose that light or dark sensitizes the shoot apex for the reception of the floral stimulus from the leaves.

Evocational events and a multicomponent floral stimulus

Well-documented changes that occur in the shoot apex of the long day (LD) plant, *Sinapis alba*, upon the arrival of the floral stimulus include increases in RNA synthesis and respiratory enzyme activity, and enhanced formation of ribosomes (Bernier, Kinet and Bronchart, 1967; Havelange and Bernier, 1974; Pryke and Bernier, 1978). Many of these events, now observed in several species (*see* Lyndon and Francis, 1984), are consistent with increased rates of cell division which often result in enlarged prefloral meristems. In many instances, such as in *Chrysanthemum*, the enlarged apex accommodates a new phyllotactic arrangement of primordia in the flower (Horridge and Cockshull, 1979).

A curious feature of floral evocation is that the increased rate of growth in the apex is often achieved by a synchronization of cell division. It is not necessary, or normal, for increased rates of cell division in meristems to occur by synchronization. The simplest mechanism for increased division rates is for the component phases of the cell cycle to shorten equally. Also, the only other well-documented occurrence of synchronization of cell division in plants is during the pre-meiotic cell cycle of meiocytes, where synchrony is achieved by a considerable lengthening of the cycle (Bennett, 1976). Why cells become synchronized in pre-floral shoot meristems is unclear but may occur as a side-effect of as yet unidentified components of the floral stimulus.

ESSENTIALITY OF EVOCATIONAL EVENTS

The essentiality of many of 'the events' has been questioned since various species, given various light–dark treatments, either fail to register a particular event yet flower, or conversely, register an event but remain vegetative. For example, synchronization of cell division was catalogued in the apex of the LD plant, *Silene coeli-rosa*, during a 24 h interval prior to sepal appearance (Francis and Lyndon, 1979). A peak in the mitotic index was followed by successive peaks in the proportions of cells in G1, S-phase, G2 and a second mitotic peak. However, exposing *Silene* to a normal inductive treatment of 7LD followed by 48 h darkness prevented synchrony yet the plants ultimately flowered (Grose and Lyndon, 1984). Even an increase in the size of the prefloral apex, central to published models of floral competence (Charles-Edwards *et al.*, 1979), is apparently not necessary for flowering in *Perilla nankinensis* (Nougarède *et al.*, 1964), *Humulus lupulus* (Thomas and Schwabe, 1970) or in nutrient-starved *Silene* (R.F. Lyndon, unpublished observations).

Conversely, increases in total RNA were observed in the shoot apex of *Silene* given a non-inductive treatment of 3LD (Miller and Lyndon, 1977), and mitotic peaks occurred in cytokinin-treated shoot apices of *Sinapis* in short-day (SD) conditions yet the plants remained vegetative (Bernier *et al.*, 1974).

Clearly no evocational event *per se* is of critical importance for flowering. However, it may be that the many events that occur during floral evocation are orchestrated both temporally and spatially so that, for example, an increase in RNA synthesis may lead to a mitotic peak in a cluster of cells. If this occurred at a particular location within the apex it would enable a change in the polarity of growth required for sepal initiation. That a particular light–dark treatment dampens a particular evocational event, but not flowering, suggests that a meristem that has received necessary components of the floral stimulus can compensate providing all other evocational events have acted in concert. Even in Grose and Lyndon's (1984) experiments, 48 h darkness following 7LD delayed flowering indicating that the apex overcame the perturbation by 'resting' until favourable conditions resumed.

MULTICOMPONENT FLORAL STIMULUS

Grafting experiments have yielded data consistent with the conclusion that the floral stimulus is a single hormonal substance-florigen (Lang, 1965). Various experiments have demonstrated the presence of a graft-transmissible stimulus which is apparently neither species- nor photoperiod-specific (Zeevaart, 1958, 1976). Zeevaart (1984) concluded that SD and LD plants share a common but not necessarily identical stimulus for photoperiodic induction.

The proposed existence of florigen has been confounded by the continual failure to isolate a chemical which results in LD or SD plants flowering in non-inductive conditions. Given the multitude of events that are triggered at the apex it seems more likely that the stimulus is multi-component. If so, an explanation is required for the remarkable inductive effect one induced donor leaf can have on a non-induced recipient plant (Zeevaart, 1958). Could it be that in such experiments a single graft-transmitted factor operated in concert with endogenous factors resulting in a floral response? For example, a simple metabolite may have been transmitted to the host which would remain quite innocuous in subsequent searches for the active ingredient.

Reception of the floral stimulus

The argument presented thus far is that the floral stimulus comprises various components which trigger a series of events in the apex. Is it necessary for the apex to undergo a period of growth and development before the stimulus can have an effect? In true day neutral (DN) plants, synthesis of the floral stimulus is not dependent on a specific environmental trigger (Salisbury, 1963) yet naturally growing DN plants flower at a particular time of the year. For example, *Impatiens parviflora* flowers 35 days after seedling emergence from the soil during day-lengths of May, but this interval is shortened by approximately one-third by growing the plants in continuous light, or doubled in 8 h days (Evans and Hughes, 1961). One interpretation of these data is that more floral stimulus is synthesized in continuous light, thereby hastening flowering, and less in 8 h days. However, the opening of the first flower in *Impatiens parviflora* is correlated with vascularization of the eighth leaf pair (Hughes, 1965) indicating that the plant reaches a specific developmental stage before flowering can commence. Furthermore, true DN plants, not requiring a specific photoperiodic trigger, may be exporting the floral stimulus continually but the target meristems only become sensitive at a particular stage in their development. If so, different species may differ in the rate at which the shoot apex acquires sensitivity.

RIPENESS TO FLOWER

There are some plants, such as *Pharbitis nil*, which can be induced to flower within 1 week of germination whereas others, such as woody perennials, must traverse a juvenile-to-mature phase before they will flower (reviewed by Bernier, Kinet and Sachs, 1981). Lang (1965) concluded that such differences are due to the ability of a plant to attain the induced state and produce florigen rather than its ability to respond to florigen. For example, Zeevaart (1962) found that juvenile shoots of *Bryophyllum* flowered when grafted onto mature flowering stocks indicating that juvenility in this species is not a property of the meristem. Conversely, when juvenile scions of *Larix leptolepis* (Japanese larch) and *Larix decidua* (European larch) were grafted on to mature plants and examined 1 year later only one out of 56 surviving scions produced cones in Japanese larch, and none out of 22 produced cones in European larch. Similarly in *Hedera helix*, only one out of 22 surviving juvenile scions flowered when grafted onto mature vines (Robinson and Wareing, 1969). These data support the idea that the cells of the shoot apex must acquire sensitivity to the floral stimulus.

Thus ripeness to flower could relate to the rapidity with which cells of the apex acquire sensitivity as well as to the capacity of the leaves to respond to an inductive treatment and synthesize the floral stimulus. Inductive light or dark may have a dual effect, resulting in synthesis of the floral stimulus in the leaves and sensitizing the shoot apex for the reception of the floral stimulus.

Sensitivity of the shoot apex of short-day plants

Bernier (1971) described changes that occurred in the shoot apex upon the arrival of the floral stimulus in five photoperiodically sensitive plants including three SD ones:

Xanthium strumarium, Pharbitis nil and *Chenopodium rubrum*. Of these three, *Xanthium* has been most extensively studied. Peaks in the mitotic index occurred in both the central and peripheral zones of the shoot meristem 36 and 56 h following a 16 h inductive dark period (Jacqmard *et al.*, 1976). The first mitotic peak was preceded by an increase in the proportion of cells in G2, shown by an increase in the G2/G1 ratio at 28 and 32 h (*see* Francis and Lyndon's (1978a) recalculation of the data of Jacqmard *et al.* (1976)). The second peak in mitotic activity was followed by a less pronounced increase in the labelling index 60 h after the inductive dark period (*Figure 21.1*). All of these peaks were suppressed, and the plants remained vegetative, if a 15 min light interruption was given in the middle of the 16 h dark period. Thus in *Xanthium* this alteration in the pattern of cell division seems to be a characteristic feature of pre-floral shoot apices.

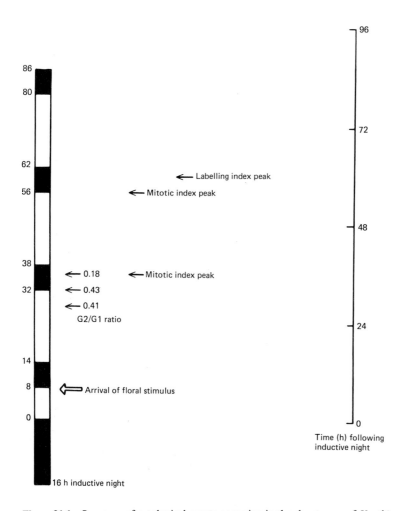

Figure 21.1 Sequence of cytological events occurring in the shoot apex of *Xanthium strumarium* during an 86 h interval following one inductive night (after Jacqmard *et al.*, 1976) and an indication of the presumed arrival of sufficient floral stimulus to evoke a flower (after Salisbury, 1955, 1963; Jacqmard *et al.*, 1976).

In *Xanthium* defoliation experiments have indicated that transport of the floral stimulus from the leaves commences during the light period following the inductive night (Salisbury, 1955, 1963; Jacqmard *et al.*, 1976). Thus the initial peak in the mitotic index occurred 28–30 h after the arrival of sufficient stimulus to evoke a flower (*Figure 21.1*). Is there any evidence for events occurring in the shoot apex of *Xanthium* before the presumed arrival of the floral stimulus? An inhibitor of RNA synthesis, 5-fluorouracil (5FU), suppressed flowering in *Xanthium* when applied to the bud at the start of a 16 h inductive long night (Bonner and Zeevaart, 1962). The data were consistent with an inhibition of RNA synthesis during the first 8 h of darkness and the effect was bud- rather than leaf-specific. Moreover, unlike the effects of another inhibitor, 5-fluorodeoxyuridine, 5FU applied at the beginning of the dark period inhibited flowering but did not result in any general inhibition of vegetative growth (Salisbury and Bonner, 1960). These observations were similar to those made on the shoot apex of *Cannabis sativa* following treatments with 2-thiouracil. This pyrimidine analogue when applied to the shoot apex daily, just before the onset of twenty one 16 h nights, severely reduced the flowering response in male plants and almost abolished flowering in female plants. Thiouracil, whilst initially retarding growth, did not have any long-lasting effects. The conclusion was that the inhibitory effect on flowering was due to a loss of responsive capacity of the shoot apex to leaf-generated stimuli (Heslop-Harrison, 1960). Given the likelihood that the effects of any metabolic inhibitor are less specific than was originally thought, the data support the idea that 5FU- and thiouracil-effects rendered the shoot apex insensitive to the arrival of the floral stimulus.

Clearly in SD plants the onset of inductive or non-inductive darkness will result in the same changes in the apex. In *Xanthium* an interaction between a sensitized apex and the bulk of the floral stimulus following a 16 h night may result in recurrent mitotic peaks and later the production of a floral apex.

Sensitivity of the shoot apex of long-day plants

The notion that early responses of the shoot apex to inductive light are important for flowering in LD plants relates to recent work on *Silene coeli-rosa*. This plant requires 7 LD for 100% flowering and 9 days elapse between the beginning of induction and the morphological appearance of sepal primordia (Miller and Lyndon, 1976). Each LD consists of 8 h of high fluence rate light from fluorescent tubes and tungsten bulbs supplemented with a 16 h photo-extension provided by tungsten bulbs (*Figure 21.2*).

Synchronization of cell division occurred 24 h before sepal appearance (Francis and Lyndon, 1979) at a time of increased growth at the apex compared with uninduced plants in SD (Miller and Lyndon, 1976). The only other occasion when the growth rate was enhanced in the apices of LD plants was during the first LD, referred to as day 0 (Miller and Lyndon, 1976; Francis and Lyndon, 1978a). The faster rate of growth was not achieved by a synchronization of cell division but by a transient shortening of the cell cycle from 20 h in SD to about 12 h in LD (Francis and Lyndon, 1978b). A feature of the shortened cell cycle was an accumulation of cells in G2 of the cell cycle, initially detected 1 h after the start of floral induction (Francis, 1981). This rapid G2 increase is due to an increase in the rate of DNA replication fork movement, initially detected at 1730 h of the first LD (Ormrod and Francis, 1986a). This remarkably rapid increase in the rate of DNA replication is the earliest reported event occurring in the shoot apex during this 7 LD treatment.

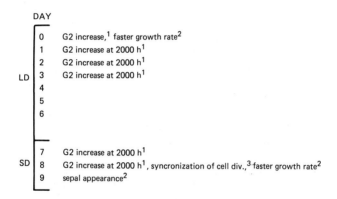

Figure 21.2   Diagrammatic representation of a short day (SD) and a long day (LD) used in the studies on *Silene* together with the unique sequence of events that occur in the shoot apex of 28-day-old plants exposed to 7 LD and then returned to SD (after 1, Ormrod and Francis, 1986b; 2, Miller and Lyndon, 1976; 3, Francis and Lyndon, 1979).

Are these cytological changes merely 'random noise' resulting from a change in spectral quality at 1700 h or are they related to flowering?

The G2 increase observed on day 0 was also observed at 2000 h of days 1–3 and 7–8 of an inductive LD treatment (*Figure 21.2*; Ormrod and Francis, 1986b). Interpolation of a dark period (di) between 1700 and 1720 of each of 7 LD suppressed flowering in *Silene* (Taylor, 1975; Ormrod and Francis, 1986b) and also prevented the characteristic G2 increases on days 0–3 and 7–8. Furthermore, 3 diLD followed by 4 LD resulted in only 10% flowering and 3 LD is totally non-inductive (*Table 21.1*). Thus the stimulation of DNA replication on day 0, and the G2 increases on days 0–3, may indicate that the apex is being sensitized during the initial 3 LD for the reception of the floral stimulus.

The inhibitory effects of the dark interruptions in *Silene coeli-rosa* are novel particularly since similar dark-interruptions in *Silene armeria* and other LD plants promote flowering (Wellensiek, 1984). The nature of the inhibition can be considered at two levels which are not necessarily mutually exclusive.

First, the dark periods could result in the synthesis of a floral inhibitor in the leaves which is then translocated to the apex. The effect would be analogous to those

Table 21.1 THE PERCENTAGE OF 56-DAY-OLD PLANTS OF *Silene* WHICH FLOWERED
WHEN MAINTAINED IN (*a*) SHORT DAYS (SD), OR IF EXPOSED, WHEN THEY WERE 28
DAYS OLD, TO (*b*) 3 LONG DAYS (LD); (*c*) 4 LD; (*d*) 7 LD; (*e*) 7 DARK-INTERRUPTED (di)
LD, OR (*f*) 3 diLD FOLLOWED BY 4 LD

Treatment	Percentage flowering
SD	0
3LD	0
4LD	17
7LD	100
7 diLD	8
3 diLD; 4LD	10

After Ormrod (1985).

ascribed to a mobile inhibitor synthesized in the LD plant *Nicotiana sylvestris* held in
non-inductive conditions (Lang, Chailakhyan and Frolova, 1977; Lang, 1980).
However, whether in *Silene* 20 minutes is sufficient for the induction, synthesis and
transport of an inhibitor, suggested by Schwabe (1984) to be an abscisic acid-like
molecule, is doubtful. However a pre-existing ABA-like molecule could be circulating
around the plant and simply drawn to the apex upon darkness, suppressing the
changes to the cell cycle and inhibiting flowering.

Second, the apex may perceive the change from light to dark rendering it insensitive
to the floral stimulus. This would suggest that in *Silene* exposed to normal LD the
change in spectral quality resulting in changes to the cell cycle is also perceived at the
apex.

There is evidence that the apex of a higher plant can perceive and respond to light.
For example, irradiation of the apex of *Pharbitis nil* with R(660 nm) light, by inserting
a single optical fibre onto the plumule, resulted in a decrease in the flowering response
(Gressel *et al.*, 1980). In *Pinus sylvestris* and *Picea abies*, piercing of buds with optical
fibres allowed natural light to bypass R-absorbing bud scales. This enabled a higher
proportion of FR light to reach the apical dome resulting in the induction of female
strobiles (Kosinski and Giertych, 1982).

In our studies, *Silene* is grown for 28 days under SD conditions and plants of this
age have, on average, three leaf pairs which are visible and the apex is enclosed in a
further four pairs of leaves. Green leaves are very effective FR filters (Bannister, 1976)
and therefore in *Silene* any light reaching the apex, being transmitted through several
leaf pairs, will be FR enriched. It follows that the FR component of tungsten
photoextension could be received by the apex bringing about rapid changes to the cell
cycle which occur on day 0.

To test whether the apex could respond to light, the apical dome and youngest pair
of leaf primordia were cultured on Murashige and Skoog medium and subjected to
LD, or non-inductive 5 min FR treatments at 1700 h of 7 SD. G2 increases were
detected at 2000 h of days 0–3 in both treatments, but the characteristic increases in
the G2 proportion on days 7 and 8 found in intact plants (*Figure 21.2*), were not
found in cultured apices exposed to FR or 7 LD. Moreover, the cultured LD-apices
when returned to SD conditions did not flower, but if kept permanently in LD they
formed small floral plantlets within the flask (J.C. Ormrod and D. Francis, unpublished observations).

Other recent experiments comprised placing black hoods over the apex of 28-day-
old plants enabling leaf pairs 1, 2 and 3 to protrude through slits on the side. These

plants were exposed to 7 LD and once again G2 increases were recorded at 2000 h of days 0, 1, 2 and 8 but not on day 7. In this treatment only about 60% of the plants flowered which is at least partly due to the hood masking the base of the older leaves since transparent hoods used in identical experiments resulted in 100% flowering (Ormrod, 1985). Thus it seems more likely that presumed signals transmitted during the early part of induction are from the leaves to the apex.

The data from both cultured- and shaded-apex experiments are consistent with the idea that during the induction of intact plants the photoextensions of LD 0–3 sensitize the apex and that during LD 4 to 7 the bulk of the floral stimulus is exported from the leaves to the apex.

The nature of the sensitivity: conclusions

It was suggested that in woody perennials, meristematic cells have to undergo a certain number of mitotic cycles before the apex becomes receptive to the floral stimulus (Robinson and Wareing, 1969). Lang (1965) and Friend (1984) suggested that derepression of floral genes in the shoot apex may require not only the arrival of the floral stimulus but also the stimulation of DNA replication. Also Wareing (1978) raised the somewhat novel idea that in meristems selective gene activation and repression could be transmitted through DNA replication and subsequent cell division. Are such changes manifest in the *Silene* apex on transfer to inductive conditions? The ideas developed in the present paper are that the altered pattern of cell division occurring in the shoot apex during early evocation marks a change in sensitivity of the apex which is required for successful interaction with the floral stimulus.

Changes in sensitivity would not necessarily rely on qualitative changes in gene expression in the shoot apex during evocation; the evidence for this is sparse (*see* Lyndon and Francis, 1984). As mentioned earlier the rapidity of early responses in *Silene* preclude induction, synthesis and transport of regulatory molecules. What could cause rapid changes to DNA replication during the onset of inductive conditions?

Phytochrome has been strongly implicated to control flowering and despite the uncertainty of its precise role, one of phytochrome's activities is as a membrane-bound effector of ion movement (Marme, 1977). Changes in phytochrome conformation upon transfer of plants from light to dark, or from one spectral quality to another, must result in changes in membrane potential in the leaves. Such changes in membrane potential could facilitate a rapid leaf-to-apex ionic signal.

Calcium movement and changes in calcium concentration ($1–10 \,\mu mol \, l^{-1}$) promote cell division and activate protein kinases in animal systems (Dunham and Walton, 1982). The activation of these enzymes leads to the phosphorylation of nuclear proteins which are associated with high rates of cell division in roots of *Pisum sativum* (Hetherington and Trewavas, 1984). Also, increased nuclear protein-kinase activity is associated with the onset of DNA synthesis in cultured artichoke tuber cells (Melanson and Trewavas, 1981). Thus elevated calcium ion levels were correlated with increased protein kinase activity and subsequent increases in DNA synthesis and cell division. Given these changes and given the rapidity of changes to the cell cycle in the shoot apex of *Silene*, the following scheme is proposed:

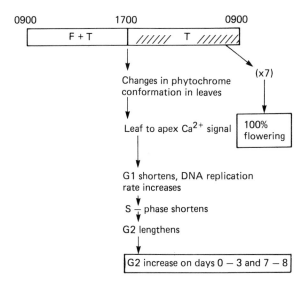

Seven dark interrupted LD suppressed these changes and resulted in only 8% flowering (Ormrod and Francis, 1986a), and extending the dark interruption from 20 to 60 min completely inhibits flowering (Ormrod and Francis, unpublished observations). Whilst there is no evidence to indicate that these cytological changes lead to flowering, hence the deliberate divergence above, they are at least markers of when important events occur.

Altered sensitivity of the apex could thus be achieved by ionic signals resulting in altered polarity of ions both between and within cells. Natural transcellular currents result in altered polarity of cell division in unicellular systems such as fucoid eggs (*see* Weisenseel, 1979) and such alterations in the apex of a higher plant may be an integral part of the flowering process.

Changes in membrane potential obviously occur throughout growth and development. Why then should these changes be part of a sensitizing effect on prefloral apices when they are presumably occurring during every cell division in the vegetative apex? Trewavas (1982) pointed out that the sensitivity of cells to external and internal signals is continually changing. Only by recognizing this can the multitude of effects that plant growth regulators have on development be appreciated. No less a case can be made for the range of effects different plant growth regulators and different light–dark cycles have on promoting or retarding flowering, even in the same species. Endogenous events within the apex if altered at a particular time, by a particular treatment, may act in concert with the various components of the floral stimulus to bring about the transition from vegetative to floral growth. The proposed causal agent responsible for early changes within the apex is an ionic signal generated from the leaves.

It remains for future research to prove, or in particular to disprove, these various suggestions and in this respect concluding comments of Vanderhoef (1980), reviewing theories of auxin control of cell extension, are salutary: 'We spend too much time defending and not enough time attacking hypotheses.'

Acknowledgement

I thank the Agricultural and Food Research Council for support through Grant No. AG 72/43.

References

BANNISTER, P. (1976). *Introduction of Physiological Plant Ecology*, 1st edn. Oxford, Blackwell

BENNETT, M.D. (1976). The cell cycle in sporogenesis and spore development. In *Cell Division in Higher Plants* (M.M. Yeoman, Ed.), pp. 161–198. London, Academic Press

BERNIER, G. (1971). Structural and metabolic changes in the shoot apex in transition to flowering. *Canadian Journal of Botany*, **49**, 803–819

BERNIER, G., KINET, J.-M. and BRONCHART, R. (1967). Cellular events at the meristem during floral induction in *Sinapis alba* L. *Physiologie Végétale*, **5**, 311–324

BERNIER, G., BODSON, M., ROUMA, Y. and JACQMARD, A. (1974). Experimental studies on the mitotic activity of the shoot apical meristem and its relation to floral evocation and morphogenesis in *Sinapis alba*. *Botanical Gazette*, **135**, 345–352

BERNIER, G., KINET, J.-M. and SACHS, R. (1981). *Physiology of Flowering*, Vol. 2. Boca Raton, Fl. CRC Press

BONNER, J. and ZEEVAART, J.A.D. (1962). Ribonucleic acid synthesis in the bud as an essential component of floral induction in *Xanthium*. *Plant Physiology*, **37**, 43–49

CHARLES-EDWARDS, D.A., COCKSHULL, K.E., HORRIDGE, J.S. and THORNLEY, J.H.M. (1979). A model of flowering in *Chrysanthemum*. *Annals of Botany*, **44**, 557–566

DUNHAM, A.C.H. and WALTON, J.H. (1982). Calcium ions and the control of proliferation of normal and cancer cells. *Biosystems Reports*, **2**, 15–30

EVANS, G.C. and HUGHES, A.P. (1961). Plant growth and the aerial environment. I. Effect of artificial shading on *Impatiens parviflora*. *New Phytologist*, **60**, 150–180

EVANS, L.T. (1971). Flower induction and the florigen concept. *Annual Review of Plant Physiology*, **22**, 365–394

FRANCIS, D. (1981). A rapid accumulation of cells in G2 in the shoot apex of *Silene coeli-rosa* during the first day of floral induction. *Annals of Botany*, **48**, 391–394

FRANCIS, D. and LYNDON, R.F. (1978a). Early effects of floral induction on cell division in the shoot apex of *Silene*. *Planta*, **139**, 273–279

FRANCIS, D. and LYNDON, R.F. (1978b). The cell cycle in the shoot apex of *Silene* during the first day of floral induction. *Protoplasma*, **96**, 81–88

FRANCIS, D. and LYNDON, R.F. (1979). Synchronisation of cell division in the shoot apex of *Silene* in relation to flower initiation. *Planta*, **145**, 151–157

FRANCIS, D. and LYNDON, R.F. (1985). The regulation of the cell cycle in relation to floral induction. In *The Cell Division Cycle in Plants* (J.A. Bryant and D. Francis, Eds), pp. 199–215. Cambridge University Press

FRIEND, D.J.C. (1984). The interaction of photosynthesis and photoperiodism in induction. In *Light and the Flowering Process* (D. Vince-Prue, B. Thomas and K.E. Cockshull, Eds), pp. 257–275. London, Academic Press

GRESSEL, J., ZILBERSTEIN, J.A., PORATH, D. and ARZEE, T. (1980). Demonstration with fibre illumination that *Pharbitis* plumules also perceive flowering photoinduction. In *Photoreceptors and Plant Development* (J. de Greef, Ed.), pp. 525–530. Antwerpen University Press

GROSE, S. and LYNDON, R.F. (1984). Inhibition of growth and synchronized cell division in the shoot apex in relation to flowering in *Silene*. *Planta*, **161**, 289–294

HAVELANGE, A. and BERNIER, G. (1974). Descriptive and quantitative study of ultrastructural changes in the apical meristem of mustard in transition to flowering. I. The cell and nucleus. *Journal of Cell Science*, **15**, 633–644

HESLOP-HARRISON, J. (1960). Suppressive effects of 2-thiouracil on differentiation and flowering in *Cannabis sativa*. *Science*, **132**, 1943–1944

HETHERINGTON, A.M. and TREWAVAS, A.J. (1984). Activation of a pea (*Pisum sativum*) membrane protein kinase by calcium ions. *Planta*, **161**, 409–417

HORRIDGE, J.S. and COCKSHULL, K.E. (1979). Size of the *Chrysanthemum* shoot apex in relation to inflorescence initiation and development. *Annals of Botany*, **44**, 547–556

HUGHES, A.P. (1965). Plant growth and the aerial environment. IX. A synopsis of the autecology of *Impatiens parviflora*. *New Phytologist*, **64**, 399–413

JACQMARD, A., RAJU, M.V.S., KINET, J.-M. and BERNIER, G. (1976). The early action of the floral stimulus on mitotic activity and DNA synthesis in the apical meristem of *Xanthium strumarium*. *American Journal of Botany*, **63**, 166–174

KOSINSKI, G. and GIERTYCH, M. (1982). Light conditions inside developing buds affect floral induction. *Planta*, **155**, 93–94

LANG, A. (1965). Physiology of flower initiaion. In *Encyclopedia of Plant Physiology* (W. Ruhland, Ed.), Vol. 15, pp. 1380–1536. Berlin, Springer-Verlag

LANG, A. (1980). Inhibition of flowering in long day plants. In *Plant Growth Substances* (F. Skoog, Ed.), pp. 310–330. Berlin, Springer-Verlag

LANG, A., CHAILAKHYAN, M. Kh. and FROLOVA, I.A. (1977). Promotion and inhibition of flower formation in day neutral plants in grafts with a short-day plant and a long-day plant. *Proceedings of the National Academy of Sciences of the USA*, **74**, 2412–2416

LYNDON, R.F. and FRANCIS, D. (1984). The response of the shoot apex to light-generated signals from the leaves. In *Light and the Flowering Process* (D. Vince-Prue, B. Thomas and K.E. Cockshull, Eds), pp. 171–189. London, Academic Press

MARME, D. (1977). Phytochrome: membranes as possible site of primary action. *Annual Review of Plant Physiology*, **28**, 173–198

MELANSON, D. and TREWAVAS, A.J. (1981). Changes in tissue protein pattern associated with the induction of DNA synthesis by auxin. *Plant, Cell and Environment*, **5**, 53–64

MILLER, M.B. and LYNDON, R.F. (1976). Rates of growth and cell division in the shoot apex of *Silene* during the transition to flowering. *Journal of Experimental Botany*, **27**, 1142–1153

MILLER, M.B. and LYNDON, R.F. (1977). Changes in RNA levels in the shoot apex of *Silene* during the transition to flowering. *Planta*, **136**, 167–172

NOUGAREDE, A., BRONCHART, R., BERNIER, G. and RONDET, P. (1964). Comportement du méristème apical du *Perilla nankinensis* (LOUR) DECNE en relation des conditions photopériodiques. *Revue générale Botanique*, **71**, 205–238

ORMROD, J.C. (1985). *The Effects of Light on Cell Division in the Shoot Apical Meristem of Silene coeli-rosa (L.) Godron in Relation to the Transition to Floral Growth*. PhD Thesis, University of Wales

ORMROD, J.C. and FRANCIS, D. (1986a). Mean rate of DNA replication and replicon size in the shoot apex of *Silene coeli-rosa* during the initial 120 minutes of floral induction. *Protoplasma*, **130**, 206–210

ORMROD, J.C. and FRANCIS, D. (1986b). Cell cycle responses to red or far-red light, or darkness, in the shoot apex of *Silene coeli-rosa* L. during floral induction. *Annals of Botany*, **57**, 91–100

PRYKE, J.A. and BERNIER, G. (1978). RNA synthesis in the apex of *Sinapis alba* in transition to flowering. *Journal of Experimental Botany*, **29**, 953–961

ROBINSON, L.W. and WAREING, P.F. (1969). Experiments on the juvenile-adult phase change in some woody species. *New Phytologist*, **68**, 67–78

SALISBURY, F.B. (1955). The dual role of auxin in flowering. *Plant Physiology*, **30**, 327–334

SALISBURY, F.B. (1963). *The Flowering Process*, 1st edn. Oxford, Pergamon Press

SALISBURY, F.B. and BONNER, J. (1960). Inhibition of photoperiodic induction by 5-fluorouracil. *Plant Physiology*, **35**, 173–177

SCHWABE, W.W. (1984). Photoperiodic induction—flower inhibiting substances. In *Light and the Flowering Process* (D. Vince-Prue, B. Thomas and K.E. Cockshull, Eds), pp. 143–153. London, Academic Press

TAYLOR, S.M.J. (1975). *Factors Controlling the Flowering of* Viscaria candida, PhD Thesis, University of London

THOMAS, G.G. and SCHWABE, W.W. (1970). Apical morphology in the hop (*Humulus lupulus*) during floral initiation. *Annals of Botany*, **34**, 849–859

TREWAVAS, A.J. (1982). Growth substance sensitivity: the limiting factor in plant development. *Physiologia Plantarum*, **55**, 60–72

VANDERHOEF, L.N. (1980). Auxin regulated cell enlargement: is there action at the level of gene expression? In *Genome Organisation and Expression in Plants* (C.J. Leaver, Ed.), pp. 159–173. New York, Plenum

WAREING, P.F. (1978). Determination in plant development. *Botanical Magazine, Tokyo*, **1**, 3–17

WEISENSEEL, M.H. (1979). Growth movement directed by light. Induction of Polarity. In *Encyclopedia of Plant Physiology* (W. Haupt and M.E. Feinleib, Eds), New series Vol. 7, pp. 485–505. Berlin, Springer-Verlag

WELLENSIEK, S.J. (1984). The effect of periodic dark interruptions in long photoperiods on floral induction in the long day plants *Silene armeria* L., annual *Lunaria annua* L. and *Samolus parviflorus* raf. *Journal of Plant Physiology*, **117**, 257–265

ZEEVAART, J.A.D. (1958). Flower formation as studied by grafting. *Mededelingen van de Landbouwhogeschool Wageningen*, **58**, 1–88

ZEEVAART, J.A.D. (1962). The juvenile phase in *Bryophyllum daigremontianum*. *Planta*, **58**, 531–542

ZEEVAART, J.A.D. (1976). Physiology of flower formation. *Annual Review of Plant Physiology*, **27**, 321–348

ZEEVAART, J.A.D. (1984). Photoperiodic induction, the floral stimulus and flower-promoting substances. In *Light and the Flowering Process* (D. Vince-Prue, B. Thomas and K.E. Cockshull, Eds), pp. 137–142. London, Academic Press

22

INITIATION AND GROWTH OF INTERNODES AND STEM AND FLOWER FRUSTA IN *SILENE COELI-ROSA*

R.F. LYNDON

Department of Botany, University of Edinburgh, UK

Introduction

The formation of a flower is first recognizable as a change in the arrangement of the primordia at the shoot apex, accompanied by a decrease in the size of the primordia at initiation, and a lack of internodes. There is a decrease in the length, at initiation, of the stem frusta that give rise to the node plus internode (Lyndon and Battey, 1985). The final lengths of internodes may therefore be related, at least in part, to the sizes of the stem frusta at initiation. The formation of flowers, in which internodes are suppressed, is very often accompanied by a simultaneous increase in the growth of internodes below the flower, suggesting that either potential internodal cells in the flower are not produced, or they may be formed at frustum initiation but do not grow and multiply.

   The problem of the flower, in terms of frustum formation and growth, is therefore: why do internodes not form? Are the necessary cells not formed at frustum initiation? If not, then the primordium plus frustum of the flower is a different morphological entity from that in the vegetative plant. Or are the frusta similar at initiation but develop differently? These questions can be answered only by finding out what happens at the earliest stages of frustum initiation and growth. Most previous work on internode growth has been concerned with the growth of internodes already several mm long at the start of measurements (Garrison, 1973; Enright and Cumbie, 1973; Maksymowych, Maksymowych and Orkwiszewski, 1985). The very earliest stages of the growth of stem frusta have, however, been followed in some plants. The frusta grew in breadth rather than length for several plastochrons after initiation in *Lupinus* and *Chrysanthemum* (Sunderland and Brown, 1956; Berg and Cutter, 1969), but in *Agropyron* older frusta showed an initial lag in growth both in breadth and in length (Smith and Rogan, 1975). Frustum growth has not been followed beyond the apical meristem and not in flowering plants. It is at these earliest stages of frustum growth, when the internode is only a fraction of a mm long, that cell division predominates and when gibberellic acid has a major effect (Sachs, Bretz and Lang, 1959). It is presumably at these earliest stages that the developmental pathways of vegetative and floral frusta diverge.

   In order to understand why internodes do not form in the flower one can pose the converse question: why do internodes form in the vegetative shoot? By comparing frustum initiation and growth in the vegetative shoot and in the flower it should be possible to pinpoint the differences in growth pattern and so gain some insight into the type of cellular changes that are associated with the transition to flowering and why internodes are therefore suppressed in the flower.

The intention here is to make such a comparison, of the growth of frusta from initiation to the later stages of development, and to compare the sizes at initiation, the rates of growth, the response to long-days, and the distribution of cell division and elongation in frusta in vegetative and flowering plants. Frustum growth was followed in *Silene coeli-rosa*, which is an obligate long-day plant, which has opposite decussate leaves, and in which the terminal apex transforms into the first flower.

Experimental

Plants of *Silene coeli-rosa* L. Godron were grown from sowing in SD (short-days) and when 28 or 30 days old, they were selected for developmental uniformity according to the length of the third leaf pair in the ways previously described (Miller and Lyndon, 1976). SD consisted of 8 h light/16 h dark. LD (long-days) were the same but with low level illumination from incandescent lights during the 16 h, otherwise dark, period. Temperature was 20 °C throughout. The day of selection was designated experimental day 0.

For sectioning, shoots stripped of their oldest leaves were fixed in 3:1 ethanol:acetic acid, then dehydrated in an ethanol series, transferred by stages to xylene and embedded in Paraplast. Serial longitudinal sections 10 μm thick, in the plane of the odd-numbered leaf pairs, were stained usually with haematoxylin and orange G or fast green.

Frustum length was measured as the distance between the axils of successive leaf pairs, the frustum for a particular leaf pair consisting of the node of that leaf pair and the internode below it. Frustum breadth was the width of the stem at the leaf axils at the base of the frustum.

Measurements for *Figures 22.2* and *22.3* and *Table 22.5* were made on plants defoliated to expose the frusta. The lengths of the frusta were measured with a ruler if they were more than about 5 mm long, otherwise they were measured under a dissecting microscope with an ocular micrometer. All other measurements were made on sections. The outlines of the sections were traced using a camera lucida, and measurements were made on the scale drawings so obtained. For counting the numbers of cells in the frusta, lines were drawn down files of cells while they were viewed with the camera lucida and the number of cells passed in traversing the length of the frustum was recorded. This was repeated for six files per frustum per apex. Only pith cells were measured.

GROWTH OF STEM FRUSTA

The growth of stem frusta is best exemplified by comparing successive frusta along the stem. Since the growth pattern is the same for plants with 9 and with 12 pairs of leaves (*Figure 22.1*) then the increase in size of successive frusta also represents the temporal sequence of development. Each plastochron is about 4 days (Lyndon, 1977), and so *Figure 22.1* represents about 20 days of development. Since frusta are necessarily exactly one plastochron apart this gives a more accurate representation of their growth than by sampling different plants at different times. The breadth of the frustum increases exponentially from initiation, which is taken to be when the frustum can be recognized as the axis associated with the youngest pair of leaf

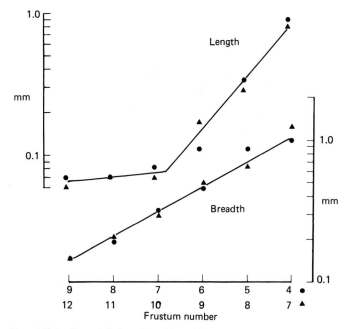

Figure 22.1 Growth in length and breadth of successive stem frusta in *Silene* plants in SD. Each set of points represents the means from three plants.

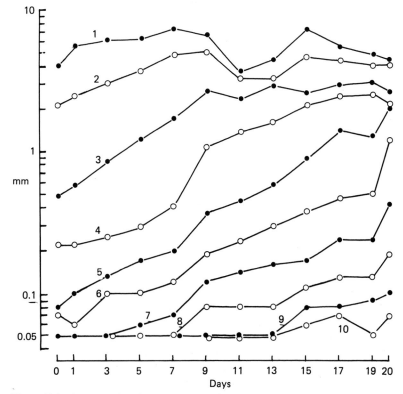

Figure 22.2 Frustum elongation in SD in *Silene*. The points represent means from 6 different plants each day. Frustum numbers shown on the graph.

primordia. Length of the frustum increases very little for the first two plastochrons, but then elongation begins and is exponential.

The pattern of growth of successive frusta is similar (*Figure 22.2*) but with a tendency for the relative elongation rate to fall with successive frusta. Growth may not be truly exponential over the whole of the growing period; the apparent S-shaped curve for frustum 4 was also found in a duplicate experiment, which gave very similar overall results.

On transfer to LD the rate of frustum and internode elongation is promoted in all frusta (*Figure 22.3*). The relative elongation rate in LD clearly increases to a maximum and then decreases; the period of exponential growth is restricted to the

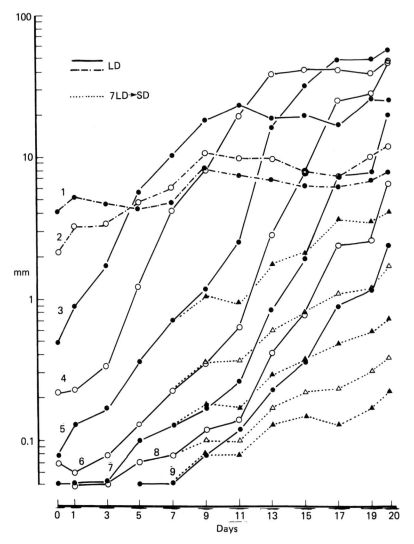

Figure 22.3 Frustum elongation in *Silene* in LD (———·—·) and in plants given 7 LD and returned to SD (..........). The points represent means from six different plants each day.

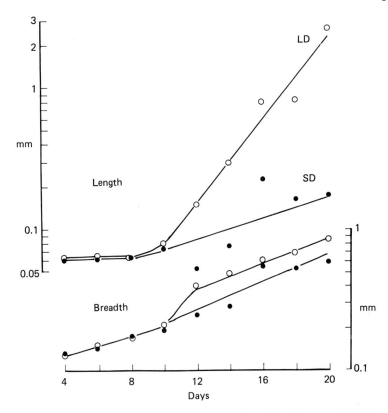

Figure 22.4 Effect of LD on growth in length and breadth of frustum 8 in *Silene*, LD (—○——); SD (—●—). Each point is the mean from three plants.

first half of the growing period. The effect of LD on the elongation of frusta depends on their stage of development at the time the LD treatment was begun. Frustum 1, which was almost at mature length in SD on day 0 (*see Figure 22.1*) was affected least, but even this frustum increased to about 7 mm instead of the 4–5 mm achieved normally in SD. The effect of LD is greater on successively younger frusta and becomes maximal in frustum 5 (*Figure 22.3*). Later frusta attained similar final lengths to frustum 5 when the plants were continued in LD until flowering. The implication is that only frusta less than about 100 μm in length at the beginning of LD treatment were able to respond maximally. This corresponds to frusta at the very beginning of their elongation phase (*see Figure 22.1*), when they are not much longer than at initiation. This conclusion is supported by data from older plants that were kept until day 20 in SD (i.e. 48 SD from sowing) and then transferred to LD. The maximal response after 21 LD was shown by frustum 8, which was the youngest frustum more than 100 μm long when the LD treatment was begun. The duration of frustum growth may be reduced slightly by LD (compare frusta 4 and 5 in *Figures 22.2* and *22.3*). The response of the frusta to LD, i.e. the increase in log final length in LD over log final length in SD, seems to be proportional to the fraction of the duration of frustum elongation left to that frustum at the onset of LD.

When plants were given 7 LD—a fully inductive treatment (Miller and Lyndon, 1976)—and then returned to SD the rate of frustum elongation reverted to that of plants continually in SD (cf. *Figures 22.3* and *22.2*). The effect of the LD treatment on growth rate did not persist for more than about 2 days after transfer to SD.

The effect of LD on frustum growth was almost entirely on elongation. The effect on all frusta was similar to that on frustum 8 (*Figure 22.4*) shown for illustration. The LD perhaps reduce the initial period of little extension from about 8 to about 4 days (cf. *Figure 22.2* and *22.3*); frusta 8 and 9) but the main effect is on increasing the rate of elongation in the main elongation phase. The breadth of all frusta was unaffected by LD except perhaps for a transient increase in growth rate which was often observed when the frusta began to elongate more rapidly in LD (*Figure 22.4*).

The growth of frusta in SD, LD and 7 LD in a duplicate experiment was similar to that reported here. The main conclusion is that frustum final length depends on the effects on elongation which operate on very young frusta when they are still only 100 μm long.

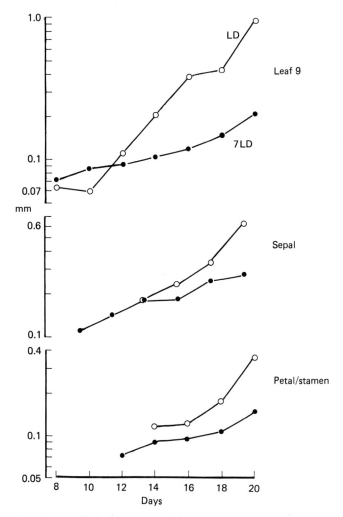

Figure 22.5 Effect of LD (—O—) on elongation of 9th stem, sepal, and petal/stamen frusta in *Silene*. Controls given 7 LD and returned on day 7 to SD (—●—). Each point is the mean from three plants.

GROWTH OF FLOWER FRUSTA

Associated with the sepal frustum in *Silene* are the five sepal primordia, and with the petal/stamen frustum five petal and 10 stamen primordia. It was not feasible to try to distinguish petal from stamen frusta as the axils of the petals are above the bases of the outer whorl of stamens.

The potential for elongation of flower frusta can be measured by comparing their growth in plants maintained in LD and in plants which have been induced with 7 LD and then returned to SD, in which initiation and growth of leaf pair and frustum 9 and the flower occur while the plants are in SD (*Figure 22.5*). The effect of LD on the sepal and petal/stamen frusta is to increase their growth rate to a similar extent to that of the frustum associated with the last leaf pair. These frusta clearly have the initial potential to elongate, but the petal/stamen frustum does not continue to do so, since internodes are not formed between the individual petals and stamens. As in the stem frusta there was little effect of LD on the increase in breadth of the sepal and petal/stamen frusta, which was slightly slower than in the stem frusta. The sepal frustum appeared to grow in length from inception and did not show an initial period of increase in breadth alone (*Figure 22.5*). The sepal frustum at inception is longer than other frusta (*Table 22.1*). This is reflected in its final length at anthesis since the pedicel (to which it gives rise) is almost invariably longer than the last internode. On the other hand the petal/stamen frustum, although it is comparable in length at initiation to a stem frustum, does not elongate markedly. The length of the frusta at maturity is therefore not determined only by their length at initiation.

The length of frustum per primordium (at initiation) does however decrease on flowering from 31.5 μm for stem frusta (two primordia per frustum) to 22.8 μm for the sepal frustum (five sepals) and to 5.1 μm for the petal/stamen frustum (15 primordia; five petals, 10 stamens).

Table 22.1 LENGTHS OF YOUNGEST FRUSTA IN *Silene*, BEFORE THE NEXT PRIMORDIUM OR WHORL WAS APPARENT

Frustum	*Length (μm)*	*No. of apices*
Stem*	63 ± 1	(50)
Sepal	114 ± 8	(9)
Petal/stamen	77 ± 3	(13)

* Frusta 7–13 inclusive. The values for different stem frusta were not significantly different.

CELL GROWTH IN FRUSTA

Differences in the growth of frusta can be found at the cellular level. In stem frusta two distinct regions are found. At the upper, nodal end of the frustum, at and just below the level of the axils of the leaves, the cells are apparently randomly packed and are not in files; below this is a region that gives rise to the internode in which the pith cells are in clear files which have frequent transverse walls. The youngest frustum associated with newly initiated leaf primordia consists of eight layers of cells which are not distinguishable from each other. However, in the second youngest frustum the lower four layers of cells can be seen to be beginning to enlarge (*Table 22.2*). This continues during the next plastochron and only in the third plastochron after initiation is transverse cell division observed, and cell number per frustum length

Table 22.2 GROWTH OF FRUSTUM PITH CELLS IN VEGETATIVE *Silene* PLANTS WITH 8 PAIRS OF LEAVES + PRIMORDIA IN SD

Frustum	Frustum length (μm)	Total no. of cells per frustum length	No. cells in:		Cell length (μm cell^{-1})		
			Upper	Lower	Upper	Lower	
8	57	7.7	7.7		7.4		All cells similar
7	73	8.3	4.0	4.3	7.4	10.2	Cells in lower part begin to enlarge but not divide
6	82	7.9	4.2	3.7	9.6	11.7	
5	157	15.1	4.4	10.7	12.0	9.8	In lower part cells in files with frequent transverse walls; also showing lateral expansion
4	348	33.0	6.3	26.7	10.9	10.2	
3	868	53.3	7.8	46.5	14.6	16.1	

Each value is a mean from three apices.

increases. This corresponds with the onset of the frustum elongation phase 2 plastochrons after initiation (*see Figure 22.1*).

Increase in cell number and hence occurrence of transverse division to give files of cells, occurs at first only in the lower part of the frustum (Frustum 5; *Table 22.2*). Although cell number in the upper part of the frustum also begins to increase (Frustum 4, *Table 22.2*), the internode, and hence nearly all the increase in length of the frustum, derives from the elongation and cell divisions in the files of cells formed from the four cell layers in the lower half of the original frustum. The internode therefore originates from the lower half of the frustum and the node from the upper half; the two halves can be seen to be growing differently from the first plastochron after initiation and before transverse cell division begins. Cell length in the elongating frustum remains similar both in its upper and in its lower parts, although elongation is almost entirely restricted to the lower half. This implies that cell division keeps pace with cell elongation so that mean cell length remains similar in upper and lower parts of the frustum (*Table 22.2*).

In the growth of the petal/stamen frustum no such distinction could be made at any stage between cells in the upper and lower part of the frustum. The cells did not obviously form files but retained a packed, random appearance like those in the upper (nodal) part of the stem frusta. Cell extension and cell division appeared to be equally spread throughout the frustum except in older frusta in which the cells towards the base of the frustum tended to be larger (*Table 22.3*). In the petal/stamen frustum there was therefore no visible differentiation of cells specialized to divide transversely and to elongate. The number of cell layers in the youngest petal/stamen frustum at initiation is about 13, or about one cell layer per primordium (*Table 22.3*).

Table 22.3   GROWTH OF PITH CELLS IN THE PETAL/STAMEN FRUSTUM OF *Silene*

Frustum length (μm)	No. of apices	Total no. of cells per frustum length	Cell length (μm cell^{-1})	
			Upper half	Lower half
80–90	(2)	13.2	6.3	6.6
115–120	(2)	16.2	7.3	7.2
135	(2)	16.2	8.4	8.4
204	(1)	22.2	8.1	10.0
324	(1)	29.8	8.4	9.0
420	(2)	25.5	12.2	14.9

As the sepal frustum grows, immediately after initiation (*Table 22.4*), the cell number does not increase but the cells elongate to about twice their original length. This occurs to the same extent throughout the frustum although the cells in the lower half are longer than those in the upper half. From initiation of the frustum the pith cells are in files which derive from the files of cells formed in the apical dome during its enlargement after the initiation of the last pair of leaf primordia and before the initiation of the sepals. When the sepal frustum has elongated to more than 500 μm, transverse cell divisions accompany extension but these occur equally in both halves of the frustum. Like the petal/stamen frustum, there is no distinction into cells forming the node and cells forming the internode. However, in the petal/stamen frustum all cells are apparently potential nodal cells but in the sepal frustum they are all potential internodal cells. When transverse cell division becomes frequent in the sepal frustum the cells in the upper half become slightly longer than the cells in the

Table 22.4   GROWTH OF PITH CELLS IN THE SEPAL FRUSTUM OF *Silene*

Frustum length (µm)	No. of apices	Total no. of cells per frustum length	Cell length (µm cell⁻¹)		
			Upper half	Lower half	
120–150	(4)	12.8	8.6	14.1	
180–240	(5)	10.9	17.7	20.6	Cell
310	(1)	13.6	20.5	25.4	elongation
640–670	(2)	27.7	27.8	21.2	Cell division and
930	(1)	38.3	27.7	21.4	elongation

lower half (*Table 22.4*). The pith of the sepal frustum becomes very regular in appearance in longitudinal section and consists of cells elongating and dividing transversely. Cell length remains more or less constant, implying that cell division keeps pace with cell extension.

GROWTH OF THE SEPAL FRUSTUM

As the flower begins to develop the sepal frustum develops in a way unlike any other frustum. This can be followed by seeing how the vascular structure of the sepal frustum changes during its growth (*Figure 22.6*). The course of the procambium is at first like that in other frusta (1 and 2, *Figure 22.6*). But as the frustum grows the points

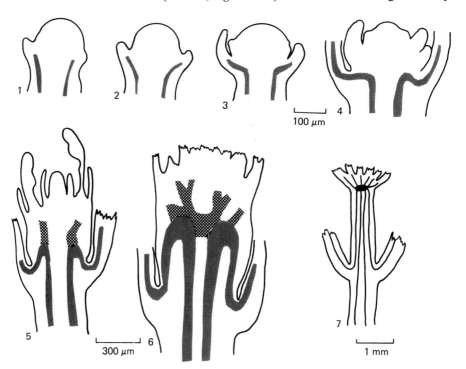

Figure 22.6   Successive stages (1–7) in the development of the sepal vascular traces from initiation (1) to anthesis (7) in *Silene*.

at which the procambium turns downwards into the stem become moved upwards above the axils of the sepals (4, 5, *Figure 22.6*). This is apparently because of the growth of the inner tissues but not the outer tissues at the sepal insertions, so that the inner part of the sepal frustum, including the pith and the vascular tissues, grows up above the sepal axils. The true petal/stamen frustum is those tissues above the uppermost points of the sepal vascular traces in the axis. The slight bulging of the outer tissues just above the sepal axils (5, *Figure 22.6*) is characteristic, and is consistent with an expansion of inner tissues above a constraining ring of outer tissue at the sepal axils. The internode which thus forms between the sepals and the petals (7, *Figure 22.6*), and which at anthesis is about 2 mm long, is therefore almost entirely derived from the sepal frustum growing up beyond the axils of the sepals. Thus there is no true internode between sepals and petals in *Silene*.

Discussion

The reason that internodes are suppressed in the flower seems to be because the cells that give rise to the internode by forming files are not formed in the petal/stamen frustum. The successive frusta constitute a sequence starting with the vegetative stem frusta, which form nodal cells and internodal cells. In the sepal frustum nodal cells are not evident and the whole frustum is essentially internodal but the cell files have a lower frequency of the transverse divisions typical of the stem frusta. In the petal/ stamen frustum all cells appear to be nodal in type and cells giving rise to files are not initiated.

The transition to flowering may therefore consist of three steps:

1. The change in primordium arrangement.
2. The suppression of internodes because the cells generating them are not formed.
3. The differentiation of the floral organs.

The suppression of the internodes seems to occur after the change in primordial arrangement because, in *Silene*, an internode is formed by the sepal frustum even though the primordial arrangement has changed from that in the vegetative plant.

A stem frustum clearly gives rise to the node, which shows little elongation, and the internode which is the main site of stem elongation. Some recent evidence suggests that the node and internode may originate from distinct cell layers when the frustum is formed. In *Sambucus* there are tannin-containing coenocytic cells which extend the length of each internode (Zobel, 1985). These coenocytes originate in a single layer of cells at the base of the apical dome. The suggestion is that these coenocytes are therefore indicators of the cell layer which gives rise to the internode. The single cell layer between successive coenocytes at the base of the apex gives rise to the nodal part of each frustum.

In *Silene* there is a maximum of four cell layers from which the internode originates (*see Table 22.2*). Although *Silene* does not contain coenocytic cells as in *Sambucus*, it does of course contain sieve elements which can be seen readily in sections stained by the periodic acid–Schiff method. Not infrequently only two sieve elements can be seen to extend through the internodal portion of a young frustum and another two through the nodal portion, suggesting that the frustum in *Silene* may originate from a total of only four cell layers at the base of the apical dome, and the internode also only from two cell layers, or one layer per leaf for the internode and one for the node. In the petal/stamen frustum of *Silene* there are about 13 cell layers at initiation (*see*

Table 22.3) and 15 associated primordia (5 petals; 10 stamens), equivalent to about 0.9 cell layers per primordium. Such a reduction to one cell layer associated with each primordium would at least be consistent with the hypothesis that one of the cell layers—that giving rise to the internode—is not formed in the flower. The hypothesis proposed here is therefore that the initiation of a leaf primordium also results in the designation of a minimum of two layers of cells as frustum, one layer giving rise to the node and one layer to the internode, and that in the flower the internodal initials are not formed and that there is only one layer of frustum initials associated with each primordium.

It is characteristic of flowers that primordium area at initiation and frustum length at initiation are both reduced compared with the vegetative apex (Lyndon and Battey, 1985). When proliferous 'flowers' were formed in *Silene* (Lyndon, 1979) the primordia were less than half the area at initiation of leaf primordia and the length of each frustum was half the length of a frustum associated with one leaf primordium in the normal vegetative plant. Judging by the congested nature of the proliferous 'flowers' the frustum layers missing were those giving rise to the internodal initials. In *Ambrosia*, when the phyllotaxis changed from decussate to spiral the length of the internode between successive single leaves was approximately two-thirds that of the internode between successive leaf pairs (Soma and Kuriyama, 1970). All of these observations are consistent with the hypothesis that the frustum and primordium are initiated together and that there is some sort of proportionality between the size of a primordium at initiation and the length of the frustum associated with that primordium. Translated into cellular terms this could perhaps mean that there is a specific number of cell layers initiated as frustum for each primordium formed.

At inception of stem frusta there is no internode present and the leaf bases extend down into the leaf axils. Only after about 2 plastochrons when the internode elongates (*see Table 22.2*) do the adjacent cells of the leaf base also elongate and divide to form the outer tissues of the internode. The sepal frustum is unusual in that the primordia are initiated towards the distal end so that the internode is present from inception. The cell files that give rise to the pedicel pith are formed directly from the cell files in the enlarged apical dome and do not arise subsequently by division as do the cell files in the pith of the stem frusta. The petal/stamen frustum resembles a stem frustum in that the primordium bases extend down into the organ axils, but differs in that extension of the bases of the primordia to contribute to internodes does not occur and so the bases of the petals and stamens remain in close contact in the flower.

The curious growth of the sepal frustum in which the inner tissues of pith and vascular strands extend upwards past the sepal axils, with compensatory growth of the cortical cells at the sepal node and subsequent extension of the cortical and epidermal cells just above the sepal axils, eventually gives rise to an internode about 2 mm long in the mature flower. The way this internode is formed very strongly suggests that the driving force for elongation of this internode comes from the internal cells, especially the pith. Indeed the visual impression from sections is that the driving force for elongation of all the internodes could come from the elongation of the files of pith cells (Sachs, 1882). Supporting evidence is that in *Silene armeria* the pith rib-meristem cells in the apex are the ones most activated by gibberellic acid, which promotes stem elongation (Besnard-Wibaut, Noin and Zeevaart, 1983).

The rate of elongation of internodes in *Silene* is promoted in LD (*Figure 22.3*) but reverts to a lower rate when the plants are transferred back to SD. Internodes growing or not yet initiated at the time of transfer back to SD do not attain the length of internodes of plants maintained in LD (*Figure 22.3*). However, when such plants returned to SD approach anthesis the distal internodes begin to extend and at

Table 22.5   INTERNODE LENGTHS AT OR NEAR ANTHESIS IN *Silene* INDUCED BY 7LD

Frustum	Internode length (mm)		Frustum
—	—	21.3	Sepal
Sepal	35.6	14.0	11
10	15.0	9.7	10
9	10.0	6.7	9
8	8.4	5.0	8
7	6.3	5.0	7
6	6.6	6.0	6
5	8.1	9.0	5
4	12.7	13.7	4
3	18.0	17.7	3
2	8.9	8.3	2
1	7.7	8.7	1
	Mean of 7	Mean of 3	

anthesis there is a gradient of basipetally decreasing internode length in the pedicel and the last three stem frusta (*Table 22.5*). Plants with an extra leaf pair below the flower also show the same pattern with three longer internodes below the pedicel, showing that this late elongation is related to the position of the flower. This suggests that as the plant reaches anthesis the developing flower stimulates the elongation of the terminal frusta, perhaps by the production of gibberellins by the stamens (Murakami, 1975).

The petal/stamen frustum, although it enlarges as the flower develops, does not increase in longitudinal cell number much beyond 30 or so cells per file (*see Table 22.3*). Restriction of growth of this frustum coincides with the development of the flower nodal vascular structure at the base of this frustum, where the traces from the petals, stamens and carpels all join with the vascular strands from the sepals. In *Silene* all vascular strands in the flower join at the same level, unlike at the leaf insertions where there is a typical leaf gap and the leaf trace joins with the stem vascular bundles one node or so below the node of insertion. Sachs (1969) has shown that whether or not new vascular traces join with older ones can depend on the relative flux of auxin through the new and old strands. A new strand will fuse with an older one if the ratio of auxin in the new to that in the old strand is high. If the fusion of vascular bundles in *Silene* is governed in this way, the fusion of all the flower traces with the strands from the sepals at the base of the petal/stamen frustum would imply that sepals, unlike leaves, are poor sources of auxin. We do not know whether the reduction of auxin production by new primordia may be one of the events of the transition to flowering. Changes in auxin production by primordia, or in auxin transport, may well be involved in the change in primordial arrangement and the formation of whorls of organs that occurs on flower initiation. Changes in primordial size and fusion of primordia, as occurs in floral whorls, can be induced experimentally by chemicals which are antiauxins or inhibitors of auxin transport (Meicenheimer, 1981).

The development of vascular tissues may also be more rapid after the transition to flowering than in the vegetative shoot, as shown by careful measurements of the rate of vascular differentiation in *Perilla* (Jacobs and Raghavan, 1962). This may also be indicative of changes in the availability of metabolites and growth substances at the shoot apex associated with the transition to flowering and early flower development. Premature differentiation of vascular tissues may also have a role to play in the control of development on flowering.

References

BERG, A.R. and CUTTER, E.G. (1969). Leaf initiation rates and volume growth rates in the shoot apex of *Chrysanthemum*. *American Journal of Botany*, **56**, 153–159

BESNARD-WIBAUT, C., NOIN, M. and ZEEVAART, J. (1983). Mitotic activities and levels of nuclear DNA in the apical meristem of *Silene armeria* (strain S1.2) following application of gibberellin A_3. *Plant and Cell Physiology*, **24**, 1269–1279

ENRIGHT, A.M. and CUMBIE, B.G. (1973). Stem anatomy and internodal development in *Phaseolus vulgaris*. *American Journal of Botany*, **60**, 915–922

GARRISON, R. (1973). The growth and development of internodes in *Helianthus*. *Botanical Gazette*, **134**, 246–255

JACOBS, W.P. and RAGHAVAN, V. (1962). Studies on the floral histogenesis and physiology of *Perilla*—I. Quantitative analysis of flowering in *P. frutescens* (L.) Britt. *Phytomorphology*, **12**, 144–167

LYNDON, R.F. (1977). Interacting processes in vegetative development and in the transition to flowering at the shoot apex. *Symposia of the Society for Experimental Biology*, **31**, 221–250

LYNDON, R.F. (1979). A modification of flowering and phyllotaxis in *Silene*. *Annals of Botany*, **43**, 553–558

LYNDON, R.F. and BATTEY, N.H. (1985). The growth of the shoot apical meristem during flower initiation. *Biologia Plantarum*, **27**, 339–349

MAKSYMOWYCH, R., MAKSYMOWYCH, A.B. and ORKWISZEWSKI, J.A.J. (1985). Stem elongation of *Xanthium* plants presented in terms of relative elemental rates. *American Journal of Botany*, **72**, 1114–1119

MEICENHEIMER, R.D. (1981). Changes in *Epilobium* phyllotaxy induced by N-1-naphthylphthalamic acid and α-4-chlorophenoxyisobutyric acid. *American Journal of Botany*, **68**, 1139–1154

MILLER, M.B. and LYNDON, R.F. (1976). Rates of growth and cell division in the shoot apex of *Silene* during the transition to flowering. *Journal of Experimental Botany*, **27**, 1142–1153

MURAKAMI, Y. (1975). The role of gibberellins in the growth of floral organs of *Mirabilis jalapa*. *Plant and Cell Physiology*, **16**, 337–345

SACHS, J. (1882). *Textbook of Botany*, 2nd edn. Translated by S.H. Vines.

SACHS, R.M., BRETZ, C. and LANG, A. (1959). Cell division and gibberellic acid. *Experimental Cell Research*, **18**, 230–244

SACHS, T. (1969). Polarity and the induction of organised vascular tissues. *Annals of Botany*, **33**, 263–275

SMITH, D.L. and ROGAN, P.G. (1975). Growth of the stem of *Agropyron repens* (L.) Beauv. *Annals of Botany*, **39**, 871–880

SOMA, K. and KURIYAMA, K. (1970). Phyllotactic change in the shoot apex of *Ambrosia artemisiaefolia* var. *elatior* during ontogenesis. *Botanical Magazine, Tokyo*, **83**, 13–20

SUNDERLAND, N. and BROWN, R. (1956). Distribution of growth in the apical region of the shoot of *Lupinus albus*. *Journal of Experimental Botany*, **7**, 127–145

ZOBEL, A.M. (1985). The internode of *Sambucus racemosa* L. originates from a single cell layer. *Annals of Botany*, **56**, 105–107

VI

Photosynthesis, translocation and flower initiation

23

ROLES OF PHOTOSYNTHESIS AND ASSIMILATE PARTITIONING IN FLOWER INITIATION

R.M. SACHS
Department of Environmental Horticulture, University of California, USA

Introduction

In 1910 the Royal Society of London invited Georg Klebs to give the Croonian lecture on the influence of environment on plant form and development. This was notable in that it contested the generally accepted view that an organism's form was the expression of its 'inner nature', with external factors only supplying material and energy to build up the organisms. Klebs' work with the fungus, *Saprolegnia*, and the flowering plant, *Sempervivum Funckii*, demonstrated clearly that environmental factors, particularly nutrition, controlled many aspects of development (expression of the inner nature). His most important findings were that high rates of carbon assimilation with low nitrogen supply accelerated the transition from the sporophytic (vegetative) to gametophytic (sexual) generation.

Although Klebs' work was extended substantially, nutritional hypotheses lost favour after the discovery of photoperiodism and evidence that supported a more specific, leaf-derived stimulus/hormone or hormone complex. Although not identified, the stimulus could not be a common photosynthetic assimilate. Defining and resolving differences between nutritional and hormonal/morphogen hypotheses, a major goal in this chapter, is a theme common to many reviews (e.g. Bodson and Bernier, 1985). The reasons for seeking synthesis are apparent on examination of the weaknesses of each hypothesis and consideration of the role of naturally occurring growth substances in the process of assimilate partitioning.

Seven kinds of observations suggest that a supply of assimilates greater than that required for vegetative growth is part of the signal for evocation and initiation. These are

1. Higher radiant energy is required for reproductive than continued vegetative development.
2. Reversion to the vegetative state is often observed in flowering plants placed at low irradiance levels.
3. Sucrose or other sugars can substitute for photoperiodic requirements for floral initiation.
4. Higher concentrations of sugars are required for reproductive than vegetative bud formation for tissues cultured *in vitro* than for vegetative development.
5. An increase in assimilate concentration or turnover in the shoot apical meristem is found before, or at the same time as, the first phases of the transition to reproductive development.

6. Moisture and osmotic stress and reduced nitrogen nutrition, used judiciously when the plant is source limited, can accelerate flowering, retard growth and result in increased carbohydrate concentration in the shoot.
7. Girdling and espalier training, that retard vegetative growth and elevate assimilates in distal portions of the shoot, accelerate flowering.

(For reviews of (6) and (7) consult Kraus and Kraybill, 1918; Sax, 1954; Allsopp, 1965; Jackson and Sweet, 1972; Borchert, 1983; Goldschmidt *et al.*, 1985.)

A role for photosynthesis in the synthesis and phloem loading of a specific floral stimulus has been proposed; this proposal, that cannot be tested until a specific stimulus is identified, serves as a counter to the general, non-specific nutritional/ assimilate supply role for photosynthesis that will be examined in this chapter.

Nutritional/hormonal hypothesis

STATEMENTS AND QUESTIONS

Nutritional, or assimilate-dependent, hypotheses propose that a morphogenetic event (e.g., flower initiation) will not occur if a target tissue (e.g., the shoot apical meristem) receives less than some threshold level of substrates. The target tissue is a 'black box' that responds in a pre-programmed fashion to the nutrient level bathing it, or the physical stresses to which it is subjected as a result of changed growth rates in neighbouring tissues (*Figure 23.1*). Nutritional hypotheses generate unique questions and propositions. The first proposition is that the activity of growth substance and environmental factors on flowering will be strongly dependent on source strength (irradiance levels). Does photoperiodic induction alter starch : sugar hydrolysis,

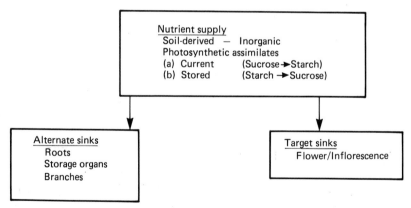

Figure 23.1   Probable nutritional relationships important for control of flower initiation. Induction as targeting: the essence of a nutrient diversion hypothesis.
Processes/substances promote flowering if they:
   1. Activate target sink.
   2. Inhibit alternate sinks.
   3. Increase source strength (starch→sugar; high irradiance).
Processes/substances inhibit flowering if they:
   1. Inhibit target sink.
   2. Activate alternate sinks.
   3. Decrease source strength (sugar→starch; low irradiance).

thereby changing sugar transport capacity of induced leaves, and in effect increase or decrease source strength (Grainger, 1938; and *see* Chapter 17)? Does assimilate supply to the target tissue increase before any other biochemical change (Bodson and Outlaw, 1985)—suggesting a feed forward control of evocation and the 'bicycle pump' theory of sink activation (Hardwick, 1984)? Since at floral evocation assimilate concentration may fall initially if demand by the developing flower or inflorescence exceeds supply (Mohapatra *et al.*, 1982, 1983), or remain unchanged if supply is equal to demand (Kinet *et al.*, 1985), is there feedback control to source tissues with a consequent rapid increase in assimilate flux (Lenton, 1984)? Is an increase in assimilate supply from source tissues mandatory for evocation to continue?

The potential for intersection of hormonal and nutritional hypotheses is clear—for example, growth substances or other compounds may activate targets by increasing the permeability of membranes to assimilates, a prospect emhasized in the review by Marre (1982), and posed as a reasonable interpretation of the morphogenetic activity of oligosaccharins in tobacco tissues (Tran Thanh Van *et al.*, 1985; Albersheim and Darvill, 1985). Photoperiodic induction or growth regulator treatments may increase invertase activity in shoot apical meristems, thereby increasing the ability of the latter to utilize sucrose. Any process or substance that inhibits floral initiation may promote activity of competing sinks, thereby reducing assimilate supply to the target tissues. The corollary proposition is that any process or substance that inhibits competing sink activity would appear as a promoter of floral initiation (Sachs and Hackett, 1983). In this view induction is considered to be 'targeting' of meristems, an integral part of a nutrient diversion hypothesis.

TUBERIZATION AND FLORAL INITIATION: PARALLEL CONTROLS

There are extraordinary parallels between the controls for floral initiation and tuberization. Hypotheses for the control of tuberization (Moorby, 1978; Ng and Loomis, 1984) concern the minimum assimilate supply for initiation of the process, growth substance-induced tuberization, day-length with its effect on naturally occurring growth substances (Palmer and Smith, 1970; Biran *et al.*, 1974; Van Staden and Dimalla, 1977; Sattelmacher and Marschner, 1978b; Kannangra and Booth, 1978; reviews by Moorby, 1978 and Chailakhyan, 1985), and high-irradiance override of day-length requirements (Bodlaender, 1963). Also, non-specificity of tuber-forming and inhibiting agents (Nitsch, 1965; Tizio and Biran, 1973; Hammes and Nel, 1975), nitrate-induced inhibition (Sattelmacher and Marschner, 1978a) and, from reciprocal grafting experiments, both the scion and receptor tissue in the assay for the tuber-inducing agents (Nitsch, 1965; Chailakhyan, 1985) are involved.

Reciprocal grafts between the non-tuber forming sunflower and the tuber-forming Jerusalem artichoke (Nitsch, 1965) show that root tuberization occurs only on the latter but may be induced by either species. Tuber formation occurs in all day-lengths when the day-neutral sunflower is the scion but only in SD when the SD Jerusalem artichoke is the scion. Chailakhyan (1985) used SD, LD and day-neutral tobacco plants, as scions on potato stem/root stocks. Potato stocks tuberize in SD when the SD tobacco is the scion, in LD when the LD tobacco is the scion, and in all day-lengths if the day-neutral tobacco is used as the scion. Hence the flower forming stimulus-complex in tobacco contains the tuber-forming stimulus for potato; the assay used defines the stimulus. Clearly, the stimulus is not a specific morphogen.

Considering other studies on tuberization in potato, it is probably a cytokinin, a mixture of growth substances, or some material that changes the sensitivity of the receptor tissues to cytokinin and other growth substances. In the presence of some threshold level of assimilates (and the stimulus), tuberization results.

NUTRIENT DIVERSION AND CORRELATIVE INHIBITION

Correlative inhibition: general

Girdling experiments gave early support to a nutrient diversion hypothesis for the control of flowering in fruit trees, since one interpretation for the observed increase in number of flowers above the girdle was that the basipetal flow of assimilates was interrupted by cutting the phloem, thereby maintaining a greater supply for potential 'fruiting' buds (Knight, 1820; Sax, 1954; Goldschmidt *et al.*, 1985). However, an alternate interpretation, based on hormonal explanations for correlative inhibition, is that girdling interrupts the flow of more specific substances that either promote or inhibit flowering.

Decapitating an orchid shoot promotes flower initiation (Goh and Seetoh, 1973), removal of young leaves (net assimilate importers), promotes flower or floret initiation in tomato (de Zeeuw, 1956), apple (Fulford, 1966), tobacco (Wardell, 1976) and bougainvillea (T'se *et al.*, 1974). Removal of competing axillary branches increases both the number of inflorescences with floret development and the rate of floret development on the main shoot of bougainvillea plants (Ramina *et al.*, 1979). Root initiation and expansion at the time of photoperiodic induction inhibit floral initiation in *Anagallis* (Bismuth *et al.*, 1979); in *Pharbitis* seedlings cultured *in vitro* in continuous light, benzoic acid derivatives that inhibit root growth promote flower initiation (Shinozaki and Takimoto, 1983). All of these phenomena are accounted for by both nutritional and hormone-inhibitor/promoter hypotheses. Although the traditional, hormonal explanation is frequently cited for root-induced inhibition of flower initiation (Miginiac, 1972; Miginiac and Sotta, 1985; Josefusova *et al.*, 1985; McDaniel, 1984), there is reason to believe that in part the proposed hormonal influences are related to changes in nutrient supply available to the presumptive floral meristems. This would seem to be the case in studies by T'se *et al.* (1974) and Ramina *et al.* (1979) for bougainvillea and Shinozaki and Takimoto (1983) for *Pharbitis*.

Alternate bearing: a special case for correlative inhibition

Hypotheses accounting for alternate bearing in fruit trees (alternating years of heavy and light flower initiation following light and heavy fruit load, respectively), invoke assimilate supply, nutrient diversion and growth substance-type control of flowering. Variation in assimilate level alone is inadequate to account for fluctuations in flowering (Stutte and Martin, 1986). The inhibiting role of seed-derived growth substances, most likely gibberellins, are often of greater import (Chan and Cain, 1967). There is evidence that growth substance inhibition is the result of induced decreases of stored assimilates preceding a critical stage of floral initiation (Growchowska, 1973). Most of these elements are combined in the model for flower bud initiation proposed by Monselise and Goldschmidt (1982). Selective girdling and variable irradiance, with naturally parthenocarpic (or de-seeded or growth substance-treated) or seeded fruit produce the required experimental combinations for testing the relative contributions of assimilate supply and seed-derived inhibitors to flower initiation.

FAILURES OF NUTRITIONAL/ASSIMILATE SUPPLY HYPOTHESES

Assimilate supply (or sugar concentration) cannot be the sole signal for floral initiation, at least not in all species nor in all conditions. Assimilate supply to the shoot apical meristem may increase in non-inductive and inductive photoperiodic treatments equally, but flowering may occur only after the inductive treatment, and assimilate level in the shoot may increase following treatments with certain growth substances that both promote and inhibit flower initiation (Ramina *et al.*, 1979; Ross *et al.*, 1984; *see* especially the review by Pharis and King (1985) for a comprehensive analysis of gibberellin and tissue specificity in the control of reproductive development). Closely related tissues from tobacco cultivars do not develop flower buds when cultured in similar, assimilate-enriched, nutritional conditions (Aghion-Prat, 1965; Kamate *et al.*, 1981). Also, the phenomena of position (floral gradient, Prat (1976)) and age-related, stable (epigenetic) changes in morphogenetic potential, i.e. questions of tissue competence and determination (McDaniel *et al.*, 1985; and *see* Chapter 5) are not readily accounted for by nutritional hypotheses (unless non-specific changes in cell permeability is 'determination'). Finally, mere assimilate supply or concentration does not account for the importance of timing of high irradiance requirements or sugar applications in flower initiation (*see* final section).

Selected experiments

POTENTIAL MISDIRECTION: CAVEATS

Since high PAR affects many plant processes (e.g. HIR) and photosynthesis affects many other processes (e.g. energy supply; transpiration), some caution is advised before assuming that assimilate supply is the major factor altered when irradiance is increased (*see*, for example *Table 2*, in Friend, 1984). Nevertheless, most studies support the irradiance–photosynthesis–assimilate connection.

In the absence of biochemical tests, evocation and initiation can only be detected after completion of at least the early stages of flower and inflorescence development, a subject that will be reviewed in detail by Halevy (*see* Chapter 26).

ASSIMILATE SUPPLY AND THE FLOWERING PROCESS

Assimilate requirements for induction

Some early studies with photoperiodically sensitive species suggested that the role of photosynthesis in the inductive process, i.e. the high-intensity light reaction, was to provide an energy supply for growth. Experiments with chlorophyll-deficient barley (*Arabadopsis*) and *Anagallis* and *Brassica* show that concurrent photosynthesis is not a general requirement for photoperiodic induction (Deitzer, 1984; Friend, 1984; Friend *et al.*, 1984) when an external carbon source is provided. There are, however, reports of more specific roles for photosynthesis during induction.

Data for flowering of *Xanthium* in winter and summer (*Figure 23.2*) suggest that photosynthesis affects the synthesis of specific floral stimuli (or their transport and stability), during the second part of a long night (Salisbury, 1963). Ireland and Schwabe (1982a, b) have presented convincing evidence for *Xanthium* and *Kalanchoe* that some early product of photosynthesis is required during induction for synthesis of the floral stimulus and not merely for energy supply. Evans' (1976) study of the timing of DCMU-induced inhibition of LD induction in *Lolium temulentum* indicates that photosynthesis is vital for phloem loading of specific floral stimuli for transport to the shoot apical meristem, or other tissues involved in the flowering system. Assimilate supply to the shoot apical meristem was effectively eliminated as a contributing factor in *Lolium*; ^{14}C transport studies revealed that apical buds of both DCMU-treated and untreated plants received approximately the same assimilate supply.

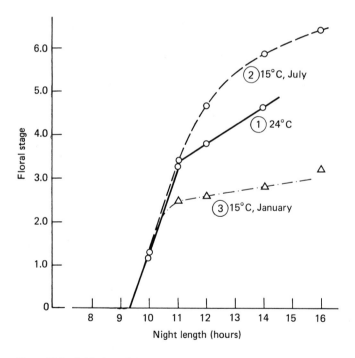

Figure 23.2   Initiation of the male inflorescence in *Xanthium pennsylvanicum* (Chicago strain) as a function of night-length and time of year at Fort Collins, Colorado. Plants were grown in greenhouses (Curves (2) and (3) for January and July experiments) in LD conditions (natural day extended to 20 h with incandescent light of 500 lux). The night of induction was in a temperature-controlled chamber. Floral stage system is described in Bernier *et al.* (1981, Vol. I); florets are not initiated until Stage 4. (Reproduced from Salisbury (1963) by kind permission of author and publishers.)

Assimilate mobilization in the induced leaf: source strength

Grainger's (1938) results with *Chrysanthemum morifolium* indicated that increased hydrolysis of starch and transport of soluble sugars from leaves during the dark period was important in the flowering process and accounted for differences in the dark requirements for flowering among cultivars. Deitzer (*see* Chapter 17) presents more convincing evidence for LD-induced hydrolysis of starch to soluble sugars in LD varieties of *Hordeum*. Another study with the SDP, *Perilla ocymoides*, reveals SD-induced increase in assimilate transport from detached leaves (Zeevaart, 1975; and *see* Chapter 19); this system is more amenable to analysis than whole-plant studies since the leaf-induced 'mobilization' and transport of assimilates cannot be confounded with photoperiodically induced sink activation in the shoot apical meristem and consequent feedback to the leaves.

Assimilate supply for floral initiation

Feed forward control

Irradiance and increased assimilate supply

Klebs (1918) found that all stages of reproductive development, from the maturation period (ripeness-to-flower) through anthesis were accelerated by high rates of carbon assimilation. His critical experiment with *Sempervivum Funckii*, the use of supplemented high-intensity radiation from incandescent lamps to obtain inflorescence initiation in greenhouses during the winter (where otherwise vegetative growth continued regardless of daylength), has been extended to many other species. In some day-length sensitive species, radiant energy may decrease or replace photoperiodic or vernalization requirements (*see* Chapter 12), and can be used with some precision as the sole environmental control of flower initiation in day-neutral species (*Table 1* in Bodson and Bernier, 1985; *Figures 23.3* and *23.4*). In woody perennials flower initiation occurs toward the exterior of the leaf canopy, rarely at the interior; e.g., flower initiation was inhibited in apples when the incident light was reduced by 80%, a level normally found about 1 m into the canopy (*Figure 23.5*). The minimum radiant energy requirements for flower initiation vary widely among species, e.g. flower initiation in the day-neutral W-38 tobacco cultivar requires a radiant energy input about 1/20 that for the SDP, bougainvillea, and about 1/2 that of the LDP, fuchsia (Sachs, unpublished observations). It is well-known that radiant energy values alone cannot give a measure of carbon balance in a plant. Assimilate partitioning as a function of radiant flux is undoubtedly a more significant relationship.

Carbon dioxide level

Carbon dioxide depletion and enrichment studies suggest that the high irradiance requirement for flower initiation reflects a requirement for increased photosynthesis (Sachs, 1979). There are, however, other factors to consider; for example, Quedado and Friend (1978) found continued promotion of flowering in *Anagallis* at radiant energy inputs above the maximum CO_2 fixation. Marc and Gifford (1984) found that although CO_2 enrichment advanced the time of floret initiation in wheat much of that advance could be attributed to a faster growth rate rather than a specific action of

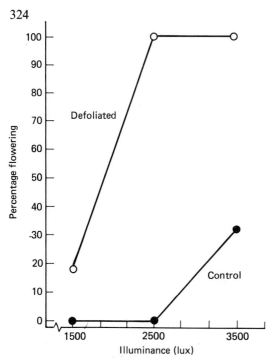

Figure 23.3 Inflorescence initiation in the day neutral plant, *Nicotiana tabacum* 'W-38', as a function of radiant energy and young leaf removal. Plants were grown in growth chambers at 19°C with continuous light (2500 lux from cool white fluorescent tubes is about 30 μmol m^{-2} s^{-1} PAR). (Reproduced from Wardell (1976) by kind permission of author and publisher.)

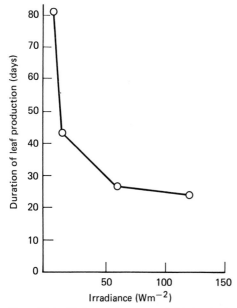

Figure 23.4 Node to inflorescence initiation in the SDP, *Chrysanthemum morifolium* cv 'Polaris' as a function of radiant energy. Plants are held in continuous light at 20°C. (Reproduced from Cockshull (1979) by kind permission of author and publishers.)

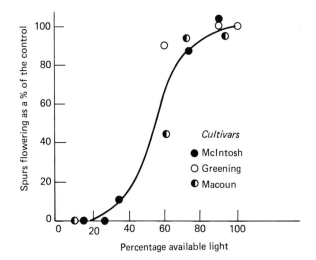

Figure 23.5 Flower initiation in spur shoots of three apple cultivars as a function of percent of incident radiation at the spur shoots, light measurements were made during the spring of the year, 1 year prior to recording data on flowering. Trees were in Geneva, NY where the total solar radiation during the growing season (May 15 to Sept 15) is about 60 000 g cal cm^{-2}. (Reproduced from Cain (1971) by kind permission of author and publishers.)

enhanced photosynthesis on floral initiation. In this same study the CO_2 enrichment treatment delayed floret development in a sorghum cultivar.

Sugar feeding studies

Seedlings, raised *in vitro* on an adequate nutritive medium with a defined carbon source, will flower in low irradiance conditions (Sachs, 1979; and *Figure 23.6*), or in total darkness, or without the environmental signals required if they had received some photosynthetically active radiation (Lona, 1949; Sugino, 1957). Sucrose or glucose is required for floral initiation in tissue pieces of tobacco (Aghion-Prat, 1965), *Sinapis* (Deltour, 1967), endive (Paulet and Nitsch, 1964) and *Plumbago* (Nitsch and Nitsch, 1967a, b) at a higher concentration than that required for vegetative bud initiation or root initiation. Growth, at least in tobacco, is probably limited at the lower sugar concentrations. Hunt and Loomis (1976) found for callus tissue from *Nicotiana rustica* a linear correlation between growth rate and sucrose concentration up to 0.1 mol l^{-1} (34 g l^{-1}) sucrose, which is the concentration required for optimal floral initiation in W-38 tobacco internode segments (Aghion-Prat, 1965).

Tissues receiving higher sucrose or glucose levels (from exogenous or endogenous sources) may be expected to develop increased invertase (Fawzi and El-Fouly, 1979; Morris, 1982), fructose 1,6-bisphosphate and glucose-6-phosphate which in turn should affect glycolytic and other metabolic systems, or systems controlling enzyme synthesis (Bodson and Outlaw, 1985). For example, Auderset *et al.* (1980) observed increased glucose-6-dehydrogenase activity per unit fresh weight in the shoot apical meristems of spinach within a few hours after the critical day-length was met. An integral part of the feed-forward concept for control of flower initiation is the assumption that sucrose and other sugars act as enzyme-inducing agents. Cumming

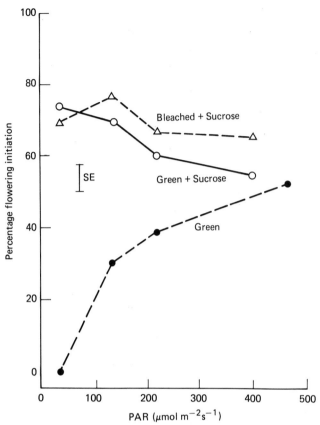

Figure 23.6 Flower initiation in the LDP, *Brassica campestris*, as a function of radiant energy and sucrose. Bleached plants were treated with Sandoz 6706, a herbicide that prevents chlorophyll accumulation, and grown on agar with 80 mmol l⁻¹ sucrose. Green plants were grown on vermiculite. (Reproduced from Friend *et al.* (1984) by kind permission of authors and publishers.)

(1967) found that glucose is more active than sucrose in promoting or inhibiting flowering in *Chenopodium* seedlings. Reproductive tissues of bougainvillea, cultured *in vitro*, require fructose or glucose, not sucrose, for floret initiation and maximum growth, whereas vegetative tissues grow as well with sucrose as with the monosaccharides (Steffen, 1986; *Figure 23.7*). Thus, one supposes that some part of the inductive signal for reproductive development in both *Chenopodium* and bougainvillea may involve activation of an invertase system (*see* Chapter 27 for an in-depth study of invertase in tomato).

Assimilate levels at the shoot apical meristem: their significance

Bodson (1977, 1984) and Bodson and Outlaw (1985) find elevated sucrose levels in the apical meristem and apical bud of *Sinapis alba*, following LD (or displaced SD) induction, before other biochemical or ultrastructural changes are noted. These are considered in the next chapter.

Low temperature, vernalizing treatments increase carbohydrate concentration in the shoot tip during or just before floral evocation (Sadik and Ozbun, 1986;

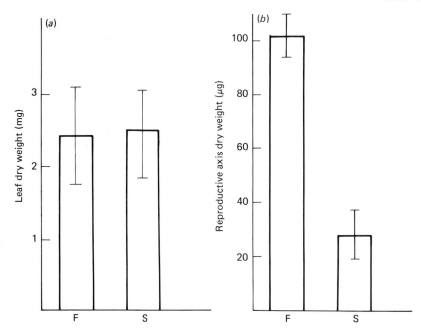

Figure 23.7 Dry weight after 2 weeks in culture on basic nutritive medium with either 3% fructose (F) or sucrose (S). (*a*) Young leaves, about 1 mm long. (*b*) Reproductive meristems, pre-floret stage. (Reproduced from Steppen (1986) by kind permission of author and publishers.)

Rodrigues-Pereira, 1962; and *see* Chapter 10). However, Fontes and Ozbun (1972) have shown in broccoli that when plants are grown continuously at high temperatures elevated sugar and starch levels are found in the shoot tip even though flowering is inhibited. As Mohapatra *et al.* (1982, 1983) observed in barley, carbohydrate levels in the developing inflorescence axis do not increase; rather they decrease, in LD conditions where assimilate demand by the inflorescence exceeds supply. Hence, high levels of assimilates (as distinct from turnover and supply) may reflect failure of the evocational processes or inflorescence development. It must be remembered, however, that the shoot tip comprises young leaves, leaf primordia and internodes besides the apical meristem and significant differences in assimilate distribution may occur between these during vernalization (*see* Chapter 10).

Sink activation, photoperiodic induction and growth substances

In bougainvillea, rapid increases in assimilate movement and accumulation in reproductive meristems are observed as a function of SD and cytokinin treatment, indicating increased sink strength of the tissues (T'se *et al.*, 1974; *Figure 23.8*). Dry weight gains of meristems (pre-bracteole stage) are detected within 24 h of the beginning of SD or high irradiance (Gallaher and Sachs, unpublished observations); hence, the specific activity (a measure of sink strength) of the reproductive tissues may not increase. Metabolic activity of shoot apical meristems increases rapidly following photoperiodic induction in many species (Bernier *et al.*, 1981; Bodson, 1984). Gressel *et al.* (1970) observed increased uridine incorporation into RNA within hours of the

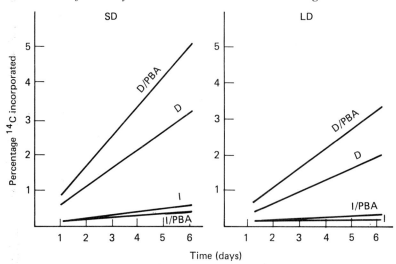

Figure 23.8 ^{14}C labelled assimilate accumulation in reproductive meristems of the SDP, *Bougainvillea* 'San Diego Red', as a function of day-length (SD, left; LD, right), young leaf removal (I = intact; D = defoliated), and cytokinin treatment (PBA). (Reproduced from T'se *et al.* (1974) by kind permission of authors and publishers.)

end of the critical night; Abou-Haidar *et al.* (1985) found that ^{14}C incorporation per unit weight increased more than two-fold for several hours following the end of induction and Thigpen and Sachs (1985) found a sharp, transient decrease in ATP concentration at approximately the same time. Together these observations suggest a rapid, if only transient, increase in sink strength and assimilate (and nucleotide) demand. Thus if source strength, say photosynthesis or stored reserves, is low for some period subsequent to induction or competing sink demand is relatively great, there is a potential for assimilate limitations for floral initiation and development (*see* review by Kinet and Sachs, 1984; and Chapter 26).

The metabolism, distribution and tissue sensitivity to cytokinins, gibberellins, auxins, and abscisins change as a function of photoperiodic induction (Nernier *et al.*, 1981). The difficulties in developing generally valid hypotheses for the role of gibberellins in reproductive development has been recognized (Pharis and King, 1985), and the same problem is encountered with other growth regulators. Studies with cytokinins are, however, probably more important for changes in source-sink relations, as noted above for tuberization and sink activation. Van Staden and Wareing (1972) and Henson and Wareing (1974, 1977) found rapid changes in cytokinin distribution and metabolism in *Xanthium* root and shoot systems during the first inductive dark period, and Kinet (cited in Bernier *et al.*, 1981) detected elevated levels of cytokinins in *Sinapis* leaves and roots shortly after the end of an inductive long day. There is, however, insufficient data to link such changes to altered assimilate or sucrose concentration in either species (Bodson, 1984). Studies by Abou-Haidar *et al.* (1985) show that plumular tissues from SD-induced *Pharbitis* become much more sensitive to an applied cytokinin and also accumulated labelled assimilates more rapidly than plumules from non-induced plants. Also, cytokinin applications promote floret/flower initiation in grapevine (Srinivasan and Mullins, 1978, 1979; *Figure 23.9*), bougainvillea (T'se *et al.*, 1974), and *Pharbitis* (Ogawa and King, 1980; Abou-Haidar *et al.*, 1985).

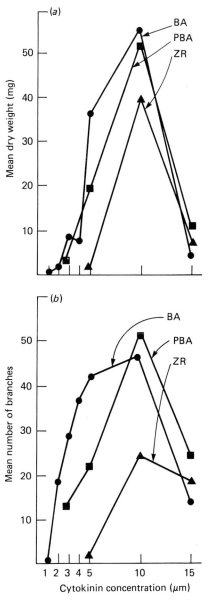

Figure 23.9 Branching of inflorescence axis of grapevine tendrils ('anlagen') cultured *in vitro* as a function of cytokinin treatment (BA, PBA, ZR). Florets are initiated at distal end of branches subsequent to cytokinin treatment. (Reproduced from Srinivasan and Mullins (1978) by kind permission of authors and publishers.)

Nitrogen supply and nutrient diversion

Klebs (1918), Kraus and Kraybill (1918), Allsopp (1965) and others found that low light combined with high nitrogen fertilization promoted vegetative growth. This suggested that the observed delay in the onset of reproductive development occurs because insufficient assimilates remain to support the reproductive transmission at the shoot apical meristem—clearly a reference to nutrient diversion (*see* discussion by Blake and Harris, 1960; and *see* Chapter 10). Unfortunately, much research has placed emphasis on Klebs' and Kraus and Kraybill's use of the C/N ratio which has proved to have little or no value in relation to flower initiation.

Research by Murneek (1948) with soybean, and by many others (Lang, 1965; Bernier *et al.*, 1981) revealed no change in node number before the first flower as a function of nitrogen nutrition. Furthermore, Murneek found no increase in C/N ratios in the critical period preceding flower initiation. In fact a significant decrease is reported, with an increase in C/N ratio only *following* the appearance of flower primordia. A common observation by this time was that improved N nutrition improved flower production, fruit set and growth in many species; indeed modern agricultural practice demands relatively high levels of N. Thus Murneek concluded that development affects nutrition, metabolism and metabolite distribution probably more than the other way round (Murneek, 1948; *see* also Hardwick, 1984 and Lenton, 1984), but he did not do the experiments required to resolve the controversy on nitrogen supply and flower initiation. The reasons seem clear; there was exaggerated emphasis on absolute values for the C/N ratio and little credence was given to concepts of nutrient diversion in plant development.

Nitrogen nutrition effects on flower initiation can be observed only *as a function of photosynthetic activity and assimilate supply*. Bunt's (1969) results with greenhouse-grown tomato show that the nitrate-induced delay in anthesis occurs only under the low-light conditions of winter. Friend *et al.* (1984) recently demonstrated the relationship between nitrate-induced inhibition of flowering and sucrose supply and day-length in *Brassica* (*Figure 23.10*); the results appear to be unequivocal in support of a nutrient diversion hypothesis. Allsopp (1965) emphasized that it is not the C/N ratio but the excess or deficiency of carbohydrate or nitrogen compounds, relative to some threshold level, that ultimately permits organ initiation and development. If photosynthesis is at a high rate, carbohydrates accumulate, even in the presence of excess nitrogen, and both tissue differentiation and growth may proceed more rapidly than under low nitrogen nutrition. This proposition fits the feed-forward hypothesis for morphogenesis. A prudent assessment is that nitrogen supply may have a regulatory role in plant development, and insofar as flower initiation is concerned, an indirect one that is dependent on carbohydrate supply (Trewavas, 1983; Naylor, 1984).

The determinate axis, plastochron stage, timing and assimilate supply: a model for floral initiation responsive to assimilate supply

THE DETERMINATE REPRODUCTIVE AXIS: INFLORESCENCES AND FLOWERS

If there is homology of floral structures across the angiosperms, then in some species with inflorescences the initial evocational event should be the formation of a

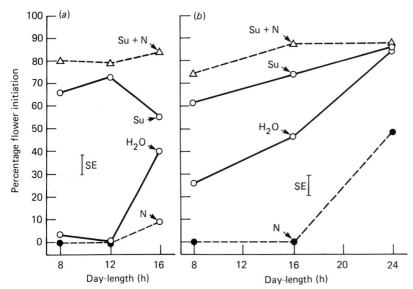

Figure 23.10 Flower initiation in green *Brassica campestris* as a function of day-length, sucrose (80 mmol l⁻¹) and nitrate (4 mmol l⁻¹). Data showing promotion by sucrose and inhibition by nitrate are from two separate experiments, *a* (8, 12, 16 h day-length) and *b* (8, 16, 24 h day-length). (Reproduced from Friend *et al.* (1984) by kind permission of authors and publishers.)

determinate shoot axis and not flower/floret initiation. Of inflorescences the morphogenesis concerned with initiation of reproductive axes, rather than initiation of florets, appears intermediate between vegetative and reproductive development. Unfortunately, there is little information on whether the physiological processes for evocation and transition from an indeterminate shoot axis directly to a single determinate flower differ from those required for evocation of an inflorescence axis with subsequent evocational steps for its florets. The steps preceding flower initiation in inflorescences, which require the formation of determinate shoots, are often experimentally separable from those required for floret initiation. This may be invaluable in defining the morphogenetic processes, and chemical or physical factors required for the formation of a determinate reproductive shoot and then the formation of florets.

Salisbury (1963) data for inflorescence initiation in *Xanthium* in winter and summer (*see Figure 23.2*) suggest that the first stages of receptable development are relatively independent of assimilate supply whereas later stages of floret initiation require a significantly greater supply. In grapevine and bougainvillea the reproductive meristem will develop a peduncle under all irradiance conditions supporting vegetative growth, but anlagen formation (grapevine) and bracteole and floret initiation require either irradiance levels more than 10-fold greater or treatments with growth substances.

PLASTOCHRON STAGE AND INDUCTION

In *Anagallis* and *Scrophularia*, transition to flowering is dependent on the stage of plastochron at the start of induction (Fontaine, 1972; Miginiac, 1972). In *Bidens radiata*, Pouhle *et al.* (1984) found that SD-induced flower initiation was optional in the first 48 h after germination and fell dramatically at the time of initiation of the second pair of leaves. Owens and Paolillo (1986a, b) observed similar age-related factors for SD-induction and initiation of flowers at terminal and axillary positions in *Pharbitis nil*. These studies suggest a correlation of the first stages of evocation with growth of the apical meristem and the developing phyllotactic pattern.

TIMING AND ASSIMILATE SUPPLY

Timing of assimilate arrival at the shoot apical meristem appears in some instances as important for floral initiation as concentration or supply. Promotion and inhibition of flower initiation are observed as a function of the timing of glucose feeding during an endogenous rhythm in *Chenopodium rubrum* (Cumming, 1967) or in *Sinapis alba* as a function of the timing of the high irradiance period or timing of sucrose feeding (Bodson *et al.*, 1979). CO_2 enrichment delays flower development in sorghum under inductive SD conditions, beginning at the earliest stages of floral initiation, although photosynthesis is increased (Marc and Gifford, 1984). Flowering in *Lemna* may be promoted by inhibiting photosynthesis or by sucrose feeding, but it is also inhibited when sucrose is added with other factors in the media (Posner, 1969), suggesting a much more complex control of the shoot apical meristem and transport processes (Sachs, 1979).

A MODEL FOR FLORAL INITIATION

There is no simple explanation for floret initiation requiring a greater assimilate supply than vegetative development. One proposal is that more assimilate is required for biosyntheses of new substances with morphogenetic information (i.e. gene derepressors) that are in turn required by shoot apical meristem tissues to cause the floral transition. Although plausible, this hypothesis is not currently favoured. An alternate proposition is that as assimilates promote growth of the dome and subtending primordia (Horridge and Cockshull, 1979; Cockshull and Horridge, 1980), entirely different physical conditions are created at presumptive sites for whorls of floret primordia or perianth parts. Lyndon (1977) and Lyndon and Francis (1984) concluded that the size of the dome need not change, but rather the critical factor for evocation in inflorescences may be the change in growth rate of the dome relative to that of the incipient floret primordia and reduced elongation of the shoot axis (*see* Chapter 22).

Models that account for the changed phyllotaxy and size relationships observed in the dome have been based on competition for assimilates between the dome and presumptive floret or perianth parts (Charles-Edwards *et al.*, 1979), new stable states for the dome and lateral primordia, and release of an inhibitor from all lateral primordia that is related to their size (Thornley and Cockshull, 1980; Lyndon and Battey, 1985). Hardwick (1984) proposed that the physical conditions required for initiation of the whorls of florets and perianth parts depend upon changes in growth pattern of the meristem and primordia at a certain plastochron stage, an idea derived from several studies of phyllotaxy (Lintilhac, 1984; Green, 1980) and flowering (Lyndon, 1977) and included in a modified form in the model presented by Thornley and Cockshull. Green (1985) has found cellulose reinforcement patterns at the dome of *Vinca* that predict sites of initiation of the first whorls of floral primordia. These reinforcement patterns on the dome surface are the result of a physical resolution of the stresses derived from young, growing leaf primordia. Further study of the appearance and orientation of microtubulin, the filamentous protein on which cellulose microfibrils appear to be oriented in the apical dome, as a function of induction and growth rates of young leaf primordia should provide a link between the biophysical and physiological systems involved in evocation.

The proposed model for floral initiation, dependent on plastochron stage and relative growth rate of recently initiated leaves, and hence on timing of events, may account for failures to correlate assimilate supply (or sucrose concentration) with evocation in intact plants or organs. Responses of subapical meristematic tissues (Owens and Paolillo, 1986a) as well as those of the leaf primordia assume a role as important as that of the apical meristem proper. The model also makes it easier to understand how more direct relationships are observed between sugar concentration and *de novo* flower initiation *in vitro* when there are no pre-existing leaf primordia or other meristematic tissues.

References

ABOU-HAIDAR, S.S., MIGINIAC, E. and SACHS, R.M. (1985). 14-C-Assimilate partitioning in photoperiodically induced seedlings of *Pharbitis nil*. The effects of benzyladenine. *Physiologia Plantarum*, **64**, 265–270

AGHION-PRAT, D. (1965). Neoformation de fleurs in vitro chez *Nicotiana tabacum* L. *Physiologie Vegetale*, **3**, 229–303

ALBERSHEIM, O. and DARVILL, A.G. (1985). The oligosaccharins. *Scientific American*, **253**, 58–64

ALLSOPP, A. (1965). The significance for development of water supply, osmotic relations and nutrition. In *Handbuch der Pflanzenphysiologie* (A. Lang, Ed.), Vol. 15/1, pp. 504–552

AUDERSET, G., GAHAN, P.B., DAWSON, A.L. and GREPPIN, H. (1980). Glucose-6-phosphate dehydrogenase as an early marker of floral induction in shoot apices of *Spinacia oleracea* var. Nobel. *Plant Science Letters*, **20**, 109–113

BERNIER, G., KINET, J.-M. and SACHS, R.M. (1981). *The Physiology of Flowering*, Vol. I. *The Initiation of Flowers*. Vol. II. *The Transition to Reproductive Growth*. Boca Raton, Fl., CRC Press

BIRAN, I., LESHEM, B., GUR, I. and HALEVY, A.H. (1974). Further studies on the relationship between growth regulators and tuberization of Dahlias. *Physiologia Plantarum*, **31**, 25–38

BISMUTH, F., BRULFERT, J. and MIGINIAC, E. (1979). Mise à fleurs de *l'Anagallis arvensis* L. en cours de rhizogenèse. *Physiologie Végétale*, **17**, 477–482

BLAKE, J. and HARRIS, G.P. (1960). Effects of nitrogen nutrition on flowering in carnation. *Annals of Botany*, **24**, 247–257

BODLAENDER, K.B.A. (1963). Influence of temperature, radiation, and photoperiod on development and yield. In *The Growth of the Potato* (J.D. Ivins and F.L. Milthorpe, Eds), pp. 199–210. London, Butterworths

BODSON, M. (1977). Changes in the carbohydrate content of the leaf and the apical bud of *Sinapis* during transition to flowering. *Planta*, **135**, 19–23

BODSON, M. (1984). Assimilates and evocation. In *Light and the Flowering Process* (D. Vince-Prue, B. Thomas, and K.E. Cockshull, Eds), pp. 157–169. London, Academic Press

BODSON, M. and BERNIER, G. (1985). Is flowering controlled by assimilate level? *Physiologie Végétale*, **23**, 491–501

BODSON, M. and OUTLAW, W.H. Jr. (1985). Elevation in the sucrose content of the shoot apical meristem of *Sinapis* at floral evocation. *Plant Physiology*, **79**, 420–424

BODSON, M., KING, R.W., EVANS, L.T. and BERNIER, G. (1977). The role of photosynthesis in flowering of the long day plant *Sinapis alba*. *Australian Journal of Plant Physiology*, **4**, 467–468

BORCHERT, R. (1983). Phenology and control of flowering in tropical trees. *Biotropica*, **15**, 81–89

BUNT, A.C. (1969). Peat-sand substrates for plants grown in containers I. The effect of base fertilizers. *Plant & Soil*, **31**, 97–110

BUNT, A.C. and POWELL, M.C. (1983). Quantitative response of the carnation to solar radiation, long days and supplemental light source. *Acta Horticulturae*, **141**, 1–6

CAIN, J. (1971). Effects of mechanical pruning of apple hedgerows with a slotting saw on light penetration and fruiting. *Journal of The American Society of Horticultural Science*, **96**, 664–667

CHAN, B.C. and CAIN, J.C. (1967). The effect of seed formation on subsequent flowering in apple. *Proceedings of The American Society of Horticultural Science*, **91**, 63–67

CHAILAKHYAN, M. Kh. (1982). Hormonal substances in flowering. In *Plant Growth Substances 1982* (P. F. Wareing, Ed.), pp. 645–655. London, Academic Press

CHAILAKHYAN, M. Kh. (1985). Hormonal regulation of reproductive development in higher plants. *Biologia Plantae*, **27**, 292–302

CHAN, B.C. and CAIN, J.C. (1967). The effect of seed formation on subsequent flowering in apple. *Proceedings of The American Society of Horticultural Science*, **91**, 63–67

CHARLES-EDWARDS, D.A., COCKSHULL, K.E., HORRIDGE, J.S. and THORNLEY, J.H.M. (1979). A model of flowering in chrysanthemum. *Annals of Botany*, **44**, 557–566

COCKSHULL, K.E. (1972). Photoperiodic control of flowering in the chrysanthemum. In *Crop Processes in Controlled Environments* (A.R. Rees, K.E. Cockshull, D.W. Hand and R.G. Hurd, Eds), pp. 235–259. London, Academic Press

COCKSHULL, K.E. (1979). Effects of irradiance and temperature on flowering of *Chrysanthemum morifolium* Ramat. in continuous light. *Annals of Botany*, **44**, 451–460

COCKSHULL, K.E. and HORRIDGE, J.S. (1980). Further evidence of a relationship between size of the Chrysanthemum shoot apex and inflorescence development. *Annals of Botany*, **46**, 125–127

CUMMING, B.G. (1967). Circadian rhythmic flowering responses in *Chenopodium rubrum*: effects of glucose and sucrose. *Canadian Journal of Botany*, **45**, 2173–2193

DELTOUR, R. (1967). Action du saccharose sur la croissance et la mise à fleurs de tissues d'apex de *Sinapis alba* L. cultives *in vitro*. *Comptes Rendues Acad. Sci., Paris*, **265**, 2765–2767

DE ZEEUW, D. (1956). Leaf-induced inhibition of flowering in tomato. *Proc. Konink. Akad. Wetensch. Amsterdam*, **59**, 535–540

DEITZER, G.F. (1984). Photoperiodic induction in long-day plants. In *Light and the Flowering Process* (D. Vince-Prue, B. Thomas and K.E. Cockshull, Eds), pp. 51–63. London, Academic Press

EVANS, L.T. (1976). Inhibition of flowering in *Lolium temulentum* by the photosynthetic inhibitor, 3(3,4-dichlorophenyl)-1,1-dimethyl urea (DCMU) in relation to assimilate supply to the shoot apex. *Etudes de Biologie Végétale*. Homage au Professeur Pierre Chouard (R. Jacques, Ed.). Gif-sur-Yvette, Paris, CNRS

FAWZI, A.F.A. and EL-FOULY, M.M. (1979). Amylase and invertase activities and carbohydrate contents in relation to physiological sink in carnation. *Physiologia Plantarum*, **47**, 245–249

FONTAINE, D. (1972). Incidence du stade de développement de point végétatif de l'*Anagallis arvensis* L. au cours du plastochrone, sur la mise à fleurs de plantes soumises à des conditions limitantes d'induction. *Comptes Rendues Acad. Sci. Paris*, **274**, 2984–2987

FONTES, M.R. and OZBUN, J.L. (1972). Relationship between carbohydrate level and floral initiation in broccoli. *Journal of The American Society of Horticultural Science*, **97**, 346–348

FRIEND, D.J.C. (1965). Ear length and spikelet number of wheat grown at different temperatures and light intensities. *Canadian Journal of Botany*, **43**, 345–353

FRIEND, D.J.C. (1984). The interaction of photosynthesis and photoperiodism in induction. In *Light and the Flowering Process* (D. Vince-Pru, B. Thomas and K.E. Cockshull, Eds), pp. 257–275. London, Academic Press

FRIEND, D.J.C., DEPUTY, J. and QUEDADO, R. (1979). Photosynthetic and photomorphogenetic effects of high photon flux densities on the flowering of two long day plants, *Anagallis arvensis* and *Brassica campestris*. In *Photosynthesis and Plant Development* (R. Marcelle, H. Clijsters and M. VanPoucke, Eds), pp. 55–73. The Hague, W. Junk

FRIEND, D.J.C., BODSON, M. and BERNIER, G. (1984). Promotion of flowering in *Brassica campestris* L. cv Ceres by sucrose. *Plant Physiology*, **75**, 1085–1089

FULFORD, R.M. (1966). The morphogenesis of apple buds. III. The inception of flowers. *Annals of Botany*, **30**, 207–219

GOH, C.J. and SEETOH, H.C. (1973). Apical control of flowering in an orchid hybrid, *Aranda* Deborah. *Annals of Botany*, **37**, 113–119

GOLDSCHMIDT, E.E., ASCHKENAZI, N., HERZANO, Y., SCHAFFER, A.A. and MONSELISE, S.P. (1985). A role for carbohydrate levels in the control of flowering in Citrus. *Scientia Horticulturae*, **26**, 159–166

GRAINGER, J. (1938). Studies upon the time of flowering of plants. I. The relation of nocturnal translocation to the time of flowering. *Annals of Applied Biology*, **25**, 1–19

GRAINGER, J. (1964). A possible mechanism for the action of floral stimuli in plants. *Horticultural Research*, **4**, 104–125

GREEN, P.B. (1980). Organogenesis—a biophysical view. *Annual Review of Plant Physiology*, **31**, 51–82

GREEN, P.B. (1985). Surface of the shoot apex: a reinforcement-field theory for phyllotaxis. *Journal of Cell Science*, Suppl. **2**, 181–201

GRESSEL, J., ZILBERSTEIN, A. and ARZEE, T. (1970). Bursts of incorporation into RNA and ribonuclease activities associated with induction and morphogenesis in *Pharbitis*. *Developmental Biology*, **22**, 31–42

GROCHOWSKA, M.J. (1973). Comparative studies on physiological and morphological features of bearing and non-bearing spurs of the apple tree. I. Changes in starch content during growth. *Journal of Horticultural Science*, **48**, 347–356

HAMMES, P.S. and NEL, P.C. (1975). Control mechanisms in the tuberization process. *Potato Research*, **18**, 262–272

HARDWICK, R.C. (1984). Sink development, phyllotaxy, and dry matter distribution in a large inflorescence. *Plant Growth Regulation*, **2**, 393–405

HENSON, I.E. and WAREING, P.F. (1974). Cytokinins in Xanthium strumarium: a rapid response to short day treatment. *Physiologia Plantarum*, **32**, 185–188

HENSON, I.E. and WAREING, P.F. (1977). Cytokinins in *Xanthium strumarium* L.: Some aspects of the photoperiodic control of endogenous levels. *New Phytology*, **78**, 34–45

HORRIDGE, J.S. and COCKSHULL, K.E. (1979). Size of the chrysanthemum shoot apex in relation to inflorescence initiation and development. *Annals of Botany*, **44**, 547–556

HUNT, W.F. and LOOMIS, R.S. (1976). Carbohydrate-limited growth kinetics of tobacco (*Nicotiana rustica* L.) callus. *Plant Physiology*, **57**, 802–805

IRELAND, C.R. and SCHWABE, W.W. (1982a, b). Studies on the role of photosynthesis in the photoperiodic induction of flowering in the short-day plants *Kalanchoe blossfeldiana* Poellniz and *Xanthium pensylvanicum* Wallr. I. The requirement for CO_2 during photoperiodic induction. II. The effect of chemical inhibitors of photosynthesis. *Journal of Experimental Botany*, **33**, 738–747, 748–760

JACKSON, D.I. and SWEET, G.B. (1972). Flower initiation in temperate woody plants. *Horticultural Abstracts*, **42**, 9–24

JOSEFUSOVA, Z., OPATRNA, J. and PAVLOVA, L. (1985). Root–shoot correlations linked with photoperiodic floral induction in *Chenopodium rubrum* L. *Biologia Plantae*, **27**, 386–391

KAMATE, K., COUSSON, A., TRINH, T.H. and TRAN THANH VAN, K. (1981). Influence des facteurs génétiques et physiologiques chez le *Nicotiana* sur la néoformation *in vitro* de fleurs à partir d'assises cellulaires épidermiques et sous-épidermiques. *Canadian Journal of Botany*, **59**, 775–781

KANNANGARA, T. and BOOTH, A. (1978). The role of cytokinins in tuber development in *Dahlia variabilis*. *Zeitschrift für Pflanzenphysiologie*, **88**, 333–339

KINET, J.-M. and SACHS, R.M. (1984). Light and flower development. In *Light and the Flowering Process* (D. Vince-Prue, B. Thomas and K. E. Cockshull, Eds), Chapter 15, pp. 211–225. London, Academic Press

KINET, J.-M., SACHS, R.M. and BERNIER, G. (1985). *The Physiology of Flowering*. Vol. III. *The Development of Flowers*. Boca Raton, Fl., CRC Press

KLEBS, G. (1910). Alterations in the development and forms of plants as a result of environment. *Proceedings of the Royal Society Series B*, **82**, 547–558

KLEBS, G. (1918). Über die Blutenbildung von Sempervivum. *Flora*, **111**, 128–151

KNIGHT, T.A. (1820). Physiological observations upon the effect of partial decortication, or ringing, the stems or branches of fruit trees. *Transactions of the Horticultural Society*, **4**, 159–162

KRAUS, E.J. and KRAYBILL, H.R. (1918). Vegetation and reproduction with special reference to the tomato. *Oregon Agricultural Experimental Station Bulletin*, No. 149

KREKULE, J. (1979). Stimulation and inhibition of flowering. In *La Physiologie de la Floraison* (P. Champagnat and R. Jacques, Eds), pp. 20–57. Colloques Internationales CNRS, Paris, CNRS

LANG, A. (1965). Physiology of flower initiation. In *Handbuch der Pflanzenphysiologie*, (A. Lang, Ed.), Vol. 19/1, pp. 1381–1536. Berlin, Springer-Verlag

LENTON, J. (1984). Are plant growth substances involved in the partitioning of assimilate to developing reproductive sinks? *Plant Growth Regulation*, **2**, 267–276

LINTILHAC, P.M. (1984). Positional controls in meristem development: a caveat and an alternative. In *Positional Controls in Plant Development* (P.W. Barlow and D.J. Carr, Eds), pp. 83–105. Cambridge University Press

LONA, F. (1949). La fioritura delle brevidiurne a notte continua. *Nuovo Giorunale Botanico Italiano N.S.*, **56**, 479–515

LYNDON, R.F. (1977). Interacting processes in vegetative development in the transition to flowering at the shoot apex. In *Integration of Activity in the Higher Plant. Society for Experimental Biology, Symposium*, **31**, pp. 221–250

LYNDON, R.F. and BATTEY, N.H. (1985). The growth of the shoot apical meristem during flower initiation. *Biologia Plantae*, **27**, 339–349

LYNDON, R.F. and FRANCIS, D. (1984). The response of the shoot apex to light-generated signals from the leaves. In *Light and the Flowering Process* (D. Vince-Prue, B. Thomas and K.E. Cockshull, Eds), pp. 171–189. London, Academic Press

McDANIEL, C.N. (1984). Competence, determination, and induction in plant development. In *Pattern Formation. A Primer for Developmental Biology*. (G.M. Malacinski and S.V. Bryant, Eds), pp. 393–412. New York, Macmillan

McDANIEL, C.N., SINGER, S.R., DENNIN, K.A. and GEBHARDT, J.S. (1985). Floral determination, stability, timing, and vast influence. In *Plant Genetics* (M. Freeling, Ed.), pp. 73–87. New York, Alan R. Liss

MARC, J. and GIFFORD, R.M. (1984). Floral initiation in wheat, sunflower, and sorghum under carbon dioxide enrichment. *Canadian Journal of Botany*, **62**, 9–14

MARRE, E. (1982). Hormonal regulation of transport: data and perspectives. In *Plant Growth Substances 1982* (P.F. Wareing, Ed.), pp. 407–417. London, Academic Press

MIGINIAC, E. (1972). Cinétique d'action comparée des racines et de la kinétine sur le développement floral de bourgeons cotylédonaires chez le *Scrofularia arguta* Sol. *Physiologie Végétale*, **10**, 627–636

MIGINIAC, E. and SOTTA, B. (1985). Organ correlations affecting flowering in relation to phytohormones. *Biologia Plantae*, **27**, 373–381

MOHAPATRA, P.K., ASPINALL, D. and JENNER, C.F. (1982). The growth and development of the wheat apex. The effects of photoperiod on spikelet production and sucrose concentration in the apex. *Annals of Botany*, **49**, 619–626

MOHAPATRA, P.K., ASPINALL, D. and JENNER, C.F. (1983). Differential effects of temperature on floral development and sucrose content of the shoot apex of wheat. *Australian Journal of Plant Physiology*, **10**, 1–7

MONSELISE, S.P. and GOLDSCHMIDT, E.E. (1982). Alternate bearing in fruit trees. *Horticultural Reviews*, **4**, 128–173

MOORBY, J. (1978). The physiology of growth and tuber yield. In *The Potato Crop* (P.M. Harris, Ed.), pp. 153–194. London, Chapman and Hall

MORRIS, D.A. (1982). Hormonal regulation of sink invertase activity: implications for the control of assimilate partitioning. In *Plant Growth Substances 1982* (P.F. Wareing, Ed.), pp. 659–668. London, Academic Press

MURNEEK, A.E. (1948). Nutrition and metabolism as related to photoperiodism. In *Vernalization and Photoperiodism* (R.O. Whyte and A.E. Murneek, Eds), pp. 83–90. Waltham, Ma., Chronica Botanica

NAYLOR, A.W. (1941). Effects of some environmental factors on photoperiodic induction of beet and dill. *Botanical Gazette*, **102**, 557–575

NAYLOR, A.W. (1984). Functions of hormones at the organ level of organization. In *Hormonal Regulation of Development. II. Encyclopedia of Plant Physiology N.S.10* (T.K. Scott, Ed.), pp. 172–218. Berlin, Springer-Verlag

NG, E. and LOOMIS, R.S. (1984). *Simulation of Growth and Yield of the Potato Crop*. Wageningen, Holland, Pudoc

NITSCH, J.P. (1965). Existence d'un stimulus photopériodique non spécifique capable de provoquer la tuberisation chez *Helianthus tuberosus* L. *Bulletin Société Botanique Française*, **112**, 333–340

NITSCH, J.P. and NITSCH, C. (1967a). The induction of flowering in vitro in stem segments of *Plumbago indica* L. II. The production of reproductive buds. *Planta*, **72**, 371–384

NITSCH, J.P. and NITSCH, C. (1967b). Néoformation de fleurs in vitro chez une espèce de jours courts: *Plumbago indica* L. *Annales Physiologie Végétale*, **7**, 251–256

OGAWA, Y. and KING, R.W. (1980). Flowering in seedlings of Pharbitis nil induced by benzyladenine applied under a non-inductive daylength. *Plant and Cell Physiology*, **21**, 1109–1116.

OWENS, V. and PAOLILLO, D.J. Jr. (1986a). The effect of ageing on flowering of the axillary buds of *Pharbitis nil* Chois. *American Journal of Botany*, **73**, 882–887

OWENS, V. and PAOLILLO, D.J. Jr. (1986b). The effect of ageing on growth and flowering of the terminal bud of *Pharbitis nil* Chois. *American Journal of Botany*, **73**, 888–893

PALMER, C.F. and SMITH, E.E. (1970). Cytokinin-induced tuber formation on stolons of *Solanum tuberosum* L. *Physiologia Plantarum*, **23**, 599–606

PAULET, P. and NITSCH, J.P. (1964). Neoformation de fleurs *in vitro* sur des cultures de tissus de racines de *Cichorium intybus* L. *Comptes Rendues Académie Scientifique, Paris*, **258**, 5952–5955

PHARIS, R.P. (1972). Flowering of chrysanthemum under non-inductive long days by gibberellins and N,6-benzyladenine. *Planta*, **105**, 205–212

PHARIS, R.P. and KING, R.W. (1985). Gibberellins and reproductive development in seed plants. *Annual Review of Plant Physiology*, **36**, 517–568

POSNER, H.B. (1969). Inhibitory effect of carbohydrate on flowering in *Lemna perpusilla*. I. Interaction of sucrose with calcium and phosphate ions. *Plant Physiology*, **44**, 562–566

POULHE, R., ARNAUD, Y. and MIGINIAC, E. (1984). Ageing and flowering of the apex in young *Bidens radiata*. *Physiologia Plantarum*, **62**, 225–230

PRAT, N. (1976). L'organongenèse florale *in vitro*. In *Etude de Biologie Végétale— Hommage au Professeur Pierre Chouard* (R. Jaques, Ed.), pp. 231–241. Gif-sur-Yvette, Paris, CNRS

QUEDADO, R. and FRIEND, D.J. (1978). Participation of photosynthesis in floral induction of the long day plant *Anagallis arvensis*. *Plant Physiology*, **62**, 802–806

RAMINA, A., HACKETT, W.P. and SACHS, R.M. (1979). Flowering in *Bougainvillea*: a function of assimilate supply and nutrient diversion. *Plant Physiology*, **64**, 810–813

RODRIGUES-PERIERA, A.S. (1962). Physiological experiments in connection with flower formation in Wedgewood iris (*Iris* cv 'Wedgewood'). *Acta Botanica Neerlandica*, **11**, 97–138

ROMBERGER, J.A. and GREGORY, R.A. (1974). Analytical morphogenesis and the physiology of flowering in trees. In *Proceedings of the North American Forest Biology Workshop*, 3rd Edn. (C.P.P. Reid and G.H. Fechner, Eds), pp. 132–147. Colorado State University

ROSS, S.D., BOLLMAN, M.P., PHARIS, R. and SWEET, G.B. (1984). Gibberell in $A_{4,7}$ and the promotion of flowering in *Pinus radiata*: Effects on partitioning of photoassimilate within the bud during primordia initiation. *Plant Physiology*, **76**, 326–330

ROSS, S.D. and PHARIS, R.P. (1985). Promotion of flowering in tree crops: different mechanisms and techniques with special reference to conifers. In *Trees as Crop Plants* (M.G.R. Cannell and J.E. Jackson, Eds), pp. 383–397. Institute of Terrestrial Ecology, Huntingdon, England

SACHS, R.M. (1979). Metabolism and energetics in flowering. In *La Physiologie de la Floraison* (P. Champagnat and R. Jacques, Eds), pp. 169–208. Colloques Internationales CNRS No. 285. Paris, CNRS

SACHS, R.M. and HACKETT, W.P. (1983). Source–sink relationships and flowering. *Strategies of Plant Reproduction. BARC Symposium No. 6* (W.J. Meudt, Ed.), pp. 263–272. Totowa, NJ, Allenheld

SADIK, S. and OZBUN, J.L. (1968). The association of carbohydrate changes in the shoot tip of cauliflower with flowering. *Plant Physiology*, **43**, 1696–1698

SALISBURY, F.B. (1963). Biological timing and hormone synthesis in flowering of Xanthium. *Planta*, **59**, 518–534

SATTELMACHEꞦ, B. and MARSCHNER, H. (1978a). Relation between nitrogen nutrition, cytokinin activity and tuberization in *Solanum tuberosum*. *Physiologia Plantarum*, **44**, 65–68

SATTELMACHER, B. and MARSCHNER, H. (1978b). Cytokinin activity in stolons and tubers of *Solanum tuberosum* during the period of tuberization. *Physiologia Plantarum*, **44**, 69–72

SAX, K. (1954). The control of tree growth by phloem blocks. *Journal Arnold Arboretum*, **35**, 251–258

SHINOZAKI, M. (1972). Floral initiation of *Pharbitis nil*, a short-day plant, under continuous high-intensity light. *Plant and Cell Physiology*, **13**, 391–393

SHINOZAKI M. and TAKIMOTO, A. (1983). Effects of some growth regulators and benzoic acid derivatives on flower initiation and root elongation of *Pharbitis nil*, Strain Kidachi. *Plant and Cell Physiology*, **24**, 433–439

SRINIVASAN, C. and MULLINS, M. (1978). Control of flowering in the grapevine (*Vitis vinifera* L.). *Plant Physiology*, **61**, 127–130

SRINIVASAN, C. and MULLINS, M.G. (1979). Flowering in *Vitis*. Conversion of tendrils into inflorescences and bunches of grapes. *Planta*, **145**, 187–192

STEFFEN, J. (1986). *C-sources Required for Reproductive Development, In Vitro, of bougainvillea Meristems*. PhD Dissertation, University of California

STUTTE, G. and MARTIN, G. (1986). Effect of light intensity and carbohydrate reserves on flowering in olive. *Journal of The American Society of Horticultural Science*, **111**, 27–31

SUGINO, M. (1957). Flower initiation of spring wheat in total darkness. *Botanical Magazine of Tokyo*, **70**, 369–375

THIGPEN, S.P. and SACHS, R.M. (1985). Changes in ATP in relation to floral induction and initiation in *Pharbitis nil*. *Physiologia Plantarum*, **65**, 156–162

THORNLEY, J.H.M. and COCKSHULL, K.E. (1980). A catastrophe model for the switch from vegetative to reproductive growth in the shoot apex. *Annals of Botany*, **46**, 333–341

TIZIO, R. and BIRAN, M.M. (1973). Are cytokinins the specific factors for tuber formation in the potato plant? *Phyton*, **31**, 3–13

TRAN THANH VAN, K., TOUBART, P., COUSSON, A., DARVILL, A.G., CHELF, P. and ALBERSHEIM, P. (1985). Manipulation of the morphogenetic pathways of tobacco explants by oligosaccharins. *Nature (London)*, **314**, 615–617

TREWAVAS, A.J. (1983). Nitrate as a plant hormone. In *Interactions Between Nitrogen and Growth Regulators in the Control of Plant Development*, pp. 97–109. British Plant Growth Regulator Group, Monograph 9

T'SE, A., RAMINA, A., HACKETT, W.P. and SACHS, R.M. (1974). Enhanced inflorescence development in Bougainvillea 'San Diego Red' by removal of young leaves and cytokinin treatments. *Plant Physiology*, **54**, 404–407

VAN STADEN, J. and WAREING, P.F. (1972). The effect of photoperiod on levels of endogenous cytokinins in *Xanthium strumarium*. *Physiologia Plantarum*, **27**, 331–337

VAN STADEN, J. and RINALLA, G.G. (1977). The distribution of cytokinins in tuberizing potatoes. *Annals of Botany*, **41**, 741–746

WARDELL, W.L. (1976). Floral activity in solutions of deoxyribonucleic acid extracted from tobacco stems. *Plant Physiology, 57*, 855–861

WAREING, P.F. and PHILLIPS, I.D.J. (1978). *The Control of Growth and Differentiation in Plants*, 2nd edn. Oxford, Pergamon Press

ZEEVAART, J.A.D. (1975). Studies on flowering in *Perilla. Annual Report MSU/DOE Plant Research Laboratory 1974*, Pp. 47. Published by MSU/DOE laboratory at Michigan State University

24

DISTRIBUTION OF ASSIMILATES FROM VARIOUS SOURCE-LEAVES DURING THE FLORAL TRANSITION OF *SINAPIS ALBA* L.

M. BODSON and B. REMACLE
Centre de Physiologie Végétale Appliquée (IRSIA), Department of Botany, University of Liège, Belgium

Introduction

During flower induction in the LDP *Sinapis alba*, an early increase in the soluble carbohydrate concentration of the apical bud has been observed regardless of the inductive treatment. A single LD, a single SD displaced by 10 h in the 24 h cycle or a single LD with CO_2 removed from the air during the day extension lighting period all produced this effect (Bodson, 1977; 1984). The increase was not therefore related to an extension of the photosynthetic assimilation period or to an increase of the photosynthetic assimilation rate in response to an inductive treatment (Bodson, unpublished observations). There is also no evidence for the apical bud attracting more assimilates exported out of a single young adult leaf during induction (Bodson *et al.*, 1977). In *Trifolium pratense*, however, an alteration of the pattern of assimilate transport to the apex from leaves of different ages has been shown to occur as a result of floral induction (Jones and Stoddart, 1973). In our growth conditions, *Sinapis* is a monopodial plant that bears about 10 non-senescent leaves at the time of induction. The distribution of assimilates has only been studied previously using a single young adult leaf as source (Bodson *et al.*, 1977). In this chapter, assimilate distribution and assimilate supply to the bud from leaves of other developmental ages during the floral transition of *Sinapis* is considered.

The export rate and the distribution of recently synthesized ^{14}C-assimilates from three leaves selected as representative of the leaf complement at the time of induction is examined. The chosen leaves were: a leaf recently emerged from the bud (LPI (leaf plastochron index) 3), a young expanded leaf (LPI 5) and an adult leaf (LPI 8).

Two questions have been considered for each source-leaf: firstly, what is the export rate and distribution of assimilates during the light period of the SD; and secondly, is there any change in export and distribution of assimilates during the floral transition induced by one LD? Three times during floral transition have been considered:

1. The period of day extension lighting, i.e. the time when the early increase of the soluble carbohydrate concentration in the bud is observed.
2. The middle of the first SD after the inductive LD.
3. The middle of the third SD after the inductive LD.

The last two times correspond respectively to the evocation of the meristem (Bernier, Kinet and Bronchart, 1967; Bernier, Kinet and Sachs, 1981) and to the initiation of the first flower primordia (Bernier, Kinet and Bronchart, 1967; Bodson, 1985).

Experimental

GROWTH CONDITIONS

Plants were grown from seeds in perlite at 20°C in S(8h)D; light from 08.30 h to 16.30 h, relative humidity 80%, illumination by light from fluorescent tubes (Phytor CRHL g tubes, ACEC, Charleroi, Belgium) providing 155 μmol m^{-2} s^{-1} PAR measured with a quantum meter (LI-140, from Lambda Instruments, Lincoln, Nebraska) at the top of the canopy. Plants were watered daily with demineralized water and once a week with complete nutrient solution. Plants kept in these conditions remained vegetative. When 49 days old, plants were induced to flower by a single L(22h)D. The environmental conditions during the LD were the same as those described above for the plants kept in SD.

^{14}C LABELLING OF ASSIMILATE

The source-leaves were selected in vegetative and induced plants depending on their position relative to LPI 1: the first leaf emerging from the bud longer than 1 cm. LPI 3, 5 and 8 were non-senescent leaves of increasing age. Their respective areas were 30, 75 and 100% of the maximal leaf area. Leaves were exposed to ^{14}CO$_2$ generated by adding 50% (v/v) lactic acid on NaH^{14}CO$_3$ (S.A. 2.15 GBq mmol^{-1}, Radiochemical Centre, Amersham). The initial CO$_2$ concentration in the feeding system was 970 ppm resulting from a mixture of NaH^{14}CO$_3$:NaHCO$_3$ (at a concentration of 5 g/100 ml) 3:2. Thirty minutes prior to feeding with ^{14}CO$_2$, and during feeding, plants were exposed to light at a photon flux density of 250 μmol m^{-2} s^{-1}. At the end of the exposure excess ^{14}CO$_2$ was removed with a soda lime column and the photon flux density was reset at 155 μmol m^{-2} s^{-1}.

^{14}C-assimilates were produced by enclosing the leaf lamina in an assimilation chamber and feeding ^{14}CO$_2$ for 10 min. Plants were harvested individually 3 h after the end of the feeding period and dissected into component parts. These were dried at 80°C and weighed. ^{14}C-activity was determined after complete combustion in an automatic sample oxidizer (Oxymat IN4101, Intertechnique, Plaisir, France). Samples larger than 100 mg dry weight were previously ground in a Wiley mill to pass a 40-mesh sieve and ^{14}C-activity was determined in an aliquot (40–60 mg) of the ground sample. ^{14}C-activity in the various plant parts was expressed as a percentage of the total ^{14}C-activity in the plant. The export rate was the ^{14}C-assimilates that moved out of the source-leaf 3 h after the exposure of that leaf to ^{14}CO$_2$, expressed as a percentage of the total ^{14}C-activity of the plant. Each treatment comprised six plants and was repeated twice. The values shown in graphs and tables are the means from both experiments.

^{14}C-assimilate supply to the bud was examined after feeding leaves with ^{14}CO$_2$ for 20 min. As specific activity is strongly dependent on rate of ^{14}C assimilation, leaves at the same developmental stage were fed simultaneously in all treatments. At various times up to 4 hours after leaf feeding, the terminal 3 cm of the shoots from four plants were harvested, fixed in liquid nitrogen and freeze dried. The apical bud was then dissected out under a stereoscopic microscope. Each bud consisted of leaf primordia 1 mm long or less and 0.1–0.2 mm of stem tissue. They were weighed with a Cahn G$_2$ electrobalance (Ventron Instruments, California, USA) and digested for 1 h in 0.5 ml of Lumasolve (Lumac/3M, Schaesberg, The Netherlands) in a water bath set at 50°C.

The ^{14}C-activity of the various samples was determined in a Packard liquid scintillation spectrometer. The experiment was repeated twice and the values reported are the means from both experiments.

Assimilate export before and during induction

When leaves of vegetative plants were labelled at three different times during the 8-h light period—09.30, 12.30 and 16.30 h—the export of ^{14}C-assimilates from different age leaves fluctuated throughout the light period (*Figure 24.1(a)*). The maximal value was observed in the middle of the day, the minimum by the end of the day. Although the pattern was similar for LPI 3, 5 and 8, the export rates were always lower for the younger leaf. Plants induced to flower were labelled 14, 28 and 76 h after the start of the LD. At 14 h the export rates were similar to those observed at the beginning of the day for non-induced plants (*Figure 24.1(b)*). Export rates remained the same at 28 h and decreased at 76 h. Comparison of these values with those recorded for vegetative plants labelled in the middle of the day, shows that, whatever the leaf age, export of ^{14}C-assimilates out of the induced leaf decreased progressively after 28 h from the start of the LD.

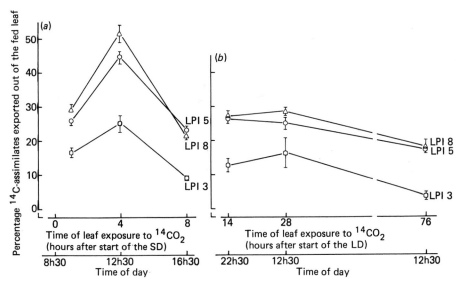

Figure 24.1 Percentage of ^{14}C-assimilates exported out of the fed leaf 3 h after the leaf exposure to ^{14}CO$_2$. (Vertical bars represent SE.)
(*a*) Vegetative plants. Leaves were fed with ^{14}CO$_2$ at different times during the 8 h light period (short day, SD).
(*b*) Plants induced to flower by a 22 h LD. Leaves were fed with ^{14}CO$_2$ at different times after the start of the long day regimen.

Table 24.1 DISTRIBUTION OF ^{14}C-LABELLED ASSIMILATES BETWEEN THE DIFFERENT PARTS OF VEGETATIVE PLANTS 3 h AFTER FEEDING THE LEAF WITH ^{14}CO$_2$ (MEANS ± SE)

Exporting leaf	Time of Leaf exposure to ^{14}CO$_2$ (h after start of SD)	Percentage of ^{14}C-assimilates in:						
		Fed leaf	Leaves above fed leaf	Stem above fed leaf	Leaves below fed leaf	Stem below fed leaf	Roots	Apical bud
LPI 3	1	83.2±1.7	1.0±0.3	0.3±0.09	0.4±0.1	13.9±1.3	1.0±0.3	0.06±0.01
	4	75.0±2.4	2.5±0.6	0.5±0.1	0.5±0.08	16.0±1.9	5.4±0.4	0.1 ±0.02
	8	91.2±0.8	0.5±0.1	0.2±0.09	0.2±0.02	8.1±1.0	0.1±0.02	0.04±0.9
LPI 5	1	70.9±1.9	3.0±0.4	3.5±0.4	0.3±0.04	17.6±1.3	4.4±0.7	0.2 ±0.04
	4	58.3±2.5	3.9±0.4	3.0±0.4	0.2±0.03	27.0±2.0	7.3±1.2	0.1 ±0.02
	8	78.6±1.1	3.1±0.4	1.3±0.2	0.2±0.03	13.4±4.1	3.3±0.4	0.2 ±0.03
LPI 8	1	73.9±1.8	1.4±0.2	2.9±0.4	0.2±0.02	13.7±1.1	3.6±1.7	0.1 ±0.03
	4	65.1±1.0	2.8±0.5	5.3±0.6	0.2±0.03	15.8±1.2	10.1±0.7	0.08±0.01
	8	77.1±2.4	1.8±0.6	1.7±0.4	0.2±0.07	11.6±4.3	5.6±0.9	0.06±0.01

Assimilate distribution

Distribution of the assimilates between the plant parts is shown in *Table 24.1* and *Figure 24.2(a)*. At any time in the SD, the largest part of the assimilates exported from LPI 8 moved down to the stem and the root system. Whilst this was also true for the assimilates exported from LPI 5, this leaf also provided a larger amount of ^{14}C-assimilates to younger leaves than LPI 8. Of the assimilates exported from LPI 3, the largest part moved in the stem below the fed leaf. The stimulation in export observed for LPI 3, 5 and 8 in the middle of the day resulted in more ^{14}C-assimilates moving to the stem and the roots. At any time of the day, the apical bud was mainly supplied with assimilates exported from LPI 5.

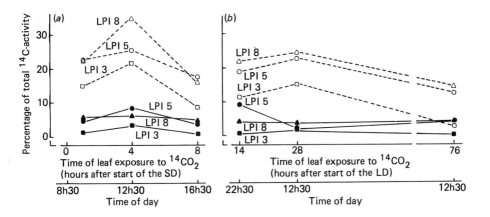

Figure 24.2   Percentage of ^{14}C-assimilates transported above (————)
(stem + leaves + apical bud) and below (– – – –) (stem + leaves + roots) the fed leaves.
(Data computed from *Tables 24.1* and *24.2*.)
(*a*) Vegetative plants. Leaves were fed with ^{14}CO$_2$ at different times during the 8-h light period (short day, SD).
(*b*) Plants induced to flower by one 22-h long day (LD). Leaves were fed with ^{14}CO$_2$ at different times after the start of the LD.

When the plants were induced to flower, there was little change in the pattern of assimilate distribution (*Table 24.2* and *Figure 24.2(b)*). Of the assimilates exported from LPI 3, 5 and 8, the larger part still migrated down to the stem below the fed leaf and the root system. Fourteen hours after the start of the LD, there was, however, a temporary increase in the percentage of ^{14}C-assimilates migrating from LPI 8 into the younger leaves and the upper part of the stem (*Figure 24.2(b)*). The decrease in export observed 28 and 76 h after the start of the LD, for leaves at the three developmental ages, was reflected mainly in a decrease of the percentage of ^{14}C-activity in the roots and the lower part of the stem. Fourteen and 28 h after the start of the LD, the apical bud was supplied principally by LPI 5, whilst at 76 h, LPI 8 provided more to the apical bud than at earlier times in floral transition.

Because of the small size of the bud, its sink strength appears low and results based on percentages of total ^{14}C-activity accumulating there do not allow changes in import of ^{14}C-assimilates there to be detected. Arrival of ^{14}C-assimilates in the bud has

Table 24.2 DISTRIBUTION OF ^{14}C-LABELLED ASSIMILATES BETWEEN THE DIFFERENT PARTS OF PLANTS INDUCED TO FLOWER BY A 22 h LD. PLANTS WERE HARVESTED 3 h AFTER FEEDING THE LEAF WITH $^{14}CO_2$ (MEANS ± SE)

Exporting leaf	Time of Leaf exposure to $^{14}CO_2$ (h after start of LD)	Percentage of ^{14}C-assimilates in:						
		Fed leaf	Leaves above fed leaf	Stem above fed leaf	Leaves below fed leaf	Stem below fed leaf	Roots	Apical bud
LPI 3	14	87.2±1.8	0.6±0.1	0.2 ±0.04	0.4±0.03	9.7±1.1	1.4±0.2	0.06±0.01
	28	83.4±5.0	1.6±0.9	0.1 ±0.06	0.4±0.1	12.8±3.4	1.7±0.6	0.05±0.01
	76	96.5±1.3	0.3±0.1	0.04±0.03	1.0±0.4	2.0±0.9	0.2±0.05	0.02±0.01
LPI 5	14	73.1±1.3	1.9±0.3	2.6 ±0.4	0.3±0.05	15.7±1.1	5.9±0.6	0.1 ±0.02
	28	71.7±1.2	1.4±0.1	2.2 ±0.3	0.2±0.02	18.1±0.9	6.3±0.6	0.1 ±0.02
	76	81.4±2.6	2.9±0.4	1.2 ±0.3	0.5±0.08	11.2±1.9	2.7±0.4	0.07±0.01
LPI 8	14	73.5±1.8	3.8±1.7	5.3±0.6	0.1±0.02	12.4±1.0	6.4±0.4	0.07±0.01
	28	74.9±2.2	0.8±0.4	1.7±0.4	0.1±0.01	15.6±1.5	6.9±1.3	0.04±0.01
	76	83.0±0.5	1.5±0.1	2.8±0.2	0.2±0.02	8.0±0.4	4.5±0.5	0.1 ±0.02

therefore been assessed by the specific activity (cpm/100 µg dry weight) of the apical bud at various times after feeding the leaf with $^{14}CO_2$. Import of ^{14}C-assimilates from LPI 3 and LPI 5 into the apical bud was studied at the time of the early increase in the soluble carbohydrate concentration, i.e. at the beginning of the supplementary light period of the LD. Plants were labelled with $^{14}CO_2$ before the end of the main photoperiod and were then either transferred to darkness (vegetative plants) or kept in light for induction. Buds were collected 1, 2, 3 and 4 h after feeding the leaves with $^{14}CO_2$. The initial rate of arrival of ^{14}C in the apical bud was similar in vegetative and induced plants for assimilates exported from LPI 3 and LPI 5 (*Figure 24.3*). These observations confirmed that there was no alteration in the assimilate supply to the apical bud early in the inductive treatment.

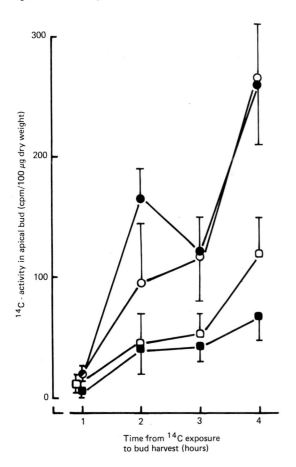

Figure 24.3   Time course of arrival of ^{14}C-assimilates in the apical bud of vegetative plants (○,□) and of plants induced to flower (●, ■). Leaves were exposed to $^{14}CO_2$ just before transfer to darkness for vegetative plants and prior to the inductive day extension light period for plants submitted to the LD. (Vertical bars represent SE and, for clarity, are reported on one side of the mean only.)
○, ● = ^{14}C-assimilates exported from LPI 5.
□, ■ = ^{14}C-assimilates exported from LPI 3.

Discussion

Apart from studies concerned with relationships between the transport of assimilates and transport of the floral stimulus (*see* Zeevaart, 1976; Bernier, Kinet and Sachs, 1981) there have been few reports on assimilate translocation during the floral transition. In the LDP *Lolium temulentum* (Evans, 1976), there is no evidence for an increased assimilate import into the shoot apex at floral evocation, while in the SDP *Xanthium strumarium* (Bodson, 1984; Mirolo, Bodson and Bernier, unpublished observations) and *Pharbitis nil* (Abou-Haidar, Miginiac and Sachs, 1985) a temporary increase in ^{14}C-assimilate arrival in the apical bud occurs during floral evocation.

The study reported here considered both the export and the distribution of assimilates during the floral transition in *Sinapis*.

EXPORT OUT OF THE LEAF

Both in vegetative and in induced plants, the export of assimilates out of the leaf increased with leaf age. There was a diurnal fluctuation in export throughout the light period in vegetative plants and a gradual decrease in export from induced leaves which began at the first SD after induction and was greatest at the time of flower initiation. As reported for *Vicia faba* (Pearson, 1974), these fluctuations in export rate are not related to modifications of the net photosynthetic rate as this remained constant in both vegetative and induced plants for up to 32 h after the start of the LD (Bodson, unpublished). Since the export rate is largely controlled by mechanisms located in the source-leaves (Geiger, 1979), marked changes in the metabolic status of the leaves must be expected to occur during the floral transition.

ASSIMILATE DISTRIBUTION

There was no modification of assimilate distribution between the plant parts examined during and after induction in *Sinapis*. This agreed well with results on *Pharbitis* which showed that the distribution of assimilates between the major sinks of the seedling was not modified after the inductive treatment (Abou-Haidar, Miginiac and Sachs, 1985). During evocation, the apical bud of *Sinapis* was preferentially supplied with assimilates exported out of a young expanded leaf (LPI 5). At the time of initiation of the flower primordia, the proportion of assimilates that moved to the bud from the adult leaf (LPI 8) increased whilst that from the younger leaf (LPI 5) decreased. These results reflect a shift in the source materials transported to the bud at the time of flower initiation, as reported also for *Trifolium pratense* (Jones and Stoddart, 1973). In *Trifolium*, however, assimilates supporting bud development were increasingly supplied by younger leaves as floral induction proceeded.

Clearly, during the inductive treatment, there was no modification of the assimilate supply for the apical bud that could account for the early increase of the soluble carbohydrate concentration in the apical bud reported earlier (Bodson, 1977, 1984). Whether such a conclusion is also valid for the apical meristem, the site of both floral evocation and an early elevation of the sucrose content (Bodson and Outlaw, 1985) is not yet known. The apical bud analysed here was a complex system where stem tissue, axillary meristems and leaf primordia constituted the largest part of the sample. Large differences exist between the growth rates of these different components of the shoot tip at floral transition (Lyndon, 1977; Bernier, Kinet and Sachs, 1981). A recent report has also emphasized metabolic differences between adjacent tissues within the shoot apical bud: the apical meristem versus the first leaf primordia (Croxdale and Outlaw, 1983).

Competition between the shoot bud components for assimilates has been demonstrated by Ross *et al.* (1984) using *Pinus radiata*. Here it was shown that allocation of ^{14}C-assimilates to the terminal bud was reduced at the time of the sexual differentiation but that there was a significant reallocation of ^{14}C-assimilates within the bud to the developing floral primordia at the expense of the pith tissue. Such a situation could also be encountered in the bud of *Sinapis alba* at floral transition. Analysis of the distribution of assimilates between the different components of the apical bud is therefore warranted. Alternatively, the increase of the soluble carbohydrates, shown to occur both in the bud and the meristem, could have originated from a modification of the partitioning of the assimilates between soluble and insoluble forms in the meristem and the other components of the apical bud. It is also possible that, at floral transition, a remobilization occurred of reserve forms of carbohydrates stored within the bud or in other plant parts. Although this last hypothesis is difficult to assess, it is clear that future work must consider the carbohydrate supply and metabolism separately in the different components of the apical bud.

Acknowledgement

The authors wish to thank Professor G. Bernier (University of Liège, Belgium) for critical reading of the manuscript.

References

ABOU-HAIDAR, S.S., MIGINIAC, E. and SACHS, R.M. (1985). ^{14}C-assimilate partitioning in photoperiodically induced seedlings of *Pharbitis nil*. The effect of benzyladenine. *Physiologia Plantarum,* **64**, 265–270

BERNIER, G., KINET, J.M. and BRONCHART, R. (1967). Cellular events at the meristem during floral induction in *Sinapis alba* L. *Physiologie Végétale,* **5**, 311–324

BERNIER, G., KINET, J.M. and SACHS, R.M. (1981). *The Physiology of Flowering*, Vols I and II. Boca Raton, Fl., CRC Press

BODSON, M. (1977). Changes in the carbohydrate content of the leaf and the apical bud of *Sinapis* during transition to flowering. *Planta,* **135**, 19–23

BODSON, M. (1984). Assimilates and Evocation. In *Light and the Flowering Process* (D. Vince-Prue, B. Thomas and K. Cockshull, Eds), pp. 157–169. New York, Academic Press

BODSON, M. (1985). *Sinapis alba* L. In *Handbook of Flowering* (A.H. Halevy, Ed.), pp. 336–353. Boca Raton, Fl., CRC Press

BODSON, M., KING, R.W., EVANS, L.T. and BERNIER, G. (1977). The role of photosynthesis in flowering of the long-day plant *Sinapis alba*. *Australian Journal of Plant Physiology,* **4**, 467–478

BODSON, M. and OUTLAW, W.H. Jr. (1985). Elevation in the sucrose content of the shoot apical meristem of *Sinapis alba* at floral evocation. *Plant Physiology,* **79**, 420–424

CROXDALE, J. and OUTLAW, W.H. Jr. (1983). Glucose-6-phosphate dehydrogenase activity in the shoot apical meristem, leaf primordia and leaf tissues of *Dianthus chinensis* L. *Planta,* **157**, 289–297

EVANS, L.T. (1976). Inhibition of flowering in *Lolium temulentum* by the photosynthetic inhibitor 3(3,4-dichlorophenyl)-1,1-dimethylurea (DCMU) in relation to assimilate supply to the shoot apex. In *Etudes de Biologie Végétale, Hommage au Professeur P. Chouard* (R. Jacques, Ed.), pp. 265–275. Paris, CNRS

GEIGER, D.R. (1979). Control of partitioning and export of carbon in leaves of higher plants. *Botanical Gazette,* **140**, 241–248

JONES, T.W.A. and STODDART, J.L. (1973). Correlative effects of leaf age on reproductive growth in red clover (*Trifolium pratense* L.). *Planta,* **113**, 67–77

LYNDON, R.F. (1977). Interacting processes in vegetative development and in the transition to flowering at the shoot apex. In *Integration of Activity in the Higher Plant* (D.H. Jennings, Ed.), pp. 221–250. Cambridge University Press

PEARSON, C.J. (1974). Daily changes in carbon-dioxide exchange and photosynthate translocation of leaves of *Vicia faba. Planta,* **119**, 59–70

ROSS, S.D., BOLLMANN, M.P., PHARIS, R.P. and SWEET, G.B. (1984). Gibberellin A4/7 and the promotion of flowering in *Pinus radiata. Plant Physiology,* **76**, 326–330

ZEEVAART, J.A.D. (1976). Physiology of flower formation. *Annual Review of Plant Physiology,* **27**, 321–348

25

INHIBITION OF FLOWERING—EFFECTS IN THE LEAF AND ON TRANSLOCATION OF THE STIMULUS

W.W. SCHWABE and M. PAPAFOTIOU
Department of Horticulture, Wye College, University of London, UK

Introduction

Environmental control over both promotion and inhibition of flowering has been under close investigation for half a century, but by far the greatest attention has been given to the promotive effects of favourable photoperiods. Lang and Melchers (1943) had reported on inhibitory effects in LD plants and interest in this has been renewed by Lang, Chailakhyan and Frolova (1977); however, the present discussion will be restricted to SD plants. In a series of experiments with *Kalanchoe blossfeldiana*, *Glycine soya*, and *Perilla ocymoides* it has been shown that the establishment of the very mechanism ('factory') for making the promotive floral stimulus in the leaf can be prevented by unfavourable day-length (Schwabe, 1956, and 1959). The fact that there is a permanent change in metabolism in the leaf has been shown very convincingly by Zeevaart (1957a, b, 1958). The evidence from the intercalation of single, unfavourable LD cycles in a sequence of SD cycles has suggested that an inhibition acting upon succeeding SDs is the result and that this is quantitative. To dismiss these results as merely confusing the rhythmic phases of the plant (King, 1984) seems somewhat improbable, especially when periods of 24 h dark do not affect flowering, while 24 h light periods do, and when moreover, an extractable inhibitor produced in LD can be demonstrated (Schwabe, 1972).

The present study was concerned with two other aspects of 'inhibition', i.e. not the establishment of the mechanisms of making the promoter, but rather with the prevention of the product from the leaf—or part of the leaf—from reaching the target meristem. The two well-established situations are:

1. When the distal part of a single leaf is induced, while the proximal part is held in the unfavourable LD (i.e. Chailakhyan, 1945; Gibby and Salisbury, 1971).
2. When an uninduced leaf in the same orthostichy is situated above the induced leaf (Harder, Westphal and Behrens, 1949).

The most popular explanation for both these effects has been for many years that the interposed leaf, especially if in LD, would serve as the predominant source of carbohydrate export to the growing tip and thus co-transport of the flowering stimulus from the induced part of the leaf or entire leaf would fail, especially when the non-induced leaf was nearer to the meristem, i.e. what may be called the 'carbohydrate competition theory' (Chailakhyan and Butenko, 1957; King and Zeevaart, 1973). However, there are other, possible, modes of action which include: prevention of the passage of the promoter through leaf tissue in the unfavourable day-length (Gregory, 1948), or interference by a specific flowering inhibitor causing its inactivation (Searle, 1965; Gibby and Salisbury, 1971).

Experimental

In the investigation described both *Xanthium strumarium* and *Kalanchoe blossfeldiana* were used. The treatments given involved different methods of preventing photosynthesis by the inhibitory leaves or parts of leaves, employing several techniques such as enclosure with soda-lime and blockage of stomata. The opposite treatment, i.e. enhancement of carbohydrate content by sucrose injection, was also tried to compete with movement of carbohydrate from the induced leaf. To test the significance of routes of transport, separation of differently treated parts of the leaf blade was attempted by making cuts between adjoining parts of the leaf blade; a technique used by Searle (1965). Finally, the application of auxin to the leaf blade as well as the auxin-transport inhibitor 2,3,5-triiodo-benzoic acid (TIBA) was employed to modify possible movement of promoters (or inhibitors) from the leaf blade. In most such experiments a single leaf was used for induction, i.e. a young, not quite expanded leaf in *Xanthium*, or two leaves in the same orthostichy in *Kalanchoe*, unless stated otherwise in the table of results. Since in *Xanthium* the intercellular spaces do not communicate with one another throughout the leaf (it is heterobaric), it is particularly suitable for the half-leaf method, so that it is possible to maintain part of the leaf in CO_2-free air without internal gas exchange. *Kalanchoe*, which is homobaric is thus most suitable for injection experiments into the intercellular spaces.

The various treatments given and the results in terms of inflorescences produced need not be detailed in the text, but can be seen in the tables, and will be described together. The degree of flowering in *Xanthium* has been expressed as a 'score' in which each male inflorescence is weighted as 1 and each female inflorescence as 2. In *Kalanchoe* the mean number of flowers is shown.

The first four experiments are summarized in *Table 25.1* and from this it is clear that exposure of the proximal (basal) half of the leaf to LD is inhibitory regardless of whether it is in CO_2-free air or not, and this is so when 1, 2 or 3 SDs are given. If the base is given SD, normal induction occurs, as it does when the entire leaf is induced by SD. But if CO_2 is excluded from the induced, basal part of the leaf, a very large reduction in flowering is caused. These results both confirm what was known since Chailakhyan's (1945) experiments, but they also indicate that withholding CO_2 does not diminish the inhibitory effect of the interposed LD portion of the leaf, although it presumably has little or no carbohydrate to export preferentially to the shoot apex.

In the experiment described in *Table 25.2* a variety of leaf blade cuts was used, again with *Xanthium*. The usual inhibitory effect of the proximal (basal) leaf part in LD is shown, though it did not prevent flowering completely. Cuts through the blade down to the midrib between the differentially treated parts of the lamina did not ameliorate the inhibition at all. Even when only 2 quarter-leaves were left on opposite sides of the midrib the inhibition was still highly significant. Clearly, living contact between the two blade parts is not relevant in this context.

Turning to the effect of an interposed LD leaf in *Kalanchoe* given an almost saturating dose of SD treatment (*Table 25.3*), an attempt was made to abolish the effect of the intervening leaf in LD by depriving it throughout of CO_2, by enclosure in a clear polythene bag with soda lime. As an alternative, the midrib of the LD leaf was

Table 25.1 *Xanthium strumarium*. THE EFFECT OF LACK OF ASSIMILATE ON THE INHIBITING ACTION OF THE BASAL-HALF LEAF IN THE UNFAVOURABLE DAY-LENGTH DURING INDUCTION. EXPERIMENT 1: 3 SD (JAN. 1984). SODA LIME APPLIED ON THE 1ST SD, FIVE REPLICATES. EXPERIMENT 2: SD (MARCH 1984) SODA LIME AND LANOLIN APPLIED 1 DAY BEFORE THE 1ST SD, FIVE REPLICATES, SINGLE LEAF PLANTS. EXPERIMENT 3: 2 SD (MARCH 1984). SODA LIME AND LANOLIN APPLIED 1 DAY BEFORE 1ST SD, FIVE REPLICATES. EXPERIMENT 4: 1 SD (JULY 1984). LANOLIN APPLIED 2 DAYS BEFORE THE SD, EIGHT REPLICATES. SCORE: INFLORESCENCES (MALE = 1, FEMALE = 2).

Experiment 1		Experiment 2		Experiment 3	Experiment 4
Treatment	Mean score	Treatment	Mean score	Mean score	Mean score
LD / SD	70	SD	203	121	186
LD / SD CO$_2$ free	15	SD / LD	61	29	32
SD / LD	1	SD / LD lanolin	57	26	30
SD / LD CO$_2$ free	0	SD / LD CO$_2$ free	37	20	
SD / LD in open bag ○	0	SD / LD in water	25		
$P = 0.05$: LSD = 23			LSD = 55	LSD = 40	LSD = 28

severed. Both these treatments did, in fact, result in higher flower numbers, but unfortunately the error variation in flower number was very high, making the result rather inconclusive.

Feeding of sucrose to the induced leaf, presumably increasing the carbohydrate for export, did not promote flowering in *Kalanchoe* (*Table 25.4*); in fact, sucrose injection gave fewer flowers than the water injection, and both treatments yielded fewer flowers than the dry controls. Feeding sucrose to petioles of *Xanthium* above the induced leaf

Table 25.2 *Xanthium strumarium.* EFFECT OF CUTTING THE LEAF BLADE ON THE INHIBITING ACTION OF BASAL PART OF LEAF BLADE, HELD IN UNFAVOURABLE DAY-LENGTHS. 2 SD (DECEMBER, 1984); EIGHT REPLICATES. SCORE: INFLORESCENCES (MALE = 1, FEMALE = 2)

Treatment	Mean score	Treatment	Mean score
LD / SD	73	LD / SD	56
SD / LD	33	SD / LD	20
LD / SD	78	LD / SD	65
SD / LD	17	SD / LD	5

P = 0.05   LSD = 15

Table 25.3 *Kalanachoe blossfeldiana.* EFFECT OF PREVENTING PHOTOSYNTHESIS OR TRANSLOCATION OF THE ASSIMILATE FROM THE NON-INDUCED INTERPOSED LEAF ON ITS INHIBITING ACTION ON THE TRANSPORT OF THE SD STIMULUS TO THE APEX. 14 SD (FEBRUARY 1984); NINE REPLICATES

Treatment

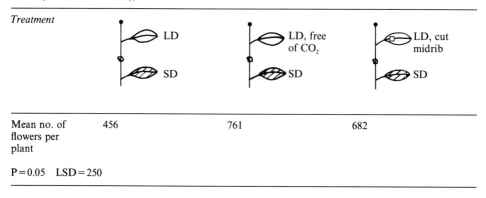

Mean no. of flowers per plant	456	761	682

P = 0.05   LSD = 250

Table 25.4 *Kalanchoe blossfeldiana* AND *Xanthium strumarium*. THE EFFECT OF ADDED SUCROSE (5%) ON THE PRODUCTION AND TRANSLOCATION OF THE FLOWERING STIMULUS

Kalanchoe blossfeldiana *12 SD (April–May 1985), Sucrose injections* *on the 4th and 5th SD. 7 replicates*		Xanthium strumarium *1 SD (May 1984), Sucrose feeding 1 day before* *the SD till 2 days after it. 10 replicates.* *Score: inflorescences (male = 1, female = 2)*	
Treatment	*Mean of no. of* *flowers at the tip*	*Treatment*	*Mean score*
sucrose 5% / SD	22	sucrose 5% / SD	54
water / SD	27	water / SD	81
SD	53		
P = 0.05 LSD = 21		P = 0.05 LSD = 28	

did reduce the score slightly, but the effect just failed to reach significance, and clearly did not prevent the inductive stimulus from reaching the terminal meristem.

In *Table 25.5* data are recorded from an experiment with *Kalanchoe* in which the inhibitory LD leaf (or its petiole) situated above the induced SD leaf, was given a series of treatments. There are differences between flower numbers produced by the terminal or axillary meristems, which are also of importance, quite apart from the total number of flowers per plant.

The results of the experiment suggest that the inhibitory effect of this interposed leaf appears to be enhanced when it is injected with a 10 ppm solution of indole-3-butyric acid (IBA). The auxin transport inhibitor TIBA injected in a similar manner at 100 ppm allowed a considerable number of flowers to be produced in the axil of the SD leaf, but not at the terminal apex. On the basis of the carbohydrate competition theory, none of these treatments should have had any effect.

In the other treatments given, the blade of the interposed LD leaf was removed and substances fed into the petiole. When 5% sucrose was fed (plus 2 ppm IBA to prevent petiole abscission), or when 10 ppm IBA alone was applied, the flower numbers were reduced to less than one-half or one-third respectively of the control, the petiole of which was left untreated. This result suggests that IBA application strongly interfered with the stimulus from the SD leaf reaching the apex. The results of the

Table 25.5 *Kalanchoe blossfeldiana.* EXPERIMENTS ON THE INHIBITING MECHANISM OF THE INTERPOSED, NON-INDUCED LEAF. 10 SD (MAY 1985); FIVE REPLICATES. WATER, SAP FROM LD KALANCHOE LEAVES, IBA AND TIBA SOLUTIONS INJECTED INTO THE LD LEAF MIDRIB, ON THE 1ST, 4TH AND 8TH SD, JUST BEFORE THE DARK PERIOD. SUCROSE AND IBA APPLIED ON THE INTERPOSED PETIOLE BY THE WICK METHOD THROUGHOUT THE 10 SD PERIOD

Treatment	Mean no. of flowers at the tip	Mean no. of flowers at the SD leaf axil	Mean no. of total flowers	Treatment	Mean no. of flowers at the top	Mean no. of flowers at the SD leaf axil	Mean no. of total flowers
LD — H₂O / SD	13	0	13	SD	27	6	34
LD — LD sap / SD	9	1	10	sucrose 5% + IBA 2 ppm / SD	13	2	16
LD — IBA 10 ppm / SD	2	3	5	IBA 10 ppm / SD	8	5	13
LD — TIBA 100 ppm / SD	1	16	18	P=0.05 LSD	11	12	14
P=0.05 LSD	11	12	14				

treatment in which 5% sucrose was applied could be interpreted as due to the IBA effect alone, but it could also represent a sucrose effect, and further experimentation is needed.

Using the half-leaf method with *Xanthium* a number of different sites of application of 100 ppm TIBA or 10 ppm IBA were tested on the export of the stimulus from the distal part of the leaf (*Table 25.6*). A few significant results may be singled out. Application of IBA to the distal (i.e. SD part of the leaf) appeared to increase the transport of the SD effect; this was significantly so when the basal, inhibitory (i.e. LD treated) part of the leaf was simultaneously treated with TIBA. Also IBA application, through a wick, to the midrib between the two differentially treated parts of the blade, was particularly inhibitory. Again there are hints here that the transport may be

Table 25.6 *Xanthium strumarium.* EFFECTS OF IBA AND TIBA ON THE PRODUCTION AND TRANSLOCATION OF THE FLOWERING STIMULUS FROM THE DISTAL HALF-LEAF. 1 SD (MAY 1985); EIGHT REPLICATES. HORMONE APPLIED TO BOTH LEAF SURFACES BY PAINTING ON: BEFORE, ON AND AFTER THE SD AT 9 am. HORMONE APPLICATION ON THE PETIOLE (WICK METHOD) 1 DAY BEFORE THE SD AND FOR 2 DAYS AFTER IT. (IBA = 10 PPM, TIBA = 100 PPM). SCORE: INFLORESCENCES (MALE = 1, FEMALE = 2)

Treatment	Mean score	Treatment	Mean score	Treatment	Mean score
SD / LD	97	SD — IBA / LD — TIBA	175	SD / LD — IBA (on petiole)	56
SD — TIBA / LD	116	SD — IBA / LD	143	SD / LD ← IBA	140
					92
SD / LD — TIBA	135	SD / LD — IBA	104	SD — IBA, TIBA / LD	

P = 0.05   LSD = 78

enhanced if it goes with auxin movement, and either promotion or inhibition can be enhanced according to the site of auxin application.

The last experiment to be described concerns IBA or TIBA application, by painting both surfaces of the induced leaf at different times, i.e. on the day before, during, or after a single day's SD induction as well as for 3 days. The most significant results, shown in *Table 25.7*, indicate that when IBA was applied *after* the SD, the flowering score was greatly increased above the water controls, but if applied *during* the SD it was reduced, while daily application for 3 days (i.e. before, during and after the SD) gave a score closely similar to the control. The response to TIBA treatment nearly always led to a reduction of the score.

In discussing these data it must be stressed that they represent somewhat preliminary results. Clearly, some need to be repeated again and with greater precision. However, *in toto* it may be said that it would not be easy to explain them on the hypothesis that an intervening LD, given to the leaf base or to an interposed leaf, merely operates as an alternative and preferential source of carbohydrate movement to the apical meristem, thus preventing the flowering stimulus from reaching its target. Previous experiments with *Kalanchoe* cited by Schwabe (1984) had shown that in *Kalanchoe* export of labelled carbohydrate from an induced leaf was not significantly reduced by the interposition of a LD leaf, yet flowering was severely reduced.

On the other hand, it would seem that auxin transport from the leaf may enhance also the transport out of the blade of the SD stimulus, and equally it may stimulate

Table 25.7   *Xanthium strumarium.* THE EFFECT OF IBA AND TIBA APPLICATION ON THE PRODUCTION AND TRANSLOCATION OF THE FLOWERING STIMULUS. 1 SD. TREATMENT 1, 2, 3: EIGHT REPLICATES. TREATMENT 4, 5, 6, 7, 8, 9: SIX REPLICATES. HORMONES PAINTED ON BOTH LEAF SURFACES AT 9 am. TIBA = 100 PPM, IBA = 10 PPM. SCORE: INFLORESCENCES (MALE = 1, FEMALE = 2)

Treatment	Mean score	Treatment	Mean score	Treatment	Mean score
Water for 3 days	116	TIBA before the SD	117	IBA before the SD	142
TIBA for 3 days	84	TIBA on the SD	80	IBA on the SD	89
IBA for 3 days	115	TIBA after the SD	97	IBA after the SD	186

P = 0.05   LSD = 41

the transport from the inhibitory leaf or part of it. Whether in this case it is actually an inhibitor molecule which is mobilized or a factor interfering with the promoter is impossible to say, and clearly a great deal of further experimentation will be needed to clarify what may be happening. Nevertheless, it would seem that further worthwhile results may yet be obtained with relatively simple experimentation. In any case, there are now serious doubts whether the carbohydrate competition theory can be maintained any longer, and the influence of auxin transported out of the leaf on promoter movement may be more important than has hitherto been appreciated.

References

CHAILAKHYAN, M.C. (1945). Photoperiodism of the individual parts of the leaf, its halves. *Doklady Academy of Sciences of the USSR,* **47,** 220. Reported by Naylor, A.W. (1953). In *Reactions of Plants to Photoperiod in Growth and Differentiation in Plants* (W.E. Loomis, Ed.). Iowa State College Press

CHAILAKHYAN, M.C. and BUTENKO, R.G. (1957). Translocation of assimilates from leaves to shoots during different photoperiodic regimes of plants. *Fiziologia Rasteniye (Soviet Plant Physiology),* **4,** 450–462

GIBBY, D.D. and SALISBURY, F.B. (1971). Participation of long-day inhibition in flowering of *Xanthium strumarium. Plant Physiology,* **47,** 784–789

GREGORY, F.G. (1948). The control of flowering in plants. *Symposium, Society of Experimental Biology II. Growth,* pp. 75–203

HARDER, R., WESTPHAL, M. and BEHRENS, G. (1949). Hemmung der Infloreszenbildung durch Langtag bei der Kurztagspflanze *Kalanchoe blossfeldiana. Planta,* **36,** 424–438

KING, R.W. (1984). Light and photoperiodic timing. In *Light and the Flowering Process* (D. Vince-Prue, B. Thomas and K.E. Cockshull, Eds), pp. 91–105. London, Academic Press

KING, R.W. and ZEEVAART, J.A.D. (1973). Floral stimulus movement in *Perilla* and flower inhibition caused by non-induced leaves. *Plant Physiology,* **51,** 727–738

LANG, A. and MELCHERS, G. (1943). Die photoperiodische Reaktion von *Hyoscyamus niger. Planta,* **33,** 653–702

LANG, A., CHAILAKHYAN, M.C. and FROLOVA, I.A. (1977). Promotion and inhibition of flower formation in a day neutral plant in grafts with a short-day plant and a long-day plant. *Proceedings of the National Academy of Sciences USA,* **74,** 2412–2416

SCHWABE, W.W. (1956). Evidence for a flowering inhibitor produced in long days in *Kalanachoe blossfeldiana. Annals of Botany,* **20,** 1–14

SCHWABE, W.W. (1959). Studies of long-day inhibition in short-day plants. *Journal of Experimental Botany,* **10,** 317–329

SCHWABE, W.W. (1972). Flower inhibition in *Kalanchoe blossfeldiana.* Bioassay of an endogenous long-day inhibitor and inhibition by (±) abscisic acid and xanthoxin. *Planta,* **103,** 18–23

SCHWABE, W.W. (1984). Photoperiodic induction—flower inhibiting substances. In *Light and the Flowering Process* (D. Vince-Prue, B. Thomas and K.E. Cockshull, Eds), pp.143–152. London, Academic Press

SEARLE, N.E. (1965). Bioassay of floral stimulus in *Xanthium. Plant Physiology,* **40,** 261–267

ZEEVAART, J.A.D. (1957a). Studies on flowering by means of grafting. I. Photoperiodic induction as an irreversible phenomenon in *Perilla. Proceedings, Koniglijke Nederlands Academie van Wetenschapen, Series C,* **60,** 325–331

ZEEVAART, J.A.D. (1957b). Studies on flowering by means of grafting. II. Photoperiodic treatment of detached *Perilla* and *Xanthium* leaves. *Proceedings, Koniglijke Nederlands Academie van Wetenschapen, Series C,* **60,** 332–337

ZEEVAART, J.A.D. (1958). Flower formation as studied by grafting. *Mededelingen Landbouwhogeschool Wageningen,* **53,** 1–88

VII
Flower development

26

ASSIMILATE ALLOCATION AND FLOWER DEVELOPMENT

A.H. HALEVY
Department of Ornamental Horticulture, The Hebrew University of Jerusalem, Israel

Introduction

Flower formation is the final stage in the ontogenetic development of the shoot meristem. Every active shoot meristem will eventually reach this stage unless its development is impeded by environmental conditions or by correlative inhibition of other organs. Both of these factors may influence flower development by directing assimilates either towards or away from the flower bud.

The well-known work of Kraus and Kraybill (1918) on the carbohydrate : nitrogen ratio in tomato plants has often been misquoted in the literature dealing with flower initiation. Their studies were concerned not with flower initiation but almost entirely with flower development and fruit set, and their findings in that connection are still valid today. Developing flowers are centres of growth which make intensive use of carbohydrates and other metabolites. Acute carbohydrate shortage often leads to the arrest of flower development or abortion of the flower buds. Environmental conditions or horticultural treatments that enhance carbohydrate levels promote flower development. Unless there is a surplus of organic metabolites, there will inevitably be competition for them between the various sinks. When several floral initials have been formed, competition for the limited substrates may occur between the developing flowers.

The subject of flower development has been thoroughly and critically examined recently (Kinet, Sachs and Bernier, 1985). Elsewhere in this book the role of assimilate distribution in floral transition (*see* Chapter 24) and in flower initiation (Chapter 23) are discussed. This chapter will focus on the effect of assimilates on the later stages of flower development. Some examples will be presented that illustrate the importance of assimilate allocation to the flower bud during flower development, as well as the possible involvement of specific carbohydrate compounds in the regulation of flower development.

Sink activity of the developing flower bud

A number of studies have shown that the young developing flower bud is a major sink for assimilates under favourable growing conditions, when the metabolites essential for its growth are in ample supply. For example, in experiments with gladiolus

364

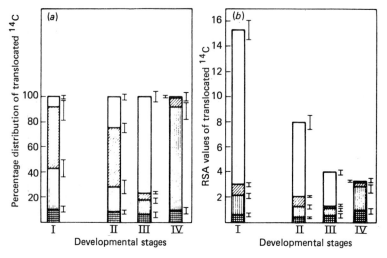

Figure 26.1 The partition of the ¹⁴C-metabolites translocated out of the source (third leaf) between the different parts of the Gladiolus plant (cv. Eurovision) at various stages of development (I, 90-day-old plants, the inflorescence still hidden between the leaves; II, 120-day-old plants, the inflorescence beginning to emerge from the leaves; III, 135-day-old plants, anthesis; IV, 150-day-old plants—inflorescence wilted). (a) Results expressed as per cent distribution of ¹⁴C; (b) results expressed as relative specific activity (RSA) values (calculated as follows according to Mor and Halevy (1979): dpm g⁻¹ in a specified part of the plant divided by dpm g⁻¹ of the whole plant, excluding the source leaf). □, inflorescence; ▨, stems and leaves; ▥, new corm; ▦, roots. Vertical bars indicate 2 × standard error. (Reproduced from Robinson *et al.* (1980) by kind permission of authors and publishers.)

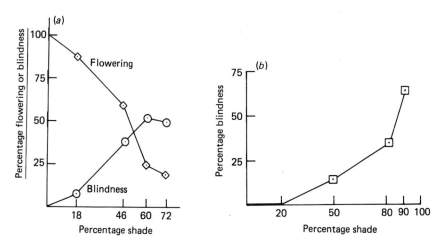

Figure 26.2 (a) Effect of shading rose plants (cv. Baccara) on per cent flowering and per cent flower abortion ('blindness') of the two upper shoots. (b) Effect of shading single rose shoots on per cent flower abortion ('blindness') on this shoot. (Reproduced from Zieslin and Halevy (1975) by kind permission of authors and publishers.)

(Robinson *et al.*, 1980), it was shown that the plant contains two major sinks, the inflorescence and the new corm. At an early stage in flower development the absolute percentage of ^{14}C assimilates translocated to the flower bud is small, but its relative specific activity (RSA), representing the relative sink activity, is already very high (*Figure 26.1*). Similar results were obtained with roses (Mor and Halevy, 1979). However, under stress conditions associated with an inadequate supply of essential assimilates, the young flower bud constitutes a weak sink in comparison with the vegetative apices, developing leaves, fruits or storage organs, and competed poorly with them for the available assimilates (Halevy, 1975, 1984). This was found to be the case under conditions of light, temperature or water stress. In plants possessing young flower buds, these environmental stresses promote abortion, blasting or abscission of the flower buds, while other organs may be only slightly affected, as discussed below. Where flower development coincides with fruit growth, the flower buds compete unfavourably with the developing fruit for photosynthates. This might be the main reason for flower bud abscission and the consequent alternate bearing in fruit trees (Monselise and Goldschmidt, 1982).

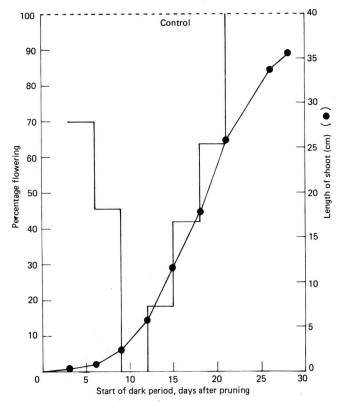

Figure 26.3 Effect of time of darkening single rose shoots (cv. Marimba) on shoot elongation and on per cent flower buds reaching anthesis (% flowering). Branches were pruned to the second five-leaflet leaf from top, and the shoot emerging from the upper bud was darkened for 12 days at various times after pruning. Percentage of shoots flowering was measured 34 days after pruning. Growth curve of control plants is shown, with points at the beginning of the dark periods. (Reproduced from Mor and Halevy (1980a) by kind permission of authors and publishers.)

The rose is a self-inductive plant in which flowers are initiated autonomously in every growing shoot after a certain number of leaves have been formed. It is well known, however, that flower production in roses is correlated with light energy. Low irradiance causes a reduction in flowering mainly because of an increase in flower abortion (*Figure 26.2(a)*). This response has generally been attributed to the effect of light on photosynthesis; however, when only one young shoot or its tip is covered while the rest of the plant is held in full light, flower bud abortion is still promoted in the covered shoot (*Figure 26.2(b)*). It has also been shown that darkness is particularly detrimental at the start of elongation of the flowering stem, and that it has little or no effect before or after this stage (*Figure 26.3*). The young shoots with their apical flower buds are totally dependent on the translocation of metabolites from mature leaves (Mor and Halevy, 1979). Reducing the amount of light reaching the developing shoot or keeping only the young tip in darkness greatly decreases the amount of ^{14}C assimilates translocated to the tip, thus promoting the atrophy and death of the young flower bud (*Table 26.1*) This clearly indicates that light acts directly on the rose flower buds themselves, enhancing their sink activity (Mor and Halevy, 1980; Mor, Halevy and Porath, 1980). Similar results have been obtained with grapevines (May, 1965). In contrast, no evidence for light-induced sink activation was found in *Bougainvillea*, tomato or chrysanthemum (Kinet, Sachs and Bernier, 1985; p. 85).

In gladiolus, flower degeneration is promoted by low light intensity (Shillo and Halevy, 1976a) as well as by low temperature and water stress (Halevy, 1962; Shillo and Halevy, 1976c). Like roses, gladiolus flower buds are sensitive to these stresses at a specific stage in their development and are affected only slightly or not at all at other stages. Even relatively slight water stress leads to a decrease in the mobilization of ^{14}C assimilates by the inflorescence and an increase in their transport to the competing sink, the corm (*Table 26.2*).

Flower blasting in gladiolus is promoted not only by low irradiance but also by short photoperiods (SD). Low-intensity light applied as night break, greatly reduces the incidence of blindness and increases the number of florets per inflorescence . As in the case of both low irradiance and water stress, the flower buds are sensitive to short photoperiod mainly during the early stages of their development (*Figure 26.4*). It was found that the photoperiod directly affects the sink activities of the two competing sinks (the inflorescence and corm), and the distribution of assimilates between them.

Table 26.1　DISTRIBUTION AS MEAN±SE % OF ^{14}C-LABELLED ASSIMILATES IN YOUNG ROSE SHOOTS (CV. Marimba) AS AFFECTED BY DARKENING A SINGLE SHOOT ON A PLANT. SOURCE LEAVES WERE PULSED WITH $^{14}CO_2$ 7 DAYS AFTER START OF DARKENING. RSA IS COMPUTED AS IN *Figure 26.1* (FROM MOR AND HALEVY, 1980)

	Control		Darkened shoot	
	^{14}C Translocated		^{14}C Translocated	
Parts of young shoot	out of source leaf	RSA	out of source leaf	RSA
Whole shoot	81.8±3.7	3.6±0.7	38.1±5.5	3.0±0.1
Shoot tip	5.1±1.0	22.8±4.1	0.6±0.3	1.7±0.5
Leaf (third from bottom)	10.8±4.7	1.9±0.6	10.0±0.7	6.7±0.5
Other parts (stem and other levels)	65.9±6.6	3.7±0.4	27.5±5.1	2.1±0.2

Table 26.2 MEAN (±SE) DISTRIBUTION OF ^{14}C-ASSIMILATES TO VARIOUS PARTS OF
WELL-IRRIGATED AND STRESSED GLADIOLUS (CV. EUROVISION) PLANTS. MEANS OF
NINE REPLICATES (FROM ROBINSON *ET AL.*, 1983)

Treatment	Water potential of the fifth leaf (bars)	Distribution of translocated ^{14}C between the differential parts of the plant (%)		
		Inflorescence	Stem and leaves	Corm
Well irrigated	−6.1±1.7	61.2±3.4	33.0±3.2	5.7±0.6
Stressed	−14.1±1.8	7.4±3.6	67.7±5.4	24.8±5.4

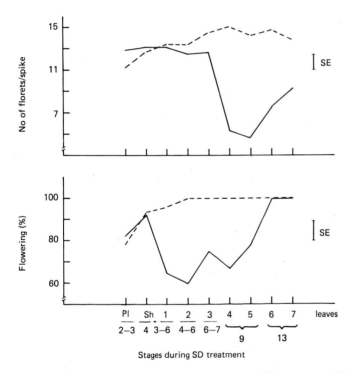

Figure 26.4 Effect of short photoperiods applied at different stages of development on
flowering of gladiolus (cv. Sans Souci). Abscissa—developmental stage at start (upper
row) and at end (lower row) of SD treatment. Pl, planting; Sh, sheath leaves; 1–8, 1–8
expanded foliage leaves; 9, spike emergence from leaves; 10, 11, spike extension and
growth; 13, half of the florets open (anthesis); 15, wilting of last floret. (Reproduced from
Shillo and Halevy (1976b) by kind permission of authors and publishers.)

The strength of the flower sink is increased in LD and that of the corm in SD (*Figure
26.5*). Short photoperiod were also found to promote corm development in the
absence of flowers (Shillo and Halevy, 1981), which may indicate that the primary
effect of photoperiod is on corm growth, thus increasing the ability of the corm to
compete with the inflorescence for assimilate in SD.

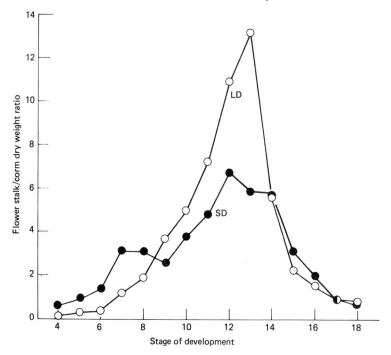

Figure 26.5   Effect of photoperiod on distribution of dry matter between the flower stalk and corm of gladiolus (cv. Spic and Span) at various stages of development (*see* legend to *Figure 26.4*). Results are expressed as the ratio of dry weight of the flower stalk to the corm at each developmental stage. (Reproduced from Shillo and Halevy (1981) by kind permission of authors and publishers.)

Flower development in many bulbous plants can be promoted by chilling the bulbs prior to planting. Such treatment enhances the hydrolysis of reserve carbohydrates in the bulbs and the consequent accumulation of starch and soluble sugars in the developing flower buds, as demonstrated in iris (Rodrigues Periera, 1962) and tulip (Ho and Rees, 1975, 1976; Moe and Wickstrom, 1979). Hobson and Davis (1978) reported that prolonged exposure of tulip bulbs to excessive cold, which results in the production of poor quality flowers, causes starch hydrolysis as in normal cooling, but prevents the mobilization of sucrose from the scales to the flower buds.

Flower blasting is common in winter-forced iris grown in the greenhouse, under conditions of low irradiance and high temperatures (Hartsema and Luyten, 1955). Vonk and associates (Mae and Vonk, 1974; Vonk and Ribot, 1982) have shown that there is a specific effect of light, which is independent of photosynthesis, on sink activation of the flower bud. Keeping the plant in darkness for 7 days at the sensitive stage markedly reduces translocation of both ^{14}C and ^{32}P to the developing flower bud. Sano (1975) showed that removal of foliage from iris plants grown in light has little or no effect on their flower development, while reduction of bulb weight greatly promotes flower blasting. This indicates that light directly affects the mobilization of metabolites from the mother bulb to the flower bud. Recently, Elphinstone, Rees and Atherton (1986) confirmed an earlier report by Hartsema and Luyten (1955) that at high temperatures and the same light integral, long photoperiods promotes flower abortion of iris. They demonstrated a direct effect of photoperiod on the distribution of metabolites between the flower bud and the daughter bulb. At higher temperatures, long photoperiods promote the sink activity of the daughter bulb, thus increasing the competition between the two developing sinks, the flower and the bulb (*Figure 26.6*). These findings are similar to those obtained with gladiolus (Shillo and Halevy, 1981).

It is well known that low light intensity promotes flower abortion in tomato plants. A low supply of assimilates at the sensitive stage, which lasts for 10 days from the time that the bud is macroscopically visible, was found to cause complete abortion of the inflorescence, without affecting the growth of the young leaves (Kinet, 1977a). At this stage the flower buds cannot successfully complete with other sinks, such as the apex, young leaves and roots, for the available assimilates (Russell and Morris, 1983). Flower abortion at low light regime can be prevented by removal of the young leaves developing below the inflorescence (Kinet, 1977b).

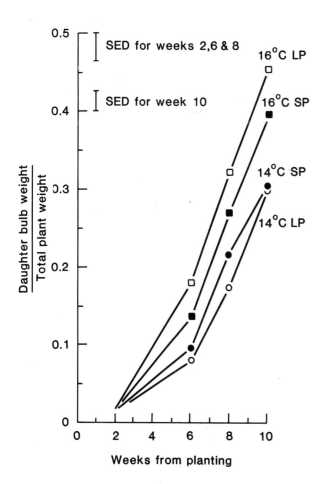

Figure 26.6   Growth curves of daughter bulb weight as a proportion of total plant weight in iris (cv. Wedgwood) grown at 14 and 16°C and long (LP, 24h) and short (SP, 8 h) photoperiods. (Reproduced from Elphinstone, Rees and Atherton (1986) by kind permission of authors and publishers.)

Heat stress also promotes flower abortion in tomato plants. Assimilate import by the flower buds was recently shown to be inhibited at high temperatures (Dinar and Rudich, 1985a, b). The effect of heat stress on assimilate partitioning is more marked in the heat-sensitive cultivar Roma VF than in the heat-tolerant cultivar Saladette. These findings suggest that the modification of assimilate partitioning at high temperatures results from a reduction in the ability of younger flower buds to mobilize assimilates.

Growth substances and sink activity of flower buds

The import of assimilates into the developing flower bud, may be regulated by the level of endogenous growth substances in the flower. Under adverse conditions, such as low light intensity or low temperatures, both of which promote flower abortion, a decline in the levels of gibberellin-like substances (GA) is observed in rose shoots (Zieslin and Halevy, 1976b). The decline is more pronounced in the lower than in the upper shoots and becomes progressively greater with the reduction of light intensity. The lower shoots are much more sensitive than the upper ones to the abortion-promoting stress conditions. Transport of ^{14}C-assimilates to the upper shoots is greater than to lower shoots on the same branch. Keeping the upper shoot in darkness increases its rate of flower abortion and decreases assimilate transport into it; at the same time flower development in and ^{14}C-assimilate transport into the lower shoots are promoted (Mor *et al.*, 1981). Treatment of shaded rose plants with GA$_3$ reduces flower abortion in the upper shoots (Zieslin and Halevy, 1976a).

When cytokinin levels were followed in the two rose shoots after the upper shoot alone was held in darkness for 8 days, it was found that flowering in the upper shoot was reduced and the cytokinin level in it was increased relative to the upper shoots of control plants (Van Staden *et al.*, 1981a). At the same time flowering and cytokinin levels increased slightly in the lower shoots which were exposed to light, when the upper shoots were darkened. This increase in the lower shoots could be partially reversed by exposing the etiolated shoots to light for 2 days (*Figure 26.7*). It seems therefore that higher endogenous cytokinin levels in roses are not correlated with reduced flower abortion or with enhanced mobilizing capacity of the flower buds. It has been suggested that the accumulation of cytokinins might result from a slowing down of their utilization, as was found to be the case in senescing leaves (Van Staden, 1977) and correlatively inhibited rose buds (Van Staden *et al.*, 1981b).

External application of benzyladenine (BA) to the lower shoots promotes flower development there (Mor and Halevy, 1984). BA application to the shaded upper shoot reverses the effect of darkness on both the flowering and the sink activity of the shoots, thus restoring the apical control of this shoot (*Figure 26.8*; Mor and Halevy, 1981).

Application of the growth retardant chlormequat (CCC) increases flower production (Byrne *et al.*, 1971) and decreases flower abortion in roses grown at low light intensity (Zieslin and Halevy, 1976a; Mor *et al.*, 1986). This effect may be explained by the enhanced transport of ^{14}C-assimilates to the second young shoot, thus promoting flower development there (*Figure 26.9*). Similar promotion of flower development (Halevy and Shillo, 1970) and assimilate mobilization (Ginzburg, 1974) has been reported for gladiolus. In this plant, chlormequat increases the endogenous levels of GA-like substances (Halevy and Shillo, 1970).

In tomato plants, endogenous cytokinin levels decrease considerably under condi-

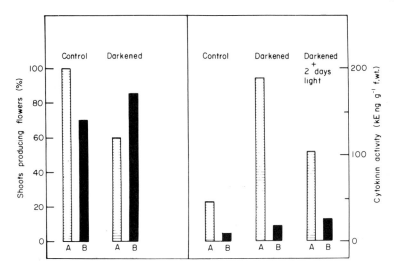

Figure 26.7 Effect of darkening the upper shoot of rose (cv. Golden Times), on per cent flowering of the upper (*a*) and the second (*b*) shoots, and on the cytokinin activity (which co-eluted with zeatin and ribosylzeatin) in their tips. (Reproduced from Van Staden, Zieslin, Spiegelstein and Halevy (1981) by kind permission of authors and publishers.)

tions of low light intensity which promote flower abortion. Endogenous GA levels, however, increase under these conditions (Leonard and Kinet, 1982). It therefore appears that, in contrast to roses, flower development in tomato is correlated with increased levels of cytokinins and reduced levels of GA. External application of BA and GA can reverse the deleterious effect of the low light intensity and considerably enhance assimilate intake by the developing inflorescence (Kinet *et al.*, 1978). Chlormequat promotes flower development in tomato plants grown at low light intensity and high temperatures, probably by reducing the levels of endogenous GA in the shoot tips and correspondingly the growth of competing sinks (Abdul, Canham and Harris, 1978; Nourai and Harris, 1983).

Ethylene production by the shoot tips of rose plants grown in the shade is lower than in those grown in sunlight. However, in shade-grown roses a four-fold increase in ethylene evolution is observed in the second shoot, which is prone to abort under these conditions (*Figure 26.10*). Application of ethephon to the developing buds enhances abortion; and this effect is more pronounced on the lower than on the upper shoots (Zieslin and Halevy, 1976b).

Ethylene seems to be the main factor promoting flower bud abortion and abscission in many plants (Halevy and Mayak, 1981; Sexton *et al.*, 1985). Ethylene production is greatly enhanced in 'Enchantment' lilies grown under low light conditions which lead to flower bud abortion or abscission. The stage at which the flower bud is most sensitive to low light is at bud length of 10–30 mm coincided with meiosis of the stamens (Durieux, Kamerbeek and Van Meeteren, 1983). The flower buds respond to shading at this sensitive stage by enhanced ethylene production. Application of the ethylene antagonists silver thiosulphate or AVG prevents flower abscission under these conditions (Van Meeteren and De Proft, 1982).

Injecting reproductive tulip bulbs with ethephon or exposing them to ethylene results in complete blasting of the flower, while growth of the daughter bulb is

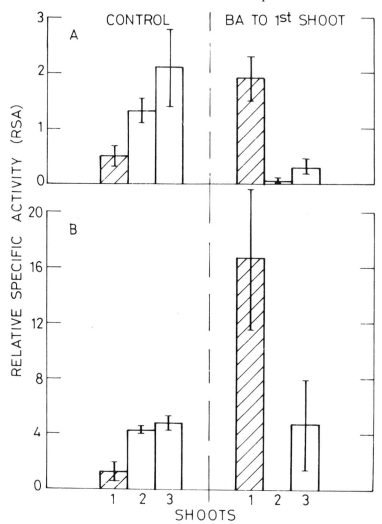

Figure 26.8 Distribution of radioactivity in terms of relative specific activity (*see* legend to *Figure 26.1*), between three young rose shoots (cv. Marimba) on the same branch. The uppermost shoot was darkened, BA (50 mg l⁻¹) was applied to the darkened shoot. $^{14}CO_2$ was pulsed to the leaf below the third shoot. (*a*) Entire shoot; (*b*) shoot tips. (1) The uppermost shoot, (2) the second shoot, (3) the third shoot from above. Means of four replicates with SE (bars). (Reproduced from Mor, Spiegelstein and Halevy (1981) by kind permission of authors and publishers.)

promoted (De Munk and Gijzenberg, 1977; Moe, 1979). The ethephon treatment inhibits the transport of ^{14}C-metabolites to the flower bud. Injection of cytokinins or GA into the bulbs partially counteracts the effects of ethylene on both flower development and the transport of carbohydrates to the flower buds. It seems that ethylene weakens, while cytokinins and GA strengthen, the sink activity of the flower bud and its ability to compete with the daughter bulb for the reserve nutrients of the mother bulb.

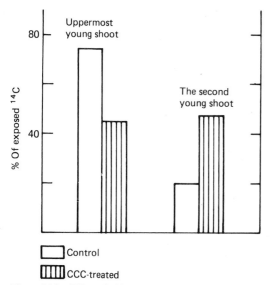

Control
CCC-treated

Figure 26.9 Effect of chlormequat (CCC) applied as soil drench (1 g per plant) on distribution of ^{14}C-assimilates in the two upper young shoots of rose plants (cv. Marimba). (Mor and Halevy, unpublished observations.)

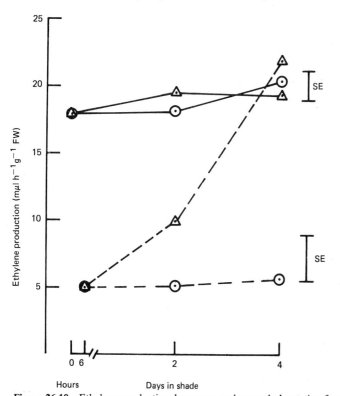

Figure 26.10 Ethylene production by upper and second shoot tips from plants held in full light or in 50% shade. ○, upper shoot; △, second shoot; ———, full light; – – – –, shade. (Reproduced from Zieslin and Halevy (1976) by kind permission of authors and publishers.)

The results presented above indicate that factors which impede the mobilization of carbohydrates from the source (photosynthesizing leaves or storage organs) to the developing flower buds impair the further growth of the buds and promote their abortion. Growth substances seem to play a role in the control of assimilate distribution between the various competing sinks. It is not clear, however, what factors determine the endogenous levels of the growth substances or how they facilitate the allocation and intake of assimilates. Furthermore, treatments that affect the levels and distribution of carbohydrate may also affect production and transport of endogenous growth substances.

It is also not clear whether the decrease in the rate of assimilate transport to the developing flower bud is the cause or the result of the processes leading to flower atrophy. Is assimilate intake controlled by the growth rate of the flower or is the growth rate determined by the rate of intake? As Bodson and Bernier (1985) recently put it: 'From the available information it is not possible to conclude whether the assimilate accumulation in the inflorescence precedes or follows the cellular and metabolic activation linked to the growth of this reproductive structure.' Detailed kinetic studies of these events in the developing flower parts are needed in order to throw light on this question.

Possible regulatory role of specific carbohydrate components in flower development

From the results presented above it is clear that conditions such as low light intensity and other factors that impede flower development and promote abortion are critical at specific stages of flower development. This may indicate that apart from the general non-specific supply of assimilates required for this process, there may be certain specific substances which are transported together with the assimilates and which play a regulatory role in flower development.

Using thin cell-layer explants from tobacco floral branches, Tran Thanh Van and associates (1985) have recently shown that certain oligosaccharides at very low concentrations (10^{-8}–10^{-9} mol l^{-1}) can induce either flowers or vegetative buds in these explants depending on the pH of the medium. These regulatory compounds have been termed oligosaccharins by Albersheim and associates, who also demonstrated their role as elicitors for phytoalexin production in plants infected by certain pathogens (Darvill and Albersheim, 1984).

There are indications that certain oligosaccharides may be involved in the regulation of flower development. Ho and Rees (1976) showed that in tulip plants small quantities of certain oligosaccharides are transported from the scales to the developing flower by the time that rapid growth is about to begin. The normal development of citrus flowers, as of other flower buds, requires a constant supply of carbohydrates, which are normally supplied by the photosynthesizing leaves. Lack of carbohydrates is a major factor responsible for flower bud abscission and alternate bearing (Monselise and Goldschmidt, 1982). However, it was recently found (Vu, Yelenosky and Bausher, 1985) that developing orange flower buds are able to fix directly CO_2 into a number of compounds. The significance of CO_2 fixation by the green flower buds is not clear, but it may satisfy the requirement for specific carbohydrates or other compounds required during the active period of flower development.

Floral malformation in mango is one of the most serious problems of this crop in India and other countries. Flowers of malformed panicles are larger than normal and are mostly male. Sugar levels were found to be significantly higher in normal flowering shoots than in malformed ones. However, the malformed flowering shoots accumulate excessive amounts of acid hydrolysable polysaccharides, which appear to be responsible for the impaired development of the flowers (Pandey, Rao and Pathak, 1977). While none of the above examples can be taken as conclusive evidence for the regulatory role of specific carbohydrates in flower development, they indicate that such a possibility merits serious investigation.

References

ABDUL, K.S., CANHAM, A.E. and HARRIS, G.P. (1978). Effects of CCC on the formation and abortion of flowers in the first inflorescence of tomato (*Lycepersicon esculentum* Mill.). *Annals of Botany*, **42**, 617–625

BODSON, M. and BERNIER, G. (1985). Is flowering controlled by assimilate level? *Physiologie Végétale*, **23**, 491–501

BYRNE, T., HALEVY, A.H., FARNHAM, D. and KOHL, H. (1971). Chemical reduction of leaf drops in greenhouse roses. *Florist's Review*, **149**, 24–26, 71–74

DARVILLE, A.G. and ALBERSHEIN, P. (1984). Phytoalexins and their elicitors—A defence against microbial infection in plants. *Annual Review of Plant Physiology*, **35**, 343–275

DEMUNK, W.J. and GIJZENBERG, J. (1977). Flower-bud blasting in tulip plants mediated by the hormonal status of the plant. *Scientia Horticulturae*, **7**, 255–268

DINAR, M. and RUDICH, J. (1985a). Effect of heat stress on assimilate partitioning in tomato. *Annals of Botany*, **56**, 239–248

DINAR, M. and RUDICH, J. (1985b). Effect of heat stress on assimilate metabolism in tomato flower buds. *Annals of Botany*, **56**, 249–257

DURIEUX, A.J.B., KAMERBEEK, G.A. and VAN MEETEREN, U. (1983). The existence of a critical period for the abscission and a non-critical period for blasting of flower buds of *Lilium* 'Enchantment'; influence of light and ethylene. *Scientia Horticulturae*, **18**, 287–297

ELPHINSTONE, E.D., REES, A.R. and ATHERTON, J.G. (1986). The effect of photoperiod and temperature on the development of Dutch iris flowers and daughter bulbs. *Acta Horticulturae* (in press)

GINZBURG, C. (1974). The effect of gibberellin A_3 and (2-chloroethyl)3 methylammonium chloride on assimilate distribution in gladiolus in relation to corm growth. *Journal of Experimental Botany*, **25**, 995–1003

HALEVY, A.H. (1962). Irrigation experiments with gladioli. In *Advances in Horticultural Science and their Appliances* II, pp. 279–287. Oxford, Pergamon

HALEVY. A.H. (1975). Light energy flux and distribution of assimilates as factors controlling the flowering of flower crops. In *Proceedings of the XIXth International Horticultural Congress*, Warszawa 4, pp. 125–134

HALEVY, A.H. (1984). Light and autonomous induction. In *Light and the Flowering Process* (D. Vince-Prue, B. Thomas and K.E. Cockshull, Eds) pp. 65–73. London, Academic Press

HALEVY, A.H. and MAYAK, S. (1981). Senescence and postharvest physiology of cut flowers, Part 2. *Horticultural Reviews*, **3**, 59–143

HALEVY, A.H. and SHILLO, R. (1970). Promotion of growth and flowering and increase in content of endogenous gibberellins in gladiolus plants treated with the growth retardant CCC. *Physiologia Plantarum*, **23**, 820–827

HARTSEMA, A.M. and LUYTEN, T. (1955). Early flowering of Dutch iris 'Imperator'. V. Light intensity and daylength. *Acta Botanica Neerlandica*, **4**, 370–375

HO, L.C. and REES, A.R. (1975). Aspects of translocation of carbon in the tulip. *New Phytologist*, **74**, 421–428

HO, L.C. and REES, A.R. (1976). Re-mobilization and distribution of reserves in the tulip bulb in relation to new growth until anthesis. *New Phytologist*, **76**, 59–68

HOBSON, G.E. and DAVIES, J.N. (1978). Influence of the extent and duration of cold treatment on the flowering behaviour, composition and metabolic activity of tulip bulbs. *Scientia Horticulturae*, **8**, 279–287

KINET, J.M. (1977a). Effect of light conditions on the development of the inflorescence in tomato. *Scientia Horticulturae*, **6**, 15–26

KINET, J.M. (1977b). Effect of defoliation and growth substances on the development of inflorescence in the tomato. *Scientia Horticulturae*, **6**, 27–35

KINET, J.M., HURDEBISE, D., PARMENTIER, A. and STAINER, R. (1978). Promotion of inflorescence development by growth substance treatment to tomato plants grown in insufficient light conditions. *Journal of the American Society of Horticultural Science*, **103**, 724–729

KINET, J.M., SACHS, R. and BERNIER, G. (1985). *The Physiology of Flowering*, Vol. III, pp. 274. Boca Raton, CRC Press

KRAUS, E.J. and KRAYBILL, H.R. (1918). Vegetation and reproduction with special reference to the tomato. *Oregon Agricultural Experimental Station*, Bulletin 149

LEONARD, M. and KINET, J.M. (1982). Endogenous cytokinin and gibberellin levels in relation to inflorescence development in tomato. *Annals of Botany*, **50**, 127–130

MAE, T. and VONK, C.R. (1974). Effect of light and growth substances on flowering of *Iris* × *hollandica* cv. Wedgwood. *Acta Botanica Neerlandica*, **23**, 321–331

MAY, P. (1965). Reducing inflorescence formation by shading individual sultana buds. *Australian Journal of Biological Sciences*, **18**, 463–473

MOE, R. (1979). Hormonal control of flower blasting in tulips. *Acta Horticulturae*, **91**, 221–228

MOE, R. and WICKENSTROM, A. (1979). Effect of precooling at 5 or −1°C on shoot growth, flowering and carbohydrate metabolism in tulip bulbs. *Scientia Horticulturae*, **10**, 187–201

MONSELISE, S.P. and GOLDSCHMIDT, E.E. (1982). Alternate bearing in fruit trees. *Horticultural Reviews*, **4**, 128–173

MOR, Y. and HALEVY, A.H. (1979). Translocation of ^{14}C-assimilates in roses. I. The effect of the age of the shoot and the location of the source leaf. *Physiologia Plantarum*, **35**, 177–182

MOR, Y. and HALEVY, A.H. (1980). Promotion of sink activity of developing rose shoots by light. *Plant Physiology*, **66**, 990–995

MOR, Y. and HALEVY, A.H. (1984). Dual effect of light on flowering and sprouting of rose shoots. *Physiologia Plantarum*, **61**, 119–124

MOR, Y., HALEVY, A.H. and PORATH, D. (1980). Characterization of the light reaction in promoting the mobilizing ability of rose shoot tips. *Plant Physiology*, **66**, 996–1000

MOR, Y., SPIEGELSTEIN, H. and HALVEY, A.H. (1981). Translocation of ^{14}C-assimilates in roses. II. The effect of shoot darkening and cytokinin application. *Physiologia Plantarum*, **52**, 197–200

MOR, Y., HALEVY, A.H., KOFRANEK, A.M. and KUBOTA, J. (1986). Forcing pot roses from own-root cuttings; effect of growth retardants and light. *Acta Horticulturae* (in press)

NOURAI, A.H.A. and HARRIS, G.P. (1983). Effects of growth retardants on inflorescence development in tomato. *Scientia Horticulturae*, **20**, 341–348

PANDEY, R.M., RAO, M.M. and PATHAK, R.A. (1977). Biochemical changes associated with floral malformation in mango. *Scientia Horticulturae*, **6**, 37–44

ROBINSON, M., HARAV, T., HALEVY, A.H. and PLAUT, Z. (1980). Distribution of assimilates from various source leaves during the development of *Gladiolus grandiflorus*. *Annals of Botany*, **45**, 113–122

ROBINSON, M., HALEVY, A.H., GALILI, D. and PLAUT, Z. (1983). Distribution of assimilates in *Gladiolus grandiflorus* as affected by water deficit. *Annals of Botany*, **51**, 461–468

RODRIGUES PEREIRA, A.S. (1962). Physiological experiments in connection with flower formation in Wedgwood iris. *Acta Botanica Neerlandica*, **11**, 97–138

RUSSELL, C.R. and MORRIS, D.A. (1982). Invertase activity, soluble carbohydrates and inflorescence development in the tomato (*Lycopersicon esculentum*, Mill.). *Annals of Botany*, **49**, 89–98

SANO, Y. (1975). Effect of light and storage nutrition on the growth and flowering in iris 'Wedgwood'. *Journal of the Japanese Society for Horticultural Science*, **44**, 66–72

SEXTON, R., LEWIS, L.N., TREWAVAS, A.J. and KELLY, P. (1985). Ethylene and abscission. In *Ethylene and Plant Development* (J.A. Roberts and G.A. Tucker, Eds), pp. 173–196. London, Butterworths

SHILLO, R. and HALEVY, A.H. (1976a). The effect of various environmental factors on flowering of gladiolus. I. Light intensity. *Scientia Horticulturae*, **4**, 131–137

SHILLO, R. and HALEVY, A.H. (1976b). The effect of various environmental factors on flowering of gladiolus. II. Length of day. *Scientia Horticulturae*, **4**, 139–146

SHILLO, R. and HALEVY, A.H. (1976c). The effect of various environmental factors on flowering of gladiolus. III. Temperature and moisture. *Scientia Horticulturae*, **4**, 147–155

SHILLO, R. and HALEVY, A.H. (1981). Flower and corm development in gladiolus as affected by photoperiod. *Scientia Horticulturae*, **15**, 187–196

TRAN THANH VAN, K., TOUBART, P., COUSSON, A., DARVILL, A.G., GOLLIN, D.J., CHEFF, P. and ALBERSHEIM, P. (1985). Manipulation of the morphogenetic pathways of tobacco explants by oligosaccharides. *Nature (London)*, **314**, 315–317

VAN MEETEREN, U. and DE PROFT, M. (1982). Inhibition of flower bud abscission and ethylene evolution by light and silver thiosulphate in *Lilium*. *Physiologia Plantarum*, **56**, 236–240

VAN STADEN, J. (1977). Seasonal changes in the cytokinin content of the leaves of *Salix babylonica*. *Physiologia Plantarum*, **40**, 296–299

VAN STADEN, J., ZIESLIN, N., SPIEGELSTEIN, H. and HALEVY, A.H. (1981a). The effect of light on the Cytokinin content of developing rose shoots. *Annals of Botany*, **47**, 155–157

VAN STADEN, J., SPIEGELSTEIN, H. ZIESLIN, N. and HALEVY, A.H. (1981b). Endogenous cytokinins and lateral bud growth in roses. *Botanical Gazette*, **142**, 177–182

VONK, C.R. and RIBOT, S.A. (1982). Assimilate distribution and the role of abscissic acid and zeatin in relation to flower-bud blasting, induced by lack of light in *Iris* cv ideal. *Plant Growth Regulation*, **2**, 93–105

VU, J.C.V., YELENOSKY, G. and BAUSHER, M.G. (1985). Photosynthetic activity in the flower buds of 'Valencia' orange (*Citrus sinensis* (L) Osbeck). *Plant Physiology,* **78,** 420–423

ZIESLIN, N. and HALEVY, A.H. (1975). Flower bud atrophy in Baccara roses. II. The effect of environmental factors. *Scientia Horticulturae,* **3,** 383–391

ZIESLIN, N. and HALEVY, A.H. (1976a). Flower bud atrophy in Baccara roses. V. The effect of different growth substances on flowering. *Physiologia Plantarum,* **37,** 326–330

ZIESLIN, N. and HALEVY, A.H. (1976b). Flower bud atrophy in Baccara roses. VI. The effect of environmental factors on gibberellin activity and ethylene production in flowering and non-flowering shoots. *Physiologia Plantarum,* **37,** 331–335

27

THE REGULATION OF ASSIMILATE PARTITION AND INFLORESCENCE DEVELOPMENT IN THE TOMATO

D. A. MORRIS and A.J. NEWELL*
Department of Biology, University of Southampton, UK

Introduction

In many plant species flower initiation terminates further vegetative development and for the remainder of its life the photoassimilatory capacity of the plant is directed towards the provision of substrates for the development and growth of the reproductive organs. In other species, however, vegetative development does not cease when flowers are initiated and successive flowers and new vegetative organs are formed and grow at the same time. In this case available photoassimilates must be partitioned between the simultaneous demands created by vegetative and reproductive sinks.

In the tomato (*Lycopersicon esculentum* Mill.) successive inflorescences, leaves and internodes develop concurrently over an extended period of time. If daily light integrals are low during the early stages of reproductive development in this species, a disproportionate reduction in the growth rate of the first inflorescence takes place compared with the growth of vegetative organs at the shoot apex (Hussey, 1963; Kinet, 1977a). Under extreme conditions, especially if temperatures are high, development of the first inflorescence may be completely arrested and abortion of the flower buds may occur (Cooper and Hurd, 1968; Calvert, 1969; Kinet, 1977a). In a natural plant population a mechanism for diverting assimilates from reproductive organs, which under the prevailing conditions may have little chance of reaching maturity, to growing leaves and internodes at the shoot apex clearly has survival value. In the commercial glasshouse tomato crop, however, such a mechanism can lead to a serious loss of high-value early yield (Calvert, 1969).

Several authors have suggested that the arrested development of the first inflorescence under low light conditions may result from its inability to compete successfully for assimilates with vegetative sinks at the shoot apex (Hussey, 1963; Calvert, 1969) and in the roots (Cooper and Hurd, 1968). Some support for this suggestion is provided by studies of the patterns of carbohydrate distribution in the plant which have revealed that shortly after its macroscopic appearance, the first inflorescence receives the bulk of its assimilates from leaves which, simultaneously, are also major sources of assimilates for the root system and for the growing apical tissues (Russell

*Current address: Department of Plant Sciences, Agricultural Sciences Building, University of Leeds

and Morris, 1982). It is becoming clear, however, that to attribute flower abortion under low-light conditions solely to the failure of the inflorescence to compete successfully with alternative sinks may be too simple an explanation. A growing body of evidence is accumulating which suggests that environmentally-induced changes in the levels and distribution of endogenous plant growth substances may be involved. Whilst these may act locally to influence sink activity (possibly by regulating phloem unloading or modulating the activity in sink tissues of enzymes involved in carbohydrate metabolism), it seems likely that growth substances exported by the vegetative sinks may act more directly to regulate the developmental behaviour of the inflorescence. The preferential diversion of assimilates from reproductive to vegetative sinks under limiting light conditions therefore may be a consequence rather than a cause of events leading to reduced flower bud growth and to abortion.

This chapter reviews evidence linking inflorescence development and assimilate partition in the tomato and speculates on mechanisms which might operate to regulate the inhibition of flower development in unfavourable light conditions.

Effects of source and sink manipulation on inflorescence development

Evidence that development of the first inflorescence in the tomato under unfavourable light conditions may be retarded or aborted as a result of interactions with major vegetative sinks is derived mainly from experiments involving source- or sink-leaf removal, shading treatments, root pruning or root restriction, and application of exogenous plant growth substances. A summary of environmental conditions and experimental treatments which can affect development of the first inflorescence in tomato is given in *Table 27.1*. Removal of young leaves at the shoot tip strongly promotes flower bud development in the first inflorescence under favourable light conditions (Kinet, 1977b; Abdul and Harris, 1978; Russell and Morris, 1982; and references cited by these authors), the greatest promotion occurring when leaves which develop at the same time as the inflorescence itself are excised. Removal of leaves initiated earlier or later than the inflorescence has less effect (Kinet, 1977b). Even under light conditions that favour normal flower development, removal of young leaves at the shoot tip can significantly increase the rate of dry-matter accumulation by the inflorescence (Russell and Morris, 1982). Kinet (1977b) concluded that excision of young leaves promoted flower development by removing the primary competing sinks for assimilates.

In contrast to the effects of removing apical leaves, treatments which reduce total assimilate production by the plant substantially inhibit inflorescence development and may induce flower bud abortion. Such treatments include the excision of source leaves (Saito and Ito, 1974; Russell and Morris, 1982), shading the whole plant (Russell and Morris, 1982; Newell, unpublished observations) and increasing planting densities (Hand and Postlethwaite, 1971; Russell and Morris, 1982). Results from an experiment in which mature foliage leaves and/or the shoot apex (all tissues above and including the first inflorescence) were shaded independently at macroscopic appearance of the flower buds have shown that the primary effect of shading the whole plant is to reduce photoassimilation by the source leaves (Newell, unpublished observations). Shading the apex alone had no effect on the progress of flower bud development compared with unshaded plants, although the rate of dry weight gain by the buds was slightly reduced. Nevertheless, shading the apex alone greatly increased its fresh weight gain and stimulated internode elongation in the apical region. When

Table 27.1 ENVIRONMENTAL CONDITIONS AND EXPERIMENTAL TREATMENTS REPORTED TO INFLUENCE DEVELOPMENT OF THE FIRST INFLORESCENCE IN THE TOMATO

Conditions that promote flower development	*Conditions that inhibit development or cause flower bud abortion*
High light intensities	Low light intensities (especially near 'buds visible')
Short photoperiods	Long photoperiods (at the same total daily radiation)
Low planting densities	High planting densities
Low temperatures	High temperatures (especially if combined with low light)
Root restriction treatments	Phosphorus deficiency
CO_2 enrichment	
Applications of cytokinins and gibberellins to flower buds	Application of gibberellins to leaves
Application of growth retardants and polar auxin transport inhibitors	

the whole plant was shaded, flower bud development was retarded and dry weight gain by the inflorescence was substantially reduced compared with plants in which only the source leaves were shaded. This suggests that when total assimilate availability is lowered by shading the source leaves, a reduction in light intensity at the apex itself may influence inflorescence growth, possibly by stimulating expansion growth in the apical tissues.

Root restriction treatments (e.g., delay in transplanting from pots to greenhouse beds) also may stimulate inflorescence development and reduce flower bud abortion (Cooper and Hurd, 1968), consistent with the observation that roots and first inflorescence receive assimilates from the same source leaves (Russell and Morris, 1983).

The observations cited above support the view that under low-light conditions the retarded development of the first inflorescence may involve diversion of assimilates to vegetative sinks. However, the mechanisms that regulate the partition of assimilates between the reproductive and vegetative sinks under different light conditions remain poorly understood. Development of the inflorescence is most susceptible to unfavourable light conditions for a relatively short period at and just after its macroscopic appearance (Kinet, 1977a), suggesting that events within the flower buds themselves may be important in determining their fate. Several recent reports have indicated that in both the flower buds and the apical leaves levels of plant growth substances may change substantially in response to treatments that modify flower development. Furthermore, applied growth substances may promote flower development under adverse conditions or retard it under marginal light conditions. The regulation of inflorescence development by light may therefore involve correlative interactions between the inflorescence and vegetative sinks which are mediated by endogenous plant growth substances.

Plant growth substances and inflorescence development

That the inhibitory effects of young leaves on flower development in the tomato might be mediated by their production of plant growth substances was suggested by Leopold and Lam (1960). The young leaves have been shown to be sources of gibberellin-like compounds capable of stimulating tomato stem extension, and the activity of these compounds is substantially lower in plants grown at low temperatures that favour flower development under low-light conditions than in plants grown at higher temperatures (Abdul and Harris, 1977, 1978). Applications of gibberellic acid (GA_3) reverse the promotive effects of low temperature on flower development in poor light conditions and reduce flower number still further at high temperatures (Abdul and Harris, 1978).

Consistent with this evidence for a regulatory role of gibberellins in flower development is the observation that several inhibitors of gibberellin biosynthesis can affect flower bud development and abortion (Abdul, Canham and Harris, 1978, and references therein). Treatment of young plants with (2-chloroethyl)-trimethylammonium chloride (CCC) and α-cyclopropyl-α- (4-methoxyphenyl)-5-pyrimidenemethanol (ancymidol) reduced shoot height and dry weight, increased flower number in the first inflorescence and greatly reduced flower bud abortion (Abdul *et al.*, 1978; Nourai and Harris, 1983). Application of GA_3 reversed these effects and CCC reduced the production of gibberellin-like substances by the shoot tip. However, CCC may also have effects unrelated to the inhibition of gibberellin synthesis. Skene (1968) reported

10–20-fold increases in the cytokinin content of xylem sap of grapevines treated with CCC. Cytokinins have been shown to be important in the regulation of flower bud development in the tomato (*see* below). Significantly, N-dimethylaminosuccinamic acid (B-9) also reduced shoot growth, but had no effect on inflorescence development or on the production of gibberellin-like compounds by the shoot tip (Abdul *et al.*, 1978).

Therefore, whilst gibberellins may be involved in the regulation of shoot growth and, by inference, the sink activity of the apical tissues, gibberellins exported from the apical leaves to the inflorescence itself also may influence flower bud development. Flower buds targeted for abortion under low-light conditions contain higher than normal concentrations of gibberellins (Leonard and Kinet, 1982). These authors suggested that gibberellins may be inhibitory in the early stages of flower development. However, when GA_3 or GA_{4+7} are applied directly to the buds they promote rather than inhibit development and may prevent flower abortion in unfavourable light conditions, especially if applied together with, or shortly after, cytokinins (Kinit, 1977b; Kinet *et al.*, 1978; Leonard *et al.*, Newell, unpublished observations).

Cytokinins appear to be important during the early stage of flower bud development and their concentrations are low in buds targeted for abortion under adverse light conditions (Leonard and Kinet, 1982; Kinet and Leonard, 1983). In such buds mitotic activity and nuclear DNA synthesis cease but both resume 16–20 h after the applications of N^6-benzylaminopurine (BAP), alone or in combination with GA_{4+7} (Kinet *et al.*, 1985). It has been proposed that cytokinins and gibberellins may act sequentially, gibberellins regulating the development of flower parts after flower initiation (Kinet, 1977b; Kinet and Leonard, 1983).

The source of the cytokinins in developing flower buds is uncertain and the reduction in cytokinin concentration following exposure of plants to adverse light conditions may be the result of a reduction in the import of cytokinins rather than a change in local biosynthesis. There is evidence that cytokinins produced in the root system are transported to tissues in the shoot (*see* references in Morris, 1981) and it has been found that the retarded inflorescence development and increased flower bud abortion in tomato caused by phosphorus deficiency is associated with a reduced concentration of cytokinins in the root bleeding sap (Menary and van Staden, 1976). Cytokinin concentrations in the xylem sap of *Perilla fructescens* was found to increase five-fold following flower induction in short days (Beever and Woolhouse, 1973). Treatments that polarize assimilate flow in the phloem also lead to the polarized transport of root-derived cytokinins (Morris and Winfield, 1972).

In addition to gibberellins, endogenous auxins also may be involved in correlative interactions between the vegetative tissues of the shoot apex and the developing inflorescence. Applications of 2,3,5-triiodobenzoic acid (TIBA) may reduce the number of mainstem leaves formed prior to flower initiation, particularly if applied at the cotyledon stage (Zimmerman and Hitchcock, 1942; de Waarde and Roodenburg, 1948; de Zeeuw, 1956). The synthetic auxin α-naphthaleneacetic acid (NAA) had the opposite effect (de Zeeuw, 1956). The effect of both compounds was reversed if the young leaves were removed. Teubner and Wittwer (1955, 1957) found that N-aryl- and N-m-tolylphthalamic acids greatly stimulated early flower initiation and growth. Promotion of flowering by morphactins has also been reported (Gauss, 1970). Since TIBA (N-m-tolyl-) and 1-naphthylphthalamic acid (NPA) and morphactins are potent and specific inhibitors of auxin transport in plants, their effects on inflorescence development in the tomato suggest that auxins produced in, and exported from, the shoot apex may be involved in the regulation of reproductive development.

There is little available information on the role, if any, of inhibitors such as abscisic acid (ABA) in the regulation of flower development and abortion in the tomato. However, the striking similarity between the effects of the shoot apex on the behaviour of the first inflorescence and the correlative inhibition of lateral bud growth in many species suggests that investigations of ABA levels in buds targeted for abortion might prove rewarding (cf. Kinet *et al.*, 1978; Tucker, 1980).

Regulation of assimilate partition during inflorescence development

The partition of assimilates between competing sinks is determined by their relative abilities to take up and metabolize or sequester sucrose unloaded from the phloem (Gifford and Evans, 1981; Ho and Baker, 1982; Morris, 1983). In species that translocate sucrose there is frequently a close correlation between the specific activity of acid invertase (EC 3.2.1.26) in sink organs (particularly those undergoing rapid cell expansion) and their rate of growth or rate of assimilate import (reviewed by Morris, 1983; Morris and Arthur, 1984a). Activities of this enzyme, and hence potential rates of sucrose hydrolysis, can change dramatically in response to light and growth substance treatments and these changes may be correlated with altered patterns of sugar metabolism and assimilate distribution (Morris and Arthur, 1984b; 1985a, b; 1986b). In developing tomato fruit the flux of sucrose import in the phloem is inversely correlated with fruit sucrose concentration (Walker and Thornley, 1977; Walker and Ho, 1977) suggesting that the hydrolysis of sucrose by invertase may rate limit import (Walker, Ho and Baker, 1978).

There are some indications that acid invertase may be involved in assimilate partition between the first inflorescence and competing vegetative sinks in the young tomato plant. Spacing, shading and source-leaf removal treatments that reduce inflorescence growth and lead to flower bud abortion also lead to a reduction in the acid invertase content of the inflorescence and a fall in its reducing sugar concentration. Conversely, removal of young leaves at the shoot apex stimulates dry matter accumulation by the inflorescence and increases its acid invertase and reducing sugar content (Russell and Morris, 1982). Shading treatments that cause flower bud abortion lead to an increase in the specific activity of acid invertase in the competing tissues at the shoot apex (Newell, unpublished observations). The inhibition of flower bud abortion by direct applications of BAP + GA$_3$ to the buds of plants grown in low-light conditions is correlated with a three-fold increase in the specific activity of acid invertase in the inflorescence (*Figure 27.1*). The activity of the enzyme in the shoot apex rose substantially in response to the shading treatment, but the increase was smaller in plants that received the growth substance treatment. This is consistent with the observation that treatment of the flower buds with mixtures of cytokinins and gibberellins reduces the rate of dry matter increase by the apical tissues (Kinet *et al.*, 1978; Newell, unpublished observations) and the rate at which they import ^{14}C-labelled assimilates (Leonard *et al.*, 1983). Such growth substance treatments lead to small but significant increases in the concentrations of both sucrose and reducing sugars in the inflorescence, but do not affect sugar or starch concentrations in the apical tissues (Newell, unpublished observations). Tests are continuing to determine which component in the growth substance mixture is responsible for stimulating invertase activity in the flower buds.

In normal light conditions, the activity of acid invertase in the flower buds increases in parallel with the increase in weight of the androecium and falls at, or shortly after,

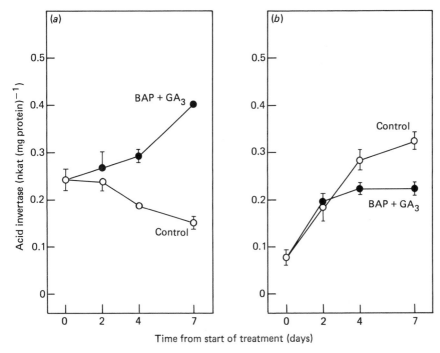

Figure 27.1 Changes in the specific activity of acid invertase in (a) the developing first inflorescence and (b) the shoot apical tissues of young tomato plants following the application of mixtures of BAP (20 mmol l^{-1}) and GA$_3$ (40 mmol l^{-1}) to flower buds. Growth substances were applied daily as 5 μl droplets to the bases of the first fiver flower buds commencing 4 days after the macroscopic appearance of the inflorescence. Ground, freeze-dried samples from 5 to 7 plants per treatment were bulked and extracted in ice-cold phosphate/citrate buffer (pH 5.0). Assay procedures were as described in Morris and Arthur (1984b). Data points are means of assays on four aliquots of the buffer extracts (± standard errors of the means).

anther dehiscence, suggesting that the bulk of the enzyme present in the flower is located in, or regulated by, the stamens (Russell and Morris, 1982). Measurements of enzyme activity in individual flower parts have confirmed the presence of high specific activities of acid invertase in the androecium (Newell, unpublished observations). Together, these observations support the suggestion that by metabolizing sucrose, acid invertase may play a key role in regulating the import of assimilates into sinks (Morris, 1983; Morris and Arthur, 1984a; 1986b) and therefore may be involved in controlling assimilate partition between the inflorescence and the tissues with which it competes. Nevertheless, more evidence is required before such a role for invertase can be established unequivocally, and the mechanism by which activity of the enzyme itself is regulated remains uncertain.

In a range of species increases in cell growth rate and/or assimilate import induced by IAA, gibberellin or cytokinin applications have been found to be closely correlated with increases in acid invertase activity (*see* Morris, 1983; Morris and Arthur, 1984a). GA$_3$ applications to intact bean plants (*Phaseolus vulgaris* L.) which drastically alter the root/shoot partitioning of ^{14}C-labelled assimilates greatly stimulate acid invertase activity in young internodes and reduce its activity in the root (Morris and Arthur, 1985b). It has recently been found that the stimulation of acid invertase activity by

IAA in bean stem segments can occur when IAA-induced cell growth is inhibited, indicating a rather direct effect of IAA on the synthesis or turnover of the enzyme (Morris and Arthur, 1986a). In view of the close similarity between correlative inhibition of axillary bud growth and the inhibitory effect of young apical leaves on the development of the first inflorescence in the tomato, it is of interest that the well-documented ability of IAA applications to replace the inhibitory effect of the shoot apex and to polarize assimilate flow (Morris, 1982; Patrick, 1982) is associated with a large stimulation of acid invertase activity in the IAA-treated tissues (Morris and Arthur, 1986b).

Concluding remarks

The observations discussed in the preceding sections suggest that the effects of daily light integral on inflorescence development, flower bud abortion and assimilate partition between vegetative and reproductive sinks in the tomato are mediated by regulatory mechanisms of considerable complexity. An attempt is made in *Figure 27.2* to summarize in the form of a schematic model possible interrelationships between vegetative organs at the shoot apex and the developing first inflorescence. It is suggested that the progress of inflorescence development may depend on the supply to the flower buds of cytokinins originating elsewhere in the plant. Should this supply decline, for example as a result of a reduction in the flux of phloem translocation to the inflorescence, then development of the flower buds may become arrested and they may abort. Whilst changes in the levels of gibberellins and auxins in the apical tissues may inhibit inflorescence growth indirectly by stimulating invertase activity and sink metabolism in the young leaves and internodes, the observed effects of auxin transport inhibitors in promoting inflorescence development suggest that auxin exported by the apical tissues may be involved more directly in regulating flower bud development. Kinet *et al.* (1978) have drawn attention to the close similarity that exists between apical control of inflorescence development in the tomato and the much-studied correlative inhibition of axillary bud growth.

Auxin transported from the shoot tip appears to be involved in both processes; both axillary bud inhibition and inhibition of flower bud development are relieved by the removal of young leaves (the putative sites of auxin biosynthesis—Schneider and Wightman, 1978); both axillary bud outgrowth and inflorescence development are stimulated by direct applications of cytokinins to the inhibited organs, and such applications promote mitotic activity (Kinet *et al.*, 1985; Nagao and Rubinstein, 1976); in both cases, continued development of the organs after initial release from inhibition by cytokinins requires the application of gibberellins and/or auxins (Catalano and Hill, 1969; Sachs and Thinmann, 1964; Kinet and Leonard, 1983); and in both cases the inhibitory effects of the shoot apex are intensified under conditions that reduce assimilate availability.

The totality of evidence strongly suggests that the regulation of inflorescence development by young leaves may be regarded as a special case of apical dominance. Although the mechanism of correlative inhibition of axillary bud outgrowth by the shoot apex is itself not fully understood, in several species (including the tomato) treatments that suppress axillary bud outgrowth cause high concentrations of ABA to accumulate in the buds or nearby stem tissues (Tucker, 1980). There is some evidence to suggest that IAA may maintain high levels of ABA in stems (Eliasson, 1975). The role of cytokinins in the developing tomato flower buds may be to counteract the

387

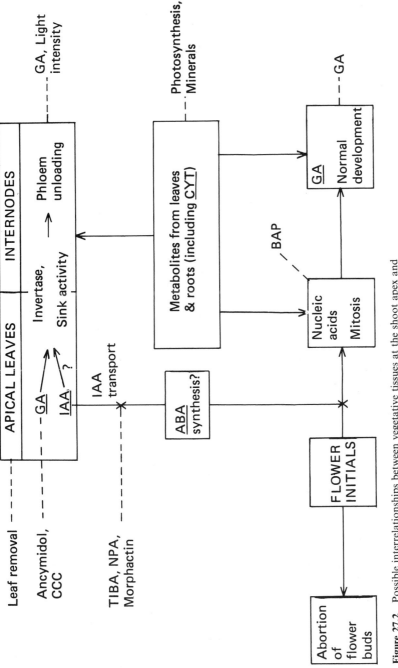

Figure 27.2 Possible interrelationships between vegetative tissues at the shoot apex and the first inflorescence in the tomato, and their modification by environmental factors and growth substance applications. For details, *see* text. Sources of endogenous growth substances are shown underlined; broken lines indicate possible sites of action of external factors and applied growth substances.

inhibitory effects on their development of ABA. It is well known that these compounds have mutually antagonistic effects in a number of developmental processes. Measurements of the concentration of ABA-like inhibitors in the tomato inflorescence during its normal development and under conditions that promote bud abortion clearly would be of considerable interest.

The dominance of young leaves over inflorescence development may therefore result in part from their auxin-mediated effects on the accumulation of inhibitors in the flower buds and in part from their ability to polarize the translocation of assimilates, including phloem-mobile cytokinins, towards the shoot apex. The effect of direct applications of cytokinins to the buds may be to replace the endogenous cytokinins diverted to the shoot apex, thereby reversing the effects of inhibitors accumulating in the buds. Once development of the inflorescence and flower buds is initiated, its continued progress may depend on local mechanisms that regulate its sink activity.

Acknowledgements

We thank Mrs R.P. Bell for assistance with some of the experiments discussed here, and Dr R. Menhenett for much helpful advice and encouragement. Financial support from the Science and Engineering Research Council and the Agricultural and Food Research Council is gratefully acknowledged. We thank the Director, GCRI, Littlehampton for the generous provision of facilities to carry out some of the work described.

References

ABDUL, K.S. and HARRIS, G.P. (1977). An agar-diffusion technique applied to the study of gibberellins in tomato (*Lycoperiscon esculentum* Mill.) plants. *Annals of Botany,* **41**, 369–374

ABDUL, K.S. and HARRIS, G.P. (1978). Control of flower number in the first inflorescence of tomato (*Lycopersicon esculentum* Mill.): The role of gibberellins. *Annals of Botany,* **42**, 1361–1367

ABDUL, K.S., CANHAM, A.E. and HARRIS, G.P. (1978). Effect of CCC on the formation and abortion of flowers in the first inflorescence of tomato (*Lycopersicon esculentum* Mill.). *Annals of Botany,* **42**, 617–625

BEEVER, J.E. and WOOLHOUSE, H.W. (1973). Increased cytokinin from root system of *Perilla fructescens* and flower and fruit development. *Nature (New Biology),* **246**, 31–32

CALVERT, A. (1969). Studies on the post-initiation development of flower buds of tomato (*Lycopersicon esculentum*). *Journal of Horticultural Science,* **44**, 117–126

CATALANO, M. and HILL, T.A. (1969). Interaction between gibberellic acid and kinetin in overcoming apical dominance, natural and induced by IAA, in tomato (*Lycopersicon esculentum* Mill. cultivar Potentate). *Nature (London),* **222**, 985–986

COOPER, A.J. and HURD, R.G. (1968). The influence of cultural factors on arrested development of the first inflorescence of glasshouse tomatoes. *Journal of Horticultural Science,* **43**, 243–248

DE WAARDE, J. and ROODENBURG, J.W.M. (1948). Premature flower bud initiation in tomato caused by 2,3,5-triiodobenzoic acid. *Proceedings, Koninklijke Nederlandse Akademie van Wetenschappen, Amsterdam, Series C,* **51**, 248–251

ELIASSON, L. (1975). Effect of indoleacetic acid on the abscisic acid level in stem tissue. *Physiologia Plantarum,* **34**, 117–120

GAUSS, J.F. (1970). Morphactin: An exciting growth regulator for the study of tomato flower development. *Horticultural Science,* **5**, 319

GIFFORD, R.M. and EVANS, L.T. (1981). Photosynthesis, carbon partitioning and yield. *Annual Review of Plant Physiology,* **32**, 485–509

HAND, D.W. and POSTLETHWAITE, J.D. (1971). The response to CO_2 enrichment of capillary-watered single truss tomatoes at different plant densities and seasons. *Journal of Horticultural Science,* **45**, 19–27

HO, L.C. and BAKER, D.A. (1982). Regulation of loading and unloading in long distance transport systems. *Physiologia Plantarum,* **56**, 225–230

HUSSEY, G. (1963). Growth and development in the young tomato. II. The effect of defoliation on the development of the shoot apex. *Journal of Experimental Botany,* **14**, 326–333

KINET, J.M. (1977a). Effect of light conditions on the development of the inflorescence in tomato. *Scientia Horticulturae,* **6**, 15–26

KINET, J.M. (1977b). Effect of defoliation and growth substances on the development of the inflorescence in tomato. *Scientia Horticulturae,* **6**, 27–35

KINET, J.M. and LEONARD, M. (1983). The role of cytokinins and gibberellins in controlling inflorescence development in tomato. *Acta Horticulturae,* **134**, 117–124

KINET, J.M., HURDEBISE, D., PARAMENTIER, A. and STANIER, R. (1978). Promotion of inflorescence development by growth substance treatments to tomato plants grown in insufficient light conditions. *Journal of the American Society of Horticultural Science,* **103**, 724–729

KINET, J.M., ZUNE, V., LINOTTE, C., JACQUMARD, A. and BERNIER, G. (1985). Resumption of cellular activity induced by cytokinin and gibberellin treatment in tomato flowers targeted for abortion in unfavourable light conditions. *Physologia Plantarum,* **64**, 67–73

LEONARD, M. and KINET, J.M. (1982). Endogenous cytokinin and gibberellin levels in relation to inflorescence development in tomato. *Annals of Botany,* **50**, 127–130

LEONARD, M., KINET, J.M., BODSON, M. and BERNIER, G. (1983). Enhanced inflorescence development in tomato by growth substance treatments in relation to ^{14}C-assimilate distribution. *Physiologia Plantarum,* **57**, 85–89

LEOPOLD, A.C. and LAM, S.L. (1960). A leaf factor influencing tomato earliness. *Journal of the American Society of Horticultural Science,* **76**, 543–547

MENARY, R.C. and VAN STADEN, J. (1976). Effect of phosphorus nutrition and cytokinins on flowering in the tomato, *Lycopersicon esculentum* Mill. *Australian Journal of Plant Physiology,* **3**, 201–205

MORRIS, D.A. (1981). Distribution and metabolism of root-applied cytokinins in *Pisum sativum. Physiologia Plantarum,* **52**, 251–256

MORRIS, D.A (1982). Hormonal regulation of sink invertase activity. *Plant Growth Substances 1982* (P.F. Wareing, Ed.), pp. 659–668. London, Academic Press

MORRIS, D.A. (1983). Hormonal regulation of assimilate partition. Possible mediation by invertase. *News Bulletin, British Plant Growth Regulator Group,* **6**, 23–35

MORRIS, D.A. and ARTHUR, E.D. (1984a). Invertase activity in sinks undergoing cell expansion. *Plant Growth Regulation,* **2**, 327–337

MORRIS, D.A. and ARTHUR, E.D. (1984b). An association between acid invertase activity and cell growth during leaf expansion in *Phaseolus vulgaris* L. *Journal of Experimental Botany,* **35**, 1369–1379

MORRIS, D.A. and ARTHUR, E.D. (1985a). Invertase activity, carbohydrate metabolism and cell expansion in the stem of *Phaseolus vulgaris* L. *Journal of Experimental Botany*, **36**, 623–633

MORRIS, D.A. and ARTHUR, E.D. (1985b). Effects of gibberellic acid on patterns of carbohydrate distribution and acid invertase activity in *Phaseolous vulgaris*. *Physiologia Plantarum*, **65**, 257–262

MORRIS, D.A. and ARTHUR, E.D. (1986a). Stimulation of acid invertase by indol-3yl-acetic acid in tissues undergoing cell expansion. *Plant Growth Regulation* (in press).

MORRIS, D.A. and ARTHUR, E.D. (1986b). Auxin-induced assimilate translocation in the bean stem (*Phaseolus vulgaris* L.). *Plant Growth Regulation*, **4**, 259—271

MORRIS, D.A. and WINFIELD, P.J. (1972). Kinetin transport to the axillary buds of dwarf pea (*Pisum sativum* L.). *Journal of Experimental Botany*, **23**, 346–355

NAGAO, M.A. and RUBINSTEIN, B. (1976). Early events associated with lateral bud growth in *Pisum sativum* L. *Botanical Gazette*, **137**, 39–44

NOURAI, A.H.A. and HARRIS, G.P. (1983). Effects of growth retardants on inflorescence development in tomato (*Lycopersicon esculentum*). *Scientia Horticulturae*, **20**, 341–348

PATRICK, J.W. (1982). Hormonal control of assimilate transport. In *Plant Growth Substances 1982* (P.F. Wareing, Ed.), pp. 669–678. London, Academic Press

RUSSELL, C.R. and MORRIS, D.A. (1982). Invertase activity, soluble carbohydrates and inflorescence development in the tomato (*Lycopersicon esculentum* Mill.). *Annals of Botany*, **49**, 89–98

RUSSELL, C.R. and MORRIS, D.A. (1983). Patterns of assimilate distribution and source-sink relationships in the young reproductive tomato plant (*Lycopersicon esculentum* Mill.). *Annals of Botany*, **52**, 357–363

SACHS, T. and THIMANN, K.V. (1964). Release of lateral buds from apical dominance. *Nature (London)*, **201**, 939–940

SAITO, T. and ITO, H. (1974). Studies on growth and flowering in the tomato. XV. Role of mature leaves and immature leaves on the development of the flower especially that of the ovary. *Journal of the Japanese Society for Horticultural Science*, **42**, 310–316

SCHNEIDER, E.A. and WIGHTMAN, F. (1978). Auxins. In *Phytohormones and Related Compounds—A Comprehensive Treatise* (D.S. Letham, P.B. Goodwin and T.J.V. Higgins, Eds), pp. 29–105. Amsterdam, Elsevier/North Holland

SKENE, K.G.M. (1968). Increases in the levels of cytokinins in bleeding sap of *Vitis vinifera* L. after CCC treatment. *Science*, **159**, 1477–1478

TEUBNER, F.G. and WITTWER, S.H. (1955). Effects of N-m-tolylphthalamic acid on tomato flower formation. *Science*, **122**, 74–75

TEUBNER, F.G. and WITTWER, S.H. (1957). Effect of N-arylphthalmic acids on tomato flower production. *Proceedings of the American Society for Horticultural Science*, **69**, 343–351

TUCKER, D.J. (1980). Apical dominance—a personal view. *News Bulletin, British Plant Growth Regulator Group*, **4**, 1–9

WALKER, A.J. and THORNLEY, J.M.H. (1977). The tomato fruit: import, growth, respiration and carbon metabolism at different fruit sizes and temperatures. *Annals of Botany*, **41**, 977–985

WALKER, A.J. and HO, L.C. (1977). Carbon translocation in the tomato: effects of fruit temperature on carbon metabolism and the rate of translocation. *Annals of Botany*, **41**, 825–832

WALKER, A.J., HO, L.C. and BAKER, D.A. (1978). Carbon translocation in the tomato: pathways of carbon metabolism in the fruit. *Annals of Botany*, **42**, 901–909

ZEEUW, D. DE (1956). Leaf induced inhibition of flowering in tomato. *Proceedings, Koninklijke Nederlandse Akademie van Wetenschappen, Amsterdam, Series C,* **59,** 535–540

ZIMMERMAN, P.W. and HITCHCOCK, A.E. (1942). Flowering habit and correlation of organs modified by 2,3,5-triiodobenzoic acid. *Contributions of the Boyce Thompson Institute,* **12,** 491

28

FLOWER DEVELOPMENT IN THE BULBOUS IRIS

E.D. ELPHINSTONE and A.R. REES
Crop Science Division, Glasshouse Crops Research Institute, Littlehampton, UK

J.G. ATHERTON
Department of Agriculture and Horticulture, University of Nottingham, UK

Introduction

The Dutch iris is a hybrid bulbous plant, in which growth and flowering can be manipulated using storage temperature treatments ('forcing') to obtain cut flowers out of their natural flowering season, which in the UK is April to June. A developmental disorder, 'blasting', or flower-bud abortion can prevent the production of a harvestable flower, particularly when iris bulbs are forced during low irradiance conditions in winter. Unfortunately this is the time when there is a great demand for high-quality iris flowers. Since each bulb planted is relatively costly, such losses cannot be tolerated by growers (Walla and Kristoffersen, 1969).

Aborted flower-buds appear papery, dry and brown. They fail to increase in length or weight (general atrophy), and flower stem extension stops. *Figure 28.1* shows a bud developing normally and one at a slightly later stage of development that has aborted. Bud abortion is usually accompanied by the drying and abortion of the two spathe leaves (*Figure 28.2*) but other leaves are not affected. No abscission of either the buds or the spathe leaves follows flower abortion.

Previous work has shown that flower abortion occurs in forced bulbs after planting, at high temperatures and low irradiances, or if plants are subjected to water stress (Hartsema and Luyten, 1955; Kamerbeek, 1969; Fortanier and Zevenbergen, 1973). In general those conditions that are thought to lead a reduced carbohydrate status of the plant following planting are known to cause flower abortion. The influence of light on flower development, however, has been shown by Mae and Vonk (1974) not to be solely attributable to the level of assimilates from photosynthesis. They investigated flower development under normal (56 W m^{-2}) or low (2.6 W m^{-2}) light and normal (0.03%) or low (0.003%) CO_2 concentration. The reduced CO_2 level allowed normal flower development, whereas reducing the light level but maintaining normal CO_2 concentration resulted in fewer flowers developing. Following investigation of the movement of ^{14}C and ^{32}P under light and dark treatments, it was concluded that light promotes the movement of carbohydrates in the direction of the developing flower bud. Mor and Halevy (1980) comment on a similar effect of light in rose.

Flower development in iris under low light can be improved by injecting cytokinin into the bud (Mae and Vonk, 1974). This treatment also increased the movement of ^{14}C-assimilates towards the bud. Vonk and Ribot (1982) detected a rise in ABA activity in buds that were subjected to a prolonged dark treatment and postulated that cytokinin binds with the ABA causing the activity of the latter to fall.

Figure 28.1   Iris flower-buds (A) aborted and (B) developing normally.

Temperature treatments given before flower initiation to obtain marketable flowers outside the natural season can also affect flower abortion. The standard treatments given to unplanted bulbs in dark, controlled temperature stores include an initial high temperature treatment (> 25°C), which allows the production of further foliar leaves and prevents the formation of a daughter bulb at the apex (Kamerbeek, 1965) followed by a cool temperature treatment (< 17°C), at which flowers initiate. Both treatments increase the rate of flower development.

This chapter describes investigations into the effects of pre-planting storage temperatures and conditions in the glasshouse during growth, on flower and whole-plant development. The aim was to elucidate the mechanism of flower-bud abortion.

The influence of pre-planting treatments on flower development

Pre-planting temperature treatments could influence post-initiation flower development in two ways:

Figure 28.2 Flower-bud abortion accompanied by drying of the two spathe leaves enclosing the bud. The other leaves grow normally.

1. Directly, by changing the way in which the flower initiates. For example, adverse temperatures during gynoecium initiation result in abnormal gynoecium formation which may affect subsequent flower development. We have observed previously that the gynoecium is the first floral organ to show signs of abortion when a bud fails. By removing parts of the flower, Vonk and Ribot (1982) concluded that the gynoecium played an important role in the promotion of stem extension.

2. Indirectly, by influencing aspects of development elsewhere in the plant, which in turn influence the flower development. For example, low pre-planting temperatures induce the formation of daughter-bulbs and subsequent warmer temperatures favour their growth (Le Nard, 1973; Sano, 1974a). This increases competition between the daughter bulbs and the flower. The lower the storage temperature, the earlier flowering occurs in the plant's development, i.e. after fewer leaves have been initiated (Blaauw, 1941; Sano, 1974b). Pre-planting

temperatures also influence the rate of leaf growth and the final leaf length. Leaf growth is stimulated by storing the bulbs at 17°C before 9°C and is reduced by reversing the treatment (Schipper, 1983). As storage temperatures are increased from 8 to 20°C the final leaf length is increased (Sano, 1974c). Leaf number and leaf growth are therefore influenced by pre-planting temperature treatments. Storage temperatures also affect the mobilization of reserves in the mother bulb and hence their availability for the flower and other sinks. Starch hydrolysis increases as temperatures fall from 25 to 10°C and then decreases again at temperatures lower than 10°C (Halevy, 1963).

The indirect influence is examined here. Previous reports have suggested that to allow a greater proportion of the mother-bulb reserves for flower growth and development, leaf growth should be reduced to a minimum (Fortanier and Zeven-bergen, 1973; Kamerbeek, Durieux and Schipper, 1980; Schipper, 1981). Increased vegetative growth, encouraged by pre-planting treatments, would therefore be expected to result in increased failure of flower development. This was tested by subjecting bulbs to a range of pre-planting cold treatments that would give rise to plants showing differing degrees of vegetative growth and possessing various sinks in major competition with the flower.

Following treatment, bulbs were planted in the glasshouse under conditions that would not, *per se*, cause abortion but would allow the influence of the pre-planting treatment to be assessed. Plants were harvested for growth analysis when either the first bud had reached anthesis or, if judged to have aborted by gentle squeezing (the so-called 'pinch' test; Vonk and Ribot, 1982), when most of the other plants from that treatment reached anthesis. Correlation coefficients were calculated to determine the relationships, if any, between the development of the flowers and the growth of various other plant parts. Comparisons of the number of buds, dry weight of the flower and stem and the number of days to anthesis were made with other aspects of whole plant growth as shown in *Table 28.1*. The only negative correlation was found between mother-bulb dry weight at harvest and the number of buds developing or flower plus stem dry weight. The relationship between the dry weight of the flower and stem at harvest, and the degree of flower development was established. The heavier the flower and stem the greater was the possibility of two or more buds per plant developing (*Figure 28.3*). This supports the findings of Fortanier and Zevenbergen (1973) who found that stem extension stopped in plants when flowers aborted.

Table 28.1 CORRELATION COEFFICIENTS (*r*) BETWEEN FLOWER DEVELOPMENT AND VEGETATIVE GROWTH

Comparison	*Logit (% bulbs with 2+ buds developing)*	*Flower + stem dry weight*	*Days to anthesis*
1. Leaf dry weight	0.75	0.89	0.85
2. Daughter bulb DW	0.39*	0.55	0.29*
3. Vegetative DW (1 + 2)	0.76	0.94	0.78
4. Mother bulb DW	− 0.63	− 0.56	− 0.43*
5. Days to anthesis	0.59	0.83	—
6. Rate of vegetative growth (3/5)	0.79	0.97	0.78
7. Stem length	0.82	0.96	0.83
8. Flower/stem DW	0.77	—	0.83

Comparisons marked * were not significant (p > 0.05).

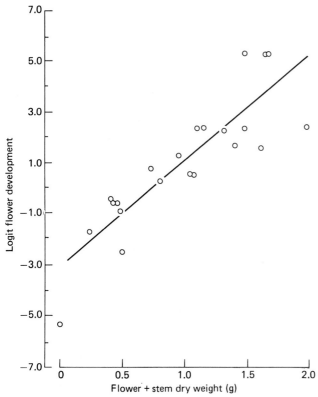

Figure 28.3 Relationship between logit percentage flower development to anthesis and the mean flower and stem dry weight for 'Wedgwood' 10+ and 8–9 cm grades over three planting dates. $r^2 = 0.73$ (p = 0.001).

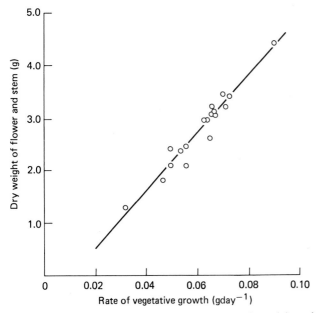

Figure 28.4 Relationship between flower and stem dry weight and the rate of vegetative growth. $y = -0.566 + 55.0x$. $r^2 = 0.94$ (p = 0.001).

There was also a strong correlation between flower and stem dry weight and leaf dry weight. No significant correlation existed between flower development and daughter bulb dry weight. When leaf and daughter bulb dry weights were combined to give total vegetative dry matter in competition with the flower and stem, a good positive correlation was found ($r^2 = 0.88$, $p = 0.001$). The rate of vegetative growth compared with the final flower and stem dry weight gave a linear relationship with even better fit (*Figure 28.4*). Hence, the more rapid the vegetative growth due to the influence of the pre-planting treatment, the more likely was the development of the flower buds to anthesis.

Effect of post-planting treatments on flower development

Having established how the relationship between vegetative growth and floral development is influenced by pre-planting temperatures, post-planting treatments were investigated. Bulbs were retarded at high temperatures for different periods to give three planting dates, following identical cool treatments for flower initiation. Plants were then forced at four different temperatures in the glasshouse under three different levels of irradiance. Mean daily temperatures above 18°C significantly reduced the proportion of bulbs in which a flower reached anthesis. Increased light integral allowed more flowers to develop even at the higher temperatures. These results are in agreement with several previous reports (Hartsema and Luyten, 1955; Kamerbeek, 1966; Fortanier and Zevenbergen, 1973).

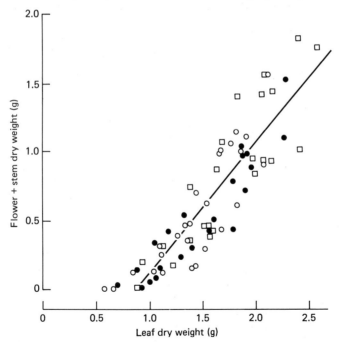

Figure 28.5   Relationship between the dry weight of the flower and stem and the dry weight of leaves. $r^2 = 0.82$ ($p = 0.001$). ○ = planting date I; ● = planting date II; □ = planting date III.

Post-planting conditions were shown to affect the relationship between vegetative growth and floral development in that the flower plus stem dry weight was again shown to increase directly in proportion to the degree of flower development. The dry weight of leaves and the dry weight of the flower plus stem were also examined for the different treatments. *Figure 28.5* shows a linear relationship between these for the three planting dates and two grades of mother-bulbs planted (10+ and 8–9 cm circumference bulbs). The number of leaves did not differ between treatments for a given planting date. It appears important therefore to obtain an increase in vegetative growth in order to achieve high flower and stem dry weights that coincide with more flowers developing to anthesis.

Distribution of ^{14}C-assimilates

The sequence of demands for assimilates by various plant parts during forcing were examined by feeding plants with $^{14}CO_2$ through the second leaf and then determining the distribution of ^{14}C-labelled assimilates exported 24 h later. *Figure 28.6* shows the distribution of these exported ^{14}C-assimilates for plants harvested 15, 28 or 42 days after planting. The relative specific activity (RSA) was also calculated according to the method of Mor and Halevy (1979):

$$RSA = \frac{dpm\ g^{-1}\ in\ a\ specified\ plant\ part}{dpm\ g^{-1}\ of\ the\ whole\ plant,\ excluding\ the\ source\ leaf}$$

where $dpm\ g^{-1}$ is the disintegrations per minute for each gram of dry matter. The RSA provides an estimate of the relative sink strength of a given plant part, independent of the size of the organs (*Figure 28.7*). Some plants were transferred to low irradiance conditions 14 days before labelling to observe the effect of low light on the distribution of assimilates and relative sink strength. The demand from growing leaves for assimilates and whether or not this coincided with demands from the flower were of particular interest in view of the results presented above.

The proportion of assimilates exported from the source leaf which were recovered in other leaves was at a maximum soon after planting, then declined with successive harvests and was negligible by day 42. The ^{14}C-assimilates recovered from rapidly growing, young leaves was always significantly higher for plants in low light than in high light (p = 0.001). Similarly, the RSA of the leaves declined between day 15 and 28 and remained low subsequently. This was unaffected by irradiance level. The percentage of exported ^{14}C-assimilates recovered in the flower and stem and their RSA followed a similar pattern in that both were reduced by low irradiance at the first harvest (day 15), and the last (day 42, p = 0.01).

The flower competes for current assimilates with various other plant parts during its development to anthesis. Soon after planting, there was significant competition from the leaves and this was more marked under reduced light. Leaf competition decreased as leaves approached their full size. Plants that were transferred back to normal light at this stage showed normal flower development. Increased competition between leaves and the flower was not as detrimental to flower development at this stage as it was later. This later, critical, stage of development had been identified previously by Hartsema and Luyten (1961), Fortanier and Zevenbergen (1973) and Mae and Vonk (1974). In the experiments described here, it occurred 42 days after planting. At this time the main competition was between the flower plus stem and the

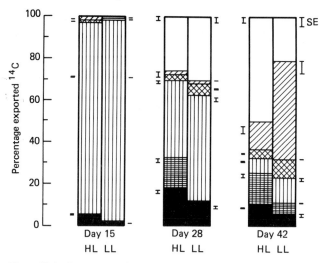

Figure 28.6   Percentage of exported ^{14}C assimilates distributed to the various plant parts under high (HL) or low (LL) light on three harvest dates from planting. (*See Figure 28.7* for key.)

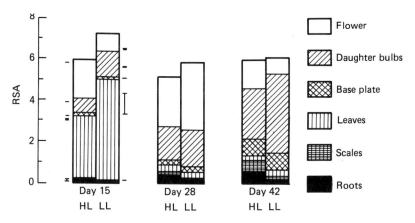

Figure 28.7   Relative specific activity (RSA) of the various plant parts under high (HL) or low (LL) light for three harvest dates from planting.

daughter bulbs. The RSA of the daughter bulbs was always greater under low light than under high. This is consistent with previous results obtained when investigating daughter bulb growth in competition with the flower (Elphinstone, Rees and Atherton, 1986).

Ho and Rees (1975, 1976, 1977) showed that current assimilates in the tulip contributed mainly to the growth of the flower plus stem and to the growth of the daughter bulbs only after anthesis. This was despite the daughter bulbs having a higher sink strength than the flower. The scales of the mother bulb were able to satisfy the carbohydrate demands of the daughter bulbs. With iris, current assimilate was detected in the mother-bulb scales at the time of the final harvest. In high light the import of assimilates into the scales started earlier than in low light. Mae and Vonk (1974) also observed movement of current assimilate into the scales of the old mother bulb at this critical stage for flower development. The scales had apparently switched from being a source to a sink. Whilst the purpose of these assimilates in the old scales is unknown, they could permit a continuous supply of carbohydrates to the developing bud, which Sano (1974a) considered necessary to avoid abortion. Mother-bulb scales could act as a temporary store for assimilates which are then remobilized during the night or during times of low light integral.

Carbohydrate analysis of the flower buds

Changes in carbohydrate composition of the developing flower under various light regimes were then determined.

Fresh flower bud material was cut into small pieces and dropped immediately into boiling absolute ethanol to which a little calcium carbonate had been added. The bud material was then extracted for a further 6 hours in 80% (v/v) aqueous ethanol. The extracts were combined and reduced by evaporation at low pressure before clarification with neutral lead acetate and sodium oxalate (Anon, 1975). Sugars in this alcohol extract were identified as mainly fructose, glucose and sucrose using HPLC with 80% acetonitrile as a solvent. After the required dilution, samples were analysed on a Technicon autoanalyser using a copper-neocuproine method (Bittner and Manning, 1967). Sucrose was then determined by acid hydrolysis of the ethanol extract and the reducing sugars again determined. The difference between the reducing sugars before and after acid hydrolysis gave the concentration of sucrose in the extract. Starch was determined in the alcohol-insoluble material which was ground and gelatinized. The reducing sugars were then determined after hydrolysis with amyloglucosidase enzyme.

Buds were taken from plants that had been grown under unshaded or shaded conditions for the previous 14 days. Effects of cytokinin on bud abortion and carbohydrate changes were also determined. Buds were injected either with benzylaminopurine (BA) 1 ml, 10^{-4} mol l^{-1}, in 0.5% DMSO or with 0.5% DMSO. Only those buds showing no sign of abortion were taken for analysis.

The carbohydrate content of the buds showed large variation within treatments making it difficult to draw conclusions (*Figures 28.8* and *28.9*). This was possibly the result of a wide range of developmental stages obtained from the single harvest.

Hexose content per gram dry weight of bud was greater under low light than high light. As the buds from the high-light treatment were heavier than those from the low light, the hexose content of buds of similar weight were not significantly different between treatments. The water content of the buds in low light was greater than that of buds grown in high light. The higher proportion of hexoses in the dry material could have had a role in maintaining a higher osmotic potential to support this greater water content. The proportion of sucrose, on both a dry-weight and a per-bud basis, was greater under high light than low. With a greater photosynthetic rate under high than low light the gradient of carbohydrate concentration between source and sink would also be steeper. Hence the movement of sucrose, the major translocated sugar, would be greater under high light. Cytokinin increased the sucrose content of the bud as a whole but did not significantly affect the proportion of sucrose per gram dry weight. Thus the supply of sucrose to the bud was increased by cytokinin but the ratio of sucrose to other dried material was not changed by cytokinin treatment. The

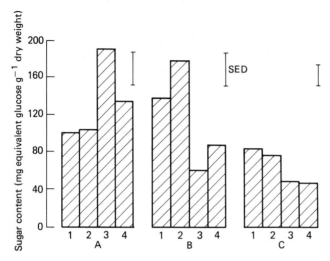

Figure 28.8   Sugar content (mg equivalent of glucose) per gram of dry bud material from plants grown under unshaded or shaded conditions, with or without cytokinin application. A = Hexoses, B = sucrose, C = starch. 1 = Unshaded without exogenous cytokinin. 2 = Unshaded with exogenous cytokinin. 3 = Shaded without exogenous cytokinin. 4 = Shaded with exogenous cytokinin.

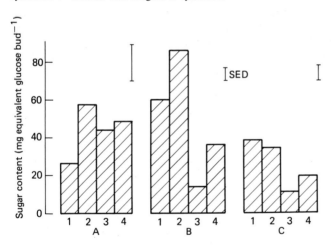

Figure 28.9   Sugar content (mg equivalent of glucose) extracted from a bud of average dry weight from each treatment, unshaded, shaded and with or without cytokinin. A = Hexoses, B = sucrose, C = starch. 1 = Unshaded without exogenous cytokinin. 2 = Unshaded with exogenous cytokinin. 3 = Shaded without exogenous cytokinin. 4 = Shaded with exogenous cytokinin.

starch content of flower buds was greater in high light than low light. The content of starch was related more to the light intensity increasing photosynthesis than to the ability of cytokinins to increase the sink strength of the bud. The proportion of starch in the dry matter remained unaltered by light or cytokinin treatments.

These results suggest that cytokinin increases the turnover and metabolism of sucrose, causing greater concentration gradients between the source (leaf) and sink (bud). Alternatively, light may increase the availability of carbohydrates but not necessarily the turnover, resulting in the storage of carbohydrates as starch. Low levels of carbohydrate production by the leaves, even when the turnover of sucrose at the bud was increased using cytokinin, did not result in heavier buds. The production of carbohydrates was then the limiting factor.

Conclusions

The major cause of flower-bud abortion in iris appears to be preferential distribution of carbohydrate to the daughter bulbs rather than to the flower. The initial mobilization of reserves in the bulb is sufficiently rapid to allow adequate leaf growth; therefore the leaves are not competing with the flower bud at the critical stage when it is most prone to abortion. Instead they are the source of assimilates essential to support the development both of the flower and of the daughter bulbs. By the critical stage for flower abortion, the old mother bulbs were importing assimilates regardless of growing conditions.

The heavier the leaves produced, the greater was the growth of the flower. The morphology of iris leaves suggests that they are poor interceptors of available light. When the leaves are short they remain erect and close to the flower stem, with a large degree of mutual shading. As the length of the leaves increases, they bend away from the flower stem exposing more leaf surface at a suitable angle allowing greater interception of available light. The more the leaf extends therefore, the greater become the chances of supplying the required assimilates for flower development.

Competition between vegetative growth and floral development has been shown to occur in other plant species, e.g. *Lycopersicon esculentum* (Kinet, 1977); *Bougainvillea* (Tse *et al.*, 1974) and *Vitis vinifera* (Mullins 1968). In such plants the initiation and early growth of young leaves, which are sinks for assimilates, occurs simultaneously with the development of the flowers. The young leaves and flowers are both competing for current assimilates, both organs being of similar sink strengths. In iris all the leaves and flower are initiated within the mother bulb utilizing stored reserves. After planting the leaves elongate first and at the time of highest assimilate demand by the flower, during stem extension, the necessity for assimilates for leaf growth is minimal.

Promotion of flower development by high irradiance appears to be mainly a result of a greater supply of assimilates following increased photosynthesis, whereas cytokinin applied to the flower appears to increase sucrose metabolism, thereby increasing the flower sink strength for sucrose.

Acknowledgements

This work was supported by a Postgraduate Studentship (E.D.E.) from the Agricultural and Food Research Council.

References

ANON. (1975). In *Official Methods of Analysis of the AOCA* (W. Horwitz, Ed.), 12th edn., p. 568. Washington, AOCA

BITTNER, D.L. and MANNING, J. (1967). Automated neocuproine glucose method: critical factors and normal values. In *Automation of Analytical Chemistry*, pp. 33–36. New York, Technicon Symposium

BLAAUW, A.H. (1941). On the relation between flower formation and temperature I. (Bulbous Irises). *Proceedings Section of Sciences Kon. Nederlandse Akademie van Wetenschappen*, **44**, 513–520

ELPHINSTONE, E.D., REES, A.R. and ATHERTON, J.G. (1986). The effect of photoperiod and temperature on the development of Dutch iris flowers and daughter bulbs. *Acta Horticulturae*, (in press)

FORTANIER, E.J. and ZEVENBERGEN, A. (1973). Analysis of the effects of temperature and light after planting on bud blasting in *Iris hollandica*. *Netherlands Journal of Agricultural Science*, **21**, 145–162

HALEVY, A.H. (1963). Metabolic changes in Wedgwood iris as influenced by storage temperature of bulbs. In *Proceedings of the Sixteenth International Horticultural Congress 1962* (A. Lecranier and A.I. Croessels, Eds), pp. 220–228. National Vegetable Research Station Library, Wellesbourne

HARTSEMA, A.M. and LUYTEN, I. (1955). Early flowering of Dutch iris 'Imperator' V. Light intensity and daylength. *Acta Botanica Neerlandica*, **4**, 370–375

HARTSEMA, A.M. and LUYTEN, I. (1961). Snelle bloei van iris Wedgwood IIIA and IIIB. Invloed van temperatuur en licht. *Proceedings of the Kon. Nederlandse Akademie van Wetenschappen (Series C)*, **64**, 600–616, 617–629

HO, L.C. and REES, A.R. (1975). Aspects of translocation of carbon in the tulip. *New Phytologist*, **74**, 421–428

HO, L.C. and REES, A.R. (1976). Re-mobilization and redistribution of reserves in the tulip bulb in relation to new growth until anthesis. *New Phytologist*, **76**, 59–68

HO, L.C. and REES, A.R. (1977). The contribution of current photosynthesis to growth and development in the tulip during flowering. *New Phytologist*, **78**, 68–70

KAMERBEEK, G.A. (1965). Temperature treatment of Dutch iris bulbs in relation to the development. In *Report of the First International Symposium on Iris, Florence 1963*, pp. 459–75.

KAMERBEEK, G.A. (1966). Influence of light, temperature and other factors on bud blast of Dutch irises. In *Proceedings of the Seventeenth International Horticultural Congress, Maryland, 1* (R.E. Marshall, Ed.), No. 233. National Vegetable Research Station Library, Wellesbourne

KAMERBEEK, G.A. (1969). Influence of light and temperature on flower bud development in bulbous irises (*Iris* cv. Wedgwood) and lilies (*Lilium* cv. 'Enchantment'). *Acta Horticulturae*, **14**, 175.

KAMERBEEK, G.A., DURIEUX, A.J.B. and SCHIPPER, J.A. (1980). Analysis of the influence of ethrel on flowering in iris 'Ideal': an associated morphogenic physiological approach. *Acta Horticulturae*, **109**, 234–240

KINET, J.M. (1977). Effect of defoliation and growth substances on the development of the inflorescence in tomato. *Scientia Horticulturae*, **6**, 27–35

LE NARD, M. (1973). Influence de la température de conservation des bulbes sur la différenciation d'organes aériens leur élongation et la bulbification chez l'iris bulbeux hollandais var 'Wedgwood'. *Annales de l'Amélioration des Plantes*, **23**, 265–278

MAE, T. and VONK, C.R. (1974). Effect of light and growth substances on flowering of *Iris* × *hollandica* cv. Wedgwood. *Acta Botanica Neerlandica*, **23**, 321–331

MOR, Y. and HALEVY, A.H. (1979). Translocation in roses I. The effect of the age of the shoot and the location of the source leaf. *Physiologia Plantarum*, **45**, 177–182

MULLINS, M.G. (1968). Regulation of inflorescence growth in cuttings of grape vine (*Vitis vinifera* L.). *Journal of Experimental Botany*, **19**, 532–543

SANO, Y. (1974a). Studies on the flowering of bulbous iris. *Journal of the Faculty of Agriculture, Shinshu University*, **11**, 93–181

SANO, Y. (1974b). Effect of temperature on the flower bud formation in iris 'Wedgwood'. *Journal of the Japanese Society for Horticultural Science*, **42**, 84–90

SANO, Y. (1974c). Relation between the physiological condition of bulbs and the effect of low temperature on the flower bud formation in iris 'Wedgwood'. *Journal of the Japanese Society for Horticultural Science*, **42**, 333–340

SCHIPPER, J.A. (1981). Rookbehandeling van irisbollen leidt tot bloeiverhoging. *Vakblad voor Bloemisterij*, **36**, 40–41

SCHIPPER, J.A. (1983). Geremde teelt van iris. *Hobaho*, **57**, 6–7

TSE, A.T.Y., RAMINA, A., HACKETT, W.P. and SACHS, R.M. (1974). Enhanced inflorescence development in *Bougainvillea*. *Plant Physiology*, **54**, 404–407

VONK, C.R. and RIBOT, S.A. (1982). Assimilate distribution and the role of abscisic acid and zeatin in relation to flower-bud blasting, induced by lack of light, in iris cv. Ideal. *Plant Growth Regulation*, **1**, 93–105

WALLA, I. and KRISTOFFERSEN, T. (1969). Some factors affecting the results of early forcing of *Iris* × *hollandica* 'Wedgwood'. *Acta Horticulturae*, **14**, 187–191

VIII

The future

29

TOWARDS A BETTER UNDERSTANDING AND USE OF THE PHYSIOLOGY OF FLOWERING

L.T. EVANS
CSIRO Division of Plant Industry, Canberra, Australia

Introduction

The title of this book emphasizes the *manipulation of flowering*: the uses to which the physiology and genetics of flowering can be put. Most scientists would hold strongly to the view that, in the long run, the most effective manipulation will come from a better understanding of the flowering process. However, we admit that much of the manipulation of flowering which has been so crucial to agriculture, and which has transformed horticulture, has been arrived at empirically. Some was known to the practical before it was recognized physiologically, as with Klippart's use of vernalization. Likewise, it was practical problems with flowering in hops and hemp, soybeans and tobacco that led first Tournois and then Garner and Allard to the realization that day-length may control flowering. Equally, however, research techniques such as night-breaks and plant growth regulators are now used on a vast scale in horticulture.

A data base search revealed that since I last reviewed the field in 1971, 26 000 papers concerned with flowering have been published, about 8000 of them on day-length and 800 on vernalization, but although our understanding of the flowering process has been consolidated in the interval, it has not been transformed. We may, however, be on the threshold of new advances, especially for our understanding of the processes of floral evocation and development, where the techniques of molecular biology should soon allow us to analyse these processes in ways that have not previously been possible. Such techniques may be less helpful with events in the leaf, yet the additional insights they bring, e.g. on phytochrome and endogenous rhythms, should help to resolve the complexities of time measurement by leaves. I am confident that while we continue to travel hopefully towards greater understanding of flowering in *Pharbitis* or *Xanthium*, we shall also arrive at more effective manipulation of flowering in many economic plants.

Lessons from natural variation

Before considering the ways in which flowering behaviour has been manipulated, several aspects of the control of flowering in wild and weedy plants deserve mention.

First, although individual species are often described as being short- or long-day plants, some encompass a wide array of response types, such as the perennial grasses

Bouteloua curtipendula and *Themeda australis*, the legume *Stylosanthes guianensis*, and weeds such as *Chenopodium rubrum* and *Lemna aequinoctialis*. With *Themeda australis*, for example, genotypes from the northern, summer rainfall region of Australia are short-day plants (SDP) while those from the southern, winter rainfall areas are long-day plants (LDP), their requirement for long days becoming quite weak in the drier inland regions, but enhanced by a vernalization requirement in the coldest regions. At intermediate latitudes some intermediate-day genotypes are found. This wide range in environmental control of flowering among *Themeda* population appears to be adaptive, although it is not always apparent how it is so. The lesson for domesticated plants is that widely adapted species may encompass within their gene pools a wide array of environmental responses for the control of flowering.

In some species, however, the populations may be all LDP though differing in day-length response, as in *Phleum pratense*, or all SDP, as in *Xanthium strumarium* where populations differ in critical night length, effect of temperature and age at ripeness-to-flower. The combination of these variations appears to be a sufficient basis for the successful adaptation of the species in many different parts of the world. The lesson from these plants is that interactions between a few environmental and plant factors influencing flowering can result in close adaptation to local conditions.

A third lesson from undomesticated plants is that although the initiation of flowers, the first step in the flowering process, is often the most tightly controlled by environmental factors, later steps may also be controlled, sometimes even more rigorously. Among the populations of *Themeda australis* for example, those from southern inland regions of Australia often had an absolute long-day requirement for inflorescence initiation whereas inflorescence development was indifferent to day-length. In other populations, however, the requirement for long days for development was as rigorous as that for initiation of the inflorescence. Also, in several populations of *Themeda*, day-length at the time of flowering determined whether reproduction was sexual or apomictic. Thus environmental controls on flowering may operate at any stage, and recognition of this is important not only for the manipulation of flowering but also to our thinking about the mechanisms involved.

Manipulation by selection and breeding

Modification of the flowering responses of domesticated plants by selection, much of it done unconsciously, has played a major role in:

1. Adapting land races and varieties to local conditions.
2. Permitting the spread of crops to new regions and environments.
3. Improving yield potential or reliability.

All three roles may be illustrated by reference to sorghum and rice.

1. ADAPTING LAND RACES AND VARIETIES TO LOCAL CONDITIONS

Garner and Allard included six varieties of sorghum in their experiments: they all flowered within a few days of one another in SD, but as flowering was delayed by longer days, varietal differences became more pronounced, and of more adaptive significance. Curtis (1968) found local Nigerian sorghums to out-perform improved varieties and other land races in their own environment, apparently because optimum performance requires flowering to occur about 2 weeks before daily rainfall begins to fall below evapotranspiration, with some variation depending on soil water-holding capacity. Over the years, small differences in sensitivity to day-length have been unconsciously selected in order to optimize the average flowering time of the land races. An equivalent example for rice is the need for close control of flowering time in deep-water varieties so that it is synchronized with the cresting of the flood waters, largely through sensitivity to day-length.

2. PERMITTING THE SPREAD OF CROPS

For SDP like sorghum and rice, the spread of their cultivation to higher latitudes has required selection for reduced sensitivity to day-length, as also in maize, cotton and soybean. The wild relatives of these crops are commonly SDP, whereas modern temperate varieties are almost day neutral. In fact, indifference to day-length has been specified as a desirable objective for global plant breeding programmes where the ability to flower at all seasons and latitudes is sought, e.g. for wheat at CIMMYT. Similarly, with tropical crops now grown under irrigation, such as rice, whereas previously it was advantageous for varieties to flower only at the end of the wet season, so that the grains grew on stored soil water and could be dried and harvested in sunny weather, now the emphasis is on using irrigation to grow two, three and soon four crops of rice per year, with the consequence that their flowering must now be insensitive to day-length.

Variation in response to day-length or temperature is also important in relation to the spread of weeds as well as of crops. *Sorghum halepense* provides one example, *Rottboellia exaltata* another. Most accessions of this latter weed are strict SDP, but we have recently found a genotype that is relatively insensitive to day-length (*see Figure 29.1*), a characteristic that could allow it to spread to higher latitudes.

3. IMPROVING YIELD POTENTIAL

The manipulation of flowering time to increase yield potential may run counter to the changes involved in selecting for wider adaptation or greater yield stability. Closer adaptation to local conditions and later flowering with more growth before it tend to enhance yield potential. In sorghum, for example, yield is positively correlated with leaf number and time to flowering under irrigated conditions. Changes over the last 70 years among Philippine rice varieties illustrate some of the cross-currents and compensating factors (Evans *et al.*, 1984). The traditional local varieties were mostly sensitive to day-length, but the pre-war introductions and bred varieties were even more sensitive, and the latest to flower in the field. As more rice was grown under irrigation, outside the wet season, varieties that were less strongly SD-requiring and that flowered faster were selected. In the 1960s the trend towards day-length-insensitivity became more pronounced, but that towards faster flowering was reversed by the selection of varieties like IR8 with a longer juvenile phase, associated with greater yield potential. However, selection is now focused on varieties with a shorter juvenile phase, so that more crops per year can be grown, but without a reduction in yield potential. These changes have all been brought about by empirical selection balancing yield, generation time, pest resistance, plant height and grain yield components.

Would better understanding of the physiology and genetics of flowering have assisted plant adaptation and improvement? Possibly. For example, the recognition of soybean as a SDP, in which a few genes control the response to day-length, maturity group, and flowering habit, has led to relatively close specification of optimal flowering in various environments, particularly when temperature is also taken into account. In sorghum, likewise, manipulation of the four maturity genes has permitted a fine tuning of varietal flowering response (Quinby, 1974). In terms of genetic control of flowering, the garden pea is probably the best understood species, and this understanding is beginning to have an impact on varietal yields. Such examples may soon multiply, but my doubts as to whether we shall really improve on empirical selection stem from two considerations. First, although adaptive value may be seen in specific characteristics, all their environmental consequences will not be known, nor how they may interact with other genes. Secondly, what may seem optimal for adaptation may not be so for yield. Empirical selection resolves such conflicts in a way that conscious selection would find hard to match.

Environmental manipulation

Whereas genetic manipulation is the most practicable way of modifying the flowering of field crops grown over large areas, environmental and chemical manipulation are at least as important with many horticultural crops. Sugar cane provides one of the few examples of environmental manipulation of flowering in field crops. This is possible because its intermediate day-length response limits flower induction to a brief period each year, the first 20 days of September in Hawaii, and exposure to light breaks on at least 5 of these 20 nights prevents flowering and raises sugar yields (Moore, 1985). In this case, work on the effects of light break timing and duration and on the intercalation of LD at various times during photoperiodic induction has led to an effective control system which is widely used although costly. An alternative is to stress the crop by withholding irrigation water for a month prior to induction.

Environmental manipulation to control the incidence, timing and quality of flowering is characteristic of modern horticulture, and has been applied with increasing sophistication and economy to a widening range of species and environmental factors since Blaauw introduced sequences of chilling treatments to control the flowering of bulbs. For example, many orchid species are controlled by day-length, even closely related ones often differing in their photoperiod requirements (Goh and Arditti, 1985). Temperature is critical for many, e.g. in *Phalaenopsis* in which cool night temperature, not day-length, is the operative factor. A fall in temperature triggers flower bud development in other orchids, such as *Dendrobium crumenatum*. High irradiance is crucial for others, such as *Vanda*, especially when coupled with cool nights in the case of *Cymbidium*, while water stress is used to control flowering in *Vanilla*.

Control of day-length has long been applied to obtain year-round production of flowers in both SDP and LDP, and horticulturists have been quick to use the results of physiological experiments to maximize the cost effectiveness of night-break treatments. Indeed, many of the environmental manipulations used in flowering physiology can be used fairly directly in horticulture, and there is considerable scope for applicable research, e.g. on the optimum timing and spectral composition of light interruptions or interpolated long days in preventing the flowering of SDP.

Chemical manipulation

The manipulation of flowering by a variety of chemicals is already used widely in horticulture and eventually may become more important in agriculture than environmental manipulation but whether 'regulants' will match herbicides in agricultural significance, as has been predicted, remains to be seen. Although there has been a great deal of empirical testing of the effects of chemicals on flowering, much of this has grown out of physiological analysis of the flowering process and as this develops, so will more powerful procedures for manipulation become available.

Only two points need to be made at this stage. A wide variety of plant growth substances is already in horticultural use, as Halevy's *Handbook of Flowering* (1985) makes clear: ethylene-generating chemicals, e.g. for the year-round production of pineapples and mangoes; TIBA on soybeans; gibberellins on many species; growth retardants; abscisic acid; cytokinins and salicylic acid on several orchids; maleic hydrazide, etc. These affect different stages in the overall flowering process and the sequential use of several plant growth regulators seems likely to be applied increasingly in the future. Secondly, greater use will probably be made of combined chemical and environmental treatments developed for specific genotypes. Potted azaleas provide a good example, where sequential use is made of light-breaks and growth retardants for uniform growth, of short days at controlled temperatures for flower initiation, and of cold storage and GA_3 for release from dormancy (Criley, 1985).

Management practices

Pruning and nutrition have long been used in horticulture for the manipulation of flowering, and improved control systems continue to be developed, such as that in Israel for bananas. There is little scope with field crops, although ratooning at the right time is used to ensure that sugar cane is still in the juvenile stage during the brief period when flower induction could occur (Moore, 1985), and may prove useful with other crops such as deep-water rice.

By and large, however, the manipulation of flowering in agricultural plants will be mainly by varietal selection, whereas in horticulture the future is bound to be characterized by increasingly specific combinations of variety, environmental control, chemical treatment and other management techniques arising directly from physiological experiments and understanding of the flowering processes. It is to aspects of these that we now turn.

Time measurement in the leaves

The adaptive advantage of photoperiodism is that it provides a seasonal signal which is relatively free of 'noise' from variations in temperature and irradiance for the control of plant life cycles. The leaves—especially the actively expanding ones in some SDP—are the main organs perceiving the day-length, but other organs may also respond directly, including the apical bud where it is exposed as in *Cuscuta* (Baldev, 1959) and *Kleinia* (Schwabe, 1970). In cases where the apical bud appears to have responded before the message has been received from the leaves, e.g. in the experiments by Gressel *et al.* (1970) with *Pharbitis*, this may have been either a direct

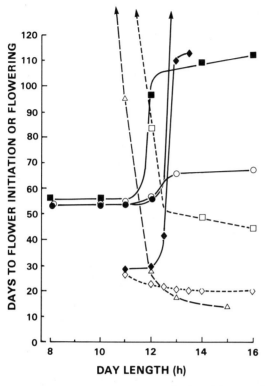

Figure 29.1   Flowering response to day-length by several plants grown in the Canberra phytotron. All received 8 h of high-irradiance natural light extended with incandescent lamps, and the response is days to flower initiation in two genotypes of *Rottboellia exaltata* (○, ●), Templar wheat (■), cowpea line 3699 (◆) and line 4552 (◇) and *Lolium temulentum* (△), and days from double ridges to anthesis in Templar wheat (□).

response by the bud to day-length—as suggested by the experiments of Gressel *et al.* (1980) with optical fibres—or because of an early message from the leaves, a distinction that needs to be explored further.

Figure 29.1 indicates the responses to day-length for flowering in some of the plants grown in the Canberra phytotron. One *Rottboellia* genotype is a strict SDP, and the Ceres *Lolium* a strict LDP. Templar wheat has a sigmoid response to day-length for inflorescence initiation, which is faster in SD but eventually occurs in LD, as does flower bud appearance in the cowpea line 3699, in the quantitative genotype of *Rottboellia* and in many other SDP, in the manner of a fail-safe mechanism. After initiation in SD, Templar wheat requires LD for inflorescence development, so it behaves as an SLDP. Cowpea line 4552 is included to represent genotypes less sensitive to day-length. These few examples illustrate part of the range in response to day-length from SDP to LDP, from qualitative via quantitative to relative indifference, and from one stage to two, but the striking feature of *Figure 29.1* is how much of the change in response is concentrated in the 11–13 h range. This might be expected for tropical plants such as the cowpea lines from Nigeria or the *Rottboellia* genotypes from Papua New Guinea, but not for the temperate plants. Halevy's *Handbook* illustrates many other examples of responses concentrated in the 11–13 h range, such as *Kalanchöe, Panicum maximum*, rice, sorghum, *Stylosanthes* and sugar cane.

This is not universally true, of course, *Xanthium* being an outstanding exception, as is the hop and some lines of soybean, all SDP where the critical dark period length may be only 8–9 h, and in LDP such as *Phleum pratense* or *Bromus inermis* the critical day-length may be up to 17 h or more (Heide, 1984). Nevertheless, there may be an important clue here to the nature of time measurement, and to the arbitrary way in which we determine the critical day-length.

For the present we remain rather schizophrenic about time measurement, not knowing how—or even whether—to combine catenary processes with endogenous rhythms. The early work, particularly with *Xanthium*, was so persuasive that the length of the daily dark period is of overriding importance, as is the fact that it has a critical length determined by the need to consummate a chain of reactions. The relative insensitivity of the critical night length to temperature in *Xanthium* and *Chenopodium*, though apparently not in *Pharbitis*, is awkward but can be got around by the concept of a temperature-compensated chain of reactions.

Far more attention has been paid to what happens at the beginning than at the end of a critical dark period, probably because a likely candidate for the first process in the chain of dark reactions was thought to be the thermal reversion of phytochrome from the Pfr to the Pr form. At first this process was believed to occupy a significant part of the critical dark period, but brief exposure to FR at the beginning of the dark period has little effect on its critical length in *Xanthium* and shortens it by only 45 min in *Pharbitis*, which can nevertheless have a marked effect on flowering. Also, even the small proportion of phytochrome set in the Pfr form by FR can reduce the flowering response in *Pharbitis* (Evans *et al.*, 1986), so complete reversion to the Pr form may be required, and would take longer. Our earlier null point estimates indicated that the proportion of phytochrome in the Pfr form after 9.5–11 h of darkness was substantially lower than that set by FR (Evans and King, 1969). However, they also suggested that the rapid fall in phytochrome Pfr involved in the flowering process did not occur at the beginning of the dark period, but only after about 5 h of darkness. Evidence for delayed reversion was also found in *Chenopodium rubrum* (King and Cumming, 1972) and in the LDP *Lemna gibba* G_3, in which Kato (1979) found evidence of a circadian periodicity in the time at which Pfr reversion appeared to occur during a 15 h dark period.

Although several criticisms can be made of the null response method on which these deductions are based (e.g. Vince-Prue, 1983), they do not, in my judgement, invalidate the broad conclusions, the most important of which is that the timing of dark reversion in at least one pool of phytochrome involved in photoperiodism may be determined by an endogenous rhythm rather than by the dusk signal. This could account for the findings that the time at which a red light break is most inhibitory during the inductive dark period is unaffected by temperature in both *Xanthium* and *Pharbitis*. Kloppstech (1985) has presented evidence that several Pfr-requiring mRNA syntheses may be driven by an endogenous rhythm, so both the appearance and the disappearance of some Pfr may not be determined only by the dawn and dusk signals. Moreover, as Lumsden *et al.* (1985) have shown, the rate of phytochrome dark reversion may vary depending on which domain of the molecule is bound to proteins.

The relations between endogenous rhythmicity, phytochrome transformations and photoperiodism may at last be on the verge of being clarified, although I suspect that J.B.S. Haldane's dictum 'Nature is cleverer than you think; nature is cleverer than you *can* think' will still haunt us. An important question still to be explored with plants is to what extent differences in the period of the endogenous rhythm may explain some of the variation in photoperiodic behaviour, because Bargiello *et al.* (1984) and others have shown rhythmicity in *Drosophila* to have a relatively simple genetic basis. The period of the circadian rhythm varies with *per* gene dosage, which controls both the circadian eclosion rhythm and the short period love song rhythm: these periods are 19 h and 40 seconds respectively in *per^s* flies, 24 h and 50–60 s in normal flies, 29 h and 80 s in *per^1* flies, and both absent in *per^0* flies, which lack the *per* gene. Besides the intriguing possibility that a comparable gene may determine photoperiodic behaviour in plants, these experiments also suggest that endogenous rhythms with periodicities which are submultiples of the circadian rhythm should also be sought.

In this context some recent experiments with *Pharbitis* have revealed an endogenous rhythm with an approximately 12 h period (hence semidian) and with a marked effect on flowering apparently by changing the critical dark period length (Heide *et al.*, 1986; Evans *et al.*, 1986). This semidian rhythm is distinct from the circadian one not only in its periodicity (*Figure 29.2*) but also by persisting in prolonged, high irradiance and by feeding forward to the dusk signal rather than referring back to it. As such it may play a role in photoperiodic time measurement either directly or indirectly through interaction with the circadian rhythm as in tidal organisms. It may also help to explain the significance of day-lengths in the 11–13 h range (*see Figure 29.1*) and it raises the possibility of defining the end of the critical dark period directly in relation to the rhythm without recourse to a chain of dark reactions. However, we have yet to find a semidian rhythm that affects flowering in other plants.

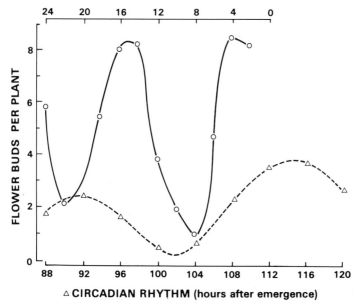

Figure 29.2   Flowering in *Pharbitis nil* as influenced by circadian (△) and semidian (○) rhythms. Circadian data from Paraska and Spector (1974, *Figure 2B*), semidian rhythm from Heide *et al.* (1986, *Figure 2*).

Transmission from leaf to shoot apex

Our understanding of what happens between photoperiodic induction in the leaves and floral evocation at the shoot apex is no clearer than of what happens before or after. Is the message to the shoot apex chemical, as we have thought, or is it transmitted biophysically? Is it a stimulus or an inhibitor of evocation, or both? Is it specific to floral evocation or not? How soon is it exported, how fast does it move, and is it translocated in mass flow with the photosynthetic assimilates? Indeed, are they the effective compounds in some cases, is the medium the message? Or are there several messenger compounds, either within one species, or differing between groups, with different translocation characteristics, only the slowest of which can be estimated? What are the message compounds, and do they act directly on the morphogenetic field of the shoot apex, or via the transcription of new genes?

The classical grafting experiments strongly suggest that—at least between graft partners that are fairly closely related taxonomically though differing in photoperiodic response (but *see* Zeevaart, 1976)—a floral stimulus is translocated from induced leaves, and that it probably moves in the assimilate stream and can act at low concentrations. Defoliation experiments with plants requiring only one inductive cycle also indicate the movement of a floral stimulus out of induced leaves in both SDP and LDP. However, the symmetries involved with indirect evidence of this kind make it difficult to distinguish sometimes between promotion and inhibition. As Sachs and Hackett (1983) point out, an inhibitor that reduced the ability of leaf primordia to direct nutrients away from the shoot apex could mimic the transmission of a stimulus. In some plants, such as strawberry (SDP) and *Lolium temulentum* (LDP), defoliation experiments have produced evidence for the translocation from leaves in non-inductive day-lengths of a transmissible inhibitor of flowering, and more recently Lang *et al.* (1977) have found comparable evidence in grafting experiments with tobacco. Both a stimulus and an inhibitor appear to be produced in *Lolium* and tobacco, and floral evocation depends on the balance between them. This balancing may shift as induction proceeds, in view of the changing effect of interpolated or simultaneous LD during SD induction of *Rottboellia exaltata* (Evans, 1962) and *Poa pratensis*.

For many plants several alternative pathways to induction have been defined. *Silene armeria*, for example, is induced by LD at 20°C, SD at low temperatures (5°C), SD at high temperatures (32°C) or GA_3. In such cases, rather than thinking in terms of such disparate conditions all producing a floral stimulus, which they appear to do, it might be fruitful also to explore the implications of the simpler view that flowering is controlled by an inhibitor produced in short days at intermediate temperatures, which could also account for the parallel changes in response to the three inductive conditions among genetically different lines (Wellensiek, 1985).

Is the medium the message?

For the last 50 years, the physiology of flowering has been dominated by Chailakhyan's concept of a floral hormone, florigen, thought to be transported along with assimilates in the phloem from leaf to shoot apex. Yet florigen remains hypothetical. I have reviewed previously the evidence against a hormone which acts solely on floral evocation, and would add here only that the translocation of such a specific hormone by mass flow with photosynthetic assimilates would be a most inefficient way of having it reach its target since only about one molecule per million would ever arrive at the shoot apex. Yet in *Pharbitis*, the effects of leaf size and indirect estimates of the speed at which the floral stimulus moves strongly suggest that it is translocated with the assimilates. Might the assimilates themselves play the controlling role? Sachs and Hackett (1983) review many cases in which the supply of assimilates to the shoot apex at floral evocation is crucial, and where a nutrient diversion hypothesis cannot be distinguished experimentally from the florigen hypothesis.

The supply of photosynthetic assimilates—as influenced by irradiance, nutrition and CO_2 level as well as day-length—is likely to influence the flowering process at many points. It may provide substrates for the synthesis of floral stimulus or inhibitor, assist their loading into the phloem, act as the medium for their translocation to the shoot apex, or possibly even as the photoperiodic message itself whether as sugars or as more specific oligasaccharins (Tran Thanh Van *et al.*, 1985). And throughout floral evocation and development assimilates will be needed as a source of energy.

Photosynthesis itself is influenced by day-length and so is the night-time remobilization of assimilates stored by day in the leaves. The proportion of assimilate which is partitioned into starch by day is much greater in SD and responds quickly to changes in day-length (Sicher *et al.*, 1982) and even to displaced SD (Britz *et al.*, 1985). Moreover, the rate at which the starch is mobilized from the leaves at night is also under photoperiodic control (Lush and Evans, 1974). Despite this metering, however, the flow of assimilates to the shoot apex is slowed after a few hours in the dark.

In species where this is a major limitation to floral evocation and development, long days will enhance flowering, particularly for plants grown under low irradiance, as *Sinapis alba* is in the Liège system (about 18 W m^{-2}, or 1–2% of full sunlight). So too will a higher CO_2 level, a displaced SD, or even 3 SD of quite modest irradiance (Bodson *et al.*, 1977). Some other LDP, such as *Brassica campestris*, behave similarly. However, in view of the attention given to photosynthesis in this book and elsewhere (Bodson and Bernier, 1985), it is worth reminding ourselves that there are also LDP which retain their requirement for LD even under high irradiance, such as *Lolium*, *Anagallis arvensis* and *Hyoscyamus* (Warm and Rau, 1982).

In these, and in some SDP such as *Kalanchöe*, flower evocation and/or development may be enhanced by high irradiance or higher CO_2 levels, but that is to be expected in view of the many possible roles for assimilates in the flowering process. In *Lolium*, for example, the flowering response increases with irradiance, and is inhibited by DCMU applications up to the time when the LD stimulus is exported from the leaf, their concentration having parallel effects on photosynthesis and on flowering (Evans, 1976). Yet high irradiance cannot replace the need for one LD. Assimilates may be necessary, but they are not sufficient for floral evocation by LD in *Lolium*, nor by SD in *Xanthium* or *Pharbitis*. Only in *Lolium*, however, is there clear evidence that the floral stimulus does not move in mass flow with the assimilates, since it is translocated at only $1–2.4 \text{ cm h}^{-1}$ compared with $77–105 \text{ cm h}^{-1}$ for assimilates measured analogously and simultaneously, and is exported from leaves that are too small to export assimilates (Evans and Wardlaw, 1966). Bernier *et al.* (1981) suggest that such an experimental approach 'requires ingenious, perhaps also ingenuous, experimenters', but their rejection of such evidence unambiguously differentiating between the floral stimulus and nutrient diversion hypotheses appears disingenuous. Similarly, while partial defoliation can be called an 'insult' it is one which is experienced by most plants in the real world, whether from pest or herbivore or pruner or flowering physiologist!

Assimilate supply to the shoot apex, as influenced by competition from young leaves, stem growth, or branching, may have a potent effect on the flowering response at all stages of development, either directly or via effects on the translocation of the floral stimulus. Sachs and Hackett (1983) favour the direct effects in their 'nutrient diversion' hypothesis, but the less direct effects of 'stimulus diversion' may be at least as important, as Ogawa and King (1979) showed with *Pharbitis*. Those LDP and other plants in which floral evocation and/or development is controlled by the supply of assimilates to the shoot apex certainly deserve further study, but it may be misleading to base our thinking about the sequence of events at evocation in truly photoperiodic plants, on those like *Sinapis*.

Morphogens or initiators of transcription

Floral stimuli or inhibitors could act directly on the pattern of activity at the shoot apex, as sucrose level might be expected to do, or they could act by initiating or inhibiting the transcription of genes involved in the flowering process.

This latter alternative could provide the requisite amplification of effect, e.g. for the floral stimulus from a small amount of grafted donor leaf, and the results obtained with inhibitors of transcription applied near the shoot apex at about the estimated time of arrival of the floral stimulus suggest that transcription then is indeed essential to floral evocation in several photoperiodic plants. We still lack evidence of new RNA transcriptions in shoot apices at floral evocation in any species, but it is being sought in several photoperiodic plants and, if found, is likely to open up the process of floral evocation to more experiment and less speculation. New transcripts and new proteins are sure to be identified at later stages of floral development, such as the possibly new proteins found by Lyndon *et al.* (1983) in the *Sinapis* apex 50–52 h after the beginning of the inductive day.

Current models of biological pattern formation (e.g. Meinhardt, 1984) require the interaction of at least two types of molecules, an autocatalytic activator and an antagonistic inhibitor. The latter may diffuse more rapidly than the activator. The range of the activator, at least, must be comparable with the size of the field. Consequently, the messenger substances from the leaves are unlikely to participate *directly* in changing shoot apical activity from the vegetative to the floral pattern. Even the slower-moving LD stimulus from *Lolium* leaves may move too fast to participate directly in pattern formation at the shoot apex. Thus any floral stimulus or inhibitor translocated from the leaves is more likely to act *indirectly* at the shoot apex, via gene activation or repression.

Bernier *et al.* (1981) present a model of floral evocation involving several sequences of events which may be initially independent but eventually interact to commit the meristem to initiate flowers. Their model is heavily based on work with *Sinapis* and may not be representative of truly photoperiodic plants. It also tends to minimize the significance of the grafting experiments, which may be only part of the story but which imply that a graft-transmissible messenger compound can activate the whole flowering sequence at a step before flower initiation in a number of more or less related plants, regardless of their photoperiodic response.

On the other hand we also know that there are several environmental pathways to floral evocation in quite a few species, and that a variety of plant growth regulators, stresses and pruning treatments as well as greater irradiance may also cause evocation. The classical florigen model tends to ignore these as 'unspecific', while the Bernier model dethrones the grafting experiments. We need a model which can accommodate both the photoperiodic highway and the alternative byways to floral evocation. The models developed for floral evocation in *Chrysanthemum* assume a switching between two stable steady states as the result of an external stimulus, like the older 'canalization' models. Thornley and Cockshull (1980) have used the equations of catastrophe theory to simulate the switch from vegetative to reproductive growth at the shoot apex, associated with a decrease in primordium size, a shortening of the plastochron and an increase in apical growth rate. Such changes occur during early floral development in many species, but in species induced by one cycle they seem to occur after the time when RNA transcription, apparently essential to flowering, occurs at the shoot apex in response to the arrival of the photoperiodic stimulus.

However, if other environmental or chemical treatments also result in some of these secondary effects of the floral stimulus, e.g. by changing the growth rate of the apical dome relative to that of the leaf primordia (Lyndon and Battey, 1985), the shoot apex may then switch to the reproductive steady state. Alternatively, we could assume that the floral stimulus leads, via gene activation, to a series of component processes, any one of which may limit floral evocation in individual species and each one of which may be initiated by alternative pathways.

Although still hypothetical and not really explanatory, such models indicate in principle how the classical florigen model and the less specific multiple pathway model of floral evocation need not be mutually exclusive, and how the bewildering variety of inductive conditions need not rule out a relatively simple and general underlying mechanism. This is important because a delight in the complexity of the phenomenology of flowering may too often be a deterrent to further analysis of the nature of evocation.

However, the greatest deterrent remains the problem of sampling enough shoot apical tissue to be able to derive and use molecular probes. *In vitro* systems like that with tobacco (Tran Than Van *et al.*, 1985) may be useful in this respect, but these too can be extremely sensitive to variety, growing conditions, pH, cytokinin, auxin and sucrose levels, as well as to oligosaccharins from sycamore cell walls. Earlier work by Aghion-Prat (1965) showed, for example, that only non-photoperiodic varieties of tobacco produced floral primordia in such a system, so its relevance to photoperiodic induction is not clear. Moreover, there is a marked gradient in florigenic activity on the plant, only tissue from the floral branches giving rise to floral primordia *in vitro*. Thus, only already floral tissue from varieties which flower in any day-length form floral primordia *in vitro*, and such material may not tell us anything about floral evocation.

Nevertheless, we need to gain a molecular foothold on the flowering process, with evidence of new transcription at the shoot apex, and although it would be preferable for this to be during evocation, even later stages would be helpful as well as earlier ones during juvenility or vernalization. Likewise, while it would ultimately best be found in meristematic tissue *in vivo*, *in vitro* systems may well provide the earliest evidence. Such work surely offers our best hope of obtaining a clearer picture of the nature of floral evocation from which we could work backwards to the message from the leaves and the inductive processes in them, and forwards to the processes of flower development. Then we should really be able to manipulate flowering more absolutely, more economically, and more elegantly. We should also be able to ask new kinds of questions about the flowering process, and to escape some of our current mythologies.

References

AGHION-PRAT, D. (1965). Néoformation de fleurs *in vitro* chez *Nicotiana tabacum* L. *Physiologie Végétale*, **3**, 229–303
BALDEV, B. (1959). *In vitro* responses of growth and development in *Cuscuta reflexa* Roxb. *Phytomorphology*, **9**, 316–319
BARGIELLO, T.A., JACKSON, F.R. and YOUNG, M.W. (1984). Restoration of circadian behavioural rhythms by gene transfer in *Drosophila. Nature (London)*, **312**, 752–754
BERNIER, G., KINET, J.M. and SACHS, R.M. (1981). *The Physiology of Flowering*, Vols I and II. Boca Raton, FL., CRC
BODSON, M. and BERNIER, G. (1985). Is flowering controlled by the assimilate level? *Physiologie Végétale*, **23**, 491–501
BODSON, M., KING, R.W., EVANS, L.T. and BERNIER, G. (1977). The role of photosynthesis in flowering of the long-day plant *Sinapis alba. Australian Journal of Plant Physiology*, **4**, 467–478
BRITZ, S.J., HUNGERFORD, W.E. and LEE, D.R. (1985). Photoperiodic regulation of photosynthate partitioning in leaves of *Digitaria decumbens* Stent. *Plant Physiology*, **78**, 710–714
CRILEY, R.A. (1985). Rhododendrons and azaleas. In *CRC Handbook of Flowering IV*, pp. 180–197. Boca Raton, FL., CRC
CURTIS, D.L. (1968). The relation between date of heading of Nigerian sorghums and the duration of the growing season. *Journal of Applied Ecology*, **5**, 215–222
EVANS, L.T. (1962). Daylength control of inflorescence initiation in the grass *Rottboellia exaltata* L.f. *Australian Journal of Biological Science*, **15**, 291–303
EVANS, L.T. (1976). Inhibition of flowering in *Lolium temulentum* by the photosynthetic inhibitor 3(3,4-dichlorophenyl)-1,1-dimethylurea (DCMU) in relation to assimilate supply to the shoot apex. In *Etudes de Biologie Végétale*, pp. 265–275. Paris
EVANS, L.T. and KING, R.W. (1969). Role of phytochrome in photoperiodic induction of *Pharbitis nil. Zeitschrift für Pflanzenphysiologie*, **60**, 277–288
EVANS, L.T. and WARDLAW, I.F. (1966). Independent translocation of ^{14}C-labelled assimilates and of the floral stimulus in *Lolium temulentum. Planta (Berlin)*, **68**, 310–326
EVANS, L.T., VISPERAS, R.M. and VERGARA, B.S. (1984). Morphological and physiological changes among rice varieties used in the Philippines over the last seventy years. *Field Crops Research*, **8**, 105–124
EVANS, L.T., HEIDE, O.M. and KING, R.W. (1986). A semidian rhythm in the flowering response of *Pharbitis nil* to far-red light. II The involvement of phytochrome. *Plant Physiology*, **80**, 1025–1029
GOH, C-J. and ARDITTI, J. (1985). Orchidaceae. In *CRC Handbook of Flowering I*, pp. 309–336. Boca Raton, FL., CRC
GRESSEL, J., ZILBERSTEIN, A. and ARZEE, T. (1970). Burst of incorporation into RNA and ribonuclease activities associated with induction of morphogenesis in *Pharbitis. Developmental Biology*, **22**, 31–42
GRESSEL, J., ZILBERSTEIN, A., PORATH, D. and ARZEE, T. (1980). Demonstration with fiber illumination that *Pharbitis* plumules also perceive flowering photoinduction.

In *Photoreceptors and Plant Development* (J. De Greef, Ed.), pp. 525–530. Antwerpen University Press

HALEVY, A.H. (Ed). (1985). *CRC Handbook of Flowering, I–IV*. Boca Raton, FL., CRC

HEIDE, O.M. (1984). Flowering requirements in *Bromus inermis*, a short-long day plant. *Physiologia Plantarum*, **62**, 59–64

HEIDE, O.M., KING, R.W. and EVANS, L.T. (1986). A semidian rhythm in the flowering response of *Pharbitis nil* to far-red light 1. Phasing in relation to the light-off signal *Plant Physiology*, **80**, 1020–1024

KATO, A. (1979). Maintenance of high Pfr level in the dark period in relation to flowering in *Lemna gibba* G$_3$. *Plant and Cell Physiology*, **20**, 1285–1293

KING, R.W. and CUMMING, B.G. (1972). The role of phytochrome in photoperiodic time measurement and its relation to rhythmic timekeeping in the control of flowering in *Chenopodium rubrum*. *Planta*, **108**, 39–57

KLOPPSTECH, K. (1985). Diurnal and circadian rhythmicity in the expression of light-induced plant messenger RNAs. *Planta*, **165**, 502–506

LANG, A., CHAILAKHYAN, M.K. and FROLOVA, I.A. (1977). Promotion and inhibition of flower formation in a day neutral plant in grafts with a short-day plant and a long-day plant. *Proceedings of the National Academy of Science of the USA*, **74**, 2412–2416

LUMSDEN, P.J., YAMAMOTO, K.T., NAGATANI, A., and FURUYA, M. (1985). Effect of monoclonal antibodies on the *in vitro* Pfr dark reversion of pea phytochrome. *Plant Cell Physiology*, **26**, 1313–1322

LUSH, W.M. and EVANS, L.T. (1974). Translocation of photosynthetic assimilate from grass leaves, as influenced by environment and species. *Australian Journal of Plant Physiology*, **1**, 417–431

LYNDON, R.F. and BATTEY, N.H. (1985). The growth of the shoot apical meristem during flower initiation. *Biologia Plantarum (Praha)*, **27**, 339–349

LYNDON, R.F., JACQMARD, A. and BERNIER, G. (1983). Changes in protein composition of the shoot meristem during floral evocation in *Sinapis alba*. *Physiologia Plantarum*, **59**, 476–480

MEINHARDT, H. (1984). Models of pattern formation and their application to plant development. In *Positional Controls in Plant Development* (P.W. Barlow and D.J. Carr, Eds), pp. 1–32. Cambridge University Press

MOORE, P.H. (1985). *Saccharum*. In *Handbook of Flowering IV*, pp. 243–262. Boca Raton, FL., CRC

OGAWA, Y. and KING, R.W. (1979). Indirect action of benzyladenine and other chemicals on flowering of *Pharbitis nil* Chois. *Plant Physiology*, **63**, 643–649

PARASKA, J.R. and SPECTOR, C. (1974). The initiation of an endogenous rhythm affecting flower bud formation in *Pharbitis nil*. *Physiologia Plantarum*, **32**, 62–65

QUINBY, J.R. (1974). *Sorghum Improvement and the Genetics of Growth*. Texas A and M, College Station. p. 108

SACHS, R.M. and HACKETT, W.P. (1983). Source-sink relationships and flowering. In *Strategies of Plant Reproduction* (W.J. Meudt, Ed.), pp. 263–272. Osmun, Allenheld

SCHWABE, W.W. (1970). The control of flowering, growth and dormancy in *Kleinia articulata* by photoperiod. *Annals of Botany*, **34**, 29–41

SICHER, R.C., HARRIS, W.G., KREMER, D.F. and CHATTERTON, N.J. (1982). Effects of shortened daylength upon translocation and starch accumulation by maize, wheat and pangola grass leaves. *Canadian Journal of Botany*, **60**, 1304–1309

THORNLEY, J.H.M. and COCKSHULL, K.E. (1980). A catastrophe model for the switch from vegetative to reproductive growth in the shoot apex. *Annals of Botany,* **46,** 333–341

TRAN THANH VAN, K., TOUBART, P., COUSSON, A., DARVILL, A.G., COLLIN, D.J., CHELF, P. and ALBERSHEIM, P. (1985). Manipulation of the morphogenetic pathways of tobacco explants by oligosaccharins. *Nature (London),* **314,** 615–617

VINCE-PRUE, D. (1983). Photomorphogenesis and flowering. In *Photomorphogenesis* (W. Shropshire and H. Mohr, Eds), pp. 457–490. Berlin, Springer

WARM, E. and RAU, W. (1982). A quantitative and cumulative response to photoperiodic induction of *Hyoscyamus niger*, a qualitative long day plant. *Zeitschrift für Pflanzenphysiologie,* **105,** 111–118

WELLENSIEK, S.J. (1985). *Silene armeria*. In *Handbook of Flowering IV*, pp. 320–330. Boca Raton, FL., CRC

ZEEVAART, J.A.D. (1976). Physiology of flower formation. *Annual Review of Plant Physiology,* **27,** 321–348

LIST OF PARTICIPANTS

Abrams, S.R.	Plant Biotechnology Institute, National Council of Canada, 110 Gymnasium Road, Saskatoon, Saskatchewan S7N 0W9, Canada
Ahamed, K.U.	University of Southampton, Building 44, Southampton SO9 5NH, UK
Alderson, P.G.	University of Nottingham, School of Agriculture, Sutton Bonington, Loughborough LE12 5RD, UK
Atherton, J.G.	University of Nottingham, School of Agriculture, Sutton Bonington, Loughborough LE12 5RD, UK
Barrett, Sarah K.	University of Nottingham, School of Agriculture, Sutton Bonington, Loughborough LE12 5RD, UK
Benson, Erica E.	University of Nottingham, School of Agriculture, Sutton Bonington, Loughborough LE12 5RD, UK
Bodson, Monique.	Université de Liège, Dépt. de Botanique, Sart Tilman, 4000 Liège, Belgium
Booth, D.	University of Leeds, Department of Plant Sciences, Agricultural Sciences Building, Leeds LS2 9JT, UK
Bowman, J.	Nickerson RPB, Rothwell, Lincolnshire LN7 6BT, UK
van Breukelen, E.W.M.	Nickerson-Zwaan, PO Box 19, 2990 AA Barendrecht, The Netherlands
Brewster, J.L.	National Vegetable Research Station, Wellesbourne, Warwick CV35 9EF, UK
Bridle, K.A.	R.J. Reynolds Tobacco Co., Bowman Gray Technical Center, Winston-Salem, North Carolina 27102, USA
Chu, N.M.	University of Yale, Department of Biology, PO Box 6666, New Haven, CT 06511, USA
Cochet, T.	Laboratoire de Cytologie Expérimentale et Morphogenèse Végétale, Bât N2, 4 Place Jussieu, 75005 Paris, France
Cockshull, K.E.	Glasshouse Crops Research Institute, Worthing Road, Littlehampton, West Sussex BN17 6LP, UK
Cogan, Diane E.	Butterworth Scientific, PO Box 63, Westbury House, Bury Street, Guildford, Surrey GU2 5BH, UK
Davenport, T.L.	University of Florida, Tropical Research and Education Center, 18905 SW 280 St, Homestead, Fl. 33031, USA
Davy, A.J.	University of East Anglia, School of Biological Sciences, Norwich NR4 7TJ, UK
Day, W.	Rothamsted Experimental Station, Physiology and Environmental Physics, Harpenden, Herts AL5 2JQ, UK
Dean, M.	Nickerson RPB, Rothwell, Lincolnshire LN7 6BT, UK
Deitzer, G.F.	Environmental Research Center, 12441 Parklawn Drive, Rockville, Maryland 20852-1773, USA
Dick, J.M.	Institute of Terrestrial Ecology, Bush Estate, Penicuik, Midlothian, Scotland

Dickens, C.W.S.	University of Natal, Research Unit for Plant Growth and Development, Botany Department, PO Box 375, Pietermaritzburg 3200, South Africa
van Dijck, R.M.	University of Antwerp, Department of Biology, Universiteitsplein 1, B-2610 Antwerpen, Belgium
van Dijk, M.J.	University of Leiden, Oudenborch 26, 2681 HZ Monster, Netherlands
Djurhuus, R.	Agricultural University of Norway, Department of Floriculture and Greenhouse Crops, PO Box 13, N-1932, AAS-NLH, Norway
Dutton, Kirsty J.	University of Aberdeen, School of Agriculture, 581 King Street, Aberdeen A89 1UD, Scotland
Ellis, P.R.	Scottish Crop Research Institute, Mylnefield, Invergowrie, Dundee DD2 5DA, Scotland
Elphinstone, E.D.	Glasshouse Crops Research Institute, Worthing Road, Littlehampton, West Sussex BN17 6LP, UK
Elston, J.	University of Leeds, Department of Plant Sciences, Leeds LS2 9JT, UK
Evans, L.T.	CSIRO Division of Plant Industry, GPO Box 1600, Canberra, ACT 2601, Australia
Feuerhelm, D.W.	Elsoms Seeds, Pinchbeck Road, Spalding, Lincolnshire PE11 1QG, UK
Ford, M.A.	Plant Breeding Institute, Maris Lane, Trumpington, Cambridge CB2 2LQ, UK
Francis, D.	Department of Plant Science, University College, PO Box 78, Cardiff CF1 1XL, UK
Green, C.F.	University of Nottingham, School of Agriculture, Sutton Bonington, Loughborough LE12 5RD, UK
Gregson, K.	University of Nottingham, School of Agriculture, Sutton Bonington, Loughborough LE12 5RD, UK
Hackett, W.P.	University of Minnesota, Department of Horticultural Science and Landscape Architecture, St. Paul, MN 55108, USA
Halevy, A.H.	The Hebrew University of Jerusalem, Faculty of Agriculture, PO Box 12, Rehovot 76–100, Israel
Hand, D.J.	University of Nottingham, School of Agriculture, Sutton Bonington, Loughborough LE12 5RD, UK
Hand, D.W.	Glasshouse Crops Research Institute, Worthing Road, Littlehampton, West Sussex BN17 6LP, UK
Harris, G.P.	University of Reading, Department of Agriculture and Horticulture, Earley Gate, Reading RG6 2AT, UK
Holmsen, T.W.	Dow Chemical Company, 2800 Mitchell Drive, Walnut Creek, California 94598, USA
Horridge, J.S.	Glasshouse Crops Research Institute, Worthing Road, Littlehampton, West Sussex BN17 6LP, UK
Ilker, R.A.	General Foods Corporation, 555 S. Broadway, Tarrytown, NY 10591, USA
Ivins, J.D.	University of Nottingham, School of Agriculture, Sutton Bonington, Loughborough LE12 5RD, UK
Jackson, J.A.	University of Edinburgh, Department of Botany, Mayfield Road, Edinburgh EH9 3JH, UK
Jaffe, M.J.	Wake Forest University, Biology Department, Box 7325, Reynolda Station, Winston-Salem, North Carolina 27109, USA
Jegla, D.E.	Department of Biology, Kenyon College, Gambier, Ohio 43022-9623, USA
Jones, T.W.A.	Welsh Plant Breeding Station, Plas Gogerddan, Aberystwyth, Dyfed SY23 3EB, Wales
De Jong, T.J.	University of Leiden, Department of Population Biology, PO Box 9516, Leiden, The Netherlands
Kadman-Zahavi, A.	The Volcani Center, Beit Dagan, Israel
Kemp, D.R.	Welsh Plant Breeding Station, Plas Gogerddan, Aberystwyth, Dyfed SY23 3EB, Wales

Kennedy, D.	Elsoms Seeds Limited, Pinchbeck Road, Spalding, Lincolnshire PE11 1QG, UK
Klinkhamer, P.G.I.	University of Leiden, Department of Population Biology, PO Box 9516, Leiden, The Netherlands
Krekule, J.	Institute of Experimental Botany, Czechoslovak Academy of Science, Ke Dvoru 15, Praha 6-Vokovice, 166-30, Czechoslovakia
Law, C.N.	Plant Breeding Institute, Maris Lane, Cambridge, UK
Lewis, D.H.	Plant Physiology Division, DSIR, Private Bag, Palmerston North, New Zealand
Lexander, K.A-M.	Hilleshog Research AB, PO Box 302, S-261 Landskrona, Sweden
Longden, P.C.	Broom's Barn Experimental Station, Higham, Bury St. Edmunds, Suffolk IP28 6NP, UK
Longman, K.A.	Institute of Terrestrial Ecology, Bush Estate, Penicuik EH26 0QB, Scotland
Lord, T.	University of Nottingham, School of Agriculture, Sutton Bonington, Loughborough LE12 5RD, UK
Luedeke, F.	University of Newcastle upon Tyne, Department of Agriculture, Newcastle upon Tyne NE1 7RU, UK
Lyndon, R.F.	University of Edinburgh, Department of Botany, Mayfield Road, Edinburgh EH9 3JH, Scotland
McDaniel, C.N.	Rensselaer Polytechnic Institute, Department of Biology, Troy, NY 12180-3590, USA
McKinless, J.	University of Nottingham, School of Agriculture, Sutton Bonington, Loughborough LE12 5RD, UK
McLaughlin, J.M.	University of Massachusetts, Department of Plant and Soil Sciences, French Hall, Amherst, Massachusetts 01003, USA
Mahklouf, M.N.	University of Nottingham, School of Agriculture, Sutton Bonington, Loughborough LE12 5RD, UK
Mancarenhas, J.P.	National Science Foundation, Programme in Development Biology, Room 332, 1800 G Street NW, Georgetown, Washington, DC, 20550, USA
Mathias, P.J.	University of Nottingham, School of Agriculture, Sutton Bonington, Loughborough LE12 5RD, UK
van Meeteren, U.	Bulb Research Centre, PO Box 85, 2160 AB Lisse, The Netherlands
Metzger, J.D.	Metabolism and Radiation Research Laboratory, State University Station, Fargo, ND 58105, USA
Moe, R.	Department of Floriculture and Greenhouse Crops, PO Box 13, 1432 As-NLH, Norway
Moir, D.L.	A.L. Tozer, Pyports, Cobham, Surrey KT11 3EH, UK
Montalli, E.F.	University of Nottingham, School of Agriculture, Sutton Bonington, Loughborough LE12 5RD, UK
Monteith, J.L.	University of Nottingham, School of Agriculture, Sutton Bonington, Loughborough LE12 5RD, UK
Morris, D.A.	University of Southampton, Department of Biology, Building 44, Southampton SO9 5NH, UK
de Munk, W.J.	Bulb Research Centre, PO Box 85, 2160 AB Lisse, The Netherlands
Napp-Zinn, K.	Botanisches Institut, Gyrhofstr 15, D-5000 Köln, 41, West Germany
Newell, A.	University of Leeds, Department of Plant Sciences, Agricultural Sciences Building, Leeds LS2 9JT, UK
Norton, C.R.	University of British Columbia, Vancouver V6T 2A2, BC, Canada
Nothmann, J.	The Volcani Center, Department of Vegetable Crops, ARO, P.O.B. 6, Bet Dagan 50–250, Israel
Ormrod, L.	Université de Liège, Département de Botanique, B22, Sart Tilman, 4000 Liège, Belgium
Ottosen, C-O.	Institute of Glasshouse Crops, Kirstinebjergvej 10, 5792 Aarslev, Denmark

Papafotiou, M.	University of London, Wye College, Near Ashford, Kent TN25 5AH, UK
Philippe, L.E.	University of Antwerp, Department of Biology, Universiteitsplein, B-2610, Antwerp, Belgium
Porter, J.R.	Long Ashton Research Station, Long Ashton, Bristol BS18 9AF, UK
Poulsen, N.	Research Centre for Horticulture, Institute of Vegetables, Kirstinebjergvej 6, DK-5792 Aarslev, Denmark
Pressman, E.	ARO, The Volcani Center, Department of Vegetative Crops, PO Box 6, Bet Dagan, Israel
de Proft, P.M.	University of Antwerp, Department of Biology, Unviersiteitsplein, B-2610, Wilrijk, Belgium
Pullan, M.R.	University of Nottingham, School of Agriculture, Sutton Bonington, Loughborough LE12 5RD, UK
Purse, J.G.	Shell Research Limited, Broad Oak Rod, Sittingbourne, Kent ME9 8AG, UK
Quiroz, L.F.	University of Antwerp, Department of Biology, Unviersiteitsplein 1, B-2610, Wilrijk, Belgium
Rajagopal, R.	Royal Veterinary and Agricultural University, Thorvaldsensvej 40, DK 1871 Copenhagen, V, Denmark
Rashid, K.A.	University of Southampton, Biology Department, Building 44, Southampton SO9 5NH, UK
Rees, A.R.	Glasshouse Crops Research Institute, Worthing Road, Littlehampton, West Sussex BN17 6LP, UK
Roberts, E.H.	University of Reading, Department of Agriculture, Earley Gate, PO Box 236, Reading RG6 2AT, UK
Roberts, J.A.	University of Nottingham, School of Agriculture, Sutton Bonington, Loughborough LE12 5RD, UK
Roelofse, E.W.	Glasshouse Crops Research Institute, Worthing Road, Littlehampton, West Sussex BN17 6LP, UK
Sachs, R.M.	University of California, Department of Environmental Horticulture, Davis CA 95616, USA
Schwabe, W.W.	University of London, Wye College, Department of Horticulture, Wye, Near Ashford, Kent TN25 5AH, UK
Semple, Jayne T.	Nickerson, RPB Limited, Rothwell, Lincoln LN7 6DT, UK
Silim, S.N.	ICARDA, PO Box 5466, Aleppo, Syria
Singer, S.R.	Rensselaer Polytechnic Institute, Department of Biology, Cogswell 130 Troy, New York 12180-3590, USA
Sobeih, W.Y.	University of Nottingham, School of Agriculture, Sutton Bonington, Loughborough LE12 5RD, UK
Srinivasan, C.	Department of Environmental Horticulture, University of California, Davis, USA
van Staden, J.	University of Natal, Box 375, Pietermaritzburg 3200, South Africa
Steffen, J.D.	University of California, Department of Environmental Horticulture, Davis CA 95616, USA
Steffens, G.L.	US Department of Agriculture, ARS BARC-West, Fruit Laboratory Building 004, Room 111, Beltsville, MD 20705, USA
Steven, M.D.	University of Nottingham, Department of Geography, University Park, Nottingham, UK
Streit, L.E.	Ciba-Geigy, R 1040 P12 Postfach, CH-4002, Basel, Switzerland
Summerfield, R.J.	Plant Environment Laboratory, Shinfield Grange, Cutbush Lane, Shinfield, Reading RG2 9AD, UK
Sussex, I.M.	Yale University, Department of Biology, PO Box 6666, New Haven, CT 06511-7444, USA
Taeb, M.	University of Nottingham, School of Agriculture, Sutton Bonington, Loughborough LE12 5RD, UK
Thomas, B.	Glasshouse Crops Research Institute, Worthing Road, Littlehampton, West Sussex BN17 6LP, UK
Thornley, J.H.M.	Animal and Grassland Research Institute, Hurley, Maidenhead, Berks SL6 5LR, UK

Tommey, A.M.	University of Newcastle upon Tyne, Faculty of Agriculture, Newcastle upon Tyne, UK
Tsao, T.H.	University of Peking, Department of Biology, Beijing, People's Republic of China
Tucker, G.	University of Nottingham, School of Agriculture, Sutton Bonington, Loughborough LE12 5RD, UK
Vince-Prue, D.	Glasshouse Crops Research Institute, Physiology and Chemistry Division, Worthing Road, Littlehampton, West Sussex NB17 6LP, UK
Wall, J.K.	University of Reading, Department of Horticulture, Earley Gate, Reading RG6 2AN, UK
Wallerstein, I.	The Volcani Center, Department of Ornamental Horticulture, P.O.B. 6, Bet Dagan 50–250, Israel
Wareing, P.F.	University College of Wales, Department of Botany and Microbiology, Aberystwyth, Dyfed SY23 3DA, UK
Wheelans, Shelagh K.	University of Nottingham, School of Agriculture, Sutton Bonington, Loughborough LE12 5RD, UK
White, Gretel	University of Nottingham, School of Agriculture, Sutton Bonnington, Loughborough LE12 5RD, UK
Whittington, W.J.	University of Nottingham, School of Agriculture, Sutton Bonington, Loughborough LE12 5RD, UK
Wightman, F.	Carleton University, Biology Department, Ottawa, Ont. K15 5B6, Canada
Williams, C.A.	University of Nottingham, School of Agriculture, Sutton Bonington, Loughborough LE12 5RD, UK
Williams, R.H.	Hurst Crop Research and Development Unit, Great Domsey Farm, Feering, Colchester, Essex, UK
Wiltshire, J.J.	University of Nottingham, School of Agriculture, Sutton Bonington, Loughborough LE12 5RD, UK
Wilson, L.A.	University of the West Indies, Faculty of Agriculture, Department of Crop Science, St. Augustine, Trinidad, West Indies
Withers, L.A.	University of Nottingham, School of Agriculture, Sutton Bonington, Loughborough LE12 5RD, UK
Wright, C.J.	University of Nottingham, School of Agriculture, Sutton Bonington, Loughborough LE12 5RD, UK
Wurr, D.C.	National Vegetable Research Station, Wellesbourne, Warwick, CV35 9EF, UK
Zeevaart, J.A.	Michigan State University, Plant Research Laboratory, East Lansing, MI 48824, USA

INDEX